# BLACKNESS IN LATIN AMERICA
## AND THE CARIBBEAN

D1572147

BLACKS IN THE DIASPORA
Darlene Clark Hine, John McCluskey, Jr., and
David Barry Gaspar, General Editors

# BLACKNESS IN LATIN AMERICA AND THE CARIBBEAN

*Social Dynamics and Cultural Transformations*

VOLUME I
Central America and Northern
and Western South America

Compiled, edited, and with a general introduction by
## Norman E. Whitten, Jr., and Arlene Torres

INDIANA UNIVERSITY PRESS
*Bloomington and Indianapolis*

This book is a publication of
Indiana University Press
601 North Morton Street
Bloomington, Indiana 47404-3797 USA

www.indiana.edu/~iupress

*Telephone orders*   800-842-6796
*Fax orders*   812-855-7931
*Orders by e-mail*   iuporder@indiana.edu

The paper used in this publication meets the minimum
requirements of American National Standard for Information
Sciences—Permanence of Paper for Printed Library
Materials, ANSI Z39.48-1984.

Manufactured in the United States of America

Library of Congress Cataloging-in-Publication Data

Blackness in Latin America and the Caribbean : social dynamics and
   cultural transformations / compiled, edited, and with a general
   introduction by Norman E. Whitten, Jr. and Arlene Torres.
      p.    cm. — (Blacks in the diaspora)
   Contents: v. 1. Central America and Northern and Western South
America — v. 2. Eastern South America and the Caribbean.
      ISBN 0-253-33404-7 (v. 1 : cl : alk. paper). — ISBN 0-253-21193-X
(v. 1 : pa : alk. paper). — ISBN 0-253-33406-3 (v. 2 : cl : alk.
paper). — ISBN 0-253-21194-8 (v. 2 : pa : alk. paper)
      1. Blacks—Latin America—History.   2. Blacks—Caribbean Area—
History.   3. Latin America—Race relations.   4. Caribbean Area—
Race relations.   5. Blacks—Race identity.   6. Social change.
7. Functionalism (Social sciences).   I. Whitten, Norman E.
II. Torres, Arlene.   III. Series.
F1419.N4B53   1998
305.89608—dc21                                        97-44093
   1  2  3  4  5     03  02  01  00  99  98

# CONTENTS

# PREFACE

The *longue durée* involved in publication of this work has puzzled many of our colleagues, including those who anonymously reviewed various drafts in various stages or who tried to purchase the work over the past four years. Accordingly, we feel it necessary to give a history of the project leading to these two volumes and to explain the initial and eventual focus.

During the summer of 1990, Howard Doddson, chief of the Schomburg Center for Research in Black Culture at the New York Public Library, wrote to invite Norman Whitten to prepare an edited volume on the subject of comparative black settlements and community patterns. The compilation, with a significant introduction, was to be part of an ambitious and important series, the Schomburg Library of the Black Experience in the Western Hemisphere, 1492–1992. In August 1990, Whitten invited Arlene Torres to participate with him in this project. The two of us then asked Doddson to expand the project to two volumes; to limit the region covered to Central America, South America, and the Caribbean; and to allow us up to 100 pages for our introduction to each volume. We completed the project for the Schomburg Library series in early February 1991 on the schedule set by Schomburg.

By midwinter 1992, serious doubts were cast on the fate of the Schomburg series, which was to have numbered between thirty-five and sixty-five volumes. Because we wanted our volumes to appear in 1992, the year of the quincentennial celebration of the European conquest, we agreed to publish independently with Carlson, the publisher-designate of the Schomburg series. It was hoped that if a series did materialize, our tomes would be reincorporated therein.

In November 1993 we talked to Joan Catapano of Indiana University Press about publishing a paperback comprising selections from the larger work. Then, as it became increasingly apparent that the work would not appear with Carlson, Indiana University Press set to the process of anonymous peer review, followed by a marketing survey to see if the Press could pull the project out of the fire, so to speak, and publish the two volumes. In the fall of 1996 Indiana agreed to bring this work out.

Originally we were charged with pulling together previously published materials on comparative black settlements and community patterns in English, Spanish, French, and Portuguese. This we did. Because we were restricted to pre-published articles and chapters, we could not commission any articles or include articles in preparation but not yet accepted for publication. In the contract we signed with Indiana University Press, we agreed to select only publications in English or to provide translations but were free to select a limited number of new contributions to Afro–Latin American or Afro-Caribbean systems of community, culture, and communication.

The agreement with Indiana University Press allowed us to do what we originally wanted to do—to provide readers with a set of chapters that range from early groundbreaking pieces to exemplars of contemporary Afro-Americanist scholarship of the late 1990s. Selections such as those of Roy Simon Bryce-Laporte on Panama, Nina S. de Friedemann on Colombia, Madeline Barbara Léons on Bolivia, Florestan Fernandes on Brazil, B. Edward Pierce on Suriname, Leo A. Despres on Guyana, and M. G. Smith on Carriacou are heavily and, for the time, appropriately "social scientific" and analytical of plural systems of social relationships. Serious ethnography of complex social processes set in nation-state contexts of inclusion and exclusion—the hallmark of later "ethnicity studies"—are the strengths of these pieces, as is serious attention to kinship and family systems unfamiliar to anthropological and sociological specialists in this panhuman domain.

Such groundbreaking and enduring presentations are complemented by many "intermediate" pieces ranging from Virginia Kerns's on Belize through those by Michael Taussig on Colombia, Kathleen Klumpp and Norman Whitten on Ecuador, Lee Drummond on Guyana, Sally Price on Suriname, Douglas Midgett on Grenada, John Stewart on Trinidad, and Frank E. Manning on Bermuda. These essays represent an interesting and creative merging of social science rigor with humanistic skills; each is grounded both in the harsh realities of being black in plural systems and in the creative adjustments and accomplishments of actors in such systems. Blackness in these "middle" articles begins to emerge as a creative force as the authors tease out the symbolic dimensions of cultural phenomena, with careful attention to social relations, including gendered interaction and symbolism, community formations, and regional and national systems. In most of the latest contributions we find a definite swing into the cultural creativity of blackness together with metaphors and movements of cultural transformation and resistance by people forging anew their positions in dynamic local, regional, national, and global dimensions. In short, this work has benefited by the four "lost" years. We hope that its readers will appreciate the mix of older, middle, recent, and brand new that these two volumes provide.

The general introduction to these volumes, "To Forge the Future in the Fires of the Past: An Interpretive Essay on Racism, Domination, Resistance, and Liberation," was prepared in 1991. It was designed and written to provide a broad framework for our selection of articles and chapters in the two volumes. The introductory chapters designed specifically for volumes I and II set forth discursive accounts of the contents of the volumes within the framework established in the general introduction. Since we were forced by circumstances of length and style to eliminate several pieces originally selected, in the introductory chapters we indicate other works, especially in Spanish and French, which should be used, when possible, to supplement these volumes. Both introductory chapters are designed to pick up and in some instances elaborate on the themes of the general introduction. The reader may want to read all three as an extended essay on blackness in Latin America and the Caribbean.

In these three introductions we try to give breadth and depth to our subject matter by understanding "blackness" and "illumination" as together constituting a dynamic, international aesthetic pattern across space and through time. We also want to help readers to rethink some deeply held but illusory notions about Latin America and the Caribbean and about the subject of blackness there. To do this we chose an essay format for all of the introductions. By use of this format we draw attention to history and geography to show how the focus on blackness among human beings transcends the boundaries imposed through nearly 500 years of cultural transformations and across some of the least known topographical spaces for most North Americans and Europeans.

We seek to challenge readers to think more about the issues raised in the introductions and thereby to appreciate more thoroughly the strengths of the varied articles and chapters that are reprinted and the three printed here for the first time. We also take readers into quotidian and ritual life, and where possible we draw attention to cosmological features of cultural significance. To do so we weave in and out of meaning in vernacular and written Spanish, as do many of the authors, to allow readers to consider seriously the nature of speech, talk, discourse, writing, and all other systems of human communication as they condition humanity's view of humanity. Inasmuch as viewpoints are also conditioned by systems of domination and hegemony in active interaction with processes of resistance and creativity, we indicate something of the local, regional, national, and international situations affecting blackness and illumination.

During 1992–93, with the celebration of European conquest and of whiteness, a veritable deluge of publications emerged on imagery and imaginations and on histories and reinterpretations of the European New World of 1492 and the shattered yet enduring indigenous worlds of 1492–1992. We have been able to incorporate but a handful of these references into this work. We hope nonetheless that our endeavors will place something of a corrective on the polarized European–Indian theme and lead those not specializing in Afro-Americana to understand that within *la leyenda negra* of indigenous destruction and black slavery is the illumination of transformed Africanity in the Americas and the creativity of freedom seized. We seek to portray the image of blackness as something not bound to skin color or stereotypes of complexion.

The subject of blackness in the Americas was given short shrift during the celebrations and lamentations of 1992, and accordingly the literature presented here did not find its way into the references and discussions of that brief period. What we offer is a critical review of blackness in systems dominated by whiteness; we argue that such domination and polarization emerged in their powerful racist dimensions sometime before 1502 and that the issues we address and which are now being addressed by more and more scholars require the sustained attention recently given to Europeans and Native American systems of response to the European conquest and colonization of the Americas.

The year 1992 did witness an upswing of serious research and publication on the subject of these volumes, though nothing came forth compared to the foci on Europeans and "disappearing Indians." An important complement to these volumes is the slim but powerful publication of the North American Congress on Latin America, *The Black Americas 1492–1992*. Also, the editors of the *Encyclopedia of World Cultures* commissioned a few chapters on blackness in the Americas, including Venezuela, Colombia, Ecuador, Bolivia, and Brazil, for its volume on South America. Nonetheless, on the volume's thirteen maps of culture areas with 456 peoples of South America presented, the only black people listed are the Saramaka of Suriname. Not a single other African American culture, community, or ethnic group is mentioned in the legends or placed on the maps. *Negreado* is the Spanish term for this common phenomenon of leaving cultures of black Americans off maps and out of history. It is a phenomenon receiving considerable attention among peoples of color in Latin America.

A serious historic complement to our work is found in *Race, Discourse, and the Origin of the Americas*, published in 1995 by the Smithsonian Institution Press. Although the book was part of the Smithsonian's program to commemorate 1492 and the voyages of the Admiral of the Ocean Sea, and although it is rich in literature on African-European and African-American experiences and histories, the foreword by Robert McCormick Adams, distinguished anthropologist and director of the Smithsonian Institution, fails to mention Africans or African Americans. Also in 1995 the Minority Rights Group in London brought forth *No Longer Invisible: Afro-Latin Americans Today*, with commissioned essays on all nation-states of Latin America. Reading this work, one is struck by the lack of attention in its chapters to contemporary people of African American descent, as well as the failure to comprehend self-liberation as a dramatic and enduring Afro-American enactment throughout the Americas.

As we complete our writing, we continue to review exciting papers on blackness in Latin American and Caribbean regions by scholars submitting their works to professional academic journals. We hope that our compilation and interpretation of materials in these volumes ignites even more attention to this critical area of African diaspora studies.

This endeavor could not have been carried out over the initial five-month period of selection, research, interpretation, and writing without significant support from the University of Illinois at Urbana-Champaign. The Research Board of this university provided assistance on two previous projects that established the foundation upon which this present project was conceptualized and carried to completion. The previous grants allowed Norman Whitten, with the support of two research assistants, Isabel Pérez and Diego Quiroga, to build a database on black, indigenous, and "mixed" people in northern South America and Central America vis-à-vis nationalist and ethnic-bloc formations and their motivating symbolic agencies. Arlene Torres also participated in this research, with the support of an Illinois Consortium for Educational Opportunity Fellowship.

In October 1990, the Department of Anthropology of the UIUC provided initial funding for copying materials. Subsequently, the Office of the Vice-Chancellor for Academic Affairs provided a shoestring grant for part-time research assistance in fall 1990 and for additional copying. We are grateful to both sources for the necessary funding.

The faculty and staff of the Afro-American Studies and Research Program at the UIUC provided valuable assistance, including reference materials, computer facilities, and technical support. Rosemary M. Stevenson and Vera Mitchell at the Afro-American and Africana Library enthusiastically furnished us with needed reference materials, particularly those pertaining to the life and work of the late Arthur Alfonso Schomburg.

Ingrid Offenbacher, a sophomore in the Campus Honors Program (in 1990), volunteered to work for us without pay as our first assistant. Soon thereafter we employed José Antonio Ruíz, a research assistant in Library Science; later, Jeffrey Vanderziel and Ricardo Herrera provided necessary technical support and assistance. As our work progressed, various colleagues submitted suggestions and recommendations for book selections or for our own reading, and we wish to thank each: Alice A. Deck, Virginia Kerns, Jill Leonard, Consuelo López Springfield, and Inga Treitler. We also thank an anonymous reviewer for Carlson Publishing, Inc., for many helpful suggestions on our introductory essay and several anonymous reviewers for Indiana University Press for valuable suggestions and for the moral encouragement to keep the project alive and to strive to publish the results.

Marvin A. Lewis helped this project in many ways over many years, and his comparative studies of Afro-Hispanic literature offer a parallel view to what we are attempting here in cultural anthropology and critical thought. In 1992, in excerpting a small part of the general introduction for publication in *The Black Americas 1492–1992*, the NACLA Report on the Americas, Mark Fried gave sustained and needed encouragement with regard to directions in analysis and presentation. As the project entered its penultimate phase in 1994, Harriet Stockanes demonstrated her remarkable talents in securing permissions from contributors. The last stage, from 1994 through January 1997, was set by Joan Catapano, with whose guidance and creative encouragement this project is now carried through to completion.

We greatly appreciate the critical readings by Pedro M. Hernández, Jill Leonard, Alejandro Lugo, Marvette Pérez, Diego Quiroga, Dorothea Scott (Sibby) Whitten,

Kevin A. Yelvington, and Marta Zambrano in the preparation of our introductions and the collegial support provided by each of them during various segments of research, writing, and editing.

Finally, we wish to express our deepest gratitude to internationally renowned Puerto Rican artist Arnaldo Roche Rabell for permission to reproduce his painting *Azabache*. In our view, *Azabache* embodies what we have tried to convey ethnographically, the power (*ase*) of blackness in the African diaspora.

Urbana, Illinois
January 1997

PART ONE

# THE BLACK AMERICAS
# AND THE AFRICAN DIASPORA
# IN THE LATE TWENTIETH CENTURY

GENERAL INTRODUCTION

# TO FORGE THE FUTURE IN
# THE FIRES OF THE PAST

## An Interpretive Essay on Racism, Domination, Resistance, and Liberation

*Norman E. Whitten, Jr., and Arlene Torres*

*Soy de carbón*
*y mis pies zapatean por liberarse de la candela de una rumba*
*soy de carbón*
*y el fósforo del bombo enciende mi cintura.*

I am of charcoal
and my feet tap to liberate them from the fire of a rhumba.
I am of charcoal
and the match of the drum ignites my waist.

—Antonio Preciado Bedoya, *Jolgorio: Poemas* (1961);
translation by Marvin Lewis (1983:121)

### Blackness, Culture, Communities, and Regions

The two volumes introduced here present essays on the social systems and dynamics of communities and regions from areas of Latin America and the Caribbean where blackness is significant in human social relations and historical and contemporary discourse. The term *black*, according to Webster, is an adjective derived from Latin constructs meaning, in a literal sense, "sooted, smoke black from flame." Its first meaning in the twentieth century is "opposite to white." The "sooted" (darkened, blackened) concept derives in an earlier (or deeper) etymology from the Latin *flagrare*, "flame," "burn" with a transformation to "flagrant." The concept of blackness, as it is explored in these two volumes, reflects again and again on the ironies of its origins. A theme running through these books is the dialectic between the darkening influences of white domination in the African diaspora and the enlightened cultural, social, and economic creativity produced and reproduced in the eternal fires of black rebellion.

These volumes deal with black culture. But that is to say, at one and the same time, too much and too little. *Culture* is an ambiguous but important term. In Spanish, the feminine article *la*, as in *la cultura*, elevates a concept to something refined, European, civilized. When one goes to an expensive opera in Bogotá, Colombia, for example, wearing "fine" clothes and speaking in a "refined manner," one is participating in *la cultura* and one is *muy culto*, very civilized. Today, in most Latin American societies, to affix *cultura* to blackness without the article *la* is to demean traditions and lifeways to something "vernacular," worthy of study by folklorists but insignificant in the processes leading to higher and higher levels of Latin American civilization.

Still worse, *cultura negra* or *una cultura negra* is something to be viewed as unrefined, inchoate, confused, fragmented, stagnant, and static. One studies *una cultura negra* (a black culture) to find "Africanisms" as scattered traits, retentions, reinterpretations, or syncretisms (e.g., Herskovits 1945, 1948, 1956) that suggest a bit of Africa retained and an enormous amount of culture lost. At the First Congress of Black Culture in the Americas held in Cali, Colombia, in 1977, black people, well aware of these stereotypes and the power of racist symbols, insisted on the article *la*, as *La Cultura Negra*, for black cultures: black, sophisticated, existential, experiential, and adaptable—entwined processes of tradition, history, and modernity moving toward higher and higher levels of black civilization in the Americas. And many (but not all) white scholars there vociferously resisted incorporation of the Spanish article that changes the culture signified from low to high.

Important developments in anthropological, historical, and literary theory in the late twentieth century with regard to the concepts of culture, according to the distinguished historian Daniel J. Boorstin (1983), resonate well with the insistence of Latin American black spokesmen and spokeswomen for *La Cultura Negra*. "'Culture' (from Latin *cultus* for 'worship') originally meant reverential homage. Then it came to describe the practices of cultivating the soil, and later it was extended to the cultivating and refinement of mind and manners. Finally, by the nineteenth century 'culture' had become a name for the intellectual and aesthetic side of civilization" (Boorstin 1983:647).

Black culture, as used in this general introduction, is that which is worthy of reverential homage by black people within their communities, regions, and nation-states; it is also the means by which the cultivation and refinement of mind and manners has been nurtured, developed, and adapted in the African diaspora of the Americas for over 500 years. Survival itself, as in the cultivation of the soil, figuratively and literally, is a critical concept contributing to the sense and reference of "black culture." Black culture is that which is illuminating to black people, and through them to others who will read, reflect, and think about blackness in settings of white domination. It is also reflected in, and contributes to, subsistence and commercial survival strategies and is adaptive to a myriad of structures of domination encountered and overcome in the African diaspora.

To discuss "communities," "regions," or "societies" in the Americas, where blackness is an important criterion for social categorization and interaction, is to plunge into contradictory ideologies of "races" to chart the currents of histories, stereotypes of moral (and immoral) topographies, and deeply held religious and aesthetic feelings. It is to delve into questions of racial separation, racial mixture, and the combined results—in structures of power and domination—of separation and mixture. This process of immersion is a richly rewarding one, as it reveals increasingly insightful and illuminating cultural experiences. These experiences became increasingly expansive, insightful, and revelatory in the wake of the European conquest's quincentennial celebration of 1992.

> *Barrio de los negros*
> *de calles oscuras*
> *preñadas de espantos,*
> *que llevan, que asustan,*
> *que paran los pelos*
> *en noches sin luna*
>
> *Barrio encendido,*
> *de noche y de día,*
> *infierno moreno,*
> *envuelto en las llamas*
> *de son y alegría.*
>
> Barrio of blacks
> of dark streets
> bursting with spooks
> that carry off, that frighten,
> that make hairs stand
> on moonless nights
>
> Inflamed barrio
> by night and by day,
> black hell
> enveloped in the flames
> of rhythm and happiness.
>
> —Preciado Bedoya, *Jolgorio: Poemas* (1961);
> translation by Lewis (1983:121–122)

*Community* was a key term in the original charge to develop these volumes. As nearly as we can see, every sociologist and anthropologist using the term has eschewed definitions offered by others and has developed his or her own definition and perspective according to the nature of the work at hand. The verb *com-*

*mune*, as "the action of communing," and the noun *community*, as "those . . .
practicing community together," are here used in their processual and dynamic
senses, as defined by the *Oxford English Dictionary*. The word *commune* stresses
"to talk together, converse; . . . to hold intimate (mental or spiritual) intercourse"
(see for elaboration Desan 1989 and Honigmann 1959:136–155). A community
may, as in the case of the Pacific Lowlands of Colombia, be a regional culture
self-aware of its ethnic status, or it may be an interaction group participating as
actors and audience in a stick fight outside a bar in Trinidad. The former community may be relatively self-contained in its internal discourses, while the latter
may commune in its collective interest in jazz from the United States and drum
rhythms from Africa.

The purpose of this general introduction is to set forth features that lead to
commonalities and broad divergences of black people in selected regions of the
Western Hemisphere. We seek to present illustrative material on the vitality of
black people in their varied social and cultural settings. The regions to which we
direct our attention share a history. They were first affected by conflict-ridden
Iberian discovery and the initiation of conquest. By the early sixteenth century,
subjugation of the Western Hemisphere had been undertaken by the rapidly
expanding colonial forces of the Spanish, Portuguese, French, Dutch, and English conquerors.

Eventually colonial rule gave way to national forces, but at that point North
America began to impose its economic and cultural will on the area. As a result of
this history, these areas are today characterized by external European and North
American domination and rampant internal underdevelopment. To allow the
reader to appreciate the selection of chapters published in these two volumes, we
first consider key concepts and then present facets of the emergence of the power
potential within what Roger Bastide (1967) referred to as *les amériques noires* and
what Stokely Carmichael (1967) called "the black Americas."

After the editors' introductory chapters, the first volume, which focuses on
Central America and Northern and Western South America, opens with a chapter by Norman E. Whitten, Jr., and Diego Quiroga about black culture of the
West Coast of Colombia and Ecuador. The second volume, on Eastern South
America and the Caribbean, closes with a chapter by Michel S. Laguerre on the
Vodún religion of Haiti and its dual role as an egalitarian liberation ideology for
its practitioners and a hierarchical organization of political control wielded by
the elite. The beginning and end of these books establish a contrast that we see
running through the history of black people with diverse lifeways in the Americas
since the time 500 years ago when the first black-Hispanic slave fled to the interior of the island of Hispaniola to live there with native Taíno Arawakans.

Those two chapters explore in complementary ways the key features that guide
the presentation of materials in the two volumes: blackness, culture, social relations, cultural continuity, radical change, structures of domination, religion, ideology, resistance, and creativity. Significantly, all the authors presented here must

somehow cope with powerful ideologies of "race" in modern, underdeveloping nation-states and with the inner essence of "being black" within aggregates of New World peoples who may be classed as Negro, mulatto, *negro, zambo, moreno, trigueño, mulato, pardo, negre, preto, cafuço, noire,* or *nengre,* or who self-identify by these or cognate terms.

### Nationalism, Ethnic-Bloc Formation, and Ideologies of Racial Cultures

In our exploration, let us begin with the crucial concept of *nationalism.* This word refers to the identity of the majority of people within a nation-state with the republic, nation, or national society as the primary reference group. A nation-state must, above all else, retain all power of sovereignty and all power of territoriality. Ideologies of nationalism are located within the cultural space of nation-state control. In Spanish-speaking, Portuguese-speaking, and French-speaking republics in the 1990s we find two complementary and one competing nationalist ideology of racial culture, often denoted by one of these symbols: racial mixture, Indianism, or blackness. We present each of them briefly, by reference to the terms in the language with which they are most commonly associated.

*Mestizaje,* the ideology of racial intermingling, is an explicit master symbol in all Latin American countries. Perhaps ironically, we take the concept of *Indianism* to be a nationalist dimension of *mestizaje. Indigenismo* is a dual concept reflecting, on the one hand, a search for the creative dimensions of nationalism through the symbolism of an indigenous past and, on the other hand, a social-political-literary symbol that conveys the mood of remorse over the living conditions of contemporary "acculturated Indians." The ideology of *mestizaje* embraces both senses of *indigenismo* (e.g., Bourricaud 1962; Pitt-Rivers 1967, 1973; Tomoeda and Millones 1992). Indeed, *indigenismo* may be thought of as a key support for the exclusion of contemporary native peoples from nation-state affairs. A third component of *mestizaje* is *blanqueamiento,* which means "whitening." We discuss this later because it is not usually an explicit component of nationalist ideology.

At the other end of the spectrum is *négritude,* a concept that denotes the positive features of blackness among people classed as, or self-identifying as, "black." This term was brought into French literary being in 1947 by the black Martiniquan poet Aimé Césaire (Coulthard 1962:58). It provides a single term by which to assert the positive power inherent in, and the positive aesthetic forces of, "blackness," leaving many avenues open for the definition of what and who is, and what and who is not, to be considered "black." Within the Americas, only Haiti has adopted an explicit nationalist ideology of *négritude,* and the literary and artistic roots of this concept provide the basis for Césaire's (and for others', such as Frantz Fanon's) literary and political creativity (Coulthard 1962:58–70).

Nationalist ideologies develop not only symbols of internal "oneness" based on concepts of "racial classification," but also ideas of oppositions using the criterion of "cultural exaggeration" as discussed by James Boon (1982). We submit that throughout the New World, the *mestizaje–négritude* contrast represents a symbolic opposition reflecting cultural exaggeration of ideologically conjoined social constructs of race, civilization, nationalist patrimony, and social movement. We develop and illustrate this argument throughout this general introduction.

Thus far we have been discussing nationalism and the dominant racialist ideological contrasts that obtain during processes of nationalist consolidation. A nation-state is also often characterized during the consolidation of its developing nationalism by what Clifford Geertz (1973:234–310) calls *ethnic-bloc formation*. An ethnic bloc constitutes a conscious reference group for those who share recurrent processes of self-identification. Ethnic blocs may be based on criteria such as common residence, language, tradition, and custom. Indeed, the bases for bloc identity may slip and slide around the criteria themselves, as the bloc itself becomes increasingly strong.

The concept *bloc* is taken from politics (as in a political bloc); whatever its bases, the power of identity and the power of representation are crucial. Such powers come into being when ethnic exclusion takes place, as when indigenous people or black people are ethnically disfranchised from full participation in the dominant society.

Other powers within ethnic blocs derive from a collective, inner sense of a oneness of a people, in contradistinction to nationalist racialist hegemony. The powers are related, but the nature of such a dynamic relationship requires careful empirical study. Whitten (1985), following Geertz (1973) and Stutzman (1981), has argued that ethnic-bloc formation is a process of contra-nationalism and that the symbolic processes of ethnic-bloc formation are similar to, or the same as, those identified in processes of nationalist consolidation. Ethnic exclusion from nationalist consolidation and ethnic perspectives and contra-nationalism from ethnic and nationalist perspectives are related in multiple manners, which are quite specific in numerous instances. But the relationships in all cases ramify through the political-economic fabric of any social order. Ethnic-bloc formation, in other words, is as international in scope as it is local in origin.

In Hispanic-American, Gallic-American, Luso-American, Anglo-American, and Creole-American communities and regions, we anticipate that black-based ethnic-bloc formations will use the ideology of *négritude* and, in so doing, will be perceived as a threat to nationalist sovereignty and nationalist territoriality.

In the processes of ethnic-bloc formation in the Americas, we can identify three master symbols of ideology, the latter two of which are potentially complementary: phenotypical, cultural, or ethnic lightening (or whitening); black liberation; and indigenous autodetermination. Again, as in nationalist ideology, we discuss these in the language in which each is most commonly associated.

*Blanqueamiento* refers to the processes of becoming increasingly acceptable to those classified and self-identified as "white." This is an ethnic movement—coterminous with socioeconomic advancement governed by the ideology of "development"—that depends upon socioeconomic and political assistance and loans from the developed (i.e., highly industrialized, highly energy-dependent) countries. Although not often recognized as such, the ideology of "whitening" is an unconscious psychological process accompanying the economic state of underdevelopment in the twentieth century. *Blanqueamiento* essentially accepts the implicit hegemonic rhetoric of the United States with regard to "white supremacy" and often blames those people classed as black and indigenous for the worsening state of the nation.

Ethnic or cultural "lightening" may occur as an ideological feature among people self-identifying as "black." One example would be nineteenth-century Haitian literary circles wherein the positive attributes of blackness (via Egypt and the Sudan) were juxtaposed to French civilization. *Blanqueamiento*, an enduring ethnic-bloc complement to the nationalist ideology of *mestizaje*, is an ephemeral feature of enduring *négritude*. To the extent that people in the Americas accept, however implicitly, northern Anglo-American standards of whiteness as attached to "developmental potential," the phenomenon of hegemony may be said to exist.

*Négritude* (*négritud* in Spanish) may express the same sets of meanings in ethnic-bloc rhetoric that it does in nationalist rhetoric. Indeed, the Haitian ethnologist Jean Price-Mars, during the United States occupation of Haiti from 1915 to 1934, conscientiously turned to the voices of Haitians for concepts of blackness, Africanness, and being Haitian. He published the results of his extended ethnographic studies in 1928 as *Ainsi parla l'oncle*. Price-Mars sought to liberate nationalist ideology from its European francophonic bases in "whitening," where the powerful, literate elite of Haiti saw themselves as mulatto (somewhat analogous to *mestizo*). It is worth pausing here to reflect on the vision of Price-Mars as described by G. R. Coulthard (1962:64):

> Price-Mars urged his compatriots to look into their folklore—into the stories, legends, proverbs, religious practices, music and dancing of the Haitian people which had been ignored or scorned during the "French" nineteenth century. He recommends the study of African civilizations and of African elements in Haitian folklore, pointing out that the mystique of Africa is still very much alive in Haitian folklore, full of reference to "Guinée." He lashes out savagely at the racial prejudices of the Haitian *élite*, its snobbish worship of everything French or foreign, its attempts at racial and cultural dissociation from the people.

From the writing of Price-Mars onward, *négritude* and its implicit and explicit cognates must be considered to have two senses: in their nationalist sense they may or may not reflect a process of "lightening," but in their ethnic-bloc sense they are profoundly populist and rejecting of nonblackness as a criterion for sophisticated self-awareness (see especially Trouillot 1990:124–136).

*Autodeterminación indígena* is the assertion that indigenous people who were deposed and disfranchised by the European conquest of the Americas must speak to New World nation-states in modern, indigenous ways which they themselves will determine. It is a proclamation of indigenous sovereignty and territoriality. This symbol of liberation specifically looks to contemporary indigenous cultures in multiple communities and societies across the Americas. It rejects the literary-based ideological component of *indigenismo* just as early twentieth century ethnographers such as Price-Mars in Haiti and Fernando Ortiz in Cuba turned away from elite academician definitions of national culture and sought out the voices of the culturally rich black poor in both urban and rural areas. Today indigenous self-determination is appealing to black people in many areas. It would seem that *négritude* and *autodeterminación indígena* are complementary constructs of ethnic-bloc ideology, both of which are contrary to *mestizaje* as nationalist ideology and ethnic-bloc ideology.

In the first chapter of the first volume and the last chapter of the second volume, the authors address the issues of blackness within three nation-states characterized by dominant, articulate ideologies of "race": *mestizaje* in Ecuador and *négritude* in Haiti. In the nonanglophonic world today, Ecuador and Haiti constitute polar nationalist opposites. In the former, the colonial dream of overcoming the barriers of racial classification linked to economic opportunities became transformed into a nationalist, democratic ideology of "racial mixture." In the latter, blackness inundated a formative New World gene pool to create the first self-liberated democratic island republic in the Americas with collective, self-conscious roots in its African and European past.

## Moral Ordering of Racialist Topography

Let us explore for a moment how these nationalist and ethnic-bloc ideologies play out in the Caribbean, Central America, and northern and western South America. We begin with one country in which *négritude* is explicitly nationalist.

Haiti has its sovereign locus on the western portion of the island of Hispaniola (named Española in 1492 by Columbus). Hispaniola is the island where Columbus established his first colony to carry on the work of the Kingdom of Castile. The island at that time was inhabited by indigenous Arawakan-speaking people, the Taíno, but became increasingly black in the interior and western region and "mixed" on the east coast as self-liberated Africans and Spaniards and their mixed progenies mingled genetically with one another and with indigenous people (Moya Pons 1986a, 1986b; Price 1979:419). Haiti is a black republic that achieved its formal independence from France in 1804. Its name was immediately changed from that of the slaveholders, Saint Domingue, to the Arawakan word for "mountains" (*haiti*), home of the native Taíno before 1492 and haven of indigenous, black, and "mixed" maroons thereafter. (Maroons were people who had escaped from the domination of European colonizers.) The eastern portion of Hispaniola became the nation of the Dominican Republic.

Blackness in Haitian ideology constitutes the sovereign and territorial locus of the inner power of its nationalism. That contrasts with the *mestizaje* ideology of the liberated lands of the northern Andes and the Spanish Main, Gran Colombia (which became Ecuador, Colombia [which included Panama until 1903], and Venezuela in 1830).

Black Haiti, the nation, looks out toward Cuba's Oriente region across the Windward Passage to the west. It was in this black region of Cuba where Fidel Castro began to form his revolutionary movement and from which he launched it in 1956 in the Sierra Maestra mountains. On March 25, 1959, Castro announced that "racial discrimination in Cuba was 'possibly the most difficult of all the problems that we have to confront' " (Rout 1976:308).

Adjoining Haiti on the east is the Dominican Republic. Santo Domingo, the first Spanish settlement in the Americas, is its capital. This section of Hispaniola did not achieve independence until 1844.

> The 1844 independence movement stressed the European, Catholic, "civilized" culture of the Dominicans over against the African and "barbarous" Haitians, and on these grounds appealed for sympathy and support to the United States and to European nations. Racialism has, in fact, played a significant part in relations between the two countries, as many Dominican historians acknowledge. (Collier, Blackmore, and Skidmore 1985:284)

Four hundred miles south of Haiti lie Venezuela and Colombia, lands also governed by *mestizaje* ideology. But in the coastal areas of Colombia and Venezuela the people are predominantly black. In the wars of liberation against European colonialism (between 1813 and 1822) led by Simón Bolívar, a Venezuelan, black troops from Haiti were used in the overthrow of colonial governments in Venezuela, Colombia, and Ecuador. As the creole nationalist spirits rose, so too did ethnic-bloc unity among black aggregates who rebelled against masters and oppressors, marched with Bolívar, then continued their struggles internally in these three nations (Guss and Waxer 1994).

Racialist ideologies influencing the complementary processes of nationalism and ethnic-bloc formation became intertwined historically in what was once the Republic of Gran Colombia, constituted of territory from the Orinoco River to the Pacific coast, and from what is now northern Peru to Panama. In literary and historical treatises on Simón Bolívar, his possible black ancestry as evidenced by his "mulatto blood" is mentioned from time to time. Whereas in Haiti this was and is viewed as a positive trait, it became a negative one in Gran Colombia.

One senses an uneasiness of white and mestizo biographers about the relationship of a mulatto as descendant of blackness and *mestizaje* as legitimate "mixture." There is an anticipated paradox to this unease, because Bolívar himself feared the worst for elite whites and mixed creoles if the energies residing in black cultures were unleashed (Wright 1990:27–29). Indeed, when black soldiers of liberation began to rally around one of his black Haitian generals, he allegedly had the general shot.

Cuba has long been the setting for dynamic African American ethnic-bloc solidarity based upon extant social relationships symbolized by African languages (especially Lucumí [Yoruba]) and religious brotherhoods such as Santería (see, e.g. Ortiz 1975b, 1975c, 1986; Cabrera 1969a, 1969b, 1970b; Brandon 1993). We are not clear on such relationships in the 1990s (compare, e.g., Moore 1988 with Pérez Sarduy 1990; Brandon 1993).

We know that black ethnic blocs in many parts of Venezuela, Colombia, and Ecuador are taking on the powerful rhetoric of *négritud* in opposition to that of nationalist *mestizaje*. In some areas of Colombia (e.g., the Department [state] of Chocó) and Ecuador (e.g., in Esmeraldas and Carchi Provinces), those developing an ethnic-bloc ideology of *négritud* and those developing an ethnic-bloc ideology of *autodeterminación indígena* are discussing alliances between black and indigenous people in opposition to the *mestizaje-blanco* barrier found in political-economic affairs. And the Chocó state formally petitioned the government of Colombia in 1989 to grant it the legal status of an "indigenous region" (*comunidad indígena*).

In Central America, especially Honduras and Nicaragua, one finds the phenomenon of the merger of indigenous and black ethnic populations. People such as the Garífuna, for example, who speak creolized Arawakan (the language of ancient Hispaniola, the Greater Antilles, and parts of the Guianas), Spanish, and English, are usually identified as Afro-American. For another example, the Miskito (from the English word *musket*) of Nicaragua and Honduras may fiercely identify as indigenous people seeking indigenous self-determination, but they are classed in Nicaragua as "indigenous" when they appear "Indian" to the nationalists and "ethnic" when they resemble the Anglo-Caribbean-Nicaraguan black people in the eyes of the dominant classifiers.

*Négritude* is not generally respected in images held of Haiti by white and *mestizo* people living in the Spanish Caribbean and the adjacent Spanish Main and down the Andes in Ecuador, Peru, and Bolivia. We must stress that the negative racialist image of Haiti is confined to those self-identifying in a nationalist manner with various doctrines of *mestizaje* that have the implicit or explicit facet of *blanqueamiento*. Nor does the image of Haiti enjoy a positive ideological image in the dominant sectors of Anglo-Caribbean politics.

The concept of Haiti as a nation within the popular culture of these regions by those self-identifying as "white" or "light" includes the idea of impoverishment to the point of creating an island of infrahumans. It also contains the imagery of revolts out of control, of a revolution not completed that could someday overwhelm the democracies of mainland South America. The imagery of black Haiti held by mainland South American whites (*mestizos*) suggests an undesirable power of blackness within *mestizaje* that is to be feared and controlled. It suggests a racialist revulsion and spiritual awe of latent and nascent power that survived the transformation from distinct gene pools into a *mestizo* "cosmic race" (*raza cósmica* Vasconcelos 1925).

Phenotypical and cultural categories within Haiti—the nation-state constituted ethnically by an ideology of descent from Africans who undertook the first act of self-liberation by active black-nationalist revolution in the Americas—are also prey to the ideological specter of "lightening" in a political-economic sense. According to Laguerre (e.g., 1976, 1982a), such lightening in stereotypic features has combined with political-economic power in a modern system where sets of urban mulatto elite have separated themselves from the rural black masses of poor people. Moreover, in downtown Port-au-Prince, capital of the Republic of Haiti, a "black ghetto" (Belair) has come into being through the historical processes of flow of power away from the black poor.

> The term ghetto refers to a sociological and economic phenomenon. Ghetto designates an urban district within which residents socially bound to each other are kept as a group in a marginal political, economic, and sometimes geographic position. I see the evolution of Belair as a satellite community tied to and largely dependent upon the development of the city itself, which, in turn, was a satellite of France during the colonial period (1625–1791) and is now more or less a satellite of the United States. (Laguerre 1976:26; for excellent discussions of the light elite–black yeoman distinctions in Haiti, see, e.g., Price-Mars 1928, Leyburn 1941, Coulthard 1962, and Mintz 1966)

The phenomenon of "lightening" is well known in Venezuela, Colombia, and Ecuador, where it is called *blanqueamiento*, or "whitening." Those pursuing a course of becoming "whiter" (people classed as *mestizo*, mixed, usually refer to themselves as *blanco*, white) refer to their "whiteness" in "cultural" terms as becoming more civilized and "conscious" than their "darker" black and indigenous national congeners. They classify some individuals, groups, and aggregates as *negro* (black), or *negreado* (darkened, blackened), implying lack of civilization and lack of culture—people without consciousness (*a los que les falta consciencia*) and hence unself-reflective and stupid. Those classed as *indio* (Indian) are regarded in the same manner.

Processes of pernicious pluralism activate and perpetuate the clash of three dynamic, paradigmatic symbols of nationalism as manifest in *mestizaje, indigenismo,* and *blanqueamiento,* on one side of the nationalist–ethnic-bloc ideological polarity. The same processes animate two vehicles of ethnic-bloc liberation—*négritud[e]* and *autodeterminación indígena*—on the other side. By "paradigmatic" here we mean that the entire complex is evoked—however implicit the evocation may be in a given text or discourse—when any one of these master symbols on either side of the nationalist–ethnic-bloc polarity is brought into discursive consciousness.

*Mestizaje* is a powerful force of exclusion of both black and indigenous aggre-gates in the Americas in the late twentieth century (see, e.g., Rout 1976; Stutzman 1981; Whitten 1985, 1986a; Friedemann 1984; Wade 1993). This exclusion mechanism is likely to continue to generate its polar opposite: black and indige-nous awareness of exclusion and a continuous struggle for ethnic powers.

These processes are especially evident in the United States territory of Puerto Rico, an island just east of the Dominican Republic. This island is the last vestige of United States colonialism in the Caribbean. Spain ceded Puerto Rico, as well as the Philippines and Guam, to the United States at the Treaty of Paris on De-cember 10, 1898, following the Spanish-American War (waged by the United States against the Spanish in Cuba and Puerto Rico in the Caribbean). In this same treaty Cuba gained its status as an independent nation-state.

In the fall of 1993 the residents of Puerto Rico voted in a nonbinding plebiscite to maintain the island's commonwealth status. On the island itself, *puertorri-queños* clearly regard their territory as a *nación* and they are as "nationalist" about their identity as are Colombians, Ecuadorians, Venezuelans, Jamaicans, Cubans, or Haitians.

Historically, the emergence of nationalist Puerto Rico as a creole colony under Spanish rule embraced the ideology of *mestizaje*. Within this ideology the *jíbaro* came to symbolize the Puerto Rican peasant, the bearer of a nascent Puerto Rican identity and culture that emphasizes a primary Spanish-indigenous heri-tage. In this mixture the sense of rural Spanish is privileged over indigenous de-scent. Although, in many areas, *jíbaros* vary in phenotype from brown to black, there is little if any "national" emphasis on the African component of Puerto Rican heritage in the conceptualization of the rural population or its significant black population.

The 1898 invasion of Puerto Rico by U.S. troops and the events thereafter give impetus there to the nationalist ideology of *mestizaje* and especially to the dimen-sion of *blanqueamiento*. This ideology was further reinforced by the view that the paternalist social order of the plantation contributed to the social integration of racial aggregates (Quintero-Rivera 1987). More than a hundred years later these ideological and literary interpretations of Puerto Rico's ethnic past and present heritage are being challenged by black urban and rural Puerto Ricans who have, since the formation of maroon groupings on the island, maintained their auton-omy. It is clear that Puerto Rico, while not a nation-state, is nonetheless charac-terized by a nationalist ideology of *mestizaje*, on the one hand, and the formation of black ethnic blocs, on the other.

Historically, social unities have developed in Puerto Rico between rural ma-roons and the urban mulatto populations. This has resulted in the creation of black ethnic blocs that have constantly redefined the Puerto Rican national iden-tity by invoking series of ascriptions attached to "blackness." Spokesmen and spokeswomen for these blocs draw on dimensions of *mestizaje* or *négritud* (or both) depending upon the social context of racialist discourse. Today, Puerto Rican migration to the mainland United States and return migration from the mainland to the island have intensified the multifaceted discourse as features of the categorization of Puerto Ricans as "minorities" and as "people of color" enter the *mestizaje–négritud* dialogue.

### The African Diaspora

The sociologist Ruth Simms Hamilton and her associates at Michigan State University, who have initiated long-range, sustained research on the African diaspora with funding from the Ford Foundation, define this subject as follows:

> the African diaspora represents a type of social grouping characterized by a historical patterning of particular social relationships and experiences. As a social formation, it is conceptualized as a global aggregate of actors and subpopulations, differentiated in social and geographical space, yet exhibiting a commonality based on historical factors, conditioned by and within the world ordering system. Among characteristics that distinguished the diaspora as a global formation from other socially differentiated groups are the following shared historical experiences: *Migration and Geo-Social Displacement: The Circularity of a People;* . . . *Social Oppression: Relationships of Domination and Subordination;* . . . *Endurance, Resistance, and Struggle: Cultural and Political Action.* (Simms Hamilton 1990:18)

There is a myth, widely held in the United States and widely printed in history books, about the progress of the African diaspora in the New World. According to this myth, Africans were first brought to the southern United States as slaves. There they lived in submission for a long time, until they were eventually liberated by white people of the North. In this myth the U.S. congressional enactment of the Fugitive Slave Law of 1850 is never mentioned.

The transformation of this myth into historical fact is well illustrated in the words of Lerone Bennett, Jr. (1987 [1962]:30): "The captain [of the Dutch slave ship] 'ptended,' John Rolfe noted, that he was in great need of food; he offered to exchange his human cargo for 'victualle.' The deal was arranged. Antony, Isabella, Pedro, and 17 other Africans stepped ashore in August 1619. *The history of the Negro in America began*" (emphasis added). The fact is that self-liberation by black people began 117 years prior to the day when that Dutch slaver brought twenty "negars" to Jamestown, Virginia. Over a century of black freedom had expanded the African diaspora throughout the Caribbean and Latin America (including the Pacific regions) and into what is now the continental United States before the date inscribed in this racialist American legend of origin. We turn now to blackness at earlier dates to understand more of the African diaspora in the Americas.

Whether black Africans or black Iberians reached the New World with Columbus on either of his first two voyages is not clear; they probably did not (Schomburg 1928:93, Alegría 1985:59). Nor is it clear whether Africans reached the New World prior to Columbus. We do know, however, that when serious European settlement began on the island of Hispaniola, African diaspora relations began in an immediate moment of self-liberation:

> With the fleet of Governor Ovando, bound for Hispaniola in 1502 to reinvigorate the faltering colony that Columbus had left behind the previous year, sailed "a few Negroes . . . brought out by their masters." (Parry and Sherlock 1965:16)

> Among them was the first Afro-American maroon, an anonymous slave who "escaped to the Indians" [Taíno Arawakans] in the mountainous interior soon after setting foot in the New World. (Guillot 1961:77, from R. Price 1979:1)

In western Hispaniola, where the French established colonial Saint Domingue, and in the interior of the Spanish territory that eventually became the Dominican Republic, *marronage* sustained a liberation atmosphere: "From the first years of slavery on the Island, Indians and [black] slaves had run away to inaccessible mountains, and throughout the colonial period, every mountain in Haiti was used at one time or another by fugitive slaves" (Laguerre 1989:41).

The Puerto Rican historian Jalil Sued Badillo (Sued Badillo and López Cantos 1986:175–189) documents the processes of slavery, self-liberation (*cimarronaje*), and indigenous and black rebellion and the consequences for people in Europe, Africa, and the New World in meticulous detail in *Puerto Rico Negro* (Black Puerto Rico). He documents the first active indigenous and black revolution in 1514 on the island of Puerto Rico. In this revolt two Taíno Arawakan chiefs (*caciques*) and their people allied with black (*ladino*) rebels to fight actively against the governmental representatives of the Spanish Crown. This was the beginning of the maroon in Puerto Rico.

Sued Badillo also documents a second major uprising in 1531 involving the enslaved black population. This represented a greater threat to the colonizers because the number of "blacks" had increased, while the "white" population had decreased. He argues (Sued Badillo and López Cantos 1986:187) that relatively little attention has been paid to these initial uprisings because the Spanish conquerors publicly supported the capture of "cannibals" (including Arawakans) as substitutes for costly African slaves. The "Caribs" were regarded as captives of "just wars" (Palencia-Roth 1993), whereas black slaves were regarded as "inferior beings." In retaliation for black Puerto Rican uprisings, the Church and Crown accused freed and enslaved black men and women of sorcery and witchcraft. In 1591 four enslaved women were hanged and burned in the outskirts of San Juan (Sued Badillo and López Cantos 1986: 151–154).

In 1522, black people revolted in Santo Domingo, the major city of Hispaniola: "Some forty slaves working at the sugar mill on the plantation of the governor, Admiral Diego Columbus (a son of the explorer), conspired with other blacks working on nearby establishments" (Rout 1976:104; see also 21 ff.). Thereafter, revolt was ubiquitous in the Caribbean and mainland South and Central America.

Wherever slavery existed, self-liberation began, and in many areas ethnic blocs of rebellious black people maintained their own sovereignty and territoriality for a century or more (see Barnet 1966; Baralt et al. 1990; R. Price 1979, 1983, 1990; Pérez de la Riva 1946, 1952, 1979; Whitten 1986 [1974]; Friedemann and Arocha 1986; Carvalho Neto 1965; Kent 1979).

Writing about Haiti, Laguerre (1989:39–40) says:

> Marronage was a central fact in the life of the colony, not only because of maroon military power and the number of slaves who constantly joined them, but also because of the danger inherent in expeditions to destroy revolutionary centers of these fugitive slaves. Any study centered upon the slaves must also consider this phenomenon of marronage; for wherever there were slaves, there were also maroons. . . . Living in free camps or on the fringes of port cities, they were a model for the slaves to imitate, embodying the desires of most of the slaves. What the slaves used to say in *sotto voce* on the plantations, they were able to say aloud in the maroon settlements.

Most of the prominent black areas of eastern and northern South America, Central America, and the Caribbean derive directly from creative processes of rebellion, self-liberation, and sovereign territoriality that were initiated and sustained by African American people. And these areas are many. They include various regions of Brazil; the *yungas* of Bolivia; the northwest coast of Ecuador; the Pacific and Atlantic coasts and Cauca Valley of Colombia; the Venezuelan *llanos* (plains) and northern coastal crescent; the interior of the Guianas; the Darién, coasts, and interior of Panama; the Mosquitia of Honduras and Nicaragua; the west coast of Guatemala, Belize, Honduras, and Nicaragua; the mountains of Haiti and the Dominican Republic; the Jamaican Blue Mountains and Red Hills regions; the Cuban Oriente region. This list is by no means exhaustive. The people of these areas have, over the years, affected the dominant colonial, republican, and nation-state systems in a variety of ways.

Although few scholars in the twentieth century have taken time to document such information (notable exceptions include Baralt et al. 1990, Cabrera 1970a, Arrázola 1970, Friedemann and Cross 1979, Ortiz 1986, R. Price 1983), self-liberation—with its awful manifestations of war, pestilence, and death—are thoroughly embedded in the dynamic historicities of African American people hemisphere-wide.

Among the Saramaka people of Suriname, for example, this information is part of a historical complex called First-Time (R. Price 1983). First-Time (*fési-tén*), refers to the time when the ancestors heard the guns of war. Saramakan speaker Tebíni, in 1976, told the ethnographer-historian Richard Price:

> Those people who didn't live to see the Peace, they must not be jealous. Their hearts must not be angry. There is no help for it. When the time is right, we shall get still more freedom. Let them not look at what they have missed. Let us and

them be on one side together, those First-Time people! It is to them we are speaking. (R. Price 1983: epigraph)

According to R. Price (1983:epigraph), who has done extensive historical work in
European and other archives, Tebíni was quoting words "first spoken in 1762."

But the African diaspora did not, as so many suppose, originate in the New
World; it began in North Africa and the circum-Mediterranean, in Europe, and
in Asia. We do not know how long black people had been traveling there or when
the first slaves were brought there. We do know that in 711, as the Muslim conquest of Iberia began, black soldiers were present in the Islamic forces. Farther
north, according to the historian Folarin Shyllon (1982:171), "Irish records suggest that during a Viking raid on Spain and North Africa in 862, a number of
Africans were captured and some carried to Dublin, where they were known as
'blue men.' " In the tenth century, black African fighters were a significant part
of the conquering army of North African Moors.

By the eleventh and twelfth centuries (and on into the sixteenth), images of
black Africans were to be found in monumental art and architecture, Christian
iconography, heraldic shields, and other aesthetic forms throughout Western
Europe (Devisse and Mollat 1979, Devisse 1979). Indeed, imagery of Africans is
pervasive in Europe between the fourth and fourteenth centuries (Devisse
1979:35; Courtés 1979). Representations of Africans in many postures and guises
occur in connection with religious ideology involving the land of Ethiopia, the
coming of the Magi, the realm and person of Prester John, the Queen of Sheba,
Saint Maurice, and the meaning of Old Testament legendary histories and
prophecies about darkness and light.

By the middle to late fifteenth century, the religious imagery of blacks in
Europe acquiesces to the power politics of the Iberian kingdoms. The African
American historian Leslie Rout is quite clear about the European correspondences that developed as Iberians recognized an inversion of imagery—black African warriors to be feared, on the one side, and black Africans as beings to be
conquered and enslaved, on the other:

> During the centuries of bitter struggle, the black African had become known to
> the Christians essentially as a soldier fighting for the Moors or as a slave laborer.
> The Portuguese, therefore, looked upon blacks as the logical answer to their prob-
> lems of a cheap source of labor after 1250, and as early as 1258 Moorish traders
> appeared at fairs at Guimaraes (Northern Portugal) offering sub-Saharan Africans
> for sale. (Rout 1976:4)

Rout is also clear about Hispanic views of black people during the period of the
Christian reconquest of Iberian territory and the subsequent expulsion of Moors,
Jews, and non-Christian blacks, which was completed between 1492 and 1502:
"Ultimately, to the white Christians of Spain, the captive from *Negrería* and/or

his *ladino* descendant were believed to be loyal, superstitious, lighthearted, of low mentality, and distinctly in need of white supervision" (Rout 1976:21–22). Rout defines *Negrería* as "the totality of western Africa occupied by black people" (335, note 80).

With the perfection of the lateen sail and other innovations such as the single rudder and caravel-designed vessel, movement farther and farther down the coast of Africa (and eventually around the Cape; see, e.g., Boorstin 1983:221) and back was made possible for Iberian (mostly Portuguese) explorers and traders.

As soon as Europeans were able to travel back to Iberia with relative ease from their ventures to the west coast ports of black Africa, the Atlantic traffic in African slavery (the ships bringing slaves were called *negreros*, "black bringers") began in earnest and the African diaspora expanded exponentially. "Between 1441 and 1550, more than half of the slaves extracted from the coast of West Africa were destined for the labor market in Europe, particularly the Iberian peninsula, or for use in the emergent plantation economies of the Atlantic islands" (Collier, Blackmore, and Skidmore 1985:138; see also Terborg-Penn 1986, Forbes 1993, Russell-Wood 1995; and see Alegría 1985:62 for an illustration of a sixteenth-century lateen-rigged slave ship in the Caribbean).

The same innovations—nurtured by the Portuguese planner known as Prince Henry the Navigator—that allowed the small, sturdy caravels to return to Iberia from West Africa also helped ships to return to Europe after traversing the Atlantic (using especially the remarkable route discovered and charted by Columbus), and, more important, to tack through islands and river channels and around reefs in Europe's New World. The African diaspora of this New World is a circum-Atlantic phenomenon that rapidly reached the Pacific region of northern South America, Central America, and Mexico.

The first slaves of Europeans in the Americas were not black people of African descent but native Americans, definitely Arawakan and possibly Cariban. Columbus brought them to Iberia on his first two voyages, and by his order many were sold into slavery. The fate of at least some of these native Americans was to become enslaved on the Canary Islands, where sugar was rapidly becoming a cash crop and where the reconquest by Iberian Christianity was nearing completion.

Two key Old World words have a great significance in the African diaspora of the circum-Atlantic as manifest in Spanish classificatory power: *ladino* and *bozal*. A *ladino* in the sixteenth century was someone not originally Christian (e.g., Jewish-Hispanic, indigenous-Hispanic), and/or non-Moorish Hispanic but not white. Black *ladinos* were Africans or African-descended people who became Hispanicized and accepted (or paid lip service to) Christianity. Also known as *negros latinos* or *negros Castilla* (Alegría 1985:60), they could be free or slave, rich or poor, but they were bound to serve whites. *Bozales* were blacks "fresh from Africa." They were slaves in the sense of being "muzzled," or tethered by a "halter." From the concept of the *ladino/bozal* opposition came the opposition of "mulatto/slave," which continues to permeate the literature in Brazil, Cuba, and

Haiti, and elsewhere. "Mulatto" may often be read as "free black" as well as "lightened black." In some areas of Latin America and the Caribbean, however, it may mean "darkened white" or just plain "darkened."

*Mulatto* (French *mulâtre*) comes from the Spanish and Portuguese *mulato*, which itself comes from "mule," progeny "mixed" by the crossing of a horse and a donkey. According to the *Oxford Universal Dictionary*, the highly uncomplimentary definition is this: "One who is the offspring of a European and a Negro; hence any half-breed resembling a mulatto." With the abolishment of slavery in the middle to late nineteenth century, the terminology transformed to "mulatto/ black" in black regions, and "white/mulatto" in regions dominated by lighter phenotypes. This transformation was facilitated in several areas (e.g., Nicaragua, Haiti, and Puerto Rico) by extended occupation by United States troops.

A popular saying of white-*mestizo* intellects in categorizing the masses of their nations in Ecuador and Peru is this: "Quien no tiene de inga, tiene de mandinga (whoever is not of [the] Inca is of [the] Mandinga)." A variant of this is "Lo que no tiene de inga tiene de mandinga (that which is not of [the] Inca is of [the] Mandinga)." The latter refers to that which is in the blood (e.g., Hurtado 1980:325). Such figures of speech—and there are many more—"halfbreedize" in a pejorative manner the darkening of national histories. For but one salient example, in the Hispanic Caribbean the word *dinga* (for Dinka) is substituted for the Andean *inga*. Isabelo Zenón Cruz (1975:256) offers the phrase "el que no tiene dinga, tiene de mandinga" as one of many that assert a universal "black blood" for people of color. Another phrase loaded with stigma is "¿y tu abuela dónde está? (and your grandmother, where is she?)," which means "you may not look black, but [the speaker knows] you descend from blackness." Arlene Torres pursues the meanings of this and cognate tropes in volume II. Writing of this process in the Chincha and Cañete valleys of Peru, the French historian and sociologist Denys Cuche (1981) has a section of his chapter on "métissage et discrimination raciale" (miscegenation and racial discrimination) on the subject of the "métis négroïde" (the black-like mixed person).

From the beginning of the African diaspora in Europe and the Americas, "whitening" and "darkening" have been dual symbolic processes of classification and identity. Dominant though it may be in nationalist rhetoric in Hispanic nation-states, *mestizaje* is not a positive ideological feature in communities and regions where people classed as *negro* (black) reside. In such communities, from a nationalist (but not ethnic-bloc) perspective, lightness as superior to darkness is the general classificatory feature, however complex the issues of lightness and darkness may be. In fact, in many regions and communities inhabited by black people, the word *mestizo* may refer to "black blood" (meaning "darkened"—*negreado*) with none of the connotations of "lightening" implied. This, by the way, is the meaning of the Portuguese term *mestiço* ("darkening" or "darkened") in many parts of Brazil and the French *métissage* in parts of the francophonic

Caribbean. The process of darkening is called *mulatización* ("mulattoization") in Cuban communities in Cuba and Miami.

Historically, a key feature in the development of African diaspora awareness in the Americas has been self-liberation, called *cimarronaje* (run-awayism) in Spanish, *marronage* (same meaning) in French. These concepts come from the New World Spanish word *cimarrón*, influenced by Arawakan (Price and Price 1993), which is also the derivation of the English term *maroon* and the French term *marrón*. Self-liberation brings with it a sense of belonging, of New World identity (e.g., Mintz and Price 1976, Price 1983, Laguerre 1989). It may or may not include a sense of being African; histories and historicities of black people in the Americas vary considerably with regard to a sense of dispersal from a common African homeland.

Today, from their own perspectives over at least the past two centuries, the self-identifying term for a full participant in black culture in the Department of Chocó, Colombia, is *libre* (free). Farther south, in the Pacific Lowlands of Colombia and Ecuador, black people regard the coastal and riverine sectors of this tropical rain forest as their original homeland. There, they say, their ancestors seized their freedom, asserted their culture, and made the productive land "theirs." Africa and the "congos," they say, are far to the north—"down the coast"—beyond the Panamanian Darién, in an undesirable location. Until very recently, black people, who constitute 90 percent or more of the population of the Pacific Lowlands of Panama, Colombia, and Ecuador, have emphatically denied an African diaspora. They have actively rejected concepts that suggest that they are lost souls separated from a distant homeland. They have insisted, and most still insist, that they are possessors of their own homeland. Like the maroons in the interior of Suriname and French Guiana, their self-conscious historicity is alive with events establishing their own communities, called *palenques*, in their own territory by their own creative volitions.

In 1990, Cuban nationalist rhetoric drew fresh allusions from the metaphor of "darkened." According to Marifeli Pérez-Stable, Cuba's political consciousness ("*consciencia*" as defined by the late Ernesto [Che] Guevara) of its nationalism is manifest in the symbol of maroon liberation.

> "The future of our homeland will be an eternal Baraguá!" Raúl Castro proclaimed on March 15 in Santiago de Cuba. To announce next year's Communist Party congress, Fidel's younger brother read a text steeped with historical allusion. Baraguá was where mulatto independence leader Gen. Antonio Maceo met with his Spanish adversary in 1878 to discuss the Pact of Zanjón, a compromise negotiated by the civilian, mostly propertied wing of the separatist movement to end the Ten Years' War (1868–1878). Maceo and his *mambises*—the guerrillas of the Ejército Libertador (Liberation Army)—refused peace without independence. . . . (Pérez-Stable 1990:32)

He argues that Maceo's protest in the name of maroon (*mambises*) liberation was "an early expression of Cuban radical nationalism, one of the principal ideologies of the island's politics, which would later inspire the 1959 revolution" (32). By this argument we can see initial Cuban regional ethnic-bloc black liberation as transforming into movements of nationalist liberation and the allusion to the dark origins of the *Movimiento veinte y seis de julio* as being sparked again in the 1990s (for background, see Ibarra 1972).

The play on themes from the various discourses and practices of "white culture" and "darkened people" took on myriad dimensions, only a couple of which we mention here. Columbus was struck by one feature of the Taíno Arawakan indigenous people he encountered: they did not wear clothes. Rather, they presented their sense of individual and collective selfhoods by such means as body and face painting, hair dressing, stone adornments in lips and cheeks, nasal and ear adornments of precious metals (gold and *guanín*). One code of the Old World immediately promulgated on the New World was to "clothe" the subjugated Native Americans in appropriate (i.e., inferior) European garb. Significantly, then, in Dutch Guiana, which was to become Suriname, one of the first things that self-liberated slaves did was to shed their European clothes. Equally appropriate, perhaps, is the call of dark people in the Caribbean, as elsewhere, when beginning the English game of cricket: "put on your whites!"

## Structures of Domination

The sociologist Max Weber (e.g., 1958, 1964), who has had far greater influence on modern symbolic and political anthropology and on neo-Marxism than many are willing to admit, argued strongly for a social-research methodology that involves three dimensions.

The first dimension of systematic research is what he calls "objective." It consists of measuring the relations of class by reference to people aggregated in society vis-à-vis their relations to the market. If poor people in a given community or region cannot afford to purchase the adequate carbohydrates and proteins while another aggregate of people in the same community or region purchases basic foodstuffs and special foods, pays for the education of its children, and builds up a stock of reserve funds, we can measure the relationships of the two aggregates to the market and state the results in terms of a "lower class" and a "middle class." If we find, as is usually the case, that a small interlocking group of people controls the local and regional markets that contribute to their superior wealth, then we can speak of an "upper class," or local or regional elite, and we can measure the economic power of this class and compare it objectively by the use of statistics to the others.

The second dimension of Weber's research strategy is to seek out the "subjective" aspects of a given community or region (or nation-state). Subjectivity refers to "status" as clearly differentiated from "class." Status is the shared style of life,

determined by the amount of social honor people have within the subjective social order. In the understanding of status one must understand classificatory
schemes that people in varied walks of life use to order the people around them,
to keep people away from them, to establish interactional bases that transcend
market forces, and to categorize people whom they know, whom they have been
told about, and whom they imagine. Matters of status are categorical and stereotypical. Ethnicity and "race relations" fall into the dimension of subjective, categorical, and stereotypical social relations.

Weber's third research method of social analysis was to see how, in the development of public policy, struggles for dominance crystallized in political arenas.
Such dominance crystallization constitutes the forces that initially shape the
structure of power.

One important dimension of power is what Weber called *Macht*, the ability to
force one's will upon others against resistance (Weber 1964:152). When one party
achieves dominance over another, it may influence the acquiescing party to
accept, however implicitly, the symbols of domination; such acceptance is the
essence of hegemony. Power always involves struggle, and the struggle is categorized by cultural conventions, motivated and shaped by magico-ideological constructs, and supported by political-economic resources.

When issues of class and status are dictated by questions of "race" or ethnic
representations, structures of domination are in evidence.

One would like to think, and many would have us believe, that in Latin America and the Caribbean there is substantial fluidity in class, ethnic, and power relationships. Such is not the case. Almost everywhere, serious research turns up a
pyramidal class structure, cut variously by ethnic lines, but with a local, regional,
and nation-state elite characterized as "white." And white rules over color within
the same class; those who are lighter have differential access to some dimensions
of the market. This is one significant manifestation of enduring structures of
domination. When a majority of black people constitutes the entire urban and
rural lower class of a region, this is another dimension of the structure of domination. Any combination of features that results in the perpetuation of lightness
as superior to darkness adds to the features of a racialist structure of domination,
with clear international repercussions.

Structures of domination appear strikingly in the structure of language; they
intensify culturally by simple rhetorical devices.

The first of these is *simile*. When a person says, "s/he sure doesn't look like a
Negro," or "el [ella] no parece como negroide[a]," a powerful statement has been
made that some other people will "look like" someone who "is" black. The "like"
(*como*), in other words, signals a conscious or unconscious awareness that there
are agreed-upon commonalities or properties that attach to persons of color. In
fact, the use in "science" or "social science" of the English suffix "oid" (which
means "like, as") is nothing more than rhetorical deployment of simile to reflect
the enduring imagery of a symbolic formation that stems from the fifteenth cen-

tury. For example, "Negroes" come from Africa and "Negroids" live in New Guinea. Although *negroide* and *négroïde* (negroid) are very common terms in New World and Old World Spanish and French discourse about "race" and even "culture," nowhere in the Spanish-speaking world does one ever encounter *blancoide* (Caucasoid, "like white"; Lewis 1983).

*Metaphor* is the second rhetorical strategy in maintaining structures of domination. When someone says "s/he is black," "s/he is descended from blacks," "s/he is part black," a metaphor is deployed. With metaphor the person, class, aggregate, group, community, or region is tagged with the cognitive and symbolic associations of a category of "darkened." These associations constitute properties of blackness that convey meaning, as though physical features, genealogy, or heritage have some real correspondences among people and categories. People of color, in other words, are signified by qualities and resemblances that belong to signifiers that stem from racialist and racist cultural constructs. Whereas, for example, black Panamanians think of themselves as *gente*, people, and black English speakers in Panama think of themselves as "people," both are tagged *negro* in Spanish and "black" in English. The properties of the signification "blackness" attached to certain Panamanians and Anglo-Caribbeans in Panama lump very different people, traditions, and customs, and garb them with attributes of convergent but false resemblance.

Structures of domination are given form, meaning, and power of repression by the rhetorical strategy of *reification*, regarding an abstraction or mental construction as though it were a real thing in the world. Reification occurs when people consciously read symbolic, religious, moral, or ideological properties into categorical social relationships, as though these properties actually "existed." In a chapter on "Humanity and Animality," the British structuralist Edmund Leach (1982:107) says, "The naming of relationships marks the beginnings of moral sanctions." This is the process of signification wherein meaning is constructed by strengthening the relationship between the signified (individuals, aggregates, groups, or categories of people) and the signifier (cognitive and symbolic associations and labels that constitute the properties of categories). When nationalist ontology and ideology reify racial mixture not only as an ideal but also as a "reality," they create objectifications of "outsidership" among indigenous and black populations of modern nation-states. People in communities and regions so objectified and morally sanctioned by undesirable attributes self-consciously reflect on such reifications and attempt to overcome the barriers imposed by racialist structures of domination. This involves symbolic as well as practical dimensions of actions of moral inversion in society. The invariable result is a reordering of visions that people hold of humanity and spirituality in the world perceived and the world imagined. When such actions spark movements of self liberation they may be said to become "flagrant." Dolgin, Kemnitzer, and Schneider (1977: 37) write: "Each action situation is the locus of such reification; and because such reification is the practical key and the ontological root of domination, every action situation is the site of negotiation for, or struggle against, domination." These authors (1977:3) open their book with a phrase from Karl Marx: "As people express their lives, so they are . . . " This is an intriguing figure of speech because it begins with a simile ("As") and it ends with a representational metaphor ("they are"). One need but classify the "they" in ethnic or "racial" terms to have a powerful reification. In circumstances where people come to express their lives in a manner corresponding with the structure of domination, the phenomenon of hegemony occurs.

Finally, in the process of formation and strengthening of structures of domination and the inevitable forces of resistance to them, we must consider the phenomenon of *hypostasis*. This word, which entered the English language by 1529, literally means "that which stands under"; i.e., a support or foundation (for other concepts). *Hypostatize*, according to Webster, means "1. to make into or consider as distinct substance; attribute substantial or personal existence to, 2. to regard as a reality; assume to be actual." A structure is a set of relatively invariant reference points that remain after a series of transformations has occurred. Hypostatized structures are those that are taken to be enduring realities. They are structures with deep historical underpinnings and supports that unite concepts of humanity and divinity and separate both from animality (see, e.g., Leach 1982).

In the ethnic formation of the circum-Atlantic structure of European domination, three relatively invariant reference points were the categories of the white (European) in superior relationship over the black (African) and the native ("Indian"). Such a categorical hypostasis established by phenotype and pigmentation constitutes, as an undergirding foundation, a multitude of ethereal and even fantastic classifications that people took to be "real" 500 years ago and still take to be "real." During the colonial, republican, and modern eras of Latin American and creole transformations, these were complemented, as we have seen, by reference to *mestizaje, blanqueamiento*, and *indigenismo* in Spanish, denoted by other cognate concepts in English, French, Portuguese, and Dutch.

This structure of domination manifests a pyramidal class structure with white people on top, masses of pluralized mestizo, mulatto, and white people in the middle, and poor, pluralized black, mestizo, and indigenous people on the bottom. It is assumed to be an unchanging, static reality by people at the pinnacle and middle of the structure. The full power of bureaucracy is wielded to solve the "black problem," find new ways to overcome the "Indian problem," and accelerate the processes of *mestizaje*. While such solutions to hypostatized problems are being sought, national, regional, and local resources flow to the top, are partially redistributed in the middle, and deprive those on the bottom of the class-ethnic hierarchy. This is a process of reproduction of underdevelopment of Fourth World people in underdeveloping Third World nations and the production of increased distance between Third World poverty and First World wealth (see, e.g. Worsley 1984).

Within any given structure of domination, we expect to find that those in power strive to maintain hegemony over those immediately below them by blaming those on the bottom (especially ethnically distinct indigenous and black people) for the "undeveloped" condition of regions and communities where they are designated by reification. The hypostatized "reality" is often inscribed in developmental reports, plans, and educational materials and in scholarly publications. At the same time, this symbolic but negatively concretized "reality" is challenged by powerful, dynamic counterideologies. The rhetoric of such counterideologies seeks to spark recognition of the falsity of the static ideological structures with their locus in white-supremacy doctrines.

Ethnic-bloc formation undertaken under the ideological aegis of *négritud* and/ or *autodeterminación indígena* strongly illustrates the challenges mounted in the late twentieth century to false yet hypostatized "reality" that has been with the New World since 1492. No wonder, then, that during the conquest quincentennial celebration many black (and mestizo) people in Latin America joined their indigenous fellow citizens in the cry "¡Despues de 500 años de dominación, autodeterminación en 1992! (After 500 years of domination, self-determination in 1992!)."

## Processes of Liberation

Understanding processes of liberation involves us at still greater depth with the elements of dominance crystallization that constitute structures of power. Structures of domination and the ways in which blocs coalesce, change, and are expressed, maintained, and transformed are highly dynamic and volatile. While hegemony may come into being, it never lasts, for people are conscious actors attuned to their life situations. Dolgin and colleagues (1977:44) summarize as follows:

> People act on the basis of belief. To study belief in action . . . is to examine the possibilities of freedom, and the roots of oppression and alienation. But these can be studied only in the context of a *practical* commitment to freedom and a determination to overcome that which stands in its way. People made it, is the principal lesson of modern anthropology; people can remake it, must become the principal lesson of our work in the future.

When discussing structures of domination we introduced briefly the idea that people are signified by signifiers as they become parts of categorical webs of signification in modern nations. The signifier *negro* (black), when wielded by whites and mestizos in the Cauca Valley of Colombia to represent people of dark complexion, expresses a series of attributes that includes laziness, danger, and "migrating" to "work" for wages from a "jungle" littered with African "superstitions." People categorized as "black" in the Cauca Valley are looked upon as morally "darkened" by history, geography, and descent. The history of the Cauca Valley is one of increasing white wealth, oppression of black yeomanry, and destruction of indigenous people.

Such white categorization stems from the conjoined legacies of slavery and self-liberation of black people, and later the white tradition of this region of importing black laborers from the adjacent Pacific Lowlands. It also stems from a deep-seated nonblack fear of free black people who have long resided there. This is a region where self-liberation came early to black slaves, and by the late eighteenth century both white-owned plantations and black *palenques* were developing not only in competition with one another but at times in collaboration (Taussig 1980). Writing of the descendants of the self-liberated black *cimarrones* there in the 1880s, Michael Taussig says:

> these black peasants were outlaws—free peasants and foresters who lived by their wits and weapons rather than by legal guarantees to land and citizenship. The fearful specter of a black state was not lost on some observers. "In the woods that enclose the Cauca Valley," wrote the German traveler Freidrich von Schenk in 1880, "vegetate many blacks whom one could equate with the maroons of the West Indies." They sought solitude in the woods, "where they regress once again slowly to the custom of their African birthplace as one commonly sees in the interior of Haiti. . . . These people are tremendously dangerous, especially in times of revolution when they get together in gangs and enter the struggle as valiant fighters in the service of whatever hero of liberty promises them booty." (Taussig 1980:58)

Being "signified" or "represented" as "black" in a white-dominated world is to be stigmatized to a position of ethnic disadvantage in a discourse of racial asymmetry. This does not mean, however, that people so stigmatized will accept a position of disadvantage or elect to describe their situation through the dominant discourse. Indeed, the black narrative modes that are all too often strung together and published as "folklore" constitute, as Price-Mars (1928), Ortiz (1975c, 1986), R. Price (1983, 1990), Taussig (1980), and Friedemann and Cross (1979) have shown, a rich embodiment of enlightened and insightful black representation of the entwined histories, presents, and futures of conquest, domination, and self-liberation. As Taussig (1987:135) puts it, "From the represented shall come that which overturns the representation." This statement relates directly to the idea of people remaking the world and being in a world refashioned from the conquered one.

For one example taken from the power of language to reformulate perspectives of being in the world, let us return to two illustrations previously presented and see them in a dialogical or confrontational manner. Black people from Ecuador who attended the First Congress of Black Culture in the Americas in 1977 were well aware of the phrase "Lo que no tiene de inga tiene de mandinga." They resented immensely its introduction as a way of asserting the *mestizo* character of

Ecuadorian "popular" or "vernacular" culture by a prominent Ecuadorian folk-lorist who was invited there to present a formal paper based on his extensive re-search on Afro-Ecuadorian "beliefs and superstitions." They immediately pointed out that the lack of the Spanish article *la* (the) before both Inca and Mandinga relegated indigenous cultures of the Americas (bound up in the word *inga*) and indigenous cultures of Africa (bound up in the word *mandinga*) to something unrefined and static. The scholar responded forcefully that this was part of "Ecuadorian folklore" and should be presented as collected among "the poor and the backward" (*los pobres y los atrasados*). Black people publicly argued back against the scholar's flawed rhetoric, and a clear insistence on the phrase *La Cultura Negra* came forth. Blackness of the past and present and toward the future was what the conference was all about. Blackness in all its flagrant dimensions is to be cultivated and understood, not "studied" as a set of scattered artifacts, they asserted. Having stressed the positive value of blackness in Ecuadorian, Colombian, and Peruvian cultures and traditions, black delegates and others called the distinguished scholar *un mestizo*, a halfbreed. This, still in confrontational context, was also significant, because the man clearly self-identified as *blanco*, white, while proclaiming the nation of Ecuador to be *mestizo*.

*Blackness* at the 1977 congress referred (and continues to refer) to that epitomizing referent worthy of a macro-identity to which communities, regions, even nations could aspire. Such a referent is transcendental; it comes from black people in black communities, but it is the polar opposite of "popular culture." In the United States and elsewhere in the Americas and the Atlantic rim, the epitomizing symbol of blackness in its transcendental character is expressed as "soul" (in volume II, see especially the chapters by Mitchell on Brazil and Laguerre on Haiti). This is an aesthetic quality that people self-identifying with human blackness and/or black cultures find and appreciate across the boundaries of specific communities, regions, nations, or traditions.

Let us now consider *travel*, for through this mechanism the circum-Atlantic cultural system of inter-regions and inter-traditions came into existence, and through this mechanism its collective vitality in remarkable diversity is constantly enriched. According to Daniel J. Boorstin (1983), Mary W. Helms (1988), and Mary B. Campbell (1988), a universal in culture is the inextricable relationship between travel and power.

The European "discovery" of America in 1492 and the rapidly ensuing conquest expanded structures of domination exponentially. Domination was the European ideological and practical issue in 1492 (as it still is) by those representing struggling kingdoms. Columbus sailed for the king and queen of Castile. His motivation was to discover a cheaper and safer route to the East Indies (all land from India eastward through Asia and the Pacific islands) and to find ways to make huge profits there. He claimed that he had done so (and that he had discovered the location of paradise) and announced his greatness to the literate world in a public "letter to a prince" in 1493.

In addition to his self-designation as "bearer of Christ," Columbus demanded and was granted the secular tide of "Admiral of the Ocean Sea." He (in error) also named the inhabitants of an entire continent of diverse native people as *indio* (of the "Indies," from which come the French *Indiens*, the German *Indianer*, and the English *Indian*), the most common representation used today in most of the world for the Native Americans burdened by the crushing weight of Old World expansionist hegemony.

Columbus clearly "marked the beginning of moral sanctions" (Leach 1982) with his designation *indio*. Not long after, Bartolomé de las Casas defended the "humanity" of the *indios* and in so doing recommended the massive importation of black Africans (*negros de Africa*) to take over the animal tasks heretofore relegated to the native inhabitants of the New World. The hegemonic morality of white power and *indio*/black forced subservience to the Church, State, and secular holders of land and people was established in the early sixteenth century in Europe and the Americas.

But there were many—including black people of many origins—who traveled far and wide in the New World. We quote here from a piece of fiction based upon archival documents (e.g., Cabeza de Vaca 1542a, 1993) to allow the reader to capture something of the flavor of such ventures in the early exploration and conquest of the Americas.

> I am Estevän, a black man from Azemmour, in Morocco. . . . After completing necessary preparations, on the seventeenth day of June, 1527, a Friday, we departed Spain in five ships—six hundred we were, a few more or less—and, except for the score or two who fell sick with the vomits and one lost in the sea, it was a fair and easy voyage to the Island of Santo Domingo, where we rested forty-five days procuring provisions and horses. (Panger 1982:34)

Estevän, a *ladino* slave, also classed as a Moor, then traveled by ship and on foot around the New World with Alvar Núñez Cabeza de Vaca, during which time he was granted his freedom. The novel *Black Ulysses* (1982), from which we quote, is based on a translation of a sixteenth-century journal (Cabeza de Vaca 1542b). This travel took place more than ninety years before the "negars" were brought by the Dutch slaver to Jamestown. The journal describes in detail the first European-African expedition to explore the southern part of what is now the United States and northern Mexico. In terms of present regions, the travelers went from Santo Domingo (Hispaniola) to Trinidad, then Cuba, on to Florida, up the west coast of the Gulf of Mexico, across the northern shores of that gulf, down to Corpus Christi, Texas, into the interior of Mexico, back up to El Paso and down to Culiacán on the west coast of Mexico. Insights brought out by the eight-year chronicle suggest relationships more than 450 years ago that might have existed beyond the pale of Spanish conquest society. The fictionalized Estevän says:

With these Indians [of west Mexico, near the Gulf of California] with whom I
dwelt for many months, I was not a slave, and because I came to them as a trader
I was permitted to go from one tribe to another, a thing forbidden to all except
this one class of beings. Because of the color of my skin and because of my profession as a trader—one who brings both commodities and messages which to
these Indians is of the highest importance—I was treated with great honor while
amongst these Charrucos, as I was by every nation to which I traveled as far distant
as fifty leagues north and even a greater distance south. (Panger 1982:363)

For individuals to venture out beyond the realm of the known and to return with
new information of great worth to those who sent them creates an increasing
"fund of power" for the travelers (Helms 1988: 169). Black people from black
Africa had long been going out and coming back to increase funds of power for
states and empires developing in Central and West Africa.

The possibility of journeys by Africans to the New World and back to the Old
is occasionally debated by a handful of scholars (e.g., Jeffreys 1971). For our purposes we can state with confidence that African-diaspora social relations began
to appear in Hispaniola at least by 1502 and soon thereafter throughout the
New World from Florida to Argentina. From that time on, activities of African-
Americans were to be partially, sometimes inextricably, bound to the upper
realms of wealth and power in New World colonies, republics, and eventually
modern nation-states.

This does not mean that freedom could not be seized. Such freedom is evident
in the sustained movements of black self-liberation found throughout the Americas. As Richard Price has written,

For more than four centuries, the communities formed by such runaways dotted
the fringes of plantation America, from Brazil to the southeastern United States,
from Peru to the American Southwest. Known variously as *palenques, quilombos,
mocombos, cumbes, ladeiras,* or *mambises,* these new societies ranged from tiny
bands that survived less than a year to powerful states encompassing thousands of
members and surviving for generations or even centuries. Today their descendants
still form semi-independent enclaves in several parts of the hemisphere, remaining fiercely proud of their maroon origins and, in some cases at least, faithful
to unique cultural traditions that were forged during the earliest days of Afro-
American history. (Price 1979:1; see also Thoden van Velzen and van Wetering
1988; Friedemann and Cross 1979)

Even in the myriad fortified black, indigenous, and black-indigenous territories, however, a close connection with structures of domination was maintained
by war, by trade, and by the creation of many mechanisms of "distance" (see, e.g.,
Taussig 1986, S. Price 1983, R. Price 1990, Thoden van Velzen and van Wetering
1988). Estevàn, for example, may have thought about remaining with Native
Americans near the coast of California (where, perhaps, a *palenque* could be de-

veloped), but instead he pressed on southward with Cabeza de Vaca, to unite with Hernán Cortés.

> Accompanied by scores of Christians met along the way and hundreds of Indians, we entered Mexico City July 25, 1536, eight years, two months and twenty five days from our landing on the coast of Florida. . . . Viceroy Mendoza came up and, after presenting me with a likeness of Christ's Mother, Mary, done in gold and jewels, declared that he was claiming me for his household. Although I forced my face to give no sign, within my heart turned to ice. Nothing Alvar Nuñez [or the others with whom he had traveled] could say altered the Viceroy's determination. Thus despite the silks I now wore, the gold and silver coins that filled my pockets, I was again a slave. (Panger 1982:400–401)

We stated that black Americans who escaped slavery in the New World were nonetheless partially bound because of the necessary links to dominant colonial, republican, and nation-state societies. This does not mean that black people were powerless because of these links. There are other dimensions of power that shape and communicate ethnic and cultural forces. As William Arens and Ivan Karp (1989:xii) put it, "The concept of 'power' as it is used by all peoples encodes ideas about the nature of the world, social relations, and the effects of actions in and on the world and the entities that inhabit it." These sources of power in the African diaspora constantly give rise to meaningful resistance, to revelation of structures of oppression, to insight into the nature of political-economic barriers, and to a sense of worth of human congeners struggling together against forces of repression. It is in these struggles that the sense of community is found.

Anthropological understanding of black cultures and traditions in the New World has often bogged down in debates about how to scale Africanisms in the aesthetics, ritual, play, theater, folklore, cosmology, music, dance, religion, and ideology of black aggregates against Europeanisms in black cultures. Some scholars have even stewed about relationships of Native American cultures and African-American cultures, and learned conferences have been held on the past, present, and future of "black Indians." Our position is that the elements and themes of cultural traditions may come from any source. Traditions are not static, and they may change radically for a variety of reasons (e.g., Shils 1981, Hobsbawn and Ranger 1983). The white Mississippians' taste for okra, which blacks brought to the Americas from Africa, is no less "theirs" in the late twentieth century than is the black Bermudans' fondness for English cricket. Emergent patterns, with very shallow time depths, nonetheless suggest relationships to the past and trajectories toward the future. Sahlins (e.g., 1981:7), as well as Kuper (1988), correctly locates *transformation* as a means of understanding traditions.

Consider human beings interacting in myriad aggregations around the globe. Now, zoom down on the circum-Atlantic as a culture region of intersystems. It is immediately apparent that the elements, complexes, and themes that compose traditions are spread and sorted variously by ongoing transactions within actual groups, communities, and regions. Cultures, we could say, embrace diversities of traditions while at the same time scrutinizing their arbitrary nature (e.g., Babcock 1978:29).

Traditional African American arts and rituals, for example, exist as objects (sculpture, carving, painting, quilting, weaving, pottery) or stylistic renditions (storytelling, joking, poetry, mythmaking, historic narrative, worship, dance, mime, music, theater) that particular people take to be part of their own past, present, and unfolding future heritage. They may also exist in the living memory of people who no longer perform the rituals or craft the arts. Absence of ongoing practice is not necessarily evidence of culture loss or "acculturation," for talk about objects, past activities, and events is a powerful mechanism of culturally sustained ability, of creativity, of power. Put differently, the discourses about past practices may be taken as a model of cultural continuity and a model for trans-formations in present ideology and cosmology. And such discourses may reveal far more about black or indigenous historical dynamics than reified inscriptions in learned volumes about the so-called "genuine but 'disappearing' Africans and Indians in the New World."

Let us again turn to the Saramaka of the interior of Suriname. In the 1970s people there cautiously told Richard and Sally Price about customs they no longer practice except in times of collective crisis, because they were associated with First-Time, a real, historic time-space of war and rebellion which, if dis-cussed, would "kill people." Using many techniques of sophisticated communi-cation, Saramaka speakers told of battles, of rituals, and of powerful artifacts while at the same time keeping the bulk of their specific knowledge diffuse and pro-tected (Price and Price 1980). In Richard Price's *Alabi's World* (1990), there is moving testimony to the strength of this tradition as maintained through the Saramakans' historical lore, and we learn about the continuing struggle against domination in the late twentieth century.

> In 1978, the Saramaka elder Peléki voiced the greatest fear of all Maroons, prophe-sying that those times—the days of war and slavery—shall come again. In 1986, after two centuries of peace, they did. Great war *óbias* that had lain dormant since the eighteenth century were dug from the earth and revivified. The blood of hun-dreds of Maroons—men, women, and children—as well as that of other Suri-namers has once again stained the ground. And as this book goes to press, the end is not in sight. (Price 1990:epigraph)

In a review of Richard Price's *First-Time* (1983), Whitten (1986b) argues that "the creative act of territorial and societal formation at the frontier of colonial-state or nation-state places cultures so formed (maroon cultures) in continuous jeopardy of reconquest. The jeopardy lurking in the present and future, in turn, motivates continuous reproduction of poignant and accurate images of the past."

The creativity of African American ethnogenesis that led to the emergence of six nations (not nation-states) of self-liberated black people in the interior of Suriname and French Guiana is an example of what we call ethnic-bloc formation. These people self-identify as Saramaka, Matawai, Kwinti, Djuka, Paramaka, and Aluku. They are collectively called *bushenenge*, "forest blacks," by Dutch-speaking outsiders and "bush Negroes" by English speakers searching for "lost Africans." Each of these peoples fought for more than a hundred years against the Dutch and the French, and they won their independence. Then, in the late twentieth century, as Suriname entered a phase of nation-state socialist nationalism, the sheer existence of peaceful black people in a "plural" nation seemed to threaten the sovereignty and territoriality of an increasingly bloodthirsty and oppressive military state. The consequence was a civil war waged in Suriname, news of which scarcely reached the metropolitan news services of industrial nations. Ethnicity emerges in sharp relief within nation-states undergoing intensive movements of nationalist selfconsciousness, where "ethnic" comes to mean something other than what nationalist ideologues proclaim is "traditional" to an "authentic past" of the nation. "*Ethnicity* labels the visibility of that aspect of the identity formation process that is produced by and subordinated to nationalist programs and plans—plans intent on creating putative homogeneity out of heterogeneity through the appropriative processes of a transformist hegemony" (Williams 1989:439).

As for ethnic power, Arens and Karp (1989), writing about black Africa, state: "Underlying much of the ritual and cosmology is a sense of power derived from different capacities and uses to act on the world." In a survey of symbolism and language of power in African societies and cultures, they find that indigenous concepts of power in Africa refer to ability or capacity, as contrasted with physical strength. They state that "there is no word for authority and duly constituted government authorities are referred to by some of the words for control" (xx), adding:

> Once we incorporate semantics, cosmology, and action, power can be understood as something significantly more subtle and meaningful than sovereignty of domination isolated at one single point in time or place. Rather, it is recognized as a pervasive social resource, which provides the ideological bases for various domestic and public relationships in Africa and elsewhere. (xx–xxi)

INTRODUCTION TO VOLUME I

# CENTRAL AMERICA AND NORTHERN
# AND WESTERN SOUTH AMERICA

*Norman E. Whitten, Jr., and Arlene Torres*

In mid-September 1996, the University of Illinois at Urbana-Champaign hosted
visits by an Afro-Colombian congresswoman, Zulia Mena, and an Afro-Bolivian
leader, Fortunata Medina Pinedo de Pérez. The first was originally from a small
town near Quibdó, the capital of the Chocó Department of the Pacific Lowlands
of Colombia, and the second from Tocaña and Coroico, in the Nor Yungas, the
deep valleys that cut through the Andes northeast of La Paz into Amazonia. Both
women were and are leaders in social movements of ethnic self-assertion in their
respective nation-states; both are now nationally prominent and becoming internationally known. Both spoke of ethnic movements in their respective nations
as involving indigenous people and black people, whose histories, they said, are
clearly intertwined. Both also spoke of the endurance and creativity of imagery
of the past, projected from a formative present into a future of hope and resilience.

Zulia Mena stressed the powers of such cultural phenomena as music, dance,
speech, and literature. Fortunata Medina stressed the same creative powers and
showed us how they came together in both political meetings and national festivals in Bolivia. In listening to and interacting with these two spokeswomen for
the cultural powers of blackness in nation-states wherein the ideology of *mestizaje*
prevails, the sense of drama of regional and ethnic phenomena came through
clearly. And with equal clarity we heard about the cultural creativity of the reclamation of the enduring traditions of their respective nation-states. Their movements were not "against the state." Rather, they sought to create ethnic space for
blackness as a creative cultural quality within their respective nations. Both of
these women stressed the forging of the future of their own cultural presence.
Nothing could be further from the notion of "popular culture." The themes expressed in our general introduction, in other words, emerged on our own campus
from insightful presentations from the heart of Afro-Colombia and Afro-Bolivia.

We begin this first volume on blackness in Central America and northern and
western South America with eleven chapters on Central America and the northern South American lowlands. Throughout this region freedom was claimed
early by black people, and as Hispanic slavery grew, so too did black alliances
with competitors of the Spanish, the British privateers, buccaneers, and pirates. If

one thinks of the African diaspora primarily in terms of the "black Atlantic" (see Gilroy 1993) one comes to deal heavily with the escalation of slavery in British, French, and Dutch domains. Such immersion in slavery literature is essential. But it can lead the scholar with Western historical orientation to view blackness itself primarily in terms of Northern European–African colonial-colonist dynamics of profit and slavery. It can skew attention away from the Spanish-Portuguese dominated situations of the fifteenth and sixteenth centuries, restricting modernity not only to Northern Europe but also to the later colonial centuries. Such a view also takes relationships between black people and indigenous people as virtually nonintersecting. This is the way much of Western history has presented and presents materials that are the substance of the essays that ensue. This introduction, together with the essays, seeks to correct this perspective.

We choose in this work to open the issues bound to blackness and by implication (and some specification) to those bound to indigenousness. We do so by presenting information drawn from serious ethnography undertaken in diaspora regions adjacent to the circum-Atlantic system proper. There are two primary reasons for this. The first is that the area of our immediate and opening concern is not well known in African diaspora studies; the second is that this region is of enormous importance to diaspora studies, providing, as it does, a rich source of information on the dynamics of blackness in the context of colonial, republican, and contemporary nation-state struggles for identity, freedom, and democracy. Inasmuch as the region is undergoing attention to the substances of our central concern in the 1990s, we try now to contextualize previous work.

In 1975 Norman Whitten and Nina S. de Friedemann drew together material on the culture and history of a significant sector of this region. Both of them had undertaken serious ethnography, Whitten in the Pacific Lowlands of Ecuador and Colombia and Friedemann in various regions of Colombia. They pulled materials on blackness in Colombia and Ecuador together and published them in an extended article, "Black Culture of the Ecuadorian-Colombian Littoral," which they published in the *Revista Colombiana de Antropología*. In this presentation they used the figure of speech *la cultura negra*. By so doing they sought to draw academic attention not only to the important cultural region known as the Pacific Lowlands Cultural Area extending from the Darién province of Panama south through the Colombian departments of Chocó, Valle, Cauca, and Nariño and the Ecuadorian province of Esmeraldas, but also to the cultural potential for ethnic pride that emerged from sustained ethnography.

That work, stressing "black culture" in a professional Latin American anthropological journal, marked a transition point in Latin American and North American scholarship applied to African American peoples of Latin America. Up until the early 1960s the few Afro–Latin American studies that existed provided data-rich, small-scale ethnographies "suspended in time" in an "ethnographic present." Such studies were treated to historical distributional analyses to determine the number and complexity of African "traits." While not denying the value of intensive studies in relatively small-scale (local) settings, on the one hand, and historical distributional analysis, on the other hand, Whitten and Friedemann wanted to stress historical factors of freedom in the face of slavery, cultural sensitivities, ethnic pride, and political-economic disadvantages and potentialities in regional and interregional perspectives of modern Latin American nation-states.

The Whitten and Friedemann piece stressed the cultural values of blackness in a region populated primarily by blacks with smaller indigenous groupings. It discussed the ways by which the historical doctrine of *mestizaje*, "racial mingling," conjoined with nationalist images and strategies of "developmentalism" to create a dynamic system of oppression against which black people and indigenous people were forced to struggle (see, e.g., Corsetti, Motta González, and Tassara 1990). In the 1970s, as before, black people had little or no outside help, and indigenous people (Emberá, Waunan, Cuna, Katio, and Chami of Colombia; Chachi and Tchachela of Ecuador; and Awá [Coaiquer] of both nations) could turn only to the oppressive "guidance" of the International Catholic Church. We mention this article as an attempt to consolidate an emergent academic perspective in the mid-1960s that tried to see global dimensions of regional systems and to thereby understand such systems in their local-level manifestations.

In 1977 in Cali, Colombia, people from many parts of the Americas and from Africa gathered at the First Congress of Black Culture of the Americas. As mentioned in the general introduction, it was there that the concept of *La Cultura Negra* rang forth as an epitomizing, charged symbol worthy of macro-identity to which black people and others could aspire. It became clear there in northwestern South America in the 1970s that a parallel perspective between those studying qualities of blackness in Latin America and those living such qualities had emerged. Although the proponents of understanding blackness in its own right and through it such intertwined, inextricable phenomena as whiteness, "whitening," and *mestizaje* constituted a minority, the "black perspectives" of Afro-Latin Americans could no longer be denied; invisibility was dissolved again from the modern historical matrix of interethnicity (see, e.g., Taussig 1978, Córdoba 1983, Arocha 1992).

In 1994 Nina Friedemann (with Jaime Arocha) and Whitten (with Diego Quiroga) were commissioned to prepare essays on Colombia and Ecuador respectively for the volume *No Longer Invisible: Afro-Latin Americans Today* (1995). In their essay, Friedemann and Arocha detail the history of Afro-Colombians, bringing us to the dramatic legislative and ethnic confrontation through which black people of Colombia, or at least some sectors of Colombia, may now be treated as equal to indigenous people in terms of land and property rights attendant on the constitutional reform wherein the nation-state was declared "multicultural, multinational, and multiethnic." To return to our opening paragraph to contextualize Zulia Mena's visit to our university, Friedemann and Arocha conclude their chapter in this way:

NORMAN E. WHITTEN, JR., AND ARLENE TORRES                                    37

One important feature comprises the recognition of Afro-Colombian ancestral territorial rights, including rights to use plant and animal resources and to mine for gold and platinum. Another involves the possibility of defending Afro-Colombian cultural and historical identities by means of special education programs, and a third concerns the influence and control that Afro-Colombian communities have gained over the planning and implementation of socioeconomic development. These advantageous developments have quickly led to political participation. Rudecindo Castro, president of the Peasant Association of Baudó, and Zulia Mena, president of the Organization of Popular Barrios—both former members of the Special Commission for Black Communities—stood as candidates in the 1994 congressional elections. Zulia Mena obtained 40,000 votes, a much larger share than that obtained by the candidates of the traditional leftist parties. (Friedemann and Arocha 1995:72)

At the beginning of Part Three of this book, the Andes, Peter Wade discusses these processes in Colombia. The cognate nations of Venezuela, Ecuador, Peru, and Bolivia manifest the same ethnic struggles as Colombia, but thus far only Bolivia has moved to declare itself legally "multicultural," in which process an indigenous person bilingual in Aymara and Spanish, Victor Hugo Cárdenas, was elected vice president of the nation in 1993 (see, e.g., Albó 1994). It was through Vice President Cárdenas, Fortunata Medina told us, that Afro-Bolivians gained access to the pinnacle of national executive power and authority. Although only the Andean-Amazonian countries of Bolivia and Colombia thus far have asserted multiculturality and multiethnicity in their national constitutions, movements are well under way in such directions in virtually every Latin American nation (see, e.g., Van Cott 1994).

We open the first part with the chapter published in 1995 by Whitten and Quiroga, which provides an academic overview of Afro-Ecuatoriana that parallels, as scholarship often does, the visions of those engaged in social movements of self-determination and transformed ethnic representation in that nation and in sister nations. Their review of ethnic terminology in vogue at the nation-state pinnacles of economic and political power reflect terminology common in northern and western South America and in Central America. They turn to the self-reflexive analysis by black people in Ecuador with regard to the Spanish language and its subtle and not-so-subtle color-coding mechanisms:

Black people in Ecuador draw specific attention to nouns, verbs, adjectives and adverbs involving double meanings of blackness. For example, the verb *negrear* (to blacken) is used socially to confer lesser status. To say that someone's life is *negreando* can mean that person is drifting toward crime, is becoming poorer or is heading toward states pejoratively associated with black people: lazy, dirty or ugly. By inference . . . *negrear* and its derivatives and near cognates (*negar*, to negate) bring all such associations to bear on the stigmatized subject of the predication. *Negrear* can also mean to make someone "disappear" as a social being of worth. For example, the verb is applied to people who have been promised a salary at one level, and then are actually given far less. Such a person is *tratado como negro*, "treated like a black," or simply *negreado*, "blackened." To contest being treated in a disparaging way one may exclaim, "¡No mi negree!" which can be translated euphemistically as "Don't deny me!" or "Don't look through or past me."

*Despreciar*, which means to "scorn," "look down on," "reject," or "set aside," is what black movements struggle against. The verb, when employed by those with wealth, high prestige, or political power, severely constricts ethnic space of those "negated." To counter the processes of *despreciado*, people in Afro-Latin American and indigenous Latin American movements seek to deploy the verb *respetar*, which means to "respect," "revere," or "honor." It is by respect of people and their cultural creativities and traditions—wherever those traditions may come from—that the citizens of a modern nation-state come to imagine a set of social relations with ample space for multiculturality. And it is in the richness of multi-culturality that black and indigenous people seek to contribute to their respective countries, and to global cultures and cultural globalizations.

Although we are dealing with blackness in Latin American settings in this volume, the role of the United States can never be ignored or underestimated. As we write, for example, powerful negotiations are going on between the United States and Central and South American nations over the former's need (or demand) for a sea-level canal to connect the Atlantic and Pacific Oceans. On December 31, 1999, the Panama Canal is to be ceded back to Panama, a nation-state formed by secession from Colombia engineered by the United States in 1903. Less than three years from now there may be a "dry canal" through the isthmus of Tehuantepec, southern Mexico, and/or through the Mosquito coastal regions (entering at Bluefields), Nicaragua, or through the Atrato-San Juan drainage of the Pacific Lowlands of Colombia.

According to the *New York Times* (Rohtner 1996), the likelihood is that Bluefields, home of thousands of black people, most bilingual in English and Spanish, and some speaking Mískito, will be the cutting point for this new canal. Ernesto Samper, president of Republic of Colombia, is quoted by the *Times* as stating that Colombia would build its own canal, as a series of lakes created by flooding the Atrato (including the home community of Zulia Mena) and the San Juan. In one fell swoop Colombia would, in this scenario, obliterate half or more of the territory now ceded to the black people and indigenous people of the Pacific Lowlands of Colombia, flood Quibdó, the capital of the Chocó, and destroy the world's richest rain forest with the greatest biodiversity on earth that is home to the densest population of people in the entire moist tropics of the Americas. Lest we "blame" the internal Colombian political economy for this pending act of ecological and ethnic devastation, note must be taken of the fact that plans in the United States have been drawn up for such a canal since at least 1950 (see, e.g.,

Whitten and Quiroga 1990, Whitten 1994 [1974]), when atomic explosives were deemed appropriate for blasting through the Serranía de Baudó.

The Colombian transoceanic canal, as currently envisaged by President Samper and his advisors, would constitute a catastrophe similar to the one that occurred more than two decades ago to the Saramaka Maroons of Suriname (R. Price 1983). No provision to protect the nearly 500-year-old landholdings of black people in the Colombian Chocó has been made. It will seriously affect about 800,000 or more black people and some 15,000 indigenous people of the Chocó Department. In the face of this threat, indigenous and black people have banded together under the auspices of the Emberá and Waunan Regional Indigenous Organization (OREWA). This organization sought the advice of the Cree First Nation of Canada, many of whose leaders have long engaged in contesting the Canadian government's policies and practices vis-à-vis massive hydroelectric projects. (The Cree are an Athabaskan-speaking native people.)

From the Whitten and Quiroga chapter we move to Panama to gain a perspective on conflict and salient social relations among black Panamanians. In "Crisis, Contraculture, and Religion among West Indians in the Panama Canal Zone," R. S. Bryce-Laporte discusses the variety of factors of migration, national identification (English-speaking black West Indians as bilingual Panamanians), structures of legal domination (U.S. Canal Zone policies and practices of racial language discrimination), community-level and regional-level occult mechanisms of resistance, and the internal clashes among black people that such mechanisms produce. The conflict between two young black men, which ramified to their families and on through the social fabric of the community, is analyzed as a microcosm of sustained contradiction between "the United States legal code and West Indian folk magic." Having established this, Bryce-Laporte considers the Canal Zone in the 1950s to be "a colonial, conflict-based plural system." We shall come to this concept of conflict-based plural system, introduced by M. G. Smith in 1965, again and again in these two volumes. The continuing focus on religious power inherent in black communities for black self-assertion and liberation in the face of substantial constraints will also arise repeatedly.

West Indian migration to Hispanic settings and ethnic discrimination within those settings constitute the primary focus of Philippe Bourgois's contribution. Writing of black communities in Costa Rica, he states: "Today Blacks are better off economically than the bulk of Hispanic and Amerindian population of Limón province, nevertheless ethnic discrimination against them persists." The structure of domination and its reciprocal—resistance and creative development of transformed black cultures—is set forth in clear relief when discussing the origins of the bilingual (Spanish-English) black people of the Limón province.

> Blacks in Costa Rica form part of a larger cultural formation spanning the entire Central American Caribbean which arose out of the economic enclaves established by North American transnational corporations beginning in the 1860s.

> Often the same individual who planted bananas or harvested cacao in Limón had previously shovelled dirt on the Panama Canal, or cut sugar cane in Cuba, and ultimately emigrated to New York City to work as an orderly in a hospital. . . . [Today] one of the effects of the persistence of ethnic discrimination against Blacks despite their upward class mobility is the preservation of Black culture.

In terms of migration and of community and regional organization, his argument that the black people in Panama and Costa Rica have come to represent a "labor aristocracy" discriminated against by poorer Hispanics bears careful reflection.

Virginia Kerns takes us to another sector of the African diaspora, to the Arawakan-speaking, Spanish-speaking, and English-speaking Garífuna of Belize (who are also known as the "Black Carib"). The important structural adjustment to "migrating cultures" of these trilingual people is brought out clearly for communities in this region: men must work outside the home, often as sailors or urban workers in the West Indies or the United States, while women work in the home and depend on remittances from their traveling men. Significantly, Kerns also makes comparisons with indigenous Mískito (Mosquito) and Guaymi peoples of the same region.

The theme introduced by Kerns is picked up in the sphere of ritual by Carol L. Jenkins. She focuses on the community of Dangriga (Stann Creek) and discusses the role of shamans, who are female, in the conducting of the two-week Dugu healing ceremony. Viewed from "outside" the community, this ceremony appears to be a great waste of money and food. Indeed, some nationalists call it a "Devil dance." Viewed from the inside, however, the ceremony is redistributive not only of produce but also of information about the networks of Garífuna and their far-flung resources and a "ritual reaffirmation of . . . identity as Garífuna."

The chapters by Kerns and Jenkins are important in another way. They orient us toward a sense of community that is pan-national. The Garífuna sense of community extends from Central America (where it continues to expand) to North America, with significant intra-communities both nucleated and dispersed in Los Angeles and New York (González 1988, McClaurin 1996).

Whitten continues the theme of ritual and community sense of "being" in chapter 6. He deals with both secular and sacred rituals to demonstrate the expressive complementarity of contexts in the Pacific Lowlands of Colombia and Ecuador as manifest in sex-role enactment. In some respects, the community structure in the Pacific Lowlands is quite similar to that among the Garífuna: "Specific households are embedded in networks radiating from male broker nodes which are strategic to socioeconomic striving. . . . Within the household the . . . matricentral cell is maintained by a mother's recruitment strategies for male support." The Garífuna have a far-flung sense of community across North and Central America and as sea-going people around the Atlantic rim, whereas self-identifying *morenos* and *libres* of the Pacific Lowlands extend their sense of community primarily within the nation-states of Ecuador, Colombia, and Panama.

Friedemann next discusses Güelmambí, a community of the Pacific Lowlands in Colombia which specializes in labor-intensive gold mining and the continued production of gold and *guanín* jewelry by means of pre-Columbian indigenous techniques. This chapter, by specifying and analyzing the details of local social organization of descent and kinship reproduction, represents the most sophisticated analysis yet of community-level black social organization in western South America (for a cognate in eastern South America, see R. Price 1975). Friedemann finds the black ramage kinship structure to be grounded in mythology (black historicity) and fortified by spatial living arrangements. Moreover, members of this community interact with ease with their more mobile brethren throughout this culture region and beyond (see, e.g., Whitten 1986a; Whitten and Quiroga 1990).

The next chapter is a comparative study of Garífuna and Seminole by Rebecca B. Bateman. Using an argument introduced by Whitten and Szwed (1970: 43–48) with regard to convergence in social formations among people with comparable pressures in their histories, she finds the community structures of these diverse people similar, the main difference being that the Garífuna "became more Indian, culturally, than the blacks did among the Seminole." Her argument is a good example of the complex processes discussed in great detail by Neil Whitehead (1988) as "ethnic recruitment" between black and indigenous people in the Americas. Our point here, as elsewhere, is that the contrast "black"/"Indian" is one coming from the *negro/indio* ideology that maintains whiteness in a superior position over both.

Berta Pérez, in chapter 9, "Pantera Negra: A Messianic Figure of Historical Resistance and Cultural Survival among Maroon Descendants in Southern Venezuela," underscores the vigor with which history and historicity of black tellers yield dynamics of marronage of their pasts that serve as vehicles of discursive resistance in the present. The Afro-American people of Aripao are descendants of Dutch plantation Maroons who migrated to and are now living deep in the rain forests of Bolívar State in southern Venezuela. Their route of migration, deeply embedded in their memory, includes the Caura River region, which extends from the foothills of the Parima and Pacarima highlands north to the Orinoco River between Ciudad Bolívar in the east and Caicara de Orinoco in the west. Historically this region contains one of the most rugged territories in South America (the highlands of the Guayana Shield, home of the well-known Yanomami native peoples) and the riverine area (the Orinoco, long controlled by Carib-speaking raiders who allied with the Dutch against the Spanish). Yekuana, Piaroa, and Panoan indigenous territories lie to the north of the Lower Caura. The story told is that of the black jaguar woman, Pantera Negra (black panther). It is inscribed in a late-nineteenth-century book as history and told through history and into the present as historicity (what people say about their pasts). In the history and historicity of Pantera Negra contradictions abound, as do resolutions. She, in "the book," is the black *mulata*, a Maroon culture hero born of the union of a Dutch plantation woman and a black foreman slave. She initiates her own freedom but holds black slaves and indigenous slaves. In the tellings of people of Aripao, Pantera Negra is the daughter of a Spanish princess and a black slave. This is but the beginning, for in other intrigues of the history and historicity of their pasts we encounter eternal love triangles involving a hunter (Carib in history, Spanish in historicity) that escalate, as myths are wont to do, into great potential alliances that reflect enduring discourses of power, inequality, enchantment, hope, and resilience. As Pantera Negra's stories—always told by men—unfold, so too does the cultural enchantment and embedded knowledge of the moral topography of this vast region of Venezuela, bounding and releasing, as it does, ethnic powers of whiteness, blackness, indigenousness, and *mestizaje*. In this topography, or sacred geography, *la pantera negra* twice undergoes the natural cycle of birth, life, and death and adds to it not one but two mythical rebirths. The first of these signals the contrast between slavery and *cimarronaje*, the second slavery and emancipation. In the powers of self-liberation, it is the former version—freedom at all costs—that prevails in Venezuelan black modernity of this region.

> *Si Dios fuera negro*
> *todo cambiaría*
> *Sería nuestra raza*
> *la que mandaría*

> "If God were black
> all would change.
> It would be our race
> that held the reins."

—(Roberto Angleró, Si Dios fuera negro; refrain of a Caribbean *salsa*)
Translation by David M. Guss (1993: 451, 467)

The penultimate chapter in this part is David M. Guss's article on the powerful performances of historical consciousness manifest in a festival in the regional community of Barlovento, northern Venezuela. This festival expresses changes and transformations of the entire Venezuelan national political economy over an extended period. Significant in such expression is that of the essence of blackness in this region of northern South America, which extends from the eastern border of Colombia west across the Caribbean Sea, linking the Andes with the Spanish Main and mainland South America with the lesser and greater Antilles. The Barlovento region of Venezuela lies two hours east of the capital city, Caracas. There *cimarronaje* is recorded as early as 1532 (Guss and Waxer 1994), and continues in the region of the festival through the eighteenth century. *Cumbe* is the term usually used for the runaway fortified village in this region; it derives from the Mandingo word "for separate or out-of-the-way place," according to Guss and Waxer (1994: 24–29), who add important information to the work of Richard Price (1979) and others:

> Usually located above river banks or in remote mountainous areas, cumbes were typically well-hidden, and housed an average of 120 residents. Such settlements were also called *rochelas* and *patucos*. *Cimarrones* were often assisted by indigenous tribes living in the area (e.g. the Tomusa in Barlovento), and *cumbe* populations were composed of not only blacks, but also Indians and even poor whites.

Guss's chapter is on *la fiesta de San Juan*, which takes place June 23–25 every year in the community of Curiepe and elsewhere in Barlovento. In the colonial era these three days were allocated to slaves as a taste of restricted freedom and to allow them to express pent-up tensions through African-American ritual. It seems that during this period of restricted freedom, slaves actually planned their insurrections and flights from bondage, giving us yet another instance of the inseparability of insurrection and *cimarronaje* from the institution of black slavery. The chapter begins with the concept of Saint John the Baptist, a figure curiously important in indigenous and African-American festival activity in many parts of Central and South America. We say "curiously" because this festival is one of the oldest of Catholic Christian ceremonies. Indeed, it may predate Christianity as an ancient celebration of the summer solstice. Next comes the manifestation of National Saint John, as celebration of a Venezuelan nationality promising freedom to all of its *razas*, including the *indio* and the *negro*. A subsequent transformation celebrated during this time is San Juan Cimarrón, which represents modern revolutionary activity in Venezuela. And finally we are treated to an analysis of Congo Saint John, where blackness in all of its Venezuelan dimensions, including the incorporation of whiteness, is revealed.

The nationalist and ethnic-bloc processes that we set forth in our general introduction are all reflected in Guss's chapter. We find cognate public and private cultural events in most if not all areas of the Afro-Latin American cultural regions discussed (see, e.g., Templeman 1994, Guss and Waxer 1994, Whitten and Quiroga 1990, 1994). This chapter offers one of several current breakthroughs in critical thought that demonstrate how scholars can work effectively in the confluence of ethnography, historical ethnography, ethnomusicology, and history.

Cartagena de Indias, also known as *el puerto negrero*, the slavers' (black bringers') port on Colombia's Caribbean Coast—the Spanish Main—was the entrepôt for the majority of black African slaves brought to the Spanish-dominated colonial Americas. Beginning with the Senegambia as its primary source in the sixteenth century, the Portuguese and Spanish moved southward and then southeastward down the coast of Africa, ravishing Guinean and then the Angolan and

Congo regions for its steady stream of chattels (see, e.g., Curtin 1969, Castillo Mathieu 1982, Russell-Wood 1995). Slaves were classed by their labor. The work of a very strong young man who recovered from the Middle Passage was a *pieza de indias*, "work unit of the Indies," and price was set accordingly. Men with lesser capacity for work, such as the older and sicker, and women and children were aggregated as *piezas de indias*, which makes census retrieval so difficult for this (as other) slave-dominated regions. Labor was vital to the Spanish colonies, but the presence of "blackness" was unwanted except for the measure of labor to bring wealth to the buyer (Curtin 1969). Columbus, by the way, used the concept *piezas* to refer to the Taíno Arawak of the Greater Antilles (Cuba, Hispaniola, Puerto Rico, Jamaica) whom he enslaved during his first, second, and third voyages (e.g., Forbes 1993:23). And Cartagena itself was the site of large-scale Spanish enslavement of its native "Caribes" people by authorization of a 1503 royal Spanish edict proclaiming the legitimacy of "just wars" to enslave "rebels." Enslaved native Cartagenans then were sent to Hispaniola (Haiti) to replace those decimated by Spanish slavery there (e.g., Forbes 1993: 32ff; see the introduction to volume II for more information on this subject).

Over the past quarter of a century two complementary phenomena are reported from modern Cartagena. The first is that learned scholars from many parts of the world who travel there find the discourse of "race" to be subsumed by the insistence on inequality as a class phenomenon. The second is that Afro-Colombians claiming a national political position on "black tickets" and Afro-Colombians writing of Colombian racism often come from Cartagena. Joel Streicker's final chapter in the first part addresses these issues directly. Like other authors in these two volumes, Streicker bases his description and analysis on firsthand, extended ethnographic field work, which he conducted for seventeen months in a poor district called Santa Ana, whose residents refer to themselves and are known as *santaneros*. Although people from other areas of Colombia and other Latin Americans and Anglo Americans would "see" *santaneros* as "black," the language of blackness does not constitute a significant dimension of *santanero* discussions about their life chances and social positions. What Streicker found was that to be classed as *negro* in Cartagena is to be relegated to the status of infrahuman, to be part of a complex of animality with purely negative connotations. It is to be placed outside of and below all class and status categories. In Cartagena, Streicker finds the discourse of "race" and that of "gender" and racially gendered discriminatory categories (blackness and femininity) to be encoded in the language of "class," which itself utilizes the common Latin American euphemism *clase popular*, or "popular (common) class," to designate rural peasants, proletarians, and the urban poor. The "popular class" is, in short, the bottom of the class hierarchy in Colombia, and strong associations are made with animality and femininity. People in this class are the poorest and the most politically disfranchised of Colombia in general and of Cartagena in particular. This chapter demonstrates with detailed force how the power of the symbols of oppression is utilized in everyday talk among a poor black people and how masculinity is clearly privileged as engendered dominance. The concept of racial discrimination discourse as embedded in other discriminatory discourses helps us understand something of the intricacies, at a local level, that are so pervasive on regional, national, and international levels.

The third part of this volume, on the Andes, features six chapters devoted to regions that are perhaps the least known to specialists of the African diaspora. We open with Peter Wade's overview, "The Cultural Politics of Blackness in Colombia," which moves us from the microcosm of embedded racism to the public, national recognition by Afro-Colombians of their common experiences and the oppressiveness of the extant male-dominated, white power structure and distribution of wealth and status. Once again we find the excitement manifest when scholarship of the academy intertwines with the cultural constructions of active movements to shape the ideology of nation-states in providing space for indigenous (here including black) voices. Wade raises significant and sweeping issues "for the understanding of the cultural politics of blackness and nationhood in Latin America and the Caribbean, and for anthropology in general." He establishes the history of the organization of Cimarrón in Colombia, which formed from a study group, Soweto, in 1976, by self-identifying black people throughout the nation, with the locus in Pereira (adjacent to Cali's international airport). He moves to the legal dimensions of "black culture," showing how it parallels those of "indigenous culture," upon which concepts it has been legally molded. He concludes with this productive and provocative statement about the role of scholarship in supporting movements of ethnic self-assertion:

> Supporting black mobilization in Colombia can take a variety of forms: destabilizing mainstream images of a mestizo nation, investigating and publicizing black history and ethnography, and participating in political negotiations. Nina Friedemann and Jaime Arocha have been active in all these fields, for example. It seems to me also useful to publicize the political conjunctures of identification as they occur so that blacks and non-blacks alike can see what is happening in Colombia as something that draws on the past. But far from being simply a recuperation of the past, a liberated expression of something present but repressed, these changes constitute something new, drawing on new political conjunctures; and these changes will be legitimated not so much by the past as by the future, not so much by what blackness was as by what it may become.

From Colombia we move to south to Bolivia to examine, in the chapter by Madeline Barbara Léons, key features of stratification and pluralism in the Yungas, homeland of Fortunata Medina. This is the semitropical region northeast of the capital city of La Paz where Spanish-speaking black people, Aymara-speaking black people, and Quechua-speaking and Aymara-speaking indigenous people, as well as *mestizo* colonists, constitute a plural system of conflict. Following M. G. Smith, Léons defines pluralism as "the segmentation of the society into social groups that possess analogous, parallel, non-complementary and distinguishable sets of social institutions. . . . The plural structure is maintained over time through the capacity of those of the dominant section to block the participation . . . of others."

This pluralism is brought to the fore again by Kathleen Klumpp in her detailed study of black traders of North Highland Ecuador. She focuses on the survival and profit-making economics of people coming from all-black Andean communities near the Ecuadorian-Colombian border. In contrast to practices by the Garífuna and Pacific Lowlanders, it is the women, not the men, of the Chota region who "go out" with their avocados to urban and rural markets, develop and endeavor to sustain tenuous alliances with buyers, and return with meager capital by which to survive and advance in a nationalist social environment that denigrates "blackness."

> Both the mestizo and Chota Negro traders fall within the lower limits of a hierarchical scale of social status. However, within these limits, the mestizos identify themselves and are identified by all other ethnic groups as higher on the scale of prestige evaluation than either the highland Negro or the Indian. Depending on the region of Ecuador and who is doing the evaluating, the Negro may be placed socially above the Indian, below the Indian, or at the same level. Trading relationships between the Chota sellers and their buyers should, therefore, reflect the asymmetry of ethnic status inequality.

We are unable to publish a chapter on blackness in Peru, for nothing exists in English with a strong ethnographic focus for this centerpiece of Andean regionalism in Western scholarship. We recommend, however, the only serious, historically oriented ethnography undertaken within Peruvian black communities. This is the monograph by the French sociologist and historian Denys Cuche (1981), who carefully details the forms of economics and social relationships that exist there, demonstrating many parallels with cognate communities in Ecuador, Colombia, and Bolivia.

Peter Wade continues the analysis of pluralism and pernicious racism in nations espousing the ideology of *mestizaje* by reporting on the phenomenon of blackness in Medellín, Colombia, a region long and erroneously conceptualized in Colombia as inhabited exclusively by a special *"antioqueño" mestizo* "race." Indeed, the *antioqueño* image is often taken outside of Colombia to be the quintessential representation of the republic itself. (Its personalized embodiment in the United States is that of Juan Valdéz, the handpicker of ripe Colombian coffee beans for the U.S. consumer). Wade specifically considers the migratory stream from the Chocó region to Medellín, dealing with black rural migrants in special enclaves in one of the more urbanized regions of northern South America. While the Chocoanos live in nucleated and dispersed communities in their homeland, they must adapt to fragmentation in housing arrangements in Medellín and make a creative adaptation to restore communal relationships through various recreational vehicles, to which they give their distinctive stamp of creative black behavior. Wade, in this previously unpublished essay, writes:

> Seeing music as constitutive of, as well as representing, social positionings is important too. If music is seen as a means of imagining communities—and thereby constituting them—then this opens up flexibility in grasping its representational role. It makes it easier to see how a given style of music can be seen as a national unity and a diversity. What music can represent is more contextual, depending on whose imaginings are operating and in what ways. . . . The process of imagining works between unity and diversity. . . . Imaginations are part and parcel of the social relations one lives and are as structured as they are. The point is that music can be a process of imagining and thus living different sets of social relations, rather than just representing them.

With this eloquent statement we are drawn to the phrase by Karl Marx cited in the general introduction: "As people express their lives . . . so they are."

The penultimate chapter of this volume, by Robert W. Templeman, owes much to the efforts of Fortunata Medina. "We Are People of the *Yungas*, We Are of the *Saya* Race" delves deeply into the expansive cultural symbol of music as a vehicle for the communication of ethnic power born of disfranchisement and bound for national and international respect. In the 1970s people in the deep valleys that run from the altiplano city of La Paz (whose international airport—El Alto—is the highest in the world, at 13,300 feet above sea level) toward Amazonas began to rescue from their cultural repertoire of knowledge that which they took to be *netamente africano*, purely African. As the movement to rescue their cultural heritage and hence their ethnic dignity grew, the call-response musical style known as *saya* reemerged as a local force, then transformed to a regional and national power. The *saya* itself is most properly the chorus of the call-response pattern, that part of the musical genre that unites black voices to sing of the salient themes of the past and present, themes that resound into a future to be filled with emergent culture.

The leader of the movement was and is Fortunata Medina Pinedo de Pérez, about whom we wrote at the beginning of this introductory chapter. Herein Templeman documents how the movement began in the yungas in the 1970s, a time when, as a young girl, Medina walked for two hours to attend a school where there were no chairs or desks. Communicating as black Bolivians through official channels was fruitless, so someone in the community decided that if normal requests fell on politically and ethnically deaf ears, then perhaps sung requests would enliven interethnic discourse. This *saya* was composed:

> Me manda a la escuela
> ¿Pero sin papel ni lápiz,
> con que voy a escribir?

> They send me to school,
> but without paper or pencil
> with what am I going to write?

Singing and playing music to make requests caught on, and an ethnic-cultural bridge was built between local people of color and faraway bureaucrats who lacked such complexion. Today *sayas* are sung about virtually everything known, from black needs to national power structures. One of the best-known *sayas* resonates with the verse from a Colombian salsa quoted from Guss's work on the Festival of St. John (chapter 10).

> Si yo fuera presidente,
> formaría un puente
> Formaría un puente,
> de Tocaña hasta la Paz

> If I were president,
> I would build a bridge
> I would build a bridge,
> from Tocaña to La Paz

And build a bridge these singers did, from gaining desks and chairs for their school in the village of Tocaña in the *yungas* to the winning of national musical competitions in Cochabamba, to an audience with the vice president of the nation (the Aymara indigenous man, Victor Hugo Cárdenas), to invitations from many nations (including adjacent Peru and faraway United States) to come and discuss their emergent and historical Bolivian Africanity.

The theme of Africanity leads us back again to Colombia, where we turn to one of the most powerful sets of imagery in the Western world: the God versus Devil polarity in Christian theology and practical ideology. An illustration of the dynamics of this imagery as it affects the entire "healing network" involving black, indigenous, and white-*mestizo* people of Colombia (and by implication all of Central and South America) is set forth in the final chapter of this volume, written by Michael Taussig.

At this point, we are going to present a little more background than we have with the other chapters in this volume. To appreciate Taussig's work let us first move outward in space to Cuba, then back in time to Africa and Europe in the

Middle Ages, then return to the Caribbean islands of Hispaniola and Cuba of the sixteenth and seventeenth centuries, before reviewing relevant literature from the Caribbean, Central America, and South America. We begin in recent, prerevolutionary Cuba.

The saying "Abasikiri osairo saiko" (Mientras hay Dios hay Diablitos) comes from the Lucumí language of contemporary Cuba (Cabrera 1970b). It introduces a theme to which we will again direct our attention in the second volume. Deriving directly from the Yoruba language of Nigeria, it is one of many refrains belonging to the Abakua religious movement. It means "Where there is God there are Tricksters."

Translation of *diablitos* as used by the Cuban Lydia Cabrera, a longtime student of Abakua religion, reminds us to be careful with facile cognates between the Spanish diminutive suffix *ito* and the standard English gloss "little." We have pointed out in these volumes that the concepts *blanquito* and *negrito* are not to be translated in the same way. When used in public discourse (as opposed to private, intrafamilial usage) the diminutive suffix of these terms constitutes an asymmetrical contrast reflecting social power bound to the concept of "color" or "race." By this is meant that *blanquito* stands for "really white" whereas *negrito* means "cute black," as when people in blackface dance in mockery of real black people. The *diablito* diminutive takes us to concepts of other cultures, other spirits, other deities, other ways of thinking about the supernatural or preternatural in strict contrast to the all-encompassing good (God)–evil (Devil) Christianity that so influenced the course of racism in the Americas from the fifteenth century to the present.

To understand the Cuban usage of *diablito* here we must turn to the African, African American, and Native American concepts of trickster. A trickster, a *diablito*, is a being who can seem to fit into the Christian pantheon as Devil or demon (*Diablo* or *demonio*) while in fact serving the role of other cultural being, such as the West African Legba (Lebba, Elegbara, Liba; see Herskovits 1941 [1958]:251ff.) or the Native American Zemi (Cimi, Cima). "We know beyond dispute that [the concept of the trickster] has carried over into the New World in the evidence cited from Brazil, Guiana, Trinidad, Haiti, and New Orleans. Here known under various names . . . he rules the cross-roads and, as an extension of his powers and duties in west Africa, 'opens the gate' for the other gods at all rituals" (Herskovits, p. 252).

Put this way, everywhere Christianity reigned in African, African-European, or African-American settings, tricksters were evoked by godly and saintly imagery and this evocation opened the gates to other deities. When we realize that Christianity entered West Africa (first in the Senegambia, then in other areas southward and southeastward) sometime around 1544 through Portuguese missions, this early evocation gives us pause for thought in our popular Western contrasts between Europe as Christian and Africa as Islamic and pagan. Indeed, in 1491, during the baptism of King Nzinga of the African state of Kongo (Congo; modern Zaire), Christian miracles were said to have occurred there (Thornton 1995: 169–172). Writing of Christian conversions in West Africa and of the significance of the Congolese in the Americas, Thornton states:

> There were state-level conversions, in which African political authorities accepted baptism and used their power and influence to spread the faith to their followers, as well as a number of individual conversions all along the African coast. Typically, these people were either the descendants of European settlers who had come to live permanently in Africa, or they were Africans who became associated with these commercial communities, either through marriage, co-residence, commercial interest, or enslavement. . . . Christian Africans, especially from central Africa, where Christianity was the most widespread, were often chosen to assist in the conversion of other Africans, especially in Catholic countries. They, in turn, helped shape the way in which Christian ideas were accepted by Africans in the Americas, often starting from the model of Christianity in Africa. (169–170).

Based on extensive research on the religious aesthetics of African blackness in Europe from antiquity to the sixteenth century, art historians and medieval scholars Jean Devisse and Michel Mollat (1979:255) write:

> From St. Jerome and fourth-century Christianity the Occident inherited two basic lines of thought and reflection. The first regarded Africa as a distant land, the home of heretics and schismatics and in time isolated by Islam. . . . The second . . . had to do with blackness as a color. Due to the lack of actual contact with Africa, blackness was available as an element in the visionary domain of theology and metaphysics . . . [in European art]. Blackness was the opposite of light, standing for all the hostile underworlds that Christianity took over from ancient tradition.

The sixteenth century was not only the age of exploration, conquest, and colonization for Iberians abroad but also the era of the Spanish Inquisition at home and in the new colonies (see, e.g., Lea 1908, Caro Baroja 1967). "The magical lore of the European was joined to that of the despised African and Indian to form a symbiosis, transformation, and adaptation of forms unknown to each group," Taussig writes (1980:41). The African peoples and Native American peoples within the time-space of *la leyenda negra* had already become attached to God's antithesis, the Christian Devil. One of the first magico-ideological acts of European clergy in viewing Native and African cultures in American settings was to represent non-European spirits, souls, beings, and icons as stemming from their Christian Devil. In 1502, for example, writing of the Arawakan Taíno of the island of Hispaniola, Gonzalo Fernández de Oviedo y Valdés voiced the official word of the Catholic Church with regard to all indigenous and black religious and secular objects. Focusing specifically on the indigenous Taíno, he says:

Among this tribe, I have found nothing more frequently painted, carved, or engraved, or so deeply respected and worshiped, than the hated and sacrilegious figure of the devil, which is frequently painted and carved with multiple tails and heads that are deformed, dog-like and frightful, showing ferocious teeth, disproportionate ears, inflamed serpent-like eyes, and many other frightening images.
On the island of Hispaniola, the *cemí*, as I have said, is what we call the devil. (Parry and Keith 1984:9–10)

West of Hispaniola on the island of Cuba, the historian and critical anthropological theorist Fernando Ortiz documented in great depth the plethora of Devil beliefs and practices projected onto black people during and after the Spanish Inquisition. In *Historia de una pelea cubana contra los demonios* (History of a Cuban Fight against Demons), Ortiz (1975c) describes in detail two facets of inquisitorial Devil searches. The source of evil, he says, comes from Europe and is projected onto people of color. The source of greatest fear for the Europeans is the awesome fusion of iron and fire in black reverential homage to their African American and circum-Atlantic culture. For example, in 1672, Cuban colonists located "the Devil himself" (*el mismísimo demonio*) in the black community of San Juan de los Remedios del Cayo and asked a Catholic curate to exorcise him and send him straight back to Hell. It was required by the Spanish Crown and clergy that the "iron and fire" of this community be destroyed. And in this destruction of a black, New World fusion of spiritual powers, the Christian Devil of the white conquest would be sent back to burn in the flames of Hell.

Ogún is the iron. Shangó is the fire. They are often manifest as patron saints in African-Catholic syncretisms in the colonies and in contemporary nation-states in the Americas. In some manifestations, Ogún carries a sword and stands for rebellion. But the fire of Shangó, in a feminine manifestation as thunder and lightning as well as erotic sensuality (e.g., Ortiz 1975c:114), when united with Ogún, produces the symbol of imminent revolt. In the community of San Juan de los Remedios del Cayo in 1672, this spiritual unity was embodied in a black woman prophet, Leonarda, and it was toward this black woman that the exorcism of the Devil was directed.

It should be no surprise that the Devil should be a powerful force not only in syncretized forms of African deities (for example as Ogún and Shangó) or indigenous spirits and spirit masters (Arawakan Cemi or Quechua Supai) but also among the white and *mestizo* people. In fact, where blackness and indigenousness fused in the Americas, whites seem to have attributed particularly powerful qualities to an active Devil. In spite of centuries of genetic intermingling that has produced widely scattered populations of "black Indians" (or people often self-identifying as *zambo* and/or called *zambo* by black and indigenous and sometimes *mestizo* people), the pervasive social-race polarity in Latin America, as we have seen, separates black and indigenous populations as opposites at the bottom of a class-ethnic national structure. The fusion of opposites may at times give rise to transcendent power.

All "Indians" are conceptualized as "descended" from native populations of the Americas. All "black" populations are conceptualized as "descended" from Africans. From the beginning of the colonial era to the present, whites and *mestizos* have viewed blacks and indigenes as dual founts of evil and as specialists in "African" and "Indian" witchcraft and sorcery. Such negative attributions are often said to be the "real sources" of physical illnesses and social unrest in the modern nations of the Americas. Black, indigenous, and *zambo* populations have been targets for accusations of insurgence by politicians and bureaucrats in nation-states with radically different political persuasions and ideologies (e.g., Sandinista Nicaragua and U.S.-dominated Honduras) and the subjects of sustained Christian evangelism for nearly 500 years. The political similes and metaphors used to characterize such peoples are usually those of negative animal features ("treacherous like a jaguar," "black and red forest-dwelling monkeys") and the Christian Devil. In Christian religion, the metaphors quickly became reified, and all indigenous and black manifestations of shamanism, numinous thought, aesthetic portrayal, and ritual activity became stigmatized as "Devil worship" at one time or another. Examples of this in this first volume include the *dugu* of the Garífuna described by Jenkins and the *currulao* of the Pacific Lowlands of Ecuador and Colombia described by Whitten. The Devil takes on both supernatural and subnatural (beastly) attributes and is attached syntagmatically to black, *zambo*, and indigenous peoples.

As colonial and contemporary Devil imagery attained iconic negativism in South and Central America, people classed as Indian, black, and *zambo* became human representations of cosmogonic associations of the "jungle," "nonwhite," and "Other"; and a transformation occurred to make them the national embodiment of all forces working against economic development and social improvement. Ironically, as these associations and representations intensified, the ancient Christian image of the Devil became imbued with new ethnic powers to heal. White and *mestizo* people have made and continue to make long journeys to visit indigenous, *zambo*, and black healers in lowland and Andean zones of South America. In the late twentieth century they pay from modest to large sums of money for ritual healing and, in the process, constantly transmit the ideology of supreme Devil power in the realm of mystical curing to the curers themselves.

It has been suggested by Taussig (1980, 1987), in research based on the analysis of folklore and shamanic performance in Colombia, that as the sheer reality of the concomitants of capitalist and socialist development strategies—poverty, illness, dependence, debt, and social unrest—permeate the environments of black, indigenous, and *zambo* healers, the healers themselves increase their occult powers in the eyes of whites and *mestizos*. In chapter 18, Taussig spells out the nature of the entire curing network. He regards it "as the material expression of a system of ideas, as a force for integrating at the same time as it is created by cultural and economic diversity, and as the source of the basic categories upon which popular culture rests." In a related work (Taussig 1980) he argues that North American capitalist expansion and the effects of underdevelopment in the Colombian plantation system of the Cauca Valley are revealed in the folklore and belief systems of black people in the regions of such capitalist expansion. Data that one might take as evidence of "retentions" of European Devil beliefs are seen by Taussig as local-level metaphors for the devouring effects of external capitalist domination by the United States in Colombia.

Our intellectual voyage of discovery of the illuminations to be found in Central America and northern and western South America has been a great one. Beginning with visits by an Afro-Colombian congresswoman and an Afro-Bolivian leader to the University of Illinois at Urbana-Champaign in the fall of 1996, we have ranged from western South America and Central America to Orinocan Venezuela (a segment of Amazonia) on down the Andes and back to Bolivia and Colombia. To understand contemporary and recent ethnography in the framework of 500 years of creative resistance and cultural transformations in the face of relentless oppression, we journeyed out to the Caribbean and on to several regions of West Africa. It has been necessary in this introductory chapter to range from the oppressive powers of the United States in Latin American nation-states to the ways by which tricksters, Devils, even shamanic healing are part of the same roiling system that unites ethnography and history as mutually reinforcing dimensions of experiencing culture and communities.

# REFERENCES FOR INTRODUCTORY CHAPTERS

Aguirre Beltrán, Gonzalo
    1946             La población negra de México (1519–1810). Mexico City: Ediciones Fuente Cultural.
    1958             Cuijla: Esbozo etnográfico de un pueblo negro. Mexico City: Fundo de Cultura Económica.

Albó, Xavier
    1994             And from Kataristas to MNRistas? The Surprising and Bold Alliance between Aymaras and Neoliberals in Bolivia. In Donna Lee Van Cott (editor). Indigenous Peoples and Democracy in Latin America. New York: St. Martin's Press and Washington, D.C.: Inter-American Dialogue, pp. 44–81.

Alegría, Ricardo E.
    1985             Notas sobre la procedencia cultural de los esclavos negros de Puerto Rico durante la segunda mitad del siglo XVI. La Revista del Centro de Estudios Avanzados de Puerto Rico y el Caribe 1:58–79.

Arens, William, and Ivan Karp (editors)
    1989             Introduction. Creativity of Power: Cosmology and Action in African Societies. Washington, D.C.: Smithsonian Institution Press, pp. xi–xxix.

Arocha Rodriguez, Jaime
    1992             Afro-Colombia Denied. In North American Congress on Latin America (1992), pp. 28–31, 46–47.

Arrázola, Roberto
    1970             Palenque: Primer pueblo libre de América. Cartagena, Colombia: Ediciones Hernández.

Babcock, Barbara (editor)
    1978             The Reversible World: Symbolic Inversion in Art and Society. Ithaca: Cornell University Press.

Baralt, Guillermo, Carlos Collazo, Lydia Milagros González, and Ana Lydia Vega (compilers and editors)
    1990             El machete de Ogún: Las luchas de los esclavos en Puerto Rico (siglo xix). Río Piedras: Centro de Estudios de la Realidad Puertorriqueña, Proyecto de Divulgación Popular.

Barnet, Miguel
    1966             Biografía de un cimarrón. Havana: Academia de Ciencias de Cuba, Instituto de Etnología y Folklore.

Bascom, William R.
1951          The Yoruba in Cuba. Nigeria 37:14–20.
1952          The Focus of Cuban Santería. Southwestern Journal of Anthropol-
              ogy 6:64–68.

Bastide, Roger
1967          Les amériques noires: Les civilisations africaines dans le nouveau
              monde. Paris: Payot.
1969a         (editor) Les amériques noires. Special issue of the Journal de la So-
              ciété des Américanistes 58.
1969b         État actuel et perspectives d'avenir des recherches afro-ambricaines.
              In Bastide (1969a), pp.7–29.

Beckwith, Martha
1929          Black Roadways: A Study of Jamaican Folklife. Chapel Hill: Univer-
              sity of North Carolina Press.

Benítez Rojo, Antonio
1989          La isla que se repite: El Caribe y la perspectiva posmoderna. Hano-
              ver, N.H.: Ediciones del Norte.
1995          The Polyrhythmic Paradigm: The Caribbean and the Postmodern
              Era. In Vera L. Hyatt and Rex Nettleford (editors). Race, Discourse
              and the Origin of the Americas. Washington, D.C.: Smithsonian In-
              stitution Press.

Bennett, Lerone, Jr.
1987 [1962]   Before the Mayflower: A History of Black America. Chicago: Johnson.

Blanco, Tomás
1985 [1942]   El prejucio racial en Puerto Rico. Río Piedras: Ediciones Huracán.

Bliss, Peggy A.
1995          Black, White, Puerto Rican All Over. San Juan Star, Wednesday,
              March 22, pp. 30–31.

Bolles, A. Lynne
1996          Sister Jamaica: A Study of Women, Work, and Households in Kings-
              ton. Washington, D.C.: University Press of America.

Boon, James A.
1982          Other Tribes, Other Scribes: Symbolic Anthropology in the Com-
              parative Study of Cultures, Histories, Religions, and Texts. Cam-
              bridge: Cambridge University Press.

Boorstin, Daniel J.
1983          The Discoverers: A History of Man's Search to Know His World
              and Himself. New York: Vintage.

Bourricaud, François
1962          Changements à Puno. Paris: Institut de Hautes Études de l'Améri-
              que Latine.

Brandon, George
    1993            Santeria from Africa to the New World. Bloomington: Indiana University Press.

Bugner, Ladislas (general editor)
    1979            The Image of the Black in Western Art. 2 volumes. Cambridge: Harvard University Press.

Cabeza de Vaca, Alvar Núñez
    1542a           Relation of Alvar Núñez Cabeza de Vaca. Translated from the original Spanish manuscript (1542b) by Thomas Buckingham Smith. New York: J. Munsell, 1851.
    1542b           La relación que dio Alvar Núñez Cabeça de Vaca de lo acaecido en las Indias en la armada donde yua por gouernador Pamphilo de narbaez desde el año de veynte y siete hasta el año de treynta y seis que boluio a Seuilla con tres de su compania. Manuscript, Zamora, Spain.
    1993 [1555]     Castaways: The Narrative of Alavar Núñez Cabeza de Vaca. Edited and with introduction by Enrique Pupo-Walker. Translated by Frances M. Lopez-Morillas. Berkeley: University of California Press.

Cabrera, Lydia
    1969a           (compiler) Refranes de negros viejos. Miami: Editorial C.R. (Colección del Chicherekú).
    1969b           La sociedad secreta Abakuá: Narrada por viejos adeptos. Miami: Editorial C. R. (Colección del Chicherekú).
    1970a           Otán lyebiyé: Las piedras preciosas. Miami: Mnemosyne, Ediciones Miami (Colección del Chicherekú en el Exilio).
    1970b           Anagó: Vocabulario Lucumí (el Yoruba que se habla en Cuba). Miami: Cabrera y Rojas (Colección del Chicherekú).

Campbell, Mary B.
    1988            The Witness and the Other Worlds. Ithaca: Cornell University Press.

Carmichael, Stokeley
    1967            Quoted in Muhammed Speaks, December 15, p. 2.

Carmichael, Stokeley, and Charles Hamilton
    1966            Black Power. New York: Vintage.

Carneiro, Edison
    1946            Guerras de los Palmares. Translated by Tomás Muñoz Molina. Mexico City: Fondo de Cultura Economica.

Caro Baroja, Julio
    1967            Vidas mágicas e inquisición. 2 volumes. Madrid: Taurus.

Carpentier, Alejo
    1974            Concierto barroco. Mexico City: Siglo Veintiuno Editores.

Carrión, Juan M.
1993        Etnia, raza y la nacionalidad puertorriqueña. In Carrión, Teresa C.
            Garcia Ruíz, and Carlos Rodríguez Fraticelli (editors). La nación
            puertorriqueña: Ensayos en torno a Pedro Albizu Campos. San
            Juan: Editorial de la Universidad de Puerto Rico.

Carvalho Neto, Paulo de
1965        El negro uruguayo (hasta la abolición). Quito: Editorial Universi-
            taria.

Castillo Mathieu, Nicolás del
1982        Esclavos negros en Cartagena y sus aportes léxicos. Bogotá: Insti-
            tuto Caro y Cuervo LXII.

Césaire, Aimé
1947        Cahier d'un retour au pays natal. Paris: Editions Bordas.
1948        Discours sur le colonialisme. Paris: Présence Africaine.
1956        Culture et colonisation. Présence Africaine N.S. (8–10):190–205.

Chamberlain de Bianchi, Cynthia
1984        La enfermedad de gubida y el sincretismo religioso entre los Garífu-
            nas: Un analysis etnosiquíatrico. América Indígena 44 (3):519–542.

Chioma Steady, Filomina
1981        The Black Woman Cross-Culturally. Cambridge: Schenkman.

Collier, Simon, Harold Blakemore, and Thomas E. Skidmore (general editors)
1985        Cambridge Encyclopedia of Latin America and the Caribbean.
            New York: Cambridge University Press.

Columbus, Christopher
1960        The Journal of Christopher Columbus. Translated by Cecil James.
            New York: Clark N. Potter.

Córdoba L., Juan Tulio
1983        Etnicidad y estructura social en el chocó. Medellín: Editorial
            Lealon.

Corominas
1961        Breve diccionario etimológico de la lengua castellana. Madrid:
            Gredos.

Corsetti, Giancarlo, Nancy Motta González, and Carlo Tassara
1990        Cambios tecnológicos, organización social y actividades productivas
            en la costa Pacífica Colombiana. Bogotá: Comitato Internazionale
            per lo Sviluppo dei Popoli.

Cosby, Alfred W., Jr.
1972        The Colombian Exchange: Biological and Cultural Consequences
            of 1492. Westport, Conn.: Greenwood Press.

1986            Ecological Imperialism: The Biological Expansion of Europe, 900–
                1900. New York: Cambridge University Press.

Coulthard, G. R.
1962            Race and Colour in Caribbean Literature. London: Oxford Univer-
                sity Press.
1968            Parallelisms and Divergencies between "Negritude" and "Indige-
                nismo." Caribbean Studies 8:31–35.

Courtés, Jean Marie
1979            Preliminary Essay. In Devisse (1979).

Crahan, Margaret E., and Franklin W. Knight (editors)
1979            Africa and the Caribbean: Legacies of a Link. Baltimore: Johns
                Hopkins University Press.

Cuche, Denys
1981            Pérou Nègre: Les descendants d'esclaves africains de Pérou des
                grands domaines esclavagistes aux plantations modernes. Paris: Edi-
                tions L'Harmattan.

Cudjoe, Selwyn Reginald
1978            Resistance and the Caribbean Novel. Athens: Ohio University Press.

Curtin, Phillip D.
1969            The Atlantic Slave Trade: A Census. Madison: University of Wiscon-
                sin Press.

Dallas, Robert Charles
1803            The History of the Maroons from their Origins to the Establish-
                ment of their Chief Tribe at Sierra Leone. 2 volumes. London:
                Straham.

Davis, Martha Ellen
1981            Voces del purgatorio: Estudio de la salve dominicana. Santo Dom-
                ingo: Ediciones Museo del Hombre Dominicano, Serie Investiga-
                ciones Antropológicas No. 15.

Deive, Carlos Esteban
1980            La esclavitud del negro en Santo Domingo 1492–1844. 2 volumes.
                Santo Domingo: Museo del Hombre.

Dent, Gina
1992            Black Popular Culture. Seattle: Bay Press.

Desan, Suzanne
1989            Crows, Community, and Ritual in the Work of E. P. Thompson
                and Natalie Davis. In Hunt (1989), pp. 47–71.

Despres, Leo
1984            Ethnicity: What Data and Theory Portend for Plural Societies. In

David Maybury-Lewis (editor). The Prospects for Plural Societies. Washington, D.C.: American Ethnological Society.

Devisse, Jean
1979        1. From the Demonic Threat to the Incarnation of Sainthood. In Bugner (1979), volume 2.

Devisse, Jean, and Michel Mollat
1979        2. Africans in the Christian Ordinance of the World (Fourteenth to the Sixteenth Century). In Bugner (1979), volume 2.

Díaz Soler, Luis M.
1965        Historia de la esclavitud negra en Puerto Rico. Río Piedras: Ediciones Universidad de Puerto Rico.

Dolgin, Janet L., David S. Kemnitzer, and David M. Schneider
1977        "As People Express Their Lives, So They Are . . . " In Dolgin, Kemnitzer, and Schneider (editors). Symbolic Anthropology: A Reader in the Study of Symbols and Meanings. New York: Columbia University Press.

Drake, St. Clair
1987        Black Folk Here and There: An Essay in History and Anthropology. Volume 1. Los Angeles: UCLA Center for Afro-American Studies Publications.
1990        Black Folk Here and There: An Essay in History and Anthropology. Volume 2. Los Angeles: UCLA Center for Afro-American Studies Publications.

Drolet, Patricia L.
1980        The Congo Ritual of Northeastern Panama: An Afro-American Expressive Stucture of Cultural Adaptation. Ph.D. dissertation, University of Illinois at Urbana-Champaign.

Fernandes, Florestan
1972        O negro no mundo dos brancos. Sao Paulo: Difusão Européia do Livro.

Fick, Carolyn E.
1990        The Making of Haiti. Knoxville: University of Tennessee Press.

Filho, Mello Moraes
1888        Festas e tradiçes populares do Brasil. Rio de Janeiro: H. Granier.

Fog Olwig, Karen
1993        Global Culture, Island Identity: Continuity and Change in the Afro-Caribbean Community of Nevis. Philadelphia: Hardwood.

Forbes, Jack D.
1993        Africans and Native Americans: The Language of Race and the Evolution of Red-Black Peoples. Urbana: University of Illinois Press.

Franco Pichardo, Franklyn J.
1970            Los negros, los mulatos y la nacion dominicana. Santo Domingo:
                Editora Nacional.

Friedemann, Nina S. de
1984            Estudios de negros en la antropología colombiana: Presencia e in-
                visibilidad. In Jaime Arocha Rodriguez and Nina S. de Friedemann
                (editors). Un siglo de investigación social: Antropología en Colom-
                bia. Bogotá: Etno.

Friedemann, Nina S. de, and Jaime Arocha Rodriguez
1986            De sol a sol: Genesis, transformación y presencia de los negros en
                Colombia. Bogotá: Planeta Colombiana.
1995            Colombia. In Minority Rights Group (editor). No Longer Invisible:
                Afro-Latin Americans Today. London: Minority Rights Group Press,
                pp. 47–76.

Friedemann, Nina S. de, and Richard Cross
1979            Ma Ngombe: Guerreros y banderos en Palenque. Bogotá: Editora
                Carlos Valencia.

Fundación Colombiana de Investigaciones Folclóricas
1977            Primer Congreso de la Cultura Negra de las Américas. Bogotá: Fun-
                dación Colombiana de Investigaciones Folclóricas.

Geertz, Clifford
1973            The Interpretation of Cultures. New York: Basic Books.

Ghidinelli y Pierleone Massajoli, Azzo
1984            Resumen etnográfico de los caribes negros (Garifunas) de Hondu-
                ras. América Indígena 44 (3):485–518.

Gilroy, Paul
1993            The Black Atlantic: Modernity and Double Consciousness. Cam-
                bridge: Harvard University Press.

Glissant, Edouard
1995            Creolization in the Making of the Americas. In Vera L. Hyatt and
                Rex Nettleford (editors). Race, Discourse and the Origin of the
                Americas. Washington, D.C.: Smithsonian Institution Press.

González, Nancie L.
1988            Sojourners of the Caribbean: Ethnogenesis and Ethnohistory of the
                Garifuna. Urbana: University of Illinois Press.

Gorer, Geoffrey
1962 [1935]     Africa Dances: A Book about West African Negroes (with a new in-
                troduction by the author). New York: Norton.

Grafton, Anthony (with April Shelford and Nancy Siraisi)
1992            New Worlds, Ancient Texts: The Power of Tradition and the Shock
                of Discovery. Cambridge: Harvard University Press.

Greenblatt, Stephen (editor)
1993        New World Encounters. Berkeley: University of California Press.

Guillot, Carlos Federico
1961        Negros rebeldes y negros cimarrones (perfil afro-americano en la historia del Nuevo Mundo durante el siglo XVI). Montevideo: Fariña Editores.

Guss, David, and Lise Waxer
1994        Afro-Venezuelans. In Johannes Wilbert (general editor). Encyclopedia of World Cultures. New Haven: Human Relations Area Files Press.

Harrison, Faye V.
1988        Introduction: An African Diaspora Perspective for Urban Anthropology. Urban Anthropology 17(2–3):111–142.

Helms, Mary W.
1988        Ulysses' Sail: An Ethnographic Odyssey of Power, Knowledge and Geographical Distance. Princeton: Princeton University Press.

Herskovits, Melville
1941 [1958]  The Myth of the Negro Past. Boston: Beacon Press.
1945        Problem, Method, and Theory in Afro-American Studies. Afroamerica 1: 5–24.
1948        Man and His Works. New York: Knopf.
1956        The New World Negro: Selected Papers in Afroamerican Studies. Frances S. Herskovits (editor). Bloomington: Indiana University Press.

Hill, Donald R.
1977        The Impact of Migration on the Metropolitan and Folk Society of Carriacou, Grenada. Anthropological Papers of the American Museum of Natural History 52 (2).

Hill, Jonathan D. (editor)
1988        Rethinking History and Myth: Indigenous South American Perspectives on the Past. Urbana: University of Illinois Press.
1996        History, Power, and Identity: Ethnogenesis in the Americas, 1492–1992. Iowa City: University of Iowa Press.

Hobsbawn, Eric, and Terence Ranger (editors)
1983        The Invention of Tradition. Cambridge: Cambridge University Press.

Hoetink, Harry
1967        Caribbean Race Relations: A Study of Two Variants. Oxford University Press.

Honigmann, John J.
1959        The World of Man. New York: Harper & Row.

Hulme, Peter, and Neil L. Whitehead (editors)
  1992          Wild Majesty: Encounters with Caribs from Columbus to the Pres-
                ent Day. New York: Oxford University Press.

Hunt, Lynn (editor)
  1989          The New Cultural History. Berkeley: University of California Press.

Hurault, Jean
  1965          La vie matérielle de noirs réfugiés Boni et des indiens Wayana du
                Haut-Maroni (Guyane Française). Paris: Office de la Recherche
                Scientifique et Technique Outre-Mer.

Hurtado, Osvaldo
  1980 [1977]   Political Power in Ecuador. Translated by Nick W. Mills, Jr. Albu-
                querque: University of New Mexico Press.

Ibarra, Jorge
  1972          Ideología Mambisa. Havana: Instituto Cubano del Libro.

Jeffreys, M. D. W.
  1971          Maize and the Mande Myth. Current Anthropology 12 (3):291–320.

Johnston, Sir Harry H.
  1910          The Negro in the New World. London: Methuen.

Kent, R. K.
  1979          Palmares: An African State in Brazil. In R. Price (1979), pp. 170–190.

Kerns, Virginia
  1983          Women and the Ancestors: Black Carib Kinship and Ritual.
                Urbana: University of Illinois Press.

Knight, Franklin W.
  1974          The African Dimension of Latin American Societies. New York:
                Macmillan.

Knight, Franklin W., and Colin A. Palmer (editors)
  1989          The Modern Caribbean. Chapel Hill: University of North Carolina
                Press.

Kuper, Adam
  1988          The Invention of Primitive Society: Transformations of an Illusion.
                London: Routledge.

Laguerre, Michel S.
  1976          Belair, Port-au-Prince: From Slave and Maroon Settlement to Con-
                temporary Black Ghetto. In Norman E. Whitten, Jr. (editor). Afro-
                American Ethnohistory in Latin America and the Caribbean. Wash-
                ington, D.C.: American Anthropological Association, Latin
                American Anthropology Group, pp. 26–38.
  1982a         Urban Life in the Caribbean. Cambridge: Schenkman.

1982b  The Complete Haitiana: A Bibliographic Guide to the Scholarly Literature, 1900–1980. 2 volumes. Millwood, N.Y.: Kraus.

1987  Afro-Caribbean Folk Medicine: The Reproduction of Healing. South Hadley, Mass.: Bergin and Garvey.

1989  Voodoo and Politics in Haiti. New York: St. Martin's Press.

1990  Urban Poverty in the Caribbean: French Martinique as Social Laboratory. New York: St. Martin's Press.

Laosa, Marilu de
1990  Abolición de la esclavitud (review essay of El machete de Ogún). El Mundo: Puerto Rico Illustrado, March 18, pp. 9–11.

Larrazabal Blanco, Carlos
1975  Los negros y la esclavitud en Santo Domingo. Santo Domingo: Julio D. Postigo e Hijos.

Lea, Henry Charles
1908  The Inquisition in the Spanish Dependencies. New York: Macmillan.

Leach, Edmund
1982  Social Anthropology. New York: Oxford University Press.

Levine, Lawrence W.
1977  Black Culture and Black Consciousness: Afro-American Folk Thought from Slavery to Freedom. New York: Oxford University Press.

Lewis, Gordon K.
1983  Main Currents in Caribbean Thought: The Historical Evolution of Caribbean Society in Its Ideological Aspects, 1492–1900. Baltimore: Johns Hopkins University Press.

Lewis, Marvin A.
1983  Afro-Hispanic Poetry 1940–1980: From Slavery to "Negritud" in South American Verse. Columbia: University of Missouri Press.

Leyburn, James G.
1941 [1966]  The Haitian People. 2d edition. New Haven: Yale University Press.

Lockhart, James
1968  Spanish Peru 1532–1560: A Colonial Society. Madison: University of Wisconsin Press.

Luciano Franco, José
1975  La diaspora africana en el Nuevo Mundo. Havana: Editorial de Ciencias Sociales.

McClaurin, Irma
1996  Women of Belize: Gender and Change in Central America. New Brunswick: Rutgers University Press.

MacLean y Esteños, Roberto
1948            Negros en el Nuevo Mundo. Lima: Colección Mundo Nuevo.

Malec, Michael A. (editor)
1995            The Social Role of Sport in Caribbean Societies. Amsterdam:
               Gordon and Breach.

Mandle, Jay R., and Joan Mandle
1988            Caribbean Hoops: The Development of West Indian Basketball.
               Amsterdam: Gordon and Breach.

Marques, Gabriel
1996            Brasil: Pasado, presente e as possibilidades futuras. Paper presented
               at the Afro-Latin American Research Association Conference,
               Bahia, Brazil.

Meennesson-Rigaud, Odette
1958            Le rôle du Vaudou dans l'indépendance d'Haiti. Présence Africaine
               17–18: 43–67.

Mintz, Sidney W.
1966            Introduction to Leyburn (1941 [1956]), pp. v–xlii.
1974            Caribbean Transformations. Chicago: Aldine.

Mintz, Sidney W., and Richard Price
1976            An Anthropological Approach to the Afro-American Past: A Carib-
               bean Perspective. Philadelphia: ISHI.

Mitchell, Michael
1996            Human Rights and the Afro-Brazilian Predicament. Paper pre-
               sented at the Afro-Latin American Research Association Confer-
               ence. Bahia, Brazil.

Moore, Carlos
1988            Castro, the Blacks, and Africa. Los Angeles: UCLA Center for Afro-
               American Studies, Afro-American Culture and Society Monograph
               Series No. 8.

Mörner, Magnus
1967            Race Mixture in the History of Latin America. Boston: Little,
               Brown.

Moya Pons, Frank
1986a           Después de Colón: Trabajo, sociedad y política en la economía del
               oro. Madrid: Alianza Editorial.
1986b           El pasado dominicano. Santo Domingo: Fundación J. A. Caro Alvarez.

Muilenburg, Peter
1991            Fate and Fortune on the Pearl Coast. Americas (English ed.) 43 (3):
               32–38.

Murga Sanz, Vicente
    1959        Juan Ponce de León. San Juan: Ediciones de la Universidad de
                Puerto Rico.
    1960        Puerto Rico en los manuscritos de Don Juan Bautista Muñoz. Vol-
                ume 1. Río Piedras: Ediciones de la Universidad de Puerto Rico.
North American Congress on Latin America (NACLA)
    1992        The Black Americas: 1492–1992. NACLA Report on the Americas
                25(4).
Nunley, John
    1988        Caribbean Festival Arts. Seattle and St. Louis: University of Wash-
                ington Press and the St. Louis Art Museum.
Ortiz, Fernando
    1975a       El engaño de las razas. Havana: Editorial de Ciencias Sociales.
    1975b       Los negros esclavos. Havana: Editorial de Ciencias Sociales.
    1975c       Historia de una pelea cubana contra los demonios. Havana: Edito-
                rial de Ciencias Sociales.
    1986        Los Negros Curros. Havana: Editorial de Ciencias Sociales.
Otte, Enrique
    1963        Cedulas reales relativas a Venezuela (1500–1550). Caracas: Edi-
                ción de la Fundación John Boulton y la Fundación Eugenio Men-
                doza.
    1977        Las perlas del Caribe: Nueva Cadiz de Cubagua. Caracas: Funda-
                ción John Boulton.
Palencia-Roth, Michael
    1993        The Cannibal Law of 1503. In Williams and Lewis (1993), pp.
                21–63.
Palmer, Colin A.
    1976        Slaves of the White God: Blacks in Mexico, 1570–1650.
Pané, Ramón
    1984        The Relación of Fray Ramón Pané. In Parry and Keith (1984). Vol-
                ume 1, pp. 18–27.
Panger, Daniel
    1982        Black Ulysses. Athens: Ohio University Press.
Parry, John H., and Robert G. Keith (editors), with the assistance of Michael Jimenez
    1984        New Iberian World: A Documentary History of the Discovery and
                Settlement of Latin America to the Early 17th Century. 5 volumes.
                New York: Times Books and Hector & Rose.
Parry, J. H., and P. M. Sherlock
    1956        A Short History of the West Indies. London: Macmillan.

Pérez de la Riva, Francisco
    1946            El negro y la tierra, el conuco y el palenque. Revista Bimestre Cu-
                    bana 58 (2,3):97–139.
    1952            La habitación rural en cuba. Havana: Contribución del Grupo
                    Guamá, Antropolgía 26.
    1979            Cuban Palenques. In R. Price (1979).

Pérez Sarduy, Pedro
    1990            Open Letter to Carlos Moore. Afro Hispanic Review 9 (1–3):25–29.

Pérez-Stable, Marifeli
    1990            In Pursuit of Cuba Libre. Report of the Americas 24 (2):32–48.

Pescatello, Ann M. (editor)
                    New Roots in Old Lands: Historical and Anthropological Perspec-
                    tives. In Black Experiences in the Americas. Westport: Greenwood
                    Press.

Pitt-Rivers, Julian
    1967            Race, Color, and Class in Central America and the Andes. Daeda-
                    lus 96 (2):542–559.
    1973            Race in Latin America: The Concept of "Raza." Archives Européen-
                    nes de Sociologie 14 (1):3–31.

Pollak-Eltz, Angelina
    1971            Vestigios africanos en la cultura del pueblo venezolano. Cuerna-
                    vaca, Mexico: Centro Intercultural de Documentación (CIDOC).
    1972            Cultos afroamericanos. Caracas: Universidad Catolica Andrés Bello.

Preciado Bedoya, Antonio
    1961            Jolgorio: Poemas. Quito: Casa de la Cultura Ecuatoriana.

Price, Richard
    1975            Saramaka Social Structure: Analysis of a Maroon Society in Suri-
                    nam. Río Piedras: Institute of Caribbean Studies of the University
                    of Puerto Rico.
    1979            (editor) Maroon Societies: Rebel Slave Communities in the Ameri-
                    cas. Baltimore: Johns Hopkins University Press.
    1983            First-Time: The Historical Vision of an Afro-American People. Balti-
                    more: Johns Hopkins University Press.
    1990            Alabi's World. Baltimore: Johns Hopkins University Press.
    1995            Executing Ethnicity: The Killings in Suriname. Cultural Anthropol-
                    ogy 10(4):437–471.

Price, Richard, and Sally Price
    1993            Collective Fictions: Performance in Saramaka Folktales. In
                    Dorothea S. Whitten and Norman E. Whitten, Jr. (editors). Im-

agery and Creativity: Ethnoaesthetics and Art Worlds in the Americas. Tucson: University of Arizona Press, pp. 235–288.

Price, Sally
1983          Co-Wives and Calabashes. Ann Arbor: University of Michigan Press.

Price, Sally, and Richard Price
1980          Afro-American Arts of the Suriname Rain Forest. Berkeley: University of California Press.

Price-Mars, Jean
1928          Ainsi parla l'oncle. Paris: Imprimerie de Compiègne.

Quintero-Rivera, Angel G.
1987          The Rural-Urban Dichotomy in the Formation of Puerto Rico's Cultural Identity. New West Indian Guide 61 (3–4) 127–144.

Rohtner, Larry
1996          Close to Panama, Dreams of Rival "Canals." New York Times, November 10, pp. 1A, 6A.

Rout, Leslie B., Jr.
1972          Reflections on the Evolution of Post-War Jazz. In Addison Gayle, Jr. (editor). The Black Aesthetic. Garden City, N.Y.: Anchor, pp. 143–153.
1976          The African Experience in Spanish America: 1502 to the Present Day. Cambridge: Cambridge University Press.

Routte-Gomez, Eneid
1996          So, Are We Racists???? A Conspiracy of Silence: Racism in Puerto Rico. San Juan Star Magazine, December-January, pp. 54–58.

Royce, Anya Peterson
1977          The Anthropology of Dance. Bloomington: Indiana University Press.

Russell-Wood, A. J.
1995          Before Columbus: Portugal's African Prelude. In Vera Hyatt and Rex Nettleford (editors). Race, Discourse and the Origin of the Americas. Washington: Smithsonian Institution Press.

Sahlins, Marshall
1981          Historical Metaphors and Mythical Realities: Structure in the Early History of the Sandwich Islands Kingdom. Chicago: University of Chicago Press.

Scarano, Francisco A.
1993          Puerto Rico: Cinco siglos de historia. Santa Fe de Bogotá, Colombia: McGraw Hill Interamericana.

Schomburg, Arthur A.
    1928            Negroes in Seville. Opportunity 6:93.
    1970            The Negro Digs Up His Past. In Alain Locke (editor). The New
                    Negro. New York: Atheneum, pp. 232–240.

Shils, Edward
    1981            Tradition. Chicago: University of Chicago Press.

Shyllon, Folarin
    1982            Blacks in Britain: A Historical and Analytical Overview. In Joseph
                    Harris (editor). Global Dimensions of the African Diaspora. Wash-
                    ington, D.C.: Howard University Press.

Simms Hamilton, Ruth (editor)
    1990a           Creating a Paradigm and Research Agenda for Comparative Studies
                    of the Worldwide Dispersion of African Peoples. East Lansing,
                    Mich.: African Diaspora Research Project, Monograph No. 1.
    1990b           Toward a Paradigm for African Diaspora Studies. In Hamilton (1990a).

Sinnette, Elinor De Verney
    1977            Arthur Alfonso Schomburg, Black Bibliophile and Curator: His
                    Contribution to the Collection and Dissemination of Materials
                    about Africans and Peoples of African Descent. Ph.D. dissertation,
                    Columbia University.

Smith, Michael G.
    1965            The Plural Society in the British West Indies. Berkeley: University
                    of California Press.

Smith, Raymond T.
    1956            The Negro Family in British Guiana. London: Routledge & Kegan
                    Paul.

Stevens-Arroyo, Antonio M.
    1988            Cave of the Jagua: The Mythical World of the Taínos. Albuquer-
                    que: University of New Mexico Press.

Stutzman, Ronald
    1981            El Mestizaje: An All-Inclusive Ideology of Exclusion. In Whitten
                    (1981), pp. 445–494.

Sued Badillo, Jalil
    1983            Guayama: Notas para su historia. San Juan: Oficina de Asuntos Cul-
                    turales de la Fortaleza.

Sued Badillo, Jalil, and Angel López Cantos
    1986            Puerto Rico Negro. San Juan: Ediciones Huracán.

Taussig, Michael T. (writing under the pseudonym "Mateo Mina")
    1975            Esclavitud y libertad en el valle del Río Cauca. Bogotá: Fundación
                    Rosca de Investigación y Acción Social.

1978          Destrucción y resistencia campesina: El caso del litoral pacífico.
              Bogotá: Punto de Lanza.
1980          The Devil and Commodity Fetishism in South America. Chapel
              Hill: University of North Carolina Press.
1987          Shamanism, Colonialism and the Wildman: A Study in Healing
              and Terror. Chicago: University of Chicago Press.

Taylor, Douglas
1977          Languages of the West Indies. Baltimore: Johns Hopkins University
              Press.

Templeman, Robert
1994          Afro-Bolivians. In Johannes Wilbert (general editor). Encyclope-
              dia of World Cultures. New Haven: Human Relations Area Files
              Press.

Terborg-Penn, Rosalyn
1986          Women and Slavery in the African Diaspora: A Cross-Cultural Ap-
              proach to Historical Analysis. Sage 3 (2):11–15.

Thoden van Velzen, H. U. E., and W. van Wetering
1988          The Great Father and the Danger: Religious Cults, Material
              Forces, and Collective Fantasies in the World of the Surinamese
              Maroons. Dordrecht: Foris.

Thompson Drewal, Margaret
1989          Dancing for Ogun in Yorubaland and in Brazil. In Sandra T.
              Barnes (editor). Africa's Ogun: Old World and New. Bloomington:
              Indiana University Press, pp. 199–234.

Thornton, John
1995          Perspectives on African Christianity. In Vera Lawrence Hyatt and
              Rex Nettleford (editors). Race, Discourse, and the Origin of the
              Americas: A New World View. Washington, D.C.: Smithsonian In-
              stitution Press, pp. 169–212.

Tomoeda, Hiroyasu, and Luis Millones (editors)
1992          500 años de mestizaje en los Andes. Lima: Biblioteca Peruana de
              Psicoanálisis.

Trouillot, Michel-Rolph
1990          Haiti, State against Nation: The Origins and Legacy of Duvalier-
              ism. New York: Monthly Review Press.

Van Cott, Donna Lee (editor)
1994          Indigenous Peoples and Democracy in Latin America. New York:
              St. Martin's Press and Washington, D.C.: Inter-American Dialogue.

Varner, John Grier, and Jeannette Johnson Varner
1983          Dogs of the Conquest. Norman: University of Oklahoma Press.

Vasconcelos, José
1925                La raza cósmica — misión de la raza iberoamericana —, notas de
                    viaje a América del sur. Barcelona: Agencia Mundial de Librería.

Verger, Pierre (editor)
1953                Les Afro-Américains. Dakar: Institut Français d'Afrique Noire,
                    Mémoire 27.

Wade, Peter
1993                Blackness and Race Mixture: The Dynamics of Racial Identity in
                    Colombia. Baltimore: Johns Hopkins University Press.
(in press)          Music, Blackness and National Identity: Three Moments in Colum-
                    bian History. Popular Music.

Weber, Max
1958                From Max Weber: Essays in Sociology. Translated and edited by
                    H. H. Girth and C. Wright Mills. New York: Oxford University Press.
1964 [1947]         The Theory of Social and Economic Organization. Translated and
                    edited by A. M. Henderson and Talcott Parsons. Glencoe, Ill.: Free
                    Press.

Whitehead, Neil L.
1988                Lords of the Tiger Spirit: A History of the Caribs in Colonial Vene-
                    zuela and Guyana 1498–1820. Dordrecht: Foris.
1993                Native American Cultures along the Atlantic Littoral of South
                    America, 1499–1650. Proceedings of the British Academy 81:197–
                    231.

Whitten, Norman E., Jr.
1965                Class, Kinship, and Power in an Ecuadorian Town: The Negroes of
                    San Lorenzo. Stanford: Stanford University Press.
1981                (editor) Cultural Transformations and Ethnicity in Modern Ecua-
                    dor. Urbana: University of Illinois Press.
1985                Sicuanga Runa: The Other Side of Development in Amazonian
                    Ecuador. Urbana: University of Illinois Press.
1986a [1974]        Black Frontiersmen: Afro-Hispanic Culture of Colombia and Ecua-
                    dor. Prospect Heights, Ill.: Waveland Press.
1986b               Review of books by Richard Price (First-Time: The Historical Vi-
                    sion of an Afro-American People and To Slay the Hydra: Dutch Co-
                    lonial Perspectives on the Saramaka Wars). Ethnohistory 33:91–94.
1996                Ethnogenesis. In The Encyclopedia of Cultural Anthropology. New
                    York: Henry Holt and the Human Relations Area Files, vol. 2, pp.
                    407–411.

Whitten, Norman E., Jr., and John F. Szwed (editors)
1970                Afro-American Anthropology: Contemporary Perspectives. New
                    York: Free Press.

Whitten, Norman E., Jr., and Arlene Torres
1992        Blackness in the Americas. In North American Congress on Latin
            America (1992), pp. 16–22, 45–46.
Whitten, Norman E., Jr., and Diego Quiroga
1990        Prefacio. In Giancarlo Corsetti, Nancy Motta González, and Carlo
            Tassara. Cambios tecnológicos, organización social y actividades pro-
            ductivas en la Costa Pacífica Colombiana. Bogotá: Comitato Inter-
            nazionale per lo Sviluppo dei Popoli, pp. 9–16.
1994        The Black Pacific Lowlanders of Ecuador and Colombia. In
            Johannes Wilbert (general editor). Encyclopedia of World Cultures.
            New Haven: Human Relations Area Files Press.
Williams, Brackette
1989        A Class Act: Anthropology and the Race to Nation across Ethnic
            Terrain. Annual Review of Anthropology. Palo Alto: Annual Review,
            pp. 401–444.
1991        Stains on My Name, War in My Veins: Guyana and the Politics of
            Cultural Struggle. Durham: Duke University Press.
Williams, Jerry M., and Robert E. Lewis (editors)
1993        Early Images of the Americas: Transfer and Invention. Tucson: Uni-
            versity of Arizona Press.
Wilson, Samuel M.
1990        Hispaniola: Caribbean Chiefdoms in the Age of Columbus. Tus-
            caloosa: University of Alabama Press.
Wolf, Eric
1982        Europe and the People without History. Berkeley: University of Cali-
            fornia Press.
Worsley, Peter
1984        The Three Worlds: Culture and World Development. Chicago:
            University of Chicago Press.
Wright, Winthrop R.
1990        Café con Leche: Race, Class, and National Image in Venezuela.
            Austin: University of Texas Press.
Zelinsky, Wilbur
1949        The Historical Geography of the Negro Population of Latin Amer-
            ica. Journal of Negro History 34:153–221.
Zenón Cruz, Isabelo
1974        Narciso descubre su trasero (El negro en la cultura puertorri-
            queña). Volume 1. Humacao, Puerto Rico: Editorial Furidi.
1975        Narciso descubre su trasero (El negro en la cultura puertorri-
            queña). Volume 2. Humacao, Puerto Rico: Editorial Furidi.

# PART TWO
# CENTRAL AMERICA
# AND THE NORTHERN
# SOUTH AMERICAN LOWLANDS

# 1. "TO RESCUE NATIONAL DIGNITY"

## Blackness as a Quality of
## Nationalist Creativity in Ecuador

### Norman E. Whitten, Jr., and Diego Quiroga

In 1992, in Ecuador, at the beginning of the presidency of Sixto Durán Ballén and well before any sense of Durán Ballén's possible successor came into existence, blackness became a national quality spanning coastal regions, Andean regions, and Amazonian regions of that country. Its ethnic nationalist expression was called *négritud*, from the French word *négritude*, coined initially by the Martinique writer Aimée Césaire. As the movement surged under such cultural rubrics as "the advancement of the black community," and as indentification of the movement among white and black intellectuals was expressed by the figures of speech *Afro-ecuatorianos* (Afro-Ecuadorians) and *Afro-Latinoamericanos* (Afro-Latin Americans), varied associations between those so identifying, and the indigenous movement of Ecuador came into being.

Spokesmen and spokeswomen for both movements stressed an end to nation-state nationalist racism, as bound to the concepts of "whitening," "blending," and denial of ethnic association (*mestizaje*) and "improving the race" (of indigenous and black people). A key phrase in these movements, which are becoming ever-more intertwined, came to be *rescate de la dignidad nacional* (to rescue national dignity).

In 1995–96 an Ecuadorian social movement, not a political party, emerged to unite all Ecuadorians who were sick of corruption and lack of dignity in national political party activities. Called Nuevo País (New Nation) by Freddy Ehlers, its founder in the Sierra, as the Andes mountains of Ecuador are called, and Pachakutik (New Earth, including unity of pasts and futures) by Valerio Grefa, its indigenous founder in the Amazonian region, the two associations attracted followers from coastal, Andean, and Amazonian sectors of the voting populace. Although Freddy Ehlers narrowly lost in his bid for the presidency on the first round of voting, six congressmen of the Pachakutik social movement, all of them indigenous people, were elected on the second round, five as provincial representatives and one—former president of the Confederation of Indigenous Peoples of Ecuador, Luís Macas—as national representative. This was the first time in Ecuador's history that indigenous people were elected to serve the nation as legislators.

In 1994, between these two periods of national ethnic transformation, Norman Whitten and Diego Quiroga were invited to prepare the following paper on "blackness in Ecuador" for the book entitled *No Longer Invisible: Afro-Latin Americans Today.* Published in 1995, a year before the national elections, this paper endeavors to summarize, for a general public unfamiliar with Afro–Latin American people, some of the issues involved in the nation-state of Ecuador. Between 1992 and 1996 Ecuadorian *négritud* shed its regional moorings in "hot, low, distant regions" and emerged as a clear issue in Ecuadorian Andean cultural life. The *currulao* of the rain forest–riverine region of Esmeraldas Province, *la bomba* from the deep Andean valley of the Chota-Mira River system, and manifestations of cultural *négritud* of urban areas such as Quito and Guayaquil not only became national phenomena but also became culturally significant in international centers where the diversity of *ecuatorianidad* was and is displayed.

In 1995 a black woman, Mónica Chalá, was elected "Miss Ecuador" by a Quiteño jury composed entirely of prominent Ecuadorian figures, all of whom identified as "white" (Rahier 1990) and in 1996 the new president of Ecuador, Abdalá Bucaram Ortíz, established the first Ministry of Ethnic Affairs (also known as the Ministry of Cultural Ethnics and Ministry of Ethnic Development) in the nation's history. It is oriented primarily to indigenous and black people and their "ethnic advancement." As of this writing, the ministry has been promised hundreds of millions of dollars from international agencies (including the International Development Bank and the World Bank) for autonomous deployment in the areas of education and health by leaders of ethnic cultures, particularly black and indigenous, in Ecuador. Its director is Rafael Pandam, a Shuar from the Amazonian region, Morona-Santiago Province.

Ecuadorians not pleased with the black movements of self-assertion in their country often deny that Afro-Ecuadorians culturally assert concepts of blackness, except as a very recent political movement that will soon stumble over its own rhetoric. To open this chapter, then, we quote from a poem written by the *esmeraldeño* Nelson Estupiñán Bass and first published in 1954. Estupiñán Bass was then, as he is now, one of the foremost literary figures in Afro–Latin American thought in the world.

> *Negro, negro, renegrido,*
> *negro, hermano del carbón,*
> *negro de negros nacido,*
> *negro ayer, mañana y hoy.*
> *Algunos creen insultarme*
> *gritándome mi color,*
> *más yo mismo lo pregono*
> *con orgullo frente al sol:*
> *Negro he sido, negro soy,*
> *negro vengo, negro voy,*

*negro bien negro nací
negro negro he de vivir,
y como negro morir.*

—Nelson Estupiñán Bass[1]

The Republic of Ecuador in western South America is a modern OPEC/
NOPEC nation that won its independence from colonial rule in 1822 and became in 1830 El Ecuador (the Equator). Colombia lies to its north, and Peru to
its east and south. Sustained ethnic clashes and, equally, sustained domination
by a white minority are salient features of Ecuador's tumultuous history. Mainland Ecuador is divided into three parts: Coast, Sierra (or Andes) and Upper
Amazonia (or Amazonian Region). Most of its 12 to 13 million people live in the
Coast and Sierra. Ecuador is now, as it has been since at least the early nineteenth
century, and perhaps since the sixteenth century, in the ongoing process of social
reproduction and cultural transformation of strongly represented ethnic categories that signify segments of its ever-expanding population.

To understand the dimensions of blackness in Ecuador, the three concepts of
*indio* (Indian), *negro* (black) and *blanco* (white) must be explained. These concepts emerged in the Americas as the kingdom of Castile and Aragón forged a
cultural hegemony of racial separation. The concept of "race" (Spanish *raza*) itself emerged in European dictionaries at the time of the rapidly expanding racist hegemony in the Americas. The racialist structure can be diagrammed as a
triangle within a triangle (see figure).

Ecuadorian social structure may be considered a class pyramid. An oligarchy,

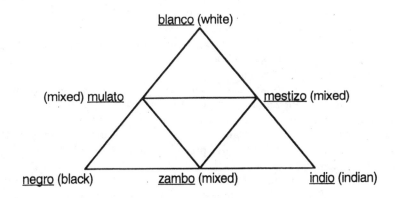

Fig. 1

known in the upper classes as *la sociedad*, and internally as *gente de bién* (or *gente bién*—proper, "right kind of" and, by extension, righteous people), constitutes the pinnacle of political power, economic control and social esteem. The *sociedad* is complemented by what we might call a new oligarchy, whose position is a direct result of accumulated wealth. All members of these oligarchies self-identify unconditionally, and are usually identified, as *blancos*. Ecuador has a significant middle class of professionals and business and service industries people who generally self-identify as *blanco*. The self-identifying phrase *buena familia* (good family) is today the most popular one among such people. It is from the elite, the educated upper and middle classes, and the military, that the concept of a united body of mixed people, *el mestizaje*, emanates. And it is among the elite, and educated upper and middle classes, that the rhetoric separating Ecuador's "races" also emanates.

Farther down the class hierarchy we find people dependent for their livelihood on commercial transactions of varying scale, none of whom self-identify as *mestizo*, except under exceptional circumstances, but who are politely tagged with various labels meaning "mixed" by those above them, or with the labels of the antipodes—*indio, negro*—when discourses reflect interaggregate or interpersonal anger signalling open conflict. Sometimes, under conditions of severe stress, those in superordinate positions use common associations for the ethnic antipodal terminology—*salvaje*, meaning savage, or *alzado*, meaning out of control—in heated discussion reflecting social conflict. Upward mobility is conceived of by those in superordinate positions of power and wealth as a process often called *blanqueamiento*, or whitening, in Ecuador, as in Colombia and Venezuela (the cognate term in Brazilian Portuguese is *embranquecimento*). The processes of *mestizaje* are also often called by the vulgar term *cholificación* in Ecuador, as in Peru and Bolivia.

People represented by those in power as *negro*, on the one side, and *indio*, on the other, are thought to be the real social antipodes of class-status relationships. Whitten has noted elsewhere that, in power politics, indigenous leaders endeavour to move a discourse about the *indio* potential for revolt directly into the realm of the status-conscious rhetoric of the oligarchies.[2] Spokesmen and spokeswomen of the *negro* potential for insurrection aim their discourse of pending disorder at the middle levels of the class and status hierarchy.

When discourses of ethnic "disorder" or "revolt" reach the mass media all subtleties of ethnic categorization are dropped in favor of unified, pejorative representations of human beings. In this process synthetic, symbolic units of racialist ideology that emerged in the Americas soon after its European "conquest"—*blanco, negro* and *indio*—bring forth a predicative link that carries the double act of assertion and denial.

Historically, there are three rural streams of Africans who became part of Ecuador's dynamic black history: those who occupy the present Province of Esmeraldas in the northwest; those of Carchi and Imbabura in the northern Andes and

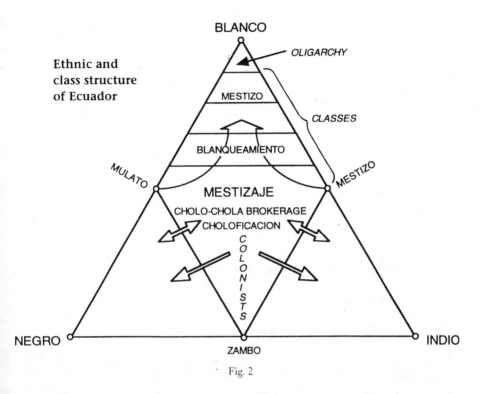

Ethnic and
class structure
of Ecuador

Fig. 2

western escarpments; and those of Loja in the south. Three urban streams also exist: those of Guayaquil, the largest city in Ecuador; those of Quito, the nation's capital; and those of Ibarra, the north's urban distribution point. Black people have also emerged in virtually every area of Ecuador through its entire history. We treat the three rural regions briefly, and then comment on the rest of Ecuador.

### Esmeraldas

Regional blackness as a force of self-liberation in Ecuador begins in Esmeraldas, and its origin occurs during a violent tropical storm and a movement of African rebellion. The documented history of Ecuador establishes the beginnings of Afro-Hispanic culture in what is now Esmeraldas, Ecuador, where a Spanish slaving ship ran aground in 1553. There a group of twenty-three Africans from the coast of Guinea, led by a black warrior named Antón, attacked the slavers and liberated themselves. Not long after, this group, together with other blacks entering the region, led by a *ladino* (Hispanicized black person) named Alonso de Illescas, came to dominate the region from northern Manabí north to what is now Barbacoas, Colombia. At this time (late sixteenth century) intermixture with indigenous peoples, to whom black people fled to establish their *palenques* (villages of self-liberated people—some fortified, some not), was such that their features were described as *zambo* (black-indigenous admixture), synonyms of which were *negro* (black) and *mulato* (mixed or hybrid black-white). Movement into Colombia by Africans was through Cartagena via the Cauca Valley, and through Panama and Pacific ports. The first black person there may have arrived with the pilot of Francisco Pizarro, Bartolomé Ruiz, on the Isla de Gallo in 1526.

There is evidence that the earliest influence on Afro-Hispanic culture in the region came from the Senegambian area of northwest Africa. Culturally, the influence of Bantu and Mande Africa (as seen in the music, especially the *currulao*) and of archaic Spain and North Africa (especially some funeral customs) predominates. By 1599 black people were clearly in charge of what was called "La República de Zambos" or "Zambo Republic." *Zambo* refers to people of color who are descendants of Native Americans and African Americans. In that year a group of Zambo chiefdoms, said to represent 100,000 or more Zambo people of Esmeraldas, trekked to Quito to declare loyalty to Spain. An oil painting of these chiefs from the emerald land of the Zambo Republic is portrayed by the "Indian artist" Adrián Sánchez Galgue; it is reportedly the earliest signed and dated painting from South America.

The Afro-Hispanic culture of the Pacific Lowlands of Ecuador and Colombia extends from Muisne in southern Esmeraldas Province, Ecuador, to the San Juan River, in Valle Department, Colombia. It is part of the greater "Pacific Lowlands Culture Area" of Panama, Colombia and Ecuador. South of this area is a distinct Manabí culture region of Ecuador; north of the area is the Afro-American Chocó region of Colombia, with black culture shared with people of the Darién Province, Panama. East of the region are the interior Andean zones of Ecuador and Colombia. The Afro-Hispanic cultural region (which is predominant) is shared with Tchachela, Chachi and Awá (Coaquier) indigenous peoples of Ecuador, and with Awá, Waunam and Emberá native peoples of Colombia.

Spanish was the language of conquest in Ecuador and Colombia, and became the language—in stylized transformations—of black people of the Pacific Lowlands. Serious linguistic work remains to be undertaken on the dialect of stylized Spanish spoken in Afro–Latin American culture of this region.

Between 600,000 and 800,000 black people occupy this region, making it the densest population in the entire lowland rainforest tropics of the Americas. About 85 percent of the population of the region shares Afro–Latin American culture. In Esmeraldas itself we estimate a figure of about 200,000 people, with the same percentage being black.

### Carchi and Imbabura (the Chota–Mira Valley)

The regions of Carchi and Imbabura, with sizeable populations of black people, are located in deep valleys conducive to tropical and subtropical agriculture. Especially prominent in this racial topography is the Chota–Mira Valley (sometimes also known locally, regionally and nationally as Coangue). This area features excellent growing conditions for commercial agricultural products sought after by such urban areas as Ibarra and Quito, and is today served by modern bus lines. Black people live in the region drained by the Chota River, which runs into the Mira River that traverses the black lowlander culture of Ecuador and Colombia, and which, in its upper course, cuts across the Panamerican highway between the Colombian border and Ibarra, capital of Imbabura Province.

Members of this expanding black population cultivate small plots of one to five hectares, upon which a large variety of foodstuffs are grown for the urban markets, for smaller villages of northern Ecuador and for internal consumption. Such small farms, drained by irrigation ditches radiating from the Chota River, were long controlled by a few huge haciendas. After the Agrarian Reform Law of 1964 black yeomen shed the status of rural share croppers and entered a system of covert and overt conflict with the power wielders of the region. They also engaged in a system of geographic and upward socio-economic mobility as their populations continued to flow from the valley to Ibarra and Quito.

The early history of the Chota–Mira Valley and its affluents and hinterlands is summarized by various authors as one characterized by ongoing open conflict between conquerors and those they sought to vanquish and turn into serfs. Between 1550 and 1610 indigenous chiefdoms were broken down, black people began entering the area, from the coast and from the Andes, and a Spanish-dominated boom in such products as gold, cotton, corn and chickens took place, but with an awful social toll.[3] The wider span of dates given, 1550–1700, subsumes a period of indigenous secular exploitation by white and *mestizo* overseers and *hacendados*, followed by a Jesuit (Society of Jesus) solution to the indigenous–non-indigenous conflicts by the direct importation of African slaves (from Africa, Iberia, the Caribbean and Colombia). Other Catholic orders and secular organizations also imported slaves for plantations in the Chota–Mira Valley.

The Jesuits ran slave-based, productive and profitable plantations in the area, and found the military means to put down slave rebellions, from their entry in 1586 until their expulsion in 1740. The strategy of the Jesuits was to focus on sugar-cane production based on black slave labor. They also introduced European grapes to be made into wines and brandies for their own local consumption. Between 1776 and 1779 Colonel calculates the *piezas de indias* (a measure of labor based on what a strong man-slave could accomplish in one day) as 1,324 for eight sugar plantations.[4] In reading such figures one must keep in mind that, the weaker the slaves became, the more it took for them to constitute one *pieza*. A recent calculation by Nelson Estupiñán Bass (1990) for 1781 is that of 2,553 slaves in the valley, divided among ten haciendas.[5]

For their part, black people, free and slave, grew other commodities for their own consumption, and eventually for the growing markets in northern Ecuador for tropical and subtropical products: avocados, tomatoes, manioc (cassava), beans, sweet potatoes, anise, papaya, watermelon, citrus fruits, plantains, bananas, grapes, cotton, coca, fibers and other crops.[6] Flight from slavery to the west (Esmeraldas), south, to the large towns and small cities of colonial rule, and east to the Amazonian Region was common. Such acts of *cimarronaje* are not documented to any significant extent in Ecuador, but we need to keep the image of an expanding web of black people in Ecuador, through runaways and their routes, in mind.

Today the population of the Chota–Mira Valley is estimated at somewhere between 15,000 and 20,000 people, of whom 97 percent or more share this regional black Ecuadorian culture.[7] We must stress here, however, that the out-migration of Afro-Chota peoples, who maintain webs of social relationships through sporadic contact with one another, is such that we should probably at least triple this figure when talking of people from the valley.

*Loja*

In Loja, southern Ecuador, Amazonian ecology winds its way through a low point in the Ecuadorian Andes. Indeed, in the *National Geographic* map of South America for "Indian" cultures, Loja is given the status of "Amazonia." Into this rich land of native peoples came conquerors and their curate scribes. One of these, Don Juan de Salinas Loyola, on his march to the tropical forests to conquer the "Jívaros" in 1557, had with him black slaves, one of whom saved his life when his canoe tipped over while trying to pass dangerous river rapids.[8] Later, in the famous (infamous) revolt of the "Jívaro" in 1579 (usually reported as 1599), it now seems clear that black people constituted part of the insurgents, as did *mestizo* people. In other words, one of the first successful revolts in Ecuador's colonial history involved the multicultural union of indigenous Amazonian people, imported and/or self-liberated black people and emerging *mestizo* people.

The slaves brought to this region were primarily household servants and gold miners. Black yeomen fanned out, especially along the Catamayo River, and black slaves were held in bondage as *piezas de indias* for killing work in the gold mines. Many fled mining and forced agricultural labor to the adjacent tropical regions, where some engaged in placer gold mining. In 1572 the lawyer Juan de Ovando described free and black people of the city of Loja as having a color just like that of the people of Guinea, West Africa.[9] There seems to have been much genetic intermingling in this region, together with an inflow of black servants and slaves from Spain, Portugal, West Africa and Colombia. Throughout the colonial era black people inhabited the Catamayo River region and engaged in rural agriculture; they also resided in a black *barrio* of the capital of Loja, also named Loja. The black population during the colonial period numbered somewhere around 5,000.

In the late 1990s we do not encounter anything resembling the concentration of black people of Esmeraldas and the Chota–Mira Valley region in Loja. Out-migration and internal genetic intermingling have changed the complexion of the area, as has the routing of the small farmers of the Catamayo River system by such modernization strategies as the development of an airport there. The twin phenomena of "development" and "whitening" are well reported in the literature on blackness in Ecuador, as elsewhere where Afro–Latin Americans live.

Slaves from all of these areas of Ecuador were legally manumitted when what is now Ecuador became part of Gran Colombia in 1824 (Colombia manumitted its slaves in 1821). But in various areas of Ecuador manumission came at different times. It supposedly came by national decree in 1854, but slavery endured in some areas until the 1860s. Slaves were freed in Loja in 1837, but in Esmeraldas and the Chota–Mira Valley some bondage still existed, now called the system of *concertaje* (often called by the Quichua phrase *huasipungo* in the Chota–Mira region), right up to the 1890s.

### Later Arrivals

The history of blackness in what is now Ecuador up to the wars of liberation led by Simón Bolívar in the north and José de San Martín in the south is that of slavery and freedom existing side by side. From about 1600 through the early 1800s slaves were brought to Barbacoas, Colombia (just north of the free Zambo Republic in Ecuador), each year. About ten *negreros* (literally, "black-bringing" ships; slavers) would arrive each year in this placer-gold-mining area, with slaves to replace those who had died and those who had fled to areas such as Esmeraldas or Chota–Mira.

In Esmeraldas Province, organizational forms of labor cooperation in raising food, exploiting forest, mangrove and sea, and panning for gold existed in remarkably similar forms in both free and slave communities. The primary cultural relationship from the sixteenth century through the twentieth is that of "racial succession" whereby black people encroach on the cultural territories of indigenous people.

In Chota–Mira the oppression of the plantation system continued, as did out-migration and sustained conflicts between black people and their wealthy white oppressors. Such conflict continues in the late twentieth century. In Loja far more absorption of black people into the general population occurred, with "racial succession" passing through generations. Also, it appears that the black people of Loja continued a pattern of out-migration.

### Ibarra, Quito and Guayaquil

Probably less than 4 percent of Ibarra is black; most of these people are from the Chota–Mira Valley and maintain their contact there. Ibarra is a residential area for black people, and it is also a springboard for migration to Quito. The concentration of the black population is found in the area of the major market and the railroad terminus. In Quito one finds from 50,000 to 60,000 black people, most of them from the Chota–Mira Valley. To this we could add about 10,000 people who might or might not be defined as black by Ecuadorian or other Latin American definitions. The neighborhoods where concentrations of black people live and work are Batallón del Pueblo, Bastión Popular Aticucho, Roldós, Carapungo and Comité del Pueblo. But they are also scattered throughout the city.

Black people have been in Quito since Pedro de Alvarado, coming from Central America with a well-seasoned army, and Gonzalo Pizarro's troops from Peru moved north to conquer it in 1534. By 1535 Quito was a Spanish colonial city, the northern sector of the administrative area of Peru, with its center in the port city of Lima. The truncation of the Inca empire was complete. The body was indigenous and black (and becoming *mestizo*), but the head was Spanish and white. Various streams of black people entered, left and stayed during its entire history. *Cimarronaje* was so prevalent in Quito that specific violent punishments (including mutilation, torture and death) for runaways were proclaimed there in 1548.

Guayaquil has a significant black population of which the largest concentration is in the *barrio* Cristo de Consuelo, with other concentrations in La Chalá and La Marimba. More recent invasions of black people from Esmeraldas have resulted in black people throughout this city of more than three million.

### Definition of the Black Minorities

*Gente morena* and *moreno* are the polite terms of reference and address in most of rural and urban Ecuador where aggregates of black people live. *Gente negra* (black people) is accepted in some areas, but is rejected in others if used by anyone not identified as black. *Afro-ecuatoriano* is an intellectual term now in favor, though it is pejorative if used colloquially. *Negro* is another intellectual term in vogue, but it is pejorative colloquially wherever black people live, when used by a non-black person. *Zambo* (indigenous–black admixture) is commonly used in black areas of Ecuador, and may or may not be pejorative if used by a non-black person. *Libre*—free in the sense of self-liberated—is not common south of the San Juan River, Colombia. It is the primary term in the Chocó north of the San Juan River and is known and sometimes used in Ecuador. On the coast, *costeño* is the primary ethnic designation for black Ecuadorians. All designations of black people are of foreign origin and designate the combination of blackness and territory. Colloquially, in Ecuador, *gente morena* (dark people) is polite usage, but intellectuals now stress the Spanish terms *negro* (black), *afro-ecuatoriano* or *afro-colombiano*, and more generally *afro-latinoamericano*.

The latter concept emerged in 1992 as nationalist ideologues stressed the Ibero–Latin American unity that excludes both blacks and indigenous people. Coincident with such stress, black leaders of movements of ethnic self-assertion came forth with the concept of *afro-latinoamericano* as an emergent idea of self-representation and self-identity for black intellectuals.

The etymology of *moreno* and *negro* seems to stem from the same root, the Latin diminutive of *maurus*, through Mozarabic and Castillian Spanish.[10] Today, however, dictionaries define *negro* as black and *moreno* as brown or brunet(te). None the less, *moreno* means black in Ecuador; it is not used to refer to people of lighter skin, or to brunet(te)s. It is used to refer to people of darker skin, or lesser status, than the speaker. In modern Ecuador the word *negro*, when used by non-black people, is pejorative, even though journalists and scholars have seized on it as the proper term for dark people. Although Ecuadorian intellectuals may disagree, if they have never lived with black people in Esmeraldas, the Chota–Mira Valley or Loja, the phrase *gente morena* is still the polite manner of speaking about dark people. One also hears *la raza morenita*, but this is not appreciated by black people, for it has a connotation of childlike and cute.

*Mulato* is also used for very light people; *zambo* refers to black–indigenous mixing but has other usages. Such terms are normally used as adjectives, not nouns. Examples include *pueblo negro* (black people) or *comunidad negra* (black community). In the 1990s the representation *negro fino* (refined black) is used in Ecuador to differentiate black people who are educated and are white-collar employees from those who are not. *Mulato* is often used in journalism to refer to a distinguished poet or novelist who usually refers to himself or herself as *negro* or *negra*. Historically, *mulato* referred to affinity between someone who was "wild" (such as an African or Native American) and "civilized" (a white person). The etymology lies in ancient Mediterranean concepts of hybridity.[11] Because of this, European colonial writers avoided drawing attention to unions between African and indigenous peoples, and substituted the term *mulato* for *zambo*.[12]

The term *negro* has repercussions in politics that demonstrate the contextual nature of this important reference point. It has recently been claimed that Esmeraldas has never had a black political representative to the national Congress. Yet Jaime Hurtado González, for many years the socialist representative from Esmeraldas (who was also a presidential candidate on two occasions), would fit all the international and national criteria of "blackness" and he was called, colloquially, in various parts of the nation, *El negro*. When confronted with such a perspective, however, black spokesmen and spokeswomen for blackness and for Esmeraldas as a black province say that he gave up his blackness by joining the power structure of Ecuador. Clearly, blackness represents more than mere skin color to those who seek a regional and human dignity through deployment of the concept.

Black people in Ecuador draw specific attention to nouns, verbs, adjectives and adverbs involving double meanings of blackness. For example, the verb *negrear* (to blacken) is used socially to confer lesser status. To say that someone's life is *negreando* can mean the person is drifting toward crime, is becoming poorer or is heading toward states pejoratively associated with black people: lazy, dirty or ugly. By inference, of course, *negrear* and its derivatives and near cognates (*negar*, to negate) bring all such associations to bear on the stigmatized subject of the predication. *Negrear* can also mean to make someone "disappear" as a social being of worth. For example, the verb is applied to people who have been promised a salary at one level, and then are actually given far less. Such a person is *tratado como negro*, "treated like a black," or simply *negreado*, "blackened." To contest being treated in a disparaging way one may exclaim, "¡No mi negree!" which can be translated euphemistically as "Don't deny me" or "Don't look through or past me." But literally it means, "Don't treat me like a nigger!"

During a public lecture in Quito during the summer of 1993, Ms. Sonya Catalina Charlá offered this definition of blackness (translated from notes taken by N. Whitten): "Who are we? We are black groups, we share history, we have our proper culture, and we have our dignity and our identity." And she went on:

> We are from Esmeraldas and from the Chota River Valley. We have distinct historical products that we know and understand. Where do we come from? We are from here. There were blacks with the conquerors, Alonso de Illescas freed us and we constituted the Republic of Zambos. We defend the liberty of the black people and indigenous people, just as did Antón from Cabo Verde in Africa, and Alonso de Illescas, the first Governor of Esmeraldas.

She then moved briefly to the Chota–Mira area, which had another origin in slavery, but with whose people "we are now one." She spoke of Guayaquil, "where the black people came as domestics and carpenters and where there are black communities today."

### Population Size and Demography

Population size and the demography of blackness in Ecuador are extremely difficult to estimate. There are no census categories to help us, and we must rely on the calculations of self-identifying black people who are working diligently on such subjects. The calculations usually proceed to take census figures from Esmeraldas and Chota–Mira, to assign a percentage to them that factors out non-black people, and then add the figures estimated for black people in Quito, the capital of the republic, and Guayaquil, the largest city on the Guayas River of the coast.

In the 31 July 1994 "Panorama" section of the conservative Quito newspaper *El Comercio*, Renán Tadeo, from the parish of Concepción of Mira Canton, in Carchi, gives us the figure of 700,000 black people in Esmeraldas, Imbabura, Carchi, El Oro and Loja, including in these figures the urban populations of black people in and on the fringes of Quito and Guayaquil. P. Rafael Savoia, who directs the Centro Cultural Afro-Ecuatoriano in Quito, Guayaquil and Esmeraldas, confirms our impression that Tadeo offers a reasonably accurate estimate of Ecuador's black population. If we figure Ecuador's national population as 12 to 13 million, we have a population that is 6 to 7 per cent black. This is within the range of a 5 to 10 per cent black population often given in Ecuador's official statistics, and by the US State Department. The concentration of black people is in northern Ecuador in a square that encloses the Quito–Muisne–Colombian-border–Ibarra points of reference (provinces of Pichincha, Esmeraldas Carchi and Imbabura).

## Cultural Forms

Spanish is the language spoken by all black people in Ecuador. A different stylization of the language is spoken in Esmeraldas than in the Chota–Mira Valley. Black people in Quito and Guayaquil, as elsewhere, are stereotyped by the way they speak, and in many places they take pains to emulate the dialects of Spanish taken to be more prestigious in certain contexts. This leads, at times, some speakers of Esmeraldas to speak with some Italian inflections due to the long association with Comboniano priests, all of whom, until fairly recently, came from Italy. Some black people from Esmeraldas speak at least rudimentary Chachi, but it is not common for them to do so.

In the Amazonian Region there are black-skinned Quichua-speaking people within Canelos Quichua culture. Some came from the Pacific Lowlands three generations ago; others came westward from Brazil and Peru during the Amazon rubber boom. Recent migrations have resulted in a substantial proportion of black people in Lago Agrio, on the Agua Rico River.

Music is a cultural form by which black people are well known in Ecuador, and in which great pride is manifest. Black musical groups are now in demand for national and regional festivals of arts and music. In Esmeraldas and the Guayas Basin international music traditions spanning the African and American continents are enlivened by all sorts of informal and formal bands. Popular music such as *gaita*, *cumbia*, *merecumbea* and now *salsa* is ubiquitous.

In Esmeraldas, as in the Pacific Lowlands of Colombia north to the San Juan River, the marimba band, sometimes called *currulao*, is an ascendant cultural expression. Two men play the marimba. One of them, the *glosador*, or another man not playing the marimba, sings long songs, some of which are improvised, at least in part, while two women, *respondadoras*, "answer" the singer. The female singers shake tube-rattles, called *guasá*, as two drummers accompany them on the *cununos*, which are cone-shaped drums like the Cuban "conga drum." The dominant beat of the marimba music is from two huge base drums, without snares, called *bombos*. The rhythms played are as African as any in the Americas, originating in the Bantu and Mande areas of West Africa.

The traditional marimba band assembles to play the music for a dance of respect (*baile de respeto*), which features a number of very different presentations, each with different rhythms, marimba melodies, *glosador* renditions and response patterns. This music and dance of respect are purely secular rituals. Powerful though these renditions are, no saints or spirits enter; the universe is restricted to respectful human interaction. Today, for national or regional festivals, the *bambuco* rhythm and dance predominate.

Another traditional music form of this area is played for the death of a child, *chigualo*, or for the festival to a saint, *arrullo*. This music is led and controlled by women, who shake maracas, and direct the rhythms of the two men playing the *cununo* and the one or more men playing the *bombo*. During the *chigualo*, the soul of the deceased child goes directly to heaven (*gloria*), bypassing purgatory. Saints and spirits may also enter from the heaven and other worlds, but those that would do harm to the celebrants are chased away by the sound of the *bombo*. Sometimes, such as during Easter festivals, an *arrullo* to a saint may be accompanied by a marimba band.

At the death of an adult an entirely different kind of music is sung. These are dirges sung by women in a style reminiscent of North African Muslim Hispanic style. Here songs are sung of the coming and going of demons and devils, as the soul of the deceased remains in the vicinity of the corpse. After nine days people again come together to sing final dirges and, essentially, dismiss the soul of the deceased to its fate in other worlds, purgatory, hell or heaven.

The most dramatic ceremony in Esmeraldas Province is that of the *tropa* (the troop or troops). This is a forceful enactment of the formation of a *palenque*, which was a village established by black people (or indigenous people) fleeing bondage. Such people were known as *cimarrones*. *La tropa* is enacted at Easter. Attendance at *la tropa* brings out-migrants from small villages such as Güimbí, an effluent of the Santiago River, back home from, especially, Guayaquil. Community ties are very important to many out-migrants, who spend considerable sums of money, and take two to three weeks out of their urban lives, to make their way up the coast of Ecuador, and thence upriver by launch, or by canoe, to attend.

*La tropa* ceremony begins in the fringes of the community as groups of soldiers run off in search of the lost Christ, but they find only the biblical thief, Barabas. They then march on the church and enter it and eventually enact the killing of Christ, his removal from the cross, the reign of the Devil, the bringing of the forest into the Catholic church of the *palenque*, the resurrection of Christ within the forest within the church, and the liberation of the people of the forest and of the church within the *palenque*.

The ubiquitous interest in globalization of their local culture manifest by black people in Ecuador was recently stimulated by a number of events that brought together black *esmeraldeños*, black people from the Chota–Mira Valley and musicians and performers from other countries, such as Cuba. One group, the Chigualeros, adapted their rhythms to *salsa* music, and introduced the marimba into the resulting dynamic renditions.

Two groups, led by Petita Palma and Segundo Quintero, have been experimenting with the globalization of their local and regional traditions for some time. A newer group, probably the most famous internationally, is Koral y Esmeralda ([Black] Coral and Emerald). Led by the dynamic *salsa* singer Carmen González, Koral y Esmeralda has played in Japan, including in its expanding repertoire the songs "Perla Negra," "Canoita" and "Chocolate." The group is also experimenting with a front-line instrumentation featuring trumpet, trombone and saxophone, while adapting rhythms, melodies and call–response pattern from *arrullo, chigualo,* and *currulao.* "This is what our ancestors told about," say some young spokespeople for this dynamic international music.

The dominant musical form of the Chota–Mira Valley is *la bomba,* also called *la banda mocha.* Traditional instrumentation features a large single-head conical drum, called *bombo,* and smaller conga drums, called *redomblantes,* together with snare drums, maracas, guitars and sometimes other instrumentation, including flutes and panpipes. Couples dance *la bomba* with stylized steps and sing stylized songs, some of them improvised. At a point in some dances each woman puts a bottle on her head and dances in an attractive, undulating manner, without disturbing the bottle. New bands dedicated to *la bomba* have played in regional and national festivals, and there is interest in many sectors to merge creatively the Afro–Latin American beats and sounds of Chota–Mira and Esmeraldas.

The cosmology of black people of Esmeraldas reflects conjunctures of Catholicism and African religion that have fused and reconfigured from the mid-sixteenth century to the present. "Dynamic" is an apt term for the religious beliefs and practices of this region of Ecuador. Other worlds exist on the sea and under, over and beyond it. The sea itself is a universe of spirits as well as a domain for visiting, travelling and shipping. Fear creatures, called *visiones* (visions, or images), are said to be encountered everywhere. Principal among them in most places are Tunda, a spiritual body-snatcher who is driven away by the sound of a base drum or shotgun, and Riviel, an especially dangerous ghost-ghoul who must be deposed by a shotgun or rifle. Other fear creatures specific to localities include "the widow" (a masked flying witch), "the headless man" and "the living dead."

This earth contains multiple entrances and exits to other worlds, including the site of a shrine to a saint, the locus of a funeral ritual for a child or an adult, and the cemetery. Heaven and purgatory seem to exist "below" the sky; saints, spirits, virgins and souls of the dead come there, and souls of the dead depart from the earth to go there. Hell is set aside from purgatory and heaven; it is the locus of the Devil, demons and the souls and spirits of dead people who expired while "hot" (that is, in a state of anger and conflict).

In the southern sector of Esmeraldas, in the area where black culture abuts the culture of the Manabí region, the cosmos is divided into two halves, called the *divino* and the *humano.* The former is the domain of the virgins and the saints (of colloquial Afro–Latin American Catholicism), and the latter is the domain of the Devil and of all the spirits and dangerous souls that can be appropriated to the Devil's domain. The domain of the *divino* is a plane of existence populated by a number of saints, including especially the Virgen del Carmen, San Antonio, Santa Rosa, El Niño Dios and La Mano Poderosa. Many people have shrines in their homes on which they light votive candles to the saints who protect them from diseases and other misfortunes. The domain of the *humano*, overseen by the Christian Devil, is the other plane of existence, populated by obscure figures such as the Anima Sola (soul by itself, lone soul) or El Mismísimo (the Devil himself).

*Curanderas* (female healers) and *brujos* (male sorcerers) are the active agents who draw from the domains of the *divino* and from the *humano*. *Curanderas* have special relationships with some saints and many of them are people who stand in for, or represent, particular saints. *Curanderas* use the power of the saints and virgins during their curing rituals. They heal illnesses such as evil eye, malignant air and magical fright. To cure patients of these afflictions, they recite secret prayers, light candles to the saints and virgins and use herbs whose names invoke the powers of important figures of the *divino*. *Brujos*, by contrast, are said to use the powers of the Devil to make people ill or infertile, or to destroy someone's business. Although most of such talk is in a "he said, she said" mode of rumor and gossip, a *brujo* will sometimes actually admit to performing acts of malign magic.

At the academic-ecclesiastical congress Compromisos por un Nuevo Ecuador held in Quito during the summer of 1994, black spokeswoman Sonya Catalina Charlá explained to an audience of more than 200 people the essence of black culture and black organization in Ecuador. Her first subject was economy. She noted with care that black people in Ecuador were not to be caught on the horns of the modernization-versus-subsistence dilemma. She said that black people knew, and scientific studies have documented, the remarkable economic adaptability of black cultures to both subsistence and market economies, the latter of which she called "global". They could take care of themselves when they needed to do so, and they could, and would, participate fully in modernization plans, if only they were not blocked from doing so by racist barriers. Drawing on the "scientific genealogical" studies of Fernando Jurado Noboa, she noted the color of Presidents past, and how an ancient "gens" (line of descent) was recently described as *zambo*, or "one-quarter black." The "gens" under discussion was that of Vicente Ramón Roca, early President of Ecuador.

Having warmed her audience with the slight allusion to blackness within an ideology of *mestizaje* in a socioeconomic class that should have been ethnically *blanco*, she defined clearly the cultural dimensions, called *la cultura* (in Spanish the definite article *la* before *cultura*, culture, elevates the concept to something high, refined and sophisticated).[13] The first of these was poetry, and she mentioned specifically Antonio Preciado Bedoya (see below), moving from the beauty of his work to the principles of blackness underscored in it. "Black people have survived, and they know how to survive," she said. She drew careful attention to the diverse skills with language which resulted from the mixing of people from various parts of Africa, and the subsequent elaborations and creative adjustments made by them and their descendants in Ecuador. Music also drew her attention, especially the marimba complex of Esmeraldas and that of the *bomba* in Chota–Mira. Finally, she turned to the strengths of black co-parentage (*compadrazgo*), to black family and to black community as structures of endurance, adaptation and creativity.

### Literature, Art and Poetry

*Barrio de los negros*
*de calles oscuras*
*preñadas de espantos,*
*que llevan, que asustan,*
*que paran los pelos*
*en noches sin luna*

*Barrio encendido,*
*de noche y de día,*
*infierno moreno,*
*envuelto en las llamas*
*de son y alegría.*

—Antonio Preciado Bedoya[14]

Black intellectuals, often identifying with, and usually representatives of, Esmeraldas Province, have contributed substantially to Ecuadorian literature and to an international or global literature. Antonio Preciado Bedoya is one such prominent poet. Adalberto Ortíz, who wrote the internationally acclaimed novel *Juyungo* (1943), is another, though he has long resided outside of Ecuador. His subsequent book, *La entundada* (1971), presages recent professional ethnography of folklore and cosmology of Esmeraldas.[15] The prize-winning novels of Nelson Estupiñán Bass, *El último río* (1966) and *Senderos brillantes* (1974), are required reading for learning about black culture in Esmeraldas, and his essay "Apuntes sobre el negro de Esmeraldas en la literatura ecuatoriana" (1967) underscores themes currently salient in Ecuador. The book by Julio Estupiñán Tello, *El negro en Esmeraldas* (1967), skilfully blends history and lore animated by literary techniques.

Constance García Barrio reviews this literature and more.[16] She clearly identifies "outsiders looking in" as a genre of literature *about* black people, and then, from the standpoint of black literature itself, identifies a number of themes, including "slavery, and flight from it," "folklore," "daily life and customs," "racial mixture–racial identity" and "conflicts of culture." Literature, including novels, short stories and poems, is a critically important window through which to understand meanings of blackness. The black writers of Ecuador have contributed significantly to this subject by drawing on local themes and understanding their global dimensions.

## Recent and Present Developments

On 30 January 1988, following some years of discussion, people in Esmeraldas formed La Asociación de Negros del Ecuador (ASONE—the Association of Ecuadorian Blacks). It included black people from the urban areas of Guayaquil, Quito and Ibarra and from other cities in the Sierra and Coast, and from the regions of Loja and Chota–Mira, as well as from Esmeraldas. One of its principal themes was, and is, "rescate de la dignidad nacional," to "rescue national dignity." This rescue is of a dignity that cannot exist while racism prevails. The movement is black ethnic nationalist and it is also nation-state nationalist. It seeks to "minimize the Spanish yoke" that has held black, indigenous and other peoples in check for a half-millennium. It seeks modernization of the economy while maintaining the skills of subsistence. Leaders currently prominent in ASONE, which is intensively involved in reversing the ecological destruction caused by lumber companies and shrimp farms, include Nel Pimentel and Simón Estrada.

Another development reported by activist Renán Tadeo, a researcher at the Centro Cultural Afro-Ecuatoriano, is significantly improved relationships between the black people of the Chota–Mira Valley and those of Esmeraldas. Relationships between such people were often characterized by suspicion and by various forms of covert and overt conflict. The will to forge black unity in Ecuador across economic, ecological and socio-political barriers is strong, as is the movement, in some sectors, to unite indigenous and black organizations. Countering this is the hiring by *hacendados* of black paramilitary bands to intimidate indigenous and other people in the rural hinterlands in various parts of the nation, including Imbabura and Carchi in particular.

According to Jacinto Fierro, who is from Borbón, in northern Esmeraldas, opportunities for black people to advance their education in secondary schools and universities have increased significantly. The movements of musical groups, mentioned above, are important, and their incorporation of more and more aspects of selected global movements (such as *salsa*), while at the same time digging deeper for their own cultural roots by reference to the musical knowledge and skills of their living forebears, is obvious.

One form of racism in Ecuador today is that of ecological transformation to the benefit of non-black people, and to the disfranchisement of black people. Since the majority of black people in Esmeraldas have been coded in economic schemes as living on "uninhabited lands" (*tierras baldías*), they have long been targeted for displacement. In Esmeraldas today the rape of the forest is well under way; in some areas black and indigenous people clash, while in others they unite.

The mangrove swamps, the most productive region for economic exploitation for subsistence and market economies for black people, are being systematically and completely destroyed by shrimp farmers, while the naval personnel responsible for protecting the swamps look on and do nothing.

There have been serious ethnic clashes in Ecuador over the past decade. In 1991 in San Lorenzo, Esmeraldas Province, black townsmen and townswomen stormed the naval base to protest against the torture and killing of a black man from Borbón; black lives were lost. News about such clashes is quickly suppressed, and very little is forthcoming from the media. In 1992 black people from Esmeraldas province joined indigenous peoples in a protest march from Puyo, in the Amazonian Region, to Quito. Later, black people from San Lorenzo vowed to initiate a black march from that port town to Quito, and they wanted the black Andeans of Imbabura and Carchi provinces to join them. As of May 1995, the march had not taken place, though the rhetoric of its imminence continues to surface. The rhetoric of the central government of Ecuador promises immediate repressive military action should such a march begin.

Black discourse at national levels stresses the positive powers of blackness, and the negative effects of white and *mestizo* exploitation and disfranchisement of Afro–Latin American peoples of Ecuador.

### Minorities and Human Rights in Ecuador

Ecuador is today governed by an ideology of *mestizaje*, which is itself driven by the spirit of *blanqueamiento*—ethnic, cultural and racial whitening. The concept of *mejor la raza* ("improve the race") has been important throughout Ecuador's history, and is stressed today as it was centuries ago. The current President, Sixto Durán Ballén, spoke of blackness and indigenization during his inaugural speech; this was only the second time that such an issue, including "blackness," was raised at this important event. But unlike the first President to raise the issue of blackness, Jaime Roldós Aguilera, who spoke of Ecuadorian pluralism and pleaded for tolerance for all Ecuadorian people during his assumption of office in 1979, Durán Ballén stressed *mestizaje*.

For nation-state nationalists and developers, those who are black and indigenous constitute a "problem" for the nation, one that can only be solved when people of color and varied cultural practices and beliefs accept the elite-generated goals of ethnic and racial intermingling. Unfortunately, such alleged intermingling leaves black and indigenous peoples—who together constitute more than 30 percent of the republic—at the antipodes of the ethnic spectrum, as illustrated at the beginning of this chapter.[17]

Ecuador is now being scrutinized by international agencies for alleged human rights violations. Data are not available on human rights activities, or lack thereof, vis-à-vis black people, and they are skimpy for indigenous people. However, the anecdotal and casual information available indicates significant prejudice of white and *mestizo* officials towards black people when any conflict of interest involving a black person and a non-black person occurs.

## Gender Issues and Children

Black women clearly vie for position as domestic workers with indigenous women. That more and more Quito households have black maids is clear. Through a combination of domestic work for black women, and other sporadic work for black men, the black population of Quito has grown significantly over the past two decades, and upward mobility in that city is also obvious. In rural areas all children have access to schooling up to the sixth grade, but after that relatively few, though perhaps in increasing percentages, can move to higher levels of education. Men and women seem to have about an even chance of securing higher education. The military presents an opportunity for some black men to gain access to higher education, and through it to higher-paying positions.

## Social Movements and Mobilizations

During the nationalist buildups to the 1492–1992 quincentennial celebrations in Ecuador and Colombia, cultural images of a distinct "Latin American–Iberian" unified identity became very important. The elite in these nations, who identify themselves as *blanco*, stressed that the national identity symbol should be that of *mestizaje* (racial intermingling) to emphasize Latin America's heritage in the 500th year since European "discovery" and "civilizing conquest" began. In direct opposition to this elite-sponsored nationalist identity emblem, black spokesmen and spokeswomen rejected "Hispanic" (Iberian) designations and stressed "Afro–Latin American culture" as their preferred designation. They also stressed the dynamics of racism built into *mestizaje* representations, and contested the use of such pejorative labels as "darkening" to refer to socio-economic processes analogous to colors of skin and other physical features.

The concept of "Afro–Latin American culture" emerged in Ecuador in 1992. It draws attention to the three emphases that characterize modern black people who maintain their dynamic and traditional lifestyles there: they are *of* "Latin America"; they stem *from* Africa; and they *are* black. "Latin American" in this context contrasts with "Anglo-American," and "Africa" contrasts with "Iberian Europe."

In Esmeraldas a small park has been established with the name of Mandela. There, every afternoon, black people gather informally to discuss the way in which blackness is perceived as inferior to whiteness. They undertake sophisticated analysis of language, talk, reference and representation. For example, they contest the phrase *mejor la raza* with another, *hacer valer la raza*. By this is meant that blackness, for black or dark people, is to be of worth, of value, and with this phrase they also call to account the discriminatory language of blackness presented daily to them through all media oriented toward "whitening." The principal contrast is that of the developers' *despreciar*, disrespect for their physical features and lifestyles, and the assertion of Afro-Ecuadorian leaders and speakers of the need for *respeto* (respect) for black people, their lifeways and viewpoints, if the nation-state of Ecuador is "to rescue its national dignity."

Use of language drawn from the domain of economics is common in the positive rhetoric of indigenous and black movements in Ecuador; it signals, among other things, that respect for the humanity of black and indigenous peoples, and the economic worth of such peoples, are inextricably bound together. This liberating figure of speech is amplified by expressions such as "Do not accept any more terms [or terminologies] against our dignity and promote the belief in our intellectual capacity."[18] This small park in Esmeraldas is emblematic of sites throughout Ecuador where small groups of black people gather to talk of their history, their present and their collective and individual fates and destinies in the futures of the various nation-states that make up the Americas.

### Prospects for the Future

The black population of Ecuador is expanding in numbers, diversifying in the sectors available for black enfranchisement and moving in search of new and better opportunities. Ties between black people in rural and urban areas are becoming stronger as the national infrastructure expands. A number of loosely articulated black movements dot the provinces of Esmeraldas and Imbabura–Carchi, and groups in Ibarra, Quito and Guayaquil engage the nationalist rhetoric of *mestizaje* with their international, national, regional and local discourses of *negritud* (blackness).

Racist barriers truncate movements, and localize them. Difficulties with access to funds for ideological and social mobilization for black people are many, in striking contrast to the pools of international money available to indigenous peoples. It is not clear whether human rights agencies are as interested in black problems as they are in those of some indigenous people. What black people have in Ecuador today they have taken for themselves, against astounding odds and adversities.

Black people say that research into their communities and cultures is lacking; international attention would be greatly appreciated. But little serious research is being done, in spite of the collaborative mood between local people of color and international scholarship that could prevail.

There are three dimensions to affirmative blackness in Ecuador. The first is in the realm of globalization of interest and concern. Do people in Europe and the United States really listen to black voices from Ecuador? If so, do they respond positively as they do with indigenous movements and movements to "save the rain forests"? We think not, although publication of this book is certainly a positive step toward the much needed globalization of information.

The second dimension is one of serious research in Afro–Latin American communities in the hemisphere. "Community studies" are not in vogue in anthropology and sociology. But people live in communities, and it is there that they talk intensively to one another, and wish their voices to be heard. A call for serious studies in communities to see what, indeed, a *comunidad negra* is in the late twentieth century, and the twenty-first century, is essential. The world needs to know how people live, what they say, what they see, feel and seek in life and in afterlife.

The third dimension is developing access to opportunity so that people who live Afro–Latin American lives, whatever those lives may be, have greatly increased opportunities for formal education so that they, at last, can undertake studies of what they deem significant. This call for research and appreciation of black lifeways in Ecuador, as elsewhere, demands an integrated and creative cross-disciplinary approach that treats seriously the ethnography, history, literature and richness of culture of Afro–Latin American peoples everywhere. The Afro–Latin Americans of Ecuador are ready and willing to participate in multiple and creative ways in such an endeavor.

## Acknowledgments

We could not have prepared this chapter without the sustained help and support of P. Rafael Savoia, Director of the Afro-Ecuadorian Cultural Center, Quito, Guayaquil and Esmeraldas, and his staff. Ana Rosa Menéndez also helped with the project that resulted in this chapter, at a preliminary stage. Our colleague at the University of Illinois at Urbana-Champaign, Dr. Arlene Torres, read and commented on a draft of this chapter. We are responsible for any errors of commission and omission that may come to light in what we hope will be sustained future research.

## Notes

1. Estupiñán Bass, N., "Canción del niño negro y del incendio" ("Song of the black child and of the conflagration"), in *Canto negro por la luz: poemas para negros y blancos*, Esmeraldas, Casa de la Cultura Ecuatoriana, 1954, pp. 50, 53.

Black, black, blackened
black, brother of charcoal,
black of blacks born,
black yesterday, today and tomorrow,
Some believe they insult me
mocking my colour,
but I myself proclaim it
with pride in the face of the sun:
Black I have been, black I am,

black I come, black I go,
black real black I was born,
black black I must live,
and as black must die.

2. Whitten, N. E., Jr, *Black Frontiersmen: Afro-Hispanic Culture of Ecuador and Colombia*, Prospect Heights, IL, Waveland Press, 4th edn, 1985.

3. E.g. Stutzman, R., *Black Highlanders: Racism and Ethnic Stratification in the Ecuadorian Sierra*, PhD thesis in anthropology, Washington University, St. Louis—Ann Arbor, MI, University Microfilms, 1974; Colonel Feijóo, F., *El valle sangrieto*, Quito, Abya-Yala, 1991, p. 19.

4. Colonel, op. cit., pp. 88, 94.

5. *Hoy*, 25 March 1990.

6. See Peñaherrera de Costales, P., and Costales Samaniego, A., *Coangue o historia cultural y social de los negros del Chota y Salinas*, Llacta no. 7, Quito, Organo de Publicación Semestral de Instituto Ecuatoriano de Antropología y Geografía, 1959; Klump, K., "Black traders of north highland Ecuador", in N. E. Whitten and J. F. Szwed (eds), *Afro-American Anthropology: Contemporary Perspectives*, New York, Free Press, 1970; Stutzman, op. cit.

7. Rafael Savoia, P., personal communication, November 1994.

8. Anda Aguirre, A., *Indios y negros bajo el dominio español en Loja*, Quito, Abya-Yala, 1993, p. 257.

9. Ibid., p. 258.

10. See Forbes, J. D., *Africans and Native Americans: The Language of Race and the Evolution of Red-Black Peoples*, Urbana, IL, University of Illinois Press, 2nd ed., 1993, pp. 67–8.

11. Ibid., pp. 131–3.

12. Ibid., pp. 93–238.

13. See p. 4, above.

14. Preciado Bedoya, A., *Jolgorio [Joy]: Poems*, trans. M. Lewis, 1983, pp. 121–2:

Barrio of blacks
of dark streets
bursting with spooks
that carry off, that frighten,
that make hairs stand
on moonless nights

Inflamed barrio
by night and by day,
black hell
enveloped in the flames
of rhythm and happiness.

15. Quiroga, D., *Saints, Virgins and the Devil: Witchcraft, Magic and Healing in the Northern Coast of Ecuador*, PhD thesis in anthropology, University of Illinois at Urbana-Champaign—Ann Arbor, MI, University Microfilms, 1993.

16.  In Whitten, N. E., Jr, *Cultural Transformations and Ethnicity in Modern Ecuador*, Urbana, IL, University of Illinois Press, 1981, pp. 535–62.

17.  In January 1995 armed border conflict again erupted between Ecuador and Peru. Two salient images of savagery and barbarism in defence of the fatherland (*la patria*) appeared on national television. One of these depicted a "Shuar" ("Jívaro") native person of the Cordillera de Condor holding a machete in his right hand, and a reduced head (monkey or human) aloft in his left hand. "This is what I will do to Fujimori" (the President of Peru), read the subtitle to this violent imagery of jungle savagery. The other image was that of huge black men, all more than six feet tall, preparing for movement to the frontier, in "dangerous Jívaro country." The announcer explained that these black people were from Esmeraldas, and specially trained in guerrilla warfare near the Taura airforce base near Guayaquil. He proceeded to explain that black people were a "race adapted to the jungle," that "they fought naked from the waist up in the jungle." The negative, racist imagery of savage (jungle-dwelling, head-taking Jívaro) and huge barbarian (jungle-dwelling, bare-chested, machete-wielding *cimarrón*)—both of which are rejected antipodes of Ecuadorian nationality during quotidian times—were raised as hyper-positive symbols of nationalism in the defence of *la patria* in the liminal space of death and destruction wherein Ecuador was engaged in sustained armed struggle with its historic nation-state adversary.

18.  See e.g. the magazine *Otra*, 18 May 1990, p. 70.

## Select Bibliography and Works Cited

Anda Aguirre, A., *Indios y negros bajo el dominio español en Loja*, Quito, Abya-Yala, 1993.
Cabello Balboa, M., *Obras*, vol. 1, Quito, Editorial Ecuatoriana, 1945 [1583].
Colonel Feijóo, R., *El valle sangrieto*, Quito, Abya-Yala, 1991.
Estupiñán Bass, N., *Canto negro por la luz: poemas para negros y blancos*, Esmeraldas, Casa de la Cultura Ecuatoriana, 1954.
Estupiñán Bass, N., *El último río*, Quito, Casa de la Cultura Ecuatoriana, 1966.
Estupiñán Bass, N., *Senderos brillantes*, Quito, Casa de la Cultura Ecuatoriana, 1974.
Forbes, J. D., *Africans and Native Americans: The Language of Race and the Evolution of Red-Black Peoples*, Urbana, IL, University of Illinois Press, 2nd edn, 1993 [1988].
García, J., *Cuentos y décimas afro-esmeraldeñas*, Quito, Abya-Yala, 2nd edn, 1988.
Girardi, G., *Los excluídos: ¿constrirán la nueva históría? El movimiento indígena, negro, y popular*, Quito, Centro Cultural Afro-Ecuatoriano and Ediciones Nicarao, 1994.
Jurado Noboa, F., *Esclavitud en la costa pacífica: Iscuandé, Barbacoas, Tumaco y Esmeraldas, siglos XVI al XIX*, Quito, Centro Afro-Ecuatoriano, Corporación Ecuatoriana de "Amigos de la Genealogía" (SAG) and Abya-Yala, 1990.
Ortiz, A., *Juyungo: historia de un negro, una isla, y otros negros*, Buenos Aires, Editorial Americalee, 1942.
Ortiz, A., *La entundada y cuentos variados*, Quito, Casa de la Cultura Ecuatoriana, 1971.
Ortiz, A. et al., *Antología de cuentos esmeraldeños*, Quito, Casa de la Cultura Ecuatoriana, 1960.
Peñaherrera de Costales, P. and Costales Samaniego, A., *Coangue o historia cultural y*

*social de los negros del Chota y Salinas*, Llacta no. 7, Quito, Organo de Publicación Semestral de Instituto Ecuatoriano de Antropología y Geografía, 1959.

Peralta Rivera, G., *Los mecanismos del comercio negrero*, Lima, Kuntur Editores, 1990.

Quiroga, D., *Saints, Virgins and the Devil: Witchcraft, Magic, and Healing in the Northern Coast of Ecuador*, PhD thesis in anthropology, University of Illinois at Urbana-Champaign—Ann Arbor, MI, University Microfilms, 1993.

Rahier, J., *La décima: poesía oral negra del Ecuador*, Quito, Abya-Yala and Centro Cultural Afro-Ecuatoriana, n.d., c.1990.

Savoia, P. R. (ed.), *El negro en la historia: aportes para el conocimiento de las raíces en América Latina*, Quito, Centro Cultural Afro-Ecuatoriano, 1990.

Stutzman, R., *Black Highlanders: Racism and Ethnic Stratification in the Ecuadorian Sierra*, PhD thesis in anthropology, Washington University, St. Louis—Ann Arbor, MI, University Microfilms, 1974.

Whitten, N. E., Jr., *Class, Kinship, and Power in an Ecuadorian Town: The Negroes of San Lorenzo*, Stanford, CA, Stanford University Press, 1965.

Whitten, N. E., Jr. (ed.), *Cultural Transformations and Ethnicity in Modern Ecuador*, Urbana, IL, University of Illinois Press, 1981.

Whitten, N. E., Jr., *Sicuanga Runa: The Other Side of Development in Amazonian Ecuador*, Urbana, IL, University of Illinois Press, 1984.

Whitten, N. E., Jr., *Black Frontiersmen: Afro-Hispanic Culture of Ecuador and Colombia*, Prospect Heights, IL, Waveland Press, 4th ed., 1985 [1974].

Whitten, N. E., Jr., *Pioneros negros: La cultura afro-latinoamericana del Ecuador y de Colombia*, Quito, Centro Cultural Afro-Ecuatoriano, 1993.

Whitten, N. E. and Szwed, J. F. (eds.), *Afro-American Anthropology: Contemporary Perspectives*, New York, Free Press, 1970.

# 2. CRISIS, CONTRACULTURE, AND RELIGION AMONG WEST INDIANS IN THE PANAMA CANAL ZONE

*R. S. Bryce-Laporte*

This paper centers on an incident which occurred in the early 1950s in a now nonexistent border town of the Panama Canal Zone.[1]

One night two young men, both Panamanian Negroes of West Indian origin, were involved in a fiery discussion during the first showing of a picture at the local movie theater. The boys exchanged insults and challenges. As soon as the picture ended both boys left with their respective entourage. The argument was resumed in the hallway of the local clubhouse. One boy struck the other on his head with a cue stick from a nearby billiard table. The victim, who later died, supposedly attempted to conceal his injury from his mother and at first gave the doctor an alibi rather than disclose the real cause.

The other boy was arrested by the Zone police (American white) but was quickly released on bail. His mother, in anxiety, sought all the assistance she could possibly obtain to influence the outcome of the pending court trial in favor of her son. In so doing she consulted, among others, the principal of the local high school (which her son attended and where she was employed as a custodian), the official public defender, her son's employers and a student leader and acquaintance of her son. All of these individuals expressed their firm opinion that in view of the circumstances of the crime and the comparative "better" reputation of her son to his victim, the sentence would be minimal. It is said that the principal (an American white) had relayed to the student leader (Panamanian–West Indian black) the firm opinion of the public defender and other judicial and police authorities (all American whites) that her son would not only receive the minimum sentence for the crime but that the sentence would be suspended for a period of probation if her son's employers (Panamanian whites) would assure them that he would continue to be in their service. It is believed that the woman obtained this assurance from the employers, who also informed her that they had already notified the zone authorities of their disposition.

Despite these assurances, the woman solicited the aid of at least two occult agencies. During the period preceding the trial she held a series of spiritual-like meetings or ceremonies at her home. They were conducted by a quasi-revivalist sect

Originally published in Norman E. Whitten, Jr. and John F. Szwed (eds.), *Afro-American Anthropology: Contemporary Perspectives* (New York: Free Press, 1970), pp. 103–18. Reprinted by permission of The Free Press, a Division of Simon & Schuster.

known locally as the "Jump-up" or "Benjinite" Church [which had apparent elements of Africanism, Catholicism, and Evangelical Protestantism in its ritual and belief systems]. In addition, she allegedly solicited the aid of an Obeah-Man (shaman) in hope of influencing the outcome of the trial in her son's favor.

It is believed by the townspeople that when the family of the deceased boy learned of her activities they solicited a similar medium, to make sure that their son's killer would pay for his crime. Neither of the two families denied these rumors nor was there any attempt made by them or the townspeople to observe complete secrecy regarding these doings.

The trial found the boy guilty. He was given the minimum period of confinement and the sentence was immediately suspended in favor of a period of probation. In the near future, however, he and his family began to experience many misfortunes and difficulties which culminated with their being ejected from the Zone. As far as the majority of the townspeople were concerned the "Thing" [as Obeah and Benjinite were sometimes called] had worked for both parties!

The major portion of this paper will be directed to answering three questions: First, why did the families of both boys resort to occult means? Second, why did they overlook their own Episcopal churches and seek the services of folk media? Third, why did their solicitations and subsequent rituals take place in relative, but not absolute, secrecy?

My effort to answer these questions requires reconstruction and *post factum* explanation. Merton (1957:93–101) criticizes such explanations on the grounds of their limited rigor and validity but concedes that they have high plausibility and are therefore revealing. I hope to draw attention to a people and to an area about which social scientists know little and to demonstrate the need for further reconsideration and modification of present concepts and methods to meet the challenges presented by these and other people in similar situations. The paper also constitutes an effort to share information from the position of a native and principal participant in a series of events rather than from the perspective of an alien investigator.

*The Canal Zone: Its Power Structure,*
*Race Relations, Plural Arrangements, and Stratification*

The Canal Zone is a strip of land which runs across the narrowest part of the Isthmus of Panama and borders the Panama Canal on both sides. Technically and geographically the Zone continues to be a contiguous territorial part of the Republic of Panama. However, for all practical and legal purposes it is under the complete and perpetual jurisdiction of the United States of America. The Canal Treaty provides for the United States to utilize the Zone for the construction, operation, maintenance, and defense of the Canal. Hence, all activities, enterprises, and organizations within the Zone are devised to comply with one or more of those functions. The following paragraphs of this section will attempt to present a picture of certain aspects of the Zone as it was even up to the mid-1950s. After that time certain marked superficial changes have become noticeable—i.e., the integration of the police force on the lower levels and the conversion of colored English language schools to "Latin American" Spanish language schools. However, many of the major structural characteristics have remained fundamentally intact.

The Canal Zone was governed by a quasi-military bureaucratic government. Its populace had no electoral vote (though Americans were eligible for jury posts and could exercise absentee voting rights). Popular voice in Zone affairs was restricted to United States labor unions and a few professional, fraternal, or patriotic pressure groups (mostly American). The Canal Zone government held totalitarian authority, jurisdiction, and control over all phases of life or organization, e.g., law, labor, capital, defense, communication and transportation, business, and services (save the churches and a few private enterprises). For all purposes, despite its non-agricultural emphasis and its principal economic functions (maritime services), the Canal Zone was a closed system reminiscent of the plantation estate which once dominated socio-economic life in most of the Circum-Caribbean (Augelli 1962:119–29; Bryce-Laporte 1962:9–91; Greaves 1959:13–22; McBride 1937:148; Mintz 1959b:42–53; Rubio 1957; Wagley 1957:3–13; Wilson 1947). Only employees of the Zone could live in the Zone, in quarters built, rented, and maintained by the Zone. Only they could purchase in its commissary stores and utilize its recreational facilities. Only they could be taught in its schools, be treated in its hospitals and clinics, and be buried in its cemeteries. Not all the employees of the Zone lived there, of course. Many lived in the terminal cities of Panama and Colón just outside its usually unmarked borders. Even these people were not fully outside the embrace of the Zone—they all treasured and utilized their "privileges" as employees to shop at its cheaper stores, to attend its more efficient and modern hospitals, to use its cleaner toilets. The Zone then was not only closed but it was also exclusive and prized.

The government pursued a rigid policy of discrimination and segregation based on race and nationality, which affected every facet of life and organization within the borders of the Zone. There were remarkably few American Negroes and few non-American whites in the civilian structure of the Zone's labor force. Hence, for all purposes the population and the labor force of the Zone fitted nearly into the two official categories: United States employee-resident (paid one rate of compensation) and local employee-resident (paid a lower rate of compensation).[2] U.S.-rate employee-residents were in general the occupants of the official, administrative, technical, professional, and skilled occupations and offices. As such they were much better paid, unquestionably privileged, and definitely allowed superior facilities. In addition, they lived in U.S.-rate towns, attended U.S.-rate schools, and utilized U.S.-rate services. Local-rate employee-residents, on the other hand, were the usual occupants of semi-skilled and menial positions, a few becoming junior clerical and supervisory personnel or semi-professionals—i.e., teachers. They were underpaid, underprivileged, and offered substandard facilities. They lived segregated from the U.S.-raters, to whom they were subordinate. The few marginal cases in either segment sought refuge in the Republic, where the economic and other material standards of living were distinctly inferior but the social climate distinctly more liberal.

The Zone situation was a quasi-caste system; its strata were rigid and the relationships between them were stable and asymmetrical. Every white American was ascribed at birth or upon entering the Zone as superordinate over every colored person, regardless of nationality, age, years of service, sex, and the like. This *de facto* relationship was an apparent extension of the *de jure* subjugation intertwined in the official structure of the Canal Zone and was undoubtedly reinforced by it in every institutional way of life in the Zone.

A glance at the judicial-police system (the official legal institution) would serve as an adequate illustration: the law and court systems were American and their implementations were reminiscent of Deep South standards. All the judicial authorities—judges, prosecutors and defenders, and jurors—were white Americans. There were only two prominent West Indian members of the Zone's bar; the remaining non-whites were minor court clerks and custodians. The police organization was all white, with the exception of prison guards. Previously, there were West Indian foot police but they could not arrest a white American even for a traffic violation in a colored neighborhood. They were assigned only to local-rate neighborhoods, never could become officers or members of motorized units, and were paid less than their white counterparts.

To a people who were migrants, or descendants of migrants, from the rural West Indies many of the laws seemed illogical, unfair, limited, strange, and contradictory to the norms of the sub-culture of the local-rate communities or the old culture of the islands. Furthermore, many of the Zone laws were contradictory to those of nearby Panama and so too the system and sentences. Furthermore, conviction, and more so, confinement, could result in the loss of one's job and the privilege of obtaining another job or other supplementary benefits of Canal Zone employment. Yet these people constituted the major part of the prison population, because their low earnings prohibited them from paying fines meted out by the court. White prisoners were rare. It was the general belief of the West Indian–Panamanian black people that the Zone law was one-sidedly severe and that on the other side it was lenient and unjust. Americans who got in trouble were often pardoned, released on bail or, after stern admonition, treated as insane or sent away quietly to the United States. When whites and blacks were indicted, the whites were used as capital witnesses against their colored cohorts and given lighter sentences and less rigorous prison duties whenever confined. Incidents to support these stereotypic beliefs formed part of the anthology of legend and folklore of West Indian–Panamanian blacks. Many local-rate teachers scolded their unruly students saying, "Why can't you be like those children over there?" (i.e., the whites).

The discrepancies between official laws and local customs had their effects even in the intimate institution of the family. The Panamanian–West Indian kinship system is bilateral and women seem central in the domestic domain. Family life was made up of a wide range of structural variations and a great deal of permissive relations. This was much more true in the Republic than in the Canal Zone, where the housing authorities and regulations imposed some far-reaching restrictions. Only legal spouse and primary relatives—parents, children, and sometimes sibling peers—were considered eligible for residence as dependents of the applicant. Only on rare occasions would the government consider a woman, even though she might be employed in its service, as an eligible holder of family quarters (that is, as the head of the household). These restrictions led to various sorts of accommodations, legal and illegal, by the local-rate residents to resolve the dilemma of maintaining Canal Zone quarters without completely disrupting the traditions of extended or compound families or matrifocal households. These housing regulations made the father's status that of recognizable head of the household or the sole "legal holder of family quarters." This status implied the role of economic locus and thereby gave him greater *de jure* authority than his West Indian counterpart.[3]

In spite of the strengthening of the husband-father role, the mother was the central figure of the local-rate family. She exercised discipline and represented the household in the absence of the father. She was responsible for the care of the children as well as for other domestic matters. In such matters she was assisted by the older children. She was considered with such reverence that any insult of her name or person was considered a dishonor to her offspring.

Children sought playmates from their peer groups at an early age, but were expected to respect all adults. Nevertheless, joking relations were most prevalent among children and non-related adults and intergenerational conflicts stemmed from differences in the standards and traditions between the old and new culture. The traditional adult-dominated relations, which never release the child, regardless of his age and status, from the dominance of parents and elders, could not persist under Canal Zone laws. People were limited in regard to how much of the law could be taken into their own hands, whether in family or non-family affairs.

### El Rabo: A Local-Rate Community as a Sociocultural System

El Rabo was a local-rate colored community within a ten-minute ride or about an hour's walk from the border of Panama City. It was located at the terminal of the Canal and the site of a ferry which connected it with the west bank of the waterway. Hemmed in on most sides by the largest and most important (white) American community in the Zone, it was typical of the segregated, sub-standard ghettos which provided residence for the local-rate employees of the Canal Zone. Its houses consisted of over-crowded, wooden, gray-colored, barrack-type buildings. Some housed bachelors and a few spinsters, but the large majority served multi-family units. All of these structures were raised from the earth by pillars varying in length from five to ten feet, which created unpaved open basements which the local people called "cellars." These cellars were utilized for every conceivable purpose, from religion to romance. All public facilities were minimal replicas of the services extended to U.S.-rate communities. Only the church buildings, the lodge-hall, and the labor union office were not subjected to the curfew regulations and surveillance of the Zone government.

The town consisted of a rather broad lower–working class (hereafter lower class) with a peripheral lower-middle-class minority. There was limited upward movement outside the class although there was almost free movement across or within the class. The limited degree of prestige differential that was attainable in the local community was made possible within the rather restrictive borders of the socioeconomic structure imposed by the Canal Zone government and the equally restrictive control system of the community itself. The few who were successful in achieving some increase in prestige often did so through a combination of education, occupation, civic-church position, and individual ambition and perseverance. A few attained some prestige through inheritance. Hence, teachers, ministers, and a few clerical or skilled supervisors, and those in close association with them, could enjoy relatively high local prestige. Such people were often called "butches" by the rest of the community.

The term "butch" connotes prestige, not popularity. The phrases "playing butch" or "acting stuck-up" imply snobbishness, social-climbing, or status-steeking—all distasteful and deviant categories vis-à-vis the larger community. It is important that one capture the subtle difference between prestige and popularity as established by the people of this community. Prestige was a classificatory attribute acquired by those who excelled in their efforts to conform to the standards of the superordinate culture—an outward orientation. Popularity was acquired by those who were considered successful or outstanding in demonstrating the "good" aspects or ideals of the subordinate culture—an inward orientation. Each carried with it a somewhat fixed range of role expectations and a corresponding set of reactive behavior patterns.

Among the qualities associated with the superordinate culture were some of definite American origin and others traceable to the "old aristocratic" culture of the middle and upper classes of the British West Indies. Those considered West Indian–Panamanian were not only those indigenous qualities of the subordinate subculture, but also those American and British traits which had been internalized or assimilated so completely by this element that they were not conceived by the community as false, foreign, nor formal—e.g., speaking with an American or British accent was considered false, foreign, and formal; playing baseball or cricket was considered normal, natural, and native!

Distinct from prestige, then, popularity was usually derived from athletic feats, public relations occupations, wealth, conspicuous friendliness, apparent freedom from bias or snobbery, and ostentatious dressing. Thus, athletes, musicians, sing-ers, delinquents, bus drivers, salesclerks, clandestine lottery vendors, drug addicts, petty criminals, and "funny" characters might be "popular." Perhaps the only ones who lacked either attribute in distinguishing measure were the "average citi-zens" or "nobodys." The few with a distinguishing measure of both were those individuals who had learned to balance or to appropriately demonstrate different traits at their respectively "proper" times. Then there were those who had both "no" prestige and "no" popularity, such as effeminate men, suspected male ho-mosexuals, girls believed to be promiscuous with white men, alleged stoolpigeons or "squealers," prisoners, and openly practicing lay members of "spirit" churches. In some cases these people with negative amounts of both attributes were often subjected to ridicule, ostracization, and persecution because they represented that which the community could not be proud of and which made the commu-nity susceptible to the ridicule of white people.

Inasmuch as these two attributes were largely aquisitive, they could be lost or threatened by the individual's overly deviating from his idiosyncratic credit (the permissible range of deviation from norms and role expectations earned or as-signed to each individual in accordance with his status). Inasmuch as the com-munity was neither simple, isolated, nor static, many conflicts arose due to incon-sistencies between status and roles perceived by those acting and those judging. Nevertheless, the apparently independent attributes of prestige and popularity seemed to constitute a sort of unwritten frame of reference within the larger norm, value, and control systems of the community. As such the attributes pro-vided guidelines for establishing status differentiation and regulating social be-havior among community members.

### Analysis

I shall now analyze the event by reinterpreting the three questions previously presented and answer them against the background of the proposed prestige-popularity situation.

1. *What social conditions seemed to be related to the effort of both families to seek the assistance of extra-legal agencies (in this case magical-religious media) to resolve what appears to be a purely criminal concern?*

To answer this question, and the others to come, one must first try to locate the two families involved along the scales of prestige and popularity. Both families were of equally low prestige. The boy who killed and his family were somewhat more popular than the victim and his family. In the town's jargon they were "popular guys" not "butches"; in the study's jargon they were much more "in-wardly oriented" than "outwardly oriented" and almost equal in status. Hence, what applies to one family also applies to the other for the purposes of this study.

These people were members of an immigrant minority which voluntarily came to the Isthmus under the auspices of an alien but superordinate American majority. The Americans created an exclusive and closed system in which their imported culture became the official norm system. This norm system was reinforced by the rigid asymmetrical power structure, race relations, and stratification system. From the very beginning the West Indian minority had no opportunity to establish their own legal institution side by side or within the official judicial-police system of the Zone. The American majority, while imposing its laws, minimized and eventually eliminated all opportunities for active political and legal participation of the West Indian minority. In a sense it was more selective giving than selective borrowing.

West Indians have been known to boast of how they were constables, soldiers, court officers, and barristers in their home government. They often decried the Zone's and Panama's legal and police system as inferior to that of the British. They even boasted that in the past when local-raters were employed as foot police there were fewer cases of crime, disrespect, and delinquency, so much so that after every major disturbance or crime these people would engage in rumor-spreading and what seemed then to be wishful thinking that colored policemen would soon be brought back into service. As the people contended, those colored policemen were men of the community, they knew the boys and their parents, would take things into their hands to chase children home, see that they went to school, whip wayward boys and complain to their parents who in turn would chastize the children again. They knew the hoodlums and their ways so well that they could anticipate their acts and capture them before they could escape. These apparently nativistic rumors expressed the yearning for more participation in law enforcement and for an avenue within the official structure to practice the kind of law and enforcement (which include close parent-police cooperation and stern corporal discipline) more in line with their own sub-culture.

They were not very trustful of the law, as can be seen from the legends and folklore of incidents which were mentioned earlier. Neither did they really understand how it worked. The very schools which were the principal agencies of acculturation, where American methods, textbooks, curricula, and administrative policies were official, were affected by the ambivalence toward acculturation. Its faculty (made up of West Indian and Panamanian blacks), while teaching American democracy and preparing their students to enter the Zone's labor force, knew only from textbooks the complicated processes and ideals behind American laws. As members of the subordinate minority they were equally subjugated to the one-sided Canal Zone system. Most of them, while ranking very high in prestige (index of high outward orientation), had doubts about the American Democratic system and resented the local situation due to the inconsistencies between what they taught and what they met as persons. They were the leaders and most militant faction of the local labor union (which at one time was allegedly Communist affiliated). But even among them there were cases of solicitations to folk magical-religious media and other extra-legal agencies in times of crisis. The school administration was never successful in getting these teachers to refrain from the use of severe corporal punishment as a means of discipline. Parents requested and supported the teachers' right to use this kind of discipline. Principals were high in the local communal power structure and like clergymen often exercised their powers as law enforcers, judges, and executors in communal conflicts.

In effect, while it is not easy to say why people would choose to solicit folk magic (or religion), it can be seen why they would find it difficult to rely solely on the Zone's judicial system. They feared, resented, mistrusted, did not understand, and were not a part of it. This was clearly demonstrated in some of the common sayings of the people. "Man can change. He is only human. He can plan and promise but you can never tell what will make him change his mind . . . Man proposes but God disposes . . . So you better do something to make sure nothing upset de plans."

The Canal Zone judiciary system simply did not have the same functions nor meaning for local-raters as it had for U.S.-raters. It reflected a different world view and rationale. It did not recognize Obeah as a social reality nor the manipulation of spirits as cause nor cure for ill-will or illness. It made no provision to prevent, protect from, nor punish the use of sorcery. In the West Indies where there was less inequality in the twentieth century, more participation in the official legal machinery, and the persecution of Obeah practitioners, these people nevertheless clung to their folk religion as an extra-judicial mechanism. It seems natural then to expect similar manifestations in the Canal Zone, where there was greater inequality, fewer opportunities for participation in legal machinery, and no direct persecution of Obeah. If the more acculturated and well-to-do "butches" often sought this medium as well as lawyers and influential friends in times of crisis, if to lose a case could mean the loss of popularity and, perhaps, a source of livelihood, then these are enough reasons for poor families (like the two involved) to seek the assistance of Obeahmen and "Jump-up" churches. From their perspective these agencies were less expensive, more readily available, more effective, and more understandable.

2. *Why did neither family, both members of the Episcopal church, consult their clergy rather than turn to other occult media?*

The community enjoyed full religious freedom, variety, and fluid choice. While the population was predominantly Protestant, the Catholic Church was strong. The formal churches were more permanent, better organized and attended, but the nativistic churches were more numerous, often duplicated, and were constantly undergoing change. It is impossible to generalize regarding the type of person or family which would belong, much less attend, one of these churches. While there are some families who subscribed to but one traditional church, in other families individual members belonged to or attended different churches. There were even cases of single individuals belonging to or attending more than one church.

The church buildings were the only public services found in multiple numbers, and, of course, they were privately owned. Consequently, they served multiple purposes or functions aside from being the sites of religious activities. The churches seemed to be involved in a similar classificatory scheme along the lines of prestige and popularity congruent with the ranking of individuals. The churches seem to range along a continuum from formal to folk. A formal church includes clergy, ritual, organization, theology, and activities governed or patterned after a larger and universal conventional religious denomination; a folk-church is governed or developed by the local minority caste and with minimal international or foreign connections. While most formal churches were considered prestige churches, it does not hold that most folk churches were considered popular, for just as there were individuals who were able to attain prestige by not being "stuck-up," some of the formal churches, being richer, better attended, and better organized, were able to sponsor or participate in activities of a "popular" nature. On the other hand, some folk churches not only had "no" prestige but were normally associated with actions considered bad, shameful, or ridiculous by even the majority of the community—hence were not popular either.

The Anglican church was the state church of the British West Indies where it was largely associated with the upper and middle classes. It was one of the few avenues from which the lower classes could derive minimal status. On the Isthmus both West Indian Anglicans and North American Episcopalians were under the jurisdiction of the American Episcopal church. In this community almost the entire population was of British West Indian nationality or ancestry, and the Episcopal Church was the largest and most populous. While it was closely related and governed by British traditions and American authorities, the local clergy was black, native, and educated. The activities of this church were of the widest variety, touching every class. It enjoyed the highest prestige and the greatest popularity among local churches. But the issue facing the two families was not solely social in nature; prestige was not involved; popularity was to some extent; but more immediately important was the need for a religious ritual to bolster their security for their respective problems. This called for either a church whose rituals and theology corresponded to that of the world view of these people or one whose atmosphere and rituals were conducive to secret participation of the nature required by the two cases. In these respects the Episcopalian Church was of little or no use.

Opposing the Episcopal and Roman Catholic churches in style, and in popularity, are the Benjinite or Jump-up sects. They do not have an elaborate or extensive formal structure. They do not embrace a large scope of the lives of their members, nor are they usually related to other national or international denominations. Some isolated churches are affiliated with or patterned after North American evangelical sects and among other isolated churches there may be visiting and irregular joint activities. In general each sect represents a small network of brethren. It is usually led by a woman called a Mother, at whose home or on whose property most of the ceremonies are celebrated. The remaining officers usually consist of a Deacon or Deaconess, a Shepherd Boy, and an Armor-Bearer.

Brothers and Sisters and a group of non-members, who range from the believing well-wishers to curious or critical observers, make up the church.

The word "Benjinite" derives from Bedwardite, an Afro-Christian revival group which was founded in Jamaica around the beginning of the twentieth century. The practices and paraphernalia of the Isthmian cult seem to approximate African-oriented West Indian cults such as myalism, kumina, convince, and pocomania (Beckwith 1923:32–45; Hogg 1960, 1964; Simpson 1956). There has been no drumming in the Isthmian cults in recent times, but there has been increasing evidence of Roman Catholic or Anglican High Church influence among the cults. West Indian pidgin English is the principal form spoken in services. While participants may dress in ordinary clothing, special habits are usually worn by women. The most common habit is generally a long white, brown, blue, or mauve dress, with a cord and a single or multi-colored turban or headwrap and regular shoes or sandals. Men usually wear black or white trousers and white shirts, but on some occasions may dress like either Christian pastors or like monks.

The Benjinite meeting begins with low-keyed prayers and singing and gradually increases in intensity and tempo as people begin to testify, shout, shake, clap, and finally prance forward and sideways in a counter-clockwise promenade. Then some individual (usually a member or officer) gets a "calling." He (or she) falls out of the group or spins into the center of the circle, starts to shake, to grunt or moan ecstatically and, as he gyrates, his body and face contort, his limbs are flung about wildly, and he is said to be "in (or catching) the spirits." The Mother, with the help of other officers, "works with him" while the brethren sing and stomp in a very deliberate and heavy tempo. As he is being "worked out of the spirits," he quiets down and slips into a trance-like state. The singing gets softer and slower as he "travels off to distant places," "hears voices," "sees visions," and "gets messages." He begins to sing or speak in "unknown tongues" or makes scribblings on the ground, and one of the participants or leaders suddenly screams out the "message" for which the entire audience and membership have been anxiously waiting. The message usually takes the form of a symbol which is interpreted as a "warning," such as "sudden death," or an indictment or caution to some *specific* person in the group. The warning usually represents "disaster" and triggers off anxieties associated with crisis situations. Sometimes the message is a "rake" which indicates a number which may be a "winner" in the various lotteries bought by Isthmian people. Sermons, singing, and feasting usually bring the official service to an end. As people leave they discuss or transmit the message or sermon to other interested parties.

In El Rabo such services were usually held at night in the open basement and were open to the public. Only day services were held indoors and the were usually to protect the ceremony from the ridicule and distractions of the larger number of passersby who would ordinarily not be present at night. In the case of the accused (discussed in the beginning of this paper) the services were held in his home even though they were carried out at night. The curtains were drawn, the ceremony itself was performed in a large inner room, and the main door to the house was closed although not locked. One of my notes describes the sessions as follows:

> As one opened the main door he encountered a crowd of curious observers, many of them friends of the accused. To get into the inner room where the ceremony took place one had to "spin his role" (turn around counter-clockwise three times under the supervision of one of the cult members) before a "seal" (a Bible with a candle and other chalk markings on the floor). Candles, flowers, Bibles, religious pictures and statuettes, crucifixes, chalk-drawings, herbs, twigs, incense, smoke, and medicated water were in abundance. The brethren performed in a circle and the accused was placed in the center. He had on a white head wrap with a candle and Bible in his hands and was promenaded and gyrated about by a presiding cult member. He perspired, gazed, and permitted himself to be led. He seemed afraid but not embarrassed. And as for the onlookers there was not time for ridicule.

The basic idea behind the ceremony was to appeal to and marshall spirits who would intercede in his behalf.

The Obeah-Man that both families allegedly visited is believed to have secret powers to deal with spirits and ghosts of "duppies" (spirits of dead people) and to be able to communicate with God, Satan, and specific dead people. He is able to get such deities to do "good" or "bad." Among the secrets he knows are the proper formulae, prayers, vows, sacrifices, and other "things" that people must do to get "things" done or to "fix" other people. He also administers baths, potions, and prescriptions, fixes penances, and makes "guards" for his clients. The Obeah-Man is regarded with awe by many Isthmians (including Americans and Latins too). The saliency of his presence is disclosed by the words of this local calypso which the accused himself had sung many times before in his heyday of popularity:

> Obeah-mancy—West and South,
> Dats how the Obeah-Man "wash dem out"
> Dey give him dey money to kill everybody;
> The people believe in too much Negro-mancy
> [necromancy].

The families resorted to these available folk media. Were such media unavailable they might have gone to the Roman Catholic Church or to a folk agency outside of town. More active, high prestige Episcopalians would have done this anyway rather than risk their prestige in a local folk-like church. In the case of low prestige families there was no need for substitution. Folk churches were available as were media where they could experiment and ritualize the latent but still surviving beliefs of their quasi-African world view without violating the local normative system. It was commonplace in the community to hear discussions, rumors, or tales of people of varying degrees of prestige who resorted to or have employed "God" and/or other supernatural beings to carry out evil as well as good.

3. *What is the function of semi-secrecy in the folk rituals?*

The community was homogeneous. There was very little preoccupation with prestige and vertical mobility, for there were few opportunities for upward movement. The community members were nearly unanimously anti-white, anti-government, and opposed to Anglo-American attitudes, for they correctly perceived themselves as being repressed by and without power vis-à-vis the white majority. The "butches" were seen as symbols of submission to or stooges for the repressive white caste. The "popular guys" were perceived as heroes, symbolically representing resistance, disrespect, or defeat of the cultural invasion and socio-economic and political imposition of the ruling white majority caste. Pressure toward conformity was strong and popularity rather than prestige was the big issue among the majority of the townspeople.

The two families involved, while not concerned with losing prestige, saw their popularity at stake. They could well afford to go openly to a folk medium, whereas a high-prestige family could not. But privacy, if not secrecy, was necessary.

The defendant's mother held the meetings in her home (rather than "under the cellar" where they were usually held) to avoid endangering the family's popularity by being mistaken for completely converted Benjinite people. Yet when rumors started to circulate neither family attempted to deny their acts. They were not violating any community norms so long as their occultism was "privately" practised. It was common to hear rumors about people of all classes and denominations employing ghosts, saints, spirits, demons, potions, and/or charms for various reason—i.e., for escape, revenge, cursing, healing, luck, power, and protection. While privacy was regarded as necessary to protect popularity, secrecy was not necessary, inasmuch as the system of norms and world view of the community reinforced sympathy toward such action. Occultism under such circumstances was expected behavior. To quote a popular saving: "Everybody does their little business when they are in a tough spot but the whole world don't have to know about it. After all, when a man is in trouble, you can't blame him for trying 'anything' to get out. . . . "

The need for continuing popularity permeates the incident. The boy who was killed accepted the challenge in the first place for fear of losing his popularity. The challenger struck his younger adversary with a cue stick rather than risk loss of popularity in a fist fight. The first boy did not want to disclose the incident even after being mortally wounded lest he be considered a "squealer" (to a white doctor) and thus lose popularity. The defendant's people struggled to win the case to avoid their son's losing popularity (and prestige) by becoming a prisoner. The town considered that Obeah and Benjinite were successful when the defendant and his family were reduced to a non-popular, non-prestige level, even though he escaped going to jail. And neither family could stand to be criticized by the community for being so "stuck up" and "stupid" as not even to try Obeah and Benjinite to "make things work out" in its respective favor.

## Summary and Conclusion

The Panama Canal Zone, up until the early 1950s, was a closed, exclusive system. Its government and organization resembled the plantation estate in that it was rigidly hierarchical, bureaucratic, pluralistic, paternalistic, authoritarian, and totalitarian.[4] The West Indian immigrants, who constituted its main civilian labor force, were in every sense subordinate to the white American majority, dependent on the Canal Zone government, and as such were exposed to the cultural standards and pressures of the latter.

The incident discussed and analyzed in this paper points to one basic area of cultural contradiction and complementarity: the United States legal code and West Indian folk magic. To complete the analysis it is necessary to discuss participation in its total setting.

The Canal Zone today may best be regarded as a colonial, conflict-based, plural system.[5] Even though West Indians have shown signs of assuming American behavior, it must be remembered that they came to the Zone as strangers to provide labor that was not forthcoming from the natives for various reasons. It was expected that each wave would be repatriated upon completion of the specific missions for which it came (Panama Railroad, French and American Canals, United Fruit Company Railroad, Third Locks Project). Inasmuch as they came in the first instance with no intentions of staying; inasmuch as one of the reasons they were imported involved their skills, attitudes, language, and cultural traditions; and inasmuch as they were led to share in the ethnocentric claim of superiority over the Panamanian natives, West Indians had no basic reason for striving to acquire Panamanian rather than American ways of life. In each instance, however, as their mission approached its end, the West Indians were discouraged from returning to their homeland by various means. They were encouraged instead either to stay in the employ of the Zone or to proceed to seek employment in various parts of the Republic, especially its two terminal cities and on the plantation and properties of the United Fruit Company. In the Canal Zone (and also in the territories of United Fruit Company) the American elite confined itself to exclusive enclaves and built adjacent "company towns." These towns were systems in which the West Indian stranger group constituted the principal employee-residents. The resulting structural asymmetry, or "two-caste" system, persisted despite shared language and tradition and despite the operation of an official school system in the Zone for training West Indians in occupations reserved for them in the Zone's bureaucratic structure. While school programs were designed to acculturate West Indians to American culture, they were not designed to prepare them for assimilation, upward socio-economic mobility, or increased participation in the power structure of the Zone.

It is generally conceded that in most societies the use of religion and magic is intimately tied up with *crisis situations*—perplexing situations in which participants experience unusually heightened anxiety because of their perceived inability to cope with or resolve a given problem. Homans (1950:321–30) in his synthesis of the Malinowski–Radcliffe-Brown controversy demonstrated that the consequence of *primary anxiety* (due to the feeling of personal inadequacy) and *secondary anxiety* (which persists until the socially prescribed religious means are utilized) are really not contradictory but complementary claims. Both forms of anxiety combine to bolster traditional religious beliefs and practices of the society in question. The incident described in this paper does not deny this relationship but rather alludes to its complication as a consequence of the Zone's social structure.

In the Canal Zone the *primary anxiety* of the West Indian stranger was not due solely to a feeling of ignorance or powerlessness but also to distrust of the superordinate and alien Americans and their judiciary system. The *secondary anxiety* did not serve to perpetuate the established (American/Anglo) religions, not even the one to which the accused overtly belonged, but rather to denigrate them in favor of older African-Antillean cultural traditions. The two families did not worry about their status (nor their "sinning") as they openly and purposefully solicited the aid of the folk media. Seemingly, their affiliation with the Episcopal (or other established) Church was not for religious but social reasons. It was necessary and expected by the community that they would have solicited such aid, and the community was willing to tolerate and even prescribe that they do so. Folklore, gossip, and rumor served to maintain the aura of awe and anxiety. They were also the media by which the community was informed of adherence to prescribed occult traditions. Thus for all reasons *some degree of obvious or advertised secrecy* rather than total secrecy or total openness was necessary.

In the Islands as well as on the Isthmus (and this includes Central America) West Indians tend to retain some of the African–West Indian traditions. Occult practices of the kind described here have been reported in fact about Afro-American peoples in various parts of the continent. Ethno-historians have argued that the widespread practice of such occultism among Afro-Americans testifies to the focal position occupied by religion in West African culture (Herskovits 1958). Notwithstanding the criticism directed toward this kind of reasoning (M. G. Smith 1965), the position of religion among West Indians, especially this particular kind of occultism, is not to be denied but further analyzed. Even if they brought this tradition from Africa via the West Indies to Panama the question arises concerning the nature of the situations which make them conducive to retention, particularly when the West Indians had an opportunity to learn and practice openly the religions of the dominant section. In other words, our question becomes: Why does *cultural* (religion) pluralism *continue* (or even take new forms) even when the subordinate carrier population is being exposed intensely to the new culture (religion) of the dominant section?

The case of the West Indians in the Canal Zone shows that they did not view themselves as *permanent* immigrants until late in their stay on the Isthmus. Even if they were educated in American culture and institutions they were denied commensurate economic access, social status, and political power to control the social determinants of their fate. They—as total dependents in a closed single-authority system—were *always* living on the *brink of crisis*. People in such situations are likely to make greater demands on their gods, spirits, and their clergy than would be expected of ordinary Protestant Christians. Consequently, most Christian (Protestant) forms could not *fully* substitute for their religions and rituals, thus perpetuating cultural-religious distinction between them as strangers and both their Panamanian hosts and their American superordinates.

In conclusion, this paper has sought to describe an occult crisis-sponsored event in such a way as to present pertinent implications which may be helpful in understanding the position of a totally dependent stranger group in a closed and stabilized plural system. The conclusions are:

1. In stabilized, asymmetrical relations within a plural society there will be a tendency for the subordinate minority to observe at least two norms of social behavior—one representing the official superordinate culture and the other representing the subordinate stratum's own subculture. In other words, such a minority is likely to become *bicultural* rather than simply *"creolized"* or *"marginal"* (cf. Polgar 1960:232–33; Shibutani 1965:282–312).

2. The subordinate stratum will tend to classify social behavior as such behavior seems to correspond to the two (or at least *three* in case of *stranger* groups) cultures. Where distance, differences, discrimination, or dislike seem to characterize the relations between the two strata, the subordinate one will tend to consider some cultural aspects of the superordinate as false, foreign, or formal and its own (or any of the superordinate or other cultures which it has assimilated) as native and normal.

   *a.* All persons and institutions of the subordinate community will be seen, categorized, and be reacted to in accordance with their status, which would be related to the degree and direction of their orientation and to their conformity to either set of norms.

   *b.* The choice of behavior of the members of the subordinate stratum would be closely related to their status when the alternatives are seen in terms of the superordinate cultural standards versus subordinate cultural standards.

    *c.* The choice of alternatives will also be related to the question of whether the institution or standard has been sufficiently assimilated by the subordinate stratum or is believed to be sufficiently appropriate to meet the demands of the situation.

3. In cases (a) where the plural society is contained within a closed, exclusive context so that the subordinate minority is localized into segregated communities, and (b) where by contact or acculturating agencies the subordinate stranger group is exposed to the culture of the dominant section but cannot at the same time experience structural advancement commensurate to their cultural acquisition there is likely to emerge among the strangers a *contra-cultural* system of values and institutions (an *underlife*).[6]

    *a.* This contra-cultural system or underlife will serve as the basis of consensus, cohesion, and guide to relationships among members of the stranger or subordinate section as well as vis-à-vis the superordinate section.
    *b.* Even if the system is characterized by parallel or common institutions these institutions will have different meanings for the subordinate strangers as compared to the dominant donor elite.
    *c.* In times of *crisis*, which in their opinions cannot be resolved adequately by the institutions or roles of the dominant or official section, the subordinate strangers will refer (openly if necessary) to their traditional institutions (which may remain active or latent) or to any new institution that they have come to assimilate into their cultural system.

## Notes

    1. I wish to acknowledge the aid extended to me by Donald Hogg, Hilda Kuper and Norman Whitten in preparing drafts of this paper.
    2. While the Canal was being built, white Americans were paid in gold coins and colored non-Americans in silver. Thus, each set of employees was known as white or "gold" employees and colored or "silver" employees, respectively. The terms "U.S.-raters" and "local-raters" or "American citizens" and "Latin Americans" are modern and more euphemistic mechanisms distinguishing basically the same divisions and eliciting similar forms of discrimination (Biesanz 1955:6). For additional social scientific treatment of the race relations in the Canal Zone see Biesanz (1950, 1951, 1953) and Westerman (1948, 1954).
    3. A perennial theme of interest in West Indian family organization has been the role of the woman as the central figure of authority and the only stable adult in the household. Details of the family life of Panamanian–West Indians are comparable to some extent to that of the Islanders (Biesanz 1955:314–23).
    4. These various contextual-structural features of the plantation and the concomitant behavior of its personnel have led to consideration of the adequacy of including it among

the category of formal-communal organization called *broad organization settlement institution* or *total institution* (Bryce-Laporte 1968; Etzioni 1961; Goffman 1961a; Hillery 1963:779–90; R. T. Smith 1967; Thompson 1959:26–37).

5. The conflict orientation of West Indian plural society is discussed by Professor M. G. Smith (1965) and other students of the area. Among the specific conceptual-methodological questions raised about Smith's work which are relevant to this paper are (1) the appropriate approach for studying social cohesiveness within individual plural segments, (2) the nature of social cohesiveness within such segments, and (3) the reasons for the perpetuation of cultural pluralism among them (Bryce-Laporte 1968:114–20).

6. The concept of *contraculture* was suggested by Yinger (1960) to refer to the culture of a subordinate or minority people which does not represent a mere sub-cultural variant but stems from frustration and conflict, in their interactions with the superordinate segment of the population. Goffman (1961a) refers to such usually elusive or illegitimate adjustive cultures among inmate populations as *underlife*. Unlike the more widely used descriptive term of *creole* or *immigrant* sub-culture (Adams 1959:73–78; Crowley 1960:850–54) which tend to emphasize acculturation and adaptation as principal sociocultural processes, the concepts of Yinger and Goffman embrace and emphasize power differentiation, control, and conflict as the influential factors in shaping the culture of stranger groups.

## References

Augelli, John D.
    1962    The Rimland-Mainland Concept of Culture Areas in Middle America. Annals of the Association of American Geographers 52: 119–229.

Beckwith, Martha
    1923    Some Religious Cults in Jamaica. American Journal of Psychology 34: 32–45.

Bryce-Laporte, R. S.
    1962    Social Relations and Cultural Persistence (Or Change) Among Jamaicans in a Rural Area of Costa Rica. M.A. Thesis, University of Puerto Rico.

Greaves, I.
    1959    The Plantation in World Economy. In Plantation Systems in the New World. Washington, D.C.: Pan American Union, pp. 13–22.

Herskovits, Melville J.
    1958    The Myth of the Negro Past. Boston: Beacon Press.

Hogg, Donald
    1960    The Convince Cult in Jamaica. In Papers in Caribbean Anthropology, Sidney Mintz (editor). Yale University Publications in Anthropology, no. 58. New Haven: Yale University Press.
    1964    Jamaican Religions: A Study in Variation. Ph.D. Dissertation, Yale University.

Homans, George C.
    1950    The Human Group. New York: Harcourt, Brace.

McBride, George
    1937    Plantation. In Encyclopedia of the Social Sciences, vol. ix. New York:
            Macmillan, p. 148.
Merton, Robert K.
    1957    Social Theory and Social Structure (revised and enlarged). Glencoe, Il:
            The Free Press.
Mintz, Sidney
    1959b   The Plantation as a Sociocultural Type. In Plantation Systems of the New
            World. Washington, D.C.: Pan American Union, pp. 42–53.
Polgar, Steven
    1960    Biculturation of Mesaquakie Boys. American Anthropologist 62:232–233.
Rubio, Angel
    1957    Las plantaciones en Panamá. Paper presented at a seminar on plantation
            systems in the New World. Washington D.C.: Pan American Union
            (mimeographed).
Shibutani, Tomotsu, and Kian W. Kwan
    1965    Ethnic Stratification: A Comparative Approach. New York: Macmillan.
Simpson, George E.
    1956    Jamaican Revivalist Cults. Social and Economic Studies 5:i–ix, 321–342.
Smith, M. G.
    1965    The Plural Society in the British West Indies. Berkeley and Los Angeles:
            University of California Press.
Wagley, Charles
    1957    Plantation America: A Culture Sphere. In Caribbean studies: a sympo-
            sium, Vera Rubin (editor). Seattle: University of Washington Press.
Wilson, Charles
    1947    Empire in Green and Gold. New York: Holt.

# 3. THE BLACK DIASPORA IN COSTA RICA

## Upward Mobility and Ethnic Discrimination

### Philippe Bourgois

> The history of the negro as a labourer is ancient and simple — perhaps more
> so than that of any other race or people. . . . With few notable exceptions, the
> negro labourer has little initiative — he is an imitator . . . experience has proved
> over and over again that only with rare exceptions has the negro been able to pursue
> theoretical studies with any degree of success. [Letter from the manager of United
> Fruit Company operations in Central America to the British Consul. June 11, 1919.]

> . . . For forty long years we Costa Ricans were displaced from the best
> jobs of the Atlantic Zone by Negroes. They were warehouse supervisors,
> chiefs of commissaries, clerks and formans [sic]. . . . They think that they
> are superior to us . . . They look down upon our language . . . [Petition by
> Hispanic banana workers to the Costa Rican National Assembly, 1941.]

Blacks of West Indian descent constitute Costa Rica's largest ethnic minority; they
reside, for the most part on the Atlantic coast in Limón province where they comprise less than 25 percent of the total population. In contrast to the Black diaspora
in most other parts of the world, Costa Rican Blacks have risen economically
relative to the dominant local population. They arrived in the late nineteenth
century as landless laborers fleeing poverty and economic crisis on their natal
islands in the West Indies. Almost all of them were employed by the United Fruit
Company in railroad construction and banana cultivation. By the 1930s most
had obtained small plots of land and/or had risen in the banana company's labor
hierarchy, replaced by Hispanic and Amerindian immigrants. Today Blacks are
better off economically than the bulk of the Hispanic and Amerindian population
of Limón province; nevertheless, ethnic discrimination against them persists. An
analysis of the history of their upward mobility can provide an insight into how
political values and ideology are formed in the context of changing class relations. It also affords a privileged perspective on the crucial importance of ethnic
discrimination in shaping a people's political and economic development.[1]

Originally published in New West Indian Guide 60:3/4 (1986), pp. 149–65. Copyright © by KITLV
Press. Reprinted by permission of KITLV Press.

## The Arrival of the West Indians

Although there was a small population of African slaves in Costa Rica during the colonial period, these early Blacks intermixed with the European and Amerindian inhabitants and no longer constitute an identifiable ethnic group. Black culture in Costa Rica today, therefore, is the product of the massive immigration of West Indians laborers in the second half of the nineteenth century through the 1930s.[2] The economic depression of the Antilles combined with the constant booms and busts of the local subsidiaries of the North American corporations active in the region, spread the Black diaspora throughout the Caribbean and coastal Central America as West Indian migrant workers were obliged repeatedly to uproot themselves from company to company and country to country in search of stable employment (cf. Davis 1980; McCullough 1977; Newton 1984; Palmer 1977). Consequently, Blacks in Costa Rica form part of a larger cultural formation spanning the entire Central American Caribbean which arose out of the economic enclaves established by North American transnational corporations beginning in the 1860s. Often the same individual who planted bananas or harvested cacao in Limón had previously shovelled dirt on the Panama Canal, or cut sugar cane in Cuba, and ultimately emigrated to New York City to work as an orderly in a hospital.

The first group of West Indian immigrant workers reached Costa Rica in 1872 (Duncan and Melendez 1981: 70–73). They were contracted by the railroad financeer, Minor C. Keith, who was later to become one of the founders of the United Fruit Company. Keith had previously unsuccessfully imported dozens of different population groups to work on the construction of the Costa Rican trans-Atlantic railroad.[3] Of all the immigrant peoples, however, only the West Indian Blacks came to tolerate the rigid labor discipline and to suffer exposure to the yellow fever, malaria and poisonous snakes which abounded in the swampy lowlands of Limón. It is reported that 4,000 Jamaicans died in the construction of the first 25 miles of the Costa Rican railroad.[4]

Although Keith imported 10,000 Jamaicans between 1881 and 1891 most of the subsequent waves of West Indian immigrants arrived on their own without sponsorship, fleeing unemployment and poverty (Rodríguez and Borge 1976: 229).[5] By 1927 there were 19,136 Jamaicans in Costa Rica, almost all in Limón province (Olien 1967: 126).

## West Indian Resistance

Most historians report that the immigrant West Indian laborers in Costa Rica at the turn of the century were fiercely loyal to their employer—Minor Keith and the United Fruit Company—and that Blacks refrained from organizing unions or provoking labor disturbances (cf. Casey 1979: 119, 125; Fallas Monge 1983: 218; Duncan & Melendez 1981: 77–78, 104).[6]

Even the publications of the Costa Rican communist party and the militant tendency within the labor union movement fail to note the participation of West Indian immigrants in the early years of the labor movement. Blacks in Costa Rica have a reputation among the general population of having always avoided labor confrontations historically. In fact, Black passivity has emerged as a racist stereotype among Hispanics in Limón.

> Blacks are conformist; they'll work for peanuts [trabajan por cualquier cochinada]. They've always been docile [han sido mancitos todo la vida]. They're pussies by nature . . . They bend with the breeze [Son pendejos: bailen el son que le locan].

Nevertheless, a closer scrutiny of the available primary sources, as well as interviews with elderly West Indian laborers from the period, refute this myth that Black laborers in Costa Rica were passive. Newspaper reports and historical archives from the turn of the century[7] abound with reference to violent strikes, labor disturbances, and attempts at union organizing (see Bourgois 1985a: 116–123; De la Cruz 1979). In fact reports of violent confrontations between Black workers and management date as far back as 1879 (Fallas Monge 1983: 218 citing *Gaceta Official*, March 1879).

Resistance by West Indian immigrants to economic exploitation and ethnic discrimination on the United Fruit Company banana plantations climaxed in the 1910s and 1920s. Their strikes were almost invariably repressed violently and usually resulted in serious casualties. Much of this resistance was channelled through Marcus Garvey's Universal Negro Improvement Association [hereafter UNIA], a worldwide organization which stressed the dignity of Blacks throughout the diaspora. Significantly, the UNIA was exeptionally strong in Costa Rica on the banana plantations. In fact, Limón is one of the few places in the world today where the UNIA formally continues to exist. The banana workers used the UNIA to organize against the racist labor hierarchy of the United Fruit Company. The organization's message was invoked in several major strikes (Kepner 1936: 180.)[8]

## Upward Mobility

The availability of unoccupied land surrounding the banana plantations provided the West Indian immigrants with an alternative to plantation wage work. During the 1910s and the 1920s increasing numbers left day labor employment and established themselves as small banana and cacao farmers. This further incited those who remained on the United Fruit Company plantations to demand higher wages and better working conditons. In short, through land acquisition,

Black immigrants had begun a process of upward class mobility; they were no longer prepared to submit to the same levels of exploitation.[9]

Emigration out of Costa Rica in the long run also played a key role in accentuating the upwardly mobile class composition of Blacks in Limón. Historically during periods of economic crisis the poorest, working class cohort of the West Indian labor force was forced to leave the region in search of employment elsewhere. From 1927 to 1950, according to national census tabulations, the Black population fell from 18,003 to 13,749 (Casey 1979: 239). A series of racist immigration and employment laws systematically propelled the working class sectors of the Black population out of the country during periods of economic crisis and prevented their re-entry during economic booms (Koch 1975: 378, 385). For example, in 1934 a law was passed forbidding the employment of Blacks outside of the Atlantic lowlands. With the dramatic reduction in employment offered by the United Fruit Company in Limón, thousands of Blacks who depended upon wage work for their survival were forced to leave the country; they were not allowed to migrate to the Pacific coast of the country where new farms were being opened up and where experienced banana workers were in high demand. The Blacks who remained behind on the Atlantic coast of Costa Rica were forced to convert themselves into full-time farmers. At first they squatted on uncultivated lands and eked out a subsistence survival in abject poverty. During subsequent economic booms, however, they were able to convert their subsistence plots into cash earning enterprises (cacao or banana farms). At the same time, during these booms working class Blacks seeking employment were prevented from entering the country by the Costa Rican immigration authorities.

In this manner, the bulk of the Black population remaining in Costa Rica left plantation employment to become small farmers. Ironically, therefore, the laws restricting Blacks to the Atlantic Coast of Costa Rica ultimately provided those who withstood the economic crises of the 1930s and early 1940s with a first choice selection of the most fertile lands closest to the transport infrastructure. With the rise in cacao prices on the world market in the mid-1950s the formerly struggling small Black farmer/squatters became comfortable landowners. By the 1960s, they constituted what anthropologist Charles Koch (1975: 378, 385) described as a ". . . rump of well-to-do peasants and old people concentrated in the best cacao districts." An increasingly large population of landless Hispanic migrants—some of whom had originally migrated out of the Atlantic region in 1934 to work on the new farms being planted on the Pacific coast—provided the Black farmers with a plentiful supply of inexpensive agricultural day labor. An ethnic occupational hierarchy emerged contrasting markedly with the pattern prevalent in the rest of the world: ". . . the Atlantic Zone [is] one of the few places in the world where bourgeois Blacks exploit an underprivileged white minority (Koch 1975: 378)."

Anthropologists who conducted fieldwork in Limón from the 1950s through the 1980s (cf. Bryce-Laporte 1962; Koch 1975; Mennerick 1964; Moock 1972;

Murillo & Hernandez 1981; Olien 1967, 1977; Purcell 1982), all report that Blacks shunned agricultural wage labor and tended to own the superior, flat alluvial lands devoted to cacao:

> The category of Black peon is almost an empty one . . . It is only in extremely rare cases that one finds a Black rural dweller who does not have access to some land, whether his own bought land or land inherited from a close kin. Most unskilled agricultural jobs are filled by Hispanics (Purcell 1982: 145).

In fact, one fieldworker in a small village in Limón in 1968 reported: "The only three negroes who did work as peons were considered mentally defective and were treated as isolates by the entire community (Moock 1972: 9)."

Nevertheless, although for the most part comfortable economically, Blacks have not emerged as the upper crust of the elite in Limón. Even at the height of their involvement in the cacao industry in the 1960s, Black farms were not large-scale, efficiently administered agro-industrial complexes oriented toward accumulating capital. The largest landholdings and the more profitable rural enterprises have always been owned by absentee landlords, often North Americans or San Jose based Hispanics. Black farmers, therefore, represent a middle level rural elite operating small or medium-sized farms.

Ironically, upward class mobility has contributed ultimately to the demise of Black farms as the new generation of educated Blacks (the children of the successful cacao farmers of the 1960s) have for the most part shunned the agricultural way of life.[10] Cacao farming is not considered a satisfactory lifestyle to college and high school graduates, no matter how successful it may appear by local rural standards. Since the mid-1970s, therefore, young Blacks have been leaving their parents' farms and going to Port Limón, San José, Panama City, or even New York City in search of better opportunities for economic advancement and more exciting urban lifestyles. Indeed the reason one sees so few Blacks performing heavy agricultural labor in Limón today is that most Blacks in their prime age for heavy manual labor have emigrated from the countryside.

Significantly, the elderly cacao farmers themselves encourage their children to leave the agricultural sector. Black parents, even those of the humblest class backgrounds, infuse their children with upwardly mobile aspirations. The emphasis is not only on getting out of wage work, but also out of agriculture *per se* and into the big cities (cf. Purcell 1982: 122; Moock 1972: 26). Farming is associated with low status. "It is considered ungentlemanly to chop bush" even on one's own farm. Younger Blacks who still reside in the countryside usually hire Hispanics to work in their cacao groves while they attend to more profitable commercial alternatives such as lobster fishing, administering restaurants, selling marihuana to tourists, working for the government, or living off remittances from kin in the United States.

The flight of young Blacks from the rural sector has led to the decay of Black-owned cacao orchards; consequently, by the early 1980s, Black-owned cacao farms on the average were older, smaller, received fewer inputs, and were more diversified than Hispanic-owned holdings (Murillo and Hernández 1981: 151). Black farmers tended to be elderly and physically on the decline. Over the past decade the pattern has been for Black rural dwellers to sell their holdings to Hispanic immigrants and either to emigrate or to "die out" (Duncan & Melendez 1981: 244–245). This process has been accelerated by a devastating leaf fungus known as moniliasis which has been destroying approximately two-thirds of the harvest since late 1978 (Murillo & Hernández 1981: 75). In fact, some of the Black cacao farmers who have been unable to emigrate have actually been forced back into agricultural wage work. Nevertheless, Blacks in rural Limón continue to enjoy an above average economic status, superior to that of most Hispanics.

In Puerto Limón, the capital of Limón Province, there are high levels of unemployment (23 percent in 1981) and there is a significant sector of working class and unemployed Blacks. Nevertheless, urban Blacks continue to occupy a slightly higher socio-economic niche than the average Hispanic; they shun the low prestige jobs. According to a 1980 survey 30.5 percent of Black workers had white collar jobs in Port Limón compared to 21.1 percent of Hispanics (Vargas & Requeyra 1983: 43, 113). For example, the street sweepers, the construction workers, and the shoe shine men are almost invariably Hispanics rather than Blacks. Blacks have been able to manipulate to their advantage a local patron-client brokerage system which affords them access to preferential employment, especially, in the public sector. When one enters a government office in Limón, the orderly sweeping the floor and emptying the garbage will almost always be a dark complexioned Hispanic; the xerox clerk (an especially "soft" task) will usually be a young Black; while the secretarial and middle-level desk positions will be occupied by both Blacks and Hispanics; and the top level administrator will, of course, almost invariably be a light-skinned Hispanic from San José.

Those Blacks who have remained on the banana plantations—especially on the farms in southern Limón spanning the border with Panama—represent a miniature labor aristocracy.[11] They generally work in semi-skilled jobs, as low level supervisors, or in the "softer" unskilled tasks. On the United Fruit Company farms, Hispanics have nicknamed Blacks "la rosca" [the groove of the screw] because they are so "tight with management." This is clearly visible in the over-representation of Blacks as mechanics, clerks, watchmen, paymasters. They are most heavily concentrated in the departments which do not require heavy manual labor such as Electricity, Transport, Engineering, or Materials and Supplies.

The largest single concentration of Black menial laborers in the plantation production hierarchy is on the docks. Significantly, however, dockworkers are better paid than farmworkers and lead more cosmopolitan lifestyles as they are located in the urban centers in the ports. Furthermore, a close examination of the distribution of jobs among dockworkers reveals that, once again, the "softer" jobs are dominated by Blacks, especially elderly Blacks. This is true, for example

of the task of "curving" [*curvear*] which involves standing at a curve point along
the loading machine to make sure that no boxes of bananas fall as they are advanced on the rollers. Similarly the worker who sits next to the power switch in
order to shut off the electricity in case of an emergency, is usually Black.

Access to alternative sources of income is at the root of Black underrepresen-
tation in the menial tasks in the banana industry today. Blacks do not shun agricultural wage work any more than do those Hispanics or Amerindians who were
also born in the plantation vicinity and who also own land and/or have access to
better jobs through seniority and contacts. The bulk of the banana worker labor
force is composed of immigrants from other provinces or countries (see Figure
3). Native born Limonenses avoid plantation wage work; they tend to have access
to land. The only difference between Blacks and Limón-born Hispanics or Amerindians is that Blacks express their distaste for plantation wage work more vocally.
They justify their rejection of agricultural day labor in specifically ethnic terms:
"I'm nobody's slave anymore. Let the Spaniards do that class of work. It's their
turn now." Blacks also explain that they avoid unskilled plantation work because
of the racism they are subjected to by Hispanic foremen.

### Ideological Implications of Upward Mobility

Land acquisition, upward mobility and the emigration of most of the poorer,
wage earning Blacks (in the 1930s and early 1940s) have contributed to the development of a conservative political ideology among Blacks. There is an emphasis on "proper behavior" and a "respect for authority" in Black culture. The pro–
North American, pro-management orientation of second and third generation
West Indian immigrants contrasts dramatically with the labor militancy of their
grandparents and great grandparents. Indeed, a political generation gap is clearly
visible in Limón today. While elderly Black immigrants who arrived at the turn
of the century enjoy reminiscing about strikes and labor union struggles, younger
Blacks insist that "First time [in the old days] our people never know nothing
about no *sindicatos* [unions], no no no." They prefer to forget that their ancestors
were severely exploited landless laborers who had to fight for their rights.

Even the poorest Black families aspire to middle class respectability. The small
minority of Blacks who are still objectively at the lower end of the local occupational hierarchy (performing machete work in the fields) identify with the conservative political attitudes and values of the more privileged members of their
ethnic group—the cacao farmers and skilled workers. Participation in unions and
antagonism toward management are viewed as alien to Black ethnic identity.
Strikes and—worse yet—"communist ideas" are abhorred as satanic values introduced by immigrant "Spaniard" day laborers of a "lower cultural level": "Strikes
come when two people can't reason and Spaniards can't reason."

This conservative political/ideological orientation has been further encouraged by the racism of Costa Rican society. Until 1949, even the second and third

generation West Indian descendants were denied Costa Rican citizenship. During the 1930s, the threat of deportation made Costa Rican–born Blacks increasingly reluctant during the Great Depression to participate in the labor movement. Their ambiguous nationality status became a Damocles sword that the United Fruit Company invoked during labor disturbances.[12] This vulnerability, combined with age-old ethnic antagonisms prevented Black workers from joining the Hispanic dominated national labor union organizations. In fact, over the years, the United Fruit company systematized an ethnically based "divide and conquer" strategy pitting Blacks against Hispanics against Amerindians (see Bourgois 1985b).[13] Frequently the strikes and union organizing drives of the original West Indian immigrants at the turn of the century were broken by the importation of Hispanic laborers.

The discrimination of the local population and the national authorities reduced the ability of Black workers to maintain antagonistic attitudes towards their employers. Costa Rican hostility towards Blacks increased dramatically, for example, during periods of economic crisis such as the Great Depression and World War II. On numerous occasions Blacks were forced to appeal to the United Fruit Company for protection from racist national authorities. This constant dependence on the "goodwill" of their North American employers and supervisors spawned a transformation in Black attitudes towards management. This was exacerbated by the legal prohibition against employing Blacks outside of the Atlantic zone in the 1930s and 1940s which augmented their dependence on the North American plantation enclave. Even those who successfully established themselves as small farmers remained largely dependent upon the United Fruit Company for their economic well-being since the Company purchased their produce. They generally did not even have legal title to their land; it was usually formally owned by the banana company.

The upward mobility of the Black population within the United Fruit Company dominated economy, consequently, has always been relatively precarious. Blacks had to remain on good terms with the transnational in order to stay in business. Those who remained directly in the employ of the Company in the "soft" privileged positions lived with the constant fear that they might be demoted at any moment should their loyalty to management be suspect. In order to maintain their position within the hierarchy of the plantation, therefore, Blacks had to emphasize their "reliability and obedience." They heightened the contrast in "culture" between them and the unruly, politically volatile "communistic" Hispanic immigrants. Today, the reputation of Blacks for apolitical passivity is their best recommendation for continued access to preferential employment.

Another important ideological influence on Blacks in Limón has been the emigration of so many of their relatives to the United States. Most Costa Rican Blacks regularly receive letters and/or visits from kin now living in New York, California, or Miami. The dramatic wage differentials between Central America and the United States make life in the North appear almost utopian from a dol-

lars and cents perspective. Photographs and descriptions of North American technology and of large urban centers accentuate the impression of United States
omnipotence. The United States is looked upon as the land of golden opportunity, as a potential savior, a *deus ex machina*. It is not uncommon to hear middle-
aged Blacks wish that "the marines would invade Costa Rica."

## Racism

There are two contradictory matrices of ethnic discrimination in Limón. On
the one hand Blacks consider themselves more cultured than Hispanics. On the
other hand Hispanics are convinced of their racial superiority over Blacks. Black
landowners employing Hispanic migrant laborers adhere to the same racist constructs typical of landowners anywhere in the world who employ landless day
laborers of a different ethnic group. Blacks often claim that "Whites"[14] are treacherous, lazy, shiftless drunkards" with "nomadic tendencies." Whites are even reputed to "smell bad" and have "cooties" [*piojos*] in their hair. It is not unusual to
hear Black farmers explain in patronizing tones how they have to be careful never
to pay their White workers on Saturday evening lest they spend all their money
on liquor before Sunday morning.

Even Blacks who work side by side with Hispanics as day laborers, ". . . in very
explicit terms, regarded themselves as superior to Hispanics . . ." (Purcell 1982:
76). Black day laborers on banana plantations refer to their fellow Hispanic workers as "less civilized." They criticize them for being loud, violent, alcoholic, and
abusive to their women. In a somewhat more poetic vein, anthropologist Trevor
Purcell (1982: 79) quotes the racist description provided by a Black woman of
her impression of Hispanic immigrant workers:

> Dey looks to me laik dey were barberians, laik dey wud kil an' iit piiple, datz di
> wey dey looks. Deze piiple wur illiterate an ignorant an wii wuz ahlweys afreeid
> av dem. If yu goin along de striit an yu si dem yu waak on di odder sa'id. Dey
> always kiari dier kutlas wid dem.

Nevertheless, the hegemony of white supremacist thought is so powerful that the
superior economic position of Blacks in the local class hierarchy has not over-
shadowed the racism lighter skinned peoples direct against them.[15] Even impoverished landless Hispanics who have worked all their lives for Black landlords,
continue to maintain the conviction that Blacks are inferior racially. For example,
the flip side to the assertion by Blacks that Hispanics are "dangerous, violent,
alcoholic savages" is that Blacks are "cowards who run at the sight of blood." The
fact that Blacks do not perform menial agricultural wage labor, is cited by Hispanics (and Amerindians) as proof that they are "lazy, ambitionless" and "afraid to
sweat." Hence the Costa Rican adage, "Where there is work there are no Blacks."
Ironically, one of the effects of the persistence of ethnic discrimination against

Blacks despite their upward class mobility is the preservation of Black culture. The obvious phenotypical differentiation of the West Indian immigrants from the rest of the Costa Rican population has prevented the second and third generations of Blacks from blending into Costa Rican society as they have risen in the local class structure. Under similar circumstances of dramatic upward class mobility, other immigrant ethnic groups would have assimilated. Although professional Blacks in Costa Rica tend to marry Hispanics and often forbid their children to speak Creole English, the racism of the host society limits the rapidity of their acculturation. Were it not for this phenotypically based discrimination, Blacks would probably no longer exist as a distinct ethnic group in Costa Rica.

## Notes

1. The information for this article was collected during one and one half years of fieldwork on the Atlantic Coast of Costa Rica and north western Panama from 1982–1983. The fieldwork was made possible by a Dissertation Research Grant from the Inter-American Foundation and by preliminary fieldwork funding from the Wenner-Gren Foundation for Anthropological Research.

2. A veritable depopulation of able-bodied laborers occurred in the West Indies at the turn of the century. For example, from 1900 to 1910, 40 percent of all adult males left Barbados in search of employment in Central America and Panama (McCullough 1977: 476).

3. In addition to small "experimental" numbers of Canadians, Dutch, Swedes, Black North Americans, Carib Afro-Amerindians, Syrians, Turks, East Indians, Egyptians, and Cape Verdians (Wilson 1947: 52, 61; Rodríguez & Borge 1976: 227), Minor Keith imported "one thousand healthy, robust Chinese of good customs and addicted to work (Costa Rican National Archives, Historical Section #1055: April 6, 1872)," and 1,500 ". . . good, humble thrifty . . . [Italians] . . . of a superior race . . . (Ibid. #1131, Feb. 23, 1888: 3)."

4. Three of Minor Keith's brothers and uncles also died while supervising the construction of the first 25 miles of the Costa Rican Trans-Atlantic railroad (Wilson 1947: 52, 59).

5. In Barbados, a day's wage was 20 cents at the turn of the century, whereas the United Fruit Company labor contractors were offering to pay the same amount per hour The unemployed were so desperate that riots erupted outside the recruiting stations of the Panama Canal Company in Barbados (McCullough 1977: 170).

6. There are a few passing references to the militancy of West Indian laborers in Costa Rica; cf. Bryce-Laporte (n.d.: 23); de la Cruz (1983: 94, 105–121); Duncan & Melendez (1981: 78); Fallas Monge (1983: 218–219); Kepner (1936: 180–181). A more detailed analysis of this issue is provided by Bourgois (1985a: 113–123) and De la Cruz (1979).

7. The newspaper archive of the National Library of Costa Rica has a valuable collection of turn of the century publications from Limón. The United Fruit Company historical archives in storage in Bocas del Toro, Panama are also an extraordinary resource: special permission to consult them must be obtained locally. One of the reasons so many

historians and anthropologists have erroneously reported that Costa Rican West Indians were passive laborers is that they relied on company reports and pro-management local newspapers which purposefully emphasized the passivity of the Black laborers in order to persuade the Costa Rican government to allow them to import larger numbers into the country. Furthermore, the comfortably established second and third generation descendants of these immigrants prefer to forget their grandparents' history of exploitation and struggle.

8. The leadership of the UNIA subsequently shunted the interests of the banana workers. United Fruit Company historical archives reveal that Marcus Garvey and his associates actually struck deals with management:

> . . . [Garvey] states that he too is an employer of labor, understands our position, is using his best endeavour to get the negro race to work and better themselves through work (UFA: Chittenden to Blair, April n.a., 1921).

> . . . Garvey was the most conservative man of any attending the meetings. He told them they should not fight the United Fruit Company . . . they must have money and that in order to get money they had to work (UFA: Chittenden to Cutter, April 22, 1921).

> Garvey's policy seems to be to keep his people industriously at work and I have told a representative here that we would aid them in any way that we could as long as this policy is maintained (UFA: Chittenden to Blair, February 27, 1922).

9. The most systematic and well documented analysis of Black upward mobility in Limón is provided by Charles Koch (1975); see also Bourgois (1985a: chapter 6).

10. Education has played a crucial role in Black upward mobility, and is part of the West Indian immigrant tradition. Today Blacks still maintain scholastic superiority over Hispanics. In 1983, while 55.4 percent of Hispanics did not finish primary school in Limón, the same was true for only 38.5 percent of Blacks (Vargas & Requeyra 1983: 44). Once again, this advantage over Hispanics has been confined for the most part to the middle-level echelons of the hierarchy, i.e., primary school and high school rather than college. Until the 1960s few Blacks reached the university level. In 1964, for example, out of the entire Limón Black population (over 10,000) there were only four Black lawyers, one civil engineer and five professors (Mennerick 1964: 50). By the 1970s, with the extended boom in the cacao economy, the children of successful cacao farmers have entered the professional occupations in disproportionate numbers; today, there are so many Black professionals dispersed throughout Costa Rica, that it would be impossible to calculate their number.

11. On the banana plantations in central Limón and on the Pacific coast there are very few Blacks of West Indian descent working in banana production. There are, however, significant numbers of workers of Afro-Hispanic descent, but they are immigrants from the northwestern province of Guanacaste. Their African descent can be traced to the slaves imported during the colonial period. They are considered Hispanic or even "white" according to Costa Rican definitions of race and ethnicity. A middle-class Black of Jamaican ancestry warned me "You may think you see Blacks working in the banana fields but don't put that in your book. They're not black Blacks: they are Guanacastecans."

12. United Fruit Company management took full advantage of the ambiguous nationality status of Blacks as is documented by the following report by an official sent to evaluate a plantation on the Panama–Costa Rica border during World War II:

> ... the Division has not been living up to the laws as regards accident pay, severance pay, and other social privileges to which laborers are entitled by law. Apparently these payments were not made ... mostly on the assumption that the Company wished to save money and *was safe in not making these payments, as most of the negroes around [here]* do not have cédulas [nationality identity cards] and cannot bring action against us in the courts (UFA: Hamer to Pollan, Feb. 1, 1943, emphasis added).

13. The most spectacular example in Costa Rica of a foreign company manipulating Black/Hispanic antagonisms within its labor force is the case of the Abangares gold mines (in which Minor Keith the founder of the United Fruit Company also had financial interests) in the province of Guanacaste (Garcia 1984: 17). In 1911 Black West Indians were brought in as foremen to supervise the largely Hispanic work force; in fact all 50 foremen at the mines were Black and Black ditch diggers were paid more than Hispanics (Ibid 1984: 57–62). One of the tasks of the foremen was to strip search workers suspected of stealing gold from the mines at the end of the day as they were leaving the pits. In 1911 this provoked a race riot. Fourteen Blacks were brutally killed by a mob of incensed workers (Ibid: 57–62, Sánchez 1971: 107–108). Although the mines were occupied by the workers and a strike was declared, their anger was vented against their immediate supervisors who were Blacks rather than against the North American owners of the mines. No workers were prosecuted for the massacre and the President of Costa Rica even publicly blamed the "foreigners" (i.e., West Indian Blacks) for having provoked the workers into killing them.

14. In Costa Rica, Hispanics are referred to as "Whites." In fact this deeply ingrained national myth that Costa Ricans are White is referred to in the scholarly literature as the "white legend" (cf. Edelman 1982: unnumbered citing Creedman 1977: x).

15. For an analysis of racism against Blacks in South America see Wade 1985.

## References

### Primary Documents and Abbreviations:

Gaceta Official, Publication of the Costa Rican National Assembly.
UFA: United Fruit Company Archives, Bocas del Toro, Panama.

*Names cited in archival correspondence of the United Fruit Company:*

Gaceta Official, Publication of the Costa Rican National Assembly.
UFA: United Fruit Company Archives, Almirante, Panama.
Blair, H. S.: Manager, Bocas Division: 1920s–1930s.
Chittenden, G. P.: Manager, Limón Division, subsequently responsible for all southern Central American operations and then vice president of the Chiriqui Land Company, Boston: 1916–1940s.
Cutter, Victor: General Manager, UFCO, Central and South American Department, subsequently vice president, UFCO, Boston: 1915–1920s.

Hamer, R. H.: Manager of Pacific Coast Divisions, UFCO, Costa Rica (Compañía Bananere de Costa Rica) and subsequently responsible for Southern Central Operations; 1940s and 1950s.
Pollan, A. A.: Executive vice president, UFCO, Boston; 1943.

*Published Sources*

Bourgois, Philippe, 1985a. Ethnic diversity on a corporate plantation: The United Fruit Company in Bocas del Toro, Panama and Talamanca, Costa Rica. Ph.D. dissertation, Department of Anthropology, Stanford University.
———. 1985b. Guaymi labor on a United Brands subsidiary in Costa Rica and Panama. Cambridge Mass. Occasional Paper No. 19 of Cultural Survival.
Bryce-Laporte, Roy Simon, 1962. Social relations and cultural persistence (or change) among Jamaicans in a rural area of Costa Rica. Ph.D. dissertation, University of Puerto Rico.
———, n.d. West Indian Labor in Central America: Limón, Costa Rica 1870–1948. Paper presented at the Spring Symposium on the Political Economy of the Black World, University of California Los Angeles, Afro-American Studies.
Casey, Jeffrey, 1979. Limón: 1880–1940. Un estudio de la industria bananera en Costa Rica. San José, Editorial Costa Rica.
Creedman, Theodore, 1977. Historical dictionary of Costa Rica. Metuchen [New Jersey], Ox.
Davis, Raymond, 1980. West Indian workers on the Panama Canal: A split labor market interpretation. Ph.D. dissertation, Department of Sociology, Stanford University.
De la Cruz, Vladimir, 1979. El Primero de Mayo de 1913. Antecedentes históricos y celebración del 1ero de Mayo celebrado en Costa Rica. Paper presented at the first meetings of the Associación Mundial de Centros de Estudios Históricos y Sociales del Movimiento Obrero (AMCEHSMO), Mexico City, 15–19 October.
———, 1983. Las luchas sociales en Costa Rica 1870–1930. San José, Editorial Universidad de Costa Rica and Editorial Costa Rica.
Duncan, Quince and Carlos Melendez, 1981. El Negro en Costa Rica. San José, Editorial Costa Rica.
Edelman, Marc, 1982. Costa Rica's threatened democracy: Economic crisis and political repression (manuscript).
Fallas Monge, Carlos Luis, 1983. El movimiento obrero en Costa Rica 1830–1902. San José, Editorial Universidad Estatal a Distancia.
García M., Guillermo, 1977. Las Minas de Abangares: Historia de una doble explotación. San José, Editorial de la Universidad de Costa Rica.
Kepner, Charles, 1936. Social aspects of the banana industry. New York, Columbia University Press.
Koch, Charles, 1975. Ethnicity and livelihoods, a social geography of Costa Rica's Atlantic coast. Ph.D. dissertation, Department of Anthropology, Kansas University.
McCullough, David, 1977. The path between the seas. New York, Simon and Schuster.
Mennerick, Lewis, 1964. A Study of Puerto Limón, Costa Rica. San José, Association of Colleges of the Midwest, Central American Field Program, Term paper.
Moock, Joyce Lewinger, 1972. The school as an arena for community factionalism. Fieldwork report, Department of Anthropology, Columbia University.
Murillo, Carmen and Oscar Hernández, 1981. El fenómeno de la reproducción de la

fuerza de trabajo: Un análisis comparativo entre pequeños productores y asalariados vinculados a la producción del cacao en la vertiente Atlántica de Costa Rica. Licenciatura thesis, Department of Anthropology, University of Costa Rica.

Newton, Velma, 1984. The silver men: West Indian labour migration to Panama 1850–1914. Jamaica, Institute for Social and Economic Research.

Olien, Michael, 1967. The Negro in Costa Rica: The ethnohistory of an ethnic minority in a complex society. Ph.D. dissertation, Department of Anthropology, University of Oregon.

———, 1977. The adaptation of West Indian Blacks to North American and Hispanic culture in Costa Rica. In Ann Pescatello (ed.), Old roots in new lands. Westport, Greenwood Press, pp. 132–156.

Palmer, Paula, 1977. 'What happen.' a folk history of Costa Rica's Talamanca coast. San José, Ecodesarrollos.

Purcell, Trevor, 1982. Conformity and dissension: Social inequality, values and mobility among West Indian migrants in Limón, Costa Rica. Unpublished Ph.D. dissertation, Dept. of Anthropology, Johns Hopkins University.

Rodríguez Bolanos, José, and Victor Borge Carvajal, 1976. El ferrocarril al Atlántico en Costa Rica. Licenciatura thesis, Department of History, University of Costa Rica.

Sánchez, José León, 1971. Picahueso. San José, Editorial Latinoamericana.

Vargas Villalobos, Martha Elena and Gabriela Requeyra Edelman, 1983. Un estudio sobre la participación del grupo negro en el empleo: Sus oportunidades y limitaciones 1981–82, Limón Centro, Provincia de Limón. Licenciatura thesis, Department of Social Work, University of Costa Rica.

Wade, Peter, 1985. Race and class: the case of South American Blacks. Ethnic and Racial Studies 8:2: 231–249.

Wilson, Charles, 1947. Empire in green and gold. New York, Henry Holt and Co.

# 4. STRUCTURAL CONTINUITY IN
# THE DIVISION OF MEN'S AND WOMEN'S WORK
# AMONG THE BLACK CARIB (GARÍFUNA)

### Virginia Kerns

### Introduction

Evidence from documentary sources, as well as recent enthnographic research with the Black Carib, show that the division of men's and women's work has not changed in any fundamental respect for nearly two centuries.[1] Women tend to work at home or in the community environs; they work largely in the subsistence sector, doing agricultural work and providing various domestic services, including food preparation and child care; although a few women work for wages, female labor is largely unpaid. In contrast, men often work at some distance from home; they participate in the subsistence sector, doing agricultural work or fishing, but they also take part in the wage economy; most of their work, whether wage labor or own-account, produces some cash income.

In this paper I suggest that structural continuity in the division of labor by sex can be explained by long-standing conditions of the labor market: specifically, by discriminatory recruitment policies of plantations and other colonial enterprises. Today, as in the past, women are largely excluded from employment in the export sector, and relatively few Black Carib women work for wages.

Discriminatory hiring practices have had several effects on the work patterns of Black Carib men and women. First, they have reinforced the traditional division of labor. By force of economic circumstance, rather than by personal or cultural preference, most women pursue their traditional tasks in the subsistence sector at home. Second, biased recruitment policies have permitted colonial enterprises to hold down wages and to hire male labor seasonally rather than permanently. Subsistence activities in Black Carib communities provide a necessary supplement to wage work in external enterprises. Many men do not earn wages sufficient to support their families fully and on a year-round basis.

In the following sections of this paper I will describe the Black Carib and the

Originally published in Christine A. Loveland and Franklin O. Loveland (eds.), *Sex Roles and Social Change in Native Lower Central American Societies* (Urbana: University of Illinois Press, 1982), pp. 23–43. Copyright © 1982 by the Board of Trustees of the University of Illinois. Reprinted by permission of the University of Illinois Press.

division of men's and women's work in the past and today. I will also present some comparative material on other, native peoples of lower Central America who participate in wage economies, and whose division of labor in some respects resembles that of the Black Carib.

The Black Carib, or Garífuna as they call themselves, are not native to Central America. Their ancestors settled there late in the eighteenth century, toward the end of the colonial era. Having been dispossessed of their land on the island of St. Vincent, their homeland in the eastern Caribbean, they were forcibly transported to Roatán, an island in the western Caribbean. From Roatán they gradually spread along the nearby coastline of Central America. Today nearly 80,000 descendants of the original few thousand émigrés live in towns and villages scattered along a narrow coastal strip facing the Caribbean Sea (see Davidson 1976, 1977). Politically, the Black Carib are divided by the national boundaries of three Hispanic republics (Guatemala, Honduras, and Nicaragua) and the British colony of Belize (the former British Honduras).

Shortly after the Black Carib arrived in Central America, the Spanish provinces declared their independence. It can be argued, however, that the Black Carib themselves remained a colonial population, separate from but subject to rule by the descendants of Europeans. They have always been a social minority, linguistically and ethnically distinct from the larger population. Today they constitute as little as 1% and no more than 8% of the national population in countries where their settlements are located.

The separation of the Black Carib from the larger society has economic and geographic dimensions as well as social ones. For well over a century Black Carib men have participated in the wage economy of Central America, working largely in non-Carib locales and foreign-owned enterprises. In Belize during the last century men were hired seasonally to extract various raw materials that were the colony's chief exports, especially timber and chicle. Today commercial export agriculture, rather than forestry, provides the colony's principal exports. A number of plantations produce sugar, citrus, and bananas for export (see Ashcraft 1973). The majority of the workers at these plantations, including Black Carib men, do unskilled, seasonal work and earn rather low wages. Given the coastal and insular locations of Black Carib settlements, at some distance from inland plantations and other economic centers, workers must migrate to find employment. Most labor migrants are men.

In the past, wage work provided a supplement to subsistence, agriculture, fishing, and trade. According to accounts from the last century, Black Carib men supplied most of the fish for the market in Belize, and the women sold yams and cassava bread there. The men also "contributed in some degree to the labor market" (Fowler 1879: 52; Fröbel 1859: 178, 185). By the 1920s however, trade seems to have declined. A resident of Belize noted then that the Black Carib "fish and farm, but little more than to supply their own needs" (Burdon 1928: 38).

During the past 50 years Black Caribs have come to depend more and more on the labor market for their livelihood (cf. Gonzalez 1969: 37). By far the major share of income from wage work is today, as in the past, earned by men. Black Carib women in Belize tend to work for wages under two circumstances: if they are educated and can earn relatively high wages (for women) as teachers or nurses, or if alternative sources of support fail. Marital separation is the most common reason that women with little education seek employment as manual workers. Most women do work for wages at some point in life, but at any given time the vast majority are not employed; in contrast, most men are either employed or seeking work.

Men's motives for seeking wage work, and the problems they encounter in finding it, are well understood (see Gonzalez 1969). Why women do not so commonly work for wages is a question that has not been addressed. Available evidence suggests that the low employment rate of women is largely due to a limited demand for female labor rather than to a limited supply. In some societies various social and cultural factors may inhibit women from seeking employment, thus restricting the supply of female labor (see Youssef 1974, Auerbach 1979). The most commonly cited factors include negative attitudes toward female employment, a lower level of education among women, and domestic responsibilities. But these have relatively little effect on the employment rate of Black Carib women. Many women state a preference for remunerative rather than unpaid work, and a large number have migrated to the United States to find employment. There is no evidence that most men attain a higher level of education than women do.[2] Finally, women who do work for wages, in Belize or abroad, can depend on kinswoman for help with child care.

Why so few Black Carib women work for wages is better explained by examining the obstacles that the aspiring female worker confronts in Belize: discriminatory hiring practices, occupational restrictions, and wage discrimination.[3] These conditions can be documented today, and there is evidence that they existed in the past. Indeed, recent research has shown that such discriminatory practices are common to the labor markets of many developing and industrialized countries.[4]

Every Black Carib household requires a cash income, and the burden of providing it has always rested primarily on male shoulders (cf. Gonzalez 1969: 56ff.). In large part this seems due to the fact that women experience so much difficulty in finding employment, particularly work that pays a living wage. This work pattern, and the problems women face in securing employment, are long-standing features of life.

*Work in the Nineteenth Century and Before*

Black Carib men already had some experience with wage work when they were transported to Central America around the turn of the nineteenth century. During the decade before their departure from St. Vincent, British planters there had hired the men individually, paying them "a Spanish dollar" a day to shuttle cargo between ship and shore (Young 1795: 106). European vessels could not easily negotiate the surf off the windward coast, but Black Caribs possessed crafts well suited to these waters and the expertise to navigate them. The colonists encouraged such gainful employment, and not only because they needed the labor of these men. They clearly hoped that the otherwise fiercely independent Black Carib might unwittingly and peacefully integrate themselves into the lower ranks of the colonial hierarchy. One discerning planter wrote, "The Charaibbs thus begin to taste of money. . . . Money civilizes in the first instance as it corrupts in the last; the savage labouring for himself soon ceases to be a savage; the slave to money becomes a subject to government, and he becomes a useful subject" (Young 1806: 275).

There is no record that Black Carib women worked for wages, as they were to do in Central America during the next century, but it was in St. Vincent that they too began to "taste of money." Cultivated plots were "worked wholly by the women," who carried their surplus produce and cassava bread to town and sold it in the marketplace (Young 1795: 26, 106).

Whether the Black Carib were yet "slaves to money" when they were deported to Central America at the end of the eighteenth century is debatable. But certainly they depended upon money to buy goods that they did not produce themselves. They were soon to acquire a reputation in Central America as a "good and useful laboring population," with a broad range of valued skills (Squier 1870: 173). During the nineteenth century Black Carib men worked at a variety of pursuits in Belize, Guatemala, and Honduras. Many worked as woodcutters. Others enlisted in military service, hired out as sailors, or worked on fruit and sugar plantations. Some earned money doing own-account work: carrying contraband, hunting deer and selling the skins, and catching fish and turtle to market in Belize.[5]

Very few nineteenth-century accounts mention men working in Black Carib communities, and for good reason. One traveler probably described most of their settlements when he said of one that it showed a "complete lack of enterprise" (Brigham 1887: 29). Another visitor to a different town explicitly remarked upon the "scarcity of men," most of whom, he learned, "were away fishing or at work" (Stephens 1841: 30). Income earning opportunities lay far afield, and those who wished to exploit them had to leave their home communities to do so. Woodcutters might be absent for six months at a time, other workers for a period of weeks or months. One nineteenth-century commentator wrote that the Black Carib were a "coast tribe," but "ubiquitous over the colony" of Belize, working at a variety of pursuits (Gibbs 1883: 166). A mid-century census supports this assertion. It shows that nearly one-quarter of the total Black Carib population was living in non-Carib locales when the census was taken (Colonial Office 1861). Most of these people were probably labor migrants.

The wage levels of male laborers seem to have been fairly uniform. At mid-century woodcutters and male agricultural workers earned about $8.00 to $10.00

per month and rations. Black Carib women, who sometimes hired their own husbands to help them with agricultural tasks, paid them comparable rates of $2.00 per week (Young 1847: 123–24; cf. Morris 1883: 120).

Women also earned money, but accounts suggest that most of it was gained from own-account work (especially as laundresses or marketers) rather than from wage labor. Those who worked for wages filled a very limited range of occupations. Some were probably employed as domestic servants in Belize (Gibbs 1883: 166). One source mentions that some women worked at sugar and banana plantations in Guatemala (Morlan 1892: 33). Exactly when women began to seek gainful employment is not precisely documented, but it may have been before mid-century. Young (1847: 107) alludes to this: "A [European] settler would find his advantage in employing Caribs to cultivate his ground," he wrote. "The women would hire themselves to attend the plantations and to make cassava bread."

When Young spoke of the advantages of hiring female labor, he referred to their wage rates as well as to their agricultural skills. After recommending the employment of Black Carib women to intending settlers, he described the men's rates for agricultural work as "too high." The latter demanded $8.00 to $10.00 a month plus rations. Women of that era could be hired for much lower rates, as little as $3.00 to $4.00 a month (Young 1847: 115, 190). A similar disparity prevailed between men's and women's wages for domestic labor. Women earned $5.00 monthly, men $10.00 (Gullick 1976: 57).

Women's work at home, like their gainful work, was largely domestic and agricultural. Although men were obligated to clear land for their wives to plant, women were otherwise largely responsible for the fields. They devoted their energies to food preparation, child care, and various other domestic tasks as well, working primarily at home or in the environs. Women also carried surplus produce as much as 40 miles to market. They retained the profits as their own, using them to purchase clothing and a wide range of other essential goods (see Roberts 1827: 274; Young 1847: 123ff.; Fröbel 1959: 185).

Since the nineteenth century the work patterns of Black Carib men and women have changed in detail but not in basic outline.

### Men's and Women's Work Today

The economic pattern of the Black Carib has always been a very broad one, and it has diversified further in this century in at least one respect: the male occupational structure, which was quite broad even in the last century, has continued to expand. In Belize, Black Carib men now hold a variety of positions in all of the agro-industries that dominate the national economy. Most are manual workers, and many still work seasonally at banana, citrus, and sugar plantations. Only a few have achieved supervisory positions. Other men work at various trades, as construction workers and carpenters, mechanics, and tailors. A number are stevedores and sailors. Some men hold positions with government, working at all ranks and in a range of departments, including the police force. A very small proportion of men are professionals, most of them teachers.

In the past, nearly all unskilled work in Belize was seasonal, but today some Black Carib men hold year-round employment. If they work in other districts, far from their home communities, their visits are occasional and brief. Men who work closer to home, within a 20- or 30-mile radius, are part-time residents of these communities, returning weekly or monthly from their work places. Relatively few men are full-time residents of Black Carib villages in Belize. Most of them are older men who have few dependents and who can afford the low returns provided by fishing and other own-account work.

The average man has little choice but to spend much of his life away from home, working for wages. Able-bodied men have few alternatives to participating in the labor market. Their primary obligation toward their spouses, dependent children, and aged parents is to contribute financially to their support. Most men sell their labor to this end. There is no compulsory age of retirement set by the government, and given a reportedly chronic shortage of male labor, able-bodied men may work into their sixties or even seventies.

Most men work at similar wage levels in the manual labor and services sector of the economy. Wages vary somewhat, but the average unskilled worker earns between $20.00 and $30.00 per week when he is employed. Beginning teachers or policemen earn only slightly more than this, but their jobs are year-round and their salaries do increase with seniority (see Labour Department 1972).

The labor participation rate of Black Carib women is far lower than men's but difficult to estimate because statistics on female employment are neither reliable nor up to date. When data on the ethnic identity and gender of workers were last collected, some 30 years ago, 25% of all Black Carib females over the age of 10 were counted as gainfully employed (CBS 1948: xxxi). This figure is somewhat misleading, however, because census returns do not specify the duration of employment. The work histories that I collected from older women suggest that many of the employed females were probably temporary, rather than seasonal or year-round, workers: that is, they were hired for a week or two to help harvest crops or pack them for shipment. Many of my older female informants spoke of having earned wages for such work as young women. There were scarcely any employment opportunities for them, they said, other than this sort of temporary work or domestic service. To judge from their work experiences, nearly all women have worked for wages at some point in life, but very often on a temporary basis.

Women, like men, tend to find work as manual laborers; unlike men, rather few women can find employment in the export sector, which has traditionally been the major employer of men in Belize. Sugar plantations recruit male work forces, save for a handful of female clerical workers. A recently established banana plantation hires women only on a temporary (one- or two-week) basis to pack fruit for shipment, and it pays them a much lower hourly rate than male field laborers earn. Gender-based wage discrimination has the sanction of tradition in Belize and is not illegal. One citrus plantation seasonally employs a relatively large number of women, many of whom are Black Carib, and it is a matter of union agreement that the women earn a lower base rate, 25% below men's. The disparity used to be greater, about 40% (see Labour Department 1972, 1973).

Most working women in Belize, including Black Carib women, are confined to a handful of disproportionately female occupations, the same ones that women filled at the beginning of the century.[6] They work principally as domestic servants and laundresses, cooks, seamstresses, shop clerks, teachers, and nurses. Most earn lower wages than men who do similar work. Seamstresses' wage rates are about 20% to 30% less than tailors', and the disparity between the wages of male and female shop clerks is roughly equivalent (Labour Department 1973). Domestic service, an almost exclusively female occupation in Belize, is the largest single occupation of women and the lowest-paid work in the country. According to official figures, nearly 30% of all gainfully employed women work as domestics, earning wages that are about one-third of those earned by men who do other types of unskilled, manual work.[7]

Black Carib women typically work for lower wages than men, and also for a shorter period of their adult lives. After the age of 45 or 50 a woman has extreme difficulty finding gainful employment, even of the lowest-paying variety. Employers say that they generally prefer to hire young women, and that the supply is sufficient for them to enforce this preference.

There is no cultural resistance to female employment. Many Black Carib women claim to be eager to work for wages, and very few men state any opposition to the notion or to the fact of their employment. As for marital status, young women whose level of education qualifies them for higher-paying jobs than average commonly continue to work after they marry. Women with dependent children and without spouses have little choice but to work for wages, no matter how dismally low. Kinswomen usually foster their children (see Kerns, forthcoming).

Although nearly every woman has been gainfully employed at some point in her life, most spend many of their adult years outside the labor force, doing unsalaried work at home. Domestic work and routine have changed rather little since the last century. Child care is still a major concern for most women. Very few live in childless households; those with grown sons and daughters often foster grandchildren or the children of other kin. Aside from child care, women also work at a variety of other domestic tasks. Many hours of the average woman's day are spent in the time-consuming work of procuring and preparing food, and laundering. The nature and extent of women's subsistence activities vary widely from one community to the next today. At the least, village women commonly collect firewood, gather wild fruits seasonally, occasionally collect crabs along the beach, and maintain small kitchen gardens. Some also cultivate larger plots at some distance from the settlement. The proportion who do so in any village depends upon a number of factors, including the distance and location of productive land and the availability of men to clear it. Very few women today market any surplus produce. They explain that there is little profit to be made, given the unreliability and cost of transportation in southern Belize.[8]

*Discussion and Comparison*

Documentary sources show that during the nineteenth century Black Carib men worked away from their home communities in a range of non-Carib enterprises and at a number of own-account, income-earning pursuits. Women were certainly not isolated or sedentary, but their work was largely unsalaried and carried out at home and in the environs. Some women were gainfully employed, but they were restricted to a narrow range of occupations with very low wage rates. Women probably earned about one-half as much as men did for manual labor.

Today many Black Carib men still spend most of their adult lives working away from their home communities. Fewer women than men are gainfully employed; as in the past, they are confined to a limited number of occupations with low wages. Many still earn wages that are about one-half those paid to men for manual labor, and they find it very difficult to obtain gainful employment after the age of 45 or 50. Despite these disadvantages, most women do work for wages at some point in their lives. When they are not gainfully employed, they work at home, where they do many of the same tasks, using virtually the same methods, as women of the last century. Nineteenth-century descriptions and photographs of the preparation of cassava bread, for example, show that the same equipment and techniques are used today (see Roberts 1827: 272–73).

Although the specifics vary, in general outline the Black Carib division of labor by sex resembles that of several other peoples of lower Central America, including the Miskito and Guaymí. The Guaymí are an indigenous Amerindian group, numbering about 50,000, who live in the mountainous portions of western Panama. The Miskito, with a population of about 40,000, are a mixed group, whose Amerindian ancestors intermarried with Africans and Europeans during the colonial era. Today their settlements extend from eastern Honduras to southeastern Nicaragua.

The Black Carib, Miskito, and Guaymí differ profoundly in many respects besides their cultural origins. They speak separate languages, have divergent religious beliefs and practices, and differ in many other aspects of culture. Yet their division of labor shows many similarities and a high degree of structural continuity, with men specializing in income-earning work (wage labor or own-account) and women in subsistence activities. Like Black Carib women, Miskito and Guaymí women tend to work at home or in the immediate environs; they work largely in the subsistence sector, doing domestic and agricultural tasks; and their labor is largely unpaid. Men participate in the subsistence sector, doing agricultural work or hunting and fishing, but they also work for wages or engage in own-account work (Helms 1971: 67, 230–31; Young 1971: 155).

One distinctive feature of the division of agricultural work is its flexibility. According to the formal division of labor, men have the task of clearing land, while women are largely responsible for the day-to-day maintenance of cultivated plots (Young 1971: 155; Helms 1971: 23, 123; Conzemius 1932: 39, 60; Taylor 1951: 55–56). If men are available, they may take part in the work of planting, weeding, and harvesting. If not, women do these tasks unassisted.

This flexibility, and women's responsibility for many agricultural tasks, allow subsistence agriculture to be carried on despite the seasonal and erratic demands of the labor market for male workers. In turn, the irregular availability of wage work, and the low wages paid, have made subsistence activities a necessary supplement to employment. Historical records indicate that Black Carib, Miskito, and Guaymí men have worked for wages for well over a century and that employment opportunities have always been highly unstable (Young 1971: 100; Helms 1971: 27; 1976).

Published accounts of the Miskito and Guaymí provide little information on female employment. Miskito women apparently do not work for wages. In the past some Guaymí women accompanied their husbands to coffee plantations and worked there seasonally (for lower wages than men earned), but most remained at home (Young 1971: 101, 155). Today a few women, unaccompanied by men, work in towns as domestics. It is difficult to determine from the information available whether cultural factors inhibit most women from seeking employment. Young (1971: 18) does mention that "far more men than women are bilingual, speaking Spanish and their native tongue." It is not clear, however, whether men have learned Spanish as a consequence of or as a prerequisite for working at plantations.[9] In any case, the fact that Guaymí women earn less than men do when they work at plantations suggests that discriminatory practices—in pay and perhaps in hiring—may limit their employment.

Such practices are common enough elsewhere in Central America (see Bossen 1979; Adams 1957: 173). Many plantations hire only men; others hire some women but pay them lower wages. Although plantations in various other areas of the world also have discriminatory hiring policies, these are by no means universal. Throughout South Asia, for example, where family recruitment policies are quite common, women and children are hired with men. In some cases women constitute as much as 50% of the plantation work force (Boserup 1970: 76). Yet in certain areas of Africa, in contrast, plantations have traditionally recruited only men.

Boserup (1970: 76ff.) argues that these differences in recruitment policy represent a means of economizing on labor costs, and vary according to the roles that men and women traditionally assume in subsistence agriculture. She points out that in many parts of Africa "the methods of food production are such that women can do nearly all of the operations unaided by men." In this circumstance, plantations and other industries in the export sector can minimize labor costs by employing only men—leaving women, children, and the elderly at home, where they are supported in part by the subsistence activities of women. In many areas of Asia, with agricultural systems in which men do a major share of the work, "the plantation owner must face the fact that the whole family must get its livelihood from the plantation." Labor costs are kept down by employing entire families (but not necessarily paying women and children the same rates paid to men). Thus, whether plantations recruit only men or whole families, they can avoid paying individual workers the wages necessary to support an entire family of dependents.

In the case at hand, there is no evidence that discriminatory hiring practices developed simply because men were considered to be more capable workers than women. Indeed, unaccustomed to subsistence systems in which women assume major responsibility for agricultural work, Europeans consistently maligned the men for their "laziness" (cf. Boserup 1970: 19, 24). Thus a colonist in eighteenth-century St. Vincent wrote about the Black Carib women: "she plants the cassava, yam, potatoes, &c., and prepares them for the indolent male," whose "sole occupation" was hunting and fishing (Davidson 1787: 11). Many nineteenth-century Euro-Americans, who saw this work pattern among the Black Carib in Central America, similarly commented on the "industry" of the women and the "laziness" of the men (Sanborn 1886: 30; Charles 1890: 114). Outsiders still tend to characterize men and women in this way (Taylor 1951: 55; Cosminsky 1976: 99).

The division of men's and women's work among the Guaymí and Miskito has been subject to the same sort of misunderstanding by outsiders, both in the past and present. Historical accounts of the Miskito are reputedly full of references to the "extremely lazy" men who "lie all day in hammocks . . . while their wives do their work" (Nietschmann 1973: 29, quoting De Lussan 1930: 287). Likewise, *latinos* in Panama still hold a stereotyped view of the Guaymí man as "an indolent vagabond who spends his time leisurely hunting and fishing, or just lying around the house while his women slave to support him" (Young 1971: 156). As Young hastens to point out, this is based on a misunderstanding of the Guaymí economic system. Hunting is scarcely a leisure activity, but one that provides needed food.

Whether these (mis)perceptions of men's work influenced labor policies in the past is debatable. Today, however, some plantation managers in Belize do try to justify both discriminatory hiring policies and low wages by reference to men's and women's work in the subsistence sector. From their perspective, Black Carib men are clearly "underemployed" at home and hence are a readily available supply of labor for work elsewhere. As for their wages, the manager of one plantation remarked to me that Black Carib men do not "need" to earn higher wages because subsistence agriculture provides some food for their families (but far less than he assumed). And besides, he said, the men are notoriously lazy (implying that they do not merit higher wages). He explained his refusal to hire women for field work as due to "force of tradition." That women should engage in agricultural work for subsistence, he suggested, was "traditional"; that they should do so for wages was not. Thus one "tradition" reinforces another.

## Conclusions

I have tried to show how long-standing labor recruitment policies in Belize have helped to sustain the traditional division of labor among the Black Carib. The discrimination that women confront in the labor market, rather than cultural factors, keeps many of them outside the wage economy and in the subsistence sector. Custom does not dictate that they refrain from gainful employment either before or after marriage. Indeed, some women worked for wages during the last century, just as their great-great-granddaughters do today. Women do not express any reluctance to work for wages, nor do men say that they are opposed to female employment. As for childrearing and other domestic responsibilities, gainfully employed women can usually depend on kinswomen to help them with these.

Still, conditions in the labor market are so unfavorable for women that, regardless of whether they are employed, they must always look to kin for their security. Unlike men, who can be economically self-sufficient when they are employed, women depend to some degree on their spouses and relatives for support throughout life. Even most gainfully employed women must receive some financial assistance from other sources if they are to maintain what is considered a normal standard of living. Few of the jobs open to women pay a living wage, and many women who wish to work for wages cannot find employment.

The effects of discriminatory labor policies on other features of social organization and culture, aside from the division of labor, remain to be briefly considered. As Bossen (1979: 42) has pointed out, "The decisions of plantation management regarding the use of female labor . . . affect not only the sexual division of labor, but also the degree of female economic dependence or independence, and the structure of the family" in the home community of labor migrants. Among the Black Carib and Miskito, as well as the Guaymí, many aspects of social life show a high degree of structural continuity (see Young 1970, Helms 1976). In the case of the Black Carib and Miskito, in particular, women act as the "keepers" of traditional customs and values. Helms (1971: 232) writes that "kinship obligations within the village are still strongly emphasized and are in the hands of the women, still the conservative element." She points out that the Miskito practice of matrilocal residence, as well as the division of labor, have permitted the Miskito to participate in the wage economy without the loss of ethnic identity, language, and traditional values. Men and women have had different degrees of contact with the outside world: "While men were free to come and go . . . women were more restricted to the confines of the village. Hence, women did not come into contact with foreigners as much as men did, and as a result became the more conservative element of Miskito society" (Helms 1971: 230). Likewise, Bort and Young characterize Guaymí women as less knowledgeable about the outside world and as "the most conservative members of the society." Most Black Carib women, in contrast, have had ample contact with the outside world and more opportunities for travel than Miskito and Guaymí women seem to have had (see Helms 1971: 67, 108). Their "traditionalism" is not due to any unfamiliarity with or antipathy toward the non-Carib world. It is simply a fact that that world offers them rather little. When women do venture forth, they find relatively few opportunities for employment, most of them very low-paying ones. It is no cause for wonder, then, that they so carefully cultivate and maintain relations with kin, and that they actively promote a morality that centers on the display of generosity and gratitude to kin. These represent women's primary livelihood, just as employment in commercial enterprises represents men's. Men, in contrast to women, have more to gain outside their home communities, and little choice but to leave and seek their fortunes there.

*Notes*

1. This paper is based on fieldwork in Belize during 1974–75 and 1976 and on research at the British Library and Public Records Office, in London and Kew, England. I wish to acknowledge the generous support of the Wenner-Gren Foundation, the Fulbright-Hays Commission, and the Department of Anthropology, University of Illinois, which made my research possible.

2. The 1970 census of Belize reveals no disparity in the current level of educational attainment of boys and girls in the southern districts, where Black Carib settlements are located (see CRP 1975: 112–13). Neither did I detect any significant disparity in the educational levels of the men and women whom I met in the course of my field research. Most of them had several years of primary education. Of the few with postprimary education, a greater proportion were male.

3. Discrimination can be said to exist "whatever market allocations are made such that nonpecuniary or extraneous factors play a role—that is, where race, religion, or sex affect the distribution of goods and jobs" (Madden 1973: 1).

4. For example, see Madden (1973), Boserup (1970: 141ff.), Oppenheimer (1970), and Bossen (1979).

5. Many nineteenth-century accounts make reference to the income-earning work of men. See, for example, Roberts (1927: 273–74), Young (1847: 124), and Fröbel (1859: 177, 184).

6. A disproportionately female occupation is one in which women form a higher proportion of the workers in that occupation than they do in the labor force as a whole (see Oppenheimer 1970: 69). Data from the 1911 census of Belize show that occupations that are disproportionately female today were so in the past as well. They include the occupations of domestic, laundress, cook, seamstress, and shop clerk (see CBS 1948: xxxvii; Department of Statistics 1960: 197ff.).

7. Figures on employment in domestic service, and wages earned by domestics, are provided by the 1960 census of British Honduras (Department of Statistics 1960: 197ff.)

and the Labour Department (1973); cf. Carey Jones (1953: 85). A higher proportion of employed women may actually work as domestics; as Ashcraft (1973: 157) points out, domestic workers are not always carefully enumerated for official reports.

8. See Ashcraft (1973) and Chibnik (1975) for a description of the internal marketing system and the problems of marketing produce in Belize.

9. Helms (1971: 176) implies that most Miskito women, like the men, are bilingual, although they rarely speak Spanish within the village. As for Black Caribs, nearly all of the men and women whom I met in Belize and Guatemala were bilingual. In the past also men and women commonly spoke another language as well as their native one (Young 1847: 123).

## References

Adams, Richard N.
    1957         Cultural Surveys of Panama—Nicaragua—Guatemala—El Salvador—Honduras. Pan American Sanitary Bureau, Scientific Publications no. 33. Washington, D.C.

Ashcraft, Norman
    1973         Colonialism and Underdevelopment: Processes of Political Economic Change in British Honduras. New York: Teachers College Press.

Auerbach, Liesa Stamm
    1979         "Women's Jobs Mean Women's Money: The Social Ramifications of the Increased Participation of Women in the Work Structure of a Tunisian Town." Paper presented at the annual meeting of the American Anthropological Association, Cincinnati.

Boserup, Ester
    1970         Woman's Role in Economic Development. London: George Allen & Unwin.

Bossen, Laurel
    1979         "Plantations and Labor Force Discrimination in Guatemala." Peasant Studies 8(3): 31–44.

Brigham, William T.
    1887         Guatemala, the Land of the Quetzal. New York: Charles Scribner's Sons.

Burdon, John
    1928         Brief Sketch of British Honduras. 2d ed. London: West India Committee.

Carey Jones, N. S.
    1953         The Pattern of a Dependent Economy: A Study of the National Income of British Honduras. London: Cambridge University Press.

Carlson, Rae
    1971         "Sex Differences in Ego Functioning: Exploratory Studies of Agency

and Communion." Journal of Consulting and Clinical Psychology 37: 267–77.

Census Research Program (CRP)
1975         1970 Population Census of the Commonwealth Caribbean, vol. 6, pt. 2, "Education." Kingston, Jamaica: University of the West Indies.

Central Bureau of Statistics (CBS)
1948         West Indian Census, vol. 1, pt. E, "British Honduras." Kingston, Jamaica.

Charles, Cecil
1890         Honduras: Land of Great Depths. New York: Rand McNally.

Chibnik, Michael
1975         "Economic Strategies of Small Farmers in Stann Creek District, British Honduras." Ph.D. dissertation, Columbia University.

Chodorow, Nancy
1974         "Family Structure and Feminine Personality." In Woman, Culture and Society, ed. Michelle Rosaldo and Louise Lamphere. Stanford, Calif.: Stanford University Press. Pp. 43–66.

Colonial Office
1861         "Blue Book of Statistics for the Colony of British Honduras," C.O. 128/42. Public Records Office at Kew, England.

Conzemius, Edward
1932         Ethnographical Survey of the Miskito and Sumu Indians of Honduras and Nicaragua. Bureau of American Ethnology Bulletin no. 106. Washington, D.C.: U.S. Government Printing Office.

Cosminsky, Sheila
1976         "Carib-Creole Relations in a Belizean Community." In Frontier Adaptations in Lower Central America, ed. Marv W. Helms and Franklin O. Loveland. Philadelphia: Institute for the Study of Human Issues. Pp. 96–114.

Davidson, George
1787         "The Copy of a Letter from a Gentleman in the Island of St. Vincent to the Reverend Mr. Clarke . . . Containing a Short History of the Caribbs." In The Case of the Caribbs in St. Vincent, ed. Thomas Coke. London.

Davidson, William V.
1976         "Black Carib (Garífuna) Habitats in Central America." In Frontier Adaptations in Lower Central America, ed. Mary W. Helms and Franklin O. Loveland. Philadelphia: Institute for the Study of Human Issues. Pp. 85–94.
1977         "Research in Coastal Ethnogeography: The East Coast of Central America." Geoscience and Man 18: 277–84.

De Lussan, Raveneau
1930         Raveneau de Lussan, Buccaneer of the Spanish Main and Early

French Filibuster of the Pacific. Trans. and ed. M. E. Wilbur. Cleveland: Arthur H. Clark.

Department of Statistics
1960 "Census of British Honduras." In West Indies Population Census. Kingston: Jamaica Tabulation Center.

Fowler, Henry
1879 A Narrative of a Journey across the Unexplored Portion of British Honduras with a Short Sketch of the History and Resources of the Colony. Belize: Government Press.

Fröbel, Julius
1859 Seven Years' Travel in Central America, Northern Mexico, and the Far West of the United States. London: R. Bentley.

Gibbs, Archibald R.
1883 British Honduras: An Historical and Descriptive Account of the Colony from Its Settlement, 1670. London: S. Low, Marston, Searle, and Rivington.

Gonzalez, Nancie
1969 Black Carib Household Structure. Seattle: University of Washington Press.

Gullick, C. J. M. R.
1976 Exiled from St. Vincent. Malta: Progress Press.

Guttman, David
1965 "Women and the Conception of Ego Strength." Merrill-Palmer Quarterly of Behavior and Development 2: 229–40.

Helms, Mary W.
1971 Asang: Adaptations to Culture Contact in a Miskito Community. Gainesville: University of Florida Press.
1976 "Domestic Organization in Eastern Central America: The San Blas Cuna, Miskito, and Black Carib Compared." Western Canadian Journal of Anthropology 6: 133–63.

Kerns, Virginia
forthcoming Women and the Ancestors. Urbana: University of Illinois Press.

Labour Department
1972 Annual Report of the Labour Department for the Years 1970 and 1971. Belize: Government Printer.
1973 Annual Report of the Labour Department for the Year 1972. Belize: Government Printer.

Madden, Janice Fanning
1973 The Economics of Sex Discrimination. Lexington, Mass.: D. C. Heath.

Morlan, Albert
1892 A Hoosier in Honduras. Indianapolis: El Dorado Publishing Co.

Morris, D.
     1883          The Colony of British Honduras, Its Resources and Prospects. Lon-
                    don: Edward Stanford.

Nietschmann, Bernard
     1973          Between Land and Water: The Subsistence Ecology of the Miskito
                    Indians, Eastern Nicaragua. New York: Seminar Press.

Oppenheimer, Valerie Kincade
     1970          The Female Labor Force in the United States: Demographic and
                    Economic Factors Governing Its Growth and Changing Composi-
                    tion. Population Monograph Series no. 5. Berkeley: Institute of Inter-
                    national Studies, University of California.

Roberts, Orlando
     1827          Narrative of Voyages and Excursions on the East Coast and in the In-
                    terior of Central America. Edinburgh: Constable.

Sanborn, Helen
     1886          A Winter in Central America and Mexico. Boston: Lee and Shepard.

Squier, E. G.
     1870          Honduras: Descriptive, Historical, and Statistical. London: Trubner.

Stephens, John Lloyd
     1841          Incidents of Travel in Central America, Chiapas, and Yucatan, vol.
                    1. New York: Harper and Bros.

Taylor, Douglas
     1951          The Black Carib of British Honduras. Viking Fund Publications in
                    Anthropology no. 17. New York: Wenner-Gren Foundation.

Young, Philip D.
     1970          "Notes on the Ethnohistorical Evidence for Structural Continuity in
                    Guaymí Society." Ethnohistory 6: 11–29.
     1971          Ngawbe: Tradition and Change among the Eastern Guaymí of Pa-
                    nama. Illinois Studies in Anthropology no. 7. Urbana: University of
                    Illinois Press.

Young, Thomas
     1847          Narrative of a Residence on the Mosquito Shore. London: Smith,
                    Elder and Co.

Young, William
     1795          An Account of the Black Charaibs in the Island of St. Vincent's. Lon-
                    don: British Library Collection.
     1806          "A Tour through the Several Islands of Barbadoes, St. Vincent, Anti-
                    gua, Tobago, and Grenada, in the Years 1791 and 1792." In History,
                    Civil and Commerical, of the British Colonies in the West Indies,
                    vol. 4, ed. Bryon Edwards. Philadelphia: J. Humphreys. Pp. 245–76.

Youssef, Nadia Haggag
     1974          Women and Work in Developing Societies. Berkeley: Institute of In-
                    ternational Studies, University of California.

# 5. RITUAL AND RESOURCE FLOW

## The Garifuna dugu

### Carol L. Jenkins

One of the key issues in contemporary anthropology is the response of societies to the decreasing availability of primary resources. Both long-term declines and short-term fluctuations in resources place a premium on the adaptive flexibility of existing institutions. In the Caribbean, as elsewhere, high fertility rates and inequitable resource distribution combine to limit available modes of livelihood for most people. It has recently been estimated that between 25 and 50 percent of all children under five years of age in the English-speaking Caribbean are malnourished (Gueri 1981), a clear indication of the poverty level of the area. Migration has become increasingly important in relieving this poverty; but at the same time, migration disrupts familial and community organization, threatens cultural integrity, and creates additional problems for those remaining behind. Traditional religious cults represent one type of institution with the potential flexibility to handle the numerous interrelated problems arising from the pressure of increasing population on limited resources (Netting 1972). The purpose of this paper is to examine the role of the Garifuna[1] (Black Carib) ancestral cult in mitigating contemporary socioeconomic problems and in providing, at least for the present, an additional option between the extremes of deprivation and permanent out-migration for the Garifuna of Belize.

The demographic situation in Belize differs from that of the rest of the English-speaking Caribbean in one major respect: as a relatively large mainland country, Belize has an average population density of only six persons per square kilometer. This figure is deceptive, however, because only 10 percent of the arable land is under cultivation or in pasture, and nearly 60 percent of the land in use is held by a small number of owners, many of whom are non-Belizeans speculating in tourism or agriculture (CFNI 1979; Stavrakis 1979). Jobs, rising incomes, and population growth characterize northern towns, but the southern Garifuna area remains largely undeveloped. Contemporary Garifuna society is marked by high levels of out-migration, decreased subsistence activities, chronic underemployment, heavy dependence on remittances from abroad, and

Originally published in *American Ethnologist* 10:3 (August 1983), 429–42. Reproduced by permission of the American Anthropological Association. Not for further reproduction.

imported food. Political and economic opportunities are further denied the Garifuna due to lingering distrust and ethnic prejudice. Within this unfortunate socioeconomic matrix, the traditional Garifuna ancestral cult has developed an expanded and pivotal role in manipulating the interrelated domains of ritual, ethnic maintenance, and economic redistribution.

Although ancestral cult activities consist of a variety of personal, familial, and communal rites, this paper focuses on the major integrative ceremony known as *adogorohani*, or *dugu*. In earlier literature on the Garifuna, the *dugu* is described as an intensification ritual, functioning as a vehicle for ethnic maintenance and reaffirming the authority of elders. Over the past decade in Belize, ethnographers have noted an apparent surge of ancestral cult activities, particularly *dugu*, despite the widespread disdain of church and medical authorities. This development is interpreted as a revitalization movement indicating completed acculturation (Sanford 1974), a means of increasing ethnic pride and visibility with political aims (Wells 1980b), a reaction to the inadequate delivery of Western biomedical care (Palacio 1973), and a mechanism for enforcing ceremonial reciprocity among kinswomen (Foster 1981). While all these factors may contribute to the recent resurgence of *dugu*, there appears to be an economic dynamic operating as well, one in which ritual functions to regulate the flow of scarce resources for the benefit of kin and community. Similar functional analyses have been carried out elsewhere by anthropologists to demonstrate the effectiveness of ritual in regulating ecological relations and food availability (Chun 1980; Ford 1971; Piddocke 1965; Rappaport 1968). In the Caribbean area, Richardson (1981) examines the economic function of funerals in channeling funds from U.S. migrants to the poor communities of their sedentary kin. In the analysis that follows, it is shown that the frequency of the Garifuna *dugu* and the necessary related expenditures are highly flexible, thus making it possible for levels of ritual activity to expand (or contract) in response to perceived levels of resource stress.

## Food Scarcity and Nutritional Status

This phenomenon was brought to my attention during a 1979 field survey of diets and nutritional status among Belizean children. Dietary assessments, based on a combination of recalls and weighed meals, indicate a serious food deficit in many households. Anthropometric analysis further demonstrates that about 25 percent of all preschool-age children show evidence of growth retardation, while another 3 percent are severely malnourished (Jenkins 1981). Calories, more so than protein, are notably lacking in children's diets. Adult diets, especially among pregnant, lactating, or sick women, are frequently deficient in important nutrients.

When survey data are analyzed by comparing rates of malnutrition and early childhood mortality across the four major Belizean ethnic groups, the Garifuna and Maya exhibit nearly twice the mortality and malnutrition of either the Creole or the mestizo (Jenkins 1980). The situation appears especially grim for Garifuna children, who experience, on average, significantly higher rates of severe and prolonged diarrhea. Consequently, these children more often exhibit both severe loss of muscle and the symptoms of kwashiorkor. Unlike the other ethnic groups in Belize, there is little difference in the prevalence of malnutrition between rural and urban Garifuna children. Differential rates of childhood malnutrition and related mortality correspond closely to the general assessment of interethnic socioeconomic status in Belize, as presented in recent economic and ethnicity studies by Ashcraft (1972), Brockmann (1977), Cosminsky (1976), Grant (1976), and Howard (1980). Garifuna rank near the bottom, only slightly above the Maya, while mestizo and Creole families are generally more prosperous and enjoy greater access to employment and entrepreneurship.[2]

## The Garifuna: Historical Background

Understanding the position of the Garifuna in Belizean society requires some historical background. The Garifuna originated as a Maroon society on the island of St. Vincent in the Lesser Antilles during the 17th and 18th centuries. Older documents report that several slave ships wrecked near the island, notably, two Spanish ships in 1635 (Calendar of State Papers [1667] quoted in Gullick 1979:451) and a British ship bound from the Bight of Benin to Barbados in 1675 (Young 1971 [1795]). The island inhabitants, of mixed Carib and Arawak stock, spoke a predominantly Arawakan tongue and were known as the Calinago, or Island Caribs (Taylor 1951). With the addition of runaway slaves, the African population grew and finally outnumbered the Caribs by 1735 (Shephard 1971). An amalgamation of West African and Calinago traits followed, and the Garifuna (Black Carib) culture developed.

During this period of population growth, the Garifuna entered a cash economy. Women marketed their produce and cassava bread (*areba*) and men sold their skills as seamen. From the Calinago, cultural traits such as language, the cassava complex, canoe technology, features of the shamanic cult, song styles, dances, and even head binding were adopted. These traits served to mark the free status of the Garifuna during the ensuing century when European settlers with thousands of African slaves attempted to build a sugar economy in St. Vincent. Contested by the territorial claims of French, British, and Garifuna settlers, St. Vincent lapsed into a period of bitter warfare in which the Garifuna maneuvered and fought to defend their autonomy. In 1797, after the British captured St. Lucia, the Garifuna lost their main source of French military support and were deported by the British to the island of Roatan, off the coast of Honduras.

During the 1800s the Garifuna population again expanded and their settlements spread along the Caribbean coast of Central America from Nicaragua to Belize. By 1833, Dangriga (officially known as Stann Creek), their largest settlement in Belize, had been established. During the century that followed, fishing and farming were the primary modes of subsistence, with intermittent supplementary activities such as wage earning and small-scale marketing of produce and prepared foods. Some men migrated to other parts of the Caribbean area for short-term work while others went to England or to the United States (Gonzalez 1969). It appears that migration was confined to younger, unmarried men, most of whom returned with savings for their families and future households. By the 1950s increasing numbers of women also migrated and return-migration began to diminish. Violent hurricanes and a stagnant economy combined to limit economic growth in farming, fishing, and commerce. In addition, political and ethnic discrimination in Belize continue to undermine Garifuna economic development (Grant 1976). Gradually, the society has become increasingly dependent on sending its sons and daughters abroad.

### Migration and Contemporary Lifestyles

Current estimates of Garifuna migration from Honduras, Guatemala, and Belize to New York City alone place the total at 10,000 (Gonzalez 1979). The Los Angeles area has a community of similar size, and nearly 2000 more Garifuna are scattered among the cities of Boston, San Francisco, Chicago, Miami, Detroit, and New Orleans. Using Davidson's (1976) estimate made in 1974 of a total population of 77,000 Central American Garifuna, we must conclude that approximately 25 percent of the entire ethnic group presently resides in the United States. Examination of the population pyramid of 1970 for the Stann Creek district (where the largest Garifuna population in Belize is found) reveals a significant decrement for the 20–45 age group, with almost as many females missing as males (Central Planning Unit 1976). Whatever the actual statistics, the demographic shift has been very great and has affected the population structures of remaining Belizean Garifuna communities.

There are few local opportunities to earn wages. A minority of women, mostly past their childbearing years, tend gardens of ground foods (root crops) and fruit trees while raising their grandchildren or other youngsters. A few of the older men do the same, in addition to fishing. Local employment for women is available in small shops or within the limited range of services offered by the government. But low wages—typically, under BZE$40 (US$20) per month—and conflicts arising over child care usually combine to make this type of employment very short-term. Some women sell home-prepared foods and wines in small quantities on a daily basis. The majority, however, are dependent on cash and other contributions from husbands, "partners," and kin. Ultimately, the greater responsibility to raise cash rests with the adult male. For a 48-hour work week in 1979, a manual laborer on the government payroll earned BZE$58 (US$29), even after 30 years on the job. Agricultural laborers on hourly wages made even less. In the citrus industry, canning factory wages were BZE$1 per hour for men and BZE$0.78 per hour for women. Nonskilled laborers such as orange pickers are seasonal workers and are paid BZE$0.40 per box; it was possible in 1979 to make a maximum of BZE$8 per day as a nonskilled laborer. At the upper end of the socioeconomic hierarchy are people with steady, well-paying jobs in the United States and a few local entrepreneurs whose businesses have been built largely on capital raised in migrant labor. At the bottom of the hierarchy are households composed of women and children with no reliable male wage earner. In some villages and neighborhoods, this type of household predominates, creating pockets of great poverty.

The lifestyles today are more varied than those of the past. Wealth and status differentials are increasing, especially between migrants and those remaining behind. Yet many families are sustained by the constant flow of cash, goods, and opportunities for visiting offered by migrants. The pressure to share is buttressed by strong family obligations and ethnic pride. But the tensions between personal acquisition and generosity, factionalism and cohesive effort, continue to bedevil interpersonal relations. While an egalitarian ethic remains valued in "onstage" behavior, envy, gossip, and threats of revenge are regular features of "offstage" behavior. Accusations of selfishness, cheating, infidelity, theft, and even murder find customary expression in theories of disease etiology and belief in obeah (Coehlo 1955; Gonzalez 1970; Sanford 1979).

An increasing frequency of garden theft discourages greater investment in farming. The ever pressing need for cash has led to an almost complete disappearance of customary seafood exchanges between kin and neighbors. With fewer fishermen, the competition for fish is often acute, and it is not uncommon for a returning fisherman to be pressured into selling at the beachside, before reaching the market, by harangues reminding him of kinship or other obligations. Groups of drummers and dancers, who have probably always been rivalrous in the past, now compete bitterly for the few yearly opportunities to earn cash by performing. Voluntary associations, based on neighborhood, sex, or religious or political affiliation, vie for members, money, and recognition. The most acrimonious conflict occurs among kinswomen as they maneuver as individuals to secure the benefit of a single wage earner's generosity. The scarcity of jobs often leads to conflict between a man's wife, his sisters, and his mother, or among half-siblings of the same father. Ancestral cult activities, by contrast, involve families spanning the entire socioeconomic spectrum and associational memberships and thus work to draw conflict-ridden kindreds into cohesive units (for a more detailed discussion of the role of kinship in *dugu*, see Foster 1981).

### The Role of the buyai in Propagating dugu

The *dugu* is a complex two-week-long ceremony honoring the ancestors (consanguineal or affinal) of someone who has experienced a serious and disabling affliction, one that is untreatable by Western doctors. The role of the *buyai* (shaman) is of central importance in determining the size and frequency of *dugu*.

Most Garifuna, whether in Belize or in the United States, seek modern medical treatment. Often, herbal and patent medicines are tried first and a medical doctor is consulted only if these fail to cure the patient. If treatment is readily effected, it is concluded that the illness had a natural cause (i.e., was given by God). Suspicions are aroused, however, if a cure is not forthcoming or if the patient suffers a relapse, as in severe childhood malnutrition, diabetes, psychiatric syndromes, or other chronic diseases, or if major surgery is advised. Spirits, either ancestral or of a humanoid variety emanating from nature, soul loss, or obeah, may be suspected as the cause. By this stage of the illness, anxiety is quite noticeable. The patient, or a kinsman, may dream that a certain ancestor is asking to be fed, and this requires consultation with the *buyai*. Even those who do not have such dreams or who ordinarily shun ancestral cult activities are encouraged by friends and neighbors to consult the *buyai* when chronically or severely ill. After a diagnostic procedure that consists of a few questions, smoke, and candle divination, the *buyai* decides if there are signs to indicate that the illness may be caused by ancestral spirits. If there are not, herbal medicines, baths, and prayers may be prescribed; alternatively, the patient may be told to see another medical doctor, for which referrals and sometimes even the necessary cash are provided. If, however, the ancestors (*gubida*) are suspected, the *buyai* calls on his or her spirit helpers (*hiuruha*) and the offended ancestors are contacted and asked to reveal their demands.

There are several ways for a family to honor its ancestors. In some homes, food and drink are regularly offered. This, however, may not be enough. When serious illness strikes, larger rituals are called for, some entailing greater expense than others. If lesser rites have already been performed, or if the case is obviously critical, a *dugu* is usually demanded. Once a commitment has been made to sponsor a *dugu*, recovery should follow, allowing, for example, the individual to return to productive activities in order to amass sufficient resources by the appointed ritual date. This date is set for some future time, anywhere from a few months to more than a year later. Any one of four grades of *dugu* may be called for (ranking from one to four: *aba, biama, oruwa, gadurulumaragari*), and each grade requires increasing amounts of food, rum, money, and labor. The largest type of *dugu* is required when an entire family is threatened with recurrent illnesses and deaths. After such a fête is held, all obligations to the offended ancestors are discharged and they will not be heard from again.

The *buyai*'s spirit helpers convey the *gubida*'s dictates regarding who must attend the rituals. The principal participants are usually the patient and one or more close relatives (consanguineal or affinal) who are also deeply concerned about the ancestor's demands. These persons are known as the sponsors or the "owners" of the *dugu*. Another group of from 12 to 35 women (in the largest type of *dugu*, men are also included) is selected by the *buyai* in accordance with the *gubida*'s wishes. This group is known as the *afunahatiu*, or ritual kindred. Each of these women must contribute at least a fowl, cassava bread, sugar, candles, and rum; they must sleep in the temple (*dabuyaba*) during the ceremony and wear a specially made uniform dyed with annatto seeds. The term "ritual kindred" is used here because these core participants may not all recognize genealogical links to the patient (Foster 1981). Fictive kinship is utilized to more widely extend the network of support and redistribution.

Even though a single ancestor is considered responsible for the patient's illness, offerings are required for other key ancestors who might feel neglected and become jealous. These ancestral dead usually represent the paternal and maternal sides of the patient's family and may include distant affines. This feature not only extends the number of living descendants who must attend but substantially increases the amount of food offerings as well.

The *buyai* informs all concerned as to what they must contribute, what they should wear, who the ritual assistants will be (fishermen, drummers, slaughterers, cooks, and food couriers), how many dories should be sent to the cays for seafood, the number of pigs and chickens that must be sacrificed, how long the ceremony will continue, and whether a new temple must be built. Special requests for favorite foods may also be conveyed through the *buyai*. It is said that if turtle or other hard-to-find meat is required, the spirits will direct the fish or turtle right into the fisherman's net. All sacrificial animals must be raised by the sponsors or their designates. Pigs are named after the ancestors being fêted and are treated with special care, being fed, in some cases, prepared foods fit for human consumption. Pigs are always male and usually number between 2 and 6, while 1 or 2 cattle may also be demanded. Between 50 and 300 fowl (always roosters and occasionally a tom turkey) are usually sacrificed at *dugu*.

Although the number of shamans appears to be increasing, most Belizeans (and many Hondurans and Guatemalans as well) prefer the ministrations of a well-known woman in Dangriga. Belizean migrants in the United States declare that only the *buyai* in Dangriga is gifted enough to carry out the *dugu* properly. Several people in New York profess to be *buyainu* and are reportedly attracting clientele at prices as high as US$400. But their expertise is not widely accepted and they are not trusted to perform the *dugu*. Several other shamans are locally recognized throughout Central America, but they are likely to hold *dugu* for their own families only (Chamberlain 1979; Kerns 1983). No *dugu* rites have as yet been held in the United States, though attempts to do so may have been made (Chamberlain 1979:92).

All informants agree that there used to be very few *dugu*, often only one per year. In some villages decades would pass without a single *dugu*. Over the past decade they have increased in Belize to a high of 11 per year, with a mean of 8, all under the control of a single *buyai*. During 1979 and 1981, at least half of all *dugu* were largely financed by migrants working in the United States, and in most cases the patients themselves were U.S. residents. A *dugu* ranked as *oruwa lumaragari*, the largest one witnessed, was almost totally financed and attended by American Garifuna. During 1980 the *buyai* informed the community that her master spirit wanted no more than one *dugu* per month in the future. Although technically a *dugu* may be scheduled at any time during the year except the Lenten and Christmas seasons, the summer months (April through September) are the most popular as they explicitly accommodate the summer vacations of working migrants. Theologically, the Lenten and Christmas seasons must be avoided because the *buyai*'s spirit helpers spend these holidays elsewhere, making it impossible and even dangerous for the *buyai* to attempt healing at these times. Thus, the number of *dugu* held under the auspices of the main *buyai* in Dangriga should not exceed 6 per year. However, her master spirit also made it clear that should a new *buyai* emerge with the recognized capabilities to heal and to perform *dugu*, the number of rites may continue to increase. No such *buyai* had emerged by the summer of 1981, but the number of *dugu* had risen to 11.

Informants suggest several different reasons for the increased frequency of *dugu* over the past decade. Some maintain that many Garifuna families no longer make private offerings to their "old parents," thereby provoking greater retribution. Frequently it is pointed out that the present *buyai* is less frightened of the Catholic Church and medical authorities than were previous practitioners, who avoided larger, public ceremonies for lesser, private rites. One *buyai* claims that the recent proliferation of incompetent shamans has required frequent and repeated *dugu* for unhealed patients. Others suggest that the ancestors are witnessing increased accumulation of wealth within many households and simply want their share. On several occasions, sponsors of *dugu* mentioned that they had been saving money for a long-awaited trip, for roof repair, or for an educational course, when the *gubida* made it known that they wanted to feast. Interestingly, one informant suggested that the current practice of feeding almost all of the sacrificed food to the living is offensive to the *gubida*, who then demand more meals for themselves. Since it is the living who give voice to the wishes of the ancestors, increased demands for sharing are clearly an expression of contemporary social stresses.

### The Preparation and Organization of dugu

Although *dugu* is a healing ceremony with periods of solemnity, it is also a joyous occasion. Garifuna ancestral spirits are quite like their living descendants, enjoying nothing better than a fine party. Food, kinsmen, drumming, singing, rum, and *hiu* (a fermented drink made of parched cassava bread and sweet potatoes) must be plentiful to guarantee success. While the living extend invitations to their kinsmen and friends, the spirits do the same and many of each are expected to attend.

The force of belief in the power of the ancestors to punish nonparticipation in *dugu* is very strong. Even among doubters, threats from elders are usually sufficient to secure attendance or the sending of contributions. Tension between the living and the dead is, however, a feature of traditional Garifuna culture, and it would be misleading to convey the impression that all who are required to attend *dugu* actually do so. The cost and, for some, the embarrassment of being seen at the temple are prohibitive. Such persons are the subjects of countless stories that recall how they or their children subsequently suffer harshly for their lack of participation. Punitive trance is the most common penalty, one that cannot be escaped simply by moving to the United States. Garifuna residents of New York or California are frequently "lashed" by the *gubida* in the privacy of their homes or at their jobs. The absence of a favorite grandchild is also a common cause for concern. At the *arairaguni* (calling down the spirits), held after the main feast is over, the family may be told that the *dugu* was unacceptable and that they must repeat the entire ritual.

Components of the ritual include the sacrifice of live animals, the presentation of considerable amounts of food and rum, ancestral spirit possession, and extensive drumming, singing, and dancing, all of which would appear familiar to students of Afro-American religions (Herskovits 1964, 1971; Leacock and Leacock 1975; Smith 1962). In addition, especially in the realm of shamanism, there are noticeable similarities between Garifuna and related Arawakan- and Carib-speaking peoples (Colson 1977; Farabee 1918; Rouse 1963). For further details on *dugu* among the Garifuna, see Coehlo (1955), Foster (1981), Kerns (1983), Taylor (1951), and Wells (1980a).

Each phase of *dugu* preparation and performance is marked by ceremonies, most of which involve food, drink, and drumming. The *arairaguni* initiates the process in a seance with the *buyai*. In the *amainahani* (preparation of a farm for *dugu*), kinsmen are expected to join in the planting and harvesting. The sponsors reward the collective labor with food and drink. *Aruguhani* (inviting) takes place after the date for the ritual is set, with the sponsor and several kinswomen, at the sponsor's expense, traveling to all communities in which concerned relatives reside. When the building of a new temple (*dabuyaba*) is demanded, wood, thatch, and vines must be secured and men must be enjoined to labor on the building. Discrete events, such as thatching the roof or attaching the *dibase* (hammock shed), are commemorated with drumming, singing, food, and drink. Although a permanent temple has been available in Dangriga for nearly a decade, private, single-occasion temples are frequently desired by the ancestor spirits of the villagers. Recently, several villages have opted to build permanent temples of their own. An additional celebration is made of the last major cassava bread baking event before the feast begins. Women sing grating songs and enjoy a meal and drinks at the sponsor's expense.

The *abelagúdahani* (bringing it all in) begins with a procession of women bearing huge tubs of *areba* (cassava bread) into the temple, accompanied by drums and singing. This phase continues until all needed items are assembled. During this phase, the *adugahatiu* (ritual fishermen) are escorted to the beach by a colorful procession, with drums, where they are dispatched in dories to secure fish and shellfish. A similar procession welcomes their return three days later.

The *hedeweihan mutu* (people's gift) is the pork distribution. Following the ritual slaughter of the pigs, the *buyai* distributes the pork in the center of the temple at a table equipped with a scale. At one *dugu* witnessed in 1981, approximately 36 kg of raw pork (valued at BZE$200) was given to the drummers, cooks, ritual assistants, and nuns from the Catholic Church (a recent innovation by the present *buyai*).

Essential ingredients of the ritual, without which a *dugu* cannot take place, include *areba, hiu*, strong raw rum, seafood, fowl, candles, drums, and costumes. Much variation exists beyond these items. In fact, there is such variability in *dugu* proceedings that few ethnographers have ever reported identical rites. Of late, the typical *dugu* in Belize includes about 60 hours of almost continuous dancing and singing, in the middle of which tables are set with food for the ancestors. In a larger *dugu* tables are filled with food on three consecutive days and dancing is not concluded until the fifth day.

Although only *afunahatiu* (ritual kindred) are absolutely required to bring offerings, other women may also make sacrifices to their own ancestors. These bowls and plates of food are set up around the main table and are later returned to their donors, who, in turn, are supposed to feed the needy with them. Today, many such offerings are actually eaten by the donors' families. Alternatively, these women may give some or all of their food to a central offering tub, which is later buried as a final sacrifice to the ancestors who did not attend. Each bowl offered in this way must be accompanied by a small fee for the temple.

Food preparations are extensive. Although emphasis is on traditional dishes, newer foods are not excluded. Morning meals (*bacháti*) of yeast or fried breads and heavily sugared coffee (sometimes made of parched ground rice or yama bush seeds) are regularly served to hundreds of people. A full meal, including meat, is not served until the first feast is prepared for the ancestors, although participants may request drinks and snacks at any time. After a full day of cooking, all is readied for the feast. Large pans and tubs filled with boiled chicken, stewed and fried fish, boiled conch, crabs, pounded plantains (*hudút*), sweet rice pudding (*bimekakule*), rice and beans, pork stewed in *recado*,[3] fish and green bananas in coconut milk (*tapáu*), a variety of porridges, and many other dishes, are brought from the kitchen and displayed. Migrants often bring food from the United States as well, such as chocolate cake, hams, liqueurs, salt cod, and candies. These different foods are then dished out in generous servings and the *adagaragúdahani* (setting of the table) begins. Each table (*madúdu*) is dedicated to one side of the family and is covered first with banana leaves and set with many pieces of *areba*. Plates of food are stacked four or five layers high, with each layer representing a single generation. An entire fowl must be offered for each sibling in the oldest generation represented. Other dishes, including pigs' heads, are placed on the floor for those ancestors too old or too small to reach the food on the table. Several sets of clothing, tobacco, and toiletry articles are laid out for the ancestors' use. While the living are served a full meal, the tables are left untouched for four to six hours, allowing the "old parents" to enjoy their feast in peace.

Following this phase is the *abayuhani* (pillaging), the only ceremony especially for children. Any child from the community may bring a bowl to be filled with generous portions of pork or chicken and rice (*hudút*), or another starchy food. From the center of the temple the *buyai* personally serves each child with an almost uncanny ability to estimate the number of children crowding around the temple and the amount of food in the tubs before her. Older customs of placing the food on leaves on the floor and having the children rush in and scramble for it (Taylor 1951) are no longer practiced. Whereas children were once kept away from the temple during most of the *dugu*, their presence is increasing noticeably. Many youngsters now enter ritual roles, including that of *afunahatiu* and trance possession. In town, between 65 and 80 children are usually fed at each *dugu*; in the villages the average is about 30. The typical diet of many Garifuna youngsters barely reaches the minimal daily requirement for energy maintenance and is clearly insufficient for normal growth. There can be little doubt that a full bowl of food (always including a sizeable portion of meat) given out during the pillaging is a welcome addition to an otherwise meager diet.

The remainder of the food from the tables is eaten by participants as well as delivered to certain old and needy people in the community. In 1979, 15 elderly people were brought covered plates of food by special couriers who were, as required, beyond the age of menopause or under the age of menarche. All *hiu* and rum must be drunk or used for massage of the head and neck, and all food must be distributed before the end of the feast. In larger *dugu* rites the food distributions discussed above are repeated daily for two or three days. Any cash deposited in the offering gourd and not used for supplies during the ceremony is donated to the hospital auxiliary fund.

### The Cost of dugu

The cost of *dugu* in Belizean terms is very high, if somewhat difficult to assess with precision. Cash outlay is usually greatest for the sponsor (or sponsors). In 1979, sponsors who were interviewed stated that their costs ranged between BZE$700 and BZE$1000. In 1981 reported figures ranged between BZE$1800 and BZE$2400. To this cost migrants must add the price of several trips to Belize, since diagnosis cannot take place over long distances. At one *dugu* witnessed in 1981, the airfares for those coming from New York City alone amounted to BZE$12,000. Additional cash outlay is required for the feeding of pigs and chickens, long-distance telephone calls, and numerous other items needed in preparation for the ceremony. The cost of travel for certain important participants also may have to be guaranteed by the sponsor. One American Garifuna who sponsored a *dugu* in 1981 stated he had spent US$6000, although the affair had been substantially supported by his siblings as well.

Table 1. Cost of *dugu* ceremonies in Belize in 1979 (in BZE$).[a]

|  | *Dugu* A (June) | | *Dugu* B (August) | |
| --- | --- | --- | --- | --- |
| Cassava bread | 30 pans @ 14.00 | 420.00 | 48 pans @ 14.00 | 672.00 |
| Rice | 30 lb @ .42 | 12.60 | 25 lb @ .42 | 10.50 |
| Flour, sack | 96 lb | 32.00 | 96 lb | 32.00 |
| Sugar | 45 lb @ .18 | 8.10 | 75 lb @ .18 | 13.50 |
| Coconuts | 10 @ .60 | 6.00 | 15 @ .60 | 9.00 |
| Limes | 24 | 1.60 | 48 | 1.60 |
| Sweet potato | 7 lb @ .40 | 2.80 | 14 lb @ .40 | 5.60 |
| Eggs | 12 | 2.80 | 12 | 3.00 |
| *Recado* | 4 pkg @ .75 | 3.00 | 6 pkg @ .75 | 4.50 |
| Coconut oil | 1 qt | 2.50 | 1 qt | 2.50 |
| Coffee/coffee beans | | 20.00 | | 25.00 |
| Mangos | | 2.00 | | 3.00 |
| Plantains | 30 | 7.50 | 30 | 7.50 |
| Green bananas | 2 hands | .50 | 3 hands | .75 |
| Pigs | 2 @ 40.00 | 80.00 | 2 @ 40.00 | 80.00 |
| Fish | 60 lb @ .70 | 42.00 | 120 lb @ .70 | 84.00 |
| Crabs | 1.5 bu | 12.00 | 2 bu | 16.00 |
| Ginger | 1 lb @ .80 | .80 | 2 lb @ .80 | 1.60 |
| Onions | 10 lb @ .60 | 6.00 | 10 lb @ .60 | 6.00 |
| Fowl | 50 @ 4.30 | 215.00 | 25 bought/died | 20.00 |
| | | | 38 @ 4.30 | 163.40 |
| Cokes, Fanta | | 5.00 | | 3.00 |
| Rum, case | | 36.00 | | 36.00 |
| Rum, offerings | | 180.00 | | 300.00 |
| Cigarettes | | 11.00 | | 11.00 |
| Candles | | 15.00 | | 15.00 |
| Annatto seed dye | | 5.00 | | 8.00 |
| Cloth | | 425.00 | | 300.00 |
| Dory rental | 1 | 10.00 | 2 | 20.00 |
| Firewood | | 25.00 | | 40.00 |
| Drummers | | 120.00 | | 120.00 |
| *Buyai* | | 60.00 | | 60.00 |
| Turkey | | 12.00 | | |
| Salt cod | 3 lb | 12.00 | | |
| Chocolate cake | | 10.00 | | |
| Wine | | 10.00 | | |
| Liquor | | 12.00 | | |
| Oatmeal | | | 10 lb @ 2.00 | 20.00 |
| Canned milk | | | 6 cans @ .72 | 4.32 |
| Sweet breads | | | 12 | 12.00 |
| Anisette | | | | 10.00 |
| | | BZE$1858.80 | | BZE$2087.77 |

|  | Dugu A (June) |  | Dugu B (August) |  |
|---|---|---|---|---|
| If the value of the dressed pork products is added instead of the cost of pigs, then |  |  |  |  |
| Pork | 80 lb @ 1.60 | 128.00 | 90 lb @ 1.60 | 144.00 |
| Lard | 15 lb @ .25 | 2.75 | 15 lb @ .25 | 2.75 |
| Morcia[b] | 10 lb | 10.00 | 10 lb | 10.00 |
| Chicharrones[c] | 15 lb | 5.00 | 15 lb | 5.00 |
|  |  | BZE$ 145.75 |  | BZE$ 161.75 |
| Expenses above less cost of pigs | (80.00) | 1778.80 | (80.00) | 2007.77 |
| Total |  | BZE$1924.55 |  | BZE$2169.52 |

[a]BZE$1.00 = US$0.50
[b]Morcia is a blood sausage made without the use of intestines as a container.
[c]Chicharrones are cracklin's, the fried residue of pork fat.

Table 1 lists the types and quantities of foods, goods, and services observed during two ceremonies in 1979. All items and services are listed at local prices for 1979. Dugu A was sponsored by a woman and her husband who had been living in New York City for about ten years. Both had well-paying jobs in large U.S. corporations and had invested in property in both New York and Dangriga. They remained in close contact with their kin in Belize, and international visits took place regularly among family members. Dugu B was given by a local woman who, as an only child raised by her grandmother, had a more restricted kin network on which to draw. Her sole source of support was her only child, a daughter working in California. It is significant that the list of afunahatiu given to this woman by the buyai included women whom the sponsor never reckoned as kin. These women participated, claiming that "sometimes dugu reveals our relatives to us." This dugu was funded almost totally by the working daughter. Both ceremonies were of the second grade (biama lumaragari), with only one day of food offerings, and both were held in the permanent temple in Dangriga.

In addition to food and rum, uniforms constitute a major expense at dugu. Each member of the afunahatiu must receive a new tailored outfit at the sponsor's expense. A special gusewe-dyed (see note 3) uniform, which the afunahatiu must obtain themselves, is also required. These can be rented or purchased but can never be worn a second time by the same woman. Each type of uniform costs about BZE$25. The cooks, and sometimes the buyai herself, must also be supplied with a second tailored outfit. At one dugu in 1981 the cost of these uniforms totaled BZE$1000.

The fishermen (adugahatiu), cooks, drummers, and ritual assistants are paid in pork, receiving about 1–1.5 kg each. All supplies, including dories, must be provided by the sponsor. Firewood and transportation of needed items from distant villages must be obtained. Drummers usually number from six to eight and receive cash and rum in addition to pork. The "heart drummer," a spirit-called role, leads much of the singing and receives double the amount paid to his sidemen (BZE$40 and BZE$20, respectively, in 1979). At some *dugu* there may be two or more "heart drummers" working in shifts of three at a time. A pint of very strong rum, locally dubbed "kill me quick," or "wash me dead," is shared by the trio of drummers after every performance of the *amalihani*, or *mali*, a complex ritual dance of great significance to the *dugu*. Since there may be as many as 30 or more *mali* performed at a single *dugu*, the drummers take the surplus rum home or drink it with their friends. Fees for the *buyai* in 1979 averaged BZE$60 and had risen in 1981 to BZE$80. At a very large *dugu* (*oruwa lumaragari*) in 1981, composed chiefly of U.S. residents, the *buyai* was paid BZE$150.

### The Image and Purpose of dugu

Sacrifice is the theological theme of *dugu*, but many local residents of Belize consider the ceremony to be a terrible waste of money. Outsiders are told it is a "Devil Dance" and that the food is thrown away. Some persons who are ethnically Garifuna but who do not participate in cult activities disdain the *dugu*. Many people over the age of 30 were beaten and ridiculed as children by nuns, priests, and schoolteachers for being seen at the temple. Decades ago, oppression was so great in Honduras that *dugu* were conducted in secret (Coehlo 1955). While active oppression has diminished, prejudice remains.

About 13.5–18 kg of generally inedible items—waste from fermenting the *hiu*; *areba* from beneath the piles of plates on the tables; the pigs' heads, feet, and offal; a few Cokes; and wet cigarettes—are discarded after each *dugu*. These are deposited in a hole by the sea, sometime before dawn, as a final sacrifice to the ancestors.

It seems likely that the great sacrifice that characterizes *dugu* results in material benefits, not losses. The flow of cash and food emanating from the *dugu* and the manner in which these are obtained reaches a large number of Garifuna households. Even non-Garifuna shopkeepers benefit as several hundred migrants return each summer for these ceremonies, buying film, drinks, local crafts, and sundry items. A conservative estimate of BZE$1500 per rite, when multiplied by an average of eight rites per year in the Dangriga area, yields BZE$12,000 brought into the area yearly, largely by U.S. migrants and their kin. This sum is equivalent to the annual spending power of 10 to 12 permanently employed wage earners.

Medical care, especially if a successful cure ensues, is also a material benefit of *dugu*. In almost every case the patient has spent a considerable sum of money seeking medical care elsewhere before turning to the *buyai*. Many have spent thousands of dollars and months in hospitals as far away as Jamaica, the United States, or Mexico. Inadequate medical care in Belize may not be the only reason for this: medical care is also frequently ineffective among migrants living in the United States. Observation reveals that this is sometimes due to poor understanding of the U.S. medical care delivery system and frequent mishandling of prescription drugs. For others, especially those with life-altering conditions such as coronary heart disease, recovery is marred by the difference in etiological premises between Western biomedicine and traditional Garifuna medical thought. Informants in New York repeatedly tell of U.S. doctors instructing their Garifuna patients to "find a doctor of your own culture." Those who seek psychiatric help are usually given tranquilizers, are seldom offered cohesive therapy, and are likely to prefer the aid of the *buyai*. In return for their financial contributions, migrants who sponsor *dugu* are given the full medical support of the *buyai*, the emotional support of family and friends, and the supernatural support of the ancestors.

There is ample evidence that the Garifuna are themselves cognizant of diminishing resources. Recent unpredictable events, such as layoffs in the United States and postal strikes in Belize, have reminded those dependent on remittances of the precariousness of their situation. One steady wage earner in the United States may have as many as six or seven dependents in Belize waiting for a postal check. Restrictive immigration quotas and the recent influx of an estimated 10,000 Salvadoreans heighten competition for the few jobs available locally. Any pressure that can be brought to bear on wealthier kinsmen to share whatever resources are available has adaptive value.

The *dugu*, as a redistributive feast, serves that purpose nicely. Productive activities are intensified for the period of preparation. Food and goods are transported from distant places and then dispensed locally. Reciprocal family obligations are emphasized and even extended through fictive kinship, making it more difficult to refuse mutual aid in the future. Inheritance rights are implicitly reaffirmed, keeping alive the cherished hope of most migrants: eventual return to Belize. Cash flow from workers abroad is stimulated and the economic boost of summer tourism is experienced in the Dangriga area. The increased presence of children is encouraged by the present *buyai* in hopes of guaranteeing the continuation of ancestral cult activities. Several villages have recently begun to build their own permanent temples to draw the benefits of *dugu* to their locales. The *buyai* recruitment process actively continues and new *buyai* hold smaller *dugu* yearly. The chief *buyai* has set the scene for flexible interpretation of the need for *dugu* and its elaborateness. As a focus for the ritual propagation of Garifuna identity, the *dugu* forms a link between migrants and their home communities, as well as a conduit through which a significant amount of real and potential resources flows.

An increasing number of Garifuna children who are born and reared in the United States no longer speak Garifuna and have never witnessed an ancestral rite. At the same time, many children born in Belize have little hope of a steady, healthy diet. The contrast helps to explain the continuance of the ceremony. The

future of *dugu* ceremonialism may ultimately rest with the willingness of the society's more productive members to invest their hard-earned capital in the ritual
reaffirmation of their identity as Garifuna.

## Notes

The fieldwork on which this study is based took place in Belize in 1979 (May to September) and again in 1981 (June to September). Further fieldwork among migrants in the
United States was conducted in 1980 (July and August) and again in 1981 (April and May).

1. Garifuna is the term used to refer to the language, the culture, or an individual; the
plural form is Garinagu. So as to avoid confusing the reader, Garifuna is used throughout
the paper.

2. While accurate in a broad sense, the class situation in Belize is considerably more
complex. In the north, some Maya families have recently experienced rising incomes due
to the cash cropping of sugar. A few Garifuna have also achieved high-status employment
in Belize, and some Creole and mestizo families are as poor as many Maya and Garifuna
families. Ritual responses to poverty among other Belizeans have not been reported.

3. *Recado* (*recardo* in Creole) is a Spanish seasoning, sometimes referred to as *achiote*,
made by combining the seed covers of the annatto (*Bixa orellana*) with other spices. The
red color of the seed cover is also the source of *gusewe* dye among the Garifuna.

## References

Ashcraft, Norman
    1972        Economic Opportunities and Patterns of Work: The Case of British
                Honduras. Human Organization 31(4):425–433.

Brockmann, C. Thomas
    1977        Ethnic and Racial Relations in Northern Belize. Ethnicity 4:246–262.

Caribbean Food and Nutrition Institute
    1979        Programs and Projects for Improving the Belize Food and Nutrition
                Situation with Particular Reference to the Agricultural Sector. Kings-
                ton: CFNI.

Central Planning Unit
    1976        Abstract of Statistics. Belmopan: Government Printers.

Chamberlain, Cynthia
    1979        Ritual Possession Trance and Ancestor Illness among the Garifuna of
                Honduras: An Analysis of the *Gubida* Cult. M.A. thesis, Department
                of Geography and Anthropology, Louisiana State University.

Chun, Kyung-Soo
    1980        Ancestor Worship and Nutrition in a Korean Village. Paper pre-
                sented at the 79th Annual Meeting of the American Anthropological
                Association, Washington, DC.

Coehlo, Roy Galvao de Andrade
1955        The Black Carib of Honduras: A Study in Acculturation. Ph.D disser-
            tation, Department of Anthropology, Northwestern University.
Colson, Audrey Butt
1977        The Akawaio Shaman. *In* Carib-speaking Indians. Ellen Basso, ed.
            pp. 43–65. Tucson: University of Arizona Press.
Cosminsky, Sheila
1976        Carib-Creole Relations in a Belizean Community. *In* Frontier Adap-
            tations in Lower Central America. Mary Helms and F. Loveland,
            eds. pp. 95–114. Philadelphia: ISHI.
Davidson, William V.
1976        Black Carib (Garifuna) Habitats in Central America. *In* Frontier Ad-
            aptations in Lower Central America. Mary Helms and F. Loveland,
            eds. pp. 85–94. Philadelphia: ISHI.
Farabee, W. C.
1918        The Central Arawaks. Museum Publications in Anthropology No. 9.
            Philadelphia: University of Pennsylvania.
Ford, R. I.
1971        An Ecological Perspective of the Eastern Pueblos. *In* New Perspec-
            tives on the Pueblos. A. Ortiz, ed. pp. 1–17. Albuquerque: University
            of New Mexico Press.
Foster, Byron
1981        Body, Soul and Social Structure at the Garifuna *Dugu.* Belizean
            Studies 9(4):1–11.
Gonzalez, Nancie Solien
1969        Black Carib Household Structure. Seattle: University of Washington
            Press.
1970        Obeah and Other Witchcraft among the Black Caribs. *In* Systems of
            North American Witchcraft and Sorcery. Deward Walker, ed. pp. 95–
            108. Anthropological Monographs of the University of Idaho, No. 1.
            Boise.
1979        Garifuna Settlement in New York. International Migration Review
            13(2):255–263.
Grant, C. H.
1976        The Making of Modern Belize. Cambridge: Cambridge University
            Press.
Gueri, Miguel
1981        Childhood Malnutrition in the Caribbean. Bulletin of the Pan
            American Health Organization 15(2):160–167.
Gullick, C. J. M. R.
1979        The Black Caribs of St. Vincent: The Carib War and Aftermath. *In*
            Actes du Congres International des Americanistes XLII, Vol. 6, pp.
            451–465. Paris: Musée d'Homme.

Herskovits, Melville, and Frances Herskovits
    1964        Trinidad Village. New York: Octagon Books.
    1971        Rebel Destiny. Freeport, NY: Books for Libraries Press.

Howard, Michael
    1980        Ethnicity and Economic Integration in Southern Belize. Ethnicity
                7:119–136.

Jenkins, Carol L.
    1980        Patterns of Protein-Energy Malnutrition among Preschoolers in
                Belize. Ph.D. dissertation. Department of Anthropology, University
                of Tennessee, Knoxville.
    1981        Patterns of Growth and Malnutrition among Preschoolers in Belize.
                American Journal of Physical Anthropology 56:169–178.

Kerns, Virginia
    1983        Women and the Ancestors: Black Carib Kinship and Ritual. Urbana:
                University of Illinois Press.

Leacock, Seth, and Ruth Leacock
    1975        Spirits of the Deep. A Study of an Afro-Belizean Cult. New York:
                Anchor/Doubleday.

Netting, Robert McC.
    1972        Sacred Power and Centralization: Aspects of Political Adaptation in
                Africa. In Population Growth: Anthropological Implications. Brian
                Spooner, ed. pp. 219–244. Cambridge: MIT Press.

Palacio, Joseph
    1973        Carib Ancestral Rites: A Brief Analysis. National Studies (Belize)
                1(3):3–8.

Piddocke, S.
    1965        The Potlatch System of the Southern Kwakiutl. A New Perspective.
                Southwestern Journal of Anthropology 21:244–264.

Rappaport, Roy
    1968        Pigs for the Ancestors. New Haven: Yale University Press.

Richardson, Bonham
    1981        Migration and Death Ceremonies on St. Kitts and Nevis. Journal of
                Cultural Geography 1(2):1–11.

Rouse, Irving
    1963        The Arawak. In The Handbook of South American Indians. Vol.
                4. Julian Steward, ed. pp. 507–546. New York: Cooper Square Pub-
                lishers.

Sanford, Margaret
    1974        Revitalization Movements as Indicators of Completed Acculturation.
                Comparative Studies in Society and History 16(4):504–518.
    1979        Disease and Folk-Curing among the Garifuna of Belize. In Actes du
                Congres International des Americanistes XLII, Vol. 6, pp. 553–560.
                Paris: Musée d'Homme.

Shephard, Charles
    1971[1831]    An Historical Account of the Island of St. Vincent's. London: Frank
                  Cass and Co.
Smith, M. G.
    1962          Kinship and Community in Carriacou. New Haven: Yale University
                  Press.
Stavrakis, Olga
    1979          The Effect of Agricultural Change upon Social Relations in a Vil-
                  lage in Northern Belize, Central America. Ph.D. dissertation, Univer-
                  sity of Minnesota.
Taylor, Douglas
    1951          The Black Carib of British Honduras. Viking Fund Publication in
                  Anthropology, No. 17. New York: Wenner-Gren Foundation.
Wells, Marilyn M.
    1980a         Circling with the Ancestors: Hugulendii Symbolism in Ethnic
                  Group Maintenance. Belizean Studies 8(6):1–9.
    1980b         Dugu, Feast for the Ancestors: The Role of an Identity Symbol in
                  Status Politics. Paper presented at 8th Annual Conference on Ethnic
                  and Minority Studies, La Crosse, WI.
Young, Sir William
    1971[1795]    An Account of the Black Charaibs in the Island of St. Vincent's. Lon-
                  don: Frank Cass and Co.

# 6. RITUAL ENACTMENT OF SEX ROLES IN THE PACIFIC LOWLANDS OF ECUADOR-COLOMBIA

## Norman E. Whitten, Jr.

Probably every Euro-American scholar to work in a black, or Afro-American, community in Latin America or the Caribbean has experienced what he regarded as exotic and prosaic rituals. The exotic all too often was classed as "sacred" and the prosaic as "mundane." Prosaic ritual received relatively less attention than the exotic, and even where exotic ritual was found to be secular, many investigators groped for evidence of past cults. The literature on Afro-American ritual life is full of the results of searches for syncretism, retention, and reinterpretation of "exotic" African forms, and is deficient in a portrayal of the range of ritual life in contemporary settings. Furthermore, the anthropological search for exotic, distinctive ritual features of ethnic units in complex societies often obscures the importance of all ritual behavior in the lives of the participants.

This paper is written as a deliberate attempt to merge the analysis of exotic and prosaic, distinctive and non-distinctive ritual with a discussion of social structure. I focus on one structural feature—sex roles.[1] Other features such as consanguinity, affinity, group formation, network maintenance, rank, stratification, and mobility are discussed in Whitten (1974).

In order to merge the study of social and ritual forms in Afro-American systems of adaptation, still more clarification is needed. Hannerz (1970: 314) recently summarized the failure of anthropology really to discuss sex roles at all in Afro-American cultures when he wrote:

> Most of what has been said about the sex roles of New World black people can find its place in one of three perspectives [represented by the work of Melville Herskovits (cf. 1941, 1943), E. Franklin Frazier (cf. 1932, 1934, 1939, 1942, 1949), and Raymond T. Smith (cf. 1956, 1963)] . . . this means that the studies only marginally involve the discussion of sex roles per se, as they are first of all studies of the family or household as an institution.

The institutional set of activities discussed as "family and household" has also been considerably garbled until recently, due to persistent failure of many scholars to distinguish the domains of activity referred to. González (1970: 223–232) recently clarified our approach to these domains:

Originally published in *Ethnology* 13:2 (1974), 129–43. Reprinted by permission of the publisher.

I suggest that we reserve the term "household" for the cooperative group which maintains and participates in a given *residential* structure, even though the contribution of any one individual may be only part time . . .

"Family" seems most usefully defined in terms of kinship networks; that is, in terms of the kinds of kinship bonds among the different individuals considered to be members of the unit.[2]

We must clearly distinguish the concepts "household" and "kinship network" from one another, and we must not automatically and unquestionably assume that they belong to the same domain of activity. I seek to understand sex roles as a component of social structure related to household, kinship, and other domains. With such clarity we should now be able to devise techniques for assembling data which will lead to a productive set of concepts about any particular Afro-American, or any other, style of life. In this paper I propose to illustrate an approach which allows for considerable synthesis of materials from various domains, and which also serves to document the breadth and complexity of one particular sex role system viewed through several ritual settings.

The area I am discussing includes the Pacific Lowland rainforest which extends from Buenaventura, west-central Colombia, to Esmeraldas, northern Ecuador.[3] The activity patterns are manifested by black people constituting the lower class in any town.[4] In this area somewhere over half a million black people make up 90 per cent or more of the population. They share a set of activities, institutions, and beliefs which are quite apparent in both secular and sacred ritual contexts. I wish to describe variations in sex role enactment in some of the ritual contexts, and to suggest the relationship of such enactment to household, kinship, community, and inter-community continuity. I refer to the structure which emerges from an analysis of contextually patterned complementary and contrastive role relationships as "Afro-Hispanic culture." I shall outline three secular contexts of sex role enactment, insert a brief discussion of some aspects of Afro-Hispanic world view in relationship to daily life, present three sacred ritual contexts, and finally indicate the relationship of ritual enactment to social structural continuity.

*Secular Contexts of Sex Role Enactment*

THE CANTINA CONTEXT

The setting is a small room in which from two to eight men gather, day or night, to drink *aguardiente* (rum) and engage in ritual exchanges of songs, riddles, *décimas*, and stories. They tell exaggerated tales of politics, travel, and sexual exploits, and relate events involving demons, phantom ships, spirits, and souls of the deceased. Children may sit on the outer steps listening, and other men and women usually loiter nearby, also listening to the stylized conversations within.

Music does not dominate this setting. When it is played it is almost always either a Mexican *ranchero*, or a ballad from the highlands of Ecuador (in Ecuador) or in a style associated with an inland area of Colombia (in Colombia). The musical aspect signals national or international identification, but the non-musical content expressed is, on the whole, characteristic of Afro-Hispanic culture. It consists of traits either not found in the interior of Colombia or Ecuador, or found in different forms, with quite different meanings.

In the *cuentos*, or stylized stories, one man relates a tale known to the others, but always with his own elaboration. The speaker endeavors to establish deep emotional tone through onomatopoeia; he imitates animals, demons, spirits, and human sounds of agony and ecstasy. Three themes dominate: extensive travel, great bouts of interpersonal combat, and amazing feats of sexual intercourse. In all cases elaborate intrigue characterizes the plot. Political discussions are greatly stylized and never fall to the level of local events; rather, high levels of national and foreign governments are elaborately described. Fear of the unknown is also communicated in this secular ritual setting, always together with means for combating the manifestations which the unknown may take at a particular time. It is in this setting that one may learn the most about the fearful creatures known as *visiones* (ghosts and spirits), *brujas* (witch-ghouls), and *brujos* (diviner-sorcerers). In all cases means of overcoming the fearful creatures through direct male physical force, proper diagnosis by men, or male trickery is stressed. Male strength, wit, and planning over female, spirit, and super-male adversaries pervade all the stories.

In the *décima*, men recite memorized poems, competing with others who may know the poem for accuracy, while in the *adivinanzas* (riddles) individuals again express their self assertion against other men, trying reciprocally to present a riddle that cannot be answered by anyone in the setting, or by answering someone else's riddle. There are enough modes of expression through the *décimas, cuentos*, brags of successful encounters with powerful adversaries or sexual exploits, and stories of inside knowledge of foreign governments so that each individual finds some mode of self assertion of his male attributes.

"Truth" has no place in the cantina context. Men pass information of emotional tone and potential social complexity, but they do not pass accurate information about economic, political, or social events. The context, it seems, asserts the primacy of the male individual in the competitive dyad: man against man, man against spirit, or man against any system.

THE SALOON CONTEXT

The saloon context takes place at night. It depends upon music, without which none of the ritual behavior described below takes place. The music is national, featuring vivacious coastal music such as *cumbia, gaita, merecumbea*, or *guaracha*, interspersed with slower *boleros, valsas*, and *rancheros*. I have described this context elsewhere (Whitten 1968). Men dominate women in the setting and use women to help solidify male-male dyads, forming chains of co-operative male associations on which any person depends for aid in work-a-day life. The idiom of kinship usually expresses such a male dyadic chain.

Groups of men actually working together sit and drink together. From time to time, one member of the group asks a woman to dance and takes her to another man in his work group, offering him the dance requested of the woman. Men not working together sit apart, or stand outside, and periodically invite a woman to dance with another man. The recipient is then obligated to close the exchange by ritual return of an acceptable token, or, as the donor prefers, to reciprocate with some form of aid at a later date.

A man who wishes to initiate sexual relations with a woman should approach the woman as she arrives at the saloon. He moves rapidly toward her walking in time to the music, swinging his arms with palms facing straight back, smiling broadly. This signals his intention not only to the woman but to all others within viewing distance. He asks her to dance with him, and during the dance makes his proposition. She may refuse to dance, or refuse when he asks her to spend the night with him; by saying nothing she consents. It is not uncommon for sexual unions, publicly signalled in this manner in a saloon, to continue, often eventuating in marriage.

Two important social adjustments relating to sex roles are enacted in the saloon context: (1) the solidifying of male social relationships (dyads and networks) through the ritual giving and lending of dance partners and alcohol, and (2) actual male-initiated household rearrangement as men begin to establish a new sexual partnership. In the saloon context ritualized male activity signals continuity in male co-operation, and the practical prerogative of men to move from one sex partner to another. Both male-male dyads and male-female dyads are expressed as co-operative, but the latter are male initiated.

## THE CURRULAO CONTEXT

The secular *currulao* or marimba dance (*baile marimba*) is performed every Saturday night on hinterland rivers, and in the all black *barrios* of large towns, but more sporadically in the smaller, less segregated towns. It provides a context in which males express assertiveness, while women express female dominance; neither male nor female sex role dominates the other, although a symbolic arena of competition pervades all aspects of ritual activity.

The *currulao* takes place in a special house—*casa de la marimba*—which contains the marimba, two large base drums (*bombos*), and two conical single-headed drums (*cununos*). It is necessary to sketch the musicians to understand the interplay between expressive roles. There are two *marimberos* who play the marimba—the *bordonero* who plays the melody, and the *tiplero* who plays a harmony. Two *bomberos* and *cununeros* accompany the marimba. A *glosador* sings the improvised verses while facing three female chorus singers, in two roles—one *solista*, or lead chorus maker, and two *bajoneras*, who harmonize with her and maintain the chorus which the *solista* begins. Two primary triads are at work in the development of marimba music. The first is formed by *bordonero* with lead *bombero* and *glosador*, the second by *solista* with lead *cununero* and *bajoneras*. The *tiplero* and other two drummers take their cues from the interplay between the two triads. The two primary triads are in continuous antagonism to one another, the antagonism expressing sex role competition over initiation of an action sequence.

The *bordonero* sets the melody and the lead *bombero* joins him; they rehearse most of an afternoon before a dance, with various *cununeros*, alter *bomberos*, and *tipleros* fitting their parts to the dominant melody and rhythm. In the towns where formal permission is necessary to hold the *currulao*, women make the arrangements. In the evening the male members of the marimba band begin to play. Men and women arrive, the men taking seats and the women greeting one another, talking loudly, and ignoring the men. Some women go through a few dance steps with one another. When the *respondedoras* arrive they move into the circle of drums, shake the tube-shakers (*guasás*) which they have brought with them, and sing a chorus of a favorite tune while the drummers and *marimberos* strengthen their beats and become more redundant. More women dance with women.

Next the *glosador* enters, standing next to the *bordonero*. The women start singing; he looks at them, listens, and then enters with a long falsetto *grito*, or call, breaking in on the chorus being sung by the *respondedoras*, and calling them to sing and to listen to him. Next he moves to a verse, which the *respondedoras* answer with a set chorus. At this time the two antagonistic triads within the marimba dance form.

Women dancers move toward men, asking them to dance. They may break their own pair and each invite a man, or the two women dancing together move toward one man, and both dance with him. A man who wishes to dance signals by standing erect, handkerchief in right hand hanging gently over his right shoulder. The woman holds her skirt slightly out to one side, swings her handkerchief from side to side, and in a distinct dance step bearing no resemblance to saloon dancing, approaches the man. The woman steadily advances, pivots, retreats, while the man becomes more excited, leaps into the air, stamps his feet in time with the *bombo*, shouts, and waves his handkerchief or hat. He may even open his arms as if to grab the woman, but as she turns to him, he retreats. (See Whitten and Fuentes 1966, Whitten 1968, Friedemann and Morales 1966–1969.)

The ambience is always tense. It is part of the relationship between *glosador* and *solista*, each the apex of an antagonistic triad of performers. The *glosador* leads in singing his verses, and the *respondedoras* harmonize with his long notes. But the chorus following the *glosador*'s verse is usually in contradiction to the intent of his verse. As the *glosador* sings and yodels about going on a trip, leaving a woman, injuring women through his great penis, or becoming the devil, the women sing back that their own men are being held or that they are not losing their men, allude to the venereal diseases in other women, and tell how the marimba chases the devil away. The music and voices get louder and louder, and the *respondedoras* and *glosador* begin to sing their phrases simultaneously, until finally all words dissolve into an intricate harmonic structure of yodels, falsettos, and glissandos up and down the scale. The *respondedoras* inevitably "win" in their struggle for dominance with the *glosador*. Before the end of the song they are loudly singing the choruses and may even take over some verses. As this happens the *glosador* may walk away from the marimba to have a drink or to dance. The music continues until the women stop singing. However, if they wait too long he may return and trick them by beginning yet another song, giving the women no rest and exhausting those particular *respondedoras*. There are many other patterns, which symbolize the same male-female struggle for initiation of a consequential set of actions. Here I have only sketched the most common *bambuco* pattern.[5]

The *currulao* normally lasts until dawn, but it may go on for two or three days. Seldom does a *currulao* end until the dancers and musicians are in a state of exhaustion, too tired to continue. By this time the singers have completely lost their voices. All participants return to their own homes, to their own spouses. Unlike the saloon context, no rearrangement of sexual partners takes place. When pushed to explain why no one initiates sexual advances or tries to leave the dance to sleep with a new partner, informants invariably, and forcefully, state that this dance is a *baile de respeto* (a ritual dance, or one involving respect role relationships).

The *currulao* presents a ritual context in which the role conflict between the male rights of self-assertiveness and mobility, and the female rights of household stability and maneuver to hold a particular man, is expressed and portrayed. In the *currulao* context male and female sex roles are equal and antagonistic as both sexes strive to dominate action sequences, and the strife is portrayed in gesture, song texts, dance styles, and the structured tension between *glosador* and *respondedoras*. A competitive, egalitarian, male-female dyad is enacted.

## The Living Walk, The Dead Wander

Before moving to sacred contexts we need some information on the integration of daily life and world view in this Afro-Hispanic culture. A structural relationship exists between mobility and social responsibility of the living, and the disposition of souls of the deceased. A boy must achieve a degree of social independence and sexual experience before he is considered ready for marriage; and his sexual relationships with a girl may obligate him to some extent to her relatives, if she becomes pregnant. Having achieved the status of father, with concomitant independence from his matricentral cell signalled by new responsibility to an affinal group, the soul of the man will tend to wander after his death, in this world and in other worlds. A woman who bears a child demonstrates a degree of social independence; her position in the mother-child dyad, and the implied position in a potential or real mother-husband dyad, both stress residential permanence, the complement to male mobility.

Let us pursue the relationship of living and dead. It is common to hear it said that a male must *andar y conocer* (literally "to walk [travel] and to know" [learn]) before he becomes a man. The phrase expresses the positive value placed on traveling and learning to cope with the environment. There is a deeper meaning, too, for *andar* means "to strut" in the black idiom. Walking in the manner prescribed for saloon giving, or for making sexual overtures to a woman, or for breaking a characteristic circling pattern during saloon dancing as an act of individual assertion is known as "walking." If one asks a black person in the Pacific littoral what he means when he says *conocer* in the above phrase he will invariably laugh, raise both hands above his head with elbows bent, fists clenched, thumbs pointing back, and move his arms and upper torso back and forth—the gesture symbolizing sexual intercourse in the wet littoral. To *andar y conocer* then also means to learn the ritual style for symbolizing co-operation and attracting a woman, and to learn the proper styles for sexual intercourse. The appropriate styles of behavior in the saloon context, it will be remembered, relate to the ritual means of signalling male-male dyadic relationships, which ramify into networks of association. The combination of *andar y conocer* is important, for it expresses the need for a man to know his way around in the social lattice of male support, as well as to know what he is about in his sexual relationships with his lover or wife.

It is said that the soul, *alma*, of a man who has died must wander. People seem less clear on whether the souls of all women must wander, but when asking about a specific woman I am invariably told that she, when young, would be found by her mother *andando con cualquiera*, "walking with anyone." This phrase applied to a specific woman means that she was having sexual affairs as a young girl. When we press further and ask if any woman avoids such sexual affairs, the answer is yes—*las vírgenes*, the virgins; and the speaker immediately lets us know that they live in *gloria*, heaven, which is part of *el cielo*, the sky. So it seems that all male and female adult souls do indeed wander, and they must be directed away from the settlement in which they lived. This is done in the *novenario*, one of the wakes for an adult.

The souls of pre-pubescent girls, and pubescent girls who everyone agrees have never had sexual intercourse with a man, and the souls of boys up to an indeterminate age when they become somewhat independent, go directly to *gloria* when they die, to live as *angelitos*, little angels, with God, Jesus, the saints, and the virgins. They alone do not wander. Their ascent is symbolized in the *chigualo*, the wake for a dead child.

Saints are also a mobile lot, and women are able to summon them from *gloria* and make requests of them. They do this by having special saints' days, at which time they sing *arrullos*, spirituals, until the spirit of the saint enters the house where the spirituals are being performed. These same spirituals are sung during the *chigualo*, and it would seem that the relationship between the living and the heaven-spirit is the same in both cases. The soul of the dead child ascends as an angel into *gloria* to the accompaniment of *arrullos*, just as the saints descend from *gloria* to help the women to the accompaniment of *arrullos*. Sometimes this latter musical context directed to saints is simply called *arrullo*, and sometimes it is referred to as *velorio*.

We return now to ritual contexts. I shall discuss, in turn, the *chigualo*, the *alabado-novenario*, and the *arrullo* to saints.

### Sacred Ritual Contexts of Sex Role Enactment

#### THE ALABADO-NOVENARIO CONTEXT

The house in which an adult dies is precariously balanced between earth (*la tierra*) purgatory (*purgatorio*), and hell (*infierno*). During the wake follow-ing death, called *alabado*, and the second wake about nine days after burial, called *novenario*, men and women from the local community cooperate in all endeavors with incoming hinterland relatives. They express equality in their roles, which are jointly oriented toward maintaining solidarity of a grouping of kinsmen around the newly deceased person, while at the same time rearranging particular kin ties so that no one can trace a relationship through the deceased. I have described this process elsewhere (Whitten 1968, 1970a). Although much attention is given to kinship in this sacred ritual context, affinity and consanguin-ity are deliberately blurred. For example, a brother of a deceased man may regard the deceased's wife as his sister during and following the *alabado-novenario*, or formally broken affinal bonds may be recalled in a re-linking of "cousins" to one another. Full co-operation between male and female sex roles is expressed: a co-operative, egalitarian, male-female dyad is enacted as the living solemnly take a position against the dead.

#### THE CHIGUALO CONTEXT

The *chigualo* context takes place following the death of a child. It is not so solemn as the *alabado-novenario*, heaven is open to the setting, and women are the interaction initiators. Most *chigualos* take place in the first two years of life, for infant mortality is very high during this time. Women attend to all matters of washing the child, seeing that it is baptized (if it has not been already), invit-ing male drummers to play during the night, and arranging with well-known *cantadoras* (women singers) to be on hand for the singing of *arrullos*. Men be-come linked in *compadrazgo* (ritual kinship) relationships if they are invited by the child's mother to help with preparations, burial, or expenses involved in the *chigualo*. Kinship terms often later replace the *comadre-compadre* terms used in the *chigualo*. When this occurs the mother of a dead child becomes the crucial locus in genealogical space for the reckoning of kinship ties.

The actual ritual is signalled by a man beating a rapid rhythm on the *bombo*, which usually begins immediately at nightfall but may begin at any time when the drummer hangs the drum. Within minutes of hearing this rhythm people come to see what woman has lost her child; some remain, some leave, such decision reflecting willingness to be included in the network of stipulated kinsmen radiating, at this time, from the mother of the deceased.

The child is placed at one end of the room, and candles surround the corpse on the table. The mother and mother's close siblings sit near the corpse, while other women assemble on one side or the other of the room. They make up a chorus, singing *arrullos* and clapping their hands for rhythm. The drummers (two *cununeros*, one *bombero*) group themselves against the opposite wall, and still other men and women sit at the far end of the room, near the main door. The scene is set for the arrival of the *cantadoras*. The female chorus has been singing since dark, and the ambience is moderately solemn but amicable. Drummers "obey" the women and "follow" their leads; men (including child's father and/or mother's husband) serve rum and coffee under the women's direction.

The chorus has been singing songs symbolizing the entry of the *angelito* (dead child) into heaven, and the *bombo* has been frightening the body- or soul-snatching Tunda apparition away, so that life within the house now opened to the sky is safe for all children, living and dead. The *cantadoras* enter around eleven or twelve at night, take up their positions, and begin to shake maracas and sing choruses more complex in rhythm and counterpoint than those sung by the general female chorus. Some of these women summon personal saints, or saints for all women, such as San Antonio, and petition things for themselves as the chorus steadfastly sings the child's entry into heaven. Sometimes the *cantadoras* will dance. If the corpse is very small, they may even pick it up and dance with it, swinging it to and fro.

After the arrival of the *cantadoras* the ambience of the *chigualo* "loosens." Adults come and go, and many take turns on the drums. Young men and women even engage in mild sex play, and children climb over everyone and everything, poking at the dead child and listening to the songs telling of the ascent of its soul into heaven. Within the house there is no danger, for the only avenue open to *el cielo* is to *gloria*—saintly spirits enter through *gloria* at the women's request. The only danger at this time, Tunda, is kept at bay by the male *bombero*. Only if children wander from the house are they in jeopardy, for Tunda could appear before them, leaving them *entundada* (frightened by the apparition), to be henceforth unable to cope with life. So the children stay and sleep in the house of the *chigualo*, within comforting range of the *bombo*, under the doors of heaven opened to them by the women.

It should be noted, in passing, that Tunda also attacks children without adult escorts who make themselves vulnerable by insulting, or being rude to, someone acting in the role of mother. Mothers threaten children with the *entundada* phenomenon, and they are regarded by boys as being capable of invoking Tunda to punish them, should the growing boy use his increasing strength, or wit, to challenge female authority. When a boy is ready to challenge his mother, he must also be ready to thwart Tunda.

The *chigualo* continues unabated until dawn, when it abruptly ends. The *cantadoras* go home, and those who have been served rum throughout the night hurriedly put the child in a little coffin (*cajita*), close the lid to the cries of the mother, and, with the drummers still beating, head for the cemetery singing *arrullos* and swinging the coffin.

A co-operative sex role relationship where women initiate interaction, dominate men, and solidify a network of kinsmen radiating from the matricentric cell (mother-dead child) is portrayed in the *chigualo*.

ARRULLO CONTEXT

The set-up for a saint's propitiation, sometimes called *velorio* (which means "wake" in standard Spanish but refers to spirit or saint propitiation in this Afro-Hispanic culture), is about the same as for the *chigualo*. The focus is a shrine, however, rather than a table used for a bier. Drummers and singers arrange themselves more or less as described above. There are usually at least two *bombos* during the *arrullo* to a saint, and there may be even more. The sound of more than one *bombo* most clearly differentiates the music of this event from that of the *chigualo*.

It is the women in a particular settlement, or *barrio* of an urban area, who undertake to organize the *arrullo* for a saint. Women must keep the dates for the saints clear and they must arrange for the *arrullo*, which means paying the male drummers for their performance and renting the drums. They must build the shrine, or pay a men to do it, and, if necessary, hide all preparation from local priests, who often regard these *arrullos* as pagan rites to be stamped out. Only women reap the general benefits of saintly aid which may occur after an *arrullo*, but men who wish to petition for luck in fishing must do so during this female-dominated sacred event.

Men attend the ritual to drink rum and *guarapo* (sugar beer) served by the women. The women often have difficulty maintaining the sacred ambience, as some men may try to turn the *arrullo* into a saloon context, described above. When men begin exchanging drinks, or try to dance, the women may even abandon the house in which the *arrullo* is held and retire without drums to shake maracas, sing, and invite a particular saint to enter the house.

The most significant saint in the Pacific Lowlands is San Antonio (Saint Anthony), and the majority of songs sung in all *arrullos* (and in the *chigualo*) are directed to him. Although his special day is June 13, all special days, in one way or another, may turn into invitations by women to San Antonio to enter the house, and to help them in their pursuit of men or their endeavors to hold onto them. In San Lorenzo, western Ecuador, for example, men say that San Antonio is the *alcahuete de las mujeres*, a pimp. Girls petition him for greater sexual attractiveness *vis-à-vis* a desirable male, just as older women petition him for the power to hold their particular men. San Antonio is also a broker or "lawyer" (see Price 1955:181) between the living and the dead, between the living and the spirits, and between spirits. He is the only saint who can work miracles on his own. He serves women in all matters, and fishermen in their exploitation of the marine environment.

Regardless of the particular day on which an *arrullo* is held, the songs to San Antonio tend to be of the longest duration and represent some of the most complicated rhythms (such as the *Bunde*). There are more than 40 of them. Frequently during a song to San Antonio the *cantadoras* engage in complicated counterpart symbolizing competition between women: one petitions one thing from San Antonio, while another petitions something else. One may be asking where San Antonio is, while a second sings: "he is under my bed." A third woman then responds: "he is having sexual intercourse with me." After such theme-counter theme textual and musical interplay the women give shouts and hug one another. By so doing they seem to symbolize a oneness of general endeavor—attracting and petitioning San Antonio—together with individuality of specific purpose.

No particular tension exists in the *arrullo*, except that provoked by men who refuse to acknowledge the importance of saints to the women's stratagems and needs. But the saints are not bothered by men's irreverence, for they are propitiated and petitioned by women, who are the sole legitimate action initiators in this context.

Saints are regarded as vain, and they are said to like ceremony. During Easter and Christmas seasons a street parade, called *Belén*, occurs, if not blocked by the clergy. Women arrange this, and they work closely with men on formal *Belén* logistics. There are often as many as twenty *bombos* and one hundred or more singers with maracas marching or strutting in a large town parade. Women set a route for the procession in terms of main streets or major trails leading past the fronts of houses; then, as the procession gets underway, the women lead it to and fro across the back yards of houses, weaving in and out and delighting the saints, who enjoy this, and frustrating the men, who are not sure where they will be led next as the women follow their day-to-day back yard visiting routes with the saints.

In the *arrullo* context women dominate everything, summoning saints into the home from heaven and leading them through their community visiting routes. They give the saints the variety and ceremony which they enjoy, and they enact both female sexual solidarity and individuality in trapping and holding men. The men in this ceremony are paid for their endeavors and dispensed with if they do not follow the female lead. Only when fishermen wish to petition San Antonio, after he is summoned by women, can a man take an active role in the *arrullo*. This is done when the women stop singing and tell a particular man to recite a sacred *décima*, called *la loa*. When the sacred petition for good fishing for another year has been made, the women see that all the men pay for the ceremony; and they then return to the patterns of behavior sketched above. The *arrullo* context portrays female-female sexual solidarity and female dominance.

### Ritual Enactment of Sex Roles and Social Structure

#### RITUAL ENACTMENT OF SEX ROLES: A SUMMARY

In the Pacific Lowlands sex role enactment ranges on a continuum from male to female initiation of interaction. These differences in role activation seem to reflect a continuum from male self assertiveness to female dominance. In the cantina context males assert their individual power over women, their mobility, and their ability to trick spirits and the dead. In the saloon context men express male network solidarity by the exchange of women as tokens, and they also express and enact actual changes of spouses. During the *currulao*, also a secular context, men express their prerogatives of mobility and allude to their relationship to the devil, while the women collectively express their prerogative to hold particular men, and seek in turn to resist male innovation in song and dance. In the sacred *alabado-novenario* context men and women express equality in sex role relationships as a human group against the unwanted dead. In the *chigualo* context women control interaction patterns and become central to intra-household reckoning of responsible kinsmen and contributors while opening the household to spirits of heaven. In the *arrullo* to saints women assume a dominant intra-community position, bringing the saints from heaven to the community and manipulating them to female bidding.

#### SEX ROLE VARIATION AND SOCIAL STRUCTURE

I have described the social system of the Pacific Lowlands elsewhere (Whitten 1965, 1968, 1970a, 1970b, 1974; Whitten and Szwed 1970b). Specific households are embedded in networks radiating from male broker nodes which are strategic to socioeconomic striving. Household maintenance tactics tap a localized kindred. Affinity, attenuated affinity, and consanguinity are all manipulated in traversing genealogical space for any ego central to household maintenance. Within the household the universal matricentral cell (cf. Fortes 1949, 1953, 1958, 1969) is maintained by a mother's recruitment strategies for male support. She uses both affinal and consanguineal dyads for such maintenance, the ramifications of these ties extending well beyond the household. Recruited men in the role of husband are the authority figures in the household, when they are actually present (Whitten 1965: 121–143; 1974: 153–157); but their responsibilities to the household involve them in constant strategies of male-male network mainte-nance outside of the household, which tap a dispersed kindred. Male mobility—horizontal, spatial, socioeconomic (see Whitten 1969)—eventually leads to po-lygyny, or serial wives. Responsibility to "abandoned" wives for aid in child rearing accrues to the husband-father's matricentral consanguines and affines.

Male self assertiveness provides continuity in Afro-Hispanic culture through mobility strategies. Female interaction initiative provides stability through house-hold permanence, and through maneuvers between households in a residential community which contribute to community permanence. Community and resi-dential permanence, in turn, contribute to male mobility by providing bases for dispersed networks. Supra-household and supra-community networks of recipro-cating males themselves are necessary for intra-household and intra-community stability in the boom-bust political economy. The male role as interaction initia-tor and the female role as interaction initiator complement one another; each contributes to social structural continuity while allowing considerable organiza-tional variety and adaptability. Women stabilize the domain of household and community; men stabilize the domain of kinship and network maintenance. Each domain is activated by maneuvers in the other domain. The specific role complementarity in the household domain leads to apparent conflict during ac-tual separation of spouses, but it provides for continuity of the household by ref-erence to the intra-household female prerogative, and male mobility prerogative.

Taken together the various ritual contexts enact the full range of sex role dif-ferentiation necessary to household, kinship network, community, and inter-com-munity maintenance. An analysis of this enactment in terms of interaction initia-tors and domain prerogatives allows us to explore sex role portrayal and its relationship to cultural continuity, whether or not rapid change is taking place.

## Notes

1. The delineation of sex role variation in the ritual contexts and its significance to daily life style and social strategy was pointed out to me by my wife, Dorothea S. Whitten, who also commented on an original draft of this manuscript. This paper is a revised and expanded version of one presented at the 70th Annual Meeting of the American Anthro-pological Association, November 21, 1971. Conrad Arensberg's incisive comments on this paper during the symposium clarified many issues. He pointed out that the interaction initiation aspect of the role relationship was the crucial feature in many of the activities which I described in the original paper. The data and themes sketched here are more fully discussed in Part II of Whitten (1974).

2. For more elaboration on these ideas see González (1965, 1969), Goodenough (1970), Whitten (1970a, 1970b, 1971, 1974).

3. The Colombian Chocó is specifically excluded from this analysis. Although data are frequently included from the Pacific Lowlands (area south of the San Juan River and west of the Cordillera Occidental) with those of the Chocó (area north of the San Juan

River, including both coastal strip and area east of the Serranía de Baudó but west of the Cordillera Occidental) I think that the differences in the two areas warrant separate treatment. I do not think that the analysis herein presented will fit the Chocó, although many of the specific elements are distributed regularly in the two areas.

4. These contexts find different specific outlets according to four niches—patterned black activity sets—governed by settlement size, which include the scattered rural dwellings, the settlement of up to around 300 people, the town of from several hundred to 3,000, and the urbanized town from around 5,000 to up to 100,000 people. The niches themselves exist in three environmental zones: sea-mangrove edge, mangrove swamp, and rain forest *tierra firma* (see Whitten 1974). "Lower class" refers to an intra-community perspective, not to national standing in regard to power over economic resources. Intra-community mobility patterns involve considerable rearrangement of behavior in specific contexts, and also a concept of ethnic lightening, regardless of actual phenotype. Whitten (1965, 1969, 1974) discusses the relationship of class and mobility to ethnic identity.

5. Other fairly common styles include the *caderona* (big-hipped woman, who symbolizes the sexually exciting woman, capable of luring men away from their homes in the saloon context). During this dance couples do a waltz-like step, loosely embraced. The *glosador* sings of his particular sexual episodes, bragging of his ability to "dry up" women, while the *respondedoras* keep singing "shake it, shake it" (*remeniate caderona, caderona vení meniate, ay vení meniate*) as a torment to the man. The *glosador* also sings of the inherent responsibility for progeny in sexual intercourse, particularly with young girls who have been certified as virgins by midwives, and the women refer to marriage resulting from pregnancy. Other dances are described in Whitten (1974).

## References

Fortes, M. 1949. The Web of Kinship Among the Tallensi. London.
—— 1953. The Structure of Unilinear Descent Groups. American Anthropologist 55: 17–41.
—— 1958. Introduction. The Developmental Cycle in Domestic Groups. Cambridge Papers in Social Anthropology, ed. J. Goody, pp. 1–14. Cambridge.
—— 1969. Kinship and the Social Order. Chicago.
Frazier, E. F. 1932. The Negro Family in Chicago. Chicago.
—— 1934. Traditions and Patterns in Negro Family Life in the United States. Race and Culture Contacts, ed. E. B. Reuter, pp. 191–207. New York.
—— 1939. The Negro Family in the United States. Chicago.
—— 1942. The Negro Family in Bahia, Brazil. American Sociological Review 7:465–478.
—— 1949. The Negro in the United States. New York.
Freilich, M. ed. 1970. Marginal Natives: Anthropologists at Work. New York.
Friedemann, N. S., and J. Morales Gómez. 1966–69. Estudios de negros en el Litoral Pacifíco Colombiano: Fase I. Revista Colombiana de Antropología 14: 55–78.
Goodenough, W. H. 1970. Description and Comparison in Cultural Anthropology. Chicago.
Goody, J. ed. 1958. The Developmental Cycle in Domestic Groups. Cambridge Papers in Social Anthropology, No. 1. Cambridge.

González, N. L. S. 1965. The Consanguineal Household and Matrifocality. American Anthropologist 67: 1541–1549.

—— 1969. Black Carib Household Structure: A Study of Migration and Modernization. Seattle.

—— 1970. Toward a Definition of Matrifocality. Afro-American Anthropology: Contemporary Perspectives, ed. N. E. Whitten, Jr. and J. F. Szwed, pp. 231–244. New York.

Hannerz, U. 1970. What Ghetto Males are Like: Another Look. Afro-American Anthropology: Contemporary Perspectives, ed. N. E. Whitten, Jr. and J. F. Szwed, pp. 313–344. New York.

Herskovits, M. J. 1941. The Myth of the Negro Past. New York.

—— 1943. The Negro in Bahia, Brazil: A Problem in Method. American Sociological Review 8: 394–402.

Price, T. J., Jr. 1955. Saints and Spirits: A Study of Differential Acculturation in Colombian Negro Communities. Unpublished Ph.D. dissertation, Northwestern University.

Reuter, E. B., ed. 1934. Race and Culture Contacts. New York.

Smith, R. T. 1956. The Negro Family in British Guiana. London.

—— 1963. Culture and Social Structure in the Caribbean: Some Recent Work on Family and Kinship Studies. Comparative Studies in Society and History 6: 24–46.

Whitten, N. E., Jr. 1965. Class, Kinship, and Power in an Ecuadorian Town: The Negroes of San Lorenzo. Stanford.

—— 1968. Personal Networks and Musical Contexts in the Pacific Lowlands of Colombia and Ecuador. Man 3: 50–63.

—— 1969. Strategies of Adaptive Mobility in the Colombian-Ecuadorian Littoral. American Anthropologist 71: 228–242.

—— 1970a. Network Analysis and Processes of Adaptation Among Ecuadorian and Nova Scotian Negroes. Marginal Natives: Anthropologists at Work, ed. M. Freilich, pp. 339–403; 609–612. New York.

—— 1970b. Network Analysis in Ecuador and Nova Scotia: Some Critical Remarks. Canadian Review of Sociology and Anthropology 7: 269–280.

—— 1971. Review of N. L. S. González: Black Carib Household Structure. Social and Economic Studies 20: 101–103.

—— 1974. Black Frontiersmen: A South American Case. Cambridge.

Whitten, N. E., Jr., and A. Fuentes C. 1966. ¡Baile Marimba! Negro Folk Music in Northwest Ecuador. Journal of the Folklore Institute 3: 168–191.

Whitten, N. E., Jr., and J. F. Szwed, eds. 1970a. Afro-American Anthropology: Contemporary Perspectives. New York.

—— 1970b. Introduction. Afro-American Anthropology: Contemporary Perspectives, ed. N. E. Whitten, Jr. and J. F. Szwed, pp. 23–60. New York.

# 7. GOLD MINING AND DESCENT

## Güelmambí, Nariño [Colombia]

### Nina S. de Friedemann

We are trees rooted in our mines
along the gold rivers.
Each trunk is a brother.
They were the founders
of our families and mines.
We are branches, limbs and twigs.
We are the descendants.

—A *miner of the Güelmambí River*

### I. Introduction

The black miners of the gold-bearing zone of the Pacific Littoral of Colombia have a social organization based on cognatic groups known as *troncos*.[1] Mining, natural environment and the socio-cultural context are critical factors for their family organization. Associated with this system of relations is an exclusive dependence on human energy and a technology so rudimentary that even the wheel has not been incorporated. Their habitat, a tropical rain forest, is one of the most humid of the world.

Troncos are defined by the miners as groups of families with rights to live, mine and do agriculture in a specific territory inherited from ancestors who took possession of the land more than 150 years ago. Each tronco claims a particular founder to whom every individual traces his line of descent through a male or female link to exercise his latent or active rights.

The miners in the Güelmambí River of the extreme southwestern corner of Colombia's Pacific littoral, are part of the South American black frontiersmen described by Whitten (1974). The tronco functions as a strategy for survival in the regional, boom or bust economy that pervades the whole society of the Pacific

Originally published as "Troncos Among Black Miners in Colombia," in Thomas Greaves and William Culver (eds.), *Miners and Mining in the Americas* (London: Manchester University Press, 1985), pp. 204–25. Reprinted by permission of Nina S. de Friedemann.

Littoral. The sporadic international demand for gold, tagua, wood, or oil has influenced their adaptation, as in the following examples:

(a)  When multinational dredges destroyed fertile land and subsistence crops in the river lowlands the miners were forced to abandon their settlements and re-establish elsewhere.[2]

(b)  When the sharp increases in labor demand in oil camps or similar venture capital enterprises attract miners to leave their own mines, the mining force becomes too small, and some local mining operations have to be closed temporarily. The remaining members of the descent group have to work in other mines.

(c)  When the rivers flood and the houses become destroyed, tile miners have to find new housing sites.

(d)  When the mining area becomes depleted, the miners have to move to other sites in search of gold.

To cope with these problems arising from the larger society, and from their own physical and social environment their tactic has been to use the resources offered by their troncos.

The Güelmambí River is located in the Barbacoas region of southwestern Colombia. The region is a wide alluvial delta formed by the deposits of the Patía River and its tributaries as they flow out of the western cordillera of the Andes toward the Pacific Ocean. The Güelmambí flows into the Telembí River, a tributary of the Patía. The upper and middle portions of almost all the waterways of the western slope of the cordillera are gold bearing. The most important gold zones are the ancient gravels of the interfluvial areas between the modern streams. Most of these gravels were deposited at the end of the Pliocene or during the Pleistocene by streams cutting through the western cordillera gold zone. They extend along a belt that runs the length of the cordillera, from the Upper Atrato River to the Colombian-Ecuadorian border. Barbacoas is located in one portion of this gold belt (West 1952, 1957).

## II. The Miners

With the arrival of the Spaniards in the sixteenth century, the Indians began to disappear rapidly, victims of epidemics, suicide, and forced labor. Although they were being replaced by black slaves in the mining centers, during the first part of this period a number of Indians worked together with blacks in the mines. The aboriginal mining technology was thus transferred to the colonial technology of mining and agricultural system and thence to the material culture of the blacks.

After abolition in 1851 many blacks dispersed over the littoral forests and settled along the banks of the rivers, much as other blacks had done before abolition, when they were allowed to buy their freedom from their masters by working on Sundays and holidays. Soon the mining center of Barbacoas became depopulated, and commercial mining was abandoned. In the forest, blacks recreated a mining economy on their own with aboriginal skills and traits, patterns from the colonial mining system, and their own cultural and social elaborations.

The various mining villages are strung out over a distance of thirty kilometers along the banks of the Güelmambí. They vary in size, the larger ones from twelve to fifty houses and the small ones from two to six. In 1980, approximately 1,200 miners lived in these settlements on the Güelmambí, i.e. 1.6 percent of the total population of the municipality of Barbacoas. Through the innumerable labyrinths of streams, swamps and rivers that flow through the soggy jungle, the inhabitants paddle their dugout canoes, the only vehicle for transportation. The rain drips continually from the palm-thatched roofs of their huts which are raised on wooden pillars two or more meters above the ground. Pigs, chickens and canoes are kept beneath the huts. Some households have a hand press for processing sugar. Others have an earthen oven for baking bread. The rocky debris left from the mining process is used to pave the areas around the house.

In the morning before adults and older children set off for the mining cuts, the women do the washing in the river. In the meantime the men and older boys work in their *chagras* (agricultural plots) and check their traps set up the night before to capture small animals such as agouti, rabbits or armadillos.

During the rainy season, mining begins at six in the morning, three days of the week in the mine of their kin group and the other days in the gold workings and fields assigned to each family. If the cut has enough water, work continues until six in the evening. When the rains slacken during the dry season, people stop going to the mines every day. When they go, they stop work between one and three in the afternoon. The division of labor tends to conform to the following pattern: men plant the crops and weed the chagras while women harvest the products and take them home; children gather fruit in the forest; and young women go to the river to catch small fish with large round nets.

At least once a month there is a *velorio*, a celebration with singing and drumming in honor of one or more of the catholic saints. The velorio starts Saturday night and lasts until dawn on Sunday and brings together people from different troncos, settlements and rivers (Friedemann 1966–9, 1974). This is an occasion to renew genealogical knowledge on troncos, ancestors, and rights. Tuesday is market day in Barbacoas and some of the miners go to sell gold dust and to buy supplies such as candles, salt, and oil.

Mining work is done with an iron bar, a digging stick, an iron spoon with a wooden handle, *cachos* (gourd scoops), a panning tray and an oblong wooden tray. Men break up the slopes or terraces with the iron bars. Stones are removed and passed from hand to hand along lines of young men and women and piled up to make terraces far from the original "cut." The finer materials are washed and the sand separated and deposited in a trench made for this purpose. Here men and women patiently stoop over the water, sand and debris, picking the remaining small stones from the mix, called *mazamorra*. From this mazamorra the women finally separate the gold dust, using slightly convex wooden panning trays that they work rhythmically to move the *jagua* (a mixture of gold dust and particles of iron oxide) to one side of the pan.

## III. Mine and Tronco

Existing literature on placer mining in the Pacific Littoral talks only about the work of groups of families and friends on public lands. The geographer, West, realized that among the miners there existed a property system regulated by descent rules, but he made only a passing reference to the system (1957: 154).

Over the last twenty years the anthropological understanding of non-unilineal descent groups with a focal ancestor has been expanded (cf Davenport 1959; Sahlins 1962; Fox 1967; Buchler and Selby 1968; Goodenough 1970; Keesing 1975), including further study of a type of non-unilineal descent group, the ramage, known especially from Polynesia.[3] The organization that has been defined as ramages in Polynesia is similar to that of the troncos in Colombia, particularly with respect to the choice between patrilateral or matrilateral affiliation alternatives and the connection of group members with a common ancestor in a chain of parents and children that is basic to the definition of ramages in non-unilineal or cognatic systems (Buchler and Selby 1968: 90; Goodenough 1970: 42). Thus, troncos in the Güelmambí may be described as consanguineal kinship groups whose members trace their descent to a common ancestor through a line of males or females in a series of parent—child links and, therefore, may also be classified as ramages.

In this article, I will analyze the San Antuco Mine, which is a *mina grande*, containing twenty-four households divided among three troncos designated Cristino, Otulio and Leonco. These names stem from the first name of the ancestor of each descent group. Traditional narratives relate the origins of each tronco and its lands, and tell of the descendants of freed slaves who came to the area, took possession of former Indian territories and formed the families that have lived there ever since.

Kinship ties are important and often discussed. At the frequent velorios genealogical histories are recounted in detail. When a man or woman arrives at the tronco's mine workings, the greeting from those at work is accompanied by remarks about the kinship tie that underlies the right and expectations on which the arriving worker's participation is based.

Each tronco owns a territory where all the family units live and work. The three troncos constitute the San Antuco Mine, known generically as a mina grande. A mina grande is composed of more than one tronco and includes each tronco's communally worked *compañía* mine, as well as the *comedero* mine alloted by each tronco to its member families, together with their agricultural plot (chagra) and house-garden-patio site.

A document exists that legitimizes the miners' claim to the San Antuco territory, dating from 1899, twenty-five years after the founders had settled in the area. However, this document, like many other property titles, is no longer regarded as valid by the national government since the miners did not keep up with tax payments and other bureaucratic requirements. Consequently, their official status is defined as squatters on public land.

There are documents for other mines in the area that bear the names of women as the ancestors of other troncos. These data are relevant for the examination of the development of the troncos as a cognatic descent system in which membership is defined by optional affiliation with a group through either a paternal or maternal link.

Most traditions on the Güelmambí also show the founders as brothers or brothers and sisters. When they were not siblings by descent, it is explained that they became siblings by settling on the same land to found the mine. Tradition tells of another instance when one of the founding brothers moved away and gave his rights to another individual who had arrived in the area. This person then became an ancestor and today is considered as having been a brother of the other founders.

Every aspect of life among the miners is in reference to the mina which includes the physical territory, the work, one's family and one's identity. The term mina applies to the complex formed by the settlement, the family chagra or agricultural plot, the family mine or comedero, and the communal mine or compañía where all the members of each tronco may exercise their rights to participate in communal mining activities.

### IV. Affiliation to Troncos: Active and Latent Rights

The actual recruitment of members in the tronco depends on the patrilateral or matrilateral affiliation that the individual chooses. Although a person can possess rights in several troncos at one time, the exercise of the right is maintained by constant participation in the communal work at the compañía mining site on the property of the tronco of affiliation, by the use of lands for his chagra and comedero, and by the preferential use of the tronco's territory in establishing his residence. Consequently a person can maintain active rights in only one tronco at a time.

The founders and the second generations of miners along the river banks maintained tronco affiliation and discrete, clearly defined parcels of land associated with each comedero, chagra and house site. This is not true today, although some people can still point out the old boundaries of the residential sites of each tronco. Some active members of San Antuco may and do, live in nearby villages.

This occurs, for example, when a woman is married to, and residing with, a man of another mina grande along the river, and it has been agreed that the family unit would affiliate with the woman's tronco. Thus, the husband, wife and children go to work the chagra, the comedero and the compañía sites using the wife's rights although their residence remains patrilocal.

As cognatic groups, the troncos can be conceived of as pragmatically restricted groups (Fox 1967: 156), since in practice the individual only exercises his active option in one mina at a time. However, this affiliation is not immutable, as seen by the maintenance of latent rights in other troncos, and their minas.

An individual can choose to affiliate with one tronco in preference to another through options provided by either a maternal or a paternal link. Each nuclear family unit also has the option of activating rights in any of the troncos to which either the man or the woman can trace ancestral lines. This optional affiliation creates a flexible system that can adjust to circumstances such as personal preference for residence, better mining opportunities, and cultivation on sites belonging to the woman's or man's tronco.

The ideal norm is that a man will have worked with his parents since adolescence on land received from them, and will continue to activate the rights received from his parental family unit. He will bring his wife to live in the territory and the tronco of his parents. In such case, the wife's rights in other troncos and often in other minas grandes remain latent in the family unit, to be exercised in case of need or to be invoked later by their grown-up children if they so desire. The preferred norm of patrilocality is changeable in cases of activation of the woman's rights by the family. When this occurs the rights of the man become the latent rights of the family unit but remain available to the husband, wife or children when circumstances require their activation. Maintenance of latent rights permits people to solve problems rapidly, as when house sites are flooded; flood victims can invoke their latent rights and acquire a new house site in a neighboring village.

The miner conceptualizes two categories of active rights within the family unit: (1) property rights to a house site, garden land (chagra), forest land and comedero mine as a member of a tronco; (2) work rights to participate in the communal mining work, the compañía. The compañía mine works on communal land that is never divided and that belongs to his tronco as a unit.

To exercise his first order rights the miner builds a house, generally overlooking the river, after having obtained approval of the group controlling the territory. He then prepares a chagra, by the slash and mulch system[4] where he plants mainly corn, beans, yuca, plantains, and sugar cane. For his comedero he makes a small water reservoir for rain water, digs a sluice and washes sand each week, a process similar to his work at the compañía level. The gold dust recovered may allow him to buy dry fish, salt, meat and staples to maintain the domestic group. The entire nuclear family cooperates in all these activities, thus exercising the rights associated with the tronco to which the unit is affiliated.

The father heads the domestic work group. He uses the iron bar to initiate the breaking up of the terrace. In domestic units of widows and children, a son is in charge of this work. If she does not have a son, the widow recruits a male worker amongst her male relatives. A rule in the mining world is "there must be a man present."

The second order of rights, those to work in the compañía, are exercised by participating in the communal mine of the tronco, where its members work together three days a week. The whole family may go to the communal mine on these days, but it is also possible for only one person to exercise rights as a member of the larger unit. The compañía names a captain to organize the workers and to assign the tasks along the trench or in the line that moves the large stones away from the cut. The captain keeps track of the days worked by each individual and at the end of the *picado*, or mining period, each worker receives a sum of money proportionate to the days he contributed. The captain and a tronco representative have the duty of exchanging the gold for money in Barbacoas. Every three months the profits are divided among the workers, who use their share primarily for the expenses of religious ceremonies, including clothing, drink and food.

In the beginning of the 1970s, the exercise of rights in one of the compañía sites of San Antuco was practiced largely by women, and male participation diminished noticeably. The same mine worked by seven men and nineteen women in 1969, had only three men and fourteen women in 1971. In recent years nearby oil fields and road construction projects have required unskilled labor, and many men have left the Güelmambí for brief periods to earn cash. While trying to get cash as workers in the larger society, they maintain their rights in their troncos and minas back in the forest and return to their families when lean times arise in the labor market. This is part of the adaptive function of the troncos, which permits the population to adjust to the boom and bust economic cycles of the Pacific Littoral.

In San Antuco, for instance, there was a period in the 1970s when the Leonco trunk had only three family units actively exercising their rights and consequently the compañía works had to close for a long time. Notwithstanding, the members spoke of their compañía mine as if the mining was being carried on regularly. By 1983, the communal mine had started operating again, with an average of seven men and ten women.

Finding gold is not easy for these miners. A group of twenty-five workers can wash the rocks and sands of a terrace for several months only to get one gram of gold dust. When this happens, the compañía group agrees to dissolve for a while. It is at this moment that its members start activating their latent rights in other compañía mines, but they must first obtain the consent of their own compañía captain and the consensus of the members of his tronco, through its representative, who is the man or woman who keeps the document of land ownership. Another option is to relocate to another site within the communal land to try their luck. If yields are promising the group may then continue together.

Table 1   Active and Latent Rights, San Antuco Families

| Family | Mine A$_1$(O) Active | Mine A$_1$(O) Latent | Mine A$_2$(C) Active | Mine A$_2$(C) Latent | Mine A$_3$(L) Active | Mine A$_3$(L) Latent | Mine B Latent | Mine C Latent | Mine D Latent |
|---|---|---|---|---|---|---|---|---|---|
| 1 | – | | | | | | | | |
| 2 | | – | – | | | – | – | | |
| 3 | | – | | | – | | | | |
| 4 | – | | | – | | | | | – |
| 5 | – | | | | | | | | |
| 6 | | | – | | – | | | | |
| 7 | – | | | | | | | | |
| 8 | – | | | – | | | | | |
| 9 | | | | | | | | | |
| 10 | | | – | | | | | – | – |
| 11 | – | | – | | | – | | | |
| 12 | – | | | – | | | | | – |
| 13 | – | | | – | | | | | |
| 14 | | – | | | – | | – | | |
| 15 | | – | | | – | | – | | |
| 16 | – | | | – | | | | | |
| 17 | | | – | | | – | | | – |
| 18 | | | – | | | | – | – | |
| 19 | | | – | | | | – | – | |
| 20 | | | – | | | | – | – | – |
| 21 | – | | – | | | | | – | – |
| 22 | | | – | | | – | | | |
| 23 | | | – | | | – | | | |
| 24 | – | | – | | | – | | | |
| 25 | | | – | | | – | – | | – |

The maintenance of latent rights is a constant feature in the daily interaction of miners, expressed through mutual aid. A person can, and does, travel to nearby villages by canoe to help repair a house, clear land, or mill sugar cane. Latent rights can also be maintained by helping in other troncos' compañía mining operations.

The Güelmambí river settlement consists of twenty-four residential units, a school and a church. The village of San Antuco is spatially distributed along the edge of the river. Active and latent rights of each family unit in the troncos rooted there could be extended to cover other minas grandes and their troncos where Otulios, Cristinos and Leoncos maintain latent rights and likewise with the latent rights that miners from other minas grandes hold in San Antuco (see Table 1). The result would be the same pattern of descent lines, spread over a larger area of the river. The system, linking people and rights across the physical boundaries

Table 2   Ancestry, San Antuco Troncos

| | $A_1(O)$ | | | | $A_2(C)$ | | | | $A_3(L)$ | | | |
|---|---|---|---|---|---|---|---|---|---|---|---|---|
| | $G_1$ | $G_2$ | $G_3$ | $G_4$ | $G_1$ | $G_2$ | $G_3$ | $G_4$ | $G_1$ | $G_2$ | $G_3$ | $G_4$ |
| 1 | F | F | M | D | | | | | | | | |
| 2 | | | | | F | M | D | | | | | |
| 3 | | | | | | | | | F | M | F | S |
| 4 | F | M | F | S | | | | | | | | |
| 5 | F | F | M | D | | | | | | | | |
| 6 | | | | | F | F | S | | | | | |
| 7 | F | F | F | D | | | | | | | | |
| 8 | F | F | F | S | | | | | | | | |
| 9 | | | | | | | | | | | | |
| 10 | | | | | F | F | D | | | | | |
| 11 | F | M | F | S | | | | | | | | |
| 12 | F | M | F | D | | | | | | | | |
| 13 | F | M | F | S | | | | | | | | |
| 14 | | | | | | | | | F | M | M | S |
| 15 | | | | | | | | | F | M | D | |
| 16 | F | M | S | | | | | | | | | |
| 17 | | | | | F | F | F | S | | | | |
| 18 | | | | | F | F | F | D | | | | |
| 19 | | | | | F | F | S | | | | | |
| 20 | | | | | F | F | D | | | | | |
| 21 | F | M | F | D | | | | | | | | |
| 22 | | | | | F | F | F | S | | | | |
| 23 | | | | | F | F | D | | | | | |
| 24 | F | F | M | S | | | | | | | | |
| 25 | | | | | F | M | S | | | | | |

Key: $G_1$ Founding generation, $G_2$ Second generation, etc.
     F = Father, M= Mother, S= Son, D = Daughter

of the minas grandes in a broad kinship network, leads the residents to correctly exclaim, "on this river we are all relatives."

Tables 1 and 2 are a summary of active and latent rights of each one of the family units within the troncos Otulio, Cristino, and Leonco. Moreover, Table 1 shows eleven units actively affiliated with Otulio, ten with Cristino and three with Leonco. Also it shows that some of the twenty-four family units of San Antuco hold latent rights in other minas grandes B, C and D along the river Güelmambí.

Table 2 specifies the male or female links used by each one of the units to affiliate actively each one with the three troncos. Here it is shown that in the fourth generation six family units (1, 5, 7, 12, 18 and 21) activated rights received through the woman, and nine family units (3, 4, 8, 11, 13, 14, 17, 22 and 24) activated rights received through the man. In the third generation five family units (2, 10, 15, 20 and 23) activated rights received through women and four units (6, 16, 19 and 25) activated rights received through men. This means that of the twenty-four houses now occupied by members of the Otulio, Cristino, and Leonco troncos, thirteen (or 54.1 per cent) of the families have affiliated by invoking rights received through men, and eleven of them (45.0 percent) have affiliated by invoking rights received through women. As these data show, the descent system has a slight patrilineal bias, possibly induced by the ideal norm of patrilocal residence.

## V. Marriage

On the Güelmambí the basic domestic and economic unit is the nuclear family. A man ideally takes his wife to live in a house he builds when they begin their life together. If he as yet has no house, he may take her to his parents' house until he obtains the wood to "raise" their own. Since both the man and woman have their own rights to a residence site, chagra and mining sites, a decision is made on the affiliation of the new family unit. The husband and wife may come from the same settlement, but each is likely to have an affiliation with a different tronco. A Cristino, for example, will marry a Leonco or an Otulio in the Mina Grande of San Antuco, or maybe someone from an entirely different tronco (here designated "X") from another mina grande. These cross-tronco marriages endow the new family unit with wider kinship links and, thus, its ability to call upon a larger set of people for reciprocal tasks.

La Mina Grande, San Antuco, is not endogamous. It is also clear that troncos C, L and O maintain control of their territories. When a C, for instance, marries someone from another mina grande, tronco X, if this person joins tronco C he or she exercises the active rights of the C spouse. The person's own rights in X are left latent for the family unit CX. Conversely, when an X brings a spouse from C to his/her mine, C joins the group with his/her latent rights for the family unit XC. The descent groups of the Güelmambí are linked in a network over a large extension of territory.

The strong preference is for marriage between people from different troncos. Tronco exogamy increases (1) the breadth of latent rights in various troncos, and (2) the number of affinal relatives of Ego, to augment the potential groups of people who may be called to work. Marriage between children of siblings is prohibited as are premarital relations, which are transitory if they do occur. Kinship terminology for first cousins reflects this rule: Ego uses the term brother/sister with the children of his parents and also the children of his father's and mother's siblings. People on the Güelmambí are emphatic that "marriage between cousins doesn't work."

Marriages in San Antuco between people of the same tronco have not lasted long. Twenty of the twenty-four marriages follow this rule. On this point it is important to observe that only ten of these marriages are between members of troncos within La Mina Grande San Antuco. Each of the other ten marriages has one spouse (six women, four men) originating in a different mina grande along the river.

On the Güelmambí, premarital relations may or may not result in a permanent relationship. If a sexual coupling concludes with the birth of a child the man might only take responsibility for the costs of the birth, the midwife and clothing for the infant. A woman involved in such a brief relationship will remain in her natal family unit and may later marry someone else. These encounters may involve youths or a single woman and a married man. In the first instance the relationship may develop into a permanent union. Community recognition of these unions is not predicated upon a formal catholic religious ceremony. Although most couples will announce their intention of going through with the ceremony some day, this may not occur until several years later. Community recognition arises from the active exercise of rights by the man and the woman as a family unit in a mina grande and in a tronco.

When an unmarried mother marries a man other than her child's father, the child remains with her parents. He adopts the grandparents' surname and exercises the rights of a child in their tronco.

In cases of prolonged sexual unions between married men and unmarried women, the woman and children of such a union form a separate family unit. The man retains sexual access to the woman, as the father of her children, and is expected to provide gifts of clothing, small sums of money for the children, occasional food to the household, and to build a house in the territory of the woman's tronco. This house becomes the property of the woman. The woman and her children remain part of her natal household. They work in that group and participate in the circle of mutual aid corresponding to it. These women may live in the same settlement or in a different one than the man with whom they are involved.

Children of such unions are known as illegitimates (bastardos), a term specifying the social illegality of their existence, and they identify themselves as "the natural child of F'" (name of father). In this way they maintain a latent paternal kinship link. During childhood and adolescence, exclusion from the descent group of the father is marked, but this may change significantly with increasing age. Today, when the emigration of young people to urban centers weakens the number of workers needed in the compañía mining, the potential human energy offered by an illegitimate offspring is welcomed. His work enables him to claim rights in his father's tronco although his social status remains that of an illegitimate.

In San Antuco there was a unit formed by a semi-invalid old woman, her illegitimate daughter, and the children of this daughter, also illegitimate. Genealogical research showed that the old woman's mother had had children in extramarital couplings with an Otulio man. She had then left the region, taking her children. She thus forfeited her children's claim to affiliation with the tronco of father or mother. The daughter of this woman who had become a semi-invalid, later returned to claim rights as a natural child of an Otulio, but they were not granted to her. Her father's brother gave her a house site within his own settlement territory but she failed in her attempt to activate any tronco rights. Her own daughter, who accompanied her, thus had no rights to offer to anyone in marriage. Like her mother, she has had children from brief sexual unions. Through her illegitimate children with another Otulio man, a member of the same tronco in which her mother attempted to claim rights, it appears that her claim might eventually succeed. When they reach adolescence they can offer their physical labor for the communal mine and mutual aid obligations within their father's tronco. If they are accepted, they will be permitted to exercise their rights within the tronco.

Once an illegitimate child is allowed to activate descent rights by working he/she establishes an affiliation just as any other member of the tronco. One man, who had previously lived in another settlement affiliated to his mother's tronco, was able to exercise rights in tronco O as the illegitimate son of an Otulio. He then married a Cristino woman and came to live in San Antuco. A few years later the relations between this man and members of the tronco were still developing. He would show a ready availability to participate in the work of his mutual aid group, and was constantly being called on.

It can be concluded that illegitimates do not represent merely a deviance from marital and family norms that can be ignored; they constitute potential human resources that can be incorporated into the tronco. In San Antuco, the mina grande from which the two sample cases were taken, there is a distinct difference in the positions. In the first case of the semi-invalid woman, not only are they not accepted in the social system, but even their existence within the physical boundaries of the community is denied. Anyone asking where the settlement begins and ends will be shown a point that specifically excludes house no. 1 from the village limits. Correspondingly, none of the persons of this household have chagra land, nor can they work in any compania. All they can do is work sand in the river, whose waters are considered property of the national government. For their support the daughter obtains periodic work in other settlements and occasional help from her lover. In the second case of the man born of Otulio, the house is located at the other end of the settlements and is included *within* its recognized boundaries. The man in this case is the illegitimate son of an Otulio with a sister of the semi-invalid old woman heading household no. 1. The rule in this instance is modified by the fact that he lives with a Cristino woman. It also highlights the importance of active work in troncos and the need of human energy.

## VI. Transmission of Property and Work Rights

To explain mining on the Güelmambí, the descent groups provide the miners with strategies of adaptation to a particular socio-economic, political and ecological environment. The potential resources and material products of their environment are secured and transmitted through tronco affiliation.

Possession of a comedero and chagra in a mina grande is subject to a process of "registration," and active residence on the part of the family unit, similar to the original occupation of the mina grande by the ancestor/founders. To "register" a plot means to obtain the approval of the tronco of affiliation to mark off within its territory a particular area for individual or family use. When the "approval" is obtained, the interested parties clear the land, cut out the underbrush, and prepare the terrain for cultivating or mining. It can then be passed on as inheritance to the next generation. It may happen that the registered plot is used for only a few years. If another aspirant of the same tronco then wants it, he can obtain it on loan from the owner of the registration. There is, then, another process of consultation and approval from the tronco. When an owner abandons the settlements and/or land without notification that he will return, a new aspirant can register it for his own use and for transmission to his heirs. Growing emigration to urban centres has increased this secondary occupation through loan and re-registration.

Houses built by a man for his family belong to both spouses. If the man dies, his wife is the sole owner and vice versa. When both parents are dead the house and all its contents are divided equally among the children. These wooden houses are easily taken apart, so each child carries away a portion. It is interesting to locate the parts of houses that belonged to the parents or grandparents and to find that the inhabitants can show the pieces and identify from whom they were received. Don Inocencio, for example, one day showed his cousin the "mother" beam of his house, inherited from his parents. His mother had, in turn, received it from the house of her parents.

House division is supervised by the eldest child, and his or her word is respected in this matter. If there are small children the eldest child also takes charge of them, receiving their portions of the house and accepting the responsibility of their care while they grow up. A child who wants to keep the entire house can have it appraised and divide its monetary value among the other children. The house can then be torn down and moved to this child's residence site, or it can be occupied where it stands. The house of an unmarried woman and her natural children is the sole property of the mother. When she dies it is divided among the children. Actions implicated in the division, appraisal, moving, or maintenance of a house in one place are matters for general discussion by everyone in the settlement and among the members of the involved troncos.

At age eighteen, children may receive land to work from their parents, and they are obligated, in return, to help the household with a portion of their harvest while they continue living in the parental house. This early inheritance of land, including trees and usable woods, induces young men and women to maintain their affiliation with their parents' tronco and to later bring their spouses there. It also permits the parents to keep their children nearby, helping in the chagra and comedero work. This redistribution of land may occur earlier if the parents are ill or are too old for active work. For example, in one of the units of San Antuco the father was old and becoming an invalid. Since most of his children were female, he gave them land to keep them and their husbands nearby when they married. In this way he managed to maintain a work force attached to the parental unit.

The lands given to children may not be used until they marry, but the new unit has to become affiliated to the parental tronco. Each tronco then makes room for new adults when they begin to exercise their rights independently of the parental domestic unit. Although each mina grande has limited land, availability of land has not been a problem, because the area is under-populated.

Both men and women work and their rights are transmitted to their children who begin exercizing them with their parents from about the age of twelve. If, as an adult, a child affiliates with another tronco these rights become latent, as explained above. When members of a group leave for long period of time they can also loan out their lands. Those who do not return eventually lose their rights. "Only the children who remain in the mina inherit," said a woman, who added "The child that does not help, does not inherit."

## VII. Discussion

This chapter has sought to describe relevant features of the tronco, a non-unilineal descent group, as an adaptive strategy for survival among blacks in a gold-mining zone of the Pacific Littoral of Colombia.

Though the system has been traced back a century, evidence suggests that its roots reach even further, to well before abolition of slavery. While cognatic groups have been the subject of study and controversy since the 1950s, this case seems to be the first one to appear among blacks living in the rain forests of South America.

Some scholars maintain that cognatic systems result from the breakdown of patrilineal systems; others feel that they are the beginning of such systems. Some theorists consider them to be an independent type that, in some cases has resulted from a breakdown of a unilineal system (Fox 1967: 153). The Güelmambí evidence shows that a definite patrilateral bias exists, induced by the ideal norm of patrilocal residence. But only a study of the changes that have taken place within the socio-economic organization of the earliest groups of freed miners, from before 1851 to the present, could help solve this question.

What this case provides is evidence of the tronco system as an adaptive strategy to cope with the use of land limited by the miners' documents, the squatter status established by the Colombian government, and also by the occurrence of such natural disasters as floods, depletion of gold and such external pressures as those posed by dredges of the multinational enclaves that rendered useless many kilometers of fertile soil along the rivers in the region. Tronco exogamy has provided the miners with a mechanism for spatial mobility, demographic adjustments and a distribution of labor force and resources within and outside the mina grande over considerable distances.

Adaptation for these people has to be understood as a process responding to fairly rapidly changing situations. It shows great efficiency at critical points, and, above all, the capability of drawing on an ample range of alternatives and resources from the physical and social environment. The role of ideology, especially that chartering kinship, marriage, and production groups, should be scrutinized in greater detail.

One notes that cognatic groups are often found among people who live in insular territories. The Güelmambí blacks, of course, are not island dwellers. Yet the pattern may still hold if we consider that these miners of continental rain forests suffer a type of isolation resultant from their historical background as forced migrants from Africa, turned slaves and then free, as well as the present social and racial discrimination they face. Furthermore, the respect given by the miners to the borders of their property surrounded by public lands may indicate their conceptualization of their territory as an island.

One might also observe that an analysis of their creativity in transforming and reinterpreting facets of the Indian society, features of the Spanish colonial society, and their African traditions into a new way of living adds a deeper perspective to the understanding of South American blacks.

## Notes

1. The basic field work for this article was carried out under the sponsorship of the Instituto Colombiano de Antropología. Further research was done under the sponsorship of CIID, IAF, FORD and FES. I would like to thank Dr Nancy Morey for her comments, as well for her help translating an early version of this article. Dr Jaime Arocha and Dr Ronald J. Duncan, having worked in the area, have contributed with discussions and suggestions. Dr Tom Greaves, who extended an invitation to join the 1982 symposium, "Miners in the Americas," in Manchester, has made valuable recommendations for this chapter. I wish to thank them all for their greatly appreciated collaboration.

2. The Colombian government has legally transferred surface soil property to other interested parties and has extended sub-soil concessions to several industrial mining enterprises. In 1937, the South American Gold and Platinum Company began exploitation in the Telembí River. In 1963 this company merged with the International Mining Corporation. The multinational enclave obtained concession rights over 1,045 hectares and requested an additional 3,168 hectares. Moreover, it rented and acquired 2,332 hectares

making a total of 6,545 hectares, or nearly 25,000 acres of river bottom land (Melo 1975: 68).

3. Cf. Firth (1936, 1957), Lambert (1966) and Hanson (1970).

4. Robert C. West (1957: 129) describes the system as evolved of Indian techniques: "seeds are broadcast and rhizomes and cuttings are planted in an uncleared plot; then the bush is cut: decay of cut vegetable matter is rapid, forming a thick mulch through which the sprouts from the seeds and cuttings appear within a week or ten days. Weeds are surprisingly few, and the crops grow rapidly, the decaying mulch affording sufficient fertilizer even on infertile hillside soils."

## References

Buchler, Ira, and Henry A. Selby
    1968    Kinship and social organization. An introduction to theory and method. New York: The Macmillan Company.

Davenport, William
    1959    "Non-unilinear descent and descent groups." American Anthropologist 61: 557–72.

Firth, Raymond
    1936    We, the Tikopia; a Sociological Study of Kinship in Primitive Polynesia. London: G. Allen.
    1957    "A note on descent groups in Polynesia." Man 57: 4–8.

Fox, Robin
    1967    Kinship and Marriage, an Anthropological Perspective. Middlesex: Penguin Books.

Friedemann, Nina S. de
    1966–9    "Contextos religiosos en un area de Barbacoas (Nariño, Colombia)." Revista Colombiana de Folklore (Bogotá) 4(18): 61–83.
    1974    Minería, Descendencia y Orfebrería, Litoral Pacífico (Colombia). Bogotá: Universidad Nacional de Colombia.

Friedemann, Nina S. de, and Jaime Arocha
    1982    "Contribución al etnodesarrollo de grupos negros en Colombia." Manuscript.

Friedemann, Nina S. de, and Ronald J. Duncan
    1974    Güelmambí: A River of Gold. Film, b/w, twenty-four minutes.

Goodenough, Ward H.
    1961    "Review of G. P. Murdock (ed.) Social Structure in Southeast Asia." American Anthropologist 63: 1341–7.
    1970    Description and Comparison in Cultural Anthropology. Chicago: Aldine Publishing.

Hanson, Allan F.
    1970    Rapan Lifeways, Society and History on a Polynesian Island. Boston: Little, Brown and Company.

Keesing, Roger M.
1975    Kin Groups and Social Structure. New York: Holt, Rinehart and Winston.

Lambert, Bernd
1966    "Ambilineal descent groups in the Northern Gilbert Islands." American Anthropologist 68(3): 641–64.

Melo, Hector
1975    La Maniobra del Oro en Colombia. Medellín: Editorial La Pulga Ltda.

Sahlins, Marshall.
1962    Moala: Culture and Nature on a Fijian Island. Ann Arbor: University of Michigan Press.

West, Robert C.
1952    Colonial Placer Mining in Colombia. Baton Rouge, Lousiana: Louisiana State University Press.
1957    The Pacific Lowlands of Colombia. Baton Rouge, Louisiana: Lousiana State University Press.

Whitten, Norman E.
1974    Black Frontiersmen, a South American Case. New York: John Wiley & Sons.

Whitten, Norman E., and Nina S. de Friedemann
1974    "La cultura negra del litoral Ecuatoriano y Colombiano: Un modelo de adaptación étnica." Revista Colombiana de Antropología (Bogotá) 16: 75–115.

# 8. AFRICANS AND INDIANS

## A Comparative Study of the
## Black Carib and Black Seminole

*Rebecca B. Bateman*

The history of European mercantile and colonial expansion in the Americas is one of destruction, dispersal, and dispossession of native populations and forced transport and enslavement of African peoples. Ironically, the very processes responsible for the decimation of many cultural groups of the Americas led to ethnogenesis, the birth of new ones. Survivors of native societies ravaged by disease and warfare recombined with others to form new cultural groups; Africans and Afro-Americans escaped bondage to form new societies on the fringes of the plantation economies in which they had been enslaved.

Black and Indians sometimes found themselves allied in a mutual fight against Euro-American domination; at other times, the "divide and rule" policies of whites pitted the two groups against each other. The contacts between blacks and Indians brought about by the expansion of the frontier also led to the ethnogenesis of new "colonial tribes" (Helms 1969), such as the Miskito Indians of Central America, the Black Carib (currently also of Central America, but with roots in the Caribbean), and the Black Seminole, whose origins lie in the southeastern United States, primarily Florida. These groups differ from one another in the nature of the relationships that existed between Africans and Indians, but all three have structural and functional similarities that can best be demonstrated through comparative study (Helms 1977: 170).

In the discussion that follows, I will deal with the last two of these examples, the Black Carib and the Black Seminole.[1] My interest in the latter has resulted in fieldwork and historical research among a community of Black Seminole, the Seminole Freedmen of Oklahoma. I was struck by the similarities in the histories of the Black Seminole and Black Carib and undertook a comparison of the histories and social structures of these two groups to increase my own understanding of the Black Seminole in particular, but also to contribute to a better understanding of the cultural and historical processes involved in ethnogenesis.

Originally published in *Ethnohistory* 37:1 (Winter 1990), pp. 1–24. Copyright © by the Society for Ethnohistory. Reprinted by permission of Duke University Press.

## Origins: Africans and Indians

### THE BLACK CARIB

Though the exact origins of the Black Carib remain uncertain, ethnohistorical evidence indicates that some blacks on the Lesser Antilles island of St. Vincent in the seventeenth century included the survivors of the wreck of a slave ship that took place in the mid-1600s, while other Africans may have been captured from slave ships and European-settled islands by the Island Carib (Conzemius 1928: 187; Taylor 1951: 18; Craton 1982: 147). Some sources suggest that the Indians enslaved the blacks (Young 1971 [1795]: 6), while others maintain that the Africans formed their own separate colony on St. Vincent, intermarrying with the Indians and adopting their language and customs (Conzemius 1928: 188).

By the time European visitors to St. Vincent first described the island's inhabitants early in the eighteenth century, the Black Carib, as they came to be called, were already more numerous than the Island, or "Red" or "Yellow," Carib. The natural increase in their population was augmented by a steady influx of escaped slaves from the neighboring islands of Guadeloupe, Barbados, and Martinique. By the early eighteenth century, the Black and Island Carib formed two territorially and politically distinct groups, the former occupying the windward side and the latter the leeward side of the island. As the century progressed, conflicts with one another and with Europeans increased as the French and English played the two Carib groups against each other to further their colonial objectives.

### THE BLACK SEMINOLE

The escaped slaves who fled into Florida in the eighteenth century encountered not one group of aboriginal inhabitants *in situ* but a diverse aggregation of native southeastern peoples. Some were survivors of native societies decimated and scattered by disease and warfare, while others were self-exiled members of the so-called Creek Confederacy. These peoples coalesced into the Florida Seminole in the mid-eighteenth century (see Sturtevant 1971 and Wright 1986 for extensive discussions of Seminole origins).

Black slaves had been escaping from the English colony of South Carolina into Spanish-controlled Florida since the late seventeenth century. A Spanish royal decree in 1693 encouraged such escapes by promising asylum to all black deserters from the British who fled to St. Augustine and converted to Catholicism. However, severe penalties for those who were caught, along with Indian slave catchers employed by the British, apparently discouraged large numbers of slaves from marooning (fleeing their owners) to Florida during this period (TePaske 1975: 3–4). Lower Creek towns were also encouraged by the Spanish to move into northern Florida to serve as buffers against British expansion to the south. Several towns did so, and all became early components of the Seminole (Sturtevant 1971: 101).

Throughout the mid-1700s, border conflicts between the British and Spanish and their respective Indian and black allies continued. Spain ceded Florida to Britain in 1763, and many of the survivors of Indian tribes indigenous to southern Florida left with the departing Spanish, as did most of the black population of Florida (Fairbanks 1974: 155–56).

During the period of British control of Florida (1763–83), and especially during the American Revolution, blacks became an important element among the Creek and Seminole (Porter 1971: 209). British agents rewarded Creeks who served in the Revolution with slaves; other blacks were captured by the Indians through raids on plantations or joined the British and their allies on promises of freedom. With the departure of the British and the cession of Florida back to Spain in 1783, slaves fleeing from South Carolina and Georgia plantations began to take refuge among the Seminole (ibid.: 207–8).

## Conflict and Removal

### THE BLACK CARIB

In 1763, St. Vincent, like Florida, had been ceded to Britain by the terms of the Treaty of Paris. At that date, the Black Carib numbered some two thousand individuals, and the Island Carib only about a hundred families. French settlers and their slaves outnumbered both the Black and the Red Carib but were confined to the leeward side of the island (Kerns 1983: 23–25).

The British immediately began to make plans to colonize St. Vincent and to sell land to British colonists. Black and Indian resistance to incursions into their territories led the British to consider a plan whereby the Carib, both Black and Red, would be shipped off to the nearby island of Bequia or be granted areas of their own choosing within a specified region of St. Vincent. They were to be compensated for their lands and given five years to relocate (Craton 1982: 149–50). Both the Black and the Island Carib rejected this offer, and conflicts with settlers continued. In 1772, the British devised a military and naval plan to force the Carib into signing a treaty similar to one signed with Jamaican maroons in 1739. News of this plan leaked out, and settlers and Carib alike became convinced that military forces were converging on the island to exterminate the Carib population. The blacks and Indians resolved to stand their ground, and the result was a "full-scale Indian war"—the First Carib War—that ended in stalemate (ibid.: 150–51).

In 1773, a peace treaty was finally signed between the Black and Island Carib and the British. Those Caribs who desired to stay would be allowed to govern themselves, to fish around St. Vincent, and to sell their produce on any British

island. They would also be required to return any runaway slaves in their possession and to refrain from encouraging any maroons to escape or harboring any
who did, under penalty of forfeiture of their lands. If they chose, Caribs could
also leave the island (ibid.: 151–52).

Two decades of peace ensued, punctuated by Black Carib participation in the
French capture of St. Vincent in 1786, but the island was returned to the British
three years later (Kerns 1983: 27). In 1795, another Black Carib–French alliance
started the Second Carib War, a revolt that ended a year later with the surrender
of more than five thousand Black Carib men, women, and children to the British
(Craton 1982: 205–6).

Along with some Red Caribs, the Black Carib were removed from St. Vincent
in 1796 to the island of Baliseau. Overcrowding, lack of fresh water, disease, and
inadequate food there reduced their numbers from 4,195 to 2,248 before they
were transported early in 1797 to Roatan Island, off the coast of what is now Honduras. The Spanish garrison there surrendered without a shot, and the British left
the Black Carib with one ship, the captured Spanish barracks, some provisions,
and expectations that they would form a permanent colony on Roatan (Gonzalez
1983: 148–49).

## THE BLACK SEMINOLE

References to blacks among the Seminole begin in 1812 with the failed attempt of the Georgia Patriots to seize control of Florida. The intervention of free
maroon settlements and blacks living among the Indians prevented the fall of St.
Augustine (Porter 1971: 209–12). In 1813–14, Andrew Jackson and his forces entered Alabama to put down an uprising by the anti-American Red Stick Creek.
After a number of military victories against Jackson, the Red Sticks and their
black allies were finally forced to flee into northern Florida.

Promises of free land in the West Indies and protection from return to their
masters attracted fugitive slaves to Florida, where British agents, with the acquiescence of the Spanish, sought to recruit an army of fugitive Indians and runaway
slaves. Many of these blacks and Indians were established at a fort built by the
British at Prospect Bluff, at the mouth of the Apalachicola River in the Florida
Panhandle (ibid.: 215–16). American slaveowners along the Florida border were
very uneasy over this "negro fort," and in 1816 it was destroyed by two American
gunboats dispatched from New Orleans (ibid.: 218–20). Black and Seminole
towns then mobilized for the First Seminole War (1817–18), and hundreds of
Red Sticks, Seminoles, and blacks began to engage American troops in skirmishes
across northern Florida. Jackson and his forces invaded Florida in 1818, destroying black and Indian towns, engaging both groups in battle, and ultimately capturing Pensacola (ibid.: 221–32).

Jackson's invasion forced the Indian and black population of Florida farther
south, into virtually inaccessible swamps. Some blacks fled to the coastal areas of

southern Florida; many continued on to Andros Island in the Bahamas by dugout canoe or were taken there by British ships (ibid.: 233–34; Porter 1945; Goggin 1946; Kersey 1981). Unopposed by the Spanish, Jackson continued to destroy Indian and maroon towns, execute British subjects, and capture Spanish forts. In 1821, Florida was formally ceded to the United States by the Spanish (Porter 1971: 234).

The years between the takeover of Florida by the Americans and the beginning of the costly and protracted Second Seminole War in 1835 saw a change in Indian policy from confining Indian tribes to reservations in the East to removing them west of the Mississippi. In 1823, some Seminole leaders were coerced into signing a treaty accepting a reservation in Florida; they were admonished to be vigilant and return any runaway slaves. In typical "divide and rule" fashion, the Indians were warned that the blacks cared nothing for them but only wanted protection from their former owners (McReynolds 1957: 98–99, 116). When Indian removal became the official policy of the Jackson administration, a few Seminole leaders were once again coerced into signing treaties, this time providing for their removal to what is now Oklahoma; but the Seminoles who signed the treaties had no real authority to speak for the majority of the Seminole. Most opposed removal, especially the blacks, for they feared that removal meant enslavement. Seminole-American relations deteriorated, and in 1835 America's costliest Indian war broke out in Florida.

Major General Sidney Jesup emphasized in 1836 that the Second Seminole War was "a negro, not an Indian War" (Porter 1971: 238). Though part of the general policy of Indian removal, the removal of the Seminole was more importantly an effort to rid Florida of the blacks. By this time, the black population of Florida included "Seminole negroes" (blacks who were closely associated with the Indians, wore Seminole dress, and fought alongside Seminole warriors) and slaves who had been captured in raids on Florida plantations, as well as recently marooned slaves. Those blacks still enslaved on Florida plantations smuggled goods to the Indians and maroons and provided intelligence regarding white activities. Some of these slaves had relatives among the Seminole and were acquainted with the Indians well enough to have acquired at least limited knowledge of their language (ibid.: 263). Recalcitrant Seminole leaders such as Wildcat and Osceola recruited heavily from the plantations, adding more and more black fighters to their ranks (ibid.: 280–84).

By 1838, many black and Indian warriors had been captured or had surrendered to American troops. Some Seminole blacks who had served as interpreters, advisors, and spies for the Seminole now cooperated with government agents to encourage hostile factions to surrender (ibid.: 258–59). The long, bloody, and costly war ended in 1842, and the majority of the Seminole and almost all of the blacks were gradually removed to Indian Territory. Attempts by the military to identify and return to their owners more recently marooned or captured blacks had to be abandoned; to do so would have prolonged the conflict and hampered removal (ibid.: 284–85; Littlefield 1977: 36).

## The Post-Removal Period

### THE BLACK CARIB

After the departure of the British ships from Roatan in 1797, the Spanish, who saw the landing of the Black Carib as a British invasion, sent a small war party from Trujillo to recapture the island. Encountering two hundred armed Caribs on the shore, the Spanish decided to parley rather than fight and negotiated capitulation terms with the Black Carib. In 1798, most of the Black Carib were transferred to Trujillo by the Spanish (Gullick 1976: 28–29). From there, the Black Carib settlements spread out to the west and eastward along the Honduran coast. As had been their custom on St. Vincent, the Black Carib established their villages in remote settings, limiting contact with outsiders. The few Europeans who did venture into their territory described the Black Carib as friendly, peaceable, and industrious, a marked change from the hostility they had exhibited toward whites on St. Vincent. Carib settlements were located close to the coast. The men hired themselves out for months at a time as mahogany and logwood cutters (Roberts 1965 [1827]: 274) and also as sailors, smugglers, hunters, and fishermen; the women cultivated cassava and other crops, some of which they sold in Trujillo and Belize to purchase clothing and other goods (Kerns 1983: 32–33), and raised hogs, fowl, and other small stock.

Having to adjust to new geographic and economic conditions, the Black Carib also found themselves affected by changing political circumstances. Two events prior to 1832 particularly affected them. First, they were classified as Negroes rather than Indians by the constitution of the Republic of Central America in 1823. Second, they became involved in the wars between liberals and conservatives in the countries that made up the Republic, principally Guatemala, Honduras, and Nicaragua. Conflicts between Guatemala and Honduras led to a continual shifting of political control over Trujillo between them. In 1832, encouraged by the Spanish, the Black Carib staged a rebellion against the governments of the formerly Spanish-controlled countries of Honduras and Nicaragua in an effort to reestablish Spanish rule. It failed, and many Black Caribs fled to British Honduras (Gullick 1976: 31).

The Black Carib came into contact with a number of different peoples following their relocation in Central America, including British and Spanish colonists, Maya Indians, blacks, and, after their flight into British-controlled areas, Miskito Indians. British colonists soon realized that the Black Carib could be valuable as military allies and laborers. Following the failed rebellion, Black Caribs who did not flee to British Honduras or Miskito territory were allowed to remain in Spanish-speaking areas of Central America, though they were regarded with suspicion. By the end of the nineteenth century, relations between the Black Carib and Spanish-speaking Central Americans could be described as indifferent, if not hostile (ibid.: 39–41). Relations between the Black Carib and other Afro-Americans were marked by conflict and mutual antagonism. Creole blacks looked upon the Carib as inferior, while the Black Carib considered themselves culturally distinct from other blacks and maintained their social distance from them (ibid.: 42).

### THE BLACK SEMINOLE

Upon occupying their assigned lands in Indian Territory, the Seminole and blacks faced still more problems. Their lands were located in the area reserved for the Creek, and many Creeks owned black slaves. Settlements of Seminole blacks were raided by Creek slavehunters; some blacks, under the leadership of Gopher John or John Horse, sought the protection of the U.S. Army at Fort Gibson, while others continued to reside near the Seminole (Mulroy 1984: 42). In 1850, a group of Indians and blacks under Gopher John and the Seminole Wildcat left Indian Territory for Mexico, hoping at last to find a place where they could live in peace (Littlefield 1977: 147; Mulroy 1984: 42). The Mexican government granted the Indians and blacks lands in exchange for their assistance in military campaigns against the so-called wild Indians (Comanche, Lipan Apache, and Tonkawa), who plagued the northern regions of Mexico (Porter 1971: 426–29). The Seminole settlers proved to be skillful fighters, but pressure groups within Mexico in the late 1850s began to agitate for the removal of both groups. By 1861, most of the Seminole Indians had returned to Indian Territory, but the blacks remained in the settlement at Nacimiento de los Negros in Coahuila (ibid.: 457–58). Their descendants continue to live there and in Múzquiz and across the Rio Grande in Brackettville, Texas.

Black Seminoles who remained in Indian Territory were next affected by the Civil War, which unequivocally ended the controversy over the status of blacks in the Seminole nation. The Seminole were divided in their loyalties during this conflict; the fullbloods remained loyal to the Union for the most part, while other Seminoles cast their lot with the Confederacy. About two-thirds of the tribe, and most of the blacks, fled to Kansas to join other refugees, while other pro-Union blacks took refuge among the Cherokee or sought protection at Fort Gibson. The Confederate Seminoles passed a law enslaving all free blacks in the Seminole nation and confiscated their property. The Confederate sympathizers took their slaves forcibly to the Red River in the Chickasaw nation to prevent their escape northward (Littlefield 1977: 183).

At the conclusion of the war, the pro-South faction continued for a while as a separate political entity in the southern part of the Seminole nation, but it finally allowed "its" blacks to move off and form their own settlements. In the meantime, the loyalist faction and the blacks with them rejoined the nation, founding settlements in the northern part of the reservation (Mulroy 1984: 601). In the treaty of 1866 between the Seminole and the federal government, the Seminole blacks, now known as the Seminole Freedmen, were granted all the rights and privileges accruing to tribal members (ibid.: 567).

After the Civil War, two events in particular greatly affected the Seminole Freedmen. The first was the allotment of the Seminole reservation under the terms of the Dawes Act in the late 1890s, and the second was the achievement of statehood for Oklahoma in 1907. Under the terms of allotment, Indians and Freedmen alike received parcels of land that totalled nearly 350,000 acres (McReynolds 1957: 344). Members of the two Freedmen bands took their allotments in the communities they had formed both before and after the war, clustering primarily around present-day Wewoka, Sasakwa, and Seminole, Oklahoma. Only a few years after allotment, restrictions that had prevented members of the Seminole tribe from alienating their lands were lifted for Freedmen and some mixed-bloods, with the result that many Freedmen fell victim to the schemes of unscrupulous white land grafters who had moved into the old reservation area in large numbers. Many Freedmen had their lands stolen from them (see also Debo 1940).

After Oklahoma became a state, Freedmen began to experience racial discrimination as Jim Crow laws were enacted by the new state government. Prior to that time, Freedman children had attended Indian or mixed schools, but the new laws classified Indians as white and prohibited mixing of whites and blacks in schools and other social settings. Freedmen found themselves lumped together with Afro-Americans whom they regarded as strangers and outsiders. Blacks had come into Indian Territory in large numbers following their emancipation, and while the Seminole Freedmen helped many of these newcomers by renting them land to farm and lending them seed and farm equipment, the Freedmen considered themselves culturally distinct from "State raised" blacks and in the early years of contact avoided intermarriage with them. Their attitudes softened in time, so that many Freedmen today are also of non-Freedman heritage (Foster 1935; Gallaher 1951).

Black Seminoles in Texas, descendants of Black Seminoles from Mexico who became Indian scouts for the U.S. Army in the mid-1800s, found themselves in a similar situation. Texas state laws also lumped the Seminole (as the Texas people call themselves) with other blacks, whom the Seminole, like the Freedmen, regarded as foreigners.[2] They also looked with disfavor upon marriages between members of their community and "American race" outsiders (Foster 1935: 49). Mexican Black Seminoles sought to maintain their distinctiveness from other peoples by using the term *índios máscogos* to refer to themselves, an indication of their Muskogean origins (Sturtevant, pers. com., 1986).

Black Seminoles in the Andros Island communities of the Bahamas, visited in 1937 by John Goggin, had retained an oral tradition of their migration from Florida that contained a reference to a long period of time during which they remained separate and aloof from the blacks of the east coast of Andros, whom they called "Congos" or "Longas." Eventually, the two groups did begin to intermarry, and Goggin (1946: 203–4) concluded that the "culture of the Andros Island Seminole is only a variation of the typical Bahaman negro culture."

*Summary and Discussion*

A point of contrast between the Black Carib and Black Seminole is that the former became more Indian, culturally, than the blacks did among the Seminole. One reason for this is that the African maroons who were the ancestors of the Black Carib were, quite literally, "just off the boat," were predominantly male, and probably had little in common, culturally or linguistically. These black men raided Island Carib villages to abduct women (Labat 1970: 137), who then raised their children according to Carib custom and in the Carib language (Bastide 1971: 82).[3]

The blacks who became associated with the Seminole in Florida most likely shared a plantation slave culture, practiced a form of Afro-Christian faith, and spoke an English-based creole language.[4] We know that this last point is plausible because linguist Ian Hancock (1975, 1977, 1980) discovered that older Seminoles of Brackettville, Texas, had retained knowledge of an English-based creole, which Hancock termed "Afro-Seminole Creole," that was very similar to Gullah. The evidence indicates that this creole was also spoken in the Oklahoma and Mexico communities, and probably in the Andros Black Seminole settlement as well. The blacks spoke Creek/Seminole with the Indians but probably the creole within their own communities. Thus, the Black Seminole, while they did adopt some Seminole cultural practices, retained a significant degree of cultural, linguistic, and political autonomy throughout their history.[5]

The status of blacks among the Seminole seems to have been one of vassalage; black *protégés*, as Kenneth Porter (1971: 302–3) has termed them, supplied agricultural products in return for protection from enslavement. While historical sources usually refer to the blacks living among the Seminole as the Indians' slaves, the relationship between the two groups never resembled the chattel slavery that existed in other slaveholding tribes. Black Seminoles settled in separate towns, both before and after removal, fought alongside Indians in the Florida wars, and were important as advisors, interpreters, spies, and go-betweens in Indian-white dealings both in Florida and in Indian Territory.

A striking similarity between the Black Carib and Black Seminole is their staunch defense of their uniqueness and independence and their resistance to outside categorizations based solely on their physical appearance. Throughout their histories both groups have fought to preserve their distinctive ways of life while adjusting to new social, political, and economic environments. Today, the Black Carib and Black Seminole recognize their affinity with other Afro-Americans: a young Black Carib man emphasizes the "Afro-Caribbean" component of his heritage (Gonzalez 1983: 161–62); a woman of the Black Seminole community of Red Bays, Andros Island, proudly proclaims, "I be Africa descended" (Sturtevant, pers. com., 1986); and Seminole Freedmen in Oklahoma prominently display portraits of Martin Luther King, Jr., in their homes. Yet these examples do not represent a loss or rejection of their Indian heritage; rather, they reflect the many years during which both the Black Carib and the Black Seminole have been treated by the larger societies in which they reside as *blacks* and have responded by forging social and political bonds with other Afro-Americans. For the Black Seminole, who have historically identified themselves as black people affiliated with but not the same as the Seminole Indians, this growing solidarity with other blacks represents an expansion of their ethnic identity.[6] For the Black Carib, their developing awareness and recognition of their African roots and their relatedness to other Afro-American societies seem like a more radical departure from their long-standing identity as an Indian group, but it would be foolhardy to predict a complete rejection or loss of their "Caribness," given their long history of fiercely protecting their ethnic uniqueness.

The ability of any group to retain its ethnic distinctiveness largely depends on its members' ability to maintain ties to one another and to their communities and thus to preserve a sense of group identity that transcends even geographic dislocations. The domestic organization of a society, the makeup of its families and communities and the relationships among its members, therefore is crucial to our understanding of how ethnicity is preserved and maintained.

### Black Carib and Black Seminole Domestic Organization

#### THE BLACK CARIB

A considerable body of literature on Black Carib domestic organization has been written, primarily by Nancie Gonzalez (1969), Mary Helms (1976, 1981), and Virginia Kerns (1983). A central focus of these writings is the presence among the Black Carib of the so-called consanguineal household, comprising related women and their children to whom men, in the roles of husbands and fathers, are attached. Helms (1976, 1981: 77), who has argued for the antiquity of this domestic form, asserts that contemporary Black Carib domestic organization, with both the consanguineal household and the practice of polygyny, shows strong structural similarities both to earlier forms among the Black Carib and to Island Carib domestic arrangements as recorded in the mid-seventeenth century. She undertook her study in response to Gonzalez's (1969: 9–11) assertion that the consanguineal household as it exists today among the Black Carib "arises in certain systems as a functional result of the group's attempt to adapt to a modern economy" and is particularly a feature of societies Gonzalez (1970) has termed "neoteric," that is, those that have supposedly "shallow cultural roots" that have formed recently (ibid.). Moreover, Gonzalez believes that contemporary Black Carib culture as a whole should be viewed as a variant of a generalized West Indian culture rather than as related to any particular Indian group (Solien 1959).

Helms agrees that the current mode of domestic organization of the Black Carib is well adapted both to the diversity of their economic pursuits and to the conditions of economic marginality necessitating such diversity, but she sees no reason to assume that current economic conditions created the consanguineal household. Rather, she views Black Carib domestic organization as traditional Carib marital and residential patterns in modern form (Helms 1981: 84–85). The problem with this emphasis on household composition is that the dynamism and adaptiveness of household membership is obscured (Ryan 1982: 126), illustrating Carol Stack's (1971) observation that the household is not always the most useful unit of study for trying to understand the actual interactions of family members. It is the fluidity of Black Carib (and Black Seminole) domestic arrangements that has enabled them to adapt to new socioeconomic conditions.[7]

Polygyny, like household composition, has historical roots among the Island Carib that extend back at least to the seventeenth century, when European observers described it. At that time most Carib men had only one wife; polygyny, though not uncommon, was practiced primarily by village and family headmen. A few of these men had several wives, some living on different islands; ideally, a husband was expected to visit his wives on a rotational basis (Helms 1981: 81). Polygyny was reported among the Black Carib from the late eighteenth through the twentieth centuries, and white observers noted that Black Carib fathers were conscientious about the care of their children, even if the mother and father had split. The husband generally kept his wives in separate houses and yards and was supposed to divide both his time and any gifts he made equally among them (ibid.: 82–83). In the early decades of this century, polygyny continued to be practiced in much the same way, with the exception that a man rarely had more than one wife in the same village. Today, some Black Carib men associate with several common-law wives, sometimes concurrently. Helms (ibid.: 84) terms this pattern "polygyny in contemporary guise."

Again, we find differing opinions on the continuity between past and present in regard to domestic forms. Gonzalez (1969: 72) refers to the taking of common-law wives as a form of "modified monogamy," because, she says, this form of "marriage" is not considered ideal by the Black Carib, and because the women involved usually do not accept each other.[8] She notes, though, that some women do like and accept the arrangement, visit back and forth, share goods, and help each other with household duties. A man is expected to recognize the children of both women equally and to assert his paternity legally by registering the children as his with municipal authorities. By doing so, he enables the children to inherit from him (ibid.: 79). If a father fails to support his children, a woman can go to court and demand a minimum allowance for each child recognized by the father (ibid.: 72).[9]

Each Black Carib community, whether in Belize, Guatemala, Honduras, or Nicaragua, is separate and autonomous from every other Black Carib community, and an individual considers his place of birth his lifetime home, regardless of where he might later live. Indeed, one's birthplace is a fundamental aspect of a Black Carib's social identity (Kerns 1983: 56). Historically, Black Carib villages, both on St. Vincent and in Central America, were established in isolated settings, and while men in particular were very mobile and pursued wage work outside the village, life inside Black Carib communities centered on food production carried out primarily by the women (ibid.: 32–33). An individual's community was a place to come back to, no matter how far he might have traveled in search of employment or how long he might have lived in another village or town.

### THE BLACK SEMINOLE

Comparable literature on domestic organization for any of the Black Seminole communities is virtually nonexistent except for certain sections in Gallaher 1951 and Mulroy 1984. The following discussion is therefore based on my own fieldwork among the Seminole Freedmen of Oklahoma and on an admittedly preliminary analysis of documentary sources, primarily census and annuity rolls and probate and civil court records.[10]

An important distinction between the Seminole Indians and the Black Seminole is the absence among the latter of the matrilineal clan system, the basis of Seminole kinship and social relations (see Gallaher 1951: 111–13). Though blacks were sometimes incorporated into Indian clans to participate in dances and ceremonials, the Freedmen, as one elderly Freedman expressed it, "didn't pay no attention to anything like that [the prohibition against intraclan marriage], 'cause we figures you ain't related unless it is blood kin" (ibid.: 112).

The most valuable sources in studying domestic organization among the Seminole Freedmen are the censuses and annuity payment rolls, where individuals were grouped according to "household." However, it is often difficult or impossible to ascertain what a household was and what social units the groups of names represent. Also, given the caveats mentioned above regarding the use of the household as a unit of study, these documents tend to reify domestic arrangements that were, like those of the Black Carib, quite fluid. They also provide few clues as to the actual interactions of people within Freedman communities or to the relationships of family members. However, when we compare these rolls with one another, we have the opportunity to see how the groupings of individuals changed through time.

Household groupings composed of related women and their children appear on these records, with no men listed; some of these women had their children by several different men. Many of these female-headed households are seen to break up as the women form new relationships with men; they and their children then appear in male-headed households. In other cases, the husbands/fathers are listed as single individuals, with other wives and children, or with their natal families.

Husbands/fathers who were non-Seminole, whether black, Indian, or white, usually do not show up on tribal censuses and rolls at all, even though they may have been present in the household with their wives and children. Thus, the assertion can be made that the consanguineal household existed among the Freedmen, and such domestic groupings no doubt were not uncommon. But the documents alone do not suggest a father's role, not do they illuminate a woman's relationship with the family or families of the man or men by whom she had children, or the assistance and support she received from her own kin. The memories of informants are much more useful for these purposes.

Some elderly Freedmen today recall growing up in large families headed by two parents, while others describe households made up of two or more generations of women and their children with no husbands/fathers permanently present. Still other Freedmen remember living in several different households while growing up, owing to the death of one or both parents or the breakup of a marriage, and being raised by relatives. Household composition, then, was fluid, while Freedman communities were characterized by sharing and cooperation among family members residing in different households.

During the period after removal and prior to Oklahoma's achieving statehood, some Freedman communities relied heavily upon hunting, fishing, and gathering, with agriculture supplying supplemental food. While the women did most of the gardening, the men helped out with the plowing and planting of large plots (ibid.: 33). Other communities relied more upon the raising of cattle and other stock. Just prior to and after statehood, the influx of white and black settlers to the area depleted the game supply, and the Freedmen came to rely more and more upon agriculture for their subsistence. As game became scarce, the men turned more of their attention to farming and tending livestock (ibid.: 35). After allotment and the massive loss of land that ensued, both men and women were forced to seek wage work outside their communities as laborers, field hands, and domestics. The family cooperation crucial in a subsistence economy based on agriculture and cattle raising now adapted itself to this new economic pattern: a woman's mother or sisters tended her children as she went off to work, and male relatives and neighbors cooperated in cutting and hauling lumber for sale. The self-sufficiency of the Freedman community prior to allotment, the result of abundant land, began to decline, however, as many Freedmen found themselves landless and what little land they retained was turned to the planting of such cash crops as cotton.

One explanation for the appearance of some of the female-headed households on censuses is the practice of polygyny among the Black Seminole, which they shared with the Indians. While most Seminole men had only one wife, older and wealthier men were frequently polygynous; in most cases the wives were sisters and resided in the same house with the husband. When the wives were not sisters, they usually were maintained by the husband in separate dwellings. Polygyny continued to be practiced by the Seminole until the early 1900s (Swanton 1928: 79; Spoehr 1942: 92). Among the Freedmen, this pattern also existed. As one Freedman put it, "As long as you put them womens up in a house of they own, and fed and take care of them, they wuz you wives, and no one else could bother them. At least, they wuzn't sposed to bother them" (Gallaher 1951: 56). Among the blacks, a man was expected to provide separate houses for his wives and their children and to visit them in turn (ibid.). He was also expected to provide for the support of his wives and children. A centenarian Freedwoman, describing the practice of separate dwellings for wives, said that if one wife got sick, the other, along with neighbor women, would go to the sick woman's house and cook, iron, clean, and wash for her. When the husband butchered a cow or hog, he would distribute the meat among the wives and their children. This informant reported "no fussin' or fightin' or nothin' " between the wives, and other Freedman similarly described cordial and even sisterly relations among wives, though no one knew of any cases in which the wives actually were sisters.

Most of the cases of polygyny I have documented come from the period between the last two decades of the nineteenth and the first decade or so of the twentieth century. The men involved fit the description of the typical polygynous male among the Seminole: all were men of some prominence and/or wealth and included band leaders and tribal council representatives, lighthorsemen, and leaders in Freedman churches. Women may have been attracted to polygynous relationships with these individuals: most of these men had jobs that paid them cash wages, and in a subsistence economy, a man with cash could provide more store-bought goods to his wives. After Oklahoma achieved statehood, Seminole Freedwomen, like the Black Carib, began to use the legal system to ensure paternal support for their offspring.[11]

Until the first decade or so of this century, marriages among the Seminole Freedmen could be made or broken with relative ease, though many lasted for many years.[12] The fluidity of relationships between men and women in Freedman communities, their tendency (until fairly recently) to avoid marriages with non-Freedmen, and the fact that, until substantial numbers of Freedmen began to leave the native communities after the First World War, children generally settled near their parents (ibid.: 63–64) all contributed to the creation and maintenance of communities made up of several large, extended families. These communities tended to be relatively insular. All individual's ties to his community were strong and remained so even if he ventured far away in search of a livelihood. Freedmen continue to return to the now mostly depopulated rural communities for church homecomings, family reunions, funerals, and their own interment in Freedman cemeteries (ibid.: 77).

The division of the entire Freedman population into just two bands for purposes of representation on the Seminole tribal council brought the residents of the various Freedman communities together to attend band meetings and discuss political action and tribal affairs. Intermarriage among the Freedman communities has also bound all Freedman to one another through complex ties of kinship. Freedmen today will say that they are all related; a glance at any individual's genealogy shows that this statement is no exaggeration.

## COMMUNITY/DOMESTIC ORGANIZATION AND ETHNICITY

The Black Carib and Black Seminole have in common aspects not only of cultural history but also, at a deeper structural level, of family composition, attachment to birthplace, and marital practice. But to what extent have these social-structural features enabled both groups historically to maintain their distinctiveness?

It should be reemphasized that among both the Black Carib and the Black Seminole (specifically, the Seminole Freedmen), communities tend to be largely separate and autonomous and their inhabitants to have a very definite sense of their superiority to, or at least distinctiveness from, those of other settlements. This is true for the Black Carib today (Kerns 1983: 6, 56–57) and, to judge from my fieldwork, also for the Freedmen historically. The residents of a community were bound to one another by complex ties of kinship, owing in no small measure to the fact that so many men and women had children by more than one mate (ibid.: 116).

The association of the Seminole Freedmen with the Seminole tribe and their representation by bands on the tribal council cut across community distinctions, and this relationship with the Seminole has served as an important integrating mechanism tying all Freedmen to one another. At times, they have found themselves at odds with the Seminole, when the political or economic interests of the Indians diverged from theirs. In fact, the relationship between the Seminole and Black Seminole throughout their history can best be described as ambivalent. There have been periods in which the Indians endeavored to separate themselves from the Freedmen by excluding them from membership and participation in the tribe. To date their efforts have all failed, because they have not been able to circumvent the 1866 treaty that granted the blacks all rights of tribal membership. Ironically, the Seminole's attempts to exclude the blacks have served to unite the Freedmen in a common cause, illustrating that their relationship to the tribe that would cast them out continues to be an important focus of their identity.[13]

Black Carib communities cooperate with each other only on one occasion each year, Settlement Day, which commemorates the arrival of the first Black Carib settlers in Belize (ibid.: 57). There are no formal ties, political or eco-

nomic, that tie the communities together (ibid.: 6). In contrast to the Black Seminole, the Black Carib do not have to struggle to maintain their ties to an Indian
group. Rather, they identify themselves and are identified by others as an Indian
people, who speak an Indian language and have cultural practices that are
uniquely the result of their Indian origins. Because so many Black Carib, particularly males, work outside their communities of birth, to return "home" is to reaf-
firm their identities as Caribs by speaking the Carib language and following
Carib cultural practices that distinguish them from "other races" (ibid.).

For both the Black Carib and Black Seminole, an extensive kin network provided a support system to rely on in times of need. Whether or not a woman had
a man to help support her and her children, she had relatives nearby who could
help her with child care or financial assistance or could take her and her children
in for a period of time. For the Black Carib, a high incidence of local endogamy,
and the tendency of women to continue to reside in their birthplace after forming unions with "strangers" from other villages, contributed to a prevalence of
mothers and daughters residing in the same community (ibid.: 109). A preliminary analysis of residence patterns for the Oklahoma Black Seminole suggests a
similar pattern, with some communities tending to be more endogamous than
others (see Mulroy 1984: 630). Couples generally resided near their families after
marriage, resulting in a similar pattern of daughters and their children remaining near their mothers.[14] In the few cases of intermarriage that did occur during
the early period of contact with "State" blacks, Freedmen rarely left their native
communities (Gallaher 1951: 89). After allotment and the massive loss of lands
among the Freedmen, a married couple sometimes was obliged to live outside
the native communities on property retained by relatives or to lease land from
white or Indian owners.

Uxorilocal residence, by providing a core of consanguineal women to tie separate families together even if husbands/fathers are absent or not members of
the group, contributes to the maintenance of cultural identity through continued
local expression of traditional forms of kinship, generosity, and general cultural
patterns (Helms 1968: 461). Kerns's (1983) work demonstrates that this is very
much the case for the Black Carib, and, as we have seen, the pattern of male
out-migration and the uncertainty of their labor and the amount and frequency
of the cash contributions they can make to their families have contributed to
the preservation of the consanguineal household, polygyny, and matrilocality
among the Black Carib (Helms 1981: 84). The Black Seminole, while not strictly
matrilocal, can also be said to exhibit a similar pattern of women playing the
important role of preservers and transmitters of cultural patterns. An individual's
identity as a Black Seminole and his band membership are inherited through
his mother, which, as Gallaher (1951: 113) has suggested, probably parallels the
matrilineal emphasis on clan membership among the Seminole. An individual whose mother was a "State" woman, for example, would not be considered

Freedman, even if his father were. In addition, strong bonds between mothers and daughters are often expressed by older Freedwomen, especially when the husband/father was not a permanent presence in the household.

## Conclusions

My purpose here has been to compare two Afro-Indian groups, though it should be quite clear that the Black Carib and Black Seminole differ substantially in the degree to which they were and are culturally Indian. The slaves who fled into Florida did not, in most cases, become culturally Indian but formed societies that were distinct blends of Afro-American and Indian cultural practices. Because the Seminole were themselves an amalgam of peoples of diverse cultural and linguistic background, the blacks who settled and allied with them became an integral part of the Seminole people (Wright 1981: 277). For the African maroons of St. Vincent, historical circumstances led to the ethnogenesis of a uniquely New World people, phenotypically African but culturally owing much to the Island Carib.[15] Continued investigation and comparative study of these "New Peoples" (Ribeiro 1968: 110) will bring ethnohistorians to a better understanding of how Europeans, Indians, and Africans interacted in the Americas to create a truly new world.

## Notes

The author wishes to thank Ken Bilby, Amy Bushnell, Michael Kenny, James Merrell, Sidney Mintz, Richard Price, and William Sturtevant for their comments and suggestions on earlier drafts of this paper, as well as Shepard Krech III and the anonymous reviewers of the original manuscript; the Wenner-Gren Foundation for Anthropological Research, for funding her fieldwork among the Seminole Freedmen of Oklahoma; and the Seminole Freedmen themselves, for their patience and hospitality.

1. "Black Carib" has been the standard designation in published ethnographic and historical works, but the names applied to the St. Vincent maroons throughout history have changed. In the eighteenth century, the British referred to the "free negroes of St. Vincent," "Black Indians," "Wild Negroes," and "Black Charibbs" (Kerns 1983: 12–13). Young (1971 [1795]: 8) states that this last term was the one chosen by the maroons themselves. Kerns (1983: 12) found that most Black Caribs she knew never used "Black Carib" among themselves but referred to themselves as Caribs or as *Garífuna*, depending on what language, English or Carib, they used. Seminole blacks have also been called various things by whites, including "Seminole Negroes," "Indian negroes," and, after the Civil War, "Seminole Freedmen." This last term, along with "native," is used by the Oklahoma blacks to refer to themselves, but other Black Seminole communities in Texas and Mexico use other terms. Richard Price and William Sturtevant have suggested that Seminole blacks in all of their communities might best be termed "Seminole maroons," an "etymological doublet" (Sturtevant 1979: 917), since both *Seminole* and *maroon* are derived from the same Spanish word, *cimarrón*. I have chosen to use "Black Seminole" mainly because,

like "Seminole maroons," it suggests that, their close affiliation with the Seminole Indians notwithstanding, the Afro-American heritage of the blacks played a strong role in the formation of a unique Black Seminole culture.

2. The Black Seminole of Texas, long separated from the Seminole tribe, use the designation "Seminoles" to distinguish themselves from other blacks and also to emphasize their pride in their unique history. These descendants of the Seminole Negro Indian Scouts, noted for their bravery and skill as scouts for the U.S. Army on the Texas frontier, are fiercely proud of their ancestors and have formed the Seminole Indian Scout Cemetery Association to maintain the cemetery near Brackettville that is the resting place of many of the scouts, including four Congressional Medal of Honor winners.

3. Michael Craton (1986: 112–13) suggests that the Island Carib first thought of blacks as intruders fit to be slaughtered or enslaved, the same as whites or Arawaks, but came to regard them as allies and by 1700, at the latest, had begun to encourage black runaways to settle with them, make common cause, and intermarry. He attributes this change in attitude to the sharp decline in the Island Carib population after 1500, as well as to a long-standing pattern among the Carib of forming alliances to resist European encroachments.

4. From his examination of advertisements for groups of runaway slaves that appeared in the Charleston, South Carolina, newspapers from 1799 to 1830, Michael Johnson (1981) has determined that many of these groups, especially those made up of slaves from rural areas, were composed of individuals who were related; the most common rural family group included a husband and wife, often accompanied by one or more children (ibid.: 433). Other maroon groups included members of the same community or work group. While it is very difficult, if not impossible, to determine whether or not slaves mentioned in these advertisements made their way into Florida, Johnson's study illustrates that maroons who did reach Florida may have arrived in family and/or community groups and been able to build their new communities around kin and their shared experiences of slave-quarter culture and language.

5. The Black Carib continue to speak an Indian language within their own communities, but few if any Black Seminoles today can speak any Seminole, and Afro-Seminole Creole survives only among a small number of mostly elderly individuals. Intermarriage with non-Seminole blacks, out-migration from Black Seminole communities, social stigma attached by outsiders to the speaking of "broken English," and, for the Oklahoma blacks, the historical process of gradual replacement of Creek/Seminole by English among both blacks and Indians have all contributed to the decline in use of these languages, making it all the more difficult for Black Seminoles to assert their distinctiveness from other Afro-Americans.

6. A quote that Kenneth Porter (1971: 3) collected from an elderly Black Seminole woman of Brackettville, Texas, succinctly illustrates this point: "We's cullud people. I don't say we don't has no Injun blood, 'cause we has. But we ain't no Injuns. We's cullud people!"

7. Helms's work suggests that this same type of dynamic composition of domestic units may have enabled the Island Carib to adapt to and survive rapid population declines as the result of European incursions.

8. Virginia Kerns (1983: 113) describes such unions as "secondary," because in cases where men support and alternately reside with two women, one has a secondary status from the community's point of view. Most women, she says, disapprove of such relation-

ships, because they nearly always lead to conflict between the two women, especially if they both have young children and depend heavily on their common husband for support.

9. Gonzalez's evidence suggests strongly that the pattern of the coexistence of monogamous and polygynous unions among the Black Carib persists, and that men and women involved in polygynous relationships have learned to use the legal system to ensure that fathers meet their obligations to their children. While polygynous unions may not be socially recognized as a desirable form of marital union, the taking of multiple spouses functions in much the same way.

10. Of the census materials, the Dawes roll, compiled when the Seminole and Freedmen lands were allotted in the late 1890s, is the most useful, because information available from the original census cards lists the parents of each individual, the band membership and owner (if any) of each individual and his or her parents, the location of the allotment, post office (a valuable indicator of residence), and age. Individuals listed together on a census card represent some sort of family or household grouping, though it is not clear in all cases whether or not these households were actually residential units. Probate court records, especially when the testimony in probate cases can be found, provide an invaluable source of genealogical information, because detailing relationships among individuals in such cases was extremely important. Heirship depositions are particularly rich sources of genealogical information, though their accuracy should always be checked with informants when possible.

11. After Oklahoma achieved statehood, polygyny became more and more problematic legally as new inheritance laws went into effect. Determining the legitimacy of the offspring of polygynous unions, especially those formed prior to statehood, created problems for local courts, so that some cases involving polygynous Seminole Freedmen went to the state supreme court. Complicating matters was the fact that no fewer than three sets of laws (tribal, Arkansas state, and Oklahoma state), plus a few special agreements made between the Seminole tribe and the federal government, were in effect at various times; each affected inheritance differently. Under tribal law, for instance, if a minor died, his or her property would be inherited by the mother or siblings and their heirs rather than by the child's father, while under Oklahoma state law, a father was allowed to inherit. Because children also received allotments of land, the right of a father to inherit from his child became quite important, so the establishment of the legitimacy of a child became a much graver issue. Fathers sought to establish their paternity legally as well, so that their children would be able to inherit from them. Mothers brought suit to have their children included in the distribution of the estate in the event that they had not been legally recognized. Figuring out what set of laws and agreements were in effect when, and which set applied in any particular case, caused headaches for the courts and must have been nearly incomprehensible to the majority of Seminole and Freedmen, who were, for the most part, illiterate.

12. Informants refer variously to the women involved in what I am terming polygynous relationships; it often depends on the informant's age. Younger individuals tend not to regard all of the women as wives but generally refer to them as a man's "women." Elderly Freedmen, on the other hand, are more likely to refer to these women as a man's wives. Individuals also differ in their attitudes toward such unions, particularly towards the men involved. Again, elderly people tend to be less critical of such relationships, while younger people find it hard to understand how the women could accept them. These differences of opinion indicate that the acceptance of polygyny as an alternative to monogamy has

declined over time, owing in no small part to the legal problems associated with polygyny (see n. 11). In addition, Art Gallaher (pers. com., 1986) has suggested that the racial discrimination aimed at the Freedman and other blacks since statehood led to their downplaying cultural practices that they feared might be considered "heathen," a reaction that might lead to even more discrimination and reprisals from whites.

13. Currently, the Freedmen and Seminole are still struggling over the disbursement of funds awarded by the Indian Claims Commission some ten years ago for lands ceded by the Seminole in Florida prior to removal. This multimillion-dollar award is to be divided between the Oklahoma and Florida Seminole (who have been unable to agree between themselves how to divide the funds equitably). The original disbursement plan excluded the Freedman, who challenged it before a congressional committee. The Freedmen contended that their ancestors were indeed an integral part of the Seminole tribe in Florida, and that therefore the Freedmen should be included in the distribution of funds. They enlisted the aid of the congressional Black Caucus and won the support of some Oklahoma congressmen. Though some groups within the Seminole tribe of Oklahoma support the cause of the Freedmen (if only to end the stalemate and get on with the disbursement of the much-needed funds), many Seminoles do not, contending that the ancestors of the Freedmen were only the slaves of the Seminole while in Florida, and that the Freedmen were not made members of the tribe until the 1866 treaty. It appears that an agreement is still a long way off.

14. While I know of no specific preference for uxorilocal residence, my informants reported that the initial aversion to intermarriage with "State" blacks was expressed particularly in regard to Freedwomen marrying non-Freedman men and thus being taken away from their families and native communities.

15. Regrettably, Nancie Gonzalez's 1988 book on Garifuna history and ethnogenesis, a major contribution to Black Carib studies, was published too late to be included in this article.

## References

Bastide, Roger
    1971            African Civilizations in the New World. New York: Harper & Row.

Conzemius, Eduard
    1928            Ethnographical Notes on the Black Carib (Garif). American Anthropologist 30: 183–205.

Craton, Michael
    1982            Testing the Chains: Resistance to Slavery in the British West Indies. Ithaca: Cornell University Press.
    1986            From Caribs to Black Caribs: The Amerindian Roots of Servile Resistance in the Caribbean. In In Resistance: Studies in African, Caribbean, and Afro-American History. Gary Y. Okihiro, ed. Pp. 96–116. Amherst: University of Massachusetts Press.

Debo, Angie
    1940            And Still the Waters Run: The Betrayal of the Five Civilized Tribes. Princeton: Princeton University Press.

Fairbanks, Charles
    1974            Ethnohistorical Report on the Florida Indians 3. New York: Garland.

Foster, Laurence
  . 1935            Negro-Indian Relationships in the Southeast. Ph.D. diss., University
                    of Pennsylvania.

Gallaher, Art
    1951            A Survey of the Seminole Freedmen. M.A. thesis, University of Okla-
                    homa.
    1986            Letter to author, December 9.

Goggin, John
    1946            The Seminole Negroes of Andros Island, Bahamas. Florida Histori-
                    cal Quarterly 24: 201–6.

Gonzalez, Nancie L. Solien
    1969            Black Carib Household Structure: A Study of Migration and Mod-
                    ernization. Seattle: University of Washington Press.
    1970            The Neoteric Society. Comparative Studies in Society and History
                    12: 1–13.
    1983            New Evidence on the Origin of the Black Carib, with Thoughts on
                    the Meaning of Tradition. New West Indian Guide 57: 143–72.
    1988            Sojourners of the Caribbean: Ethnogenesis and Ethnohistory of the
                    Garifuna. Urbana: University of Illinois Press.

Gullick, C. J. M. R.
    1976            Exiled from St. Vincent. Malta: Progress.

Hancock, Ian
    1975            Creole Features in the Afro-Seminole Speech of Brackettville, Texas.
                    Society for Caribbean Linguistics Occasional Papers, No. 3. Mona,
                    Jamaica: Society for Caribbean Linguistics.
    1977            Further Observations on Afro-Seminole Creole. Society for Carib-
                    bean Linguistics Occasional Papers, No. 7. Mona, Jamaica: Society
                    for Caribbean Linguistics.
    1980            Texan Gullah: The Creole English of the Brackettville Afro-Semi-
                    noles. In Perspectives on American English. J. L. Dillard, ed. Pp.
                    305–33. The Hague: Mouton.

Helms, Mary
    1968            Matrilocality and the Maintenance of Ethnic Identity: The Miskito
                    of Eastern Nicaragua and Honduras. In Verhandlungen des achtund-
                    dreißigsten internationalen Amerikanisten Kongresses. Pp. 459–64.
                    Stuttgart.
    1969            The Cultural Ecology of a Colonial Tribe. Ethnology 8: 76–84.
    1976            Domestic Organization in Eastern Central America: The San Blas
                    Cuna, Miskito, and Black Carib Compared. Western Canadian Jour-
                    nal of Anthropology 6: 133–63.
    1977            Negro or Indian? The Changing Identity of a Frontier Population. In
                    Old Roots in New Lands: Historical and Anthropological Perspec-

tives on Black Experiences in the Americas. Ann M. Pescatello, ed.
Pp. 155–72. Westport, CT: Greenwood.

1981        Black Carib Domestic Organization in Historical Perspective: Tradi-
            tional Origins of Contemporary Patterns. Ethnology 20: 77–86.

Johnson, Michael
1981        Runaway Slaves and the Slave Communities in South Carolina,
            1799–1830. William and Mary Quarterly 38: 418–41.

Kerns, Virginia
1983        Women and the Ancestors: Black Carib Kinship and Ritual. Urbana:
            University of Illinois Press.

Kersey, Harry A., Jr.
1981        The Seminole Negroes of Andros Island Revisited: Some New
            Pieces to an Old Puzzle. Florida Anthropologist 34: 169–76.

Labat, Jean-Baptiste
1970        The Memoirs of Père Labat. John Eaden, trans. and ed. London:
            Frank Cass.

Littlefield, Daniel F., Jr.
1977        Africans and Seminoles: From Removal to Emancipation. Westport,
            CT: Greenwood.

McReynolds, Edwin
1957        The Seminoles. Norman: University of Oklahoma Press.

Mulroy, Kevin
1984        Relations between Blacks and Seminoles after Removal. Ph.D. diss.,
            University of Keele.

Porter, Kenneth
1945        Notes on Seminole Negroes in the Bahamas. Florida Historical
            Quarterly 24: 56–60.
1971        The Negro on the American Frontier. New York: Arno.

Ribeiro, Darcy
1968        The Civilizational Process. Betty J. Meggers, trans. Washington:
            Smithsonian Institution Press.

Roberts, Orlando
1965 [1827] Narrative of Voyages and Excursions on the East Coast and in the In-
            terior of Central America. Gainesville: University of Florida Press.

Ryan, Kathleen
1982        Black Carib Household Structure: A Study of Migration and Mod-
            ernization, by Nancie L. Solien Gonzalez [review]. L'Homme 22:
            125–27.

Solien, Nancie
1959        West Indian Characteristics of the Black Carib. Southwestern Jour-
            nal of Anthropology 16: 144–59.

Spoehr, Alexander
    1942          Kinship System of the Seminole. Field Museum Anthropological Se-
                  ries 33: 37–113.

Stack, Carol
    1971          All Our Kin: Strategies for Survival in a Black Community. New
                  York: Harper & Row.

Sturtevant, William
    1971          Creek into Seminole. In North American Indians in Historical Per-
                  spective. Eleanor B. Leacock and Nancy O. Lurie, eds. Pp. 92–128.
                  New York: Random House.
    1979          Africans and Seminoles: From Removal to Emancipation, by Daniel
                  F. Littlefield, Jr. [review]. American Anthropologist 81: 916–17.
    1986          Correspondence with author, November 15.

Swanton, John R.
    1928          Social Organization and Social Usages of the Indians of the Creek
                  Confederacy. In Bureau of American Ethnology Forty-second An-
                  nual Report, 1924–25. Pp. 23–472. Washington: U.S. Government
                  Printing Office.

Taylor, Douglas
    1951          The Black Carib of British Honduras. Viking Fund Publications in
                  Anthropology, No. 17. New York: Wenner-Gren.

TePaske, John
    1975          The Fugitive Slave: Intercolonial Rivalry and Spanish Slave Policy,
                  1687–1764. In Eighteenth-Century Florida and Its Borderlands.
                  Samuel Proctor, ed. Pp. 1–12. Gainesville: University of Florida
                  Press.

Wright, J. Leitch, Jr.
    1981          The Only Land They Knew: The Tragic Story of the American Indi-
                  ans in the Old South. New York: Free Press.
    1986          Creeks and Seminoles: The Destruction and Regeneration of the
                  Muscogulge People. Lincoln: University of Nebraska Press.

Young, William
    1971 [1795]   An Account of the Black Charaibs in the Island of St. Vincent's. Lon-
                  don: Frank Cass

# 9. PANTERA NEGRA

## A Messianic Figure of Historical Resistance and Cultural Survival among Maroon Descendants in Southern Venezuela

*Berta Pérez*

Structuralist analyses of non-Western peoples such as the descendants of Vene-zuelan Maroons often negate history or historical consciousness of social realities. People such as the Maroons are thereby presented as passive recipients in the making of history vis-à-vis Western society. The work of Claude Lévi-Strauss (e.g., 1966), wherein he sets forth his distinction between "cold" (mythic) and "hot" (historical) societies, exemplifies such thematic tendencies. By contrast with Lévi-Strauss's structuralism, the historical orientation of such scholars as Jan Vansina (1965), Richard Price (1983), and Jonathan Hill (1988, 1996) provides a dynamic means by which to analyze myth as historicity wherein people drama-tize their pasts to communicate key reference points (hence "structure") across generations. Terence Turner writes:

> The work of Lévi-Strauss and other structuralist writers on lowland South Ameri-can cultures has perpetuated certain romantic notions about the nature of social consciousness in these societies, such as that they lack a notion of history, either of themselves or of their contact with Western society, having instead a totally "mythic" formulation of social reality . . . [this "mythic" formulation tends] to give way to, or decay into [a "historical" formulation] when the native social order, conceived as an internally static, unselfconscious system in its pristine, precontact state, is disrupted by the irreversible historical changes imposed from without by Western society. (Turner 1988a:195)

An assumption that people in non-Western societies are incapable of historical consciousness of social reality, either of themselves or of their contact with West-ern society, or that their first experience of history (based on conflict, contradic-tion, and change) arises from an imposed contact by Western society is sharply contested by many ethnographers. The assumption of human and cultural inca-

Printed by permission of Berta E. Pérez.

pacity with regard to history and historicity obscures the possibility of examining the "historical counterdiscourses" created by non-Western peoples that give insights into processes of ethnic empowerment and resistance over Western hegemony (Hill 1992, 1996).

There has been an increased concern over the last two decades among many anthropologists to reexamine the nature of social consciousness of people living in what are often called "non-Western societies." Emphasis has been directed to the study of non-Western cultures as being historically situated and grounded in any given set of political economic conditions. This has, in turn, allowed anthropologists to view human subjects as active social agents in the interpretation, construction, reproduction, and transformation of their experience with agents of Western society.

The findings from this redirected approach suggest "that the 'savage mind' is capable of historical consciousness and can even bring mythical consciousness to bear on the historical fact of colonization" (Beckett 1993:676). Non-Western peoples are active social agents; they certainly possess historical consciousness. Indeed, they merge historical consciousness with their mythic formulations to act in all sorts of situations involving other people.

Contemporary anthropological studies contend that mythic and historical formulations of social reality among non-Western societies are not contradictory; rather, they are compatible and complementary modes of discourse (Asad 1987, Beckett 1993, Bricker 1981, Comaroff and Comaroff 1987, 1992; Farris 1987, Friedmann 1992, Guss 1986, 1993; Hill 1988, 1992, 1993, 1996; Hugh-Jones 1988, McGuire 1992, Price 1983, Urton 1990). Roger Rasnake explains:

> The subjects' model addresses the present situation with a consciousness of transformation as well as an awareness of the past. Symbolic forms, and especially myths, thus picture the past as an arena in which the present situation of paradox was created. Myth becomes history—the mythic vision becomes imbued with a consciousness of time and transformation—and at the same time, history becomes myth—"real" events of the past . . . are modified and shaped not only to conform to principles of order in a particular cultural tradition but also to express the contemporary perception of the meaning of past events; and this is done in such a way that the remembered transformation creates a contradiction, or a paradox, that is yet to be resolved. (Rasnake 1988: 139–140)

Rasnake states that this paradox becomes clearer in the connection between social order and shared systems of meaning, and that with contradictions there is a push towards dialectical resolutions.

Colonialism entailed for the colonizers and the colonized a paradox that evoked a push toward dialectical resolutions of contradictions. Both the colonizers and the colonized were trapped in a double paradox. The colonizers needed to distinguish non-Western peoples as the "other," and also to incorporate them within their sociocultural system of domination. The colonized, for their part, needed to distance themselves from this domination as it threatened their own autonomy. The second paradox enters because the colonized were also forced to recognize themselves as "other" in order to create mechanisms of historical resistance and cultural survival (Beckett 1988:675). Such a historical push-and-pull gave impetus to non-Western peoples to become active agents of their own destinies within an imposed social order, rather than generating passive recipients of such "order."

## The Aripaeños

Aripao is a community formed by descendants of runaway black slaves, for which I use the English word "Maroons," living on the east bank of the Lower Caura River in the northwestern region of Bolívar State, Venezuela (Figure 1). The existence and, indeed, the persistence of Aripao as the sole community of blacks within a vast geographical area that covers much of Bolívar State presents an intriguing case for anthropological studies of history and historicity.

The story of the Pantera Negra, "black panther," which in the Americas refers to the huge black jaguar, comes to the foreground as Aripaeños recount the origin and history of Aripao. Some of their statements are these: "Pantera Negra was the base of the people of Aripao." "The blacks of Aripao are descendants of that history." And, "Pantera Negra and her people are the ancestors of the people of Aripao."

This chapter discusses one segment of Aripao's past, the phenomenon of *la pantera negra* (black panther, as feminine). Whether a historical reality, a legend, or a myth; whether part of the greater Caura region or native to Aripao, the phenomenon of Pantera Negra forms part of the genesis narratives of this community that focus on the colonial period. The data are drawn from two sources: a historical written account (López-Borreguero 1875) and the oral versions (historicity) of the Aripaeños (collected by the author since 1993). The analysis of both sources suggests that Pantera Negra is a messianic figure that forms part of the historical resistance and cultural survival of the Aripaeños against Western hegemony. The phenomenon of Pantera Negra shares the characteristics of messianic myth and reveals a major level of awareness of historical events.

According to Turner, there are variations in mythic and historical consciousness among non-Western societies. He identifies messianic myth as

> the inversion of the unequal relationship between the native and Western society in the existing situation of contact. This may take the overt form of a triumph of native over Western exemplars in some magical or military contest, or of the direct integration of native society into Western society on equal terms, or of the integration of Western goods and technology as cargo into native society. (Turner 1988b:262)

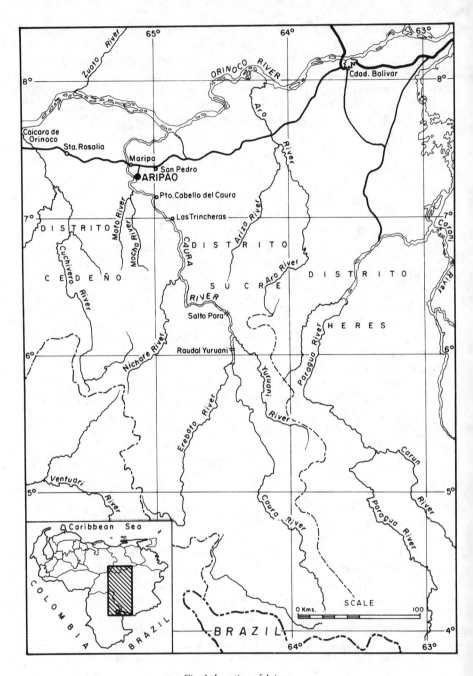

Fig. 1. Location of Aripao.

By "major level" of historical consciousness Turner means

> the conception of historical events and processes as bringing about changes in the sociocultural structure itself. . . . Major historical consciousness is that which formulates the existing social order as a whole, or some significant aspect of it, as a contingent product of an ongoing stream of action, events and forces that, just as they gave rise to it, can and will also transform it. (Turner 1998b:253–254)

I argue that the story of Pantera Negra reveals a historical inversion of the unequal relationship between Aripaeños' ancestors and colonizers. Bestowed with magical and military powers, Pantera Negra reflects resistance against colonial forces and represents changes in the social order as she becomes an agent of transformation of Western hegemony to black empowerment.

I also suggest that the Aripaeños' society, as an isolated black community and a product of the African diaspora, parallels the anthropological findings of the indigenous South American societies of the Amazonian and Andean regions. For example, as in indigenous South American narratives, Aripaeños actively evoke (or incorporate) mythic features into solidly grounded past events in the construction of ". . . shared interpretive frameworks for understanding the social situations of contact and historical processes of coping with a dominant, external society" (Hill 1988:9). In essence, Aripaeños have merged myth, historicity, and history as modes of social consciousness through which to interpret situations of their ethnogenesis in developing mechanisms for historical resistance and cultural survival.

### Cultural-Geographical and Historical Setting

Aripao, with a population of about 300 people, is the most recent settlement established by the ancestral Aripaeños. Aripaeños affirm that their ancestors were maroons.[1] But the origin or port of departure of their ancestors within the new continent is obscured to many of them. One "cultural tutor,"[2] in particular, claims that

> there were white people . . . Europeans, who highly mistreated black slaves. These blacks rose up, killing many slave owners; then they fled, crossing the Essequibo and Venturi Rivers, and other rivers as well, while fleeing from their white captors. They reached the Upper Caura River; and once they took its course they traveled down river as they were being pursued. Sometimes they would have to disembark in order to cross rapids. They formed or founded . . . [several settlements].[3]

According to information gathered from a few sources (Acosta Saignes 1954, Chaffanjon 1986, Humboldt 1991 [1941], López-Borreguero 1875, Ramos Pérez 1946, Whitehead 1988, Wickham and Crevaux 1988), the ancestors of the Aripaeños were probably Dutch-owned fugitive slaves. One particular reference indicates that the people of Aripao are descendants of runaway black slaves who fled from the plantations of Demerara (Wickham and Crevaux 1988:46).

For many present-day Aripaeños, their memory of the past takes them back as far as the Upper Caura River. They state that their ancestors moved their settlement at least four times within that region—from San Luis de Guaraguaraico to Corocito, then to "Pueblo Viejo de Puerto Cabello" (the Old Village or Town Grove of Puerto Cabello), "Mata de Pueblo Viejo" (the Old Village or Town Grove), and Aripao (see figure 2).[4]

In a recent article (Pérez 1995), I proposed that present-day Aripaeños have a historical vision that is represented and reflected in their landscape. Their landscape becomes the scenario through which Aripaeños express and identify themselves with their past and present condition. Accordingly, I presented their landscape as a historical discourse of significant elements that provides Aripaeños with a sense of continuity and wholeness of their past and present state of being. The realm of what I call the "historical landscape" of the Aripaeños ranges from the immediate surrounding of Aripao, such as the Mata de Pueblo Viejo about one kilometer away, to faraway sites such as San Luis de Guaraguaraico, which is about 230 kilometers up the Caura River from Aripao.[5]

According to my research with documented history, San Luis de Guaraguaraico, Corocito, and Pueblo Viejo de Puerto Cabello correspond to the era of slavery and marronage of their ancestors—what I refer to as the *distant past*—whereas Mata de Pueblo Viejo belongs to the era of emancipation, which I refer to as the *recent past*.

When Aripaeños themselves recount the origin and history of Aripao, the story of Pantera Negra comes to the foreground. As an ancestral figure of the Aripaeños, Pantera Negra permeates the historical landscape with mythic (and almost magical) features solidly grounded in historical events that mark the heritage and identity of the Aripaeños. I earlier wrote: "Together, the oral and written versions of Pantera Negra unveil a cyclical transformation of her life cycle [birth, life, death, and rebirth] in a temporal continuum of the Aripaeños' historical landscape" (see figure 3; Pérez 1997).

The death of Pantera Negra does not signify for the Aripaeños her demise or complete disappearance. She is reborn once to continue as an active persona in the era of slavery or marronage; and she is reborn a second time to become a passive force in the era of emancipation.[6] In essence, Pantera Negra, through her persona, deeds, and domain, leads her people from slavery to freedom.

Her historical importance and cultural relevance are reflected by this cyclical transformation and further reinforced by her second rebirth, which also signifies a gateway for embarkation—a symbolic opening or bridge that unifies Aripaeños' ancestral and present-day territories. Pantera Negra gives meaning to and represents Aripaeños' historical landscape. She is the epitome of historical consciousness.

She demarcates the historical landscape into a distant past that corresponds to the era of of slavery and marronage and into a recent past that pertains to the

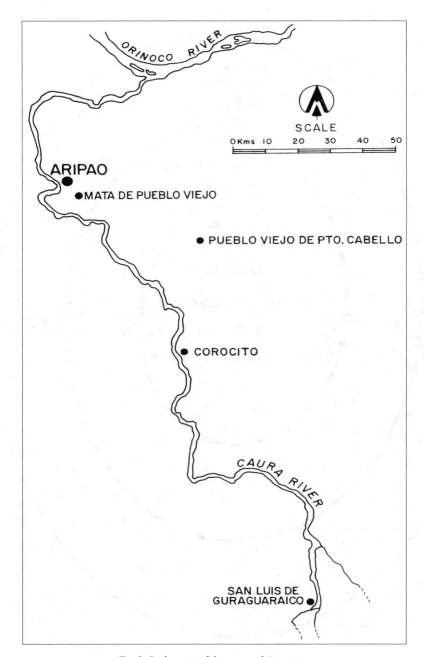

Fig. 2. Settlements of the ancestral Aripaeños.

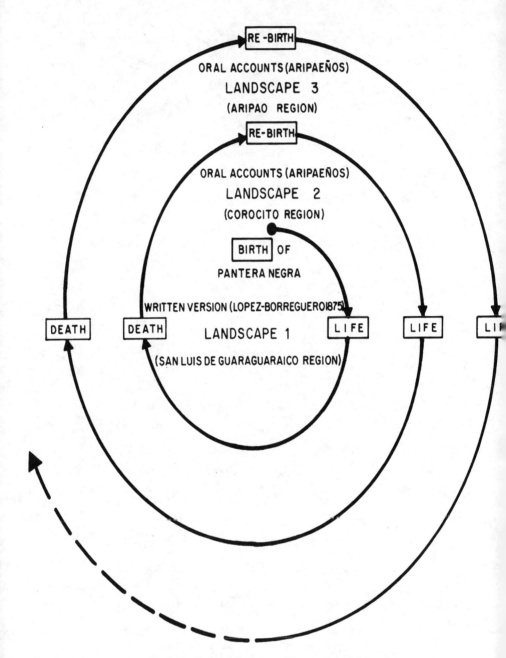

Fig. 3. Cyclical transformation of Pantera Negra's life cycle.

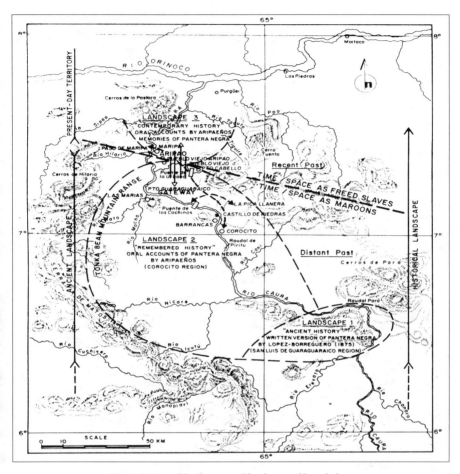

Fig. 4. Historical landscape and landscape of knowledge.

period of emancipation and freedom for the forebears of the Aripaeños. While
the distant past incorporates ancient and remembered histories that form Aripaeños' ancestral landscape, the recent past envelopes contemporary history that
molds Aripaeños' present-day territory (figure 4). She conjoins, through the cyclical transformation of her life cycle, matrices of space, time, and human action that bring about a discourse of the significant elements for the Aripaeños. In
her totality, Pantera Negra represents a permeable, free-flowing gateway for Aripaeños to move freely through their ancestral and present-day territories. Her legacy, which still lives in the minds of the present-day Aripaeños, is characterized
by her second rebirth as a passive force of emancipation.

Pantera Negra is one of the many significant discourse elements of the historical and cultural landscape of the Aripaeños. But she is precisely the one who

imparts a vitality through her persona, deeds, and domain; she has historical importance and cultural relevance as an ancestral as well as a messianic female figure.

### Pantera Negra: Historical and Mythic Modes of Social Consciousness among Aripaeños

I learned from my cultural tutors about the Pantera Negra through my inquiries about the history of Aripao.[7] In their oral accounts, however, some Aripaeños point to the existence of a book about Pantera Negra (López-Borreguero 1875). One Aripaeños man, for instance, says, "The story of Pantera Negra appears in a book." Another man states, "It is a thick book that the Spaniards put out." And still another man asserts, "Francisco used to tell the story; he had the book on Pantera Negra." They mentioned that since the story was very long and their memory of all the details was lacking, the book would be a way for me to gather the whole story and its details. The reference by various Aripaeños to the book is, perhaps, a means to reveal that which they do not wish to "tell," that which they simply do not remember, or that which they never knew.

While oral accounts told by contemporary Aripaeños and the written version of Pantera Negra differ in content, they are similar in structure. The structure is what makes the story of Pantera Negra a messianic myth. Nonetheless, the content of the story is what provides the dynamics of the cultural context(s) at work in conjunction with the structure. The content varies mainly in the ethnicity of the characters and in the setting. I suggest that the difference in setting connotes a cyclical transformation of Pantera Negra's life cycle from birth through life to death and on to rebirth according to a specific context of time and space within a temporal continuum of the historical landscape of the Aripaeños (figure 3).

Particular attention to the ethnicity of the characters in both the written and oral versions reveals the existing context of contact of the Aripaeños' ancestors with Europeans and indigenous peoples, as they moved through the cultural and historical landscape. More specifically, the messianic structure of the story is not disrupted by the transformation of ethnicity of the characters to "fit" the existing context of contact that changes through time and space within a temporal continuum of the historical landscape of the Aripaeños. Significantly, the written and oral versions differ in content (ethnicity and setting) by virtue of the change in time and space. Accordingly, the content provides clues to the existing context of temporal history.

In agreement with Jan Vansina (1965), oral traditions provide historical information and are as valid as any other sources available. I distinguish between two types of story: the written version (history) is a "snapshot" frozen in time; the oral accounts (historicity), by contrast, are symbolic continuations or transformations of the written version. Both types, when examined separately, suggest an equivalent relationship within a power struggle wherein the resolution remains ambiguous or incomplete between the ancestors of the Aripaeños and colonizers vis-à-vis indigenous peoples. Taken separately, the written version and the oral accounts are mirror images of each other. Each replicates the other on the sociocultural patterns they convey. Accordingly, each reflects a "minor level of historical consciousness" (Turner 1988b:253). But when both versions are considered together, they reveal "a major level of historical consciousness" (Turner 1988b:253–254). Together, the two versions bring about changes in the sociocultural structure itself through the symbolic rebirth of Pantera Negra. To this day, the rebirth of Pantera Negra, as implied in the oral accounts, offers the prospect and hope of black empowerment over western hegemony.

*Pantera Negra: Written Version and Oral Accounts*

The story of Pantera Negra from López-Borreguero's book, condensed and paraphrased, is as follows:

There was a dreadful, male-like woman known as Pantera Negra, who governed a colony of Africans that fled from the Dutch colonies of the Guianas. This colony was called San Luis de Guaraguaraico, located on the east bank of the Caura River on the land that was given to them by the Spanish Crown of Guayana. Aurelia was Pantera Negra's real name; she was a twenty-four year old *mulata*, with beautiful features and a complexion as white as a pearl; the child of an African man and a Dutch woman. The father of this beautiful woman was an arrogant slave, who the Governor of Dutch Guiana had assigned as foreman (*capatáz*) of all the slaves he owned in a sugar plantation near the Surinam River. The daughter of the Governor fell in love with this arrogant foreman and became pregnant by him. She fled with her lover, in the company of other black slaves, from the plantation and they wandered for months through the mountains and virgin forests. After they crossed the mountains of the Guianas, they arrived at the Upper Caura River. While embarked on their extensive travels, the daughter of the Governor died in labor, leaving behind a baby girl, named Aurelia. This girl would later become known as Pantera Negra. Upon her father's death, Aurelia took charge of the black population that now inhabited the settlement of San Luis de Guaraguaraico. These blacks built a hut for her near the town. When she was not hunting or stalking a wild animal or some poor indigenous person, she would enter San Luis de Guaraguaraico through an underground tunnel that connected her hut to her palace in the colony. Pantera Negra seemed to possess all the venom and hatred built up by her people during their times of enslavement by white colonists. Her father had taught her to hate the whites who were to blame for the death of her mother; she also disliked the indigenous peoples for their superstitious beliefs. She showed contempt and little respect for the blacks, who were now her subjects, army, and slaves and who, nonetheless, shared her African blood. Tadeo, her first cousin and lover, was her liaison to govern the black people of San Luis ·de Guaraguaraico. Near this town was an ancient Spanish colony named Santa María that was inhabited by Carib Indians and had a Carib Indian ruler (*cacique*) known as Panchito. Panchito met Pantera Negra on one of his hunting trips; she was bathing naked in a river pond. When Panchito approached her, he saw that a tiger (Spanish *tigre*, jaguar) was ready to pounce on her. Panchito killed the tiger with one gunshot. Panchito immediately fell in love with Pantera Negra because of her beauty; and Pantera Negra, taking advantage of the situation, did not kill him as she had done in the past with other intruders. He had saved her life and knowing the power he had as a ruler, she decided to include him in the plan that she and Tadeo had devised to conquer and dominate Santa María as well as other Spanish colonies. She asked Panchito, "Have you, sometimes, ever dreamt, *cacique*, of the glory that you would attain if your army would conquer the Spanish cities and establishments that lay defenseless and unsuspecting before you?" Her aim was to entice Panchito to fight and defeat the Spaniards with the help of his people and subsequently, to relinquish to her his chiefdom (*cacicazgo*) of Santa María. Panchito was enchanted by Pantera Negra; yet, he was hesitant to betray the Spaniards (as he was raised by a Spanish couple) and was much less willing to betray his people. Estrella de la Mañana, a Carib indian woman who loved Panchito, discovered that Pantera Negra and Tadeo were planning to double-cross Panchito due to his reticence. The plan was to kill his people and consequently, Panchito. Estrella de la Mañana decided to help him and so she continued to spy on Pantera Negra until Pantera Negra shot and wounded her. But Estrella de la Mañana was able to reach Panchito and to warn him about the plan that Pantera Negra and Tadeo had devised to betray him. In disbelief, Panchito went to her hut and saw Pantera Negra with her cousin Tadeo. Panchito shot and killed Tadeo; but before he died, Tadeo lunged with his knife and killed Pantera Negra. In the end, Panchito married Estrella de la Mañana. (López-Borreguero 1875:290–357)[8]

The story of Pantera Negra according to the oral accounts told to me by contemporary people of Aripao goes as follows:

A couple from the Spanish Crown had a daughter who fell in love with a black slave and became pregnant. Afraid of being reprimanded for making the European blood impure, they fled with all their people and came to the Caura River where they founded Corocito. The couple had a mulata baby girl, who was known as Pantera Negra. She was raised there and became very powerful. The Queen Pantera Negra was very beautiful. The old people used to say that she attracted a lot of men, who would fight for her. She used her feminine qualities to entice and enchant men. But she also mercilessly killed anyone who crossed her or who she did not like; she was always armed. She did atrocious things; that is why she was called Pantera Negra. She was evil; the Spaniards killed her mother and Pantera Negra wanted to take revenge; she became evil for her hatred against the Spaniards. She was a princess and had her own kingdom with blacks and indigenous slaves; she was the ruler (*cacica*) and richest woman of the Caura region; she had diamonds and gold. Pantera Negra was a loner; she lived in an underground hut in Barrancas across from Corocito, her colony. She used to come out, through a tunnel, to bathe in her river pond, known as El Castillo de Piedras. She traveled throughout the region. She took the paths of Paso de los Cochinos, Pica Llanera, and Paso de Maripa to reach Barrancas, El Castillo de Piedras [her bathing pond], Corocito, Las Marías (a town or tonka bean station), and Pueblo Viejo de Puerto Cabello (subsequent ancestral Aripaeños' settlement). One day, a man named Panchito, a Spanish hunter, went hunting and saw a tiger that was about to attack Pantera Negra, who was bathing in her pond. Panchito killed the tiger; Pantera Negra was about to kill Panchito, but decided not to do so because he had saved her life. Although Panchito fell in love with Pantera Negra, she was to marry Federico, her black lover and first cousin. But Panchito threatened to kill her people if she did not marry him. Pantera Negra, in turn, decided to kill Panchito. Each had an army. Panchito had 14,000 Spaniard men and Pantera Negra had 9,000 Maroons and slaves. Estrella de la Mañana, a Spanish woman and friend of Panchito, heard about Pantera Negra's plan and told Panchito. Panchito went to visit Pantera Negra. He found her with Federico. He proceeded to kill Federico with one gunshot and Federico killed Pantera Negra with a knife.

Some Aripaeños claim that some of the places that Pantera Negra left behind can still be seen, but are enchanted. Her bathing pond is said to be filled with pigeons of all colors. They live there, but they cannot be shot even if one tries; they are enchanted. Aripaeños even try to avoid going near the area of the pond, as they are afraid of it. Her hut and castle can be seen, but one cannot get there even if one tries; they too are enchanted. It is said that Pantera Negra is, at times, seen sitting on pure gold near the castle, but no one can reach her or get the gold even though the person tries; they are enchanted.

### Discussion

Marronage for the ancestors of the Aripaeños was a form of historical resistance and cultural survival. Both types of story tell of this flight from European oppression (the Dutch in the written version and the Spanish in the oral version). Pantera Negra was born into this crucial moment of Aripaeño history, which set the stage for Pantera Negra as a messianic female figure.

When examining the written and oral versions separately, the structure of each reveals an equivalent relationship within a power struggle. An inherent contradiction is formed between one group and another: Maroons and colonizers vis-à-vis Carib Indians. Both Pantera Negra (whether a Dutch/Spanish and African descendant *cacica* [queen, or princess]) and Panchito (whether a Carib *cacique* with Spanish alliances or a Spanish hunter) had an army by which to conquer, dominate, and rule the Caura region. Pantera Negra, however, had an additional power, which was her ability to entice and enchant men for her own purposes. Her use of this magical power put Panchito at a disadvantage. He was lured by Pantera Negra to the point of almost relinquishing his power to her. But when Panchito kills the tiger to save Pantera Negra's life, he counteracts that additional power of Pantera Negra.

The killing of the tiger, which is about to kill Pantera Negra, signifies an ethnic (blacks/Spaniards/indigenous peoples) and gender (masculine/feminine) battle for power. The act shows that Pantera Negra is vulnerable in spite of her secular and magical powers. The tripartite ethnic conflict and bi-gender conflict involved in the historical colonial power struggle is dynamically balanced. But the contradiction of their relationship—both Pantera Negra and Panchito are in a position of power to conquer, dominate, and rule the same region—pushes the narratives toward a dialectical resolution. On the one hand, the direct integration of either society (that of Pantera Negra's or Panchito's) into one chiefdom signals dominance of one system over the other. On the other hand, the death of either leader becomes imminent with the demise of that chiefdom. The death of Pantera Negra resolves the contradiction of the dialect, and the equivalent relationship within a power struggle is disrupted. Her death, though, connotes the triumph of Western hegemony, and consequently the historical disempowerment of a maroon community.

The identity of the killer of Pantera Negra brings about different resolutions than those stated above. Tadeo (in the written version) or Federico (in the oral accounts), who is her black lover and first cousin, rather than Panchito, murdered Pantera Negra. She was killed by one of her own consanguineal and ethnic kind. This in itself is an inversion that forms another contradiction: the death of Pantera Negra, as a *mulata* and thus a product of European hybridity, symbolically portrays the defeat of Western hegemony as well as the cleansing of the impureness of her blood. This resolution, however, is neither complete nor sufficient to empower the black community under Pantera Negra to rise against Western hegemony.

The written version remains a snapshot of an incomplete cycle that provides a minor level of historical consciousness. Pantera Negra dies and leaves behind an ambiguous relationship within the power struggle. Its outcome, Western hegemony, neither triumphs, nor is defeated in this historically inscribed version.

Although the oral accounts share a similar structure with the written version, they are about the first rebirth of Pantera Negra, which takes place in a new setting and changes the ethnicity of the characters. The theme of rebirth conjoins both types of story into a transformation of Pantera Negra's life cycle. Furthermore, this rebirth becomes a symbolic continuation or transformation of the written story that now reveals a major level of historical consciousness among the Aripaeños. Aripaeños are active agents in the making of history through the transformation of Pantera Negra's death into a symbolic rebirth.

While her initial death connotes an ambiguous outcome of triumph or defeat of Western hegemony, it is Pantera Negra's first rebirth that generates the black empowerment over Western hegemony. Her rebirth implies a perseverance to defeat colonial forces as well as the prospect and hope of black empowerment as a form of historical resistance and cultural survival. Although it may be viewed as contradictory, she is reborn as a *mulata* (or *mestiza*) with transformed power that this racial mixing (*mestizaje*) bestows upon her to use both cultures on behalf of her people. Although she dies, she is reborn once again. It is in this second rebirth that she leads her people from slavery to freedom. The prospect of black empowerment endures and is strengthened even more.

The confluence of the written version and the oral accounts reflects a change in the setting, from San Luis de Guaraguaraico to Corocito. It also represents a transformation of ethnicity of the characters: (1) Pantera Negra is transformed to a Spanish-African descendant from a Dutch-African offspring, and (2) Panchito and Estrella de la Mañana change from Caribs with Spanish alliances to Spaniards. The continuity of the story, as it is repeated from one region (or setting) to another, suggests the cyclical transformation of Pantera Negra's life cycle: birth, life, death, and rebirth (Pérez 1997). It also indicates the transformation of ethnicity of the characters based on the existing context of contact through time and across space within the historical landscape of the Aripaeños.

In the written version, Pantera Negra is portrayed as a Dutch descendant and her people as Dutch-owned black slaves. Their interactions with the Spaniards, at the time, were most likely to have been minimal or non-existent. However, as they fled from Dutch Guiana (now Suriname) over the rugged mountains to the Upper Caura River region, their interactions with Carib people were inevitable.[9] Once they settled in San Luis de Guaraguaraico, their interactions with indigenous Caribs were likely to continue and their contacts with the Spaniards were likely to increase. Panchito and Estrella de la Mañana, for instance, are depicted as Caribs who, in turn, had a great loyalty to the Spaniards in the Caura region.[10]

In the oral accounts Pantera Negra is depicted as a Spanish descendant and her people as Spanish-owned black slaves. At the same time, Panchito and Estrella de la Mañana are no longer portrayed as Caribs. They are now portrayed as Spaniards. I argue that this transformation of ethnicity reflects the existing context of colonial contact determined through time and across space. As this Maroon society remained in the Caura region and continued to move toward the Lower Caura River region, its interactions with the Spaniards were likely to increase while its contacts with the Dutch were likely to diminish.

It is important to emphasize the ambiguity of Panchito and Pantera Negra in the story. On the one hand, Panchito is either a Carib (with Spanish alliances) or a Spaniard. In the written account he becomes a Spaniard through the process of child rearing as he is raised by a Spanish couple who saved him, as a child, from being killed by the indigenous Cabres, an Arawak-speaking group (López-Borreguero 1875:11). In the oral versions he is a Spaniard through a symbolic transformation. In each narrative version he represents the Spanish Crown or colonial power.

On the other hand, Pantera Negra is depicted as a descendant of a European woman (a Dutch in the written version and a Spaniard in the oral accounts) and a high-ranked black slave (*capatáz*, foreman); she is *la mulata* of European-African descent. In both versions of the story, Pantera Negra represents the African or Afro–Latin American community. Despite their own ethnicity, Panchito and Pantera Negra are "almost" Europeans—Panchito through a cultural process of child rearing or symbolic transformation and Pantera Negra through a natural process of racial mixing. As ambiguous figures in the narratives, Panchito and Pantera Negra transport themselves from their own culture to a European culture. Their consequent association with the colonial culture places them in an equivalent relationship within a power struggle. This in itself is a double contradiction: the first contradiction is the subordinate population sharing an equivalent relationship of authority with a European colonial power; and the second contradiction is the empowerment of the subordinate population to a superordinate relationship with colonial society.

The written version and the oral accounts share a similar structure; one that reveals "the inversion of the unequal relationship between the native and Western society in the existing situation of contact" (Turner 1988b:262). This inversion, however, takes the overt form of an equivalent relationship within a power struggle between the native and Western society; one in which either society can claim victory or defeat without bringing about major changes in the sociocultural structure.

When Pantera Negra is symbolically reborn for the first time both types of story conjoin to represent a complete inversion in which Pantera Negra becomes an agent of change by transforming Western hegemony into the prospect and hope of black empowerment. Her death does not imply her demise or disappearance. She is reborn once again, but as a passive force rather than as an active persona. Her legacy is still in the minds of present-day Aripaeños.

In essence, Aripaeños have manipulated and transformed the phenomenon of Pantera Negra through time and across space. While the structure of each version, the written and the oral, remains congruent with the other, the content is altered or transformed to fit each existing situation of contact. But most importantly, the conjunction of both versions is what allowed changes in the sociocultural structure or social order. Pantera Negra is a messianic figure through which Aripaeños have merged myth and history as modes of social consciousness to assert historical resistance and cultural survival in colonial and post-colonial times.

## Conclusion

The paradox of colonial culture existed through time and across space between the Maroon community of Aripao and dominant Western society. The inherent contradictions within the colonial system evoked a push towards dialectical resolutions among Aripaeños. Beckett writes, "I would also see [the colonized] alternately contesting the attributed otherness that structures domination and embracing it as a basis for resistance; again, they may contest incorporation as a threat to their autonomy or embrace it as a basis for making claims on the new order" (Beckett 1993:675). The phenomenon of Pantera Negra has been one of the mechanisms by which Aripaeños have resolved contradictions of colonial and post-colonial times as a basis for resistance and as a basis for making claims on the new order.

Pantera Negra, as a messianic figure, portrays the inversion of the unequal relationship between the Maroon society of Aripao and Western society. Her rebirth, which conjoins the written version and the oral accounts, transformed the inversion to take the overt form of a "triumph" by the Maroon society over Spanish colonial power, achieved through Pantera Negra's use of her magical and military powers. The resolution of the contradiction, an equivalent relationship within a power struggle between the native and Western society, was the death of Pantera Negra rather than the direct integration of Pantera Negra's society into Panchito's chiefdom. The subsequent resolution of the contradiction, either the triumph or defeat of Western hegemony created by the previous resolution, was Pantera Negra's symbolic rebirth(s). Another contradiction, "black empowerment" over Western hegemony, is then created. Pantera Negra still reflects the historical resistance of Aripaeños against external, dominating forces and respresents changes in the social order to assure their cultural survival.

The phenomenon of Pantera Negra strongly suggests that Aripaeños are active agents of their own destiny, rather than passive recipients of an imposed social order. Pérez Sarduy and Stubbs (1995) highlight the importance of studying black people and black communities as active agents in shaping their own history. They claim that Africa and Africans, for example, have been depicted as passive victims of colonialism, when Africans have, instead, created new and complex societies in the Americas that differ from their African pasts (Pérez Sarduy and Stubbs 1995:5). This foregrounds the possibility of examining the phenomenon of Pantera Negra as a "historical counterdiscourse." The analysis of the structure and content of both the written version and the oral accounts of the phenomenon of Pantera Negra reveals processes of ethnic empowerment and resistance over Western hegemony.

Black empowerment is defined through Pantera Negra's rebirth, which revived ancestral Aripaeños' society. Her rebirth enabled ancestral Aripaeños to confront new situations of contact. Her first rebirth as an active persona led them through an era of marronage, which was their mechanism of historical resistance and cultural survival; and her second rebirth as a possible force allowed them to maintain their autonomy once they passed through the transition from slavery to freedom. As Marcus and Fischer explain,

> Most local cultures worldwide are products of a history of appropriations, resistances, and accommodations . . . [that demands] a view of cultural situations as *always* in flux, in a perpetual historically sensitive state of resistance and accommodation to broader processes of influence that are as much inside as outside the local context. (Marcus and Fischer 1986:78)

Although present-day Aripaeños still live in a marginal state (or "peripheral situation" [Turner 1986]), they have their own models, strategies, and networks through which they resist and survive within the external, dominating order of Western society. Pantera Negra illustrates such resistance and survival in a particular black Venezuelan people's historical consciousness.

The comparison of the written version and the oral accounts allows us to observe that not only Aripaeños' vision of their history changes through time, but more importantly, that Aripaeños' vision of historical landscape also changes through time. Lowenthal may be correct when he explains that "Our immediate past landscapes will be less consequential to our descendants, for whom our imminent future will have become an important element of their past" (Lowenthal 1975:24). This can be the case of present-day Aripaeños in relation to the written version, a version that they refer to as a means by which to reveal what they simply do not remember, what they do not know, or what they do not wish to divulge.

Pantera Negra continues to be a culturally significant historical and symbolic force who empowered the ancestral Aripaeños and continues to empower the present-day Aripaeños. She provides continuity that transcends time and space through her importance, potency, and power. The existence and perseverance of the Aripaeños as a singular black community in the vast geographical area that covers much of Bolívar State may be considered proof of the living legacy of *la pantera negra*.

## Notes

1. Since the sixteenth century, the word *maroon* (from the Arawak-Spanish *cimarrón*) referred to Afro-American runaway slaves. Marronage was a form of resistance to colonial enslavement. Many of these fugitive black slaves were successful in forming long-lived settlements known in English as "maroon communities," which represented a threat to colonial power.

2. The term *cultural tutor* is a substitute for the word *informant*. In my Ph.D. dissertation (1990), "cultural tutor" was proposed because it is not just information that the people give to an anthropologist; they also become his/her advisors and teachers of their culture.

3. All quotes from cultural tutors have been translated from Spanish to English by the author.

4. *Mata* is a grove characterized by its formation of a dense, rounded crown or umbrella and visibly pronounced in contrast to its surroundings of grass plains.

5. I define *historical landscape* as "the physical existence of certain elements of nature, such as trees, water resources, and animals, and in nature, such as material culture, that embraces "events of the past" and gives Aripaeños a sense of oneness, while embodying new landmarks of their present affairs" (Pérez 1995:13).

6. Passive force is defined as the absence of Pantera Negra's persona, deeds, and domain in the historical landscape of the Aripaeños' last two settlements (Mata de Pueblo Viejo and Aripao) at the time of their migration. Pantera Negra as an active persona was

no longer needed as their migration meant the transition from when they were Maroons to when they became freed slaves. Therefore, they were subject to fewer risks or dangers through changes and accommodations due to the new status.

7. It is primarily Aripaeños men who talk about the Pantera Negra. Only two elderly women mentioned having heard of her, but claimed not to know about her or the story.

8. The written version of Pantera Negra was condensed and translated from Spanish to English by the author.

9. The Guianas were known to be under the control of indigenous Carib people. In fact, the Caribs had highly developed river routes in the region, which they fiercely defended from the control of the Spanish Crown.

10. This relationship between Caribs and Spaniards was unusual, as Caribs made alliances with the Dutch. Whitehead (1988), for instance, states that as early as 1663, the Dutch had the Carib as allies to combat the Spanish threat as well as slave hunters to capture Dutch owned fugitive black slaves. Although the Caribs were a threat to runaways, the possibilities of alliances made in various forms or degrees, between the Caribs and Dutch-owned black Maroons cannot be excluded. As Whitehead observes, "it would be misleading to suggest that all Caribs everywhere were potential slave catchers for the Dutch. There were instances of Caribs being warned against sheltering runaways and, even, occasionally being brought to Essequibo to answer charges for so doing" (222n.17).

*References*

Acosta Saignes, Miguel
   1954          Etnología Antigua de Venezuela, Caracas: Publicaciones de la Facul-
                 tad de Humanidades y Educación. Caracas: Universidad Central de
                 Venezuela.
Asad, Talai
   1987          Are There Histories of Peoples without Europe? A Review Article. So-
                 ciety for Comparative Study of Society and History 29:594–607.
Beckett, Jeremy
   1993          Walter Newton's History of the World—or Australia. American Eth-
                 nologist 20:675–695.
Bricker, Victoria R.
   1981          The Indian Christ, the Indian King. Austin: University of Texas Press.
Chaffanjon, Jean
   1986          El Orinoco y el Caura: Relación de viajes realizados entre 1886–
                 1887. Caracas: Fundación Cultural Orinoco.
Comaroff, Jean, and John Comaroff
   1987          The Madman and the Migrant: Work and Labor in the Historical
                 Consciousness of a South African People. American Ethnologist
                 14:191–209.
   1992          Ethnography and the Historical Imagination. Boulder: Westview
                 Press.
Farris, Nancy J.
   1987          Remembering the Future, Anticipating the Past: History, Time, and

Cosmology among the Maya of Yucatan. Society for Comparative Study of Society and History. 29:566–593.

Friedman, Jonathan
1992         The Past in the Future: History and the Politics of Identity. American Anthropologist 94:837–859.

Guss, David M.
1986         Keeping It Oral: A Yekuana Ethnology. American Ethnologist 13:413–429.
1993         The Selling of San Juan: The Performance of History in an Afro-Venezuelan Community. American Ethnologist 20:451–473.

Hill, Jonathan D.
1988         (editor) Rethinking History and Myth. Urbana: University of Illinois Press.
1992         Contested Pasts and the Practice of Anthropology. American Anthropologist 4:809–815.
1993         Response to Comments by E. N. Anderson and Takami Kuwayama on the Contemporary Issues Forum. American Anthropologist 95:707–710.
1996         (editor) Culture, Power and History: Ethnogenesis in the Americas, 1492–1992. Iowa City: University of Iowa Press.

Hugh-Jones, Stephen.
1988         The Gun and the Bow: Myths of White Men and Indians. L'Homme 28:138–155.

Humboldt, Alexander von
1991 [1941]   Viaje a la Regiones Equinocciales. Caracas: Montalbán Editores.

Lévi-Strauss, Claude
1966         The Savage Mind. Chicago: University of Chicago Press.

López-Borreguero, Ramón
1875         Los Indios Caribes. Madrid: Imprenta de T. Fortanet.

Lowenthal, David
1975         Past Time, Present Place: Landscape and Memory. Geographical Review 65:1–36.

Marcus, George E., and Michael Fischer
1986         Anthropology as Cultural Critique. Chicago: University of Chicago Press.

McGuire, Randall H.
1992         Archaeology and the First Americans. American Anthropologist 94:816–836.

Pérez, Berta E.
1990         Ideology of the Animal Rights Movement. Ph.D. dissertation, University of Minnesota (Anthropology).
1995         Versions and Images of Historical Landscape in Aripao, a Maroon

Descendant Community in Southern Venezuela. America Negra 10:129–148.

1997   Pantera Negra: An Ancestral Figure of the Aripaeños, Maroon Descendants in Southern Venezuela. History and Anthropology 10(2–3):219–240.

Pérez Sarduy, Pedro, and Jean Stubbs
1995   Introduction. In No Longer Invisible: Afro-Latin Americans Today. London: Minority Rights Group, pp. 1–18.

Price, Richard M.
1983   First-Time: The Historical Vision of an Afro-American People. Baltimore: John Hopkins University Press.

Ramos Pérez, Demitrio
1946   El Tratado de límites de 1750 y la expedición de Iturriaga al Orinoco. Madrid: Consejo Superior de Investigaciones Científicas.

Rasnake, Roger
1988   Images of Resistance to Colonial Domination. In Rethinking History and Myth, Jonathan D. Hill (editor). Urbana: University of Illinois Press, pp.136–156.

Turner, Terence
1986   Production, Exploitation, and Social Consciousness in the Peripheral Situation. Social Analysis 19: 179–217.
1988a   History, Myth, and Social Consciousness among the Kayapó of Central Brazil. In Rethinking History and Myth, Jonathan D. Hill (editor). Urbana: University of Illinois Press, pp. 195–213.
1988b   Commentary. Ethno-Ethnohistory: Myth and History in Native South American Representations of Contact with Western Society. In Rethinking History and Myth, Jonathan D. Hill (editor). Urbana: University of Illinois Press, pp. 235–281.

Urton, Gary
1990   The History of a Myth: Pacariqtambo and the Origin of the Inkas. Austin: University of Texas Press.

Vansina, Jan.
1965   Oral Tradition: A Study in Historical Methodology. Chicago: Aldine.

Whitehead, Neil
1988   Lords of the Tiger Spirit. Dordrecht: Foris.

Wickham, Henry A., and Jules Crevaux
1988   El Orinoco en dos direcciones. Caracas: Fundación Cultural Orinoco.

# 10. THE SELLING OF SAN JUAN

## The Performance of History in an Afro-Venezuelan Community

### David M. Guss

*Si Dios fuera negro*
*todo cambiaría.*
*Sería nuestra raza*
*la que mandaría.*

—Roberto Angleró, "Si Dios fuera negro"[1]

Even the most casual perusal of anthropological literature over the last 15 years will reveal an increasing, if not obsessive, preoccupation with what some have called "the selective uses of the past" (Chapman, McDonald, and Tonkin 1989).[2] The growing awareness that histories (and not merely History, writ large) are more than simply static traditions inherited from a neutral past parallels an equally significant realization that the most common subjects of anthropological study (that is, oral-based tribal cultures) actually possess historical consciousness. Functionalism's long-dominant view of Primitive Man as an ahistoric, mythic being has therefore gradually given way to one of contested realities in which any purported absence of history becomes suspect as part of a privileged construction of it. In this sense, the acknowledgment of history or, inversely, its denial, is not about the accuracy of memory, it is about the relationship to power. While Arjun Appadurai, in a 1981 article, attempted to rein in what he called the "widespread assumption that the past is a limitless and plastic symbolic resource," he neverthe-less insisted that it is through the "inherent debatability of the past" that cultures find a way not only to "talk about themselves" but also to change (1981:201, 218).

This view, that history is primarily about the contemporary social relations of those who tell it, has important repercussions for the way in which any group defines itself in relation to another. It is for this reason, Raymond Williams writes, that "much of the most accessible and influential work of the counter-hegemony

Originally published in *American Ethnologist* 20:3 (August 1993), pp. 451–73. Reproduced by permission of the American Anthropological Association. Not for further reproduction.

is historical: the recovery of discarded areas or the redress of selective and reductive interpretations" (1977:116). There is perhaps no example for which this observation could be more true than the experience of the African-descended populations of the Americas. Brought to the New World under brutal conditions that quickly severed them from all ethnic, linguistic, and familial ties, these populations have been systematically denied the histories that others accept as a birthright. Yet many of these groups have shown, using often brilliant and resourceful strategies, that the past *is* recuperable and that proud and autonomous histories may be hidden within it. One such group that has demonstrated this is the Afro-Venezuelan community of Curiepe, a village located just two hours east of Caracas. For them, the dramatic vehicle with which to tell their history has been the performance of a three-day drum festival dedicated to San Juan.

### San Juan el Bautista

The Fiesta de San Juan, known in English as either St. John's Day or Midsummer Eve, is considered one of the oldest of all church festivals (James 1963:226). Strategically placed six months before Christmas, it celebrates the birth of St. John the Baptist, herald of the New Era and, as Jesus said, "the greatest prophet among those born of women" (Luke 7:28). But San Juan, falling as it does on the 24th of June, also celebrates the summer solstice and thus has led many to speculate that it predates the Christian era by many centuries. St. Augustine, writing in the 5th century, saw the advantage of locating this holiday on a date already widely celebrated throughout Europe. He discouraged the church from attempting to prohibit the inclusion of pagan elements, foreseeing that their appropriation could accelerate Christianity's growth (Fuentes and Hernández 1988:6). This openness resulted in not merely one of the most widely diffused holidays, but also one of the most syncretic. Dominated by rituals of fire and water, typical San Juan celebrations also included divination, fertility rites, matchmaking, harvest ceremonies, and even carnivalesque inversions (Burke 1978:194–195; Frazer 1953 [1922]:720–732).[3]

With such a wealth of associations, San Juan was easily transported to the New World. In each country throughout Latin America, it was adapted to the particular character of the population that developed there. In Argentina, for example, with its principally European population, descended mainly from Spaniards and Italians, the festival was celebrated with little variation. Bonfires were lit for couples and individuals to jump over and eventually, when the flames died, to walk through. The forms of divination were also the same: eggs dropped in glasses, mirrors read in the dark, cloves of garlic placed under beds, hair cut at midnight, gunpowder and melted tin sifted into water (Coluccio 1978:74–76).

In the Andes, with its predominantly Indian population, however, San Juan took a decidedly different turn. In Bolivia the saint was known as Tata, or Father,

San Juan and was revered as the protector of cattle, llamas, and sheep. While he also served this function in Peru, his identification with the Inca solstitial celebration of Inti Raymi provided the Catholic church with an expedient mode of appropriation (Morote Best 1955:169–170). Yet in Ecuador, the festival developed in still another direction. Seen as an opportunity to momentarily reverse both economic and social oppression, it became the occasion for a carnivalesque satire in which all members of the community participated. Indians dressed and performed as whites, while the latter assumed the subservient role of those they normally dominated. So important was this counterhegemonic performance of political subversion that Muriel Crespi refers to San Juan as "the Indian Saint" and the zone surrounding Cayambe-Imbabura in northern Ecuador as a "St. John culture area" (1981:488, 501).[4]

In Venezuela, it was neither the mestizo population nor the indigenous one that adopted San Juan. Rather it was the large black population inhabiting the many coastal plantations stretching west of Caracas to Yaracuy and east to an area commonly known as Barlovento. However, it was with the latter region, settled in the 17th century by cacao growers and slaves, that San Juan became most closely associated. A pie-shaped piece of land bounded by the Caribbean on the north and mountains on the south and east, Barlovento is less a political or geographical entity than a cultural one. While it covers more than 4,500 square kilometers, its name, derived from a Spanish nautical term meaning "whence the wind comes," rarely appears on any map or legal document. Nevertheless, its population, descended principally from the African slaves brought there in the 17th and 18th centuries, reveals a striking uniformity both economically and culturally. Despite improved access to Caracas, which can now be reached in less than two hours, and a dramatic rise in beach-front speculation, Barlovento is still an agricultural area dominated by small landholders.[5] And while each community has its own patron saint and local celebrations, the region as a whole shares a cultural heritage, as witnessed in the performance of such seasonal rites as the Easter Week processions, the Cruz de Mayo, and the Parrandas de Navidad. But of all of these, none has become so thoroughly identified with Barlovento as has that of San Juan. In fact, so widespread and passionate is the cult among these coastal communities that San Juan has become commonly known as "the saint of the blacks" (Monasterio Vasquez 1989:107).

Unlike the northern Ecuadorean celebrations of San Juan, which joined landowner and Indian in a parody of quotidian life, the celebrations in Barlovento have always been performed solely by the blacks. This does not mean, however, that the festival was not also converted into an important expression of resistance. The time allotted for San Juan was the only free time allowed the slaves, who were compelled to work 6 1/2 days a week, 362 days a year. It was a time when they were able to gather freely not only to dance and play drums, but also to conspire and plan revolts. As the only moment of freedom given them during the entire year, the festival could not help but become associated with the reversal of an oppressive social order. As Bernardo Sanz, a leading drummer in the community of Curiepe, recently observed:

> The Festival of San Juan isn't just a festival. The Festival of San Juan has its meaning. It was the three days given the slaves. And you know why the 25th of June is so popular? For the following [reason]. . . . As they were about to end the days given them to celebrate freely, they cried and jumped all over. That was the most joyous day of all . . . because they thought, "*Caramba*, let's take advantage of this, because from now till the end of next year. . . . Look, let's go. We're not going to serve that man or that one or that one over there anymore."
>
> And I'd flee. I'd go up to one of those mountains there, and then the next year I'd come down just for those days. Because on those days no one was put in jail. They were free.
>
> And that's the way people would run off, taking advantage of that chance. And that would be the day to enjoy and let loose. And some would cry because it was the last day of freedom they gave us.

Recognizing these dangers, colonial authorities tried to prohibit the mingling of slaves and free blacks during the festival. Yet as threatening as these occasions may have been to the slaveholders, outlawing them altogether was considered even more dangerous. It was seen as essential to give the slaves some "illusion" of freedom, some release from their insufferable social condition, some connection to an African past of dignity and meaning (Acosta Saignes 1967:201, 205).

But why was San Juan chosen as the saint to be celebrated? Was it, as Whitten and Monasterio Vásquez suggest, that as the prophet of a new era San Juan symbolized "the transformation from savage (sinner) to civilized (absolved Christian)" (Whitten 1981:502; also see Monasterio Vásquez 1989:108)? Or was it that his festival evoked the memory of an African solstitial ritual in a climate not unlike that of Venezuela? Certainly the cacao harvest and the initiation of the rainy season encouraged the celebration of a holiday at this time. And as some have suggested, "along with Carnival, San Juan is the most plebeian festival on the ecclesiastical calendar" (Liscano 1973:66). Its use of divination, amulets, baths, and fires was easily absorbed into an existing African tradition. It was also, as St. Augustine had observed centuries earlier, a convenient means by which the church could sanction and hence incorporate behavior that would otherwise be repellent. For San Juan, in keeping with his syncretic and adaptive history, appears to have been added to this celebration like a new frame through which to experience it. Isabel Cobos, a teacher and organizer in Curiepe, explained it this way:

> The 23rd, 24th, and 25th [are] San Juan. And they were given to the slaves to celebrate their saint. They played their drums and sang *malembe*.[6] The whites, they had no idea what saint that was. And so they said, "You want a saint? Okay, here, take this." And they set down San Juan.

Some have suggested that San Juan may actually be Shangó, the Yoruba god of thunder, whose color, like that of San Juan, is red.[7] But the importation of slaves to Venezuela ended long before the Yoruba began arriving in the New World. This, along with the fact that Venezuela's slave population was much more heterogeneous than that of countries like Cuba and Brazil, makes it difficult to ascribe any prior native identity to the saint (Brandt 1978:7–9; García 1990:87; Liscano 1973:69). What is not difficult to ascribe is the African origin of most of the festival's performative elements. For while certain features, such as bathing, divination, church liturgy, and propitiation of the saint, do recall its Spanish heritage, the principal elements remain those imported from Africa.

Beginning at noon on the 23rd of June and continuing almost nonstop through the night of the 25th, the festival's activity focuses on two different sets of drums. The first, called the *mina*, perhaps in memory of the area in Ghana from which it came, is composed of two drums, the mina proper and the *curbata*. The mina itself is a six-foot-long hollowed trunk placed upon a cross brace of two poles. It is played with sticks on both the body of the drum and its deerskin head and is accompanied by the smaller, upright curbata. The second set is composed of three cylindrically shaped, double-skinned drums called the *culo e' puya*. Of probable Bantu origin, these three-foot-long instruments are nestled between the legs of a drummer who plays them upright with a stick in one hand and the bare fingers of the other.[8]

The corpus of rhythms, dances, and songs of each of these ensembles is completely different, as is its structural relation to the saint. It is the music of the drums that satisfies the "promises" to be repaid during the three days and nights of the festival. These *promesas*, which may be based on any favor granted by San Juan, require that a *velorio* be offered, with the sponsoring household paying for all the alcohol and food consumed. During the velorio, which lasts an entire night, the image of San Juan, dressed in red and covered with flowers, is installed in a place of honor. Immediately in front of it, the culo e' puya drums are played, while outside in the street another group dances and sings to the mina and curbata. These velorios continue from house to house until the conclusion of the festival.

### San Juan Nacional

While local colonial authorities may have seen an advantage to encouraging this unusual celebration of San Juan, the earliest written records reported it with horror. Not only were the borders between San Juan and the African deities he seemed to represent dangerously blurred, but so were those between male and female. In short, the celebration appeared too erotic. Hence, when Bishop Mariano Martí visited the parishes of Barlovento in 1784, he concluded that all such festivities should be strictly prohibited. Of Curiepe in particular he wrote:

These people are led by a passion for dancing, not just at parties or celebrations on holidays or when some baptism occurs but also at what they call *velorios*, both for dead children[9] and on the eves of festivals, all of which leads to a sorry disorder, with men and women in a confused mess, especially at night. And they go on this way during these festivals with endless dancing for nearly the whole night, so that they wake up worn out and tired, incapable, and prohibited from satisfying the Precept of Mass, burdening their consciences, and, knowing the risk to which they expose themselves, still do not avoid these ridiculous and earthly diversions. Therefore, in order to end these so-called disorders, we must of course prohibit under penalty of excommunication such *velorios*, in which wild dances and other suspect gatherings occur; and we must send and order that the priest of that congregation in frequent sermons and exhortations make his parishioners understand the pernicious effects resulting from such dances, of which one Church Father has said, "They are a circle whose center is the Devil and circumference his Ministers." (Cited in Chacón 1979:33)

Of course such behavior was not entirely new to the Catholic church. As Enrique González points out, a fundamental role of saints had always been as substitutes for ancient deities.[10] In medieval Europe in particular, they provided not only a more direct access to God but also, through the dances with which they were celebrated, a critical reaccess to the body (González 1989). The church, then, would seem to have vacillated between tacit acceptance of such rites and, as Bishop Martí implores, unequivocal repression. As Taussig noted in his work among African-descended groups in neighboring Colombia, such ambivalence between license and restraint led to "almost insuperable contradictions that made social control difficult for colonialists everywhere" (1980:44). It also led to the paradox of dominant groups appropriating the very magical powers they were purportedly trying to destroy—the image of the Inquisitor with his African healer (1980:42). Yet most significant of all were the consequences of this attempted repression. With numerous examples from throughout Latin America, particularly the Andes, Taussig has shown how religious repression, time and again, has stimulated cultural creativity, leading to the fashioning of new forms of resistance from old structures of belief. And so it is too that despite the interdictions of Bishop Martí, the celebration of San Juan has continued in Barlovento to the present day, responding rather than yielding to the changing conditions in which it is performed.

It would be nearly 160 years from the time of Bishop Martí's unflattering report of the festival until any other written mention of it appeared. In 1939, however, a young poet from Caracas named Juan Liscano began making regular journeys to the village of Curiepe in the heart of Barlovento. Curiepe had changed little since the bishop's visit there in the late 18th century. One still had to go by either mule or foot or take a steamer to the port of Higuerote, located just kilometers away. Its population too had changed little, rising to just over 3,000 people

(Acosta Saignes 1959). As in Martí's time, they were mainly farmers with small orchards of cacao, citrus, and avocado. And festivals too were still times for social ties to be renewed, for families who spent much of the year isolated in the mountains to come to town to visit friends and to pay debts, both religious and otherwise. They were also times for people to drum and sing, activities for which Curiepe was said to be the very best. It was for this reason that Liscano went there, dragging his antique record-making machine with him.

Liscano had grown up in France and Switzerland. His stepfather, who had an enormous influence on him, had been the Venezuelan ambassador to the League of Nations. When Liscano returned home as a young man in 1934, Venezuela was like a foreign country to him. After studying law for three years, he decided to dedicate himself entirely to literature, associating with a movement known as "Nuevo Mundismo." In response to the chaos engulfing Europe, the members of this movement sought to discover a new spiritual ideal disengaged from both war and politics. The New World for these artists and intellectuals was to be an "Americanist Utopia," free from all the contaminating ideologies now destroying the Old (Machado 1987:40–41). It was the desire to discover an authentic American experience that led Liscano to Curiepe and the investigation of its Afro-Venezuelan music and lore. While his work is now credited with initiating the scientific study of folklore in Venezuela, Liscano insists that such was never his intention. In a 1987 interview, he stated:

> I began studying folklore as a real life experience, in order to get close to the primitive, down-to-earth man, to what I thought to be that "integrated" Venezuelan, because he was integrated with nature and tradition. (Cited in Machado 1987:47)

Given this predisposition, it is little surprise that the Sanjuanero described by Liscano was strikingly similar to that portrayed by Bishop Martí a century and a half before. But his sexually liberated celebrants were not objects of scorn to be condemned. Rather, they were ideals for a newly emerging urban population who, dominated by European culture, perceived in them an unrepressed and joyous alternative. As Liscano wrote in *La Fiesta de San Juan el Bautista:*

> Among the blacks of Venezuela, the celebration of San Juan has lost almost all religious inspiration and has been overcome by rhythmicity, orgiastic power, and drunken energy. . . . The vital release achieved through frenetic dances, collective songs, *velorios*, and processions [relieves] the tensions created by an exploitative social regime. (1973:47, 51)

Liscano's views, reinforcing not only the rupture between spirit and body but also the stereotype of black eroticism and licentiousness, were to have an important impact on both the future of Curiepe and the celebration of San Juan. Continuing to work in the area of folklore, Liscano was selected to head the Servicio de Investigaciones Folklóricas when it was formed by the revolutionary junta in the fall of 1946. And then two years later, when Rómulo Gallegos was inaugurated as the first popularly elected president in Venezuela's history, Liscano was asked to organize a five-day folklore festival to commemorate the event. Called the Fiesta de la Tradición, it was to feature the most representative groups from throughout the country. Of course, at this time the notion of "groups" was foreign to those who performed out of religious devotion in small and isolated rural communities. But Liscano, with the help of a choreographer and dress designer, succeeded in presenting 17 different acts. There were Indians from the Guajira, Tamunangueros from Lara, the Parrandas of San Pedro, the Giros of San Benito, comparsas, jinetes, Diablos, Chimbangueles, and of course the drums of San Juan. The event, held in a Caracas bull ring and attended by thousands of people, was an extraordinary success. It was as if Venezuela had suddenly discovered itself and, responding to the need of a new democracy, created a people.[11] None of the groups presented had been known nationally or even outside the particular regions in which they resided. Yet as a result of the Fiesta de la Tradición, they had embarked on a long transformation into national identity.

Within ten months, Gallegos was in exile in Mexico and the dictatorship of Marcos Pérez Jiménez installed. Liscano would renounce his position at the Servicio and then, four years later, also flee. But the image of San Juan, and particularly that associated with Curiepe, had become part of the national consciousness forever. The changes brought about by this new association were nearly imperceptible at first. A group was formed to represent the community nationally. Called the Conjunto Folklórico San Juan de Curiepe, it played at festivals in Caracas and elsewhere. In 1950 the first paved road was completed, allowing people to journey to and from Caracas in a single day. Four years later electricity arrived. Dancers like Yolanda Moreno created arrangements based on San Juan to be performed on television. Articles, records, and even books appeared (Aretz 1953, 1955; Liscano 1947, 1950; Liscano and Seeger 1947; Ramón y Rivera 1951, 1963a, 1963b; Sojo 1943, 1959, 1986). The media began to refer to the entire month of June as the "Days of San Juan," treating it as if it were a national holiday. And little by little, tourists began to appear. By 1960 there were so many that the customary velorios held in private households could no longer be performed. As a result the community, under the leadership of a local doctor, decided to construct a cultural center in which the saint would be housed. They called it the "Casa de Folklore Juan Pablo Sojo, Hijo," after the man who had assisted Liscano and been the first to write about local folklore.

San Juan would no longer be an intimate celebration, sponsored by grateful individuals repaying "promises" to a miraculous saint. It would now, befitting its new national status, be a public event organized by the community at large and open to all. The three culo e' puya drums would still have a privileged position beside the saint, but it would be in front of the stage at the Casa de Folklore. The mina and curbata meanwhile would remain a half block away on a corner of the plaza. The structural relation of the two drum ensembles would remain the same. However, the space in which the performance occurred would move from the inside out—that is, from private to public or household to square. While the new manner of presenting the festival was certainly a radical change, it was but a prelude to even greater transformations about to come.

### San Juan Monumental

Not all the tourists who began arriving in Curiepe for the celebration of San Juan were drawn by interests that articles or television programs had generated. Many were actually Curieperos who had migrated to Caracas and were now returning to experience contact with their regional heritage. Even blacks from other Barlovento communities began coming to Curiepe, convinced by both media and friends that this was the festival's most genuine expression. The fact that so many participants were emigrants on an annual pilgrimage to their homeland mediated San Juan's adaptation to its new conditions. The increased popularity of San Juan, unlike other festivals that have been converted from local and subregional holidays to national and even global ones, did not result in what John Kelly refers to as a "heritage spectacle" (1990:65), a staged event with a small core of "traditional" performers surrounded by a sea of passive onlookers. Here the majority of those labeled "tourists" did not come to observe and take photos. They came to participate, to dance, to be transported from a life of enforced marginalization to one of active centrality.[12]

While Barloventeños had been migrating to Caracas for generations, it was not until the mid-1950s that this movement took on large-scale proportions (Pollak-Eltz 1979:34). Attracted by new jobs in services and construction, immigrants attempting to re-create the conditions of family and support they had left behind began to fill up whole neighborhoods. One such neighborhood was San José, located just blocks above the Pantheon (a monument dedicated to the memory of Simón Bolívar). It was here that the great majority of those arriving from Curiepe settled. And it was here too that a group of them began to meet in 1969 to discuss ways to "help their community." It was still the era of the Alliance for Progress. Venezuela, like the rest of Latin America, was obsessed with the notion of development. Yet unlike its neighbors, Venezuela was on the verge of an enormous boom. The price of oil alone, Venezuela's main export, would rise by over 700 percent between 1970 and 1974 and then double again over the next eight years (Ewell 1984:194). The group of Curieperos meeting in the barrio of San José in Caracas thought it unconscionable that their native community should be bypassed by this economic miracle. Their philosophy, as stated by Pedro Roberto Ruíz, the self-proclaimed leader of the group, was simple: "A village that does not progress will live abandoned forever. Which is to say, communities must progress.

It's obvious." Yet exactly how to incorporate their remote agricultural community into the growing economy of the rest of the country was not clear.

After several months of discussion, Ruíz's group concluded that Curiepe's main resource was culture, and particularly the Festival of San Juan. They believed that it would be possible, with proper organization and publicity, to promote this festival to the rest of the country. If they were successful, enough tourists would arrive to generate a permanent infrastructure of hotels, restaurants, and jobs. The group dreamed of opening an enormous "drum park," so that tourists, as Ruíz put it, "could view the festival in an orderly fashion, with better execution and preparation." Drummers would be brought from all over Barlovento and at the end of each festival prizes would be handed out. Of course Curiepe had—and indeed still has—no accommodations for tourists whatsoever. But the Curiepe Prodevelopment Center (Centro Prodesarrollo de Curiepe, or CEPRODEC), as Ruíz's group came to be known, felt the most important thing was to first put the village on the map.

The nine-member core of Ruíz's group included individuals uniquely situated to mount a national publicity campaign. Two were journalists while another worked in advertising and still another in the census bureau. Ruíz himself was an officer attached to the accounting office of the air force.[13] It was, therefore, not difficult for him to gain access to the highest levels of government. After winning support from both the national and the state congresses, he entered into an agreement with the National Tourist Board (Corporación Nacional de Turismo, or CONAHOTU), which had just adopted a policy to promote festivals and other manifestations of local culture as tourist attractions. They decided that the San Juan celebration in Curiepe would be the centerpiece of an enormous folklore festival rivaling that organized by Juan Liscano in 1948. It would be promoted both in Venezuela and abroad and would be known as San Juan Monumental, the greatest San Juan ever held.

Working together, they designed a poster that would soon become the symbol of the festival. It showed three drummers playing culo e' puya. Shot from below like three giants, they were dark and sweaty, the image of the black *campesino* caught in a moment of authentic celebration. But the poster, which won a national award for photography, was by no means the only form of advertising. Ruíz went on a tour throughout the country, speaking to local groups and government officials. Ads appeared on television and radio. There were articles in magazines and newspapers. Cars with loudspeakers circulated throughout Caracas and other cities. And handbills floated through the streets everywhere. As Ruíz recalled:

> We were really proud of the advertising we did. It got all the way to Japan. The Venezuelan ambassador there contacted us to say that the word was reaching them and that the people there were really interested in finding out more about San Juan Monumental.

The advertising campaign was so successful that it brought over 100,000 people to the village of Curiepe in the course of an eight-day period. For San Juan Monumental included much more than the three days of traditional drumming. It was to be a Semana Cultural, a "Culture Week," with groups performing from every region of the country. As in the Fiesta de la Tradición, there were Diablos from Yare, comparsas from the Oriente, and the Parrandas of San Pedro. There were also performers who had not appeared there, such as Luis Mariano Rivera, a famous folksinger from Carupano, and the Calypso from El Callao. And in the center of all these acts were the drums of San Juan, playing nonstop for three entire days. As described by one of the festival's organizers:

> It was much greater than 1948. What we did was much more extensive. Of course we respected that one, yes. But what we did was to put a type of parentheses around our own folkloric tradition, which was on the 23rd, 24th, and 25th of June, the days of the drums of San Juan. There were no other folklore groups performing then. The days they performed were the 20th, 21st, and 22nd and the 26th and 27th. Because the 27th of June, by coincidence, fell on a Sunday. And so that day we presented Flor García, a popular lyrical singer, who closed San Juan Monumental at nine in the evening, singing his lyrical songs.

The strategy of locating the festival at the center of a new national culture effected a brilliant recontextualization of meanings. From a local saint's day celebrating both religious piety and ethnic heritage the festival was converted into the main act of a national variety show. The "parentheses" within which it was now enclosed formed an essential part of the new meaning the festival organizers were trying to construct. Illustrating what Goffman has characterized as the problem of "brackets" in relation to spectacles and games, San Juan Monumental had encased one ritual event (the game) within another (the spectacle). The resulting ambiguity as to "whether the outer or inner realms [were] of chief concern" (Goffman 1974:261–269) was one the village of Curiepe was not yet ready to confront. For those who had organized the event, however, the festival had been an unqualified success. Their goal had been simple: to incorporate the community into the national economy. Yet their strategy had been to start with the culture and to relocate it as squarely as possible at the center of the national one. While San Juan Monumental clearly achieved this end, its effect on both the festival itself and the local economy was one neither the organizers nor the villagers had foreseen.

The following year, 1971, the festival was celebrated in much the same way. A new committee, composed entirely of people living in Curiepe, took over its organization. To differentiate their events from those of the year before, they renamed the week of cultural activities San Juan Sensacional. For most Venezuelans, this name evoked one of the country's most popular television shows, an eight-hour extravaganza of variety acts broadcast on Saturdays and called "Sábado

Sensacional." This link to the state media was but one more step in the nationalization process begun by Juan Liscano in the 1940s. The government also continued its contribution to this process by naming Curiepe the "National Folklore
Village" and at the same time instituting a system of nominal payments for many
of the festival's drummers. Of course this system tied local performers not simply
to the government's patronage, but, in a more dangerous way, to the particular
party that was giving it out.[14]

   While San Juan Sensacional was not quite the success of the previous year's
event, it nevertheless established the festival as an annual attraction for people
throughout the country. Hence, when the Culture Week program was suspended
altogether in 1972, there was little impact on the number of visitors who came
to Curiepe to celebrate. Many of those who came, however, were attracted less
by an interest in folklore than by what they perceived as an African bacchanal
dedicated to drums, drugs, and free love. It was the image Liscano himself had
fabricated 25 years earlier, of a people "overcome by rhythmicity, orgiastic power,
and drunken energy" (1973:47; also see Liscano 1947, 1950). These stereotypes
of black hedonism and sensuality generated a new audience for the festival,
which in turn imposed its own carnivalesque definitions. Visitors from Caracas
regularly spent the day at the beach and then in late afternoon appeared scantily
clad in bikinis or shorts. They replaced the traditional dance, in which couples
gracefully moved forward and back, with long chains of whirling groups, all howl-
ing and shouting in unison. Motorcycle gangs began to arrive, and knifings and
fights were not uncommon. Villagers were scandalized, and by the mid-1970s
were spending most of the festival sheltered in their homes. As Angel Lucci, a
community organizer who was then a young man growing up in Curiepe, recalled:

> In the final years people didn't even participate. Motorcycle gangs came and took
> over the town. It was an incredible disaster. . . . No one could sleep. My mother
> and grandmother hid. They were totally terrified because it had become really
> ugly. Curiepe had handed its San Juan over to the tourists.[15]

   But it was not merely the tourists who had invaded San Juan. Commercial
interests had begun to arrive as well, particularly tobacco and beer companies.
On the days preceding the holiday, they sent groups to hang posters and pennants, not simply to advertise their products but to associate their names as closely
as possible with that of the saint. As the tourists entered, they passed beneath
enormous banners welcoming them to the drums of San Juan, courtesy of either
a cigarette or a rum. And the drummers were now dressed in T-shirts with the
name of a beer on the front and that of San Juan on the back. Those setting up
stalls to sell alcohol and food were not from Curiepe either, and none of the
profits they made remained in the community. The vision of Ruíz's group had
not materialized. The village, which numbered less than 3,000 people (Brandt

1978:10), still had not a single hotel or restaurant. And instead of enjoying the economic miracle it had been promised, Curiepe now braced itself once a year to be invaded. Those studying the festival at this time all wrote of its serious decline, predicting that if changes were not made, it would likely disappear (Brandt 1978:333–338; Chacón 1979:110; Liscano 1973:52).

### San Juan Cimarrón

The mid-1970s was a time of enormous change not simply in Curiepe but throughout Venezuela. The tremendous influx of foreign currency caused by the rapid inflation of world oil prices was resulting in a massive demographic and cultural transformation. In her book *Venezuela: A Century of Change*, Judith Ewell says that this period witnessed a "petrolization of the national problems" (1984:193–226). It gave birth, she notes, to a long list of new programs and organizations initiated by the governments of both Carlos Andrés Pérez and his successor, Luis Herrera Campíns. Many of the programs, such as the formation of the Biblioteca Ayacucho in 1974 and the Consejo Nacional de la Cultura (CONAC) the following year, were attempts to distribute this new wealth to the cultural sector.

Other programs, however, were responses to the various forms of social dislocation that had accompanied the economic boom. One such program, sponsored by the Ministry of Justice, was the "Cultural Division of Crime Prevention." Despite its somewhat inauspicious name, this small pilot program was a type of urban Peace Corps, sending out small cadres of idealistic men and women to targeted marginal neighborhoods. Their plan was to create "centers of activity" that in turn would generate community leadership, pride, and autonomy. Although Curiepe fell outside the urban mandate for this project, one of the organizers, Jesús Blanco, suggested that it nevertheless be included.[16]

Blanco was aware from previous visits to Curiepe that its youth were extremely disaffected from any organized cultural activities. In fact, the predictions of Brandt (1978:335) and others concerning the future of San Juan were based on the lack of participation or interest of the younger generation. Blanco began with an ambitious sports program, bringing young people together to compete on basketball, volleyball, and other teams. It was the first time that such sports had been introduced in any organized way, and the youth of Curiepe responded with enthusiasm. Once these groups had been formed, Blanco had little trouble in translating their energy into other cultural realms. Many of those participating in the new sports program had been upset by the invasion of tourists and the exploitation it had engendered. With Blanco's help, they developed a plan that would not only limit the impact of these visitors but also restore the community's control over the festival. The group, with 22 core members, would eventually become known as the Centro Cultural y Deportivo de Curiepe, the Curiepe Culture and Sport Center.

The initial activities of this group, which began with the celebration of 1975, were both educational and supervisory. They believed that if tourists were only informed of the festival's history and religious significance, much of the destructive behavior would disappear. They distributed lengthy pamphlets with histories of the community and detailed descriptions of each aspect of the festival. A small museum was created in an old house just off the plaza. Brigades were formed to patrol the village and to enforce a new dress code that would be more respectful of a religious holiday. Shorts and swimwear were now forbidden, as was the use of alcohol in the presence of the saint. The group also attacked the festival's commercialization, and when attempts to discourage the hanging of pennants and banners failed, members pulled them down themselves.

In time, the sale of food and alcohol was also controlled. In order to prevent profits from leaving the community, the organizers restricted concessions to local charitable and educational groups. And when drummers were finally convinced to reject all government stipends, a system of food and beverage coupons was established. It was a brilliant rerouting of reciprocity, giving the traditional velorio system new life. Instead of being paid directly by a family sponsoring the velorio, drummers now registered with the festival directorate and, after playing, were given vouchers they could use at the concessions of other village members, who were in turn receiving payments from tourists. It took several years before these innovations were fully in place. In fact, it was only after Jesús Blanco left in 1978 that the Curiepe Culture and Sport Center finally assumed total control of the festival, replacing the board that had directed it since the time of Pedro Ruíz.

One of the first decisions of the new leadership was to revive the Semana Cultural, or Culture Week. The group's intentions, however, could not have been further from those of Ruíz and his San Juan Monumental. Instead of trying to recontextualize the festival within a larger, national framework, the Culture Week of 1979 would attempt to restore it to its original one. As such, there were to be no "parentheses," only a single bracket or arrow pointing to what its organizers called "its true meaning." The events presented, therefore, would all precede San Juan, making it clear that the festival should be understood as an end in itself. They would also help to firmly relocate it within a single community and people. The groups invited would no longer be a sampling of Venezuela's most popular folkloric acts. Instead, they would be a carefully orchestrated demonstration of what the festival would now represent. For the Culture Week was no longer meant to be a simple entertainment devised to attract as many tourists as possible. It was now meant to be a heuristic tool, as the slogan heading the program unequivocally announced:

COMRADE
WE INVITE YOU TO PARTICIPATE
IN A FULL WEEK OF WORK AND RECREATION
JOIN AND STRUGGLE

A wide range of activities was now presented, including movies, plays, lectures, and even a book party.[17] Yet all of them shared a vision of regional and ethnic autonomy. A special symposium on the question of "indigenism" was held, and the film Yo hablo a Caracas was shown. The film, which Carlos Azpúrua had just completed, was a dramatic appeal by the Yekuana Indians to have their land and culture respected (Azpúrua 1979).[18] This show of solidarity with the indigenist movement underlined the feeling of many that Barlovento's culture had also been colonized and was in the same need of protection as the Indians'. The language included in the Culture Week program borrowed heavily from the indigenist literature just starting to circulate at that time. The culture now in danger, however, was the Afro-Venezuelan, as statements such as the following made clear:

> The cultural manifestations of the Barlovento area, which is to say those of Afro-Venezuelan origin, have been heavily attacked—at times to the point of disappearing—by so-called civilization. . . . We have seen how the drum festivals of Barlovento have taken on a cheap and commercial meaning, instead of those of solidarity and struggle. At the same time, we have seen how our cultural and moral values have been replaced by cultural values different from those of our Afro-Venezuelan identity. All of which shows the transculturation and domination by other cultures. (Centro Cultural y Deportivo de Curiepe 1979)

The Culture Week would now attempt to reassert Afro-Venezuelan values. Surrounded by a series of aggressively regionalist, Afro-Venezuelan performances, the festival would be symbolically recast. It would shed its image as a national extravaganza and be "re-Africanized." If Curiepe was experiencing a crisis caused by both the loss of citizens through emigration and the influx of strangers through tourism, then the festival would be a tool in consolidating its identity once again.[19] The aspects of San Juan that would be emphasized were those of liberation and resistance. For the Barlventeño, the festival would soon be as much a historical performance as it would a religious celebration. Thus, the focus would now be less on the saint and more on the drums. Or, as the statement commonly quoted that year from the local writer Juan Pablo Sojo went, "The drum is the cross of the black Christ" (1976[1943]:154).

Drums, of course, had served as images of resistance not only in Venezuela but throughout the Caribbean. In neighboring Trinidad they had become the symbol of a Carnival that had been transformed from "a high-society affair of elaborate balls" (Hill 1972:10) to an ecstatic celebration of emancipated slaves. When the former European masters had attempted to suppress these new expressions of liberation, they had done so by outlawing the use of drums, a strategy that was to have disastrous though ultimately unsuccessful results. It is interesting that when the steel drums that replaced the originally suppressed ones began appearing in London's Notting Hill Carnival in the early 1970s, their symbolic power was much the same. As Abner Cohen notes, however, there was also an appropriate transformation:

> The steel band has acquired a powerful symbolic significance well beyond the making of loud rhythms. . . . In the first place, there is a feeling of pride and ela-tion at its invention, and many Carnival leaders emphasize that the pan is the only musical instrument invented in the twentieth century. . . . At the same time, with its rust, rough edges, and clumsy appearance, the pan is the symbol of poverty and social disadvantage, a protest that in lands of plenty, endowed with so many so-phisticated musical instruments, a people should be forced to pick up abandoned shells to express their artistic feelings. (1980:71)[20]

The close symbolic connection of drums to expressions of freedom and protest, particularly during Carnival, has led more than one government to convert this holiday into a celebration of political independence. In Cuba, for example, Car-nival has been moved to the beginning of January, where it now commemorates the overthrow of the Batista government by Fidel Castro. And in Antigua, it is celebrated not during the days before Lent but rather on the 1st of August, the date on which the slaves were emancipated. It is not therefore surprising that its celebration is characterized, as Frank Manning notes, by "regional awareness [and] expressions of racial solidarity" (1977:269).

While the Festival of San Juan should not be confused with Carnival, its his-torical relation to the experience of liberation and slavery is similar to that of many New World Carnivals. In designing the program for the new Semana Cul-tural, its organizers were attempting to highlight this relation and to present a past not of docile submission but rather of proud, resolute resistance. For them, San Juan embodied this history, and the performance of the festival was a sacred re-creation of it. The performance was not simply the fulfillment of a promesa or the reenactment of an ancient fertility rite. It was a magical return to a moment of origin, and such a return is, as Duvignaud notes (following Eliade [1959] and Caillois [1959]), what "gives life to history" (1976:21). The transformation of the festival into such a "paradigmatic event" (Eliade 1959:34) depended on the in-vocation and recharging of a number of symbolic associations. Most of these de-rived their power, however, from a concept known as *cimarronaje*.

Difficult to translate into English, particularly as the closest word we have, "maroon," is already a Spanish cognate, cimarronaje is the quality or ethos of a *cimarrón*, an escaped slave. In Venezuela as elsewhere in the New World, the es-caped slave, whether in a *cumbe, quilombo, palenque*, or free village, was a source of inspiration for those still in bondage (García 1990:53).[21] He or she represented a refusal to submit either physically or culturally to the brutalizing institution of slavery, for the cimarrón communities hidden away in the mountains and swamps of the Americas often still maintained a rich African cultural heritage (García 1989, 1990; Guerra Cedeño 1984; Price 1983; Price and Price 1980). When invoking the concept of cimarronaje today, the Afro-Venezuelan refers not merely to history but to a living tradition still determined to resist the domination of a European ruling class. The concept recognizes that the black Venezuelan remains a marginalized, economically oppressed citizen who must find solutions within his or her own community.

Conversely, when elements of Afro-Venezuelan culture have already been absorbed into the centralized system of power, it is claimed that the community must *cimarronear*, or "cimarronize," them, which is to say, they must "re-Africanize" them, repositioning both their control and their meaning in the society that generated them. This of course is precisely what the new directors of the San Juan festival were now trying to do. They were attempting to "cimarronize" it by showing the festival's direct links to an ongoing tradition of autonomy and resistance. Several of the strategies used to connect the contemporary reality of Barlovento to that of its cimarrón history have already been mentioned. With its performances, lectures, and conferences, the Culture Week, which has continued with brief lapses up to the present, sought to effect this recontextualization and to provide the people of Barlovento with a new language in which to speak about both their traditions and themselves.[22] It was not long, therefore, before people began to speak of the festival, as Bernardo Sanz did, as a commemoration of the three days of freedom that the slaves had had in order to plan either rebellions or individual escapes.

Even the origin of the festival was firmly relocated in the cimarrón experience. Participants claimed that the songs and other musical aspects of the celebration derived from an escaped slave named José Larito. Larito, also known as José Hilario or Calvarito, had arrived in Venezuela on a French slave ship from the Gold Coast. With him was an African prince who, upon discovering that he was about to be sold into slavery, took a piece of tin and slit his throat. As the prince lay dying, Larito reached down and scooped up the blood, quickly covering his own body with it. After a brief period of enslavement, during which he was particularly abused, Larito fled into the mountains and formed his own cumbe. But on the 23rd of June each year he would appear in Curiepe for the celebration of San Juan, leading the drumming and singing, and then on the evening of the 25th would escape once more with a new group of cimarrones. The Spanish of course did all they could to catch him. But the power of the prince's blood allowed Larito either to become invisible or to take another form.

The tale of José Larito, which exists in both written and oral versions, is a perfect example of the "cimarronizing" process (Sojo 1959; Uslar Pietri 1975). By locating the germinating force of the festival in the deeds of a culture hero such as Larito, it transfers the locus of power from that of a Catholic saint's day to one of historical remembrance.[23] This is particularly significant when one realizes that the name José Larito is directly derived from that of Don Joseph Hilario Tinoco, the priest sent to Curiepe in November 1731 to establish the first church there (Castillo Lara 1981a:144; Chacón 1979:21). Thus, on another level, the tale is also "cimarronizing" the community's origin, converting the priest credited with its founding into a cimarrón hero. But of all the attempts to identify the festival with an African past of struggle and liberation, none has been so important as the Africanization of San Juan himself

## San Juan Congo

The pale-skinned San Juan Bautista with his burnished red cheeks and painted nails was not always the figure carried through the streets of Curiepe and sung to for three days and nights. In fact, Curieperos, though reluctant to speak of it, acknowledge that this saint is something of a newcomer. Until at least 1870, there was another San Juan, the one claimed to have been the original. Referred to as San Juan Congo, this figure was also carved of wood and coated in plaster. Yet unlike the one he replaced, San Juan Congo was said to be black. He also had a phallus, a common feature for many African figures but totally unknown for a Christian one. Like many other icons, San Juan Congo was the personal property of a single family, who on the saint's day lent him to the community to be celebrated.[24] Toward the end of the 19th century, possession of "the Congo," as he is commonly known, passed to a local doctor named Nicomedes Blanco Gil. It was then—the precise date is difficult to ascertain—that San Juan Congo suddenly stopped appearing. Some say he vanished because an indiscretion was directed at the doctor's wife as she was walking through the streets. Enraged by such disrespect, Blanco Gil decided to punish the entire community and refused to lend them the saint from that moment on. Others, however, claim that the church, upset by the saint's phallus, pressured the doctor to retire San Juan Congo.

Faced with the dilemma of having no saint with which to celebrate their festival, members of the community approached the family of Enrique Moscoso, who had just arrived from Birongo and was the owner of a much-admired image of San Juan. This image now became the official one of Curiepe, and while San Juan Congo was still celebrated on the fourth of August for several years, he was soon almost entirely forgotten. Passing into the hands of Blanco Gil's illegitimate daughter, María Poncho, the saint remained an almost hidden figure. And then in the late 1970s, nearly a century after he had been replaced, a group decided to ask Poncho if they could borrow her San Juan and hold a velorio.

While the velorio coincided with the other innovations surrounding the celebration of San Juan, it was held not during the festival itself but rather four days later, on the Day of San Pedro. By doing so, the organizers avoided the intrusion of any tourists and succeeded, as they had hoped, in re-creating the celebration as it had existed before the arrival of Liscano and others. It was to become, as people said, "our festival," "the one of the village," "the real one," and since 1979 it has been held in relative secrecy, without any publicity or national attention. For while substantial changes could be made in the organization and performance of the festival as it occurred from the 23rd to the 25th of June, the tourists and national celebrity they represented were now a permanent (and not entirely unwelcome) part of it.[25] The velorio to San Juan Congo, on the other hand, permitted the village to complete the cycle of historical recuperation already under way. The symbols surrounding this event, therefore, were a powerfully orchestrated return to origins.

Instead of celebrating the velorio in the plaza, the participants held it in the ruins of Curiepe's former church, called the Capilla, or "chapel." Sitting atop a hill overlooking the main square, the Capilla was Curiepe's sole church from the earthquake of 1811 until the construction of a new one in the village center in 1959. At one time, members of the community planned to construct a new school in its place, but after tearing down most of the old structure and rebuilding some walls, they simply left it as a shell. Today it sits as a symbol of the surrounding neighborhood of the same name, a neighborhood associated with Curiepe's poorest citizens and best musicians. "The people above" (el pueblo arriba), as they are known, have developed a certain resentment for those they call "the people below" (el pueblo abajo), the town's more well-to-do and powerful citizens, living in the larger homes around the square. For many years, the people of La Capilla had complained that the celebration of San Juan was too restricted, that it should not be limited to the main square but should also be performed in the upper part of the village. Now, with the new velorio of the 29th of June, "the people above" feel that they have finally gotten their own San Juan. María Poncho herself lives in a small house within two blocks of the "chapel," and consequently it is this neighborhood that takes sole responsibility for organizing the night-long event.

At two o'clock in the afternoon, a mixture of people, old and young, men and women, begin to arrive to decorate the remains of the church. They place palm fronds against the walls both inside and out and create a thatched ceiling from which a selection of local fruits, seeds, and nuts is hung. Above the altar where the saint will be installed is placed the most important, cacao, and then spiralling out in an improvised hierarchy are all the other locally cultivated plants: a bunch of bananas, a long curved pod of guamo, shoots of sugarcane, pineapple, passion fruit, guanábana, almonds, cashews, coconut, and a score of other rich tropical fruits that reach back to the entranceway, covering the entire ceiling. A few lights are run from a lamppost, and the altar is modestly decorated with flowers and a painted velvet hanging. At dusk a young boy arrives, nearly unnoticed, with the saint. A group close to the altar begins to play the culo e' puya and sing. And outside, 20 yards from the church entrance, others start on the mina and curbata. Both ensembles will continue playing throughout the night, with people coming from the entire village to dance, drum, sing, and drink. And, of course, to see San Juan Congo, to touch him, to ask him for a favor, to simply stand and silently pray.

It is significant that this velorio, held annually since 1979, has escaped the attention given the preceding three days of celebration. For if the consistent arrival of outsiders converted the original Festival of San Juan into a public event to be held in the village plaza, the new velorio has restored it to a private (and for those participating, "authentic") one. It has also returned the celebration to its original location, the Capilla, where for generations Curieperos worshiped and met. This "return" is especially meaningful given that the move from the Capilla to the new church coincided with the construction of the Casa de Folklore and, hence, the move of San Juan from individual home to public square. Both of these restorations, to private space and primary location, must be seen as contributing to what is perhaps the fundamental restoration—that of the original community.

But the most important element in this obvious primordialization of the festival remains its return to the original saint, San Juan Congo. As with the events surrounding the new Semana Cultural, the symbolism underlying this restitution was also powered by its relation to cimarronaje, although not simply because San Juan Congo was said to be black and hence African. The story of his origins also linked him to a past of liberation and struggle, just as the story of the festival linked it to the cimarrón hero José Larito. In the version recounted by Juan Pablo Sojo (1986:168–172), two African princes, who were also brothers, arrived in the port of La Sabana to be sold into slavery. They were brought to a plantation in Curiepe owned by a hacendado named Blanco. Once there, they showed a remarkable if not uncanny skill in the growing of cacao. Although treated with particular deference because of this, the younger of the two brothers grew increasingly melancholy and finally took his own life. The surviving brother continued to bring prosperity to his master and then one day was suddenly given his freedom along with a small piece of land. Soon after, Blanco died and the former slave took his name. The fortune and prestige of the new Señor Blanco continued to increase, with slaves and free blacks coming to him for support and advice. Then, just before the celebration of San Juan, he proposed that they form a society to purchase the freedom of two or three slaves a year. He began by contributing enough to buy the freedom of at least three of the most expensive. Moreover, he commissioned a carver to make a saint for the new order, a San Juan, said to cost 2,000 pesos and to include gold dust as well.[26]

While this tale may exemplify what John Watanabe refers to as "myths of saintly origins [that] complete the localization of . . . once-Catholic figures" (1990:138), it nevertheless contains many verifiable historical elements. In the record of his visit in 1784, Bishop Martí writes of a slave freed by Don Alejandro Blanco Villegas in order to clear and settle the area around Curiepe (García 1985:5). And documents brought to light in 1981 by the historian Lucas Guillermo Castillo Lara verify that the village was indeed founded by a group of free blacks. The leader of this group, which arrived in Curiepe a full ten years before Father Joseph Hilario founded his church, was named Juan del Rosario Blanco (Castillo Lara 1981a, 1981b).[27] But even more significant perhaps was the existence, not only in Venezuela but throughout the Caribbean and Brazil, of what were known as "liberation banks." These "emancipation credit unions," as Sheila Walker refers to them, were set up by both slaves and free blacks in order to make funds available for the purchase of "free papers" (1986:29–30).[28] It is precisely this form of sanctioned subversion which Blanco and his collaborators set up in Curiepe and for which San Juan Congo was to serve as a symbol. In the fusion of the history of this liberation movement with the origin of the saint, San Juan is not simply Africanized, he becomes the ultimate expression of cimarronaje, a precursor not simply of Jesus but of freedom.

Because of my awareness of the special esteem in which San Juan Congo was held and the role that his "blackness" played in creating this esteem, I was somewhat stunned when I finally had the opportunity to see him. For in reality he was not black at all, a bit darker perhaps than the porcelain-skinned San Juan of the Moscosos but certainly not black, not at least like Venezuela's other black saints, such as San Benito de Palermo and San Martín de Porres. In fact, in addition to being light-skinned and having Caucasian features, the two-foot-high San Juan Congo had curly blond hair. When I discussed this issue with friends of mine in the community, they appeared quite shocked. How could I not see that he was black? Yes, perhaps a restorer had been a bit overzealous in cleaning him, they confided. Nevertheless, it was still clear that he was black. After several of these discussions, I began to realize that the issues of blackness signified by San Juan Congo were much more profound than simple pigmentation. In fact, I eventually came to understand that it was actually the absence of color that made San Juan such a powerful symbol of it. For the blackness he represented was that of poverty and oppression. It was the economic and social marginalization that had defined the African condition since the arrival of the first slaves in the early 1500s. And indeed, while San Juan Congo might not have appeared black, he was certainly poor. His broken fingers, his lack of any toes, his irregular skin, all were in sharp contrast to the elegance of his wealthy namesake celebrated by "the people below."

But like all "dominant symbols," the color of San Juan is loaded with contradiction and ambiguity (Turner 1975). Hence, it also speaks directly to Venezuela's resolute denial of any color at all. In what might be called the myth of *mestizaje* or "mestizo-ness," historians, philosophers, writers, and even anthropologists have consistently claimed that in Venezuela the issue of race does not exist, that all ethnic groups have blended together in a harmonious and indistinguishable new entity called the mestizo. As Juan Liscano, one of the first to write about African cultures in Venezuela, stated:

> Racial differences were absorbed in the cruel process of our national formation, and today there is no "black problem" as there is in the United States, with its unforgivable discrimination. What exists is a class problem, just as there is everywhere. [1950:86]

This commonly held view, that discrimination is the result not of race but rather of class, is the focus of Winthrop Wright's recent study, *Café con Leche:*

*Race, Class, and National Image in Venezuela* (1990). In it, Wright makes a distinction between what he calls the "creed of racial democracy," which maintains that no discrimination based upon color exists, and the "idea of racial equality" itself, a belief somewhat less realized (1990:111). It is this "seeming paradox" that Wright addresses, showing that if blacks were able to emerge from both racial and economic oppression, they were able to do so not through acceptance but rather through miscegenation. For as Wright claims, "the myth of racial democracy's basic premise [was] that blacks achieved great things in Venezuela only as they whitened themselves and their offspring" (1990:115).[29] Racial democracy, then, was not the absence of prejudice, it was simply the license to transform one's ethnic identity. The awareness of any prejudice based on color was effectively masked by a belief system that did not recognize racial diversity. Instead, it insisted that anyone discriminated against was selected because he or she was poor. But as Wright points out, such reasoning was hopelessly circuitous, for "the majority of blacks were poor because they were black" (1990:5).[30] So widespread was this colorblind view of Venezuelan society that even social scientists subscribed to it, insisting that even those identified as black did not necessarily consider themselves to be. As one of Venezuela's leading students of Afro-American traditions, Angelina Pollak-Eltz, wrote:

> In Venezuela there is little racial consciousness or discrimination due to skin color. The fact remains, however, that the majority of Afrovenezuelans belong to the lower strata of society. This is due to class differences, lack of educational opportunities for the rural sector, and little spatial mobility until recently. Africa has no meaning for Barloventeños, who consider themselves "criollos" just like Venezuelans elsewhere. (1979:31)[31]

For those of Barlovento, such statements, along with the pattern of denial they represent, are but another step in the systematic erasure of the Afro-Venezuelan's cultural and racial history. The fact that San Juan Congo is such a powerful symbol of blackness without actually being black, therefore, reveals much about the issue of race itself in Venezuela. To those celebrating at the Capilla, San Juan Congo is clearly black. Yet his is a blackness that only they appear able (or willing) to perceive. Like the cimarrones who continue to inspire it, it is dissembled and hidden. But the power of San Juan Congo, like that of all religious experience, is the power to make the unseen visible.

## Notes

Research for this work was begun with a Mellon Grant for Non-Western Studies administered through Vassar College and continued with a Social Science Research Council Grant. The writing of the article itself was undertaken while I was a Mellon Faculty Fellow in the Humanities at Harvard University. An earlier version of the article was given at

Harvard's Mellon Seminar. I am grateful to all of its participants for various important ideas, but in particular to Ernest Brown, Walter Fluker, and Allan Gallay. In addition, Laurie Kain Hart, Ken George, and Rosalind Shaw all read this work and made valuable contributions to it. And finally, to the *campañeros* of Curiepe and Barlovento; the members of the Centro de Investigación y Documentación de la Cultura Barloventeña (CIDICUB), Angel Lucci and Tomás Ponce; and the Sanjuaneros who go on drumming and believing—*gracias por todo*.

1. The refrain of a salsa composition popular throughout the Caribbean during the late 1970s, these verses may be translated as:

If God were black
all would change.
It would be our race
that held the reins.

2. For more on the growing body of literature regarding the manner in which competing social interests help to generate new and varying versions of the past, see Brow (1990), Crain (1990), Hall (1981), Handler (1988), Handler and Linnekin (1984), Hobsbawm and Ranger (1983), Lincoln (1989), and Williams (1977).

3. As Sir James Frazer noted in *The Golden Bough*, "a faint tinge of Christianity has been given by naming Midsummer Day after St. John the Baptist, but we cannot doubt that the celebration dates from a time long before the beginning of our era" (1953 [1922]: 720). Tracing its spread throughout Europe and even Muslim North Africa, Frazer cited three elements he believed to be common to all its versions: "bonfires, the procession with torches round the fields, and the custom of rolling a wheel" (1953 [1922]:720–721). These dominant features led him to classify San Juan as a fire-festival.

4. Crespi makes the interesting observation that as distinctions between Indian and non-Indian groups have diminished, so has the significance of this festival in the Cayambe-Imbabura area (1981:497). For a view somewhat different from Crespi's, see Crain (1989), who believes the festival has actually increased in importance with both the elimination of other celebrations and the new inequities of a more market-oriented economy.

5. The 1985 census listed the population of Barlovento's four districts as 133,000, or 58.5 percent of the state of Miranda (Monasterio Vásquez 1989:8–9). For more on the geopolitics of this area, see Acosta Saignes (1959), Castillo Lara (1981a, 1981b, 1983), Ponce (1987), and Estado Miranda (1981).

6. The *malembe* is a special song played on the final afternoon of the festival. The sadness commonly associated with it is claimed to derive from its role as a farewell song to the saint. García has even suggested that this final stage of the festival, known as the *encierro*, is analogous to a wake:

This is a drumbeat performed with round drums known as *culo e' puya*. The bearers [of the image] would make the saint dance very gently, as is suggested by the word *malembe*, which, in Bantu-Lingala, means "less fast" or "slowly," and so they would proceed all the way to the small chapel where the wake was to be held. [1985:5]

Sojo also attaches special importance to the word *malembe*, claiming that it is derived from the name for an African deity and actually means "All Powerful." In discussing malembe's role in the San Juan celebration, he explains that it "represented a cult of liberation through death—death by one's own hand before the slaveowner's henchmen could lay on their fatal lashes once again" (1986:172).

7. Bastide points out that in Brazil and Trinidad, Shango, the god of thunder, is explicitly identified with San Juan and that the connection of each to fire may well explain their union. He also suggests that the common belief that San Juan must sleep through his own holiday, rather than come down to earth and destroy it, is derived from stories about Shango (Bastide 1971:156–159, 1978:274). This tradition is also found in Venezuela, where Sanjuaneros sing:

| | |
|---|---|
| *Si San Juan supiera* | If San Juan knew |
| *cuando es su día* | it was his day, oh boy, |
| *del cielo bajará, caramba,* | he'd come down from heaven |
| *con gran alegría* | with such great joy. (Adam 1981:28) |

8. It is difficult to ascertain the origin of the term *culo e' puya*. Culo is quite literally "asshole," while puya refers to a sharp stick used to clean out gourds or logs. Such terms suggest a clear sexual association. However, the term may also derive from the drums' hourglass-shaped interiors. For detailed descriptions of these drum traditions see Liscano (1970), Ramón y Rivera (1971), Brandt (1978), and García (1990).

9. The special velorio for dead children not yet baptized is the *mampulorio*. As the Lipners claim, this velorio is considered a happy occasion, "for people strongly believe that the child has gone to heaven to pray for its parents, and no sorrow should be shown" (Lipner and Lipner 1958:4).

10. Bastide refers to this phenomenon as "Catholic-fetishist syncretism" (1978:142).

11. The poet Andrés Eloy Blanco, writing about the Fiesta de la Tradición, quipped, "Columbus may have discovered America, but Liscano just discovered Venezuela" (cited in Machado 1987:49). For a detailed account of the preparation, execution, and reception of this festival, held on February 17–21, 1948, see Liscano (1950).

12. In discussing the political dimensions of Trinidad's Carnival and the various interests it arbitrates, John Stewart makes a useful distinction between visitors who are "returnees" and those who are "tourists." He claims that because they are detached from any community "encumbrances," it is the visitors in both categories who actually enjoy the event most (1986:314). For more on the concept of the "heritage spectacle," see Acciaioli (1985), Crain (1992), Karp and Lavine (1991), and Kirshenblatt-Gimblett (1991).

13. Ruíz has retired from the air force and is currently a district councilman for the opposition party, the Comité de Organización Política Electoral Independiente (COPEI).

14. The issue of patronage in local festivals, or, as Benito Yrady describes it, "negative interventions" (personal communication, 1990), was not limited to Curiepe. Begun by the Instituto Nacional de Cultura y Bellas Artes (INCBA) and continued by its successor, the Consejo Nacional de la Culture (CONAC), these small stipends tie performers to whatever political party is in power. Hence, when parties lose elections, musicians sometimes refuse to play at festivals because their payments are discontinued by the new parties in office.

15. A song popular in Barlovento at the time, credited to a farmer named Aureliano Huice, effectively captured this feeling of being overrun by tourists. In the principal refrain one fish sings to another:

| | |
|---|---|
| Lebranche le dijó a Guabina, | Lebranche said to Guabina, |
| "Vámonos para pozo hondo. | "Let's get deep down in the water. |
| Allá vienen los turistas | Here come the tourists |
| Con su destrucción en el hombro." | With destruction on their shoulders." |

16. In addition to working for the Ministry of Justice, Blanco was a professional drummer with Yolanda Moreno's Danzas Venezuela, a group that has been adapting traditional dance forms for stage and television since the early 1950s. It was through this dance troupe that Blanco became familiar with Curiepe's unique drum tradition and thus interested in returning to the village in 1975 with the ministry's new program.

17. The publication of Alfredo Chacón's *Curiepe: Ensayo sobre la realización del sentido en la actividad mágicoreligiosa de un pueblo venezolano* (1979) was celebrated in Curiepe during the Culture Week of 1979.

18. Azpúrua's film was part of a national campaign seeking both to redefine government policy toward indigenous peoples and to evict the North American–backed New Tribes Missions (Guss 1989:19–20; Luzardo 1988; Mosonyi 1981).

19. For an indication of how radical this shift in self-perception was, consider the findings of Max Brandt, who, while doing research in this area only several years earlier, had noted that most Curieperos defined themselves as well as their drum traditions as "Indian" rather than African (1978:5).

20. Historical instances of the repression of drums are to be found throughout the Americas, from the response to the Stono Rebellion in South Carolina in 1739 (Wood 1974) to Rafael Trujillo's more recent attempt to prohibit their inclusion in Dominican *merengue* bands. And while drums were not outlawed in the United States during the 1950s, congas and bongos served as the symbol of resistance for an entire generation of beats. As Dick Hebdige observed in writing about reggae and Rastafarianism:

> The voice of Africa in the West Indies has traditionally been identified with insurrection and silenced wherever possible. In particular, the preservation of African traditions, like drumming, has in the past been construed by the authorities (the Church, the colonial and even some "post-colonial" governments) as being intrinsically subversive, posing a symbolic threat to law and order. These outlawed traditions were not only considered antisocial and unchristian, they were positively, triumphantly pagan. They suggested unspeakable alien rites, they made possible illicit and rancorous allegiances which smacked of future discord. They hinted at that darkest of rebellions: a celebration of Negritude. They restored "deported Africa," that "drifting continent," to a privileged place within the black mythology. And the very existence of the mythology was enough to inspire an immense dread in the hearts of some white slave owners. (1979:31–32)

21. *Cumbe, quilombo,* and *palenque* were the terms used for cimarrón communities in Venezuela, Brazil, and Colombia respectively. The term *cimarrón* (from *cima*, or "mountaintop") was originally used for domesticated cattle that had returned to the wild. But as

Richard Price observes, "by the early 1500s, it had come to be used in plantation colonies throughout the Americas to designate slaves who successfully escaped from captivity" (1983:1).

22. Elsewhere I discuss a recent open-air performance about the life of one of Barlovento's greatest cimarrón heroes, Guillermo Rivas (Guss 1992).

23. A process similar to that in which San Juan has been absorbed into the cimarrón experience is to be found in Brazil, where black practitioners of Umbanda have placed the leaders of former *quilombos* at the head of a hierarchy of spirits. As John Burdick writes:

> The most well-known version of Umbanda situates the slave at the bottom, beneath the Indian and while in the hierarchy of spirits. But this version is adhered to mainly by whites and mulattos. Blacks in Umbanda worship a spirit unrecognized by either whites or mulattos: Zumbi, one of the chiefs of Palmares, the great maroon society that survived for almost a century in the backlands of Alagoas, until finally destroyed by the Portuguese in 1697. (1992a:27)

24. Saints may be owned by individuals, the church, or communal orders. While there is always the possibility that a saint will be manipulated for particular political ends, ownership by a communal order or *cofradía* reduces the likelihood of such behavior.

25. Although the events of 1979 and earlier reflect a great deal of dissatisfaction with the tourists, actual sentiment was quite ambivalent. People enjoyed the attention and national celebrity as well as the increase in movement and activity. The reinstitution of the San Juan Congo velorio, therefore, permitted Curieperos to experience the best of both worlds—a public, tourist celebration and a private, village one. For some interesting comparisons with tourism's effects on other local festivals, see *Power and Persuasion: Fiestas and Social Control in Rural Mexico*, in which Stanley Brandes traces the transformation of the "Night of the Dead" celebration on the 1st and 2nd of November from a small family celebration to a large tourist one. Despite busloads of tourists and a series of pageants, plays, and fairs all orchestrated by the government, Brandes claims, the Tzintzuntzan remain delighted:

> For the most part, villagers appreciate the changes that have come to the Night of the Dead. They like the liveliness, the outside attention, the influx of money, the government support and exposure. Not once, and despite some discreet probes on my part, did I ever encounter a complaint about noise, impoliteness, or sacrilege as a result of tourism. . . . Most discussions about the fiesta concern changes needed to accommodate even more tourists. (1988:108)

26. The extraordinary price of this image is underscored by the fact that the most expensive slave at the time was estimated to cost 400 pesos (Sojo 1986:171). It should also be remembered that much of the power attributed to the new saint derived from his phallus, thus connecting him not only to the Bantu Nkisi tradition but also to one of San Juan's most essential functions, that of fertility.

27. The details of Curiepe's founding came to light only at the beginning of the 1980s, when the historian Castillo Lara gained access to a collection of unarchived colonial documents in the Casa Simón Bolívar in Caracas. They proved that a mixed company of free black soldiers and *luangos* (escaped slaves from the Antilles), led by Captain Juan del

Rosario Blanco, founded Curiepe on what Castillo Lara claims was the day of San Juan, 1721 (1981a:57; also see Monasterio Vasquez 1989:17).

28. Walker notes that certain religious societies in the Bahian community of Cachoeira, Brazil, served the express purpose of providing funds for the purchase of "free papers." While she explains how the groups that were organized to celebrate the Festa da Boa Morte, or Feast of Good Death, secretly conspired to liberate those still enslaved, she emphasizes that this was by no means unique:

> The Brotherhoods and Sisterhoods were organizational structures within which Africans and later Afro-Brazilians could organize under the aegis of the Catholic church to oppose the system of slavery, and in which free Blacks could collaborate with their still enslaved brothers and sisters to increase the ranks of the free. (1986:30)

29. The myth of mestizaje or the myth of racial democracy is not unique to Venezuela but is found throughout the Caribbean and South America. As Whitten and Torres emphasize, "*mestizaje*, the ideology of racial intermingling, is an explicit master symbol of the nation in all Latin American countries" (1992:18). It is also, they point out, "a powerful force of exclusion of both black and indigenous communities in the Americas today. As a consequence, black and indigenous awareness of exclusion and continuous struggle for ethnic power will remain constant" (1992:21). For further discussions of what Arthur Corwin refers to as "the great national illusion" (1974:389) and its effects on all Latin America, see Toplin (1974) and Burdick (1992b). Like Whitten and Torres, Burdick makes the point that "whitening," as opposed to *négritude*, or the celebration of blackness, "meant eliminating the racial heritage of Africa by overwhelming it with miscegenation, the importation of Europeans, and restrictions on the immigration of blacks." He goes on to say that "if 'racial democracy' has any meaning at all, it refers to the fact that Latin American societies make some provision for better treatment of people of visibly mixed ancestry" (1992b:41).

30. Perhaps no institution more clearly demonstrates the way in which this purportedly colorblind ideology has confounded the issues of race and class than the "*gracias al sacar*." Translatable as "thanks for the exclusion," the phrase refers to papers permitting mestizos and blacks who could pay for them the right to be classified as white (Wright 1990:24). While Wright notes that the ruling class in colonial Venezuela expressed opposition to this institution, "certificates of whiteness" were nevertheless common to many parts of the Americas (Burdick 1992b:42).

31. There are numerous other examples supporting this position that race is simply not an issue in Venezuelan society. For many people, such as Guillermo Morón, president of the prestigious Academia Nacional de la Historia, the transcendence of race is a symbol of pride, attesting to Venezuela's enlightened, if not superior, state:

> It is true that there exists no negro problem in any Spanish-speaking country today, because the negro has been assimilated into society without any trouble. In Venezuela this phenomenon of complete assimilation, social, political, and economic, is of the greatest importance. Venezuela has a tradition of liberty and equality for all which in some other nations has still to be evolved. The negro of colonial days,

a slave, and therefore inferior, has given way to the educated man, the "creole" negro, who is one of the unifying links of the Venezuelan people. (1964:54)

And many others, such as the celebrated author and philosopher Arturo Uslar Pietri, feel that to speak of race is to be "un-Venezuelan":

Whoever speaks of blacks or whites, whoever invokes racial hatred or privileges, is denying Venezuela. In Venezuela, in political and social matters, there are neither whites nor blacks, neither *mestizos* nor Indians. There are only Venezuelans. (Cited in Wright 1990:122)

Until recently, among the few who had tried to expose the inconsistencies in these racial views were Juan Pablo Sojo and Miguel Acosta Saignes. While Sojo's influence as a folklorist and writer was felt primarily in the communities of Barlovento where he lived, Acosta Saignes is often credited with being the founder of Venezuelan anthropology. In work after work (1961, 1962, 1967), he documented the history and legacy of Venezuela's African-descended peoples, inspiring a whole new generation of what Gramsci might have called "organic intellectuals" (1971). Like the Sanjuaneros of Curiepe, these young Afro-Venezuelan scholars and activists are also challenging the ideology of invisibility that has dominated all discussions of race up to the present. As Jesús García, one of the most prominent figures among them, recently wrote:

Up till now, the study of the African presence in Venezuela has hardly existed for investigators. In fact, one sometimes has the impression that they would like to erase the past and opt for the cliché that we are all mestizos, without recognizing, in a profound way, that to arrive at this *"mestizaje,"* or rather what could be called our "Venezuelan-ness," we had to pass through a long struggle between dominant and dominated groups, between Europeans, Amerindians, and Africans, a process in which the African presence was a catalyzing factor in these conflicts waged for five centuries. (1990:72)

## References

Acciaioli, Greg
    1985        Culture as Art: From Practice to Spectacle in Indonesia. Canberra
                Anthropology 8(1):148–172.
Acosta Saignes, Miguel
    1959        La Población del Estado Miranda. *In* El Estado Miranda: Sus
                Tierras y Sus Hombres. Pp. 91–109. Caracas: Ediciones del Banco
                Miranda.
    1961        La Trata de Esclavos en Venezuela. Caracas: Centro de Estudios
                Históricos.
    1962        Estudios de Folklore Venezolano. Caracas: Universidad Central de
                Venezuela.

1967          Vida de los Esclavos Negros en Venezuela. Caracas: Hesperides Edi-
              ciones.

Adam, Henriette
1981          Barlovento: Cacao y Tambores, la Historia de Panaquire. Caracas:
              Biblioteca de Trabajo Venezolana.

Appadurai, Arjun
1981          The Past as a Scarce Resource. Man (n.s.) 16:201–219.

Aretz, Isabel
1953          Expresiones Negras en el Folklore Musical. Boletín del Instituto de
              Folklore (Caracas) 1(3).
1955          La Fiesta de San Juan en Cúpira. Boletín del Instituto de Folklore
              2(2):57–61.

Azpúrua, Carlos, director and producer
1979          Yo Hablo a Caracas [film]. Caracas: Caralcine (distributed in the
              United States by Cinema Guild).

Bastide, Roger
1971          African Civilizations in the New World. P. Green, trans. New York:
              Harper & Row.
1978          The African Religions of Brazil: Toward a Sociology of the Interpene-
              tration of Civilizations. H. Sebba, trans. Baltimore, MD: Johns Hop-
              kins University Press.

Brandes, Stanley
1988          Power and Persuasion: Fiestas and Social Control in Rural Mexico.
              Philadelphia, PA: University of Pennsylvania Press.

Brandt, Max Hans
1978          An Ethnomusicological Study of Three Afro-Venezuelan Drum En-
              sembles of Barlovento. Ph.D. dissertation, Queen's University of Bel-
              fast, Northern Ireland.

Brow, James
1990          Notes on Community, Hegemony, and the Uses of the Past. Anthro-
              pological Quarterly 63(1):1–6.

Burdick, John
1992a         Brazil's Black Consciousness Movement. NACLA: Report on the
              Americas 25(4):23–27.
1992b         The Myth of Racial Democracy. NACLA: Report on the Americas
              25(4):40–43.

Burke, Peter
1978          Popular Culture in Early Modern Europe. New York: Harper and Row.

Caillois, Roger
1959          Man and the Sacred. Glencoe, IL: Free Press.

Castillo Lara, Lucas Guillermo
1981a         Curiepe: Orígenes Históricos. Caracas: Biblioteca de Autores y
              Temas Mirandinos.

1981b        Apuntes para la Historia Colonial de Barlovento. Caracas: Biblioteca
             de la Academia Nacional de la Historia.
1983         La Aventura Fundacional de los Isleños. Caracas: Biblioteca de la
             Academia Nacional de la Historia.

Centro Cultural y Deportivo de Curiepe
1979         Programa de la Semana Cultural de Curiepe. Curiepe, Venezuela:
             Centro Cultural y Deportivo de Curiepe.

Chacón, Alfredo
1979         Curiepe: Ensayo sobre la Realización del Sentido en la Actividad
             Mágicoreligiosa de un Pueblo Venezolano. Caracas: Universidad
             Central de Venezuela.

Chapman, Malcolm, Maryon McDonald, and Elizabeth Tonkin
1989         Introduction. In History and Ethnicity. Association of Social Anthro-
             pologists Monographs, 27. E. Tonkin, M. McDonald, and M. Chap-
             man, eds. Pp. 1–21. London: Routledge.

Cohen, Abner
1980         Drama and Politics in the Development of a London Carnival. Man
             (n.s.) 15:65–87.

Coluccio, Felix
1978         Fiestas y Celebraciones de la República Argentina. Buenos Aires:
             Editorial Plus Ultra.

Corwin, Arthur F.
1974         Afro-Brazilians: Myths and Realities. In Slavery and Race Relations
             in Latin America. R. B. Toplin, ed. Pp. 385–437. Westport, CT:
             Greenwood Press.

Crain, Mary
1989         Ritual, Memoria Popular y Proceso Político en la Sierra Ecuatori-
             ana. Quito: Abya-Yala.
1990         The Social Construction of National Identity in Highland Ecuador.
             Anthropological Quarterly 63(1):43–59.
1992         From Local Cult of the Virgin to Media Rite: The Cultural Politics
             of Transformation and Visual Re-presentation in an Andalusian
             Romería. MS, files of the author.

Crespi, Muriel
1981         St. John the Baptist: The Ritual Looking Glass of Hacienda Ethnic
             and Power Relations. In Cultural Transformations and Ethnicity in
             Modern Ecuador. N. E. Whitten, Jr., ed. Pp. 477–505. Urbana, IL:
             University of Illinois Press.

Duvignaud, Jean
1976         Festivals: A Sociological Approach. Cultures 3(1):13–25.

Eliade, Mircea
1959         Cosmos and History: The Myth of the Eternal Return. New York:
             Harper & Brothers.

Estado Miranda, Venezuela
1981        XI Censo General de Población y Vivienda. Caracas: Oficina Central de Estadística e Informática.

Ewell, Judith
1984        Venezuela: A Century of Change. Stanford, CA: Stanford University Press.

Frazer, James G.
1953 [1922]   The Golden Bough: A Study in Magic and Religion. Abridged edition. New York: Macmillan.

Fuentes, Cecilia, and Daría Hernández
1988        San Juan Bautista. Revista Bigott 12:2–39.

García, Jesús
1985        Saint John the Baptist and Saint John Congo: Reinterpretation and Creation of African-Inspired Religion in Venezuela. In Culturas Africanas. UNESCO, ed. Paris: UNESCO.
1989        Contra el Cepo: Barlovento Tiempo de Cimarrones. Caracas: Editorial Lucas y Trina.
1990        Africa en Venezuela, Pieza de Indias. Caracas: Cuadernos Lagoven.

Goffman, Erving
1974        Frame Analysis: An Essay on the Organization of Experience. New York: Harper & Row.

González, Enrique Alí
1989        Ritmos, Plegarias y Promesas: La Música en las Festividades Populares. Paper presented at a conference sponsored by the Fundación Venezolana para la Investigación Antropológica, Caracas, June.

Gramsci, Antonio
1971        Selections from the Prison Notebooks. Q. Hoare and G. N. Smith, eds. and trans. London: Lawrence and Wishart.

Guerra Cedeño, Franklin
1984        Esclavos Negros, Cimarroneras y Cumbes de Barlovento. Caracas: Cuadernos Lagoven.

Guss, David M.
1989        To Weave and Sing: Art, Symbol, and Narrative in the South American Rain Forest. Berkeley, CA: University of California Press.
1992        Cimarrones, Theater, and the State. MS, files of the author.

Hall, Stuart
1981        Notes on Deconstructing "the Popular." In People's History and Socialist Theory. R. Samuel, ed. Pp. 227–240. Amsterdam: Van Gennep.

Handler, Richard
1988        Nationalism and the Politics of Culture in Quebec. Madison, WI: University of Wisconsin Press.

Handler, Richard, and Jocelyn Linnekin
1984          Tradition, Genuine or Spurious. Journal of American Folklore
              97:273–290.

Hebdige, Dick
1979          Subculture: The Meaning of Style. London: Methuen.

Hill, Errol
1972          The Trinidad Carnival: Mandate for a National Theater. Austin, TX:
              University of Texas Press.

Hobsbawm, Eric, and Terence Ranger, eds.
1983          The Invention of Tradition. Cambridge: Cambridge University Press.

James, Edwin O.
1963          Seasonal Feasts and Festivals. New York: Barnes and Noble.

Karp, Ivan, and Steven D. Lavine, eds.
1991          Exhibiting Cultures: The Poetics and Politics of Museum Display.
              Washington, DC: Smithsonian Institution Press.

Kelly, John
1990          Japanese No-Noh: The Crosstalk of Public Culture in a Rural Festiv-
              ity. Public Culture 2(2):65–81.

Kirshenblatt-Gimblett, Barbara
1991          Objects of Ethnography. In Exhibiting Cultures: The Poetics and
              Politics of Museum Display. I. Karp and S. Lavine, eds. Pp. 386–
              443. Washington, DC: Smithsonian Institution Press.

Lincoln, Bruce
1989          Discourse and the Construction of Society: Comparative Studies of
              Myth, Ritual, and Classification. New York: Oxford University Press.

Lipner, Ronnie, and Stu Lipner
1958          Dances of Venezuela. New York: Folkways Records.

Liscano, Juan
1947          Las Fiestas del Solsticio de Verano en el Folklore de Venezuela.
              Separada de la Revista Nacional de Cultura, 63. Caracas: Ministerio
              de Educación Nacional.
1950          Folklore y Cultura. Caracas: Nuestra Tierra.
1970          Lugar de Origen de los Tambores Redondos Barloventeños de Vene-
              zuela. Folklore Americano (Lima) 17/18(16):134–139.
1973          La Fiesta de San Juan el Bautista. Caracas: Monte Avila Editores.

Liscano, Juan, and Charles Seeger
1947          Folk Music of Venezuela. Washington, DC: Division of Music, Li-
              brary of Congress.

Luzardo, Alexander
1988          Amazonas: El Negocio de Este Mundo, Investigación Indigenista.
              Caracas: Ediciones Centauro.

Machado, Arlette
1987        El Apocalipsis según Juan Liscano. Caracas: Publicaciones Seleven.

Manning, Frank E.
1977        Cup Match and Carnival: Secular Rites of Revitalization in Decolo-
            nizing, Tourist-Oriented Societies. In Secular Ritual. S. F. Moore
            and B. Myerhoff, eds. Pp. 265–281. Amsterdam: Van Gorcum.

Monasterio Vásquez, Demetria Casimira
1989        Curiepe: Teatro y Danza en Barlovento. M.A. thesis, Universidad de
            Havana, Cuba.

Morón, Guillermo
1964        A History of Venezuela. London: George Allen and Unwin.

Morote Best, Efraín
1955        La Fiesta de San Juan, el Bautista. Archivos Peruanos de Folklore
            1(1):160–200.

Mosonyi, Estaban Emilio, ed.
1981        El Caso Nuevas Tribus. Caracas: Editorial Ateneo de Caracas.

Pollak-Eltz, Angelina
1979        Migration from Barlovento to Caracas. In The Venezuelan Peasant
            in Country and City. L. Margolies, ed. Pp. 29–54. Caracas: Edicio-
            nes Venezolanas de Antropología.

Ponce, José Tomás
1987        El Espacio Geo-histórico de Barlovento. Anatema 1(1):62–80.

Price, Richard
1983        First-Time: The Historical Vision of an Afro-American People. Balti-
            more, MD: Johns Hopkins University Press.

Price, Richard, and Sally Price
1980        Afro-American Arts of the Surinam Rain Forest. Los Angeles, CA:
            Museum of Cultural History, University of California, Los Angeles.

Ramón y Rivera, Luis Felipe
1951        Tambores de San Juan. Revista del Estado Miranda 1(3):14–17.
1963a       Cantos Negros en la Fiesta de San Juan. Boletín del Instituto de
            Folklore (Caracas) 4(3):109–153.
1963b       Música Folklórica y Popular en Venezuela. Caracas: Ministerio de
            Educación.
1971        La Música Afrovenezolana. Caracas: Universidad Central de Vene-
            zuela.

Sojo, Juan Pablo
1943        Temas y Apuntes Afro-venezolanos. Caracas: Tipografía La Nacíon.
1959        José Larito: Negro que no Quiso Ser Esclavo. In El Estado Miranda:
            Sus Tierras y Sus Hombres. Pp. 305–314. Caracas: Ediciones del
            Banco Miranda.
1976 [1943] Nochebuena Negra. Los Teques, Venezuela: Biblioteca Popular
            Mirandina.

1986              Estudios del Folklore Venezolano. Caracas: Biblioteca de Autores y
                  Temas Mirandinos.

Stewart, John
1986              Patronage and Control in the Trinidad Carnival. *In* The Anthropol-
                  ogy of Experience. V. Turner and E. Bruner, eds. Pp. 289–315. Ur-
                  bana, IL: University of Illinois Press.

Taussig, Michael
1980              The Devil and Commodity Fetishism in South America. Chapel
                  Hill, NC: University of North Carolina Press.

Toplin, Robert Brent, ed.
1974              Slavery and Race Relations in Latin America. Westport, CT: Green-
                  wood Press.

Turner, Victor
1975              Symbolic Studies. Annual Review of Anthropology 4:145–161.

Uslar Pietri, Arturo
1975              Baile de Tambor. El Vigía, Venezuela: Ateneo "Dr. Alberto Adriani."

Walker, Sheila S.
1986              The Feast of Good Death: An Afro-Catholic Emancipation Celebra-
                  tion in Brazil. Sage 3(2):27–31.

Watanabe, John M.
1990              From Saints to Shibboleths: Image, Structure, and Identity in Maya
                  Religious Syncretism. American Ethnologist 17:131–150.

Whitten, Norman E., Jr., ed.
1981              Cultural Transformations and Ethnicity in Modern Ecuador. Ur-
                  bana, IL: University of Illinois Press.

Whitten, Norman E., Jr., and Arlene Torres
1992              Blackness in the Americas. NACLA: Report on the Americas
                  25(4):16–22.

Williams, Raymond
1977              Marxism and Literature. Oxford: Oxford University Press.

Wood, Peter H.
1974              Black Majority: Negroes in Colonial South Carolina from 1670
                  through the Stono Rebellion. New York: Knopf.

Wright, Winthrop R.
1990              Café con Leche: Race, Class, and National Image in Venezuela.
                  Austin, TX: University of Texas Press.

# 11. POLICING BOUNDARIES

## *Race, Class, and Gender in Cartagena, Colombia*

### *Joel Streicker*

In this article I examine the connections among class, race, and gender in the everyday discourse of *santaneros*,[1] popular class residents of the neighborhood of Santa Ana in Cartagena, a city on Colombia's Caribbean coast. Most santaneros, like most other *cartageneros*, perceive little racial prejudice or discrimination in Cartagena; this view is common in many parts of Afro-Spanish America (Benítez Rojo 1984; Casal 1979; Rout 1976; Wright 1990).[2] Instead, the dominant view in Cartagena holds that class is the most salient social division, and thus santaneros' everyday discourse on inequality and social identity focuses on class. Here, however, I argue that it is precisely in the process of forging their class identity that santaneros discriminate racially.

I show that santaneros' discourse about class encodes racial concepts that are seldom explicitly articulated or discussed in everyday life. As an unacknowledged but pervasive language of race, class discourse promotes racism while enabling santaneros to believe that little or no racial prejudice or discrimination exists in Cartagena. These people, who do not think of themselves as racially prejudiced or discriminatory, and most of whom North Americans would consider black, by and large identify blackness with acts that contradict normative popular class identity. Ironically, a class identity that the poor see as providing strength and dignity in opposition to ruling class values also enforces racial hierarchy. At the same time, disparaging blackness in this way has the effect of discrediting what might be considered an incipient expression of pride in blackness and African-identified culture.

I also contend that santaneros use racial concepts as a language for talking about class and gender. Although the work of scholars such as Verena Martinez-Alier (1989[1974]) has been important in examining race and class in Afro-Spanish America, these writers treat race primarily as a symbol of class relations. In contrast, my analysis suggests that race is not reducible to other categories, even though it also symbolizes class standing and gender attributes. In particular, I hold that blackness acts as a source of naturalized meanings for describing and

Originally published in *American Ethnologist* 22:1 (February 1995), pp. 54–74. Reproduced by permission of the American Anthropological Association. Not for further reproduction.

stigmatizing people who are said to transgress class and gender norms. As other analysts have observed (Bourdieu 1977; Connell 1987; Stolcke 1981), naturalizing inequalities is a powerful means of representing them as legitimate or even inevitable. At the same time, however, santaneros also see blackness, and race in general, as socially constructed.

My analysis seeks to advance our understanding of racial dynamics in Afro-Spanish America by examining the intersection of race with other social identities such as class. It thus builds on the strengths of previous works dealing with race and class in the region (Schubert 1981; Wade 1985; Whitten 1986[1974]) while arguing more forcefully for the importance of gender in constructing race and class identities. In particular, I show that notions of gender are central to the meaning of class and race: for santaneros, an important means of establishing an individual's class and race identity is to measure that person's actions against standards of gender conduct. In so doing, I demonstrate the fruitfulness of the feminist insight that any given social identity is formed within a web of diverse social relationships rather than principally in the domain that folk and social scientific theories assign to its production (for example, gender as produced in the family, class in economic relations) (Ginsburg and Tsing 1990; M. Rosaldo 1980; Sacks 1989; Yanagisako and Collier 1987). Moreover, just as we must understand that santaneros construct their notions of class and race in oppostion to alternative notions, so must we also recognize the relational character of efforts to legitimate gender conceptions: santaneros form and assert images of normative masculinity in relation to competing notions of masculinity as well as in opposition to femininity, while the converse holds for femininity. This perspective permits a more nuanced account of gender than is possible in works that either present masculinity as stable and homogeneous or ignore it altogether.

Furthermore, I argue that the dominant representation of class, gender, and race among santaneros tends to support the authority of men, and especially of older men, within the popular class. Given the specific ways in which race connects with gender and class identities in Santa Ana, racial discrimination aids men (particularly older men) in representing as general what are in fact sectional interests. While hardly new, this strategy of domination has recently been the focus of a number of sociocultural analyses (Asad 1990; Dominguez 1989; Fraser and Nicholson 1990; Moraga and Anzaldua 1981; Mosse 1985; Pratt 1984; R. Rosaldo 1989; Joan Scott 1988; Wittig 1980).

A word on the vocabulary of class—both mine and that of santaneros—is appropriate here. "Popular class" is a term borrowed from the Latin American political vocabulary (*clase popular*, sometimes in the plural form: *clases populares*) and broadly includes peasants, proletarians, and the urban poor, the latter two categories partially, though not always wholly, synonymous. The popular class occupies society's most subordinate social, economic, and political positions (Cotler 1989; Galin et al. 1986; Lancaster 1988a:28–32). As we shall see, in santaneros' usage, "class" (*clase*) incorporates both social and economic stratification, combining notions of wealth, status, social honor, and other criteria of rank. I will use the term "class" in the same way.

I will also collectively call the santaneros the "popular class" in order to suggest the subordinate social, economic, and political standing that they attribute to themselves. Where "popular class" usually suggests "the lowest class," however, santaneros often distinguish themselves from "the lower class" (*la clase baja*) below them. Thus, santaneros call themselves the "middle class" (*la clase media*), "the poor" (*los pobres*), "the people" (*el pueblo*) or, less frequently, la clase baja, all but the last being conceptually opposed to both la clase baja and "the rich" (*los ricos*) or "the upper class" (*la clase alta*). As being black is considered tantamount to being de clase baja (lower class), employing this notion of blackness creates pressure for santaneros to conform to class norms. As we shall see, the dominant notion of class identity among santaneros invokes gender norms, the violation of which tends to define the violator as black. Thus, the interrelation of class and gender norms helps construct blackness as the inferior category par excellence.

### Class and Gender Identity in Santa Ana

"Respectable" santaneros (*los respetables, los que respetan, los de respeto*) support the class, gender, and race identities dominant in Santa Ana. In these people's view, the pursuit of self-interest at the expense of respect and solidarity is a major reason for what they see as the collapse of a formerly orderly social world. Self-interested action is evidence of "corruption" (*descorrompimiento, corrupción*), causing "disorder" (*desorden*) because it disrupts the exchange of obligations between subordinates and superordinates upon which order—class, gender, and age hierarchies—was based.

Questions of class identity are particularly acute for santaneros right now. Cartagena, a city of about one million people on Colombia's Caribbean coast, has undergone wrenching economic change in the past 20 years. Once a sleepy port, Cartagena now boasts a major petrochemical complex (Nichols 1973) and depends heavily on international tourism (Lemaitre 1983; Strassman 1982). The traditional commercial and cattle-ranching bourgeoisie has expanded into industry, running its varied enterprises along much more clearly capitalist lines than previously. Money from the marijuana and cocaine trades has also been funneled into the construction of expensive hotels and tourist enterprises; luxury apartments have sprung up to cater to a mixture of old elites and the new class whose wealth derives from the drug trade. At the same time, poor neighborhoods proliferate beyond the capacity of the city's already over-taxed public services network. Male unemployment and subemployment have risen, women have increasingly sought work outside the home, and most people contend that real wages have declined.[3]

Most santaneros (especially older ones) talk of these changes as having under-mined their formerly cordial and beneficial relationships with the rich. As em-ployers of artisans and domestic servants, the wealthy purportedly paid good wages and, just as important, could be counted on to help economically in a crisis or to intervene with authorities on behalf of workers. Over and above strictly economic concerns, *patrones* (bosses) felt bound to employees by sentimental ties. In turn, workers (so the story goes) served the same *patrón* for years, linked by a sense of loyalty and affection. In short, most people claim that in the old days the wealthy placed meeting their economic and social obligations to the poor above narrow self-interest. These people consider fulfilling obligations a sign of being motivated by sentiment, solidarity, and respect.

In contrast, they say, today the rich have forsaken these paternalistic relations and instead seek only personal advantage. Santaneros use this image of the past to construct a class identity that contrasts the desire of the poor to help others, and to fulfill obligations to others, with the pursuit of individual gain by the rich. The poor see themselves as feeling (*condoliente*[4]), solidary (*solidario*), and respecting (*respetan*), and the rich as self-interested (*interesado*) and unfeeling (*indoliente*). As Rosa, a middle-aged housewife who used to work as a domestic servant, put it,

> The rich don't sympathize with the poor any more. A poor person sympathizes [*conduele*] with another poor person. You yourself are the one who patches things together with another poor person because . . . now the rich don't want you to work, now the rich don't want you to study, so that everyone will be in slavery—we've got slavery. So how does a poor person get by? With help from another poor person.

Or, she added, by stealing. Note that the selfishness of the rich causes division, not only between rich and poor, but among the poor themselves; santaneros are understandably more concerned about crime among the poor than about crime against the rich. Santaneros claim that the pursuit of self-interest by the rich ex-tends to all domains of social life, including work, religious sentiment and prac-tice, politics, celebration of the city's Independence and patron saint's day fiestas, marital decisions, and conjugal and filial relations.

The theme of self-interest is also central to santaneros' concepts of gender. Acts that contravene dominant definitions of manhood and womanhood violate popular class identity. According to "respectable" santaneros (that is, those who support this identity), self-interest also motivates young popular class men and women to challenge established gender ideals. The respectable sharply criticize young men who do not fulfill their obligations to support spouses and children and to help parents. Young men's selfishness generates discord, reversing the flow of traditional economic obligations: parents support their grown sons and women support their husbands. As Antonio, an older man, said,

We [men] worked when we were little, selling kerosene, candy, and other things in the street. And what we earned was to buy rice, coconut, butter, for our parents. Now, if a young man works, he doesn't give anything to his parents, he spends the money on drugs or he eats it up. Before, one gave to one's parents, now one expects one's parents to give to one. . . . We've always first met our obligations to our women and children, whereas these young men would rather drink or take drugs than support their families.

Popular class masculine self-image exalts men's enjoyment of sensuous experience—drinking, dancing, sexual conquests—but only after a man has met his obligations to his family and to others (friends or creditors, for example) may he legitimately pursue enjoyment. Neither younger men nor wealthy men participate in this ideal, say respectable santaneros: younger men renege on commitments to their families, while the wealthy refuse to recognize any obligations to the poor and at the same time are insufficiently manly to resist their wives' attempts to curtail their enjoyment.

Young women who flout feminine ideals—particularly ideals of remaining virgins until, and monogamous within, marriage or common-law union, and avoiding male arenas and male activities—are said to act out of self-interest and to cause division. These women enter into sporadic or stable sexual relationships with men, purportedly in order to satisfy their sexual desires or in exchange for economic support, rather than out of "love" (amor). "Love" in this context means that a woman's courtship and marriage decisions are overseen by parents and are based on the latter's assessment of the man's character as well as of that of his family. According to the respectable, young women who pursue sex or money create conflict between themselves and their parents and lose reputation in the community's eyes.

The respectable at times blame young people's disrespect and lack of solidarity on the self-interest of the rich. As Antonio put it, "The crisis today is the fault of the rich, because for them money is the only thing that matters. . . . The rich are guilty—they oblige people to become thieves. Corruption comes from the top and works its way down [La corrupción viene de arriba para abajo]." At other times, however, some respectable people (like Antonio) lay the blame for young popular class people's transgression of proper behavior squarely on the young people themselves, without invoking mitigating factors. "The world today is corrupt [descorrompido] because young people don't respect," one older woman said. "The children hit the mother, the father—one doesn't know who's the mother, who's the father, who's the child."[5]

What the respectable lament, in part, is that challenges to this order are supposedly more acute than in the past, and that they are increasingly difficult to contain. We should also keep in mind that the challenges threaten to keep older men from enjoying the authority that they thought would be rightfully theirs with age, as the reference to children hitting parents indicates. This is one reason why older men's talk so notably revolves around the theme of self-interest and respectability. Older people in general most actively promote the notion that respectability characterized both class and gender behavior in the old days. Because older people grew up during that mythical time, they can convincingly represent themselves as respectable while claiming that relatively few young people today have achieved this status. I would also stress, however, that most younger respectable people share their elders' view of the past.

At the same time, the notions of respect and solidarity so central to popular class identity are most easily realized by men, especially by older men. The acts that are publicly recognized as solidary are those that are considered the men's province and, fittingly, take place in the street, the preeminent male space. Such acts include labor exchange in house building and repair, sharing of information on employment and entrepeneurial opportunities, loans, reciprocity in drinking, contributing ingredients and labor to the cooking of improvised soups as part of drinking bouts, and the rivalry and camaraderie of sports and board games.

In contrast, respectable women concern themselves primarily with domestic duties, avoiding male spaces and activities. Respectable santaneros charge that a woman who willingly strays beyond the physical and social constraints of the household destroys the delicate ties of obligation between herself and her husband, parents, and children. "Women in (or of) the street," as in the common phrase, are variously accused of neglecting their duties, gossiping, performing witchcraft, and stealing other women's husbands, all of which challenge social order by defying male authority and violating norms for women's conduct. For example, one young woman noted with disapproval that women use witchcraft "to dominate [dominar] the man, to make it so the woman can be with a lot of men, go to dances, and leave the man at home like an old rag." (Indeed, the respectable may consider that a woman "in the street" passes into the category of a "woman of the street," meaning a "whore," if they suspect her of illicit sexual relations.) In respecting, women isolate themselves from the spaces and activities in which the respectable recognize solidarity as being primarily constructed, thereby reinforcing their circumscription to the domestic realm in a dependent relation to men (husbands, fathers, grown sons).

Women's gathering in the street are rare and socially disapproved. Of course, women do get together informally, for example, while making purchases at the neighborhood stores. This is an important means for women to talk among themselves without giving the appearance of meeting for meeting's sake, as women go to the store in the line of domestic duty. Yet these encounters are not recognized as acts constructing solidarity, since women feel the need to mask the sociality of the occasion with the justification of domestic necessity. Failure to do so would open them to charges of gossiping. The dominant definition of the situation excludes even these acts of women's sharing (if only conversation) from the conceptual domain of solidarity. Indeed, women's actions that verge on gossip are seen to threaten solidarity. The same concerns motivate respectable women to avoid spending much time in other women's homes. Women commonly say that they only go to someone else's house when there is a *novedad,* something noteworthy, like an illness or a death, implying that women normally do not visit one another's homes.

Restrictions on women's movements and injunctions against their gathering reduce the opportunities for women to share food or drink. While women are never supposed to share alcohol like men, the Holy Week tradition of preparing desserts for neighbors does provide a chance for women to share food. Ironically, this publicly sanctioned act of women's food-sharing is fraught with danger: many santaneros (including women) claim that they accept but do not eat female neighbors' desserts for fear that the desserts bear witchcraft material.

Younger men are also disadvantaged in this system as it is held that they are, in general, self-interested and disrespectful, not solidary. The respectable partly attribute this alleged stance to the susceptibility of younger men to the ideology of self-interest advanced by the wealthy. At the same time, the respectable also recognize that younger men have less opportunity to realize solidarity because their economic situation is by and large more precarious than older men's as a result of recent economic crises; this makes it more difficult for them to participate as equals in solidary relations. In sum, popular class emphasis on what santaneros recognize as solidarity, sentiment, and respect privileges men's interests over women's, and older men's over younger men's, as in each case the dominant group is in a better position to embody or realize these characteristics. Enforcing class norms therefore also effectively shores up men's (and, in particular, older men's) authority.

As we will see, one who breaks with dominant notions of gender not only violates class identity but is considered to be—or to be like—a "black" (*"un negro"*), a "lower-class person" (*"una persona de clase baja"*), or a *"champetudo"* (see ensuing discussion). Respectable people's use of these three labels is one means of countering what they feel is an assault on a supposedly harmonious social order: to avoid being considered a bad man or woman, or a lower-class person, one must act like a non-*negro.* Likewise, to avoid being called *"negro,"* which most santaneros consider a stigma, one must adhere to gender norms, which are simultaneously class norms.

Before dealing in detail with race and its connection with class and gender, it is important to discuss briefly the fieldwork situation. Although I eventually met and interacted with a wide range of santaneros, my best friends and informants tended to be older men who considered themselves respectable. Most men and women, of all ages, regard the prevailing sexual division of labor and space as desirable, and their sense of propriety, their "respectability" as men and women, rests on upholding this division. This social and spatial segregation is intended to make it difficult for men outside the household to gain access to the household's women, and in general I found it effectively enforced. Though in some cases I feel that I managed to break down or elude this barrier quite well, especially where I was close to the male household head or where an older woman headed the household, in many others my presence was always somewhat awkward for all concerned.[6] Thus my field experience was skewed toward men: I was more easily included in male activities, I talked informally with men more than with women, and 44 of the 78 formal interviews I conducted were with men (17 individuals) as opposed to 30 interviews with 20 women.

Respectable people draw a sharp distinction between themselves and the disreputable, stigmatizing the latter in discourse that seems intended to keep the weaker within their own ranks from defecting. As it became increasingly clear to me during fieldwork that the issue of "respect" (*respeto*) was so crucial to understanding respectable santaneros' views of recent changes and current conflicts both within their class and vis-à-vis the dominant class, I decided that to seek disreputable friends and informants would jeopardize my standing with the respectable people with whom I had initially aligned myself. For example, had I begun talking with *viciosos* (drug users), the respectable would have been reluctant to accept me since they have staked their reputation on excluding and opposing viciosos and other disreputable people. Most cartageneros are aware of drug use among young North Americans, often blaming Colombia's drug problems on North American consumers' demands. Some santaneros, claiming to have witnessed drug use by North American tourists in Cartagena, tell lurid tales that reinforce the image of *gringos* as viciosos. For santaneros, at least initially and probably enduringly, my fair skin, education, and relative wealth made me much closer to the city's elite than to mainly darker-skinned and less educated popular class men. Given the popular view of both gringos and the young rich as viciosos, I was doubly prone to be seen as a potential if not actual vicioso. In light of this, I steered clear of viciosos. Similarly, I avoided associating with champetudos (most of who are also considered viciosos). Thus I met few people who considered themselves beyond the pale of respectability, though I was friendly with a number whom others regarded as borderline cases.

I consider the problem of access to women and the disreputable to have been less a limitation on "data collection" than an inevitable part of the positioning within fieldwork and, consequently, writing that confronts all social analysts (Abu-Lughod 1986; Clifford and Marcus 1986; Kondo 1990; R. Rosaldo 1989). I was subject to the same social pressures as others resident in Santa Ana, though to a lesser degree, and this obliged me to choose how I wanted others to view me. My account thus reflects, even as it analyzes, the social vision of respectable santaneros. In the conclusion I deal briefly with the consequences of this fact.

### Race in Cartagena

Cartagena was a major slave entrepôt and the capital of a slave-holding province until emancipation in 1852 (Meisel Roca 1980). Sexual relations among Spaniards, Africans, and Indians produced a large population of mixed descent that, in turn, generated a complex system of social stratification based on ancestry, skin color, wealth, degree of "education" (*educación*, that is, "knowing how to act"), and slave versus free status for African-descended people (Juan and Ulloa 1978[1735]:40–42; Posada 1920[1883]:334–344). Today, the vast majority of cartageneros are (from a North American perspective) of noticeable African descent (Solaun and Kronus 1973).[7]

In Cartagena, the term "*blanco*," white, seems originally to have referred to any Spaniard or person descended exclusively from Spaniards (Juan and Ulloa 1978[1735]; Posada 1920 [1883]). By the beginning of the 20th century, however, "*blanco*" came to mean only a member of the dominant class. While this class was comprised mainly of light-skinned people of exclusively Spanish descent, some wealthy, darker-skinned individuals, particularly the illegitimate sons of *blanco* men with non-*blanca* women, had entered the dominant class and thus were labelled "*blancos*." Older santaneros still sometimes refer to the rich as "*blancos*" and to the poor as "*negros*." Younger people seldom use "*blanco*" and "*negro*" in this way, as class terms.

Most santaneros agree that "*blancos*" refers only to dominant class people, no matter their skin color, hair type, or facial features. By the same token, santaneros call a poor person "*claro*" (fair, light), rather than "*blanco*," even if that person's skin color and other physical characteristics are typically "*blanco*." As one young woman put it, "I'm *clara* [fair], but I'd be *blanca* if I had money. You can be *moreno* [brown], but if you've got money then you're *blanco*."

"Moreno" is a category between *claro* and *negro*. (Other categories exist, but they are less frequently used than those discussed here.)[8] Morenos are said to have lighter skin, straighter hair, thinner noses and lips, and higher cheekbones than *negros*. However, the decisive criterion is often behavioral rather than phenotypical: people called moreno rather than *negro* are considered to act more in accord with class and gender norms. For example, during a conversation with two teen-aged girls who considered themselves morenas, the topic of boyfriends came up. Lupe teased her cousin about having a *negro* boyfriend. The cousin bridled, disputing the charge. Lupe sat back in her chair and sighed, "I want to have a really white son [*un hijo blanquito*], with straight hair and blue eyes." "You'll have a fat, *negro* one with kinky hair," her cousin laughed. I asked them why people have such a quarrel with *negros*. "It's not that we have any quarrel," Lupe said, "but have you realized how they are? They walk around all disorderly [*desordenados*], they talk like this," and here she shouted, her voice "thick" (*gruesa*, or what North Americans might call "rude"), "and they're vulgar [*son vulgares*]. They don't sweet talk the girls in a good way, they . . . " She stopped. She and her cousin looked at each other and laughed. "They're *vulgar*," Lupe said, leaving the content of their vulgarity to my imagination. Given the negative connotations of being considered *negro*, it is not surprising that nearly all santaneros self-identify as moreno or claro—even (or especially) those whose physical characteristics are, for santaneros, typically "*negro*."

Yet santaneros do not use race terms often. I believe that they are reluctant to use race terms in part because the terms carry a heavy emotional charge, as indicated above and as will become clearer below. This is consistent with santaneros' denial of racial discrimination in Cartagena. Nearly all santaneros claim that the poor do not discriminate racially, a sentiment that embodies santaneros' self-image as solidary. At the same time, most people argue that societywide discrimination is based on class rather than race, though nearly all agree that the elite informally bars blacks from the Navy and from residence in the city's wealthiest sector. Note that santaneros here again portray the wealthy as divisive.[9]

Santaneros also seem to avoid describing each other as *negro*, a tendency consistent with santaneros' self-definition as solidary. A person may have physically *negro* traits, and may be poor, but, unless known to "act like a *negro*" (or unless the speaker wants to imply this), that person will usually be called moreno. A brief consideration of the context of the conversation among Lupe, her cousin, and me, reveals something of the practical effect of explicit racial discourse, illustrating the reasons for its strategic though infrequent intervention in daily life.

Before our conversation, the three of us were sitting with Lupe's mother, Dalia, and her grandmother, Cándida, in the latter's yard when Aurelio arrived. Aurelio is a *carretillero*, a man who travels from neighborhood to neighborhood selling fruit and vegetables from a hand-drawn cart. While bantering with Cándida, Aurelio declared in jest that he was going to set up house (that is, enter into common-law union)[10] with Lupe. Cándida and the others laughed. "No way!" Cándida exclaimed. "Why would she set up house with you, you're so black!" "Never with a *negro*," added Lupe. "If I came home with a *negro* my dad would kill me." It is important to point out that the women's negative evaluation of Aurelio's blackness also surely included his lowly occupation. Carretilleros are generally held to be the least educated, most vulgar men, and the job itself involves hard labor and meager earnings. Parents often admonish their sons about the necessity of studying so that they will not remain ignorant (*ignorantes*) and have to become carretilleros, while warning daughters that if they do not study or are otherwise disrespectful they will be fit only to marry carretilleros. In this case, Lupe's mother and grandmother clearly intended to reinforce the lesson—already stressed by her father—that she should not set up house with or marry a *negro*. Lupe's subsequent comments to her cousin and me indicate that she apparently accepts the lesson.[11] Thus, the older women mobilized a racial discourse in order to discourage Lupe from even contemplating a match that they deemed inappropriate at least in part on class grounds (that is, Aurelio's poverty and low social standing); Lupe's father is a small-time building contractor and her mother is a nurse.

In part, the women's disparagement of Aurelio's blackness also rested on the assumption that to be *negro* is to be ugly. As noted, santaneros generally avoid discussing blackness and claim not to discriminate racially. Indeed, santaneros can avoid using explicitly racial terms because their language contains an implicit racial hierarchy, with *negros* on the lowest rung. In particular, santaneros' descriptions of beauty define whiteness as pretty in opposition to blackness as ugly, all without recourse to explicitly racial terms. In most of the Spanish-speaking world (including Cartagena), *simpático* means "genial, likeable, nice"; it does not refer to physical appearance. In Cartagena, however, simpático also means "good-looking." Cartageneros' use of simpático in these two senses indicates that what is considered pleasing to another person is one's physical appearance. Moreover, in Cartagena to be simpático means to have features associated with Europeans or *blancos*: a straight nose, thin lips, and high cheekbones. For cartageneros, an ugly person has a flat nose, thick lips, and low cheekbones, all features that santaneros associate with African or *negro* ancestry. In Cartagena, *maluco* is the most commonly used word for "ugly." In most of the Spanish-speaking world, including Cartagena, maluco also means "slightly sick" or "indisposed" and sometimes connotes a feeling of regret or mild shame for having disappointed or upset someone. Thus to be ugly in Cartagena is to be more *negro* than *blanco*, and to feel slightly sick or ashamed. To be good-looking is to be more *blanco* than *negro*, and to be pleasing to others.

Another pair of terms describe the same opposition. The features of *una persona simpática* are also said to be *"finas"* (fine). "Fine" in cartagenero Spanish also refers to "refinement" or "exquisiteness." In contrast, the features of *una persona maluca* are *"ordinarias"* (ordinary), having the sense of "common," "coarse," "vulgar." These two terms for physical appearance also encode a covert color/class component because the rich/whites are associated with both physical and spiritual refinement (the latter understood as "greater culture"), while the poor and *negros* are said to be more "common" in both aspects. Thus the language of physical appearance in Cartagena exalts European/*blanco* standards of taste while denigrating those of non-European origin.[12]

### La Champeta

More crucial, santaneros discriminate racially by using the terms "champetudo" and "clase baja" (lower class) as euphemisms for *"negro."* Santaneros use all three labels to refer to people who violate dominant gender and class ideals.

*La música champeta* or *champetuda* (a pejorative form of the word *champeta*) is African and African-influenced dance music from the non-Spanish-speaking Caribbean and even North America. This music began arriving in Cartagena in the 1960s and is currently popular among poor youth. Non-Spanish lyrics (commonly thought to be "African") and a good dance beat are the main criteria for calling a song champeta.[13] The music gets its name from the "champeta," a Bowie-shaped kitchen knife about a foot long. Cartageneros named the music "champeta" because those who dance to it are reputed to fight frequently at dances, and the easily concealed champeta was (and is) a favorite dance floor weapon. I say "easily concealed" because male champetudos typically dress in

baggy pants and shirts—a style the respectable consider "outlandish" (*estrafalario*), "scandalous" (*escandaloso*), and "disorderly" (*desordenado*).
Dances featuring champeta are said to attract blacks. The respectable hold that champeta dancers transgress gender ideals. Young men reportedly drink to excess, use drugs, and provoke bloody fights, all of which, the respectable allege, indicates that they pursue self-interest at the expense of respect. The respectable complain that young men waste money on these disreputable and dangerous entertainments instead of supporting their spouses and children and helping elderly or indigent parents. Moreover, the frequent fights at the dances are viewed as proof of these men's divisiveness.

Young women who attend these dances are accused of sexual promiscuity. First, the music and the dance steps are said to be sexually provocative. As one young man told me, "Take a look and see if that's dancing or if it's something else," the "something else" being "making love with your clothes on." Second, the presence of alcohol and drugs is thought to lead women to premarital or extramarital sex, which most respectable santaneros consider morally reprehensible for women. Finally, women's reputations suffer by their being present at these dances because they enter a male space without the protection of parents or brothers; these dances are considered part of the street, which is the quintessentially male space. Women who attend the dances, and who therefore are supposedly promiscuous, are thought to act out of self-interest—the desire for sex— instead of "respect" (that is, concern for their standing as reputable women). Typical is the following remark by a young man: "Those women are plebeian, bandits [*bandidas*, a euphemism for "whores"]—no decent woman would go to one of those dances." Indeed, the respectable claim that some *champetudas* (women who dance to la música champeta) commit the worst offense of which a woman is capable: neglecting her children.

Some respectable people equate *negros* with champetudos (both male and female). Most santaneros, however, simply describe *negros* and champetudos in identical terms, implying an equivalence between the two. A young friend of mine, Rogelio, who considered himself moreno and respectable, illustrated how santaneros equate "*negros*" and "champetudos" in describing *negros*: "They dress scandalously [escandalosos], they wear a red shirt, blue pants, green shoes. And they dance all disorderly [desordenados]—they *are* disorderly. And they talk 'thick' [grueso]. They're vulgar, champetudo. The moreno dances cool because he carries the rhythm in his blood, but when a *negro* comes and dances, shit, you know there's going to be a fight."

The respectable male and female champetudos' actions repudiate the respect upon which social order, and thus men's and elders' authority, is based. At the same time, anyone who violates gender norms may now be branded "champetudo," regardless of whether the violation in question involves dancing to champeta. Thus, a young man who is irresponsible toward his family is called champetudo, while a woman who others think spends too much time in the street or in men's company, or who is otherwise "disrespectful," is called champetuda. For example, when Rosa's daughter-in-law Gloria insulted her, Rosa called Gloria a champetuda, impugning her reputation by implying that only a champetuda would be so disrespectful as to insult her mother-in-law. In short, violating dominant conceptions of proper manhood and womanhood is to act like a champetudo, which in turn is to act like a *negro*. Class and gender attributes are central to the definition of blackness. Labeling all these transgressors "champetudos" is one way of repelling the perceived attack on social order, since the label evokes powerfully stigmatizing racial terms without explicitly specifying them.

Such stigmatizing has tangible effects. Many young women try to avoid being called champetudas by staying away from champeta dances, thereby ensuring that they spend little time in the street, and by otherwise fulfilling the role of dutiful daughter or wife. The respectable are particularly sensitive to the implications that champetuda behavior can have for daughters, arguing that champetudas' actions ultimately prevent them from keeping their spouses. Indeed, calling Gloria a champetuda was part of Rosa's and her husband's strategy for persuading their son to break up with Gloria. Similarly, parents attempt to discourage champetudo tendencies in sons by spending much time and energy criticizing champetudo music, dance, and behavioral dispositions. Thus, the respectable use the fear of being labeled "champetudo" to induce conformity to dominant gender, class, and, thus, race identities.

I would also point out that calling the music "champeta," and the disrespectable and disorderly "champetudos," underlines the notion that champetudos are *not* solidary with their classmates, but are instead divisive: the words "champeta" and "champetudo" draw attention to the knife (*la champeta*), which is a metonym for violence. Classifying the music as "African" also links blackness to violence and divisiveness and so suggests that blackness contradicts popular class identity. In turn, blackness and being champetudo are strongly identified because santaneros consider champeta to be "African" music.

Ironically, the assault of the respectable on the champetudo phenomenon discredits an apparently budding Afro-Colombian cultural movement. In a context in which blackness and African heritage are consistently belittled, champetudos defiantly celebrate "African" music. In contrast, the city's white elite derives its musical and dance tastes largely from white Anglo-American rock. English in Cartagena is the language of cultural cachet and economic dominance, a link with the desired world of hipness to which many young cartageneros aspire, but to which only the wealthy have access, through such resources as vacations in Miami, bilingual schools, and secondary studies in the United States.[14]

Champetudo music confounds the cultural and linguistic hierarchy, proclaiming that what is *really* cool is "African" and thus unintelligible to the elite—but not to the champetudos, who sing the champeta tunes phonetically. (In a fitting irony, some of the tunes they "sing" are in English.) Respectable santaneros occupy a cultural middle ground, preferring regional Spanish-language musical varieties such as *vallenato* and *salsa*. In putting down the champetudos, then, the respectable attempt to neutralize a cultural force that champions "Africanness," blackness, in opposition to European, white standards of taste. (The elite, in different ways, also directly opposes the champetudos.) Indeed, for respectable popular class people the champetudo phenomenon, with its alternative vision of gender, work, generational relations, and culture, represents a bid to redefine popular class identity in terms much "blacker" or more African-identified than the respectable find palatable. The dominant way of defining popular class identity, then, excludes those who would exalt blackness. Again, it is worth stressing that this notion of popular class identity, like the gender and race concepts underwriting it, reinforces the authority of men over women and of older men over younger men.

## The Lower Class

Santaneros also use the same qualities that stigmatize *negros* and champetudos to construct a "lower class" beneath their own class. Thus I heard desperately poor people talk of themselves as "middle class" while calling "lower class" others who were better off economically but who did not act from respect. For example, a young woman who considers herself morena and middle class claimed that the poor are not necessarily "lower class." In contrast to the "middle class," the "lower class" is *cochina* (dirty, piggish), *puerca* (again, dirty, piggish), and *desordenado* (disorderly). The example she cited—lower class women's failure to maintain clean, orderly homes—implies that these women do not do their housework because they are outside the home, meddling in other people's affairs, perhaps being unfaithful to their spouses, or using witchcraft ("piggish," puerca, implies both uncleanliness and the use of witchcraft). Abandoning domestic duties and entering the world of the street are considered actions based on self-interest, creating discord between spouses and between neighbors. In one act, then, these women show themselves to fail both as women and as "middle class" people: they are labeled "bad" women and "de clase baja."

Others more directly describe "lower-class" people as disorderly and quarrelsome (*peleoneros, problemáticos*), often citing the champetudos as a prime example. The president of the neighborhood council, a man in his early 70s, told me that when la música champeta first arrived in Cartagena it was greeted with enthusiasm by "low class people": "The majority of the people who went to those [champetudo] dances were very low class guys [*tipos de muy baja clase*]. . . . That attracts very low class people. So fights started, deaths, stabbings."[15] To anticipate my argument below, I quote a young man on the same subject: "La champeta began as music for lower class people [de clase baja] . . . and it continues to be [in the eyes of the rich and of respectable santaneros alike] the music of the low [*del bajo*], the poor person [*el pobretón*], those without culture [*sin cultura*]."

Class, gender, and racial identities are based on the opposition of respect, solidarity, and sentiment to self-interest and divisiveness. Thus, when santaneros invoke any one identity, they necessarily evoke the others. To label people *"de clase baja,"* *"champetudos,"* or *"negros"*—nearly synonymous terms—is a way of calling them violators of normative class and gender identities alike and of repelling the challenge that violators' actions represents to the status quo of male (and especially older male) domination of popular class life.

### Race: Symbol of Class or Irreducible Category?

In arguing that class, gender, and racial identities are mutually constructed, have I reduced race to a symbol of class difference, as Verena Martinez-Alier (1989 [1974]) did for 19th-century Cuba? Or is there a core meaning to race, something irreducible to other categories such as gender and class? These two positions are in fact not mutually exclusive. Martinez-Alier maintained that race discourse both masked and implied class differences, as a slaveholding elite tried to preserve the association between blackness and servile labor. I have demonstrated the converse, namely, that talk about class implies racial difference.[16] Nevertheless, as in Cuba, the negative qualities that santaneros generally consider inherent to *negros* partially serve to justify class domination. Because lower class people share the same characteristics as *negros*, for lower class people these characteristics acquire an aura of immutability that defines—and helps maintain—their subordinate position. At the same time, santaneros associate blackness with allegedly inherent characteristics that manifest themselves in certain types of action. From their persective, race is not reducible to other categories.

What I am arguing is that santaneros naturalize difference: santaneros see *negros*, champetudos, and la clase baja as naturally rather than culturally determined: their actions flow from (and are expressed in) their physical makeup. This notion of the natural as determining the three overlapping identities is also opposed to the cultural in another way: *incultura*, lack of culture, is imputed to *negros*, champetudos, and the lower class, while *cultura* is held as the hallmark of respectability—of people who are middle (or upper) class, moreno (or claro or *blanco*), and not champetudos. "Culture" here means knowing how to act appropriately.

For santaneros, what distinguishes the cultural from the natural is the capacity to control one's desires, channeling them toward the collective good. Those with the most cultura, those who know how to act, receive recognition as such because they are seen to act out of solidarity, sentiment, or respect—that is, out of obligations toward others—rather than out of self-interest.[17] *Negro*, champetudo, and lower-class men have certain characteristics that the respectable admire and that are part of the popular class male self-image, such as physical strength and sexual potency. Like their female counterparts, however, these men's putative inability to harness their desires to serve others and thus produce social order gives the respectable license to consider them naturally determined and to consider them ignorant of the correct ways to act.

The use of animal images to portray blacks is an especially important means for santaneros to deploy this contrast between culture and nature. This practice is most evident when discussing *palenqueros*, who occupy the very bottom of the social hierarchy in Cartagena. Palenqueros are natives of the village of el Palenque de San Basilio, a settlement founded by runaway slaves in the 17th century. Long isolated from the outside world in an inaccessible area only 70 kilometers from Cartagena, the palenqueros developed a Bantu-Iberian creole language (called *palenquero*), still spoken by older palenqueros, and they retain certain practices, especially in funerals and marriages, that distinguish them from the surrounding coastal culture (Arrázola 1970; Friedemann 1987 [1979]; Friedemann and Patino 1983). Cartagena has a large palenquero community, part of which lives on the edge of Santa Ana; the neighborhood also has a fair number of palenqueros residing in its less desirable, hilly sections. Santaneros seem more comfortable in talking about palenqueros as blacks than about non-palenqueros as blacks, probably because palenqueros are ethnically distinct, thus lessening the risk of offending interlocutors sensitive to being considered *negros*. At the same time, for santaneros, palenqueros are the archetypal *negros*: blackness is defined in terms of approximation to the palenquero pole of the racial spectrum.[18]

My friend Rogelio, who described *negros* in the same terms as champetudos, provided a good example of the "animalization" or "naturalization" of palenqueros. Rogelio likened palenqueros to donkeys:

> They eat a ton, whole pots of rice with cassava and plantain and potato [the latter three are foods said to confer physical strength and sexual potency]. But they also work more, they're like donkeys. Even the women, they carry those basins of bananas on their heads [to sell], and those things are heavy. And the men are well-endowed, they've got big pricks; the women are also voluminous. That's why you don't see a palenquero take up with a woman from here, because he'd do her a lot of damage.

Palenqueros' physical excesses mark them as being closer to the animal than to the human world. Because they exaggerate masculine qualities (sexual potency, work capacity, healthy appetite), male palenqueros are perceived as dangerous (their huge sexual organs do damage to non-palenquera women) and thus are banished to the animal kingdom, where they may be both admired and despised but in any case not treated as equals. Indeed, santaneros condemn palenqueros for their purported stupidity ("donkey" is also commonly used as a synonym for "stupid"), ignorance, lack of culture, laziness, and violence, claiming that palenquero youths are particularly disrespectful toward parents and irresponsible toward spouses.[19]

Palenquero youths are also held to be champetudos. Aside from the negative characteristics we have already seen associated with champetudos, I should point out that people also use animal imagery to talk of champetudos in general. Thus, one young man who liked champeta but who did not consider himself a champetudo complained that people "want to put [the champetudo] down as if he were a dog, they want to put one down on the ground [for being] an uncultured guy," and potentially a *ratero* (thief, from the word "rat").

Respectable santaneros also use animal metaphors to vilify poor people who renege on the obligations of class solidarity and respect for gender norms. For instance, the respectable delighted in the downfall of a poor man who struck it rich and then abandoned his poor friends, claiming that he "died like a dog" in poverty and isolation. And, as I have mentioned, women who neglect their domestic obligations are labelled puercas, pigs, while sexually promiscuous women are frequently called *perras*, female dogs, a synonym for "whores."[20]

The stress on animal qualities highlights the body, including the body's packaging. Discourse on what I will call "the low"—that is, on *negros*, champetudos, and the lower class—is about physicality, about presence and appearance. This is evident in descriptions of genital size and the "coarseness" (*lo ordinario*) of blacks' bodies and faces, as well as in portrayals of blacks and champetudos as "disorderly" (desordenados) in appearance, uncombed and unkempt, "extravagant" (*extravagantes*) or "outlandish" (estrafalarios) in dress, wearing baggy clothes to accommodate weapons that proclaim their aggressive disposition. For the male champetudo, baggy clothing is a sartorial reminder of the bellicose origins of his very name. His female partner equals him in (supposedly) exhibiting her intentions in her dress: she is said to sport sexually provocative clothing, her very presence disordering the spatial and social boundaries of female propriety. Indeed, by the semiotics of their bodies and dress, the effect, if not the intent, of "the low" is to disorder the gender and class discourses dominant within the popular class.

Dance is at the center of discourse on "the low." Here, again, respectable santaneros associate the exaltation of the body and sexuality in dance by "the low" with sexual impropriety, and thus with moral and social disorder. This link has deep roots in Cartagena; throughout the colonial period, church officials were scandalized by the "lascivious" dances that popular class people held (Bensusan 1984). The threat from disorderly, dark lower class bodies and sexuality is grave enough for respectable people to equate them with social and moral chaos, while banishing these bodies' owners to the lowest level of the social hierarchy.

The physicality of "the lows" is accentuated by their reputed inarticulateness. As Antonio claimed, "people of low culture don't understand things with words but with violent deeds . . . They swell with pride when they take that determination to say certain barbarities to others who don't deserve it because they lack culture, they don't have the facility with words to convince a person of this or that and so they do everything by force, they say very ugly words to goad you to get on their level." The opposite of physical force or rude words is verbal ability. Knowing "how to express oneself" is considered an admirable quality, one that demonstrates cultura.[21]

Most santaneros arrange the universe of capable speakers in a hierarchy. Not surprisingly, santaneros believe that the rich are better able to express themselves verbally than are the poor, while poor men stand above poor women. For instance, Antonio discouraged me from interviewing his common-law wife by claiming that "she doesn't know how to express herself." Though his real reasons may have been different (perhaps she would have expressed herself only too well), it is telling that he seized upon what he probably assumed was my acquired knowledge of this hierarchy of speakers. Santaneros say that compared with cartageneros, and with coastal dwellers in general, the *cachacos* (light-skinned inhabitants of Colombia's interior) speak "better Spanish," that is, they are able to express themselves more clearly. The Spanish themselves occupy a higher position, while English speakers as a whole sit at the top of the heap as the possessors of what santaneros call a "more developed culture."

We have seen that some santaneros hold *negros*, like the poor, to be less articulate than other people: they talk "thickly" (grueso) (or have "thick," coarse voices) and are vulgar in speech. *Negros* are thus located below the poor in general in the linguistic hierarchy. Palenqueros are considered to be at the lowest end of the scale, both for speaking "poor" Spanish (*"hablan mal el español"*), as santaneros have it, and for speaking palenquero, which santaneros tellingly label "African."[22] The linguistic peculiarities of champeta music further align the champetudos with the inarticulate: champeta songs are unintelligible to nearly all cartageneros since the words are not in Spanish but in "African." Most respectable santaneros, particularly older ones, complain that no one can even understand the words to the champeta songs. What really irritates the respectable, I think, is that la champeta extols inarticulateness (or an alternative articulateness) by deliberately seizing on songs whose words are unintelligible, and thus announces dance, with its sexual connotations, as the songs' motivation. To like champeta is, in a sense, to drop any pretense to an interest in lyrics and, instead, to exalt body movement for its own sake or as an incitement to sex. To celebrate the body and disdain verbal intelligibility is to carry popular class masculine self-image to an unacceptable extreme that the respectable handle by dehumanizing the offenders, symbolically locking them away in an inferior social status—"the natural," "the animal," "the uncultured," "the low." Women's celebration of the body and sexuality sparks a similar reaction: champetuda women are considered perras, female dogs, that is, "whores." Again, the champetudos' uncultured, animal-like, gender- and class-transgressing qualities are coded as black because (among other things) champeta is considered "African" music.

Blackness appears as the supreme category of "naturalness" in Cartagena because of the historical stereotype of Africans as bearers of a less-developed culture and as therefore driven by their passions rather than by considerations of social good (Friedemann 1984:512–515).

A recent incident dramatizes the persistence of this association. A newspaper reporter described the common people's participation in the main parade of the city's independence festivities in 1988 as "a demonstration of the worst lack of culture and lack of respect . . . putting us at the level of some African tribe or at the lowest rung of the stone age," as something certainly not characteristic of "civilized places" (*El Universal* 1988b:6).[23]

In this sense, race is irreducible: origins or physical traits are thought to cause certain behaviors. African origin and blackness are equated with the uncultured, the barely human. At the same time, blackness also symbolizes class standing, not because of its association with slavery (as Martinez-Alier demonstrated for 19th-century Cuba), but because blackness acts as the source of naturalized meanings for describing the champetudos and la clase baja, providing the language in which to cast them as uncultured animals and thus implying that they are naturally suited to occupy their low social position.

Nonetheless, while santaneros endow blackness with essential, inherited characteristics, my analysis shows that they also acknowledge that it is socially constructed (at least for non-palenqueros): blackness depends to a large degree on what one does, not what one is. Yet being called *negro* on the basis of what one does tends to slide into being considered *negro* on the basis of what one is. This occurs precisely because respectable santaneros see the behavioral aspects of blackness as naturally rather than socially determined. For the respectable, what makes an act typical of blackness is that it is evidence of motivation by self-interest rather than by the social good, by one's innate passions rather than by socially approved norms. It is an act more typical of an animal than a human, of those closer to nature than of those closer to culture.

## Conclusion

Much recent academic literature has argued that analysts, political actors, and ordinary citizens have often minimized the racial discrimination against blacks in Spanish America by privileging the class dimension of blacks' oppression (Moore 1988; Wade 1985; Whitten 1986 [1974]; Wright 1990). To understand this racial discrimination, I suggest we must examine the sustaining dynamics of racism in these societies as well as the content of the racial categories themselves. To do this means looking not only at larger economic and political inequalities based on race but also at how race intersects with other social identities, particularly class and gender, in everyday life. The nonconflictual surface impression of race relations that scholars of the area have often noted (Rout 1976; Solaun and Kronus 1973; Wade 1989) demands that we look for racial politics in novel areas. As I have shown, assertions of an oppositional popular class identity are also statements about gender and racial identity. In other words, race is embedded in class and gender discourse. We have found race (and gender) where others see only class.

   Thus, the kind of symbolic analysis attempted here can help to expose otherwise opaque connections among different dimensions of inequality. In particular, close attention to everyday discourse reveals how language embodies the normative ordering of social relations and identities. Santaneros' language suggests
that the interdependence of class, race, and gender identities and inequalities
relies crucially on the naturalization of difference, a powerful means for immo-
bilizing social arrangements and individual subjectivities (Bourdieu 1977; Connell 1987:85–87; Stolcke 1981).
   As feminist scholars have recently pointed out (Ginsburg and Tsing 1990;
M. Rosaldo 1980; Sacks 1989; Yanagisako and Collier 1987), this endeavor necessitates viewing the creation of any given social identity as occurring through
relationships in diverse areas of life, not merely in those arenas that folk and academic wisdom have privileged as the production site for that identity. Thus, for
example, we have seen that santaneros will call a woman "lower class" rather than
"middle class," not because of her wealth or her relation to the means of production alone, but because of gender-linked qualities such as her reputation for being a responsible housekeeper and a sexually faithful spouse. In much the same
way, race is partially determined by conformity to class and gender norms. In
Cartagena, the connections between race, class, and gender cannot be ignored:
popular class people's use of racial terms relies on and enforces normative class
and gender identities, just as those who assert an oppositional class identity and
advocate gender norms supporting it thereby reinforce the notion that to be *negro*
is to be socially inferior.
   I have also shown that understanding gender involves an examination of both
masculinity and femininity and of how people think about and enact masculinity
in relation to femininity and to competing masculinities; the converse, of course,
holds for femininity. Thus, the notion of masculinity at the center of normative
popular class identity is constructed not only in opposition to femininity but also
in opposition to competing masculinities—namely, those of *negros*, champetudos, and lower class men, and that of rich men (who are more "feminine" because they are self-interested and because their wives restrict their enjoyment
of drinking, dancing, and sexual conquests). In this way, the analysis avoids
the tendency of some literature either to ignore masculinity or, what amounts to
the same thing, to assume that it is stable and homogeneous. Moreover, I have
pointed out that a generational dimension is crucial to how people form their
class and gender identities: older santaneros have succeeded in convincing others
that their conceptions of the past should serve as the measure for the notions of
respectability and solidarity at the heart of these identities, notions that those labeled "*negro*," "champetudo," and "lower class" challenge.
   In this way, the particular configuration of class, gender, and race depicted
here support ways of being that tend to legitimate older people's authority, particularly that of older men, a well as of men in general. As I have argued, privileging this particular form of popular class identity also underwrites men's author-

ity over women by isolating them socially and maintaining the expectation that women be dependent on men. Like certain nationalist (Asad 1990; Dominguez 1989; Mosse 1985; R. Rosaldo 1989), working-class (Joan Scott 1988), feminist (Moraga and Anzaldúa 1981; Pratt 1984), and philosophical (Fraser and Nicholson 1990; Wittig 1980) discourses that represent sectional interests as general ones, santaneros' discourse of class identity subordinates part of the group it purports to represent, namely, women and anyone who challenges gender norms or who celebrates blackness. To paraphrase James Scott (1985), if the success of a system of domination can be measured by the degree to which members of the subordinate classes exploit and oppress one another, the system in Cartagena works admirably. We have seen that the system's racial dimension is crucial to its operation.

The success of the strategy of the respectable, whether conscious or not, to meet challenges from "the low," and thus to preserve their own position, relies partly on their ability to define the standards and boundaries of class, race, and gender identities. One important means of achieving this is by excluding the voices of "the low" from debate as much as possible while roundly condemning their actions. The respectable attempt to force "the low" into silence by proscribing contact with them. Of course, social isolation cannot be completely effective because these people remain sons and daughters, siblings, and neighbors. The price of fraternizing too much with these rebels and outcasts, however, is steep in a community in which personal identity is tightly linked to perceptions of the character of those with whom one socializes. "The low" therefore have fewer opportunities to present their case, and little chance of getting a sympathetic hearing when they do. The success of this containment strategy is also evident from the absence of these people's voices in the present article: by allowing the respectable to exert pressure on me, I conducted fieldwork mainly among the respectable and have thus presented *their* case largely without challenge. Imputing a contestatory impulse to the champetudos' actions does not remedy the exclusion of their views or of those of other disreputable groups. I hope, however, that my account of the injustices of this situation will somewhat compensate for the silence it has created.

*Notes*

The Fieldwork on which this article is based was carried out from October 1988 through March 1990 with support from the National Science Foundation (BSN 8812808). I would like to thank Deb Amory, Evie Blackwood, Don Brenneis, George Collier, Jane Collier, Ethan Goldings, Ted Hardy, Bill Maurer, Laura Nelson, and the *American Ethnologist*'s anonymous reviewers for their comments and encouragement.

1. Throughout this paper I use *santaneros* and other Spanish masculine plural nouns to include both men and women. Use of the masculine singular noun will refer exclusively to men (or the masculine), while both the plural and singular feminine nouns will refer

to women (or the feminine). Santaneros' names in the article are pseudonyms, as is "Santa Ana" itself.

2. Even some authors who clearly recognize the existence of racism virtually efface race relations by placing class struggle at the center of analysis (for example, Taussig 1980). Much recent work on Afro-Hispanic America deals almost exclusively with race (Friede-mann and Arocha 1987; Moore 1988). Exceptions to these trends include works that take race as their primary focus while also treating it as part of a structure of inequality featuring class (Taussig 1987; Wade 1985, 1989; Whitten 1986 [1974]).

3. Women's participation in the workforce rose from 26 percent in 1951 (DANE 1956) to 42 percent in 1988 (DANE 1988). Figures on male unemployment and subem-ployment are shown in Table 1. Berry (1980) shows that real wages for working class and self-employed people declined in the early 1970s. Urrutia (1985) argues that real wages as a whole rose in the late 1970s; though he concedes that they probably declined for the poor in the first half of the 1980s. The nation's largest labor federation, the Central Uni-taria de Trabajadores, claims that purchasing power for working class Colombians de-clined 8 percent between 1986 and the end of 1988 (*Latin American Weekly Reports* 1988:5). (Other sources contend that during the 1980s, real wages increased slightly, or that their evolution has not been unidirectional. See, for example, Reyes Posada 1988.)

Table 1. Unemployment and Subemployment in Cartagena, 1973–88.

|        | Male Unemployment | Total Unemployment | Male Subemployment | Total Subemployment |
|--------|-------------------|--------------------|--------------------|---------------------|
| 1973[a] | 9.7%              | 15.6%              | —                  | —                   |
| 1983[b] | 7.0%              | 12.7%              | 8.5%               | 8.7%                |
| 1988[c] | 9.8%              | 13.3%              | 18.1%              | 15.7%               |

[a] DANE 1973
[b] DANE 1983
[c] DANE 1988

4. *Condoliente* comes from the verb *condoler*, meaning, literally, "to feel pain, hurt with." While it functions like the English "to sympathize," condoler has a stronger con-notation of urgency and suffering because *doler* means "to feel pain, hurt."

5. Whether a respectable person blames the rich or young popular class people for the failures of these two groups depends largely on the context of discourse. These people's judgments are usually harsher when discussing a concrete case involving a young per-son more closely associated with the discussants' social circle. Conversely, the respectable tend to emphasize more strongly the larger political and economic determinants of young people's inappropriate actions when talking of young people or of political economy in more abstract terms.

6. It is worth pointing out that the restrictions are aimed at preventing relations be-tween heterosexuals and/or heterosexual relations. Had I been perceived as gay, I might have had more contact with women, since gay men—being above suspicion of sexual interest in women—seem to enjoy freer access to women of other households. Local no-tions of male homosexuality are consistent with the literature on other Latin American societies (cf. Alonso and Koreck 1989; Lancaster 1988b).

7. There are no official census data on race in Colombia today; the government

stopped including racial classifications in censuses after 1918 (Smith 1966), most probably in order to avoid the embarrassing (from an elite perspective) quantification of the country's non-European heritage (Arocha 1984; Pineda Camacho 1984:206–211). This is not unusual in Latin America (Andrews 1991; Rout 1976).

8. These terms include *triqueño* ("wheat-colored"), *acanelado* ("cinnamon-colored"), *indio* ("Indian"), and *chino* ("Chinese"). I heard the first term used only once, the second slightly more often. The last two terms are synonyms and are almost exclusively used to refer to someone with straight hair, or to refer to the hair itself. The few people flatly called indios are indigenous people who have recently settled or currently live in Cartagena, such as the few Indians from the Putumayo region who sell saints' portraits, sorcery counters, and love potions downtown and in the market. People with *pelo indio* (Indian hair) are subsumed under the other major categories: *claro, moreno,* and (less often) *negro*. In a 1973 study, Solaun and Kronus (1973:165) noted 62 different color terms used by people of different classes.

I never heard anyone apply the term *mulato* or *mulata* to a person; the terms were frequently used in Cartagena, at least during the colonial era, and are still current throughout Spanish America. Interestingly, cartageneros call a type of large, brown bird common to the city *Maríamulata*, "María mulata." I believe that the bird probably gained this name both because of its light chocolate coloring and because of its presence in large numbers. While the "mulata" part of the name may allude to the color of the bird, it may also call attention to the bird's ubiquity, much as does "María," a very popular name in Cartagena. This reflects or reinforces the notion that those of intermediate color, being neither *blanco* nor *negro,* form the largest sector of the population. The bird's unspectacular appearance, which contrasts with the dazzling plumage of the wild birds that many cartageneros trap and cage, may also have influenced the choice of a name that connects color, judgments of physical beauty and ugliness, and social status. As we will see, santaneros associate beauty with *blancos'* physical features and ugliness with those of the *negro*; the moreno comes somewhere in between.

9. Santaneros rightly view the Navy as the branch of the armed forces most removed from combat. Santaneros believe that being barred from entering the Navy prevents *negros* from making a decent living in the service branch that affords the greatest physical safety (it seldom combats the guerrilla groups) and that is least oppressive to the poor (it is seldom involved in human rights abuses or in forced recruiting). This contrast between rich and poor regarding combat is made sharper by the fact that in Cartagena the Navy shares a base with the Marines, the service branch that most poor cartageneros are obliged to enter and that suffers high combat casualties.

I should also point out that talk about society-wide racial discrimination usually emerged in casual conversation rather than in response to my direct questioning. This suggests that santaneros are conscious of more racial discrimination than they are disposed to acknowledge (at least to outsiders and at least in formal discussion of race).

10. *Comprometerse con,* literally, "commit himself with," Lupe.

11. Incidentally, Cándida also said, "I'm *negra,* but not like you," suggesting behavioral if not physical superiority vis-à-vis Aurelio.

12. The superiority of light skin is enacted each year during the National Beauty Contest held in Cartagena. The contestants, mainly from upper or upper-middle-class families, are light skinned, considerably more so than the majority of the residents of the departments they represent. Just before the independence festivities under whose auspices the

National Beauty Contest takes place, the city holds its Popular Beauty Contest. The Popular Beauty Contest showcases morenas and *negras* from the city's poor and middle-class neighborhoods. Once an important event in the city's independence celebration, government and upper-class neglect in recent years has subordinated the status of the popular contest to that of the national one; the former is now a low-budget imitation of the latter. The popular contest's inferior status dramatizes the inferior race and class status of its participants. For the poor, new, self-interested attitudes on the part of the rich are evident in their promoting the National Beauty Contest and gradually marginalizing the events of the independence celebration—events that encourage popular participation: the notoriety and tourism attendant on the contest enhances the prestige and wealth of the rich, as hosts to illustrious visitors and as organizers of this high-profile event and as owners of hotels and related tourist enterprises.

13.  Paul Simon's song "I Know What I Know," from the *Graceland* album, was a popular champeta song in Cartagena in 1988. Cartageneros called it "The Turkey" because the female chorus sounded to them like a turkey gobbling. Because most champeta songs are pirated, arriving in Cartagena unencumbered by such niceties as liner notes, cartageneros invent their own names for songs.

14.  English is spoken on Colombia's Caribbean islands of San Andres and Providencia, which at one time were British possessions. Despite being a short flight from Cartagena, the islands are perceived by the city's upper class as inferior culturally to both mainland Colombia and the United States, not least because the islands' "natives," descendants of African slaves, are *negros*. Indeed, most cartageneros do not consider the isleños' language to be English, but rather *patois*, a "dialect" inferior to English.

15.  This man noted proudly that the council, composed of other (mostly older) men, had avoided bloodshed at Santa Ana's annual patron saint's day celebration by hiring a brass band rather than a disk jockey with a sound system. Most sound systems prominently feature champeta music in their repertoire and consequently attract "low class" and champetudo people. Brass bands attract mainly older people because their repertoire is based on songs native to the coastal region, the majority of which were hits before most champetudos were born.

16.  Although origins and/or physical features were the primary markers of status during the initial colonial years, by the early 19th century the calculus of social classification also included wealth, occupation, level of "education" (*educación*—manners, knowing how to act), and legal status (slave versus free) (Posada 1920 [1883]:334–343).

17.  Curiously, santaneros consider the rich "cultured" (*cultos, de mucha cultura*) even though the latter renege on their obligations to the poor. I believe that the polysemy of the term "cultura" enables santaneros to remain untroubled by this seeming contradiction. Santaneros conceive of the rich as cultured because they are well-educated; they possess *una gran cultura*, as the phrase there goes. At the same time, the rich are held to be more cultured than the poor in the sense of being polite, knowing how to act effortlessly in most social situations. In the view of one older man, a staunch critic of the exploitativeness of the wealthy, even when the rich "discriminate" (on the basis of wealth and culture, not race, as he clarified) they do so "diplomatically."

18.  Norman Whitten and Grace Schubert, working in the predominantly *negro* lowland town of San Lorenzo, reported in the late 1960s and early 1970s, respectively, that transplanted highland *blancos* similarly de-humanized *negros*, also sometimes likening them to animals (Schubert 1981:572–577; Whitten 1986 [1974]:192). Schubert's account

suggests that most *negros* implicitly accepted the assertion that *blancos* are "more civilized" (*mas civilizados*) than *negros*, despite the fact that most *negros* also explicitly reject the devaluation of blackness and the putative superiority of whiteness.

19. Michael Taussig's (1987) recent work on shamanism traces out this ambivalence—the mixture of fear, hate, and imputation of supranormal powers—toward colonized inferiors. Insofar as santaneros talk of non-palenquero *negros* in similar terms, this case suggests that such ambivalence can also exist when the inferior group is not a colonial or ethnic minority.

20. Cachacos, light-skinned natives of Colombia's interior departments, considered by cartageneros to be selfish, heartless, and hypocritical, are put down in a similar way in a popular saying: "There are three ungrateful animals: the cat, the pigeon, and the cachaco."

21. In the official story of the early 17th-century founding of Cartagena's Convent of La Popa, dedicated to la Virgen de la Candelaria, the colored masses' inarticulateness appears as a sign of their impiety. On the hill of La Popa, directly behind Santa Ana, a group of Indians worshipped the devil in the form of a goat. At the end of the "demonic ceremony" those present "danced a *dans macabre* [sic], at the end of which the Indians fell, exhausted with fatigue, in a confused mob, setting the place athunder with weird shouts and coarse monosyllables" (Delgado 1972 [1912]:47). Under la Virgen de la Candelaria's injunction, the intrepid priest Fray Alonso de la Cruz Paredes expelled the Indians from la Popa in 1608 and constructed a church in la Virgen's honor. Of course, knowing the "word of God" constituted, and continues to constitute, the priesthood's primary claim to authority. This may be one reason that popular class anticlericalism centers on the disparity between priests' words and deeds.

22. Non-palenqueros' disparagement of the palenquero language has caused many young palenqueros residing outside Palenque to abandon the language altogether. Palenquero and non-palenquero intellectuals, as well as ordinary palenqueros, told me that, because of such stigmatization, most palenqueros born and raised outside Palenque today refuse to speak or even to learn palenquero.

23. The independence celebration is the highlight of Cartagena's festival season, providing popular entertainment and a chance for the city—as host to Colombia's National Beauty Contest—to represent itself to a domestic and international audience in attendance or watching on television. Given Cartagena's economic dependence on tourism, the city's display of cultura during the festivities is crucial to its image as a desirable tourist destination. Hence the heated debates in the local press and among the populace at large after the 1988 celebration, when rumors circulated that the National Beauty Contest organizers were threatening to move the contest site from Cartagena in 1990 if the public in 1989 was as disorderly as it had been the previous year.

Another journalist linked the "disorder" of recent parades to the uncontrollable passions of the champetudos. He saw the celebration in former years as

> an admirable expression of public-spiritedness . . . representing the friendly behavior of the entire participating community, founded on respect, social integration [of class, not race], decency, solidarity, and good manners, with which healthy coexistence—which is nothing more than the exercise of freedom up to the point at which the rights of others begin—is guaranteed. Contrary to those who think that the *fiestas* grant them the faculty to do whatever they please, in open stupidity

constituting libertinism, the cause of so many outrages and misfortunes. And, precisely, to this is due the bitter experiences of the last few years, hurricane gusts of disorder and confusion, favorable to looting, destruction, and assaults on physical integrity and modesty. A reflection of a depressing spectacle, not apt for decent people but for the *"champe"* [champeta] multitudes of every condition, who converge with morbid hunger upon the banquet of their debauchery and frustrations, leaving in their clumsy actions the miserable imprint of a sickening vulgarity. (*El Universal* 1988a:4)

## References

Abu-Lughod, Lila
    1986      Veiled Sentiments: Honor and Poetry in Bedouin Society. Berkeley: University of California Press.

Alonso, Ana M., and Maria Teresa Korek
    1989      Silences: "Hispanics," AIDS, and Sexual Practices. Differences 1(1):1–24.

Andrews, George Reid
    1991      Blacks and Whites in São Paulo, Brazil, 1888–1988. Madison: University of Wisconsin Press.

Arocha, Jaime
    1984      Antropología en la historia de Colombia: Una visión. (Anthropology in the History of Colombia: One Vision.) *In* Un siglo de investigación social: Antropología en Colombia. (A Century of Social Investigation: Anthropology in Colombia.) Jaime Arocha and Nina S. de Friedemann, eds. Pp. 27–130. Bogotá: Etno.

Arrázola, Roberto
    1970      Palenque: Primero pueblo libre de América. (Palenque: America's First Free Town.) Cartagena: Ediciones Hernandez.

Asad, Talal
    1990      Multiculturalism and British Identity in the Wake of the Rushdie Affair. Politics and Society 18(4):455–480.

Benítez Rojo, Antonio
    1984      La cultura Caribeña en Cuba: Continuidad versus ruptura. (Caribbean Culture in Cuba: Continuity versus Rupture.) Cuban Studies/Estudios Cubanos 14(1):1–15.

Bensusan, Guy
    1984      Cartagena's Fandango Politics. Studies in Latin American Popular Culture 3:127–134.

Berry, R. Albert
    1980      The Effects of Inflation on Income Distribution in Colombia: Some Hypotheses and a Framework for Analysis. *In* Economic Policy and

Income Distribution in Colombia. R. Albert Berry and Ronald Soligo, eds. Pp. 113–133. Boulder, CO: Westview Press.

Bourdieu, Pierre
1977    Outline of a Theory of Practice. Cambridge: Cambridge University Press.

Casal, Lourdes
1979    Race Relations in Contemporary Cuba. In The Position of Blacks in Brazilian and Cuban Society. Pp. 11–27. London: Minority Rights Group.

Clifford, James, and George E. Marcus, eds.
1986    Writing Culture: The Poetics and Politics of Ethnography. Berkeley: University of California Press.

Connell, Robert W.
1987    Gender and Power: Society, the Person and Sexual Politics. Stanford, CA: Stanford University Press.

Cotler, Julio, ed.
1989    Clases populares, crisis y democracia en América Latina. (Popular Classes, Crisis, and Democracy in Latin America.) Lima, Peru: Instituto de Estudios Peruanos.

Delgado, Camilo S.
1972 [1912]    Historias y leyendas de Cartagena, 1. Bogotá: Ministerio de Educación Nacional, Instituto Colombiano de Cultura.

Departamento Administrativo Nacional de Estadística (DANE)
1956    Censo de población de 1951. (1951 Population Census.) Bogotá: Imprenta Nacional.
1973    XIV Censo nacional de población y III de vivienda (Departamento de Bolivar). (Fourteenth National Population Census and Third National Housing census.) Bogotá: DANE.
1983    Encuesta nacional, etapa 41 (Septiembre). (National Survey, 41st Stage [September].) Bogotá: DANE. Microfilm.
1988    Encuesta nacional, etapa 31 (Septiembre). (National Survey, 31st Stage [September].) Bogotá: DANE. Microfilm.

Dominguez, Virginia R.
1989    People as Subject, People as Object: Selfhood and Peoplehood in Contemporary Israel. Madison: University of Wisconsin Press.

Fraser, Nancy, and Linda J. Nicholson
1990    Social Criticism without Philosophy: An Encounter between Feminism and Postmodernism. In Feminism/Postmodernism. Linda J. Nicholson, ed. Pp. 19–38. New York: Routledge.

Friedemann, Nina S. de
1984    Estudios de negros en la antropología Colombiana. In Un Siglo de Investigación Social: Antropología en Colombia. Jaime Arocha and Nina S. de Friedemann, eds. Pp. 507–572. Bogotá: Etno.

1987 [1979]    Ma Ngombe: guerreros y ganaderos en Palenque. (Ma Ngombe: War-
               rior and Cattle Ranchers in Palenque.) Bogotá: Carlos Valencia.

Friedemann, Nina S. de, and Jaime Arocha
1987           De sol a sol: Génesis, transformación y presencia de los negros en
               Colombia. (From Sunrise to Sunset: Genesis, Transformation, and
               Presence of the Blacks in Colombia.) Bogotá: Planeta.

Friedemann, Nina S., and Carlos Patino Rossel
1983           Lengua y sociedad en el Palenque de San Basilio. (Language and So-
               ciety in Palenque de San Basilio.) Bogotá: Instituto Caro y Cuervo.

Galin, Pedro, Julio Carrión, and Oscar Castillo
1986           Asalariados y clases populares en Lima. (Salary Workers and Popular
               Classes in Lima.) Lima, Peru: Instituto de Estudios Peruanos.

Ginsburg, Faye, and Anna Lowenhaupt Tsing
1990           Uncertain Terms: Negotiating Gender in American Culture. Boston:
               Beacon.

Juan, Jorge, and Antonio de Ulloa
1978 [1735]    Relación histórica del viaje a la América Meridional. (Historical Nar-
               rative of the Trip to Southern America.) Madrid: Fundación Universi-
               taria Española.

Kondo, Dorinne K.
1990           Crafting Selves: Power, Gender, and Discourses of Identity in a Japa-
               nese Workplace. Chicago: University of Chicago Press.

Lancaster, Roger
1988a          Thanks to God and the Revolution: Popular Religion and Class Con-
               sciousness in the New Nicaragua. New York: Columbia University
               Press.
1988b          Subject Honor and Object Shame: The Construction of Male Ho-
               mosexuality and Stigma in Nicaragua. Ethnology 27(2):111–126.

Latin American Weekly Reports
1988           Siege Rules Used to Quash Strike. November 10 (WR-88-44).

Lemaitre, Eduardo
1983           Historia general de Cartagena. Tomo IV: La república. (General His-
               tory of Colombia. Vol. 4: The Republic.) Bogotá: Banco de la
               República.

Martinez-Alier, Verena
1989 [1974]    Marriage, Class and Colour in Nineteenth-Century Cuba: A Study
               of Racial Attitudes and Sexual Values in a Slave Society. Ann Arbor:
               University of Michigan Press.

Meisel Roca, Adolfo
1980           Esclavitud, mestizaje y haciendas en la provincia de Cartagena:
               1533–1851. (Slavery, Race Mixture, and Haciendas in the Province
               of Cartagena.) Desarrollo y Sociedad 4:228–277.

Moore, Carlos
1988        Castro, the Blacks, and Africa. Los Angeles: Center for Afro-American Studies, UCLA.

Moraga, Cherie, and Gloria Anzaldúa, eds.
1981        This Bridge Called My Back: Writings by Radical Women of Color. Watertown, NY: Persephone.

Mosse, George L.
1985        Nationalism and Sexuality: Middle-Class Morality and Sexual Norms in Modern Europe. Madison: University of Wisconsin Press.

Nichols, Theodore E.
1973        Tres puertos de Colombia: Estudio sobre el desarrollo de Cartagena, Santa Marta y Barranquilla. (Three Ports of Colombia: A Study of the Development of Cartagena, Santa Marta and Barranquilla.) Bogotá: Biblioteca Banco Popular.

Pineda Camacho, Roberto
1984        La reivindicación del Indio en el pensamiento social Colombiano (1850–1950). In Un Siglo de Investigación Social: Antropología en Colombia. Jaime Arocha and Nina S. de Friedemann, eds. Pp. 197–252. Bogotá: Etno.

Posada Gutierrez, Joaquín
1920 [1883]  Memorias histórico-políticas, 2. (Historical-Political Memoirs, 2.) Madrid: Editorial América.

Pratt, Minnie
1984        Identity: Skin Blood Heart. In Yours in Struggle: Three Feminist Perspectives on Anti-Semitism and Racism. Elly Bulkin, Minnie Bruce Pratt, and Barbara Smith, eds. Pp. 9–63. New York: Long Haul Press.

Reyes Posada, Alvaro
1988        Evolución de la distribución del ingreso en Colombia. (Evolution of the Distribution of Income in Colombia.) Desarrollo y Sociedad 21:37–52.

Rosaldo, Michelle Zimbalist
1980        The Use and Abuse of Anthropology: Reflections on Feminism and Cross-Cultural Understanding. Signs: Journal of Women in Culture and Society 5(3):389–417.

Rosaldo, Renato
1989        Culture and Truth: The Remaking of Social Analysis. Boston: Beacon.

Rout, Leslie B., Jr.
1976        The African Experience in Spanish America: 1502 to the Present. New York: Cambridge University Press.

Sacks, Karen Brodkin
1989        Toward a Unified Theory of Class, Race, and Gender. American Ethnologist 16(3):534–550.

Schubert, Grace
  1981        To Be Black Is Offensive: Racist Attitudes in San Lorenzo. *In* Cultural Transformations and Ethnicity in Modern Ecuador. Norman Whitten, Jr., ed. Urbana: University of Illinois Press.

Scott, James
  1985        Weapons of the Weak: Everyday Forms of Peasant Resistance. New Haven, CT: Yale University Press.

Scott, Joan W.
  1988        Women in the Making of the English Working Class. *In* Gender and the Politics of History. Pp. 68–90. New York: Columbia University Press.

Smith, T. Lynn
  1966        The Racial Composition of the Population of Colombia. Journal of Interamerican Studies 8(2):213–235.

Solaun, Mauricio, and Sidney Kronus
  1973        Discrimination without Violence: Miscegenation and Racial Conflict in Latin America. New York: John Wiley & Sons.

Stolcke, Verena
  1981        Women's Labours: The Naturalisation of Social Inequality and Women's Subordination. *In* Of Marriage and the Market: Women's Subordination Internationally and Its Lessons. Kate Young, Carol Wolkowitz, and Roslyn McCullagh, eds. Pp. 159–177. London: Routledge & Kegan Paul.

Strassmann, W. Paul
  1982        The Transformation of Urban Housing: The Experience of Upgrading in Cartagena. Baltimore: Johns Hopkins.

Taussig, Michael
  1980        The Devil and Commodity Fetishism in South America. Chapel Hill: University of North Carolina Press.
  1987        Shamanism, Colonialism, and the Wild Man: A Study in Terror and Healing. Chicago: University of Chicago Press.

El Universal (Cartagena)
  1988a      Historia del reinado. (History of the Pageant.) November 11:20.
  1988b      Las tristes fiestas. (Sad Fiestas.) December 12:6.

Urrutia, Miguel
  1985        Winners and Losers in Colombia's Economic Growth of the 1970s. New York: Oxford University Press.

Wade, Peter
  1985        Race and Class: The Case of South America Blacks. Ethnic and Racial Studies 8(2):233–249.
  1989        Black Culture and Social Inequality in Colombia. Tunbridge Wells, England: Institute for Cultural Research Monograph Series No. 28.

Whitten, Norman E., Jr.
    1986 [1974]    Black Frontiersmen: Afro-Hispanic Culture of Ecuador and Colom-
                   bia. Prospect Heights, IL: Waveland Press.
Wittig, Monique
    1980           The Straight Mind. Feminist Issues 1(1):101–111.
Wright, Winthrop
    1990           Café con Leche: Race, Class, and National Image in Venezuela.
                   Austin: University of Texas Press.
Yanagisako, Sylvia Junko, and Jane Fishburne Collier
    1987           Toward a Unified Analysis of Gender and Kinship. In Gender and
                   Kinship: Essays Toward a Unified Analysis. Jane Fishburne Collier
                   and Sylvia Junko Yanagisako, eds. Stanford, CA: Stanford University
                   Press.

PART THREE
# THE ANDES

# 12. THE CULTURAL POLITICS
# OF BLACKNESS IN COLOMBIA

## Peter Wade

### Introduction

A decade ago, Benedict Anderson made this claim: "The dreams of racism actually have their origin in ideologies of *class*, rather than in those of nation"
(1983:136). In Latin America and the Caribbean, however, ideas about race—
that is, about people labeled as blacks, indians,[1] whites, and mestizos—have long
been important in representations of nationhood (cf. Gilroy 1987:44). Certain
ideas about race are commonly privileged at the expense of others, however:
the idea of a racial democracy in Brazil, the Jamaican national motto of "Out of
Many, One People," the Trinidadian national anthem's "Here ev'ry creed and
race find an equal place," or the view that Colombia is, or will become, an essentially mestizo nation. In all these cases, equality and/or racial and cultural
fusion are official and often popular representations. Blackness and indianness
are not necessarily ignored: both have long histories and often form part of national representations. But colonial values that privilege lightness of skin color as
a sign of social status or as the putative national destiny are still pervasive.[2]

In many countries other voices have contested these images, claiming discrimination exists against blacks and indigenous people and asserting "black power" or
"indigenous authorities" (Findji 1992); these social movements self-consciously
draw on roots of resistance that reach back into colonial times.[3] In Colombia, the
mobilization of black people around issues including human rights, racial discrimination, history, and land has flowered in the last few years; the state has also
created some institutional space for blacks and consolidated that for *indigenas*,
indigenous peoples. This raises issues for the understanding of the cultural politics of blackness and nationhood in Latin America and the Caribbean, and for
anthropology in general. First, how has such a mobilization come about in a
country where the "invisibility" (Friedemann 1984) of blacks was so entrenched
and where pervasive race mixture had apparently blurred racial boundaries to the
point where mobilization was structurally inhibited?[4] How does black mobilization relate to indigenous peoples' organizations and to a state involved in rede-
fining official representations of Colombia as a primarily mestizo nation? Sec-

Originally published in *American Ethnologist* 22:2 (May 1995), pp. 341–57. Reproduced by permission of the American Anthropological Association. Not for further reproduction.

ond, how are anthropologists to relate to this kind of mobilization? In recent years there has been much debate about the invention of culture and the deconstructions of invention. Minority peoples seeking a space in national arenas of culture and power may resent anthropologists' assertions that their traditions and self-representations are "inventions." Ethnic mobilization seems to trade in the essentializations and reifications of identity and culture that anthropologists are determined to deconstruct, especially when these involve reference to "race." Various solutions have been proposed to this dilemma, but I think none of them engage sufficiently with the political nature of the process they analyze.

In this article I look at the recent growth of the black movement in Colombia, tracing its history and its interaction with indígena mobilization and with the state, and analyzing the various competing representations of blackness that have emerged. This, in turn, lays the basis for a discussion of the issues I have enumerated in this introduction.

### Early Black Organization in Colombia

Colombia has one of the largest black populations in Latin America. Especially notable is the concentration of black people in the poor, underdeveloped Pacific coastal region, where they form perhaps 80–90 percent of the population. The literature on blacks in Colombia is important but still relatively sparse, and even less exists on recent political mobilization.[5]

Blackness as a concept in Colombia predates the Spanish conquest, since black Africans, slave and free, were part of Iberian populations long before 1492 (e.g., Saunders 1982). Black slaves in Colombia and elsewhere were often simply called negros and slavers sometimes called negreros (Jaramillo Uribe 1968; Levine 1980). There is rather little evidence on how black people in colonial Colombia referred to themselves, but by the 19th century the black poet Candelario Obeso refers straightforwardly to negros (Friedemann 1984:524). Generally, however, the term negro was stigmatized in colonial and postcolonial society (Jaramillo Uribe 1968; Mörner 1967) and, for example, free blacks in the northern Pacific Coast region called themselves libres, free people, a usage that continues today (Sharp 1976; West 1957; Whitten 1974).

In the 1970s and with the emergence of organizations that alluded more assertively to blackness, some people began to use the term negro in a rather different way. These developments were mainly the work of a small urban intellectual elite of university students and graduates who identified vigorously as blacks and were influenced by radical movements in Latin America and elsewhere. A number of small and often transient movements appeared during the seventies, but two organizations still exist and are quite representative of the scene: the Center for the Investigation and Development of Black Culture, and Cimarrón (the National Movement for the Human Rights of Black Communities in Colombia). The first, based in Bogotá, was formed by students and other educated people from the

Pacific Coast region. The organization became known for the production of a monthly newspaper, *Presencia Negra* (financed mainly by UNESCO) and for annual seminars aimed principally at *personal docente en cultura negra*, teachers of black culture. A number of books were also produced, mainly by the movement's leader, Amir Smith-Córdoba. Smith-Córdoba also gained notoriety by selling his newspaper in the city center and loudly addressing people whom he regarded as black (using a more North American than Latin American classification), calling out *"¡Hola, negro!"*—a practice that provoked hostile reactions from individuals. The Center for the Investigation and Development of Black Culture still functions, but with minimal funding, especially since UNESCO withdrew its financial support. The organization's platform is clearly the product of Smith-Córdoba's perception of North American civil rights movements that have mobilized around blackness.

The second organization, Cimarrón, has had a wider influence because of its more decentralized structure. It stemmed from a study group, Soweto, formed in 1976 by university students from the Pacific region living in Pereira, a provincial capital of the interior of the country. Cimarrón itself was formed in 1982 and consisted of study groups that were established all over the country under the auspices of the national headquarters in Pereira, and were comprised of people who identified themselves as black. The organization has even less funding than Smith-Córdoba's agency and, consequently, produces only photocopied circulars and bulletins. It takes as its icon the *cimarrones*, runaway slaves of the colonial era who are cast as a symbol of the struggle for freedom and human rights, but it also takes as a model those aspects of North American movements—such as Black Islam, the Black Panthers, and Martin Luther King Jr.'s Southern Christian Leadership Conference—that members perceive as salient.

Both Cimarrón and Smith-Córdoba's organization have had a limited impact: they never involved the mass of people who might be classified—or classify themselves—as blacks: many of these were isolated in the Pacific region and were illiterate and poor, while others subscribed to the official image of Colombia as a mestizo society and a racial democracy. Nevertheless, these movements are important in understanding how people have organized as blacks in Colombia and in analyzing the gradual changes in the representations of "black culture" that this involved.

The context from which these movements emerged involved both national and transnational elements (Fontaine 1981). In the 1970s in Colombia, regional indigenous movements were growing fast against a background of proposals for land reform, the reform of church-state relations, and the emergence of left-wing guerrilla groups (Findji 1992; Gros 1991; Pearce 1990). The civil rights and Black Power movements in the United States were also major influences, and both the Center for the Investigation and Development of Black Culture and Cimarrón make explicit reference to black U.S. leaders such as Martin Luther King Jr. and Malcolm X. Of course, U.S. movements had already had an impact in

Jamaica, Trinidad, and Guyana (Craig 1982; Nettleford 1970; Waters 1985): the Colombian organizations were part of a Caribbean-wide change. Also influential were the independence movements of various African states and the work of Léopold Senghor, president of Senegal (1960–80) and proponent of the ideology of négritude.[6]

Although the national context of political change was important, these organizations looked to other experiences and notions of blackness to inform their own positions. This created some difficulties. There were major differences between the militant separatist nationalism of the Black Muslims or the Black Panthers and King's more integrationist approach. Some of these movements overtly posited ideas of a black nation, however, thereby challenging standard notions of "American" nationhood, and all employed North American notions of blackness, which played on the relatively clear-cut definition of "black." On the other hand, references to African independence struggles also invoked specific ideas about national self-determination, the freeing of avowedly black identities from the colonial yoke, and the rediscovery of autochthonous African values.

The problem was that such a construction of blackness resonated poorly with the Colombian situation, even among many people who identified as blacks. Since the time of Colombian independence the official and widely accepted image of Colombia has been that of a nation of mestizos with, perhaps, remnants of "pure" blacks, indians, and whites, often seen as being absorbed into a steadily lightening mestizo majority (Friedemann 1984; Stutzman 1981; Wade 1991, 1993; Whitten 1974, 1985). The exclusive nature of this ideology was, of course, one target of black (and indigenous) social movements, but juxtaposing reifications of North American or African "black nations" with the official Colombian "mestizo nation" was liable to tip in favor of reaffirmations of Colombian nationhood; and any mention of black separatism—then as now—immediately drew accusations of "racism in reverse" not only from those who did not identify as blacks, but from many of those who did.

Out of this dilemma came the development of the ideology of cimarronismo by the organization Cimarrón. Cimarrón in Spanish literally means "feral" and is typically applied to something domesticated, like cattle, that has "run wild." In colonial times it was applied to runaway slaves or maroons (Price 1979:1). All over the Caribbean and Latin America, runaway slaves established fortified villages (called palenques in Colombia); in North America, where control over slave runaways was greater, however, these communities had a lesser presence—perhaps their presence was less notable in the historiographical literature than in reality.[7] The perception that palenques played a greater historical role outside North America meant that they were more easily taken as symbols of Latin American experience.

Cimarronismo[8] took the cimarrón and the palenque as symbols of resistance to oppression and the continuity of African traditions, since palenques were relatively insulated from Hispanic society. Palenques are famed for their resistance, generally because they crop up in colonial records when the authorities mounted expeditions to crush them, and the martial overtones of cimarronismo harmonize nicely with African independence struggles and with the militancy of the North American and Caribbean black power movements—a clenched black fist is one of the images Cimarrón uses in its publications. Palenques tended to form in certain areas, and there are indications that links existed between them, so the image is more of a network of communities than of a nation. Indeed, cimarron-ismo goes further than this with the Cimarrón slogan, "Let us make of every com-munity an organized palenque and of every black person a cimarrón": it is a net-work of individuals as well as of communities.

The symbols associated with maroons were not confined to Colombia: it had international connotations. In Jamaica, an organization called Abeng (from *abeng*, the cowhorn bugle used by 18th-century maroon warriors) was formed in 1969 in the heat of the Black Power movement there (Nettleford 1970:131; Waters 1985:95); in Brazil, from the late seventies Quilombismo drew on the image of the *quilombo*, or Brazilian maroon community (Nascimento 1980); and in Haiti in 1968, Duvalier had erected a monument to the *marron inconnu* (Nicholls 1979:229). In Colombia, however, the image of the palenque was all the more powerful because of Palenque de San Basilio, a village near Cartagena where the black descendants of a historically identifiable maroon community still live, speak a unique creole language, and remember their ancestors (Friedemann 1979; Friedemann and Patiño Rosselli 1983).

Cimarronismo constructs a history of Colombian palenques that is somewhat at odds with that decipherable from historical sources. These sources suggest that palenques were a richly varied set of communities. Some had trade relations with nearby haciendas, some requested priestly visits for religious purposes, some ne-gotiated their own freedom with the colonial authorities. Occasionally, the term *palenque* was applied to very heterogeneous communities outside Spanish con-trol: these included people identified by contemporary observers as indians and mestizos. In general, maroons did not fight for the abolition of slavery as such. Their struggle was ultimately waged in pursuit of their own freedom. But organi-zations such as Cimarrón represent a tradition of *cimarronaje*, in which all the palenques were crucibles of cultural resistance and a struggle for human rights. Although the cimarrones were not numerous compared to the slave population, the ideology of cimarronismo invokes a "community of suffering" (Werbner 1991:26), which invites people to connect certain aspects of their pheno-type (their physical "blackness") to a history of oppression that is initially national but also continental and even global. This is what James Carrier (1992:198) calls a process of "ethno-Orientalism," that is, an essentialist construction by blacks of their own history and society. It is worth noting here that ethno-Orientalism is not necessarily a collective process. Not all Colombians who call themselves blacks identify with cimarronismo: to many it still smacks of separatism and op-poses their vision of a future characterized by increasing integration and homo-

geneity; they subscribe to the widespread notion that the mixing process—understood in this view as the dissolution of all distinctions—is a democratizing process. This raises the issue of "authenticity" and "invention" to which I have already
alluded.

### Recent Developments in Black Organization

During the 1980s, a rather different current of organization began to develop,
accelerating rapidly around 1990 and still strong today. The representations of
blackness involved, although overlapping with the previous ones, have been influenced by indígena and state agendas. The effect of such influences reflects the
complex dialectics at work in these cultural politics that go beyond the simple oppositions between colonizer and colonized. To understand these developments,
two areas of background need to be sketched in.

THE PACIFIC: A "NEW DIMENSION" FOR COLOMBIA

Especially since the mid-1980s, the Colombian government has taken mea-
sures to increase linkages to the global economy. The Pacific coastal region,
mostly abandoned by the state since the abolition of slavery in 1851, has assumed
a new importance in this context. This region has been consistently exploited for
natural resources such as gold, platinum, and timber. Most of these resources
were ultimately controlled by foreign multinationals or by entrepreneurs from
the interior of the country, often via networks of debt-credit relationships: these
people would generally identify, and be identified by locals, as mestizos or whites.
At the same time, large areas of the region had been declared a national reserve
in a 1959 decree and the ownership of land is still largely unregulated (Wade
1993; West 1957; Whitten 1974; Whitten and Friedemann 1974).

Geopolitical dominance is reportedly shifting from the Atlantic to the Pacific,
and Colombia wants to take full advantage of the change. Grandiose development plans for the Pacific region have been presented; these fundamentally consist of infrastructural projects: roads, ports, pipelines, railways, electricity grids,
and an interoceanic canal.[9]

Existing forms of natural resource exploitation intensified during the 1980s,
and this affected relations between blacks and indigenous people in the region.
Since emancipation the former have steadily pushed the latter into the headwa-
ters of the region's myriad rivers: relations have not been openly hostile, but neither have they been free from tension. Each group maintains fairly definite ethnic boundaries. In the Chocó province in Colombia's northern region, for
example, blacks may refer to themselves as *libres* (free people), as *morenos* (brown
people), or as *gente negra* (black people). All these are categories that are for
blacks conceptually and referentially clearly distinguished from *cholo* or *indio*,
their common terms for indigenous people. Relations between the two groups

are mediated by occasional intermarriage and by relations of exchange and *compadrazgo* (godparenthood). The blacks are more closely tied to the cash economy, via gold mining and timber extraction, and to the local bureaucracy; they often act as a channel through which indigenous peoples may gain access to these spheres. In turn, indigenous people may loan the blacks land, sell them agricultural products, and provide them with traditional medical treatments (Córdoba 1983; Whitten 1974). As exploitation of natural resources intensified, those black people connected to the cash economy and seeking timber and gold began to encroach on lands that had previously been rather insulated from market forces. This created ethnic conflict with indigenous people. In a few areas, houses and canoes were burned.

The church was an important mediator in this conflict. Its Indigenous Pastoral Program had been instrumental in setting up organizations lobbying for the land rights of indígenas, notable among them OREWA, the Regional Organization of Emberás and Waunanas, formed in 1986 in the Chocó province of the northern Pacific region. It had also set up peasant organizations. While the names of these organizations—for example, ACIA, the Integral Peasant Association of the Atrato River, formed in 1984—included no overt references to blackness, they were set up by the church's Afro-American Pastoral Program to help "Afro-American" peasants organize in the face of rapid change and colonization. OREWA organized meetings in order to defuse the ethnic conflicts: in 1989 the First Meeting for the Unity and Defence of Indigenous and Black Communities took place and a joint organization, ACADESAN, the Peasant Association of the San Juan River, was born.

This alliance between blacks and indigenous people has been tenuous but significant. "Indians" have a rather different place than do blacks in the social order of Colombia. While Colombia is officially a mestizo nation, indígenas have always had a particular—though by no means privileged—institutional and intellectual place, as exemplified in an 1890 law that defined them as minors to be "protected" and ratified separate *resguardos* (reserves) and local *cabildos* (councils) for them. Equally, indigenous history and ethnography are the focus of state institutions such as the Gold Museum and the Colombian Institute of Anthropology. The possibility of state recognition of the separateness of indígenas has therefore been greater than for blacks, who have never had this kind of status (Wade 1993:29–37). Modern indigenous political organization began earlier and, crucially, has better financing and advisory backup from national and international sources (Findji 1992; Gros 1991). As I will explain in greater detail, this discrepancy has prompted some Pacific coast black leaders to associate themselves politically with indígenas in an implicit effort to create an "indian-like" identity in the eyes of the state.

In sum, the intensification of development processes in the Pacific region created local protest and also engendered a tenuous but significant alliance between people organizing as indígenas and as blacks.

POLITICAL REFORM

Colombia's political system has been characterized by two-party rule since independence. Other parties have mounted transient electoral challenges to this arrangement, but guerrilla groups, formed from about the mid-sixties onwards, were the main threat throughout the seventies and into the eighties (Bushnell 1993; Pearce 1990).

In the early eighties, beginning with the government of Belisario Betancur, the state began a series of attempts to demobilize guerrilla movements and incorporate them into traditional politics. To date—and despite murderous repression of nonviolent left-wing organizations by paramilitary and, reportedly, government forces—several guerrilla movements have in fact demobilized; the best known was M-19, which became a political party in March 1990. One of the concessions that the government offered to guerrilla movements to facilitate the "peace process" was constitutional reform: the Constitution, in force since 1886, was rigid and restricted institutional change despite various reforms during the 20th century.

This process of political reform was not aimed overtly at what the state might have called ethnic minorities. On the contrary, in the negotiations that had taken place between the government and M-19 before the latter's demobilization, "there was no debate at all about the rights and territories of ethnic groups" (Arocha 1989b:14). Similarly, the government's National Rehabilitation Plan, another measure aimed at alleviating poverty and reducing violence, did not "propose solutions to violence [directed] against ethnic minorities" (Arocha 1989a:36). These initiatives did not include people classed as indígenas, much less people labeled as blacks. Some of the violent insurgence against the state, however, had been carried out by organizations such as the Quintín Lamé guerrilla movement, which took the name of a famous early 20th-century Paéz rebel and represented itself as an indigenous movement: indígenas thus had political leverage vis-à-vis the state (Findji 1992; Gros 1991; Pearce 1990). More generally, frontier colonization in Colombia has tended to encroach on blacks' and indigenous peoples' land. Issues of violence, the development of peripheral areas of the national territory, and the growth of ethnic protest were linked, pressuring the state to consider concessions to minority populations, and perhaps thus facilitate frontier development by defining some of the sources of conflict in those areas. In short, the process of constitutional reform created a vital forum for issues of ethnicity and nationality (Arocha 1989b; Findji 1992).

*The Process of Constitutional Reform*

The process of reform consisted of the deliberations of a Constituent Assembly, elected in December 1990. In the pre-assembly phase, groups such as Cimarrón lobbied those commissions coordinating preliminary discussions. New groups also emerged. The First Meeting of Black Communities was held in July 1990, and from this was born the so-called Coordinator of Black Communities. More peasant organizations were set up in the Pacific region. Members of Cimarrón were involved in these organizations and in the Coordinator.

A document was produced by the Subcommission on Equality and Multiethnic Character in response to lobbying by black spokespeople and by academics who had studied *los negros* in Colombia and spoken up for their rights (e.g., Nina de Friedemann and Jaime Arocha). The document talked about "indigenous peoples, blacks and other ethnic groups" and made proposals for their rights to be protected by the new constitution. This document dispensed with the common academic and official practice of limiting the term "ethnic group" to people classed as indígenas.

During this preliminary phase, a number of black candidates for election to the Constituent specifically mentioned blackness or the Pacific region as part of their platform. Several candidates aligned themselves with traditional Liberal party politics. On the other hand, Carlos Rosero, an anthropology student from the Pacific region, represented the Coordinator; another candidate, Juan de Dios Mosquera, a mainstay of Cimarrón, occupied a lowly place on an alliance ticket formed around candidates of the Patriotic Union party, the legal political wing of FARC, the Colombian Revolutionary Armed Forces guerrilla movement.

Not one of these delegates was elected: funding was insufficient, and the vote for a black platform was divided among the candidates. Underlying these factors was the weak politicization of the issue of blackness in general. Two indigenous delegates were elected, and one of these, Francisco Rojas Birry, an Emberá from the Chocó, had campaigned from a platform that addressed both indigenous peoples and blacks in the Pacific region who, he said, faced common problems of colonization, land loss, and environmental degradation. Many people from the Pacific region voted for him because his platform was regional rather than "racial" in orientation and because the greater solidity of indigenous organizations made his candidacy a safer bet. Lorenzo Muelas, the other indigenous delegate and a Guambiano from the Cauca region, had been a signatory to the subcommission document that had broadened the definition of "ethnic groups" to include blacks. Both delegates had several black advisers, two of them members of Cimarrón.

During the deliberations of the Constituent Assembly, the weakness of the ethnic alliance between people organizing around indianness and around blackness became obvious as the subcommission document was ignored: Lorenzo Muelas denied all knowledge of it, and then produced another document with an M-19 delegate, Orlando Fals Borda, which did not mention "blacks" at all and restricted its proposals to "indigenous peoples" (*pueblos indígenas*) and "ethnic groups," without defining the latter term.[10] The general tone of the assembly denied that people labeled as "blacks" had any status as an ethnic group. Other delegates asked how many ethnic groups there were among the blacks, a question based on notions of ethnicity drawn from the history of politicization of indianness—and one that Muelas or Rojas would have easily answered in that context. The head of the Colombian Institute of Anthropology declared that *los negros* were not an ethnic group but were peasants and proletarians.

The new Constitution, ratified on July 5, 1991, contained clauses recognizing the "multiethnic and pluricultural" character of the nation, which theoretically helped the cause of people seeking to push blackness into the political arena (Article 7). "Indigenous communities" won concrete prizes, such as the right to elect two senators to Congress (Article 171). One concession, however, was made to "black communities." This was Transitory Article 55, requiring the promulgation of a law (subject to study by a government-created special commission) that "in accordance with their traditional production practices, and in areas to be demarcated by the same law, recognizes collective property rights for black communities which have been occupying *tierras baldías* [public or state lands] in the rural riverine zones of the rivers of the Pacific Basin." The law had also to establish "mechanisms for the protection of the cultural identity and rights of these communities, and for the promotion of their economic and social development." The law also specified that its provisions might apply to other regions of the country which "presented similar conditions," without clarifying how this could transpire (see Presidencia de la República, 1991:162–163). The article dictated that Congress had to pass the law by July 5, 1993.

### After the New Constitution

Not surprisingly, following the ratification of the new constitution, political organization in the Pacific region intensified: the main aims were to publicize the article and to get representatives from the region's black communities onto the Special Commission formed to draft the requisite law. Although some of the individual blacks involved were not from the Pacific region, community organization was centered there. The church, Cimarrón, and the old Coordinator (now renamed the Organization of Black Communities) were all active in the process, and government development organizations also became marginally involved as community organizations that took an interest in the article sprang from their development programs. In this efflorescence of association, land rights were the main focus of attention but a cultural and ethnic dimension generally also appeared. Some of the priests involved were local members of Cimarrón. The community-based didactic workshops arranged for peasant associations by Cimarrón, the church, the Organization of Black Communities, and even the government development corporations, devoted some time and resources to the history of Africans and their descendants in Colombia, showing videos with titles such as "The African Presence in Colombia" or playing recordings of songs called "Roots" or "Black Claims."

Throughout this phase, organizers presented the past suffering and resistance of black people as part of the reason why black people should organize to pro- mote new claims to land rights and recognition of cultural specificity. One of the central tenets of groups such as Cimarrón and Smith-Córdoba's organization— and of more academic supporters of black mobilization (e.g., Friedemann 1984)—is that blacks have given but have not received: they have suffered the injustices of slavery and have helped build the nation by contributing to its cul- ture and material fabric, but have been objects of discrimination or—at best— have simply been ignored. The issue of ownership follows naturally from this ob- servation of inequity: blacks have a right to a part of their nation by virtue of their historic labor and suffering, but in the Pacific region they rarely own legal title to the land they have been working since before abolition (cf. Williams 1991).

Detailed work remains to be done on the construction of local collective iden- tities, but it is clear that recent initiatives often fall on fertile ground. Around Tumaco, in the southern Pacific region, land conflicts have been violent at times as capitalist shrimp-farmers destroy mangrove swamps and let saltwater waste run onto peasants' farmland in their attempts to cash in on a booming interna- tional market. Since the shrimp-farmers are mostly whites and mestizos from out- side the region, while local peasants are blacks, the notion of fighting for rights for black communities harmonizes easily with local experiences. I interviewed women who had started small production cooperatives in the same area with the support (advice and funding) of governmental agencies and nongovernmental agencies. Training programs (*capacitación*) involving these women include work- shops on women's rights and on black identity and history; through workshops they form links with many other women's groups in the region. Notions of black identity thus intertwine with everyday economic activity, local and regional social relations, and gender issues.

On the official front, after some heel dragging the Ministry of Government issued a decree on April 1, 1992, that defined the Special Commission's mem- bership. It listed a host of community organizations that would be allowed to elect 12 delegates to the commission. Other delegates named were the vice-minister of government, officials from various government institutions (land reform agency, natural resources institute, geographical institute, and so on), plus a handful of party politicians and academics.

The progress of the commission was uneven and involved some confrontation. By the beginning of November 1992, black organization delegates signed a docu- ment refusing to assist at further meetings until they considered that the govern- ment had fulfilled its obligations as stated in the new Constitution and fully guar- anteed the real participation of their communities. Negotiations resumed, and a bill agreed upon by both black delegates and the government was finally rati- fied by the president as Law 70 on August 27, 1993 (see Ministerio de Gobierno 1993). The law recognizes black communities as an ethnic group (although only in one sentence) and focuses on defining the titling of collective land rights

to whole black communities on the specified rivers of the area defined as the
"Pacific basin." The law also nominally covers other zones of the country where
black communities occupy rural riverine public lands. The uncomfortable balance between regional specificity and national coverage is obvious: the law applies to all black communities living in specified conditions, but the emphasis on
the Pacific zone reveals the primary focus. In terms of content, the law first awards
landholding rights to black communities but then excludes community control
over natural resources, subsoils, National Park areas, zones of military importance, and urban areas; it prescribes the ecologically sustainable use of resources
by the communities (although resource use by others is not directly mentioned
in this respect). Second, the law contains articles designed to improve education,
training, access to credit, and material conditions for black communities: black
community participation in these spheres is ensured via proposed black representatives on the National Planning Council, regional planning corporations, and a
Consultative Commission to be created for the purpose of following the progress
of the law; the Ministry of Government will also create a division for black community affairs. Discrimination against black communities is outlawed, and cultural specificity was ruled a requisite component in education for black people.
Finally, the law establishes a special constituency to elect two representatives to
Congress from the black communities.

The image of black society and culture exemplified in Transitory Article 55
and its consequent law is modeled on the indígena experience of political negotiation with the state.[11] Neither the article nor the law claim to represent something called black culture: they principally specify land rights for certain communities, giving limited material benefits to people whom most would identify as
black; although they mention national coverage, this is equivocal and "ethnic
group" is defined in terms of black communities living in specified legal and economic conditions. But since the article and Law 70 are to this day the only official
statements that mention "black communities" explicitly, and since they have become the focus of political organization around blackness, it is necessary to examine how they implicitly reify an image of "black culture."

As it is represented by Law 70, black culture has a number of representative
elements (Article 2): (1) the black community, defined as a "collection of families
of Afro-Colombian descent which possess their own culture, share a history and
have their own traditions and customs" that "reveal and conserve consciousness
of identity that distinguish them from other ethnic groups" (the grammar of the
clause, reproduced here, is full of confusions); (2) communally occupied land,
defined as "ancestral and historic settlement"; (3) traditional production practices, or specified activities used "customarily"; and (4) the Pacific region itself.
Blacks in the region are also given official status as invaders occupying *tierras
baldías*, public lands. Cultural identity is located as secondary and derivative of
elements relating to geography and economics.

This representation of black culture mirrors in many ways an image of the constituent elements of native American society in Colombia: the established indígena community, communally held land, and production practices dating from time immemorial. The emphasis is strongly on historical rootedness, and black communities as defined in the law are officially charged with the protection of the environment, just as indigenous peoples are seen, and claim themselves, to be the guardians of the land. As with the politicization around indianness, the central feature is land rights, and it is no coincidence that in the Constituent Assembly, whatever the weaknesses of the indígena-black alliance, it was an Emberá and a Guambiano who were partly responsible for lobbying for rights for people from the Pacific coast. The critical differences were the inclusion of a regional focus and the institutionalization of the blacks as invaders, in contrast to indigenous peoples who have always had *original* land rights.

As with cimarronismo, the representation of blackness is guided by a specific political agenda and is partial. The locals' production practices are notoriously varied, spatially extensive, and nearly always include logging or mining in ways shaped by the changing cash economy. To specify "traditional" production practices in this case is difficult and became a point of contention between government advisers and black delegates. Commerce, for example, was not included as a "traditional" practice, despite delegates' arguments. Again, rootedness is a difficult point given that people are highly mobile in this region (Wade 1993; Whitten 1974). More to the point, of course, the image of black culture portrayed tends to exclude all black people who live outside the Pacific region: those who live in the Atlantic region or in the Cauca valley—not to mention the growing number living in cities in the interior of the country—have entirely different settlement and production patterns. Whereas cimarronismo invokes a national or even international community of blacks who share a history of suffering, the article addresses "black communities" with a common regional history of settlement and production and, more implicitly, of recent threats from exploitative colonization.

This official representation of blackness in Colombia has emerged through a complex set of relationships. Organizations push for recognition of their claims about blackness from the state, in ways often mediated by the church and other institutions, and largely following models of ethnicity set up by organizations that talk about indígenas and their history of relations with the state. State officials at many levels are interested in developing the peripheral areas where blacks and indigenous peoples live, creating an image of ecological responsibility (which it partially devolves to indígena and black guardians), and legitimating state power as democratic. All these state interests can be furthered by concessions made to blacks and indigenous peoples, and won, in part, through protest and resistance. For blacks, therefore, specific institutions within the state open a concessionary space that these institutions also try to control, using a preexisting indígena model, limiting the issue to regional land rights, and restricting the definition of "ethnic group" to a specific type of black community. Werbner (1991:15–17) out-

lines a scheme in which political organization proceeds from a growing network of affiliation, reaches an ideological convergence in which common goals
and interests are defined vis-à-vis the state, and may then become a public protest movement. In a sense, organization around blackness in Colombia has already reached the second stage while the first stage is still nascent. This has
occurred because, as Werbner rightly stresses, the process of politicization is in-
herently a dialectic, with the state generally constituting the main interlocutor
and controller.[12]

In the new "multicultural and pluriethnic" nation there is still reason to think
of Columbia as a mestizo nation with black and indigenous adjuncts located on
special reserves (usually in peripheral areas). Indígenas have long occupied this
position, and *some* blacks have now officially been incorporated into this model.
Of course, this was not a simple imposition by the state: black community organizations, including many Cimarrón members, were instrumental in the negotiations, and the notion of community fits well with that of palenque. Nevertheless,
some blacks in the Cauca valley region, for example, expressed little interest in
the article since private ownership of land has been "traditional" there (Taussig
1980). Not all black communities agreed on this representation of blackness.[13]

Blacks are no longer as "invisible" as they once were (Friedemann 1984); the
"smooth maintenance" of racial inequality has been disrupted (Hasenbalg 1979;
Winant 1992); and while blackness has not entered mainstream politics in the
same way as in Jamaica, Guyana, or Haiti, it has entered the political arena, albeit
in a marginal position. Centuries of race mixture do not, then, necessarily para-
lyze ethnic mobilization by blurring the boundaries of a potential membership.
As I mentioned in my introduction, some scholars have emphasized the structural ambiguities undermining black politicization: no one can agree on who is
and is not "black," therefore it is impossible to mobilize a well-defined mass (see
note 4).

In contrast, I argue that we must shift the focus to the "political economy"
(Fontaine 1980, 1985) of cultural struggle. The emphasis is not now on the apparently simple structural "fact" of ambiguous collective identities, but on the
political contexts in which identifications are made. The relationship of indigenous peoples and blacks to the state in Colombia has been very different from
the conquest on: indigenous identity was institutionalized, black identity was not.
It is this—more than the simple existence of race mixture—that has defined the
possibilities of black and indigenous mobilization. These possibilities can change
as people's identifications alter in new political contexts, and Colombian blacks
now occupy an institutional place of sorts—a place partly won, partly conceded.
The political economic context in this case includes the increasing colonization
of frontier zones where blacks and indigenous peoples live, the state's interest in
the Pacific as a geopolitical focus, and the need for an official image of ecological
sensitivity to secure international development loans. It also includes ethnic mi-

nority mobilizations continentwide that set the tone for new definitions of demo-cratic nations. Blacks and indigenous peoples directly affected by all these de-velopments have mobilized in protest at land loss, environmental degradation, and discrimination. In response to such protests, the state is prepared to engage in redefinitions of nationhood and to open up spaces for ethnic minorities. The state is also, however, attempting to control ethnic minorities and indeed to chan-nel them in directions that serve specific interests. A struggle over cultural poli-tics ensues, and the result is increased black mobilization and the promulga-tion of Law 70. It is interesting to note, however, that Amir Smith-Córdoba, with his tactic of calling out *"¡Hola, negro!"* to people on the street, today encounters fewer hostile reactions than ten years ago.

While black mobilization can proceed in a context of structural ambiguity about who is "black," it seems to depend on representations of identity that tend to reify "blackness." To use Taussig's words in a different context, mobilization then becomes one of those things that "take on a life of their own, sundered from the social nexus that really gives them life, and remain locked in their own self-constitution" (1992:88).

One of the tasks of anthropological analysis is to show these constitutive proc-esses at work, not as an end in itself, but because by their very nature these proc-esses hide the basis of their construction and because they may exclude certain categories of people and even perpetuate essentialist notions of race. This decon-struction of cultural "inventions" may also undermine ethnic mobilizations that, as anthropologists, we support on the basis of equality and human rights. Some anthropologists tackle this dilemma by emphasizing that inventions are not in-valid. Jackson (1995) encourages anthropologists to reject value judgments about culture as either genuine or spurious, and Clifford (1988:336–343) resists an em-phasis on cultural wholeness and historical continuity in assessing whether iden-tities are "valid." Neither author really addresses people's possibly hostile reac-tions to anthropologists' deconstructions of their traditions any more than does Hall (1992:24) with his view of the "production" and the simple recovery of iden-tity as equally valid. Hanson (1989) emphasizes that all culture is invented so deconstruction need not invalidate. This argument did not prevent antagonism from some Maori people whose "inventions" were the subject of his analysis. Later, he contended that "invention" was a "systematically misleading" term (Hanson 1991:450). Linnekin advocates applying the "thesis of cultural inven-tion to Western discourse" (1991:448), and Gable et al. emphasize that "main-stream traditions are equally invented" (1992:802). The latter suggestions are especially valuable for the Colombian case, where there are two competing rep-resentations of blackness, one more state-sponsored or mainstream than the other. If I deconstruct the minority construction of blackness as continuous resis-tance, then I am bound to unveil the state-directed alternative of blackness as a regional rooted-in-community phenomenon. Rather than just reveal the fact of "invention"—which, as Hanson notes, is ubiquitous—the point is to uncover the political agenda and the political consequences of each construction: why and how it has emerged, whom it empowers, and whom it excludes.

This emphasis on political context is helpful in another way, because some of the efficacy of these constructions seems to lie precisely in their tendency to essentialize and even naturalize, excluding certain sectors of the black population and, in the case of cimarronismo, implying that "if you're black, your real nature is to resist." If I can reveal the construction of "blackness" as a *properly political process*, rather than something determined by the geographical concentration of blacks in the Pacific region (as in Law 70) or by the supposedly resistant nature of a reified construct called black culture (as in cimarronismo), then there is the possibility of destabilizing essentializations without losing the political force of mobilizations. People can find the motive force of their actions in their politics rather than in their or others' natures or in reified histories. Ideas about essences and ancestral history are bound to be important in ethnic mobilizations and challenges to mobilizations, but the significance attached to them may be lessened by an emphasis on the objective at which people are *aiming* rather than the place from which they *have come*.[14] This approach is as liable to find favor with the people mobilizing—as with anthropologists who, although loath to accept essentializations, support human rights and cultural autonomy.

This is all the more important when representations are connected to ideas about "race." To accept the identification between phenotype and history that cimarronismo makes runs the risk of colluding in the tendency of this ideology to essentialize blackness with its easy connection between an unproblematic physical appearance called "black" and a continuous history of resistance. As an anthropologist I may support cimarronismo's demands for cultural autonomy and a shift in Colombia's mestizo image that favors the reaffirmation of difference. As an antidote to the essentialization of blackness I can contribute an understanding of the complex political context in which affirmations of difference are made. For example, I can emphasize how the change in a person's self-identification from "mulatto" to "black" is not a recuperation of a "natural" identity, a return to the fold, but is instead a result of changing social contexts, a choice made in the light of perceived common interests with other people making similar identifications. The problem here is that the deconstruction of racial identifications may be seen as part of a "postmodern critique of the 'subject' [that surfaces] at a historical moment when many subjugated people feel themselves coming to voice for the first time" (hooks 1991:28) and may thus be thought to silence this voice. This is a real dilemma, but I think it is possible to resist essentialist notions of an authentic black identity by showing the political contexts in which people choose, or are forced, to identify as black in different and varied ways. Not only can we articulate, we can also actively empower the basis on which people have formed collective identities by emphasizing how they have "actively constructed an elective community of belonging through a variety of practices" rather than expressing a "fully constituted, separate and distinct identity that was always already there" (Mercer 1992:33).

Supporting black mobilization in Colombia can take a variety of forms: destabilizing mainstream images of a mestizo nation, investigating and publicizing black history and ethnography, and participating in political negotiations. Nina de Friedemann and Jaime Arocha have been active in all these fields, for example. It seems to me also useful to publicize the political conjunctures of identification as they occur so that blacks and non-blacks alike can see what is happening in Colombia as something that draws on the past. But far from being simply a recuperation of the past, a liberated expression of something present but repressed, these changes constitute something new, drawing on new political conjunctures; and these changes will be legitimated not so much by the past as by the future, not so much by what blackness was as by what it may become.

## Notes

Research on which this article is based was carried out during the summer of 1992 with a grant from the British Academy. This supplemented earlier research throughout the 1980s. Earlier versions of this article were given at the Centre of Latin American Studies, Cambridge, England, and the Department of Social Anthropology, Manchester. I am grateful to my colleagues there for their comments. Thanks are also due to the many people in Colombia who provided me with assistance and information during research. Thanks also to the anonymous readers of *American Ethnologist*.

1. I purposely do not capitalize "indian" in order to parallel my, and others', use of "black," since they seem to me to be categories of the same order: neither is a national grouping, and both are culturally constructed and varying over space and time.

2. The literature on race and nation includes, on Latin America: Graham 1990; Skidmore 1974; Stepan 1991; Stutzman 1981; Taussig 1987, 1992; Wade 1993; Whitten 1974, 1981, 1985; Whitten and Torres 1992; Winant 1992; and Wright 1990. For the Caribbean: Brown 1979; Craig 1982; Deosaran 1987; Heuman 1981; Kuper 1976; Lewis 1983; Márquez 1989; Nettleford 1970; Nicholls 1979, 1985; Palmer 1989; Ryan 1972; Waters 1985; and Williams 1991.

3. I will not detail here the literature on indigenous resistance, but useful guides to texts on black resistance include Beckles 1988, Heuman, ed. 1986, Price 1979, and Whitten and Torres 1992. See also, for example, Campbell 1988; Price 1983, 1990; and Taussig 1978, 1980.

4. Analyses of Brazil by Degler (1971), Hasenbalg (1979) Skidmore (1972), and Toplin (1971) suggested that black mobilization was unlikely. In contrast, see Andrews 1992, Burdick 1992, Fontaine 1985, and Winant 1992.

5. Early texts include Escalante 1964 and West 1957. Whitten has written extensively on the Pacific coast region (e.g., 1974), and Taussig on the Cauca valley region (e.g., 1980). Nina de Friedemann has been very prolific (for example, her review of 1984, and Friedemann and Arocha 1986). Wade 1993 also contains a full bibliography. Arocha 1992 and Arocha and Friedemann 1993 have information on recent political developments.

6. See, for example, Nicholls 1979 on négritude.
7. However, see Price 1979:420 on North American marronage. See note 3 for literature on slave resistance generally. For Colombia, see Borrego Pla 1973; Friedemann 1979; Friedemann and Patiño Rosselli 1983; Taussig 1978, 1980; and other references in Wade 1993:Ch.5.
8. The term *cimarronaje* is generally used to refer to the practice of slave flight (although see Jaramillo Uribe 1968); the term *cimarronismo* is used to refer to the modern ideology that takes the *cimarrón* as its icon (Mosquera 1985).
9. In 1989, the Presidency of the Republic published *The Pacific: a New Dimension for Colombia*, outlining a plan that has not yet received funding. Road construction continues apace regardless. In the more recent *Plan Pacífico*, published by the Departamento Nacional de Planeación (DNP) in 1992, over 40 percent of the projected budget goes to infrastructure: energy, roads, and telecommunications. This supplemented the previous *Plan de Desarrollo Integral para la Costa Pacífica*, published in 1983 by the DNP and a government regional development corporation, a plan that had operated unevenly until then (Wade 1993:144).
10. For the text of this document, see Fals Borda and Muelas 1992. For the text of the subcommission proposal mentioned earlier, see Jimeno 1992.
11. A telling sign is Article 37, which specifies that the state should use, where necessary, "the languages" of the black communities. Since Palenque de San Basilio is the only Colombian black community that has a non-Spanish language, the use of the plural here is highly suggestive of an "indian" agenda.
12. In fact, in its definition of the Special Commission the government included Pacific region community organizations (apparently named by church leaders and other black organizations) that did not yet exist—"imagined communities" indeed!
13. Nevertheless, some of the black delegates on the Special Commission came from the Cauca valley and the Atlantic coast regions. There is perhaps an analogy with what Jackson (1991) observed in the Colombian Amazon, where lowland indians are having to represent themselves with images purveyed by highland indians who have more experience of political organization.
14. Of course this cuts both ways: we can challenge the racist link between essence and behavior, without thereby dismantling racists' hatred of blacks as a "different" group. This must be contested in moral and political terms.

## References

Anderson, Benedict
  1983    Imagined Communities: Reflections on the Origin and Spread of Nationalism. London: Verso.
Andrews, George Reid
  1992    Black Political Protest in São Paulo, 1888–1988. Journal of Latin American Studies 24:147–171.
Arocha, Jaime
  1989a    Democracia ilusoria: El plan nacional de rehabilitación entre minorías étnicas. (Illusory Democracy: The National Rehabilitation Plan and Ethnic Minorities.) Análisis Político 7:33–44.

1989b   Etnicidad, conflicto y nación posible. (Ethnicity, Conflict and a Possible
        Nation.) El Espectador, Magazín Dominical 329:14–21.
1992    Los negros y la nueva constitución colombiana de 1991. (Blacks and the
        New Colombian Constitution of 1991.) América Negra 3:39–54.
Arocha, Jaime, and Nina de Friedemann
1993    Marco de referencia histórica-cultural para la ley sobre los derechos étni-
        cos de la comunidades negras en Colombia. (Historical-Cultural Refer-
        ence Framework for the Law on Ethnic Rights for Black Communities in
        Colombia.) América Negra 5:155–172.

Beckles, Hilary
1988    Caribbean Anti-Slavery: The Self-Liberation Ethos of Enslaved Blacks.
        Journal of Caribbean History 22(1–2):1–19.

Borrego Pla, María del Carmen
1973    Palenques de negros en Cartagena de Indias a fines del siglo 17. (Palen-
        ques of Blacks in Cartagena de Indias at the End of the 17th Century.)
        Seville, Spain: Escuela de Estudios Hispanoamericanos.

Brown, Aggrey
1979    Color, Class, and Politics in Jamaica. New Brunswick, NJ: Transaction
        Books.

Burdick, John
1992    Brazil's Black Consciousness Movement. NACLA Report on the Americas
        25(4):23–27.

Bushnell, David
1993    The Making of Modern Colombia: A Nation in Spite of Itself. Berkeley:
        University of California Press.

Campbell, Mavis
1988    The Maroons of Jamaica, 1655–1796. Granby, MA: Bergin and Harvey.

Carrier, James
1992    Occidentalism: The World Turned Upside Down. American Ethnologist
        19:195–212.

Clifford, James
1988    Identity in Mashpee. In The Predicament of Culture: Twentieth-Century
        Ethnography, Literature, and Art. Pp. 277–348. Cambridge, MA: Harvard
        University Press.

Córdoba, Juan Tulio
1983    Etnicidad y estructura social en el Chocó. (Ethnicity and Social Structure
        in the Chocó.) Medellín, Colombia: Lealón.

Craig, Susan
1982    Background to the 1970 Confrontation in Trinidad and Tobago. In Con-
        temporary Caribbean Society: A Sociological Reader. Susan Craig, ed. Pp.
        385–423. St. Augustine, Trinidad, and Tobago: Susan Craig.

Degler, Carl
1971    Neither Black Nor White: Slavery and Race Relations in Brazil and the
        United States. New York: MacMillan.

330 THE ANDES

Deosaran, Ramesh
1987    Some Issues in Multiculturalism: The Case of Trinidad and Tobago in the
        Post-Colonial Era. Caribbean Quarterly 33(1–2):61–80.

Escalante, Aquiles
1964    El negro en Colombia. (The Black in Colombia.) Bogotá, Colombia:
        Facultad de Sociología, Universidad Nacional.

Fals Borda, Orlando, and Lorenzo Muelas
1992    Prospuesta de articulado. Título especial: De los pueblos indígenas y
        grupos étnicos. (Article Proposal: Special Title: Of Indigenous Settlements
        [or Nations] and Ethnic Groups.) América Negra 3:220–223.

Findji, María Teresa
1992    From Resistance to Social Movement: The Indigenous Authorities Move-
        ment in Colombia. In The Making of Social Movements in Latin Amer-
        ica: Identity, Strategy and Democracy. Arturo Escobar and Sonia Alvarez,
        eds. Pp. 112–133. Boulder, CO: Westview Press.

Fontaine, Pierre-Michel
1980    The Political Economy of Afro-Latin America. Latin American Research
        Review 15(2):111–141.
1981    Transnational Relations and Racial Mobilization: Emerging Black Move-
        ments in Brazil. In Ethnic Identities in a Transnational World. John F.
        Stack, ed. Pp. 141–162. Westport, CT: Greenwood Press.
1985    Blacks and the Search for Power in Brazil. In Race, Class, and Power in
        Brazil. Pierre-Michel Fontaine, ed. Pp. 56–72. Los Angeles: Center of Afro-
        American Studies, University of California.

Friedemann, Nina de
1979    Mangombe: Guerreros y ganaderos en Palenque. (Cattle: Warriors
        and Cattleherders in Palenque.) Bogotá, Colombia: Carlos Valencia
        Editores.
1984    Estudios de negros en la antropología colombiana. (Studies on Blacks in
        Colombian Anthropology.) In Un siglo de investigación social: Antro-
        pología en Colombia. (A Century of Social Investigation: Anthropology in
        Colombia.) Jaime Arocha and Nina de Friedemann, eds. Pp. 507–573.
        Bogotá, Colombia: Etno.

Friedemann, Nina de, and Jaime Arocha
1986    De sol a sol: Génesis, transformación y presencia de los negros en Colom-
        bia. (From Sunup to Sundown: The Genesis, Transformation and Pres-
        ence of Blacks in Colombia.) Bogotá, Colombia: Planeta.

Friedemann, Nina de, and Carlos Patiño Rosselli
1983    Lengua y sociedad en el Palenque de San Basilio. (Language and Society
        in Palenque de San Basilio.) Bogotá, Colombia: Instituto de Caro y
        Cuervo.

Gable, Eric, Richard Handler, and Anna Lawson
1992    On the Uses of Relativism: Fact, Conjecture, and Black and White Histo-
        ries at Colonial Williamsburg. American Ethnologist 19(4):791–805.

Gilroy, Paul
1987    "There Ain't no Black in the Union Jack": The Cultural Politics of Race and Nation. London: Hutchinson.

Graham, Richard, ed.
1990    The Idea of Race in Latin America, 1870–1940. Austin: University of Texas Press.

Gros, Christian
1991    Colombia indígena: Identidad cultural y cambio social. (Indigenous Colombia: Cultural Identity and Social Change.) Bogotá, Colombia: CEREC.

Hall, Stuart
1992    Identity and the Black Photographic Image. Ten.8 2(3):24–31. (Special Issue, Critical Decade: Black British Photography in the 80s).

Hanson, Allan
1989    The Making of the Maori: Culture Invention and Its Logic. American Anthropologist 91(4):890–902.

Hanson, F. Allan
1991    Reply to Langdon, Levine and Linnekin. American Anthropologist 93(2):449–450.

Hasenbalg, Carlos
1979    Discriminação e desigualdades raciais no Brasil. (Discrimination and Racial Inequalities in Brazil.) Rio de Janeiro: Graal.

Heuman, Gad
1981    Between Black and White: Race, Politics, and Free Coloreds in Jamaica, 1792–1865. Oxford: Clio Press.

Heuman, Gad, ed.
1986    Out of the House of Bondage: Runaways, Resistance, and Maronnage in Africa and the New World. London: Frank Cass.

hooks, bell
1991    Yearning: Race, Gender, and Cultural Politics. London: Turnaround.

Jackson, Jean
1991    Being and Becoming an Indian in the Vaupés. In Nation-States and Indians in Latin America. Greg Urban and Joel Sherzer, eds. Pp. 131–155. Austin: University of Texas Press.
1995    Culture, Genuine and Spurious: The Politics of Indianness in the Vaupés, Colombia. American Ethnologist 22:3–27.

Jaramillo Uribe, Jaime
1968    Ensayos sobre historia social colombiana, 1. La sociedad neogranadina. (Essays on Colombian Social History, 1. New Granadian Society.) Bogotá, Colombia: Universidad Nacional.

Jimeno, Myrian, ed.
1992    Propuesta general de la Subcomisión Igualdad y Carácter Multiétnico, de la Comisión Derechos Humanos. (General proposal of the Subcommis-

sion on Equality and Multiethnic Character, of the Commission on Human Rights.) América Negra 3:213–219.

Kuper, Adam
   1976     Changing Jamaica. London: Routledge and Kegan Paul.

Levine, Robert
   1980     Race and Ethnic Relations in Latin America and the Caribbean: An Historical Dictionary and Bibliography. Metuchen, NJ: Scarecrow Press.

Lewis, Gordon
   1983     Main Currents in Caribbean Thought: The Historical Evolution of Caribbean Society in Its Ideological Aspects. Baltimore, MD: Johns Hopkins University Press.

Linnekin, Joyce
   1991     Cultural Invention and the Dilemma of Authenticity. American Anthropologist 93:446–449.

Márquez, Roberto
   1989     Nationalism, Nation and Ideology: Trends in the Emergence of a Caribbean Literature. In The Modern Caribbean. Franklin Knight and Colin Palmer, eds. Pp. 293–340. Chapel Hill: University of North Carolina Press.

Mercer, Kobena
   1992     Back to My Routes: A Postscript to the 1980s. Ten.8 2(3):32–39. (Special Issue, Critical Decade: Black British Photography in the 80s.)

Ministerio de Gobierno
   1993     Ley 70 del 27 de Agosto de 1993 por la cual se desarrolla el Artículo Transitorio Número 55 de la Constitución Política de Colombia de 1991. (Law 70 of the 27th of August of 1993 in which the Transitory Article Number 55 of the Political Constitution of Colombia of 1991 is developed.) Bogotá, Colombia: Ministerio de Gobierno.

Mörner, Magnus
   1967     Race Mixture in the History of Latin America. Boston: Little, Brown.

Mosquera, Juan de Dios
   1985     Las comunidades negras de Colombia. (Black Communities in Colombia.) Medellín, Colombia: Editorial Lealón.

Nascimento, Abdias do
   1980     O quilombismo. (Quilombism.) Petrópolis, Brazil: Editora Vozes.

Nettleford, Rex
   1970     Mirror, Mirror: Identity, Race and Protest in Jamaica. Kingston: William Collins and Sangster (Jamaica).

Nicholls, David
   1979     From Dessalines to Duvalier: Race, Color and National Independence in Haiti. Cambridge: Cambridge University Press.
   1985     Haiti in Caribbean Context: Ethnicity, Economy and Revolt. London: Macmillan and St. Anthony's College, Oxford.

Palmer, Colin
    1989    Identity, Race and Black Power in Independent Jamaica. *In* The Modern
            Caribbean. Franklin Knight and Colin Palmer, eds. Pp. 111–128. Chapel
            Hill: University of North Carolina Press.

Pearce, Jenny
    1990    Colombia: Inside the Labyrinth. London: Latin American Bureau.

Presidencia de la República
    1991    La Constitución Política de Colombia, 1991. (The Political Constitution
            of Colombia, 1991.) Bogotá: Presidencia de la República.

Price, Richard
    1979    Introduction and Afterword. *In* Maroon Societies: Rebel Slave Communi-
            ties in the Americas. Richard Price, ed. Pp. 1–30 and 417–431. Garden
            City, NY: Anchor Books.
    1983    First Time: The Historical Vision of an Afro-American People. Baltimore,
            MD: Johns Hopkins University Press.
    1990    Alabi's World. Baltimore, MD: Johns Hopkins University Press.

Ryan, Selwyn
    1972    Race and Nationalism in Trinidad and Tobago: A Study of Decolonization
            in a Multiracial Society. Toronto: University of Toronto Press.

Saunders, A. C. de C. M.
    1982    A Social History of Black Slaves and Freedmen in Portugal, 1441–1555.
            Cambridge: Cambridge University Press.

Sharp, William
    1976    Slavery on the Spanish Frontier: The Colombian Chocó, 1680–1810.
            Norman: University of Oklahoma Press.

Skidmore, Thomas
    1972    Toward a Comparative Analysis of Race Relations since Abolition in Brazil
            and the United States. Journal of Latin American Studies 4(1):1–28.
    1974    Black into White: Race and Nationality in Brazilian Thought. New York:
            Oxford University Press.

Stepan, Nancy Leys
    1991    "The Hour of Eugenics": Race, Gender, and Nation in Latin America.
            Ithaca, NY: Cornell University Press.

Stutzman, Ronald
    1981    El Mestizaje: An All-Inclusive Ideology of Exclusion. *In* Cultural Transfor-
            mations and Ethnicity in Modern Ecuador. Norman E. Whitten, ed. Pp.
            45–94. Urbana: University of Illinois Press.

Taussig, Michael
    1978    Destrucción y resistencia campesina: El caso del litoral pacífico. (Destruc-
            tion and Peasant Resistance: The Case of the Pacific Littoral.) Bogotá, Co-
            lombia: Punta de Lanza.
    1980    The Devil and Commodity Fetishism in South America. Chapel Hill: Uni-
            versity of North Carolina Press.

1987    Shamanism, Colonialism, and the Wild Man: A Study in Terror and Heal-
        ing. Chicago: University Press.
1992    The Nervous System. New York: Routledge.

Toplin, Robert Brent
1971    Reinterpreting Comparative Race Relations. Journal of Black Studies
        2(2):135–156.

Wade, Peter
1991    The Language of Race, Place, and Nation in Colombia. América Negra
        2:41–66.
1993    Blackness and Race Mixture: The Dynamics of Racial Identity in Colom-
        bia. Baltimore, MD: Johns Hopkins University Press.

Waters, Anita
1985    Race, Class, and Political Symbols: Rastafari and Reggae in Jamaican Poli-
        tics. New Brunswick, NJ: Transaction Books.

Werbner, Pnina
1991    Black and Ethnic Leaderhips in Britain: A Theoretical Overview. In Black
        and Ethnic Leaderships in Britain: The Cultural Dimensions of Political
        Action. Pnina Werbner and Muhammad Anwar, eds. Pp. 15–40. London:
        Routledge.

West, Robert C.
1957    The Pacific Lowlands of Colombia. Baton Rouge: Louisiana State Univer-
        sity Press.

Whitten, Norman E.
1974    Black Frontiersmen: A South American Case. New York: John Wiley and
        Sons.
1981    Introduction. In Cultural Transformations and Ethnicity in Modern Ecua-
        dor. Norman E. Whitten, ed. Pp. 1–41. Urbana: University of Illinois Press.
1985    Sicuanga Runa: The Other Side of Development in Amazonian Ecuador.
        Urbana: University of Illinois Press.

Whitten, Norman, and Nina de Friedemann
1974    La cultura negra del litoral ecuatoriano y colombiano: Un modelo de
        adaptación étnica. (Black Culture of the Ecuatorian and Colombian Litto-
        ral: A Model of Ethnic Adaptation.) Revista Colombiana de Antropología
        17:75–115.

Whitten, Norman, and Arlene Torres
1992    Blackness in the Americas. NACLA Report on the Americas 15(4):16–22.

Williams, Brackette
1991    Stains on My Name, War in My Veins: Guyana and the Politics of Cul-
        tural Struggle. Durham, NC: Duke University Press.

Winant, Howard
1992    Rethinking Race in Brazil. Journal of Latin American Studies 24:173–192.

Wright, Winthrop
1990    Café con Leche: Race, Class and National Image in Venezuela. Austin:
        University of Texas Press.

# 13. STRATIFICATION AND PLURALISM
# IN THE BOLIVIAN YUNGAS

## Madeline Barbara Léons

### Introduction

Bolivia is one of the few Latin American countries to have undergone a social revolution in the twentieth century.[1] The coming to power of the Movimiento Nacionalista Revolucionario (MNR) in 1952 was truly revolutionary in that it presaged major structural alterations in Bolivian life. Nationalization of the mines, sweeping land reform, universal education and suffrage, and political incorporation of the Indian (now called *campesino*) population through the organization of peasant syndicates have altered the structure of Bolivian society. Although the system of social stratification was not directly addressed in the legislative program of the MNR, it was obviously affected by the destruction of the economic base of the old landed aristocracy and the redistribution of political power within the state.

The primary purpose of this paper is to analyze the impact on the society of the province of Nor Yungas, Department of La Paz, of the social, political, and economic changes that followed in the wake of this revolution.[2] In this context regional patterns of stratification and pluralism will be examined, as well as the internal ranking within the rural communities. In this introductory section the usage of certain key concepts will be outlined. Although the body of the paper is addressed primarily to a specific region, it is believed that the conclusions will demonstrate the more general implications of the discussion.

Two analytic approaches must be combined in studying the social and cultural distinctions that are found within a complex society like that of Bolivia. Bolivian society is differentiated on the basis of social stratification; that is, on the ranking of individuals and identifiable sub-groups along hierarchically graded continua, based on criteria of occupation, class, status, and power (Mills, 1963:306). In a slowly changing society, as Bolivia was before 1952, the hierarchical rankings determined by these diverse criteria generally coincide with one another more

Originally appeared in Walter Goldschmidt and Harry Hoijer (eds.), *The Social Anthropology of Latin America* (Los Angeles: Latin American Center, University of California, 1970), pp. 256–82. Copyright © by The Regents of the University of California. Reprinted by permission of the UCLA Latin American Center.

closely than in a rapidly changing society. To the extent that these rankings do coincide, we may speak of social strata.

Social differentiation within many complex societies may be understood by reference to social stratification alone. In societies that are not culturally or racially homogeneous, social distinctions made on the basis of cultural or racial differences may also prove to be important. The analytic framework proposed to deal with this second type of social differentiation is that of pluralism. Pluralism has received considerable attention from students of Caribbean society (cf. Rubin, ed. 1960; M. G. Smith 1965). In studies of other Latin American societies, however, the term has rarely been utilized. Topics of the same order have been discussed under the headings of caste (cf. Tumin 1952) or of racial and cultural differences per se (cf. Wagley and Harris, 1958). The concept of pluralism is utilized here in order to enhance structural clarity.

Pluralism may be defined as the segmentation of the society into social groups that possess analogous, parallel, non-complementary and distinguishable sets of social institutions.[3] Social groups differentiated on this basis may be called *plural sections*. Plural sections are frequently, but not necessarily, culturally distinct from one another. Following Pierre van den Berghe (1967:9, 10), we shall refer to social groups that are socially defined on the basis of cultural criteria as *ethnic groups*. We speak of *ethnic pluralism* in reference to the type of plural society in which the sections are distinguished primarily on this basis. Ethnic pluralism is invariably simultaneously expressed in social pluralism, but the reverse is not always true. It is possible to have social pluralism in the absence of cultural distinctions.

Plural sections are frequently racially distinctive as well. Ethnic differences may or may not be associated with racial differences. When placement of individuals within the plural structure is made primarily on the basis of racial criteria, the situation is one of *racial pluralism*.

Social stratification and pluralism are not seen as independently varying dimensions, but as structurally interconnected; no plural society can be understood exclusively in terms of its plural character, but only in conjunction with the patterns of social stratification of that society. The plural structure is maintained over time through the capacity of those of the dominant section to block the participation or acculturation of others. This capacity is not inherent in the structure of pluralism itself, but rather must be referred to the dominant section's privileged position in the cross cutting system of social stratification and its consequent ability to manipulate rewards and sanctions (Léons 1967b).

### The Yungas

The Yungas are semi-tropical valleys cutting down from the cold, arid *altiplano* to the tropical eastern lowlands. Nor Yungas is one of two Yungas provinces in the Department of La Paz. Before 1952, Nor Yungas was an area of small haciendas worked according to the traditional *colono* system, by which the hacienda laborer is given usufruct rights for a stated number of days' labor per week in the fields of the *patrón* (owner) and the performance of other traditional services. In the program of land reform these estates were broken up. In general, the former hacienda *colonos* were given title to small holdings of variable size, while the former owners kept the land that had previously been cultivated directly for the hacienda (a small proportion of the total land of the estate) (Léons 1967a). In the wake of the revolution, the *colonos* of each community were organized into local peasant syndicates, and universal suffrage for all males and females over twenty-one, without literacy requirements, was instituted. Schools built in each community and staffed by a teacher appointed by the government created widespread educational opportunities where none had existed before.

Two "old towns" were established in Nor Yungas during the colonial period. These are Coripata and Coroico, the capital of the province.[4] Coca, the most important cash crop of Nor Yungas, is cultivated most intensively in the Coripata area; coffee is of relatively greater importance around Coroico. Citrus fruits are a supplementary cash crop in both areas.

The system of stratification and pluralism of the province does not differ significantly in broad outline from that of the country as a whole, and reflects the traditional supra-national stratification patterns common to the Andean countries, all of which have large identifiable Indian populations. In Bolivia, three major ethnic groups are recognized by the society at large and identified by the racial labels of *blanco* (white), *mestizo*, (mixed), and *indio* (Indian). These ethnic groups are hierarchically ranked in terms of prestige. The conceptualization and expression of this tripartite division in racial terms may have been justifiable at one time, but now the differences among all three categories are predominantly cultural rather than racial. Although blancos and mestizos are not culturally identical, mestizo culture is basically a modification of colonial and folk Spanish patterns, and mestizos identify with the dominant blanco minority. Blancos and mestizos thus make up a single Hispanic American plural section, though one that is subdivided on the basis of what has been termed "style of life."

The Hispanic American section is counterposed structurally to a subordinate Indian section. Since individual placement in one section or the other is made predominantly on the basis of cultural criteria rather than on outward physical characteristics alone, we have a system based on ethnic pluralism. Contemporary Indian culture represents a cultural blend of folk Hispanic and pre-Conquest elements that stabilized in the late colonial period. The Indian population of Bolivia is subdivided into two major linguistic groups, the Quechua and the Aymara. In Nor Yungas those of the Indian section are all Aymara.

In the Yungas of La Paz a third plural section is also evident, that of the Negroes who were originally brought into the area as slaves on certain estates. Bolivia has a small Negro population, but it is concentrated primarily in this area. The Indian and Negro sections of the Yungas are not hierarchically ranked in respect to one another but rather constitute coordinate parallel elements.

The entire range of national stratification based on class and political power can be viewed within the Hispanic American section. Those of the Indian section, however, are restricted to a narrow range at the bottom of that stratification system. Many poor mestizos are economically no better off than Indians and are equally denied access to political power. However, in terms of prestige, under the traditional system any member of the Hispanic American section is by definition superior to all Indians.

In traditional Bolivian society, socially stable since the Republican period, the stratification hierarchies based on economic, political, and status criteria all tended to reinforce one another and to be correlated with the plural distinction separating the Indian from the Hispanic American. The traditional expression of this system and the impact of the reforms recently initiated by the national government has not been precisely the same in the towns as in the surrounding rural areas; therefore, town and countryside will be examined separately.

### The Countryside: The Pre-Reform Hacienda

In the rural areas of the Yungas during the hacienda period, the most simplified version of the stratification system was institutionalized. The hierarchical grading of social, economic, and political prerogatives were all corollary to one another. Administrators and owners were members of the dominant Hispanic American section: mestizos typically were overseers, administrators, and craftsmen, while blancos owned the estates. The labor force of the haciendas, occupying the lowest position in the economic, political, and prestige continua of stratification, was divided among two racial groups: Indian and Negro.

With the abolition of slavery the Negroes, who had been brought in to form the work force on certain haciendas, were simply transmuted into *colonos* on these estates. Most Negroes live in all-Negro communities, but some have moved into predominantly Indian settlements. Although the Negroes speak Spanish as a first language and many do not even understand Aymara, they dress in Aymara style and share many aspects of Aymara culture. This includes not only technology and associated economic patterns but also Aymara folk religion. Negroes exhibit more group consciousness than do Indians.[5] Although ties of friendship and *compadrazgo* are maintained between Indians and Negroes, especially those living in mixed communities, intermarriage is infrequent. Elaborate intermarriage networks have grown up linking rather far-flung Negro enclaves.[6]

In a structural sense, the Indian and Negro sections are completely coordinate. Indians and Negroes consider themselves to be different from, but not better than, the other group. When, in this presentation, reference is made to the position of the Indian population, it should be understood to apply to the Negro minority as well.

Under the hacienda system the *colonos* were regarded as something akin to necessary and valuable beasts of burden. They were accorded no social value, were impotent politically, and were subservient to a legal system in the hands of those of the dominant section. All Indians owed unconditional respect, marked by deferential behavior, to all mestizos.

This system was not without advantages to the *colono*. The advantage of a stable social system is that it is predictable; the security provided was the security of paternalism. Ideally, the *patrón* looked out for the interests of his *colonos* if they got into trouble with outside authorities, disciplined and rewarded them like a father, gave consent to their weddings, and formalized the relationship by becoming *padrino* of their marriages and a *compadre* through baptizing their children. Owners of Yungas haciendas were often absentees, who lived in La Paz and visited their property perhaps once or twice a year. Under these conditions the role of paternalistic mentor of the community was filled by the mestizo *mayordomo*, and it was the *mayordomo*, not the *patrón*, who usually became linked to the *colonos* by bonds of ceremonial kinship. When the owner of the estate maintained permanent residence in one of the Yungas towns, his impact on the community was more immediate. Not surprisingly, the reciprocal obligations involved in ceremonial kinship were phrased in hierarchical and paternalistic terms rather than in equalitarian terms when contracted with a *patrón* or *mayordomo*.

Despite the fact that all the *colonos* occupied the same disadvantaged social position, they did have their own informal internal social organization and system of social ranking. Within the community, different individuals received differing ascriptions of social honor from their peers. The concept of an internal prestige system based on individual achievement of status position, which was originally formulated by Beals to apply to independent Indian communities (1953:333), is pertinent as well to the internal organization of the Yungas hacienda community.

A *colono* achieved prestige within the community through a combination of the seniority accompanying advancing age, approved moral qualities, and ceremonial expenditure for the community. The *ancianos* or elders were highly respected, if informally organized, and were influential in matters of traditional wisdom. But respect for age per se was always qualified by the reflection of the moral and economic evaluation achieved by a man in his mature years. Among the moral qualities which were valued in a man was his ability to get along with his neighbors, to live quietly and steadily with his wife, whether legally married or not, to support the children he conceived, and not to engage in flagrant sexual misconduct. The most crucial moral evaluation, however, was linked to community judgment concerning whether or not an individual was hardworking or lazy. An individual who was judged to be lazy, no matter how quietly he lived, could never aspire to high prestige. The accusation of laziness compounded any crime; likewise, if a man was a hard worker, he was excused from a multitude of sins.

Most Yungas haciendas contained more than adequate land reserves, and a *colono* could normally receive the right to work as much land for himself and his family as his time, ambition, and family resources permitted. *Colonos* on Yungas haciendas also employed temporary migrant labor from free communities of the *altiplano* to assist them on their usufruct lands. On many estates the *colono* was

even allowed to provide such a substitute to fulfill his work obligation to the hacienda. Since the right to work more than an understood minimum of land was
a privilege bestowed by the hacienda administration, the ambitious *colono* had to
remain on good terms with the *patrón* and *mayordomo*. The *colonos* often ingra-
tiated themselves by gifts of eggs and vegetables to the occupants of the hacienda
house.

As a result of these manipulations, the amount of land controlled by each
*colono* family was not the same and there was a considerable wealth differential
among *colonos* even under the hacienda system. The more hardworking *colonos*
controlled more land and were economically better off. Those *colonos* who controlled greater economic resources displayed some of this wealth in the form of
personal items of conspicuous display, such as fiesta clothing, but basic differences in standards of living among the *colonos* were not implied. Rather, as in
independent Indian communities throughout Latin America, wealth differences
were leveled by the sponsorship of fiestas requiring considerable expenditure of
cash reserves. In the long run, the wealthier *colonos* did not live much better than
the poorer ones, but acquired more social prestige through ceremonial expenditure.

In order to administer the hacienda, one or two *jilicatas* (depending on the size
of the estate) were chosen from the *colono* group to act as assistant overseers. The
*jilicatas* kept track of the work obligations of all the *colonos* and administered
punishment by whipping to those who were slack or remiss. *Jilicatas* were chosen
for terms of varying length by the *patrón* or *mayordomo*, usually from among the
mature men who enjoyed good standing in the internal prestige system of the
community. Because of their high status, they could best organize and secure
compliance from the workers. At the same time, these were the individuals who
had the most respect for the hacienda administration, since they were dependent
on its favor for the privilege of working additional land. *Jilicatas* notoriously identified with the interests of the *patrón*, and were often gratuitously zealous in their
policing duties.

### The Countryside: The Ex-Hacienda

Since the land reform, the residential community corresponding to the former
hacienda has been called, interchangeably, ex-hacienda or *estancia*. The criteria
for high standing within the internal prestige system of the ex-hacienda has survived almost intact the transition from hacienda community to post-reform peasant community, despite the fact that these criteria are now applied to a changed
social reality. Under the hacienda system, the ambitious man could usually receive permission to work an ever-expanding usufruct holding for himself. Thus
the hardworking man who was valued so highly in the moral system was in a
position, barring unforeseen misfortune such as illness, to better his economic
position and consequently his standing within the community. The land reform,

by granting the *colono* title to his own small-holding, solidified a previously flex-ible system of land tenure. Except on estates that had such an excess of land that each former *colono* received the largest small-holding permissible under the law, each ex-*colono* received title to the amount of land he had under cultivation at the time of the reform.[7] Inequalities in land holdings among the *colonos* were thus frozen and perpetuated. The *campesinos* consider this practice to be entirely just, but it poses a problem for the presently maturing generation who no longer have access to land simply on the basis of will to work.

The land reform destroyed the local hacienda-based social system of the com-munity on many estates. The *patrón* and *mayordomo*, representatives of the upper social strata and dominant plural section, were effectively eliminated from the scene as the hacienda became an *estancia* of independent peasant producers. The resulting organizational void was swiftly filled by the elected peasant syndi-cate, which replaced the hacienda administration as the agency of local govern-ment and justice. The syndicate, rather than a superordinate administration, now represents the articulating link between the community and the large society.

The Secretary General has become the most important official in the local community. Although he heads a roster of twelve or thirteen officials, only the Secretary General, and those few additional secretaries who have the political interest and personal capacity, are administratively active. The extent to which this practice is followed varies with the personal qualities of the Secretary Gen-eral.

The role of Secretary General is modeled after a combination of the roles of the administrator and the *jilicata*. Individuals who become Secretaries General are not chosen from the ranks of the *ancianos*; rather, they are usually chosen on the basis of those qualities previously associated with the *jilicata*, and many im-portant officers are ex-*jilicatas* or sons of *jilicatas*. Like the *jilicata*, the Secretary General oversees communal work projects and administers punishments. More importantly, like the administrator, he is responsible for the moral and economic welfare of the community, for representing the community to the larger society, and for maintaining internal peace by settling disputes.

Unlike the hacienda administrators, however, the Secretary General is not in a position to make dictatorial decisions that would bind the community to one course of action over another. Such decisions are made in a meeting of the en-tire syndicate that includes all the adult landholders in the community. A Secre-tary General may be in a position to influence an essentially democratic deci-sion making process, but he cannot compel a community against the will of a majority.

The organization of the peasant syndicates has not meant the emergence of a new superordinate class within the local community, except in a few instances. Political office rotates annually or biennially. Particularly in the smaller commu-nities, all mature men are eventually tapped to fill some office or another. Like-wise, for a man to be out of office generally means that he is out of power. Although the range of responsible positions in the community that are open to the *campesino* has increased, the offices are still subsumed within the context of the internal prestige system of the community. A Secretary General who is politically ambitious tends not to remain in that office, but goes on to positions in the regional syndicate organization, though under such circumstances he will continue to have informal influence within his home community.

Perhaps the most important innovation of the MNR reform program for accelerating culture change has been the introduction of rural schools, if only because they teach the children to speak Spanish. Before 1952, schools were not maintained on the haciendas. A few children of *colonos* did manage to attend school in the towns, but this practice was often actively discouraged by the hacienda owners. At the present time, almost all the children are learning Spanish, and a few have continued in secondary schools outside the community. Many of the younger men now often speak Spanish among themselves.

It is likely that in the future many of the more educated young people will go to the city, but education has also become a potentially significant differentiating factor among *campesinos* who remain in the countryside as well. There are positions opening up in the *estancias* and the *campesino* towns for which the ability to speak Spanish and a functional degree of literacy are required. Such positions include teachers, notaries, and recording secretaries in the syndicates. As a result, younger men are now holding positions solely on the basis of their literacy, whereas traditionally all comparable positions of authority were reserved for mature men.

The revolution has served to accelerate other culture changes among the Indian ex-*colono* of the countryside. Under the hacienda system acculturation to the patterns of the dominant group was not encouraged and often was directly punished. These barriers to acculturation have been lowered as well; sanctions have been toned down. A *campesino* who wears shoes to town or who goes to night school need no longer fear being beaten up by town youths.

Since the incorporation of Indians into the mainstream of Bolivian life has been one of the official goals of the Bolivian government since 1952, various agencies of the national government are explicitly encouraging *campesinos* to emerge from their cultural isolation. At the same time, the agrarian reform has given most *campesinos* the economic means of acquiring new items of mestizo culture. Men wear shoes on Sundays, buy transistor radios, and build mestizo-style town houses. The norms of mestizo life have become attainable models of aspiration for the *campesinos*, to an extent that was never before possible.

Acculturative changes are not affecting all aspects of culture equally. Items of material culture are readily accepted, but basic familial and religious institutions, as well as value orientations, are not being reformulated after mestizo models. Although Yungas *campesinos* are trying to improve their standard of living, they are not trying to make themselves into mestizos. In a real sense they take pride in being *campesinos* rather than mestizos, but they prefer to be prosperous *campesinos*. Given the means, they desire to emulate mestizo standards of consumption. Education is valued as a means of upward mobility.

In the Yungas this process of rapid culture change is not unconscious. Most people are clearly aware of the situation and considerable ambivalence of feeling is apparent. Among some, there is uneasiness about the *campesinos* trying to improve their social status above that which had been presented as pre-ordained under the hacienda system. Although it is becoming more common for *campesinos* to own trucks, one hears the typical comment that some people buy trucks in order to be *caballeros* (i.e., high status Hispanic Americans), but when they have accidents it is seen as a punishment from God. Thus, on the one hand, a *campesino* should not try to act like a *caballero*, on the other, current changes are hailed as part and parcel of the emancipation of the *colono*.

We have seen that while many of the outward trappings of culture are being replaced, a core of distinctive institutional elements assures the perpetuation of a distinctively Indian way of life for the time being. Nevertheless, significant changes have already occurred, not always along the lines premeditated by the *campesinos*. The work of Richard Adams in Central America suggests that modifications in material culture and language represent the flat level of chance toward more complete cultural assimilation, while changes in social organization occur at a later stage (1956:895). The cultural gap between the Indian section and the Hispanic American section has in fact narrowed, and there is every indication that it will continue to narrow in the future. One man told us, "Our children will speak good Spanish and become *caballeros*, but I will die before that time."

### The Countryside: The New Campesino Towns

One of the most tangible manifestations of the acculturation process in the countryside has been the formation and growth of *campesino* towns. This desire of peasants to become townsmen is a reflection of the degree of culture change in the countryside. The style of house and community plan of these new towns is clearly patterned after the mestizo model.

The settlement pattern of the Yungas hacienda was not nucleated. The houses of the *colonos* were located at considerable distances from each other, and were connected to each other and to the hacienda house by paths and trails. The houses were rarely within sight of one another. In order to sell their own products and buy products from outside the region, the *colonos* had to travel to one of the old towns.

After the land reform, the former *colono* had the right to move and to build a house where he would. The *colonos* expressed sentiment favoring nucleated settlement almost immediately, and they soon acted upon it. They built houses in town not only to take advantage of town services and social life, but also to enhance personal prestige. Most of the town houses are permanently occupied, though some are used only on Sundays and holidays, while the family continues to live in the country house close to the fields.

In Nor Yungas, several *campesino* towns have come into being since the land reform. The emergence of these towns has given *campesinos* services that are associated with the mestizo towns, combined with control by and for *campesinos*. Concomitant with the growth of these towns has been an increased social differentiation among the *campesinos*.

The largest of these new towns is Arapata. Arapata has always been the administrative seat of a *cantón*[8] and had maintained a small population of mestizo petty officials, usually hacienda employees, and craftsmen. After the reform, *campesinos* from two neighboring ex-haciendas began building houses in Arapata, and the population of the town rose from 24 in 1950 to 751 in 1964.

Since Arapata was already a political center before the reform, it contained the national political offices of *corregidor* and judge. Now the town serves as headquarters for a roster of political officials, municipal, national, and syndical, whose jurisdictions go beyond the town itself. These offices, with few exceptions, are filled by local *campesinos* who, on the regional level, constitute the emerging political elite. In the case of the office of *corregidor*, there has been a direct departure from pre-reform precedent, when the position was always filled by a mestizo. Arapata political officials are among the more acculturated *campesinos*; they usually speak some Spanish and have become politically sophisticated and adept. They are involved with national political networks and mediate the impact of national policy to the dependent communities. The officeholders of the peasant syndicates, particularly, have access to manipulative political power on a national scale.

The two other large new towns of Nor Yungas, Cruz Loma and Trinidad Pampa, younger and smaller than Arapata, have coalesced around newly established nuclear schools: well-staffed rural schools that are responsible for coordinating rural education in a given jurisdiction. These new towns, like Arapata, have become the locales of the regional syndicate and thus have become nuclei of regional political power.

Despite the residents' insistence that their towns are *campesino* towns, the mestizos are not completely absent. In Trinidad Pampa and Cruz Loma the mestizo school directors are very influential. In Arapata three mestizo families are disproportionately influential and have occupied political office. At the same time, in Arapata the position of the mestizos in town is precarious and mestizo families have left town in previous years.

Arapata, located on the main road connecting Coroico and Coripata, has become an important regional market and economic center. Cruz Loma is probably too close to Coroico ever to develop an independent market, but it is not inconceivable that Trinidad Pampa may take on more economic importance in

the future. In Arapata, stores are run by the resident mestizos and more acculturated *campesinos* from Yungas towns and the *altiplano*. Several local *campesinos*
have opened small stores, which they run on a part-time basis.

Concomitant with its growth as an economic center, Arapata has seen an influx of more sophisticated *campesinos* from the *altiplano*. They have entered as
traders in *altiplano* foodstuffs, as craftsmen, and as dealers in Yungas products,
primarily coca, which was previously nearly a monopoly of mestizos in the nearby
towns. *Altiplano* traders carrying on minor trading in Yungas products had been
common in the hacienda period, but after the revolution they were in a position
to expand greatly the scale of their operations. Those who have become large
scale middlemen in the coca traffic occupy a position of economic leverage over
the local *campesinos*. Several have amassed considerable wealth and are sometimes resented as "new exploiters." Nevertheless, there is no question of their
*campesino* affiliation. They share language and custom with Yungueño *campesinos* and are tied to them through bonds of kinship and marriage.

These traders, even those who have taken up permanent residence in Arapata,
do not share in local political power, except insofar as their greater acculturative
experience permits them to deal more effectively with national institutions. This
primarily involves manipulating the market for Yungas products, evading tax collection, and maintaining their position as economic middlemen. Purely political
power in the local setting lies primarily with the syndicate organization, and the
merchants fall outside this system.

## The Towns: Social Groups

The complete range of regional stratification is represented in the towns of
Coroico and Coripata. One of the features that differentiates regional stratification patterns here from urban national stratification is a constriction of the upper
stratum, represented by the metropolitan elite and associated with blanco status.
This relative absence of representatives of the national elite was accentuated after
the revolution of 1952 when several blanco families left town. There remain several families in both Coroico and Coripata who consider themselves to be blancos.[9] In Coroico these blancos, who continue to form the apex of the social pyramid, are primarily professionals, owners of tourist facilities, and proprietors of
what has remained to them of their haciendas after the land reform. They travel
often to La Paz and maintain strong ties with the city.

The blanco groups resident in Coroico have been impoverished in recent
years. This situation reflects the national trend, in which the blanco stratum was
exceptionally hard-hit by the land reform. After the revolution many of the dispossessed hacienda owners left Coroico permanently. None of the remaining
prominent families can be considered particularly prosperous by national standards, although most are better off than other townsmen. Those who do not

have the resources to maintain a leisured style of life on what remains of their estates have become economic middlemen, enhancing their income by purchasing crops locally and remarketing them in La Paz.

Coroico and, to a lesser extent, Coripata are tourist and recreational centers. A luxury hotel located on the outskirts of Coroico attracts a steady flow of wealthy Bolivians and foreign tourists. However, they rarely mingle with the townspeople, and make no discernible impact on the life of the town.

The line between blancos and mestizos is not carefully drawn in the Yungas towns, either culturally or socially. This merging of blancos and mestizos into a common category, the *gente decente* (decent people), is one of the prominent post-revolutionary trends in national stratification (Patch 1967:122). In the Yungas the basis for this merging was present in pre-revolutionary society. As elsewhere in Latin America, blancos do not work with their hands, but even before 1952 no occupations were reserved exclusively for blancos. Mestizos could own estates and occupy political office. Indians applied the respectful designation *caballero* to blanco and successful mestizo alike.

Despite the presence of acknowledged blanco families, this amalgamated upper stratum can best be thought of as mestizo rather than blanco, although they refer to themselves as blancos.[10] Coroico and Coripata are referred to as mestizo towns. When Indians use ethnic terms, as they do in reference, they are far more likely to refer to members of the superordinate group in general as mestizos rather than as blancos.

Though the distinction between *indio* and mestizo is made on the basis of cultural rather than physical criteria, the use of racial terms to designate these groups implies a static popular conception of the stratification system and the slim chances for mobility within it. It is therefore significant that the term *"indio"* with its specifically racial referent has been officially and popularly eliminated following the 1952 Revolution and replaced by the term *"campesino,"* which literally means a rural or rustic person. In political contexts the term is used synonymously with peasant, as in *Ministerio de Asuntos Campesinos* (Ministry of Peasant Affairs). Socially, however, *campesino* has become a euphemism for *indio*.[11] Mestizos will generally distinguish between Negroes and *campesinos*. Nevertheless, the widespread usage of the term *campesino* does point to a significant improvement in the position of that group. The term *indio* at the present time has assumed pejorative connotations. Mestizos continue to use the term in its insulting sense when talking about *campesinos*, but not when talking to them, out of a healthy respect for the new political power of the Indian peasants.[12]

Not only are racial characteristics an uncertain guide to social classification, but other outward characteristics, such as mode of dress, are equally misleading. Yungas *campesina* women wear the *pollera* (full skirt), shawl, derby hat, and braided hair that are also characteristics of the Aymara-speaking Indians of the La Paz region. Since all clothing is purchased, there are no distinctive homespun patterns. However, although all women who are *de vestido*—that is, who wear modern-type clothes—are mestizas, all women who are *de pollera* are not *campesinas*. There are mestiza women who also wear the *pollera*.[13] Their identity as mestizas is nonetheless universally acknowledged.

Clothing is even less a differentiating factor for men. Since the Chaco War, *campesino* men have ceased to wear long hair and a distinctive regional costume of the kind that still characterizes Indian men of more isolated sections of the *altiplano*. In the Yungas they wear the same cheap manufactured clothes as the poor mestizo.

There inevitably exist some outward clues to status that reflect the systematic cultural and institutional distinctions that separate the two groups. The most important differentiating criterion is language. The *campesino* is monolingual in Aymara or speaks Spanish imperfectly and with a characteristic accent. Less important, but also diagnostic, is that the *campesino* male will never be seen in public without his hat; the mestizo often goes bareheaded. Although the *campesino* may wear shoes for dress occasions he usually wears rubber sandals (*abarcas*). No mestizo will ever wear sandals unless he is downwardly mobile and living among *campesinos*.

Occupation is another point of differentiation, although it is not without its exceptions. Under the hacienda system, Indians were characteristically *colonos* on the estates, and only Indians were *colonos*. Mestizos who might work for the estate belonged in a different category. Being directly involved in working the land threatened loss of status for a mestizo. In Coroico, where sectional boundaries remain rigid, this continues to be the case. No mestizo, no matter how impoverished he may be, will take agricultural wage work, and few will consider working personally on their own land. In Coripata this restriction is beginning to break down.

In Yungas towns mestizos are traditionally artisans. Among the trades represented are carpentry, tinsmithing, and shoemaking. Poor mestizos may take in washing, bake and sell bread, sell small quantities of goods from their houses, or hire themselves out for wages to the more affluent. Many of the mestizos in the towns, especially those without trades, are far more impoverished than the *campesinos* who are affiliated with ex-haciendas in the countryside and who now own land.

Even before the agrarian reform, a few Yungas *campesinos* who had managed to break their ties with the land settled in the towns. These locally born individuals did not go into commercial activities, but tended to become artisans. Although they speak good Spanish and have suitably mestizo occupations and life styles in Coroico, they are not recognized as mestizo because the other townsmen continue to remember their *campesino* origins. One such carpenter of our acquaintance characterized himself as neither mestizo nor *campesino*, but as an *obrero* (worker).[14] Such individuals would probably be recognized as mestizo if they migrated to the city or to another community where their origins were not directly known. This is the mechanism by which a small flow of individuals has achieved sectional reclassification and upward mobility in the past.

We see that the cultural boundary between plural sections was not completely impermeable, even under traditional conditions. It was possible to bridge the gap, but such reclassification normally required several generations. The actual ethnic continuum that links the Indian section with the Hispanic American section facilitates upward mobility. This continuum is the result of interbreeding and the steady, though restricted, intersectional mobility of the past.

Since the Revolution, the opportunities for reclassification in terms of plural section on a national scale have greatly increased. If a *campesino* still cannot make an acknowledged transition from *campesino* to mestizo in Coroico or Coripata, he can achieve the transition if he leaves the community. It is best accomplished in the more anonymous surroundings of the city. Once there, many young men deny their *campesino* origins and birthplace and change an easily identifiable Indian surname, such as Choque, Mamani, or Quispe, to one that would pass for Hispanic.

Although, as previously indicated, not all mestizas are dressed *de vestido*, the wearing of modern style clothing has come to take on increased significance. Probably as a move to validate their mestizo status, the mestizas in Coroico who continued to wear the traditional garments cut their daughters' hair and saw to it that they dressed *de vestido*. However, such a changeover must be accompanied by the daughter's ability to speak perfect Spanish, or she and her family will be ridiculed. Consequently, the parents' adoption of modern dress for their daughters is likely only when the parents themselves are fluent in Spanish. The local *ex-colonos* have not yet attempted to dress their daughters *de vestido*, but one can observe changes in style of dress in town *campesino* families.

*Altiplano*-born *campesinos* constitute a distinctive intermediate group in the towns. Most speak good Spanish. As in Arapata, their impact is primarily economic. These *altiplano campesinos* were an important part of the Coroico market before 1952, but since the Revolution their numbers have augmented and their significance has increased. They now virtually control the daily market, are active in buying local agricultural products in competition with mestizos, and much of the trucking of the town is in their hands.

Members of this group have been classified as *cholos* by Muratorio (1966:9). The way in which the term is used in this region strikingly demonstrates the ambiguous position of the group. Although the term *cholo* (and its feminine counterpart, *chola*), are reported to be widely used in Bolivia, it is not always used consistently. In Cochabamba, for example, the term is used synonymously with mestizo (Leonard, 1948:11). In the Yungas, *cholo* is rarely heard except when *campesinos* use it for mestizos as a derogatory term. The feminine, *chola*, on the other hand, is in frequent usage. It designates a woman who speaks good Spanish but is *de pollera* and who usually is engaged in commercial activities of some sort.

*Campesinos* generally use the term in an inclusive way to take in both the mestiza *de pollera* and the market *campesina*, while the townsmen are more likely to distinguish conceptually and verbally between the two. Change in style of dress for female children is now common among the *cholas* of the Coroico market.

A large group of *campesinos* who work the land also live in the Yungas towns. Their classification is in no way ambiguous. These *campesinos* fall into two groups, those who have residences in the town and land elsewhere, and those who are landless. Most *campesinos* who are resident in Coroico come from La Communidad. This community adjoins Coroico, and having a house in town is considered prestigious. La Communidad was one of the few independent communities that existed in Nor Yungas during the hacienda period. The inhabitants were independent small landowners. Many had been *colonos* at one time, but had managed to break the relationship and buy their own small parcels of land here.

The town of Coripata has no adjoining free community, but even before the land reform some well-off *colonos* from nearby haciendas had acquired houses in town. Since the agrarian reform this trend has been greatly accelerated in Coripata, and the number of *campesinos* who own houses has increased substantially. Not all of these houses are permanently occupied, especially by those for whom the distance from house to fields would be too great to walk daily.

The small number of landless *campesinos* who live in the towns hire themselves out, primarily to landed *campesinos*, for a daily wage. The majority are unattached women, but there are a few men who have chosen or have been forced to leave their home communities. The landless *campesinos*, particularly women with children to support, are often very poor.

### The Town: Post-Revolutionary Continuity and Change

The changes following the Revolution of 1952 have disrupted the previous fit among all the criteria of stratification in the towns. Nevertheless, the boundaries of the two plural sections, Hispanic American and Indian, remain defined as before.

The correlation of income with other stratification indices was not perfect before 1952 and is now much more anomalous. The economic position of the *campesino* peasant has greatly improved since he became owner of his own parcel of land, and in general he has more income than the poorer mestizos. At the same time, the economic position of townsmen in general has worsened. Hacienda owners lost most of the traditional income from their estates; mestizo overseers lost their relatively lucrative salaried positions and were thrown back on the scanty resources of the towns; town mestizos lost their virtual monopoly in the purchase of *campesino* products. Townsmen see the more prosperous pre-reform period as a golden age.

Despite the Revolution, power and office have never left the hands of blancos and mestizos. When the MNR took over nationally, one set of urban intellectuals and bureaucrats replaced another, while in the provinces, MNR supporters succeeded to office. Nevertheless, the bases of support of the new government had altered. The old landholders, who were primarily blancos, were deprived of their power base and were no longer influential in determining the policies and activities of the state as they had previously. Although many mestizos who were intimately connected with the estate owners shared in their downfall, others who were not personally affected by the land reform were able to step into many of the positions vacated by blancos who were deposed or who left the community.

Campesinos benefited from the political realignment, since the MNR party depended on campesino support to remain in power. The newly organized campesino syndicates were quick to realize the political leverage that they gained from this dependency. They are now for the first time in a position to put considerable pressure on the government, at both the national and local levels, to formulate policy along the lines of perceived campesino interest.

Bureaucratic offices in the Yungas towns (outside of the syndicate system) remain the monopoly of those of the Hispanic American section. In Coroico, where most remaining blancos and mestizos do not affiliate with the MNR, mestizos from outside the town have been appointed to local office. These mestizo officeholders have an interest in perpetuating the privileges of mestizos in confrontation with Indians. Mestizos in general also maintain an advantage over campesinos in that they are familiar with governmental bureaucracy through long experience, while campesinos are only beginning to function independently in the bureaucratic world. Justice, as exemplified by the national judicial functionaries stationed in the towns, continues to be mestizo justice.

On the other hand, mestizo officeholders must express at least nominal adherence to the MNR and be responsive to the collective wishes of the campesinos as a group, even at the expense of entrenched mestizo interests. Thus the political power of individual mestizos is directly tied to their choice between affiliating with the MNR and playing political roles or not. Those who choose the MNR have considerable power. Those who remain neutral or who identify with the opposition are relatively powerless. It must be remembered, however, that this analysis applies to 1964. Given the nature of Bolivian political reality, the political balance has already shifted.

The character of interpersonal relations of blancos and mestizos with campesinos has been drastically reordered. The former colono has been liberated, given a productive economic base, and invested with political importance. Hat-in-hand servility has been relegated to the past, but it does not go unlamented. Not only do mestizos revile the indios for not respecting their betters but even a few older campesinos complain that people have lost respect for one another since the agrarian reform. For the most part, however, the campesino has been more than willing to claim his place as a man. The mestizo, on the other hand, has not been so willing to put aside the superiority of caste in the name of justice and equalitarianism.

In this respect, it is interesting to note the extremely different reactions of the two old towns of Nor Yungas to the reorientation of life after the reform. In Coroico, an intense effort has been made to preserve the old stratification system as rigidly as possible in the face of change. The open hatred between mestizos and campesinos is potentially close to violence here. The campesino is reviled as lazy, stupid, and treacherous; the campesinos' characterization of mestizos is equally harsh. Most members of the Hispanic American segment of Coroico affiliated with opposition political parties. Because the town was alienated from the party in power, it received little assistance from the national government, and such municipal services as it previously had offered (electricity and hospital facilities) fell into disrepair and no longer functioned.

In Coripata, on the other hand, the good relations between mestizos and campesinos are boasted about, and the town's good reputation in this regard is known far afield. Here most of the mestizos have gone over to the MNR and do not identify with opposition parties. Most give lip service to the goals of the agrarian reform, although they may bemoan in private the manner in which it was accomplished. Normally they give to the campesino the treatment as a person that he now demands, and campesinos place great emphasis on the fact that Coripata mestizos "are not ashamed to work in the fields." The growth of Coripata, the result of town house construction by campesinos from nearby ex-haciendas, is a reflection of good relations between campesinos and mestizos to be found here. Such recent growth has not been paralleled in Coroico. Although Coripata is a smaller town than Coroico, it has benefited from its political stand by enjoying considerable governmental aid for municipal services and plaza construction.

Even in Coripata, however, the relationship between mestizos and campesinos is an ambivalent one. The resentments of campesinos who were exploited for so many years were legitimized through governmental propaganda, and the campesinos were simultaneously freed from the most onerous and obvious forms of this exploitation. But the bitterness of remembered serfdom remains. This underlying hostility is always present and is likely to find release through name-calling and violent confrontations when campesino men are intoxicated.

Despite the periodic release of usually repressed hostility, traditional social patterns have not been completely obliterated. Campesinos are still respectful, if no longer servile, toward mestizos and are expected to be so by mestizos and campesinos alike. Mestizos still deal with individual campesinos in basically paternalistic ways. In Coroico as well as in Coripata, campesinos still seek out mestizos to baptize children, sponsor marriages, lend money, and give advice.[15] Mestizos are more likely to be educated and they still fill the appointed positions in the towns. Even though they may be good party men, "mestizos stick together." Mestizos, in fact, although their situation has altered, are still in control and in a position to take advantage of campesinos.

It is apparent that the greatest continuity between pre-reform and post-reform stratification lies along the continuum of social prestige. Members of the Hispanic American section continue to enjoy higher prestige than *campesinos*. Nevertheless, as C. Wright Mills points out (1963:310), prestige involves two distinct components. The first involves the raising of the status claim and the second is the honoring of the status claim. Mestizo status claims are now far more grudgingly honored than they were before, and ambivalent or hostile feelings toward mestizos are now likely to be expressed under provocation rather than repressed. The prestige gap between *campesinos* and mestizos has already narrowed and it may be expected that the differential of prestige will shift further, albeit slowly, to bring it more in line with the actual distribution of wealth and power in the area.

*Summary and Conclusions*

In Nor Yungas, with somewhat different expression in town and countryside, the plural structure of the society has been demonstrably modified in the face of the disruption of the traditional bases of social stratification which followed the economic, political, and educational reforms of the early fifties. The old social order, predicated on the hacienda and dominated by the land-owning class and its retainers, has collapsed, and a new order is emerging.

Nevertheless, in this region continuity is also obvious. The plural sections remain defined as before with the Hispanic American section clearly dominant over the Indian. Economic, political, educational, and military institutions are still controlled on the national scene by members of the Hispanic American section, and in this region the same situation prevails. The organization of peasant syndicates has for the first time given the *campesinos* a voice and some influence in politics, but through mestizo intermediaries. Regionally, *campesinos* have not replaced mestizos in the key positions in the towns. Some members of the Hispanic American section have lost power and wealth. Their loss opened the way for other members of the same section to gain these goals, primarily on the basis of party politics.

Despite the striking evidence of continuity, it is also undeniable that *campesinos* have considerably improved their position. The gap between the two sections has narrowed and there is considerably more ambivalence involved in the maintenance of their boundaries. Members of the Indian section have sharply increased their assumption of many elements of Hispanic American culture, particularly in the realm of material acquisitions. Undoubtedly, one reason is that the economic situation of the former *colonos* has improved, and consequently they have more cash available to build new style houses and buy shoes and radios. It is also clear, however, that in the past, members of the dominant section discouraged the assumption of outward characteristics of mestizo behavior because they had an interest in maintaining social distance between *indios* and mestizos.

One of the major ways in which acculturation to Hispanic American patterns was blocked for the *colonos* in the countryside during the hacienda period was by denial or restriction of access to schools. The construction of rural schools following the revolution and the younger generation's rapid acquisition of Spanish will undoubtedly serve to accelerate acculturative change in the future.

Opportunities for social mobility and reclassification have increased considerably. The barrier separating the Indian and Hispanic American sections has become more permeable. These sections are hierarchically ranked in a prestige sense; therefore, crossing the boundary automatically makes for upward mobility. This is an old pattern, but the movement has greatly accelerated. Since cultural and linguistic shifts are prerequisite to such reclassification, townsmen and traders are more likely to be involved, but peasants are also affected. Some young *campesinos* have moved to La Paz, where they run small shops or work for wages. Others, with better education, are becoming school teachers and minor government functionaries.

A second pattern of mobility is greatly increasing in importance. For the first time, significant upward mobility along the continua of economic class and political power can be achieved without prior transfer from the Indian to the Hispanic American section. Instead, there is an increasing differentiation within the Indian section, both regionally in the Yungas and nationally. This is most visible in the political sphere where local *campesino* leaders can wield national influence; a few have even risen to occupy national office. In the Yungas, *campesinos* of *altiplano* origin have broadened their commercial activities and taken over many of the lucrative middleman positions previously occupied by mestizos. This increased range of stratification within the Indian section also serves to bridge the economic, political, and prestige gap between it and the Hispanic American section. Those who rise along the continua of class and power tend to maintain their identification as *campesinos*, while those who acquire an education and an occupation (such as teaching school) that carries social prestige are more likely to engage in intersectional mobility.

In the province of Nor Yungas, then, the past fifteen years has witnessed the weakening of the rigidity of the plural structure of the society. This weakening has been expressed in three ways: (1) increasing acculturation of the members of the subordinate section to the cultural and social norms of the dominant section; (2) increasing mobility across sectional boundaries; and (3) increasing social differentiation and stratification within the subordinate section. It may be suggested as a hypothesis that in ethnically plural societies of the Bolivian type, when the traditional bases of the dominance of the superordinate social stratum are undercut, the structure of pluralism will tend to be modified as above.

It may be noted that the last two trends are implicitly contradictory. Increased intersectional mobility implies the elimination of the plural nature of the society through the gradual absorption of those of the Indian section into the Hispanic-American section. Increased differentiation within the Indian section, rather than transfer to the Hispanic American section, implies maintenance of the plural structure, albeit modified in content. In Bolivia the two are occurring simultaneously, but they are not unrelated. The children of those Indians who have risen in the stratification hierarchy have the possibility of acquiring an advanced education leading to their reclassification in successive generations (Patch, 1967:123).

If acculturation and mobility should continue at the present rate, unchecked by political reaction, we should expect the plural divisions of Bolivian society to decrease steadily in importance, as they have in Mexico. In the absence of clear-cut racial boundaries, a system of social pluralism would be difficult to maintain as ethnic differences are minimized. Nevertheless, the elimination of pluralism is not imminent in Bolivia. Considering that Indians constitute a majority of the population, the sheer magnitude of the task, even at an accelerated pace, will ensure the perpetuation of pluralism for a long time to come.

## Notes

1. The field work upon which this paper is based was carried out from September, 1963 to November, 1964 and was supported by a grant from the Foreign Area Fellowship Program. The views and conclusions expressed in this paper are those of the author and are not necessarily those of the Foreign Area Fellowship Program. This paper has benefited from criticism and comments by William Léons, Arthur Tuden, Pedro Carrasco, and Walter Goldschmidt.

2. One *caveat* must be emphasized at the outset. Observation of social conditions in Nor Yungas, upon which this report is based, was made in 1963 and 1964. The description of social alignments as they existed at that time represents but one moment along a continuum of rapid change; it is not implied that the 1964 situation was a static one or that it represented the achievement of a new social equilibrium, despite the use of the ethnographic present. The process of realignment that was set in motion by the Revolution of 1952 has implications which will not be fully realized until the next generation. In addition, I was not in a position to observe the subsequent impact of the fall of the MNR government in November, 1964.

3. This is a modification of the definition offered by Pierre van den Berghe (1967:34).

4. The third important town of the province, Caranavi, is the center of a more tropical interior region, which only recently has been opened up to large-scale colonization. This region is not included in the scope of this paper.

5. Interestingly enough, an impressionistic view of the modal personalities of Negroes and Aymara Indians shows extreme contrast. Negroes are outgoing, amiable, and relatively unrestrained in their emotional expression. The Aymara, on the other hand, are well characterized as *cerrado* (closed). They are restrained and suppressed in their emotional expression, with an undercurrent of mutual suspicion and potential violence that always lies just beneath the surface. An Aymara, for instance, may turn away or cover his face in embarrassment when watching the typically unrestrained and exuberant behavior of Negroes at a fiesta.

6. The few genealogies collected from Negroes lead me to suspect that Negroes trace bilateral kinship ties much further, both horizontally and vertically, than do their Aymara

counterparts. Apparently, a much greater value is placed on keeping track of one's relatives, despite considerable residential separation.

7. In the Arapata area the ex-*colonos* received title to the scattered plots of land that they had acutally worked. Dwight Heath informs me (personal communication) that in the Coroico area the scattered holdings of each individual *colono* were consolidated.

8. Formerly a vice-*cantón*.

9. This evaluation may not necessarily be shared by everyone in the community.

10. Blanca Muratorio (1966) also notes this blurring of the line between blancos and mestizos, but she absorbs the mestizo into the blanco group.

11. The occupational term in use signifying agriculturalist is *labrador*.

12. Characteristically enough, on the day of the 1964 coup that toppled the Paz Estenssoro government we saw a drunken mestizo in Coroico go up to a *campesino* and shout "Piss on you, *indio*, they've killed your father."

13. Patch also confirms this for "conservative" mestizo women in the city of La Paz (1961:3).

14. William Stein notes the use of the term *obrero* under similar circumstances in Peru (1961:232, note).

15. Often the former *patrón* or administrator of a hacienda is sought out in this way. However, many have left the area. Those who remain are likely to be those who had relatively good relations with the *colonos* prior to the reform.

## References

Adams, Richard N.
  1956.    Cultural Components of Central America. American Anthropologist, 58:881–907.

Beals, Ralph Leon
  1953.    Social Stratification in Latin America. American Journal of Sociology, 58:327–339.

Leonard, Olen E.
  1948.    Canton Chullpas: A Socioeconomic Study of the Cochabamba Valley of Bolivia. Foreign Agriculture Reports, no. 27. Washington: U.S. Department of Agriculture.

Léons, Madeline Barbara
  1967a.    Land Reform in the Bolivian Yungas. América Indígena, 27:689–713.
  1967b.    Stratification and Pluralism in a Changing Society. Paper presented to the American Anthropological Association, Washington, D.C.

Mills, C. Wright
  1963.    The Sociology of Stratification. In Power, Politics, and People, edited by Irving Louis Horowitz. New York: Ballantine Books.

Muratorio, Blanca
  1966.    Changing Bases of Social Stratification in a Bolivian Community. Paper presented to the American Anthropological Association, Pittsburgh, Pa.

Patch, Richard W.
  1961.    Bolivia Today. American Universities Field Staff Report, March 17.

1967.    Peasantry and a National Revolution: Bolivia. In Expectant Peoples, edited by K. H. Silvert. New York: Vintage Books.

Rubin, Vera (editor)
1960.    Socio-cultural Pluralism in the Caribbean. Annals of the New York Academy of Sciences, vol. 83.

Smith, Michael Garfield
1965.    Plural Society in the British West Indies. Berkeley and Los Angeles: University of California Press.

Stein, William
1961.    Hualcan: Life in the Highlands of Peru. Ithaca: Cornell University Press.

Tumin, Melville
1952.    Caste in a Peasant Society. Princeton: Princeton University Press.

Van den Berghe, Pierre L.
1967.    Race and Racism. New York: John Wiley & Sons.

Wagley, Charles, and Marvin Harris
1958.    Minorities in the New World. New York: Columbia University Press.

# 14. BLACK TRADERS OF
# NORTH HIGHLAND ECUADOR

*Kathleen Klumpp*

The manner in which the various social segments of the peasant population of highland Ecuador are linked to the national economy is related to the degree of dependency on the sale of something for a livelihood and to the nature of the channels through which distributive activities take place.[1] The sale of agricultural produce within a market place organization is the primary means by which the rural Chota Valley Negro population of the northern Ecuadorian Andes is tied to and integrated into the national economy. This article will focus on the internal marketing system in which the highland Negro peasants of Ecuador are involved and on the nature of the interpersonal relationships which are initiated through trading activities.

While providing the primary means for the exchange of material goods, an internal market system is also an important mechanism through which the relationships between various social and ethnic categories may be expressed. Sidney Mintz (1959:20) has discussed an internal market system as a "mechanism of social articulation" suggesting that it may be viewed as a basic set of economic processes in which societal segments intersect. Ecuador is an ethnically plural society and production and distribution for money constitutes an important focus for interpersonal and structural relationships between various ethnic segments. Through an inquiry into the interactive situations of the marketing process one may be provided with knowledge of the economic roles of these ethnic segments and, in addition, with important insights about how members of these segments perceive themselves and one another. In the north highlands, the three ethnic groups which interact in the internal marketing system are Negro, mestizo,[2] and Indian, each being represented by different economic capacities. The concept of "social race" as used by Wagley (1965) parallels my usage of the term "ethnic."

An internal marketing system will refer to the processes and activities involved in getting material goods from the producer to the ultimate consumer, and not to a network of market place sites or centers of exchange as the term has been previously employed (Mintz 1959). It is important to keep this distinction in mind because the unit of analysis will be the nature of the relationships initiated

Originally published in Norman E. Whitten, Jr. and John F. Szwed (eds.), *Afro-American Anthropology: Contemporary Perspectives* (New York: Free Press, 1970), pp. 245–62. Reprinted with the permission of The Free Press, a Division of Simon & Schuster.

in the process of cash-oriented exchange, whether or not this exchange takes place within actual market places. It will be demonstrated that the nature of highland Negro peasant marketing behavior is characterized by varying patterns of action and circumscribed by quite different sets of restraints at the local level of intracommunity exchange than at the national level of market place trade.

Market place studies by virtue of the unit chosen have viewed the relationships of participants within the arena of the market place site as the basis for statements characterizing peasant marketing behavior and the extent to which it may be set forth through reference to the market model. Several difficulties emerge in this approach. First, concentrating on the market place obscures the importance of alternative exchange channels through which distributive activities take place and in which the economic relations between the participants may be influenced by other social considerations. Ortiz's (1967) article on Colombian peasant marketing behavior is an illuminating example of the differences which emerge in interactions in the market place and in stores. Second, marketing studies have neglected a consideration of the peasant productive sector as a fundamental part of an internal market system. Statements describing the extent to which marketing behavior is similar or dissimilar to that postulated by the market model cannot be convincingly made without considering the behavioral patterns of the producers at local levels of exchange. The market place site cannot be considered as if it were a closed microcosmic unit in which the applicability of formal economic theory to peasant exchange may be tested without reference to the total range of patterning of market behavior in the exchange network.

The first part of this article will deal with the ecological and ethnic contexts of trading in the Chota Valley and on a national scale and will consider the nature of the marketing system at the local level of intracommunity exchange. The second part will focus on the interpersonal relations between buyers and sellers within the context of a large urban market place site in Quito, Ecuador's capital city, and consider the relative influence of ethnic identity in shaping these relations. Throughout both sections, the influence of social and economic considerations in price formation will be discussed.

*Ecological Context of Marketing*

The Chota Valley is located in the northern highlands of Ecuador in the provinces of Imbabura and Carchi, approximately 105 miles by road north of the nation's capital, Quito, and 21 miles northeast of Ibarra, the provincial capital of Imbabura. The valley is divided by the Chota River which provides both the natural and the political boundary between the two provinces. Along the river, in the valley floor, runs the Pan American Highway, which is the only highland thruway connecting northern and southern Ecuador. All traffic from Colombia and the north highlands must pass through the Chota Valley by means of this cobblestoned road in order to reach Quito and points further south. The Negro settlements, which are located on the valley floor either directly on or very near to the highway, thus have ready access to transportation facilities going in either direction at almost every hour of the day and night. There are more than eight commercial bus lines in addition to many trucks which are willing to pick up passengers and their cargo. By bus the trip to Quito, traveling by night as the traders must do, takes about 9 hours. The excellent transportation facilities possessed by the Negro population of the Chota Valley is a very important factor in understanding why these cultivators are able to market their own produce directly in the largest urban centers of the highlands. They do not have to organize special transport facilities, although the members of some settlements have done so, nor do they have to rely on outside intermediaries to marker their produce. A few non-local middlemen do buy in the valley. However, the Chota peasants are in no way dependent upon them as a means of distributing their produce.

Between the Colombian-Ecuadorian border and Quito there are only two highland river basins which at their depths are characterized by a tropical climate (Teran 1966:185). From north to south respectively these are the Chota and the Guayllabamba River basins. The two basins are remarkably similar in crop production, cultivating many of the same fruits and vegetables. Most important is that these basins are the only north highland source of the avocado. The activities of the individual traders from these two valleys is essential to the task of leveling out regional differences in climate, altitude, and crop specialization. From the Chota Valley, produce moves north to the regional market centers of San Gabriel and Tulcán and reaches many of the smaller outlying towns and villages. The southern destinations of produce originating in both the Chota and the Guayllabamba valleys is Quito, Latacunga, Ambato, and Riobamba.

The Chota Valley is characterized by a semi-arid, warm climate with a mean annual rainfall at the base of only 293.5 mm. (Teran 1966:193). The area of most extensive cultivation is at the base of the valley along the River Chota where irrigation canals are run into the fields. This is also the area of the densest Negro population, with the smallest plots of land, and with the heaviest emphasis on a wide variety of cash crops. The size of the average family plot is between $2^{1}/_{2}$ and 5 acres. Although there is variation from one village to another in crop production, the inventory for the settlements located on the valley floor includes the tomato, sweet manioc, bean, sweet potato, anise, sugar cane, avocado, cotton, cucumber, papaya, lemon, orange, plantain, cabuya, melon, and carrot. The settlements located directly on the Pan American Highway devote approximately three-fourths of the family plot to cash crops of a rapidly perishable nature which are not subsistence staples. The settlements located off the main highway, however, grow a larger proportion of crops intended primarily for self-consumption such as the bean, sweet potato, sweet manioc, and the plantain, although small amounts of these products and cotton and sugar cane are sold. Sugar cane is marketed directly at a mill in the valley. Two settlements in the valley are national custom control points where all vehicles are inspected for contraband goods from

Colombia. The existence of these stops has resulted in an important internal market for immediately consumable foods. With the exception of sugar cane and the produce sold in these two settlements, all other produce is taken to market places, the most important of which are located outside the Chota Valley itself.

Until 1964 most of the Negro small holdings pertained to one of the *haciendas* in the valley. Before the Agrarian Reform Law of 1964, the majority of the Negro agriculturalists were *huasipungueros*; that is, serfs tied to a particular *hacienda* through usufruct rights to a plot of land (the right to use the property of another without changing or damaging its substance) in return for three to four days weekly labor cultivating the *hacienda* lands plus a small monetary remuneration of approximately S.05 (0.05 sucre) daily. The Agrarian Reform Law has meant the rupture of all traditional obligations between the *huasipungueros* and *hacienda*. A man is now free to sell his labor to any contractor and the *hacienda* is not under any obligation, as it was preceding the Reform, to continue to utilize the resident population as its labor source. The Agrarian Reform has not as yet affected the patterns of marketing. Although the agriculturist now owns the plot of land from which produce is sold, ownership was not a prerequisite before the Reform to engage in trading activities. The marketing patterns of today developed with the use of motorized transport.

The large market centers in the Ecuadorian highlands are located in the municipal townships and are under the legal jurisdiction of the city government which imposes taxes and other regulations. Throughout Ecuador, most of the trading activities are dominated by mestizos, although Indians may be found who are both retail sellers and wholesale intermediaries especially in certain specializations such as cattle-raising, textiles, and meat-slaughtering. However, mestizos form the large body of non-agricultural specialist intermediaries who dominate the main arteries of trade, both to the rural areas and away from them, and in the distribution from the producer to the consumer. It is the mestizos who are most often the country buyers, the truckers, the wholesale distributors, the processors, and the retailers. Whereas the mestizo is important in the internal marketing system in his role as a middleman, retail seller, and consumer, the Indian participates in the market system primarily in the economic capacity of original producer and consumer, although, of course, not all Indians gain their livelihood in agricultural pursuits. The position of highland Negroes will presently be made clear.

### The Process of Trading

The combined roles of cultivator and country wholesale buyer occupied by the Negro peasants from the Chota Valley is an unusual pattern in highland Ecuador and must in part be understood by ecological factors of readily available market places and a high demand for sub-tropical produce, especially the avocado, in the highlands.

In order to understand that aspect of the internal marketing system in which the Chota producer and producer-trader take part, the exchange of the avocado will be taken as the starting point. It is one of the most important cash crops upon which most of the trading activities are concentrated. The category of trader will be defined to include only those who buy produce from the plots of others to resell. It will not include those peasants who occasionally take small amounts of produce from their own plots to market without initially buying.

During the months of June, July, and August, between 50 to 65 individuals, the large majority women, buy avocados weekly to sell either in Ibarra or in Quito. Over 90% of the traders have access to land from which a minimal supply of avocados is obtained. Those who do not own a small plot are usually able to obtain a basic supply through sharecropping. Paying a yearly land rent does occur, but infrequently.

The process of marketing begins with the initial buying of avocados from other members of the same community. The traders living in the various settlements are not identified primarily by their occupation by either nontraders or themselves—that is, traders are thought of as primarily agriculturists who have taken up trading activities as one of several alternative ways of obtaining enough cash to buy food staples and other household necessities. However, there is a relative ease of movement in and out of trading activities. Other alternative sources of income are derived through fattening pigs and raising chickens to resell, carrying contraband, or selling avocados in the orchard. During the harvest season when market prices for avocados are extremely low, there is a tendency for some traders to switch from buying avocados to selling them in their own settlements until prices rise again. There are two sorts of traders who decide to switch from buying to selling: (1) those with small-scale operations who cannot survive three or more months of trading with accumulating decreases in the amount of capital available for weekly expenditures on avocados, and (2) those who do not lack sufficient capital with which to buy avocados, but feel that the effort expended is not worth the resultant cash income. The latter category includes those who have relatively larger plots of land from which they derive a substantial amount of avocados. Moreover, the selling prices in the orchard are often not much below those received in the market place in the same week. It is evident that the point at which the rewards are less than the effort required is necessarily a subjective evaluation subject to the intensity of the need for the small amount of cash received through selling in the market.[3] In addition to the economic factors mentioned in the decision to trade in the market place or not, a crucial element seems to be whether the individual enjoys the activity. Many women say that they are easily bored spending long periods of time in the home, and that they enjoy the freedom entailed in trading along with the hustle and bustle of the cities.

In the various Negro settlements, both the buyers and the sellers are rural cultivators who share not only a similar socio-economic position and cultural heritage but, more importantly, are linked by kinship, friendship, and *compadrazgo* (ritual co-parenthood) ties. Although the interactive patterns of the Chota buyers and sellers are necessarily founded in mutual economic need, they are strongly influenced by these enduring and often multiple social ties. The expectation of mutual favors entailed in these social relationships not only structure the buyer-seller interactive performance, but restrict the sorts of economic choices available to the Chota trader as well. It is to intracommunity buyer-seller relationships that we now turn.

Buying and selling avocados in the valley is carried out in a casual and relaxed atmosphere, in sharp contrast to the tenseness characterizing the market place exchange. The traders leave their households early in the morning to meet the sellers in the orchards. The sellers gather up the avocados and then pack them into large sacks which are carried to a clearing near the orchard entrance where the buyers are waiting. Although avocados are bought through bargaining both in the Chota Valley and in the market place, intracommunity bargaining differs significantly from that observed in the market place. Both parties to the transaction in the Chota Valley accede more easily to the other's terms. Attempts are made to bargain in mild and subdued tones in order to avoid the possibility of offending one's partner. The elements of antagonism, with buyer and seller pairs aggressively vying with each other, is minimized in bargaining within the valley. Buyer-seller quarrels are likely not only to terminate an incomplete transaction but also to create social tensions outside of the buyer-seller situation itself, especially with kin, friends, and *compadres*. Market place transactions as well may not be completed when one of the bargaining pairs is offended. There are, however, two different conceptions of what constitutes an offense. Aggressiveness with harsh verbal bantering manifested while bargaining in the market place is not sufficient cause for offense, although in the Chota Valley communities similar bargaining behavior closely approximates what Sahlins (1965: 148–49) terms "negative reciprocity" and is considered by the participants as unsociable and conflict-laden. Thus, while interactive relationships in the country exist in order to exchange material goods they also take place within a personal network and are greatly influenced by social evaluations exterior to the actual social situation.

Although dissembling about selling price is a bargaining strategy employed by the mestizo intermediaries in the market place, it is not commonly practiced by the buyers in the Chota Valley because both the traders and the sellers are well aware of last week's market prices. Equal access to market knowledge results from country producers and their buyers living in the same settlements, which also facilitates discussion of the state of the market. The Chota producer-seller is at no disadvantage at the local level due to the effective network of communication.

The Negro trader selling in Quito, at the national level, is at a greater disadvantage in acquiring market information than her mestizo client who remains in the city during the week. Because of rapidly fluctuating prices and the lack of a means by which rapid assessment of marketing conditions may be made, being physically present in the market place is the *only* way that knowledge of a particular supply-demand situation may be gained. Therefore both the traders and their suppliers are equally ignorant of market conditions at the time when such information is needed—that is, while transacting in the countryside.

Although both the producers and the traders agree that the latter should make some "profit," expressed in terms of the difference between the purchase price of the avocados and the price at which they are sold,[4] there is no concept of a customary or "just" profit margin regulating price determination, as exists among Jamaican traders (Katzin 1960:310). In fact, the notion of a profit margin in itself is not operative. Because avocados are generally bought in non-assorted size lots, classified, and then sold according to size, a direct ratio between the prices paid per hundred while buying and those received in the market place may not exist. Nevertheless, the trader does make a general overview of the spread between per hundred buying and selling prices. The price of avocados which the traders are willing to pay depends only in part upon the selling price in the market the previous week. It also depends upon expected long-range price levels for the time of year and on the expectation of receiving a certain price at the market the following week. A sudden drop in market prices (which is a common occurrence) does not necessarily influence the next week's buying prices unless such drops become continuous over time as in seasonal fluctuations. Whether or not the wife of the cultivator is receiving enough for the sale of avocados depends on (1) what she previously has sold for during this time of year, (2) what others are selling for that particular day, and (3) her subjective estimate of what she thinks the trader can sell for the next day.

A large part of the Chota traders' possibility of making a profit lies in their ability to estimate proportions in an unassorted lot. There is a fairly precise estimation on the part of the transacting pair of the various proportions of each size present. If it appears to contain more "thirds" than "regulars" or "large" then the lot will be bought cheaply, at about S/8 or S/11 per 100. The larger, preferred avocados will be bought at about S/15 to S/18. The proportion of sorted avocados carried to market is usually three-fourths of the medium and small sizes and one-fourth of the large. Although transportation costs are greater for the larger sizes because the charge is per sack, the largest proportion of the total income per sack is derived from sale of the large sizes. In fact, the traders usually make very little profit and at times actually lose on the smaller sizes if the cost of a mixed lot exceeds the total income from the separate sale of different sizes. Although the Chota traders recognize this, a particular loss does not seem to affect the next week's decision about what sizes to buy. Choosing to continue to buy the smaller sizes is not "irrational," though; rather, it must be understood through a consideration of the nature of the restrictions on alternatives, for it would be inconceivable for the trader to refuse to buy anything except the larger sizes from a seller with whom she shares strong social ties. To do so would involve both a social and an eventual economic cost which the trader could not bear. Traders rely primarily on their relatives, friends, *compadres*, and neighbors to sell them avocados and to extend essential services. Only the mestizo traders who buy in the local settlements are free from these social expectations and buy in proportions of three-fourths large and one-fourth medium and small. By continuing to buy the poorer avocados, one may argue, the Negro traders obviate social conflicts and thereby not only insure their source of supply but their continuity as traders as well. However, the traders themselves do not engage in a conscious strategy of decision-making in which all the possible consequences of different courses of action are explored nor do they verbalize any of these functional ends. "We buy the smaller avocados because they are selling them," people say. The fact that alternatives are foregone through the fulfillment of buyer-seller behavioral expectations should not be confused with a process of conscious maximization.[5]

During the months when prices in the market place drop, the Chota traders must rely heavily on their ability to secure credit or cash loans. The sellers themselves are usually willing to give the trader avocados on credit. The value of credit may extend up to S/300 (U.S. $15.00), but the specific amount will be influenced by the seller's estimation of the buyer's ability to pay for the goods the day after the buyer returns from the market. There is an expressed sense of pride in having and maintaining good credit relationships because it reflects on one's ability to manage successfully in trading activities. This ability is not only dependent on the skill of the trader within the market place, but also on the way cash is managed within the family. Women generally handle family finances, apportioning money as they wish, but with the tacit consent of the male head of the household. In families in which the wife does not market, the husbands tend to have more direct control over money uses.

Cash loans are extended by friends, relatives, *compadres*, fellow traders from one's own settlement, and occasionally by the mestizo traders who buy in that settlement. Those who extend the loans are themselves frequently indebted to others. Many prefer not to ask relatives for a loan because "one should not so inconvenience relatives," but in fact they *do* ask for help. With the exceptions noted above, borrowing within the community is normally done with extreme reluctance. "Those who loan you money will gossip, telling everyone that you are poor, that you have nothing because you are wasteful. A poor person is despicable!" Retail shopkeepers who are patronized by Chota traders and non-Negro *compadres* who live in the towns are also potential outside sources of loans.

### Social Relations within the Market Place

The market place of San Roque is only one of several large municipal market places in Quito. Like most municipal markets located in large regional centers, it is highly regulated by the city government on both the retail and wholesale levels. There is a complex system for obtaining retail stall space, monthly taxes on the stalls, vending taxes for those categorized as *ambulantes* (non-permanent mobile sellers, country wholesalers), fines, sanitation and food quality controls, officials to maintain peace and order, distinct wholesale and retail sections, and price controls. Price controls consist of the establishment of retail ceilings on all agricultural produce sold in the market place. Price ceilings are usually set to accommodate seasonal fluctuations in supply of agricultural produce, especially for perishables, but also for non-perishables, since storage facilities for all produce are seriously lacking. In San Roque, if the scarcity of avocados pushes the price up along the chain of intermediaries, forcing the retailer to exceed the fixed upper level, the market *control* will force the price down to the level of the country wholesale trader.

Most of the city buyers live and work in Quito as retailers and as secondary wholesalers of perishable produce. Many have permanent stalls in the market place. Other buyers come from the nearest large cities to the south of Quito.

The close spatial arrangement of the Chota traders into village clusters in the wholesale section of the market place facilitates the flow of price information. Bargaining is loudly carried out so that when one buyer is advancing bids, the others can overhear the transaction. Thus, no one seller is at a disadvantage through lack of access to information. Moreover, the spatial distribution also encourages animated verbal exchange among the Chota sellers. In contrast, the mestizo buyers rarely interact verbally—each goes about the business of acquiring stock quite independently. The buyers, although acting as autonomous units, do tacitly cooperate. Each adheres to the rule of separate bidding and buying, each completing a round of bargaining with the potential seller before the next buyer approaches. The practice of completing the round of price negotiations regardless of whether it results in an impasse or a sale is an obvious means of avoiding disagreements between buyers over potential sellers. This system, of course, can only function in conjunction with the sellers who do not compete overtly with one another for potential buyers.

The overall framework and rhythm of bargaining in San Roque varies with the seasonal fluctuations of sub-tropical produce. Depending on the ratio of the buyers to the sellers, the amounts which each seller has to offer, and the amounts which the buyers are able to purchase, either the buyers or their sellers will have more influence in shaping the course of the transaction. At no time, however, does either member of the transacting pair have the power to dictate the terms under which she is willing to buy or sell, although the mestizo buyers, during the harvest season, approach this state more than the Chota sellers. Although the perceived conditions of supply and demand operating at any day in the market place will set the upper limits to which a partner will have the advantage in bargaining power, such factors as skills in marketing and the nature of the buyer-seller relationship will affect the actual price reached.

There are three stages in bargaining: (1) initial probes in which the buyers and the sellers obtain an idea of each other's perception of the supply-demand conditions that particular day; (2) serious haggling in which the range of buyer-seller bids are narrowed down; and (3) completion of the transaction. The patterns of buyer-seller interaction during the second stage differ significantly according to whether the Chota traders' desire to sell is greater than the buyers' apparent interest in their avocados, giving rise in both cases to an imbalance in perceived power. When the plaza is slow for the Chota traders, they actively seek out buyers. Buyers, moreover, effectively employ words and gestures indicating indifference and self-confidence as a strategy geared to impress upon the seller her defensive position. When avocados are scarce, the performers of the defensive-offensive positions are reversed.

The final stage in completing the transaction is the most interesting because it is during this time that personalistic elements in the buyer-seller relationship manifest themselves. If the seller feels that she has less bargaining strength than the buyer, she will initiate the final interaction, calling the buyer back with a plea of "How much will you pay me for them?" However, when the advantage lies with the seller, it is the buyer who returns and asks for a quotation of the "last price" (el último) below which the seller supposedly will not go. Both these requests, by either the buyer or the seller, are different from past bids in that the solicitor is asking for a realistic and serious evaluation of the price she thinks would be fair, considering the general market conditions that day. Concessions below the statement of the "last price" are made according to an estimation of one's partner as a "good customer" (buen cliente). The buyer will consider primarily whether her client has consistently supplied her with avocados during the seasons of scarcity, giving her preference over other buyers, whereas the seller will take into consideration the regularity of the buyer in glut seasons and whether she has been willing to extend other important services to be discussed below.

Both buyer and seller consider whether they have had any previous disagreements over suspected dishonesty in handling money or over the sacks owned by both. Often, in the hopes of encouraging a good price concession, one of the transacting partners will explicitly remind the other of favors extended in the past. Although the reciprocal obligations which develop in the market place between the Chota traders and their clients endure over time, they are not fulfilled through a structure as rigid as that entailed in a trading partnership. There is no need for unvarying weekly attendance on the part of either the sellers or the buyers nor an agreement, tacit or overt, that transactions will be made with the same individuals each week. The Chota traders complete final sales with usually from 2 to 4 buyers each. Most of these buyers are considered to be "good customers," but some share a more personalized relationship than others and are therefore able to obtain a price below the "last price" with greater ease. If the Chota trader does not share a sense of amicability and cooperation with the buyer, she will refuse to make further price concessions below either her first or second statement of the "last price."

## Sources of Conflict and Cooperation in
## Market Place Buyer-Seller Relationships

There are two major sources of conflict in the buyer-seller relationship: one of which is embodied in the rules of bargaining behavior, and the other of which is inherent in any marketing system lacking an effective and standardized means for identifying goods. The sources of cooperation lie in the participants' attempts to buffer the otherwise shattering effects of seasonal fluctuations in supply through the establishment of personalized exchange relationships involving a set of long-term reciprocal obligations.

The nature of these personalized economic relationships corresponds in many ways to what is known as "pratik" among Haitian market women (Mintz 1961). However, in Ecuador, the personal elements in market place buyer-seller relationships do not appear to be as extensively developed as among Haitian market women, although their basic functions appear to be similar.

Stealing and lying are not only allowable but expected bargaining behavior, within limits, in the market place. Both parties to the transaction must look out for their own interests and, therefore, if one is deceived, the fault lies not with the offender, but with the recipient. Distrust is especially prevalent in buyer-seller relationships which are irregular, but even among preferred customers a participant may attempt to deceive her partner if she thinks that she will succeed. However, one of the most important functions of the "good client" relationship is to introduce an element of reliability and trust. If blatant dishonesty occurs, the relationship will most likely terminate.

The ownership of avocado sacks is one of the most frequent focal points of quarrels between buyers and sellers. These disagreements are not only related directly to the expectation of deception, but also to an imprecise system of ownership identification which allows the deception to occur. If an argument over a missing sack arises between a buyer and seller who have built up a relationship of relative trust and confidence, it is usually resolved through a mutual count without violent and harsh verbal displays. When serious arguments do arise, it is most often, but not always, with buyers with whom the seller has not regularly transacted and involves direct accusations of dishonesty. Each shouts charges that the other is a "thief" and "without shame." A buyer with a reputation for frequent and serious attempts at deception will simply be refused as a client by some of the Chota sellers even though he may not have previously transacted with this individual. Another important source of conflict is over money. It arises most frequently in the payment stage of the transaction when, after a mutual agreement on a certain price, the buyer short-changes the seller. Such occurrences are commonplace. Far from outraging the seller, they are regarded as little more than necessary and expected annoyances even though the seller suspects that the error was intentional.

Among Chota market women, the existence of a personal economic relationship is entailed in the statement that a particular buyer is a "good customer." A good customer shows a willingness to grant priorities in the market place. However, as already pointed out, quarreling is not absent even among those who consider one another "good customers." Nevertheless, even when arguments do occur between regular customers, the cause is more readily attributed to an unintentional mistake and quietly solved. There is the mutual expectation that each deal honestly with the other, and if a flagrant violation of this trust occurs, the relationship is permanently shattered.

Between customers, the term *comadre* or *compadre* is the accepted form of address, and between good customers, the first name is added. The Negro Chota sellers, however, do *not* share in *compadrazgo* relationships with their mestizo buyers, though they *do* extend the *compadrazgo* terminology across ethnic lines. The extension of such terms to include casual acquaintances is particularly prevalent in highland Ecuador when the social relationship is between members of two distinct ethnic groups such as between Indian and mestizo, Indian and Negro, and Negro and mestizo. This broadening of the usage of *compadre* terms is especially developed in market place trading (which has a high frequency of inter-ethnic and stranger relationships) and appears to introduce a personal tone into an essentially impersonal activity. Moreover, between "good customers" the diminutive is added to the first name, thereby stressing the element of friendliness in the relationship. When some of the Chota traders were asked why they addressed the buyers as *compadres* and vice versa, one perceptive informant answered "to put one in a mood of greater trust."

Having and maintaining good customers is exceedingly important both from the point of view of the buyer and the seller. The buyer in times of scarcity is assured that her good customers will sell to her during these times. The Chota seller, likewise, during times of glut must depend upon her good customers not only to buy from her but also to extend other types of favors.

During peak productivity, the seller risks the danger of not being able to dispose of all her produce even when her customers buy from her. It would be unheard of to pay the transportation costs to haul the produce back to the Chota Valley or to Ibarra to sell. The perishability of avocados necessitates that she dispose of them that day. There are two alternatives open to the seller when faced with this situation: first, she may trust the avocados to a buyer; and second, she may face the humiliation of selling very cheaply in the wholesale warehouse of the market place. The second alternative is taken only when the first fails.

The system of entrustment (*dejar fiado*) consists of leaving the avocados with a trustworthy buyer to sell during the Chota trader's absence. If the buyer, already supplied with her necessary stock for the week, decides to extend this assistance to the seller, the worth of the avocados is determined that day by both participants. The buyer usually attempts to be just and establishes the value according to the average prices being paid that day in the plan for the same size category.

During the intervening week, she will sell the avocados and pay the predetermined amount of money the following week to the seller. The entrustment system functions to the advantage of both buyer and seller. The direct advantages to the buyer lie in the possibility of making a greater profit than normal in the event that prices rise during the intervening week and in selling without having had to secure the necessary capital with which to buy. An indirect, but nonetheless important advantage is in reinforcing the set of reciprocal obligations between the buyer and the seller. The buyer is thus securing a future supply of stock during the scarcity season, and in addition, will be able to manipulate this favor in obtaining a good price concession. If the seller were not able to entrust her goods, she might be forced to discontinue as a trader. The entrustment system may be viewed as a means by which the seller is shielded from the full force of sudden price drops. The Chota trader, however, is not protected from paying extremely low prices when selling her avocados in the warehouse. During the months of peak productivity, with many of the Chota traders operating largely on credit anyway, such a loss weighs heavily and is especially difficult to recover from.

Other forms of cooperation and mutual assistance expressed through the giving of priorities include the giving of an "extra bit" (*yapa*) of produce to the buyer, and the occasional granting of a cash loan to the seller. The extension of loans to sellers is infrequent, but when it does occur, is interest free.

Friendliness among buyers and sellers is better manifested in inter-active patterns during non-bargaining interludes. During these periods of time, the occupational role identity of "buyer" and "seller" is not sustained. Rather, other identities such as age mates, friends, or members of the opposite sex predominate and define the interaction situation. While the particular pair is engaged in serious bargaining, the dominant interaction element is conflict and opposition in which each participant is attempting to maximize her profit. Although the object of the bargaining is to outmaneuver the other, the relationship is not completely anonymous for the identities of the participants as market place friends is still operative. By definition, however, these identities cannot predominate. The personal relationships shared by the participants in market place exchange is one of the basic resources to be manipulated in bargaining. After the completion of a sale, though, the two are no longer contenders, and their identities as friends comes to the fore through patterns of joking and teasing.

### Ethnic Identity and Monetized Exchange

The nature and extent to which ethnic identity shapes interpersonal behavior in the market place must now be examined. The relations between Negro sellers and *mestizo* buyers who belong to different ethnic groups will serve to initiate a discussion of some significant variables in the role of ethnic identity in monetized exchange throughout highland Ecuador.

Both the mestizo and the Chota Negro traders fall within the lower limits of a hierarchial scale of social status. However, within these limits, the mestizos identify themselves and are identified by all other ethnic groups as higher on the scale of prestige evaluation than either the highland Negro or the Indian. Depending on the region of Ecuador and who is doing the evaluating, the Negro may be placed socially above the Indian, below the Indian, or at the same level. Trading relationships between the Chota sellers and their buyers should, therefore, reflect the asymmetry of ethnic status inequality.

The ethnic identity of each participant in a monetized transaction may be considered to form the setting or the stage for performing buyer-seller roles. The expectations comprising the roles of buyer-seller are well defined and serve quite adequately as guides to action in most situations, whereas the behavioral expectations of ethnic identity are far too generalized to serve as concrete guides to behavior. Monetized exchange in itself does not preclude the entry of ethnic factors, however. There is a set of prescriptive behavior entailed in buyer-seller roles which must be performed in order that the transaction be completed, but within these limits there are differential possibilities for ethnic identity to shape the actual exchange. It is suggested that these possibilities vary with the degree to which the buyer-seller relationship is personalized—whether the exchange is through bargaining or non-bargaining—and the presentation of self by the parties in bargaining encounters.

During the process of reaching a mutually satisfactory price, the relative status positions accorded to the Chota Negroes and their buyers do not appear to be especially significant for understanding the content of the actual interactive performance. Although ethnic identity rarely appears in the content of verbal exchange, this is not to say that it is not significant or that its influence is not felt in bargaining. The individual's self-image as *Negro* or as mestizo and the other's perception of him seem rather to set the broad limits on the sorts of behavior which will be regarded tolerable or acceptable.

It is precisely through instances of an infraction of the parameters of acceptable behavior that the limits themselves become manifest. Such instances occasionally occur in the market place if the transaction process is unusually stressful, as for example when a serious imbalance in supply and demand is perceived. When the market conditions are very unfavorable to either member of the bargaining pair, serious disagreements easily arise between participants who do not share a personalized exchange relationship.

*It is in situations of tension that ethnic identity may be brought into play in the interaction.* For example, a Chota trader was quarreling bitterly with a non-regular mestiza buyer over the ownership of a sack. The potential buyer, in the heat of the argument, called the Chota trader a "thief," and said disgustedly as she began to walk away, "What an ugly nigger!" (¡Que negra tan fea!), the Spanish term for "ugly" having the denotation of being unpleasing both in personal conduct and appearance. The trader shouted angrily back to her, "I am not just anybody, I am a lady! Because I am black, you think you can treat me this way?"—the trader's sarcastic retort to inform the buyer that she had clearly exceeded acceptable behavior. This example is also significant because it summarizes in an interactive context statements by both mestizo buyers and Negro sellers of an ideal that ethnic identity be irrelevant in buyer-seller relations. As Goffman (1959:9–10) has well pointed out, attempts are made to reach an interactional *modus vivendi*: "Together the participants contribute to a single over-all definition of the situation which involves not so much a real agreement as to what exists but rather a real agreement as to whose claims concerning what issues will be temporarily honored."

It is suggested then, that status evaluations based on ethnic identity will be suppressed by the superordinate member of an interaction if expression of asymmetrical evaluation easily leads to open conflict. For those who share an enduring exchange relationship, the consequences of an ethnic offense weigh heavily both in terms of the psychological satisfactions of a market place friendship and mutual economic benefits. The attributes of ethnic membership thus figure as elements in the interaction between "good customers" if only as a determinant of what actions or tactics should not be employed. Ethnic identity, then, proscriptively structures personalized buyer-seller relations by prohibiting the entry of status considerations.

*In impersonal buyer-seller relations involving bargaining, the manner in which the ethnically subordinate individual presents himself bears centrally on how ethnic identity structures the interaction.* The self image presented by the individual is less important in fixed price transactions than the actual social status accorded to the ethnic group. In bargaining, however, in contrast to fixed price transactions (discussed below), the interplay of presented self image and ethnic group status is very important in determining whether ethnicity enters or is excluded from the transaction.

There are stereotyped expectations in highland Ecuador about how members of different ethnic groups behave in interpersonal relations. These expectations constitute the initial information possessed by the participants about each other. The manner in which the individual presents himself—submissively or assertively—offers additional information which either reaffirms or contradicts the ethnic group stereotype. The Chota Negroes are characterized as being assertive in their relations with members of a dominant status group and "volatile" (*impetuosos*) when offended.

Such characterization suggests an incongruence between an inferior social status and non-subservient interethnic behavioral patterns. With the exception of certain regional groups, Indians (unlike Negroes) are expected to behave with deference in the presence of status superiors. These stereotypes are significant in all social relationships but especially so in negotiated price-making.

Bargaining requires that the participants manage an impression of strength, both verbally and through posture or stance. Any signs of submissiveness, even if it simply be a hunched over stance with the head bowed, will be taken advantage of in bargaining. It is not uncommon that sales with Indians be completed in spite of verbal and/or non-verbal ethnic abuse. Examples seen within market places occur most frequently between Indian sellers vis-à-vis aggressive mestizo buyers. Verbal abuse in such transactions stresses the Indian's status inferiority. For example, he may be called a "dirty, piglike Indian" (*indio sucio, puerco*). A bargaining strategy of intimidating one into a hurried unprofitable sale is the frequent result.

Such tactics are only attempted by the dominant partner when there is a good possibility of coercing a sale or when an otherwise silent and submissive Indian has refused to meet the mestizo's price demands. An Indian who does not convey a self image of inferiority is more likely to be treated with respect in bargaining.

When the image conveyed about the individual reaffirms an ethnic stereotype of assertiveness, ethnic status infrequently enters into the exchange. Assertiveness to the point of aggression in bargaining informs the status dominant partner that the Chota traders' concept of acceptable behavior must be honored or no sale will result.

Different from bargaining is the system of fixed price transactions. Impersonal transactions in which some good or service is purchased at a fixed price are interpreted by the Chota Negroes as those situations in which ethnic discrimination most readily appears. One of the most frequent sources of complaint is to be assigned to the last row of seats on a bus after having purchased one's ticket before any of the passengers sitting up front. Buses in highland Ecuador are a symbolic representation of the status differentiations accorded to the various ethnic categories: "whites" sit in the very first rows; a variety of mestizo types are found up toward the front, middle, and back; and Indians and Negroes occupy the last rows of seats.

One Chota Negro, not being able to obtain a seat, volunteered the perceptive comment that "the money of the poor Negro is worthless!" In fact, it is not effective in securing for him adherence to the ideal expressed by the bus personnel of "first come, first serve." Other common complaints are directed toward those who make them wait until last when buying in a store, while mestizos and "whites" who had arrived later are attended to first. Similar differential treatment is found in post-offices and other governmental establishments.

Interestingly enough, when ethnic discrimination is perceived, the Chota Negroes, unlike many Indians accorded similar treatment, do not remain silent. It is because of their candid and forthright public expression of resentment that they share the reputation among Ecuadorian non-Negroes, especially the mestizos, with whom they interact the most, as being aggressive and rude (*mal educados*).

Usually a common element in fixed price transactions is differential treatment symbolized by status ranking. The Chota Negro comes last because there are others of higher social status. Here the status ranking is more important than the self-image which is projected. Fear of losing the Chota traders' business does not appear to be an important sanction in part because ticket salesmen and office personnel are not infrequently salaried petty bureaucratic officials. However, even when there is the possibility of losing the Chota Negroes' business, more business may be lost by not serving the higher status people first. Regardless of economic interest, ethnic discrimination may result through the superordinates' attempts to maintain their ego status and the self-image of other customers.

As has been suggested, these forms of discrimination result from the widespread attitudes of prejudice towards Negroes in the social race sense—i.e., by virtue of being at the bottom of the socio-economic system along with the Indians, and perhaps in some cases to simply being biologically Negro. In any case, at this point in time, the Chota traders' own perceptions of the determining factors do not involve a separation of the biological and the social.

## Summary

This paper has attempted to demonstrate that the study of trading is a useful means of gaining insight not only into the position of the Chota Valley Negroes within the larger context of an ethnically plural society, but also into the patterning of peasant marketing behavior in highland Ecuador. By viewing an internal marketing system as a distributive process, it has been shown that the marketing behavior of the Chota traders cannot be understood with reference only to the patterns which predominate in the arena of the market place. Equally important is the nature of mutual behavioral expectations of buyers and sellers at the level of intracommunity exchange. It is apparent that two sets of behavioral patterns are in operation, each with a different set of rules, but both embracing bargaining activity and personal relationships. Interpersonal relationships in both the rural villages and in the market place are instrumental in that they arise out of a mutual economic need which the exchange of cash for goods may fulfill. However, there are important differences in the nature of this exchange. The ties linking the Chota trader to the producer are enduring and often multiple, exist extrinsically to the exchange relationship itself, and strongly channel the participants' perception of the alternative courses of action which may be pursued. The influence of social ties in decision-making is especially apparent in buying patterns. Although the greatest demand in the market place is for the large avocados, the traders buy all sizes. The mestizo buyers in the valley, free from these restrictions, can directly economize, refusing to buy other than their size preference. The basis for granting priorities (credit, price and quantity concessions, and time extension on payment) arises out of the obligations and expectations, both of an economic and social nature, entailed in the formal ties of kinship, fictive kinship, and the informal ties of friendship and neighborliness. These priorities may be considered part of a wider network of favors and debts of gratitude permeating the social life of the community. Both the traders and the producers from a single village see themselves as sharing a common cultural identity, inevitably interacting with and dependent upon one another. The village is the main point of identification among the Chota peasants, and its separateness from other communities is symbolized in the market place by the village cluster spatial arrangement of the Negro traders.

The interaction patterns in the market place are shaped by both recurrent and non-enduring "stranger" relationships. The former are personalistic ties which introduce an element of trust and minimize conflict. The origin of the buyer-seller personal bonds is occupational in nature and market place friendships are considered to be a major resource to be manipulated in achieving price concessions and other services. The benefits of giving and receiving priorities are mutual for they not only protect the seller from the impact of sudden price fluctuations, but also guarantee the continuity and security of the relationship by cementing the sets of reciprocal obligations. Relationships between non-regular buyers and sellers do not exhibit the personal factors, price concessions are not necessarily given, and it is expected that forms of dishonesty will be attempted. Serious quarrels are prevalent and are not so readily attributed to a possible "mistake" as they are among "good clients."

It is evident that both the buyers and the sellers are influenced by the forces of supply and demand operating in the market place, although neither the price nor the quantity of produce brought to the market is entirely determined by these impersonal forces. Incorporated within the internal marketing system are price concessions and other priorities which introduce "non-economic" factors into the determination of price. Through the system of entrustment the city traders help the sellers receive a price for their avocados above that which they would have received in the market place had they been forced to sell. Moreover, there are attempts by the municipal government to enforce retail price ceilings on produce, thus interfering with the forces of supply and demand that are operating.

Wolf (1966:43) and others point out that there are limitations which are inherent in the peasant type of life inhibiting a capacity to participate flexibly in that part of the economy operating largely through supply and demand. These limitations can be clearly seen in the case of the Chota cultivators who cannot quickly modify production patterns to meet changes in the market price of avocados. However, the personalized economic relationships present at all levels of the marketing process in addition to the alternative occupational role of seller establish a certain resiliency whereby the economic shocks of a monetized market system may be more readily absorbed.

## Notes

1. The writer is grateful to the University of Illinois Department of Anthropology for funds which made the field research for this paper possible and especially to Joseph B. Casagrande of the Department of Anthropology, University of Illinois, for valuable criticism and guidance.

2. The term "mestizo" refers to an ethnic category. It refers to someone who is not recognizable in terms of dress or speech as an Indian, but yet does not belong to the highest socioeconomic stratum of "white." Mestizos may be rural cultivators and non-agricultural specialists. The majority live in urban centers and small villages and are to be distinguished sharply from the Indian in cultural outlook and self-identity.

3. On this point, see A. V. Chayanov 1966. The Russian economist postulates that the key to understanding peasant economic behavior lies in the factors which determine the balance between the urgency of family needs and the drudgery of labor.

4. The value of all other resources used in production, such as the trader's labor, land, and materials, is not considered in his "cost" as quantifiable entities. The labor involved in buying and selling in the orchards, in sorting and packing avocados, and in the long trip to the market is not hired, and therefore not allocated by price. There is very little productive equipment which has to be bought and even that which is, is simply not deducted from the total income. Furthermore, the value of land does not affect "cost" considerations. The Chota peasant does not think of his land in terms of a monetary value recently imputed to it by the Agrarian Reform Institute. It is now possible for the Chota small-holder to mortgage his land to a national credit and development bank for a cash loan, although he still cannot sell his plot on an open land market. However, land was not and is not today viewed as a productive factor in the capitalistic sense; that is, whether or not the selling of avocados is "profitable" to the cultivator and trader has no relation to the market value of his own piece of land. This is not the case with peasants, however, who are paying rent on the land from which they derive produce to be marketed. That owned land is not viewed as a factor of production can be seen by the fact that the trader does not include the value of the produce taken from his land to be sold in the market place in his "cost." Thus, "cost" for the trader is reduced to the amount spent on buying avocados from the plots of other peasants.

5. For a discussion of the assumption of maximizing behavior and its relationship to the processes of decision-making see Joy 1967.

## References

Chayanov, A. V.
   1966    The Theory of Peasant Economy. Homewood, Ill.: Dorsey.

Goffman, Erving
   1959    The Presentation of Self in Everyday Life. Garden City, N.Y.: Doubleday.

Joy, Leonard
   1967    One Economist's View of the Relationship between Economics and Anthropology. In Themes in Economic Anthropology. Raymond Firth (editor). A.S.A. Monograph No. 6. New York: Praeger.

Katzin, Margaret
   1960    The Business of Higglering in Jamaica. Social and Economic Studies 9:297–331.

Mintz, Sidney W.
   1959    Internal Markets as Mechanisms of Social Articulation. Intermediate Socie-

ties, Social Mobility, and Communication: Proceedings of the Annual
Spring Meeting of the American Ethnological Society. Verne F. Ray (editor). Seattle: American Ethnological Society, pp. 20–30.

1961    Pratik: Haitian Personal Economic Relationships. In Patterns of Land Utili-
zation and Other Papers: Proceedings of the Annual Spring Meeting of the
American Ethnological Society. Viola E. Garfield (editor). Seattle: University of Washington Press, pp. 54–63.

Ortiz, Sutti
    1967    Colombian Rural Market Organization: An Exploratory Model. Man
2:393–414.

Sahlins, Marshall D.
    1965    On the Sociology of Primitive Exchange. In The Relevance of Models for
Social Anthropology. Michael Banton (editor). New York: Praeger.

Teran, Francisco
    1966    Geografía del Ecuador. Quito: Editorial Colón.

Wagley, Charles
    1965    On the Concept of Social Race in the Americas. In Contemporary Cul-
tures and Societies of Latin America. Dwight B. Heath and Richard
Adams (editors). New York: Random House.

Wolf, Eric R.
    1966    Peasants. Englewood Cliffs: Prentice-Hall.

# 15. MIGRANTS IN MEDELLÍN

## Peter Wade

### Working in the City

The migration of Chocoanos to Medellín has a double aspect. On the one hand, the majority of them are simply poor migrants to the city, and they face the same problems of housing, work, transport, health, and coping with urban institutions as any other migrant of similar means. In this sense, then, they participate in national processes of rural-urban migration and urbanization. On the other hand, these processes are part of the increasing spatial integration of the national territory in which regions that occupy different positions in the hierarchies of race, power, and culture are brought more closely into contact. In Quibdó, Antioqueño migrants are nonblack entrepreneurs in an underdeveloped black city; in Unguía, Chocoanos lose their tenuous grip on the area to encroaching Antioqueño society. In Medellín, the Chocoanos are blacks in a nonblack city—and nonblack with the vengeance of a region with a whitewashed black history. They are not simply migrants but come from a region classified nationally not just as rural, in the way rural Antioquia is contrasted with urban Medellín, but as unremittingly and completely rural, primitive in its backwardness. Blackness therefore tends to suggest to nonblacks images of the most gauche country bumpkin—an evocation that has to be fought with "civilized" behavior—and this is linked to other stereotypes of blacks as inferior, nonprogressive, lazy and disorganized, images that can survive the overcoming of a rustic identity. As a result of this, the Chocoanos form a specific group with their own ways of adapting to the urban environment, even though these are within the overall pattern of migrant adaptation. The encounter of the Chocoanos with the Antioqueños in Medellín is not just a rural-urban one but also another step in the historical dynamic of being black in Colombia, of coping with a dominant nonblack world by engaging in a dialogue with it in which blacks, understanding the image of them held by nonblacks, try to subvert that image, adopting the discourse and behavior of the nonblack world. Or, equally understanding the image, they try to create or rather re-create their own black world with its distinctive discourse and behavior—a response understood by the nonblack world as confirmation of their impression that the blacks refuse to "integrate."

CHOCOANOS AS MIGRANTS IN MEDELLÍN: BASIC PATTERNS

Medellín, *ciudad de la eterna primavera*, city of the eternal spring. It was once a small colonial town where wooden houses thatched with palm leaves surrounded the central market square, the muddiness of which was only cobbled over in 1857. Now Colombia's second city, with nearly one and a half million inhabitants, it is a major commercial and industrial center whose central square, the famous Parque Berrío, is towered over by several vertiginously high multistory banks and submerged in the constant exhaust fumes of a hundred buses that pass through the cramped city center en route to distant neighborhoods, the destination also of the migrants who leave the countryside and smaller towns of Antioquia to swell the city's population in search of economic betterment. Medellín has a growing and dynamic economy, partly because it is also a major center for the country's cocaine economy; and between the mafiosos and the common thieves and muggers—not to mention the increasing violence of right-wing death squads—the city has acquired a reputation as one of the more dangerous places in Colombia.

On 23 October 1850, the emancipation of the slaves was celebrated in the Parque Berrío, when 133 of them were given letters of freedom (Olano 1939). Nowadays the blacks who congregate there on Sundays are mostly domestic servants, Chocoano women who work in middle- and upper-class Medellín homes. Their black Antioqueño cousins are forgotten in the image of the city, because the Parque Berrío is the symbolic center of the *raza antioqueña*, birthplace of "all self-respecting Antioqueños who are worthy of the name" (*El Colombiano*, Tricentenary Collection, 30 October 1975). In terms of the country's cultural geography, Medellín is also *la capital de la montaña*, the capital of the mountains, where blacks are strangers from the hot lowlands and where the *ritmo paisa*, the *paisa* rhythm, holds sway, imbuing commerce and industry (and death) with a fast-moving efficiency.

Chocoanos in this city deal with employment and housing in ways characteristic of migrants in general. They generally find work in the types of jobs which occupy most migrants to the city: domestic service for women, the construction industry for men, and the "informal sector" for both sexes, specifically the sale of food and drink on the street. Like other migrants, they try to consolidate their economic position and, when possible, educate their children. Some achieve a certain upward mobility into a relatively secure working-class position, while others remain at a more precarious level; some return home. In any case, they make use of networks of contacts with relatives, friends, paisanos, and neighbors to help them in their strategies for survival and progress, as do other migrants. Equally, like other migrants of similar economic status, a minority of Chocoanos solve their need for housing by invading unused land in ecologically marginal locations or by renting rooms in tenement blocks and other low-income dwellings. More commonly, they buy small plots sold by landowners or semilegal urban developers who subdivide larger holdings; or they buy a skeleton dwelling from a "pirate urbanizer" whose products do not conform to municipal regulations; or they may get a plot or a house through the government housing agency, the Instituto de Crédito Territorial (ICT), which they pay off in installments; some also save enough money to buy a house outright. These processes place the majority of Chocoanos in working-class neighborhoods that exhibit varying degrees of consolidation, from newly formed shantytowns to areas with paved roads, public services, and houses with plastered facades. A minority have the means to buy or rent a house in a middle-class neighborhood. As homeowners of all kinds, they—like others—construct or improve their dwellings in a piecemeal fashion, usually with their own labor and helped by relatives, friends, and neighbors.

Yet factors specific to the Chocoanos make their position different. They suffer a certain amount of discrimination in the employment and housing market; they sometimes form certain nuclei of settlement, often where a Chocoano-run dance hall functions or used to function and which are points of congregation where Chocoano culture holds sway, if only temporarily; they have a particularly strong and dense network of mutual aid and information which goes beyond kinship and local ties of city neighborhood or Chocoano river/village loyalties to include all Chocoanos as an ethnic-racial group. This ethnic network has certain key concentrations, including the nuclei of settlement and also certain bars, city locations, and one or two associations. The network also has more rarified parts where families or individuals maintain few links with other Chocoanos: as is the case with many migrants, with the passage of time they integrate into the city and lose contact with original networks and old paisanos from their home territory. In the case of the Chocoanos, however, this process is viewed by them not simply as adaptation to the city but also as assimilation to the nonblack world; as a process of *blanqueamiento*, it may attract criticism and accusations of betrayal and desertion. This is frequently connected with economic consolidation such that upward mobility, even on a small scale, tends to take on meanings that belong to a discourse of race and ethnicity.

METHODS AND SOURCES IN MEDELLÍN

I lived in Medellín for about a year. I started out renting a room in a city center house, once the home of a middle-class Medellín family, which had been converted into rooms-to-let: the owners occupied a couple of the best rooms at the front, and there were nine other rooms with a total of about twenty-five people in the house. Some rooms were cubicles partitioned off with hardboard, and a couple of retainers who did cooking and cleaning slept on the floor in the kitchen. From there I moved into a rented room in La Iguaná, an invasion settlement near the city center which had a significant Chocoano population. Despite being an invasion settlement, it had some parts dating from the 1940s which were well consolidated—although not, for all that, better regarded by the middle-class housing that surrounded it and saw it as a den of crime, vice, and poverty. The house I was in belonged to a Chocoano, Luis Urrutía, and his wife, Delfa, the oldest Chocoano residents of the settlement. It was a two-story house with piped water and electricity, and the lower story, at least, had plastered walls and tiled floors. From there, I moved into an outlying consolidated working-class barrio (neighborhood) called Aranjuez where I rented out a flat with Carlos Pino, his wife Noris, and their two children. Carlos was a black from Turbo, his father a Chocoano, and his mother a local Turbeño woman. Noris was also from Turbo but was more mixed in appearance, with long black hair and light brown skin, a person who would not readily be classed as "black" in Medellín or elsewhere. In this house, everything was legal, power cuts were only occasional, and bills for water, light, and telephone were delivered monthly—in contrast with La Iguaná, where power cuts were frequent, many people paid for electricity by an ad hoc system of charging, many did not pay at all, and there were only a couple of public phones and no mail deliveries. If I had stayed in Medellín, doubtless I would have participated in the next stage of the housing process which occurred when Carlos got his own house from the government's Instituto de Crédito Territorial: it was a structure in *obra negra*, an unfinished state, which could then be improved by plastering the walls, tiling the floor, painting, adding another story, and so on.

The Chocoano presence in Medellín was very varied, and I gathered data on a number of fronts. Through a number of contacts, made originally via friends in Unguía, I visited Chocoano families in their homes all over the city and carried out interviews on their life histories, social networks, and experiences in Medellín. I focused on specific sites of Chocoano nucleation by living in La Iguaná, a locale with probably the highest concentration of Chocoanos in the city, and there I interviewed both Antioqueño and Chocoano families. I also interviewed families in other barrios with obvious concentrations of blacks, usually pursuing contacts made via different city authorities, some involved directly in housing, some in other forms of community organization. I had particularly close contacts with Desarrollo Comunitario, the Community Development office of the municipality which dealt with upgrading low-income settlements. Planeación Social (the municipal social planning office) and Colcultura (the local branch of the Colombian Institute of Culture) also proved a useful source of contacts and information. I had contacts with black- and white-run organizations for domestic servants, the former of which was also a meeting place for Chocoanos from all walks of life. And living with Carlos Pino was an invaluable entry into the Chocoano and Costeño networks in the city. Gradually, my own network expanded so that it included Chocoanos and Antioqueños all over the city and from a variety of classes. For example, knowing Chocoanos in La Iguaná was a fairly sure way of finding a mutual connection with a great many of the Chocoanos in Medellín, at least the poorer ones: if they didn't live there themselves, or hadn't done so in the past, there was a good chance they'd have friends or relatives there.

At the same time, from a mixture of written and oral sources, I learned about the city as an urban place and set of processes, about the construction industry, domestic service and other "informal sector" activities, about local politics and education, about bars, clubs, and music—all this was necessary to conceptualize the Chocoanos in the city.

A brief account of statistical sources is also necessary here, since this and the next chapter rely on a common statistical basis. A principal source for statistics has been the government's 1981 Estudio de Población, which took a 10 percent sample of the city's households and quizzed their occupants on general and labor characteristics. The Departamento Administrativo Nacional de Estadísticas (DANE) sold me a copy of this data set, and I have been able to rework it to analyze the position of Chocoanos in the city. The survey collected a total main sample of 122,000 people. For convenience, I picked out all the households containing a person born in the Chocó and cut the households containing no Chocoanos to a quarter of their original number, giving a total sub-sample of 31,704 people, of which 55 percent were born in Medellín, 34 percent in other areas of Antioquia, and 9 percent elsewhere. The 712 Chocoanos were 2.2 percent of this sub-sample and 0.58 percent of the main sample. Of these 712 Chocoanos, 670 were over 12 years old and thus subject to questions about labor force participation; 415 were actually working at the time.

Other statistical sources for Medellín came from censuses carried out by Desarrollo Comunitario, a municipal agency dealing with "subnormal" barrios. They had information on two city center invasions that also happened to have substantial Chocoano populations, La Iguaná and Moravia, and which they planned to upgrade. Again I was able to rework these censuses for my own purposes. La Iguaná, censused in 1985, had, out of a total of 1,130 families, 141 Chocoano families (12%), and I took a third of all non-Chocoano households for purposes of comparison: data were recorded for each dwelling, for the head of each household in the dwelling, and for their spouse/companion. Moravia, censused in 1983, had a total of 3,031 families with 108 Chocoano families (4%): data were recorded for each dwelling and all its occupants, although often only reliably for the head of household.

The city sample and the Iguaná sample are internally differentiated in ways that affect comparison of the Chocoanos with others. In the city sample, the Chocoanos represent a younger group (41% under 25, compared with 25% of immigrant Antioqueños) and a poorly educated group (65% with primary education or less, compared with 56% for immigrant Antioqueños). Unfortunately, no data were available for time spent in the city. In La Iguaná, their educational status was similar to that of Antioqueños, immigrant or otherwise, but they were a more recently arrived group, both in the city as a whole (62% Chocoanos vs. 56% Antioqueño immigrants had less than ten years city experience, the difference being greater for women) and in the barrio (84% of Chocoanos vs. 60% Antioqueño immigrants had been in the barrio less than ten years). They were also a younger group (58% were under 30, vs. 26% of immigrant Antioqueños). These differences had to be borne in mind when assessing the Chocoanos' occupational and income-earning position. In the city sample, the Chocoanos were a poorer group on average, and this also had to be taken into account when assessing their housing situation. In the Moravia data, the Chocoanos' profiles with respect to age, education, time in the barrio, and income are broadly similar to all others: with these data it was not possible to separate out Antioqueño immigrants from city-born people and other immigrants. In analyzing all these data, I try to give as accurate a picture as possible, making appropriate comparisons and controlling for variables where feasible, without presenting scores of tables. I do not give levels of significance but, unless otherwise stated, only present results that are taken from tables in which the chi-square test shows a significance level of 0.05 or less. This is a limiting factor particularly for the Iguaná and Moravia data, where n is small for the Chocoanos and controlling may reduce it even further for, say, a specific age group.

## DOMESTIC SERVICE

Domestic service is one of the principal occupations for Chocoanos in Medellín. In general, in Latin America, domestic service occupies many women relative to other Third World countries, and, according to Boserup (1974), this is due to the availability of cheap female labor plus a middle and upper class for which domestic technology is still rather costly and yet which is large enough to create a high demand for service. It is also the case that women urban migrants in Latin America often outnumber males, and the job market in domestic service may be a causal factor here. The close juxtaposition of the Chocó, a poor region inhibited by blacks who since colonial times have fulfilled service roles, with Medellín, a city with a quite large commercial and industrial middle and upper class, clearly encourages the migration of black women, who as blacks and as women fit neatly into ideologies that define service as both a black and a female role (cf. Cock 1980; Radcliffe 1990; Gaitskell et al. 1983; Chaney and García Castro 1989, 7). In fact, there are more Chocoano women than men in Medellín, and, although a skewed sex ratio is common for the city as a whole, it is much more biased for Chocoanos than for other immigrants to Medellín. Related to this is the fact that Chocoanos are overrepresented in domestic service, even when compared with Antioqueño immigrants of the same age and educational status.

In the city sample, women were 67 percent of all Chocoanos, while only 58 percent of Antioqueño immigrants were female, compared with 54 percent of all city dwellers. This bias was more pronounced among working Chocoano women, who outnumbered working Chocoano men sixty to forty, roughly the obverse of the ratio for the working Antioqueños, immigrant or city born. Of the approximately 2,740 people counted as "domestic employees" in the main sample, 159 were Chocoanos (6%), and of these, the vast majority were young (under 25) women. Of the 415 Chocoano workers, male and female, nearly 40 percent were female domestics; of the 261 working Chocoano women, 60 percent were domestics. Comparative figures for Antioqueño immigrants are a mere 9 percent and 24 percent, respectively. Controlling for the fact that, relative to working Antioqueño women, working Chocoano women are generally badly educated and that many are young, their relative overrepresentation remains pronounced: significantly, it is greatest among women with primary or some secondary education, which means that even Chocoano women with some education concentrate more heavily in domestic service than Antioqueño women with the same education. The Iguaná sample of household heads indicated that a biased sex ratio is more characteristic of low-income settlements than of the city at large. For household heads and their partners, women outnumbered men by fifty-four to forty-six for immigrant Antioqueños, and by sixty-one to thirty-nine for Chocoanos. Despite more equal sex ratios, Chocoano concentration in domestic service was even more pronounced, with 51 percent of the 59 Chocoano women household heads in domestic service compared with 19 percent of the 37 Antioqueño women household heads. (If all women are included, not just household heads, the figures are 31% for Chocoanos and 6% for Antioqueño immigrants.) Again, controlling for the fact that the Chocoano women are more recent immigrants and are a much younger group than their Antioqueño counterparts does not alter the size of this difference, and even older Chocoano women or those who have been longer in Medellín proportionally outstrip their Antioqueño counterparts, although by a lesser margin (31% vs. 13% for women with more than ten years in Medellín; 40% vs. 17% for women over 25). Thus, although some Chocoano women leave service as they grow older, many remain. The Moravia data again reinforce this picture, with females outnumbering males among both Chocoanos (fifty-nine to forty-one) and others (fifty-two to forty-seven), but with 52 percent of all Chocoano women in service compared with 26 percent of other women over 18 years old. (Inexplicably, occupational data were not recorded for people under 18 in these data.)

Chocoano women who work as domestics generally leave the Chocó for economic reasons (Mena 1975), a combination of difficulties at home, plus the possibility of earning a cash income in Medellín: sending remittances home is common practice (Mena 1975). In addition, for the younger ones, their work frequently gives them their first opportunity to dispose of at least some money as they please, and this independence, albeit severely limited, is attractive. It was not unusual among the women I interviewed, who were or had started out as servants, to find that they had migrated because they "felt like it." In a great many cases, domestic service was a kind of entry into the urban world: a young woman could get to know the city and find her way around from the relative security of a middle-class home. As she became more experienced, she could pick up positions that paid more or had better conditions or perhaps allowed her time off for school or vocational classes. In the great majority of cases, the women lived in their employers' houses and at some point would contract some kind of relation with a man, nearly always another Chocoano, and have a child. This led to a number of possibilities. She might leave live-in domestic service and set up home as a housewife with her man, almost certainly in low-income housing. From home she might continue to work on a daily basis in domestic service or selling cooked food in the streets, a generally more flexible arrangement for a mother; if her man left her, she would be forced to do this, at least until she found another partner. This horizontal move from domestic service to street selling is a common strategy and has been noted in other countries (Bunster and Chaney 1985; Smith 1989). Coping with children under these circumstances is clearly a major problem, in the resolution of which women often made recourse to neighbors, friends, or relatives; it was not rare, however, to shut children in the house all day, with the eldest sibling in charge. Frequently, children would be taken back to the Chocó and brought up there by the woman's family; this would leave her free to carry on as a live-in domestic. Some women would also pay to have their children looked after by another woman and see them only on Sundays. In general, for the women I interviewed who lived with their children in their own accommodations, whether or not a man was present, life in the city had started in domestic service and progressed—as they saw it—to a situation in which they had a family and usually a dwelling, albeit in some cases an illegal shack in an invasion settlement. In many cases, the progression was tangible—having started with nothing, they now had consolidated dwellings and children at school, even at university; in these cases, however, a man with a steady job had usually been present. In this sense, domestic service is a mode of incorporation into urban life, as Jacklyn Cock (1980, 307) observes for South Africa, and it may also be a channel for upward mobility, as Margo Smith found for Lima (Smith 1973; cf. Smith 1989). Nevertheless, there is no way of knowing how representative these women are of all the Chocoano women who enter domestic service: after all, some return to the Chocó, and many continue to work in domestic service even as mothers. In effect, about a third of Chocoano domestic servants have been in service for fifteen years or more.

Statistical data on domestic service were also obtained from the Colombian Association for Population Studies (ACEP) which had a legal aid program for domestics. Their archive had basic data for some 1,120 women, collected mostly between 1984 and 1986, out of which I selected all the Chocoanos (103) for comparison with a sample (228) of the rest, of which 84 percent were Antioqueño immigrants. The Chocoanos were about 9 percent of the total sample. (It is pertinent to observe that the women who register with ACEP are a self-selected sample.)

These data showed that Chocoano domestics were roughly the same as the others in terms of education (about 80% had primary education or less), income (about 90% earned less than the minimum legal wage, with about a third earning less than half that), and age (although, since Chocoanos over 40 are underrepresented among immigrants in general, they are underrepresented among servants too). However, the Chocoanos had some specific features.

1. More Chocoano women had been working in agriculture or mining before entering domestic service (45% vs. 15%); in contrast, while 61 percent of Antioqueños had previously done housework, another 16 percent had had a more urban occupation (e.g., waitress, cleaner, operative) prior to service, compared with only 2 percent of Chocoanos.
2. A further difference was that many more of them (80%) were live-in servants than the others (54%).
3. Yet fewer of them (33%) were single than the others (53%). Instead, they more frequently had relations of *unión libre*, common-law marriage, with a man (17% vs. 6%) or were single mothers (34% vs. 22%); marriage was almost the same for both groups (12% vs. 10%).
4. In agreement with this, fewer (33% vs. 55%) had no children, and more (49% vs. 27%) had more than two.

Regional differences in gender relations here mediate women's relation to the class system (cf. Gaitskell et al. 1983). In Chocoano gender relations and family structures, unions are often more consensual than in other areas of the country, and these unions are not necessarily permanent. People, especially men, tend to be quite mobile as they move around exploiting changeable and unstable income opportunities, and they may change their partner several times during their life span, giving rise to what Whitten has termed "serial polygyny" (Gutiérrez de Pineda 1975; Friedemann 1974, 1985b; Whitten 1974). Thus women tend to head families and have to work independently of men more frequently than in Antioquia, where marriage for a woman more frequently means withdrawal from the paid labor force and dependence on a husband (see also Bohman 1984). Chocoano women are thus often obliged to earn a living, and one option is to continue to work as domestic servants, despite having children or being in a union with a man. Since only 8 percent of them said they lived with their children, versus 24 percent of others, they clearly either sent their children back to the Chocó or had them with other relatives, or possibly in paid care, in Medellín.

For all domestic servants, personal contacts are vital for finding work: for the Chocoanos this assumes particular importance, and they make very limited use of employment agencies. Virtually all of them find a position through an aunt, a cousin, a sister, or, failing those, a Chocoano friend. In a great many cases, their first visit to Medellín is in the company of an older female relative (classified as *tía*, aunt) or a female relative of the same generation (classified as *prima*, cousin), who takes them along after a visit home at Christmastime. There is a tight network involving the black servants and, parallel to this, another network linking white middle- and upper-class women to their friends, neighbors, relatives, and colleagues. Each "maid-madam" relation is a point of articulation between these networks, and this creates a very direct link between Medellín's upper and middle classes and the rivers and villages of the Chocó.

The network linking the Chocoano women—which is, of course, part of the Chocoano network in general—does more than find them an initial position. The women change jobs quite frequently, looking for better conditions or to escape a household they dislike, and the network functions as an ongoing employment exchange. The congregation of black women in the city center on Sundays is an important focus in this respect, but this function of the network is also a more continuous process carried out over telephones, in Chocoano households and in the houses of *las patronas*, the employers. The network is also a source of aid and support: friends and relatives can supply a place to live while looking for work, lend money and clothes, give advice and support in case of problems with a *patrona* or a boyfriend, and, crucially, it can help with child care. Here the fact that the network stretches back into the Chocó is of vital importance, since many women take their children back to the Chocó to be looked after. The women maintain fairly close links with the Chocó, generally returning there over the Christmas period.

The position of domestic servant, while it may be an entry into the urban world and, perhaps, social mobility, is ultimately a degrading one. Of course, there are cases in which the maid is treated as "one of the family" and given a certain amount of freedom, but she is a junior member and largely subject to the disposition of her employers. Generally speaking, the pay is bad and the hours long; women may be fired without warning, and the shadow of sexual harassment always looms. If this leads to pregnancy, a maid is almost invariably made to leave. Lack of information and education, plus the ease of replacing servants, means that these women can rarely enjoy the legal protection that exists for them (García Castro 1989; León 1989). The position is ultimately a servile one, and white images of blackness strongly associate black people, and above all black women, with the servant role. Several Chocoano women described domestic service as *humillante*, humiliating work, in which they occupied a role that was clearly inferior, even if generally they felt that they were reasonably well treated *as domestic servants*. In one extreme case, a black maid was fired ostensibly for having the same name as the employer's daughter; in other cases, the *patrona* rebuked the maid for wearing smart clothes to go out or for putting on perfume: *la muchacha*, the girl/maid, was "getting above her station." Part of this is due simply to status differences between maid and *patrona*, but there is also a strong idea that black women in Medellín are servants and should remain so: young black women students, for example, recounted that Antioqueños sometimes automatically assumed that they were domestic servants. This is to some extent a reaction that stems from the most public face of the Chocoano female presence in the city. As one newspaper article put it (*El Mundo*, 2 March 1986, 5), "By eleven o'clock [on a Sunday morning] the Parque Berrío is theirs." But there is evident exaggeration here, since the blacks only form a small percentage of the total crowd in the Parque Berrío. Again, the director of the ACEP program estimated that 30 percent of her clients were Chocoanos and that this underestimated their participation in domestic service: in fact, the figures from the ACEP 1984–86 data and the citywide 1981 sample are 9 percent and 6 percent, respectively. The Chocoano female presence in domestic service is exaggerated in people's perceptions, and this is due not simply to the overall visibility of blacks in Medellín, specifically black women servants, but also to the idea that all black women are domestics and that domestic service is an appropriate domain for black women.

In terms of political economy, domestic service is not just a luxury but, like all domestic labor, plays an important part in the reproduction of the social body. It is socially necessary labor, even if the so-called domestic labor debate has generally concluded that it cannot legitimately be termed "productive" in the strict Marxist sense of contributing to the creation of surplus value: domestic labor produces use values that are consumed within the household (Smith 1978; Vogel 1983, 23; García Castro 1982; cf. Burton 1985). Nevertheless, it is necessary to view domestic service in a wider perspective. In domestic service, women (and sometimes men; see Hansen 1986) are paid to do other households' domestic labor; in doing so, they free these households' women from some of the domestic labor culturally assigned to them in the sexual division of labor. These women can engage in simple leisure or a variety of roles in the sphere of cultural or economic production: Saffioti's (1978) Brazil study showed that many female employers take paid jobs. They can do this to the extent that domestic service is cheap. Obviously, the economic roles these women may perform when released are ones that the domestics cannot perform due to lack of skills or education (or because they are discriminated against) and are ones that earn more than domestic service costs. From the employing household's point of view, the benefits of domestic service can include more leisure for its female members, the social status that accrues from having servants, an increase in the family income if the women members work, and an increase in family status due to the women's social and cultural activities (anything from giving dinner parties to charity work). It may also be the case that the release of women into certain segments of the paid labor force depresses wages there, while middle-class discontentment is defused by the possibility of wives working for salaries that are many times greater than the wages they pay their servants (García Castro 1989, 117). All this depends on the cheapness of domestic service and thus on the exploitability of the people who do it. The stage is set for this by traditional definitions of domestic labor as women's work and thus as nonproductive (in the popular, as well as strictly Marxist, use of the term) and nonremunerative. The group that does this work for others consists of, most typically, females whose rights, earning power, and education are legally and/or socially restricted; migrants from rural backgrounds, whether in a national or international context, whose qualifications and skills are low and whose rights may be restricted; and ethnic and racial minorities, who often suffer discrimination. Quite frequently, these populations coincide, as in South Africa (Cock 1980), or overlap, as in Medellín, where about 80 percent of domestic servants are female migrants and 6 percent of them black female migrants from the Chocó.

We can now see the role played in Medellín by the Chocó and its women. In essence, the supply of Chocoano women on the domestic service market helps keep the cost of service down, with the results noted above. Significantly, although Chocoano domestics are frequently mothers, they need to work, and they can remain on the domestic service market in Medellín because the kinship-based subsistence economy of the Chocó maintains a good many of their children. In this sense, the Chocó acts as a labor reserve that supplies cheap labor to Medellín, allowing mothers to stay and work in the city and also absorbing some of the cost of reproduction of a labor force, part of which will itself work in Medellín at a later date. (See Wolpe, 1972, for an analogous argument for the South African Bantustans.) In Medellín, Chocoano women have increased their representation in the domestic labor force: fifty years ago there were virtually none; now they are heavily overrepresented there compared with immigrant Antioqueño women. There are two basic factors behind this. On the supply side, the ability to off-load children onto the Chocó gives Chocoano mothers who have to work a competitive edge that increases their participation in domestic service. On the demand side, the prevalent image of black females as servants opens this particular job market to Chocoano women, just as it makes it harder for them to enter any other. This is not necessarily expressed in outspoken preferences for black maids: the important point is the pervasive idea of the appropriateness of blacks, and especially black women, for providing service.

STREET SELLERS

According to the citywide sample, after domestic service, Chocoanos are most frequently employed in a certain sphere of the commercial sector, to wit, the sale of cooked food, fresh fruit, and drinks in public places, a category popularly known as *ventas ambulantes* or ambulant sales (Bunster and Chaney 1985). It is usually a matter of a small barrow with a few crates of beer and *gaseosa* (fizzy soft drinks) and perhaps a bottle or two of *aguardiente*, served out by the shot with green mango or orange slices as a chaser; or a small stall with a charcoal brazier on which are heated *chuzos* (kebabs) and corncobs, or with a pan of oil for frying fish, *empanadas* (corn-flour and meat pastries), and *patacones* (slices of plantain), or with a gas-heated hot-plate on which are fried *chorizos* (sausages) and *arepas de chócolo* (sweet corn cakes); or a trayful of watermelon, mango, papaya, and pineapple, sliced into handy chunks. Sometimes there are slightly larger enterprises with chairs, tables, and awnings which provide a variety of food and drink, and occasionally one sees a small stall selling sweets and cigarettes, but the small-scale sale of food is most typical. These enterprises locate themselves in different ways. Generally they congregate around places of public diversion such as El Estadio, Medellín's largest football stadium and sports complex; the Palacio de Exposiciones, where shows and events are held; the Parque Bolívar, a small city center plaza with monthly art and craft markets; the Parque del Norte, an amusement park; or the Pueblito Paisa, a tourist reproduction of a rural Antioqueño village. Some enterprises have a regular spot in these places, while others move from place to place; still others cater to the ordinary city center trade or to more suburban night spots. Wherever they go, the sellers of chuzos and chorizos have an irregular timetable, usually most active on weekends, with occasional midweek events. Some sellers go farther afield, visiting nearby towns and villages on the occasion of their annual patron saint festivals.

The citywide sample has no specific categories that select this type of activity, but next in importance for the Chocoanos after domestic service is a category that includes *ventas ambulantes* with other shop employees (8% of the employed Chocoano work force). There is also another 4 percent under the rubric of "merchant-owners": since most of these people run enterprises classified under "small-scale commerce and the distribution of food," and since virtually no Chocoanos in Medellín have their own shops, these are almost certainly people with their own small operations selling cooked food. In the citywide sample, the Chocoanos are not overrepresented in either of these categories, even though the activity is an important one for them.

In the Moravia and the Iguaná samples, domestic service still employs the greatest number of Chocoanos (47 and 44 people, respectively), despite being samples of people with their own or rented accommodations. In second place came the construction industry (with 36 and 44 individuals), and in third, *ventas ambulantes* (with 20 and 28 people in each barrio). Only in La Iguaná were the Chocoanos overrepresented in *ventas ambulantes* compared with others (17% of Chocoano household heads vs. 8% of Antioqueño immigrant household heads), but there are indications that this drops out when education and time in the city are controlled for (the numbers become too small to allow significant comparisons). La Iguaná is located very near the Estadio sports complex, and many of the Chocoanos, and the Antioqueños, in the barrio go there to sell food and drink on weekends.

There are several reasons why the Chocoanos tend to concentrate in this particular activity within the whole range of street sales, and within the informal sector as a whole. First, it is an activity that requires little investment or risk. Although some of these stalls, those with chairs, tables, several stoves, and a wide selection of meats and other fried foods, do represent a substantial investment, few Chocoanos own such enterprises, and instead they tend to concentrate on smaller-scale endeavors due to their general status as poor immigrants. Second, the sale of cooked food is an intermediate step between the domestic sphere and commerce proper: the elements and skills needed in it are easily commanded and easily reintegrated into the domestic sphere should the enterprise fail or a change in occupation take place. The sale of cooked food represents a half step into the commercial world, without confronting a host of unknown risks and processes. Third, and connected to this, the sale of street food is particularly apt for many Chocoano women who come to Medellín: this is partly because such an activity is like an extension of the kitchen in terms of skills and experience and partly because it is a fairly flexible occupation that can be adapted to the lifestyle of a single mother who has to look after her home and children. The Moravia and Iguaná samples, although not the city sample, show that Chocoano women are more frequently employed in this kind of activity than Antioqueño women, compared with their menfolk: for the Chocoanos, roughly equal proportions of working women and men are in this activity, while for the Antioqueños the percentage of women involved is about half that of men. In my experience, both in these barrios and citywide, the sale of food in public places is typical of poor, single Chocoano mothers. Clearly for these women, subsistence may be precarious: I came across families that survived on what the mother made one or two days a week.

Given the overall economic and social position of the majority of Chocoanos, the sale of street food represents a viable strategy: it requires minimal investment and risk and permits a good deal of flexibility. Equally, however, the returns are low and unstable and the hours long and antisocial, often involving work on Sundays and long into the night. They are, of course, joined in this position by many Antioqueños, immigrant and city born, who sell prepared food and drink on the streets, although many of this group also make up the other categories of street merchants, offering newspapers, vegetables, clothes, shoes, pens, nailclippers, flowers, bootleg music cassettes, secondhand ironmongery, a shoeshine or shoe repair, cigarettes, sweets, posters, books, magazines, balloons, toys, cheap jewelry, umbrellas, stationery, lottery tickets, or a chance to weigh yourself on a bathroom scale.

## CONSTRUCTION INDUSTRY

The third major source of employment for Chocoanos in Medellín is the construction industry, in which they are proportionally overrepresented compared with Antioqueño immigrants of roughly their age and educational status. Within this industry there are several levels, and the Chocoanos tend to concentrate in some and not in others. At the lowest level is the *ayudante* or helper, equivalent to an unskilled laborer. Next comes the *oficial*, or general-purpose builder, who is able to lay bricks, plaster walls, tile bathrooms, and so on. Also located at this level are electricians, plumbers, carpenters, and painters. Usually there are no qualifications to define this level: an *ayudante* may learn on the job until he feels confident enough to start on his own. Above these is the *maestro de obras*, or general foreman, usually an ex-*oficial*, who gives the *oficiales* their orders, and at the top is the *ingeniero* (engineer) or an architect who is in charge of the whole operation. Within this schema are the *contratistas*, contractors and subcontractors, who range from large-scale businessmen who subcontract out to more specialized contractors who run smaller building firms, to individual *oficiales* who seek out small jobs on a site or in private houses; *contratista* is also used to refer to unskilled individuals who, for example, get contracts digging huge holes with picks and shovels for the foundations of buildings more than five stories in height.

Chocoanos are, in the great majority, *ayudantes* and *oficiales*, the latter generally being small *contratistas*, rather than employees of a building firm. Typical is the small *oficial* with a few *ayudantes* who does small private building jobs or small contracts on a site. The unskilled *contratista* who gets digging contracts is also a common figure. Significantly, the foundation holes that the gang digs are referred to as *pilas*—the same term used in the Chocó for the artificial reservoir dug above a mine working to provide running water for a *mina de agua corrida*— and there are obvious parallels between the *cuadrilla* mining gang and the digging gang. These *paleros*, shovelers, may also be day laborers who stand at certain spots—just by La Iguaná, for example—where dump trucks pass by to collect them for work shifting earth and debris. Almost no Chocoanos are maestros, and I came across no Chocoano *ingenieros*.

Work as an *oficial* or *ayudante* is very unstable: a man would count himself lucky to work as many as six months in a year; *paleros* sometimes spend whole days waiting in vain for a truck to pick them up. In this situation, contacts and information are vital, and the building trade has its own spots in the city center where people meet to exchange news, pick up tips on work, and find *ayudantes* or *oficiales* to do contracts. Naturally, the Chocoano network also operates here, and it is very common for a Chocoano *oficial* to have other Chocoanos as his *ayudantes* and for a Chocoano *contratista* to have Chocoano *paleros* on a digging contract. This is partly because other Chocoanos are part of the immediate social network, but there is also a positive preference: "There's greater understanding between paisanos, especially in the language: you can talk fast and they understand you," said one Chocoano builder. And there is some distrust of Antioqueños: "The Antioqueño thinks he's really smart, so when he works with a Chocoano, he tries to put one over on him." However, it is also true that, in a city in which Chocoano-Antioqueño relations are typically those of subordinate to superior, the construction industry does present occasional examples of the opposite, when a Chocoano *oficial* employs Antioqueño *ayudantes*.

The citywide sample shows an overrepresentation of employed Chocoano men in the construction industry compared with employed male Antioqueño immigrants (20% vs. 11%). The Iguaná data reflect this even more strongly (49% vs. 17%), and the Moravia data also confirm the pattern (18% vs. 6%), although they can only compare the Chocoanos with all others, not just immigrants. The latter data break construction workers into maestros, *oficiales*, and *ayudantes* and show that workers split roughly equally between *oficiales* and *ayudantes* for both categories. There is just one Chocoano maestro. If age and education are controlled for in the city sample, the Chocoano overrepresentation remains in a slightly more marked form for people under 40 years old and for those with less than completed secondary education. On average, Chocoano men in Medellín are older and better educated than Chocoano women, so controlling in this way is less necessary and has less impact on patterns of overrepresentation. In the Iguaná data, controlling for age and time in the city again does not diminish the basic pattern of Chocoano overconcentration in construction.

The construction industry is an expanding one, both nationally, where the population occupied in it has risen from 3.5 percent of the economically active population in 1951 to 6.9 percent in 1985, and in Medellín, where the proportion of the employed male population in this activity rose from 9 percent to 13 percent between 1977 and 1985 (Camacol 1986; DANE's National Household Surveys) and where the area under construction has risen steadily, doubling between 1980 and 1986 (Camacol 1986). This reflects a number of trends: rural-urban migration and a growing urban population create more demand for housing, and even the urban poor employ some paid labor for their housing needs. The reorganization of the city center and the municipality's construction of housing schemes also generate new demand. And the cocaine trade, centered on Medellín, also generates a demand for luxury housing. The construction industry absorbs a great deal of unskilled labor and gives excellent opportunities for learning on the job; there is almost no control on qualifications, and building firms subcontract out between 60 and 70 percent of their work: this represents a fairly open market. Nevertheless, there is an oversupply of unskilled compared with skilled labor, and firms have a problem fulfilling their need for skilled people (Camacol 1986). So, although the construction industry is theoretically easy to enter, there is strong competition within it. An indication of this is the fact that wages in construction are consistently only 70 percent of those in manufacturing industry. The influx of black male migrants from the Chocó clearly plays a role in all this: they are part of the oversupply of unskilled workers and of builders with basic skills, and their presence helps keep wages in the industry down, maintaining a pool of cheap labor for the expansion and remodeling of the city.

OTHER OCCUPATIONS: TEACHERS,
POLICEMEN, AND PROFESSIONALS

Domestic service, *ventas ambulantes*, and construction are the major occupations for Chocoanos in Medellín, but in smaller numbers Chocoanos are also to be found in other occupations. There is a handful in manufacturing industry, which is otherwise the sector that employs most men and women in the city: generally, the Chocoanos do not have the experience and the skills needed to work in industry. An even smaller number work in commerce, outside the *ventas ambulantes* field: I came across just two who worked as sales representatives in established commercial firms. However, there are two occupations in which the Chocoano presence is notable: teaching and the police force.

In the days when Diego Luis Córdoba and Vicente Barrios revolutionized education for blacks in Quibdó, several *escuelas normales*, or schools designed to produce teachers, were created, and since that time many Chocoanos, taking advantage of one of the few opportunities open to them, have trained as teachers and found work either in the Chocó or very often outside their department: they are often found in the most isolated and distant regions, such as Guainía and Meta in the Amazon basin. At one point in the mid-1980s, eleven of the fourteen *jefes de núcleo* (a person in charge of several schools in a district) in Meta were Chocoanos. In Medellín, too, there are a good many Chocoano teachers, without their being overrepresented in this category, according to data in the citywide sample (4% of Chocoanos vs. 4% of immigrant Antioqueños vs. 3% of city-born people). Being a *profesor*, or teacher, carries a certain amount of status, and it is clear that, economic considerations apart, this is attractive for the Chocoanos, who in this fashion chip away at the racist stereotype of the black as primitive and uncultured. During much of my stay in Medellín I lived with Carlos Pino, who was a *profesor*, and I learned that, whatever the status involved, a teacher's salary gave little room for maneuver, partly because it is low by any standards and partly because the government is notorious for delaying payment and holding back extras for months on end: there are constant strikes just to get the basic salary paid. I used to socialize with Carlos and his other teacher friends, Chocoanos and other blacks from Turbo, who would meet in the center of town in the evenings for a drink or two and to exchange rumors on whether that month's pay was coming through.

Interestingly, there are clear gender differences between Antioqueños and Chocoanos in their participation in the teaching profession. For the immigrant Antioqueños, teaching is a mainly female profession, occupying 8 percent of women in the city sample and only 2 percent of men. Comparative figures for city-born Antioqueños are 5 percent of women and 2 percent of men. For Chocoanos, however, 5 percent of men teach compared with only 3 percent of women. One explanation may be that men tend to monopolize occupational positions that, from their point of view, are seen as advantageous (cf. Beavon and Rogerson 1986). For Chocoanos, teaching is a good option, hence men tend to enter into it where they can; for Antioqueños, it is relatively less so, and it becomes a feminine occupation.

Rather like teaching, the police force represents a good economic opportunity for a Chocoano man: with a little secondary education and a six-month training course, he can have a steady, if modest, income and the status of authority. In the Chocó itself, this represents an important advance, and the Chocoano trainees who go to the police training school in Medellín generally like to return to the Chocó if they can; the Antioqueño lieutenant in charge of training there in 1986 said: "To be a policeman in the Chocó is like being a professional here: they say so themselves." In that year's course, the graduate trainees were 11 percent Chocoano, 48 percent Antioqueño, and 41 percent from other areas of the country: clearly, the police force was an attractive proposition.

The small nucleus of Chocoano professionals is an interesting case: they are well-educated people, not infrequently quite light skinned, usually from families in Quibdó which have some resources there and which have been able to finance their children's studies up to university level, generally in such fields as law, medicine, dentistry, and accounting. The unusual thing is that they are not significantly underrepresented in the city sample in the various professional categories (5% for both Chocoanos and immigrant Antioqueños vs. 7% for city-born people). This is a reflection of the importance of education for the Chocoanos and also of how education for the Chocoanos tends to draw people out of the Chocó: in order to qualify in these professions, Chocoanos have to study in the interior, and since the opportunities for employment in the Chocó are limited, they often try to work in the cities of the interior as well.

THE CHOCOANOS' POSITION IN MEDELLÍN

From the citywide sample, two things at least are clear. One, the Chocoanos are a rather younger and somewhat less-educated group compared with Antioqueño immigrants. Two, the women concentrate heavily in domestic service and the men in construction compared with Antioqueño immigrants, even when age and educational status are controlled for. Both domestic service and construction yield low and/or unstable incomes, as indeed do *ventas ambulantes*, but the data on income are very hard to interpret. In the city sample, between 40 and 50 percent of working respondents declared zero income, and anyway accuracy and candor in this matter are always in doubt. The available data show the Chocoanos as a low-earning group, with a third earning below the minimum wage compared with a mere 5 percent of immigrant Antioqueños, but removing domestic servants from the sample (whose low wages are partly, but not wholly, due to many being live-in employees) almost removes this disparity, suggesting that the Chocoanos outside domestic service earn practically as much as other Antioqueño immigrants, within the limits of trustworthiness of these data. It is significant that removing domestics from the sample also balances the Chocoanos and the Antioqueño immigrants almost completely with respect to age and education.

For La Iguaná and Moravia, settlements on the lowest rungs of Medellín society, where the Chocoanos are broadly matched with other residents in terms of education (although they form a younger, more recent group in La Iguaná), the data show the same occupational patterns, although most of the domestic servants in these samples are day, not live-in, workers. Again the Chocoanos' income profiles roughly match those of Antioqueño immigrants in La Iguaná or those of all others in Moravia. In the Iguaná data at least, the great majority of household heads declared some income, although in Moravia 70 percent of respondents declared no income. If we take the data on income seriously, along with the other data, there are a number of conclusions. One, a small minority (about 10%) of well-educated Chocoanos are well placed as professionals or somewhat less well placed as teachers. Two, given their education and experience, a majority (about 50%) of Chocoanos enter the job market in its lower echelons but compete and achieve reasonably equally relative to Antioqueño immigrants at those levels, although they · concentrate in specific sectors within them. Three, a large minority (about 40%) of Chocoanos are female domestic servants, often young women, and, although they are on equal terms with other domestic servants, the burden of child care is greater for them, and they depend more on kinship and ethnic networks to cope with this. If we reserve judgment on the income data, the above conclusions hold, except that we have no idea as to how equally the Chocoanos are in fact performing: the data on housing quality in the next chapter may indicate that they are in fact performing slightly worse.

There are two more general considerations. The first is that the vast majority of Chocoanos can only compete, especially initially, at the lower levels of the occupational ladder: nearly 70 percent are employed in domestic service, construction, and *ventas ambulantes*. This is clearly connected to their background and the historically determined social and economic characteristics of the Chocó. In this sense, the Chocó as an underdeveloped region is clearly providing cheap, unskilled labor to the developing urban economy of Medellín. While migration from the Chocó to Medellín may represent a step up the ladder of regional value, being a move into a relatively developed, urban, central, and nonblack locale, the chances of significant upward mobility are limited. Chocoanos enter what has often been referred to as the "informal sector," and although there was at one time a vogue—still current in some circles (see De Soto 1989)—for seeing this "sector" as a thriving center of potential capital accumulation, critics have tended to concentrate on the exploited and subordinate position of many people working in this type of activity. This approach points out that the informal sector, or more precisely, certain specific groups within this heterogeneous and vaguely bounded descriptive category, have positive functions for the so-called formal sector, or again more precisely, for certain dominant capitalist or state sectors (Roberts 1978; Burgess 1979; Moser 1979; Bromley 1979). This line of argument can verge on a teleological functionalism that reifies the "needs" of capital and ignores possible contradictions between different capitalist and state interests (Gilbert 1986). However, recent work has given greater rigor to the concept of the informal economy, and clearly a sector of the economy which escapes official regulation, whether due to the absence of such legislation or the lack of its enforcement, does have specific relationships with, and functions for, specific interests in the regulated sector and in the state bureaucracy (Portes, Castells

and Benton 1989). For example, self-help housing and community servicing saves
government expenditure on these services and reduces housing costs for the urban labor force, keeping wages down (Gilbert and Gugler 1981, 113). Some industries use an outwork subcontracting system or use dependent workers disguised as independent workers in order to pay lower wages and eliminate costs
associated with secure, permanent employees (Roberts 1978, 116; Bromley 1979;
Portes, Castells and Benton 1989). Street vending of food has a less obvious role
to play here, but it arguably reduces the cost of reproduction of the labor force,
both manual and white-collar. In any event, this type of approach severely under-
mines the idea that work that escapes official regulation is an open road to upward mobility: much of it remains at the level of subsistence because of its subordinate relation to the regulated economy.

The second consideration is that racial discrimination may be restricting the
access of Chocoanos to occupational opportunities. This is, of course, hard to
prove. For example, the fact that Chocoano men concentrate heavily in construction, much more so than immigrant Antioqueño men of similar age and education, is not in itself proof of racial discrimination. Although construction is an
unstable occupation, the income data cannot support the contention that Chocoano men earn less than Antioqueño men. Therefore Chocoanos may concentrate there due to preference and the operation of the ethnic network. However,
there is a strong argument that the concentration of Chocoano workers in domestic service indicates a relative exclusion of them, especially the men, from other
occupations. This is a contentious issue, since it might be objected that this concentration could be more related to unspecified factors internal to the Chocó
which push more women out to Medellín than men, and to Chocoano family
structures that tend to engender a relatively large number of single-mother families in which the woman is obliged to find work to support her children. Rather
than Chocoano men being excluded, Chocoano women are simply working
more than Antioqueño women, who instead tend to be housewives. This is undoubtedly partly the case, but there are three factors that support the exclusion
hypothesis. First, according to 1973 census figures, Chocoano men are as numerous as Chocoano women in Antioquia, if Medellín is excluded: they went at that
time, and still go, in large numbers to the Urabá zone banana plantations where
they worked principally in the heaviest manual labor, the digging of drainage
ditches (although it appears that nowadays they are less specialized). Men leave
the Chocó on a par with women, but they do not end up in Medellín. If opportunities were open in Medellín, as they were for women in domestic service,
surely they would also have migrated to the city in larger numbers. In fact, the
main opening for them then, as now, was construction and *ventas ambulantes*,
notoriously unstable activities. Second, Chocoano women who are married to,
or living with, a man work more frequently than Antioqueño immigrant women
in a similar position, and although this could be due simply to different attitudes
towards women and their role in the home, or to the different contributions men

make to the family budget, it also suggests that Chocoano men are at a disadvantage in the job market and depend more on women's earnings. Third, there remains the very obvious concentration of Chocoano women in domestic service. They do not participate in other occupations as much as immigrant Antioqueño women: for the latter, white-collar administrative jobs, commercial activities, industrial jobs, and seamstressing all occupy greater proportions than for Chocoano women, even when age and education are controlled for. This certainly suggests the impact of racial discrimination, since domestic service is unquestionably a low-earning and low-status occupation.

This is not conclusive evidence. Counterarguments would (a) attack the absence of data on time spent in the city, which would be an important control factor in the citywide sample; (b) point out the generally agreed-upon inferior quality of the Chocoano education system compared with the Antioqueño system; and (c) note how ethnic networks can create concentrations in certain occupations. But the evidence presented here has to be taken in conjunction with the evidence of the Chocoanos themselves.

One black woman student, born in Medellín of Chocoano parents, reported that she was rejected at an employment agency with the words, "We don't place blacks here." Previously, when unsuccessful in job applications, she had always thought of other reasons for her failure, although the specter of racism was in the back of her mind, but this time, "I felt as if a bucket of cold water had been thrown over me." For her, it was a particular case: the agency a disreputable one, the man in charge rude and ill-mannered; she did not see it as a symptom of a more widespread phenomenon. A Chocoano physician, however, was more skeptical: "Things are difficult in Colombia, and above all in Medellín; you have to fight your way through. There's a structural aspect that nowadays is quite clear." He was referring to the Antioqueños' ethnic exclusiveness, which limited the access of the Chocoanos to the institutions, public and private, which they controlled. He had studied medicine in a university in Medellín, teaching as he studied, and after a practical year in the Chocó he found himself unable to get his foot back in the door, despite the necessary qualifications and good political contacts in the right places: he could get only short-term replacement contracts from the Social Security Department until he became a partner in a practice established by another Chocoano physician. He admitted that Antioqueño exclusiveness probably affected other non-Antioqueños apart from Chocoanos, but, while this is true, it is also a fact that the Chocó is the fourth largest source of immigrants to Medellín, after Valle del Cauca, Risaralda, and Bogotá. Since Risaralda and the northern Valle del Cauca are within the Antioqueño cultural sphere of influence, it is Bogotanos and Chocoanos who are liable to bear the brunt of *paisa* exclusiveness. In addition, Antioqueño exclusiveness is hardly separable from their ideas about the *raza antioqueña*, which defines itself in opposition to blacks, so it is inevitable that ethnic exclusiveness based on regional identity overlaps into racism.

Instances of direct, overt discrimination are fairly unusual, and it is clear that discrimination is not systematic and generalized. Indeed, some Chocoanos denied that racism existed at all. Others, however, were certain that it did, or had. In the words of one Chocoano woman,

> [In the 1950s,] people looked at a black person like something strange, like a ghost or something from another world. But nowadays there's not much [racism] because people of 20 or 25 years old have lived among the blacks . . . it's not strange for them. There are still one or two people [who are racist], but. . . . You have to understand that in those days, in a rich barrio, you didn't feel bad; but you went to a poor barrio and you felt more like sinking into the ground. But people have changed.

Nevertheless, people still reported deprecatory remarks, looks, and attitudes. There is a basic assumption that a black person is of low social status, and this has to be specifically contested. Carlos Pino, for example, found that in the school where he taught he was more than once mistaken for the janitor by Antioqueño parents: "They denied me a certain social position simply because of the color of my skin." Equally, young black women found themselves identified as domestic servants irrespective of their real status.

By the nature of the racial order in Colombia, racial discrimination against blacks is not systematic. There are, however, strong indications that Chocoanos are generally admitted to servile and manual occupations and that they encounter dissimulated resistance when they try to break out of these roles. This would help account for the striking concentration of Chocoano women in domestic service, which is otherwise hard to fully explain. It also fits in with what many Chocoanos reported on the assumptions made about blacks which classed them as low status, uneducated, and so on. The critical problem here in amassing evidence of racial discrimination is, of course, the nature of the racial order itself. Individual mobility is accepted conditionally, and discrimination is not systematic. Blacks are seen as inferior, but the qualifications and background of the vast majority in any case only suit them for the type of work which is assumed by many nonblacks to be appropriate for them. The tiny number of blacks who challenge these preconceptions can be accommodated on an individual and conditional basis. Thus overt discrimination is only likely to occur where not only is there relative clarity about blackness and nonblackness, but there is also a competitive relation between aggregates who can identify each other in these terms, or there is a perceived attempt by a "black" to challenge what are felt to be the conditions of acceptability. Competition was perhaps clearest in Unguía, where an Antioqueño frontier mentality involved clearly racist elements; but as the next chapter shows, it has also occurred in specific contexts in low-income settlements in Medellín, although the competition was about territory and cultural authority rather than jobs or wealth.

## Living in the City

Although Chocoanos tend to concentrate in certain types of employment, the black presence tends to manifest itself more plainly in the realm of consumption rather than production. Concentrations of people easily identifiable as "black" in the Medellín context occur in certain locales, and where this has happened, confrontations and antagonism have sometimes developed. When faced with black community taking an assertive and vocal stance, the working-class Antioqueño reaction has been hostile and has generally pushed blacks into adapting their behavior. The majority of Chocoanos, however, do not live in such locales and instead are widely dispersed around the city.

### CHOCOANOS IN THE URBAN SPACE OF MEDELLÍN

The history of Chocoano migration to Medellín largely mirrors the overall processes that characterize the growth of the city. After about 1920, Medellín began to grow rapidly, spurred first by industrialization in the city, then by the 1930s depression and low coffee prices, and later, after 1948, by La Violencia, the waves of civil violence between warring Liberal and Conservative factions which affected the whole country. Equally, the classic causes of rural-urban migration, such as polarization of landholding and the concentration of resources and services in the city, had a continuous effect. Within the city, from about 1920, a split began to develop within El Centro, the city center, between a traditional, more upper-class area around the Parque Berrío (prior to 1892 a typical provincial town marketplace) together with its neighbor, the Parque Bolívar, and a newer, brasher, dirtier, and more lower-class area around Guayaquil, the location of the new marketplace, the train station, the bus terminals, and hundreds of cheap hotels, pensions, tenements, brothels, small shops, and bars. Here was the arrival point for the new immigrants, and it was an area looked down upon by the "ancestral Medellín" (Viviescas 1983). Nevertheless, both zones partook of and contributed to *paisa* identity: the Parque Berrío continued to be a symbolic center of Medellín and Antioqueño identity, where any "self-respecting" Antioqueño was born, figuratively at least; but Guayaquil, now a *zona de candela*, a zone of fire (gunfire and heat), was also the "synthesis of the mightiness of a race" (Upeguí 1957), bursting with Antioqueños of rural origin, teeming with commercial ventures and wheeling and dealing.

Around 1950, the city decided to implement a Pilot Plan, designed by foreign architects, which envisaged the transformation of El Centro, in search of a city center that would "personify the driving spirit of the Antioqueños" (José Luis Sert and Paul Weiner, cited in Planeación Municipal 1980). Fundamental to this was the breaking up of Guayaquil, dispersing its transport and market facilities to more distant locations, building new roads and avenues through it, and construct-

ing a new administrative center on a spot known as La Alpujarra, a zone surrounding the now disused railway station and occupied until 1982 by a small
shantytown invasion settlement also known as La Alpujarra. The whole area of
Guayaquil acquired commercial value, and the cheap hotels, tenements, and
pensions began to be replaced by workshops, ironmongeries, and auto-parts
stores—a transformation that is still in progress today. The low-income dwellers
of the area took several different routes. Some went into nearby city center areas
that had escaped these changes, converting them into tenement zones. Many
went to a neighborhood called Barrio Antioquia, just outside the city center,
which in a rather absurd 1952 decree had, without warning, been declared the
only official red-light district in the city and was taking over some of the functions
of the old Guayaquil. And many more dispersed to the more peripheral barrios,
where they invaded, bought plots of land or skeleton dwellings, or rented accommodations (CEHAP 1986, 81). The inhabitants of La Alpujarra shantytown, along
with other city center invaders, were moved into municipal housing schemes
in various outlying barrios, where they paid for dwellings, if they were able, in
monthly installments. This dispersal coincided with the increasing growth of the
city's *barrios populares*, a euphemistic term covering consolidated working-class
areas, peripheral invasions, and pirate urbanizations. By 1930, invasions, illegal
subdivision, and sale of urban lots had already begun, and from 1940 their number increased rapidly, fed by rural migration as well as by the poor displaced from
the city center. Today, the city is surrounded on most sides by ever-growing low-
income settlements of various kinds; only in the southeast is this ring broken by
the elite suburbs that house the rich families who once reigned over the ancestral center of Medellín but retired in the face of noise, pollution, insecurity, and
overcrowding. The city authorities estimated in 1985 that there were some fifty
thousand people living in what they term *barrios subnormales* (Mosquera 1976;
Planeación Metropolitana 1985).

Chocoano emigration focuses in order of importance on Medellín and Cali,
the Urabá banana zone, Bogotá, and the Atlantic coast cities (DANE 1985b, 122–
28). Migration to Antioquia in significant numbers has been quite recent: as late
as 1930, most of the journey had to be made by mule, and a reasonable dirt road
did not open until about 1946. According to the national censuses, there were
3,811 Chocoanos in Antioquia in 1951; 10,174 in 1964, and 18,490 in 1973, rising from 0.3 percent to 0.6 percent of the total population. Figures on Chocoanos in the municipality of Medellín are very scarce: the 1973 census gives
a figure of 5,978 (0.5%), and a 1981 population study of a 10 percent sample of
the city (DANE 1985b, 126) gave an expanded figure of 7,423 (0.6%), with another 885 estimated in neighboring municipalities within the Metropolitan Area
of Medellín. The accuracy of these figures is, of course, open to question, and it
is quite possible that they are underestimates. Nevertheless, the 1981 study does
cover all barrios, including peripheral and illegal ones, and does explicitly in-

clude live-in domestic servants, both categories that would include many Chocoanos and that one might otherwise suspect would be badly covered.

In the 1950s, the Chocoanos had small concentrations of settlement near the
Guayaquil area—specifically in an area called La Bayadera—in small zones of
tenement buildings; this area was also a center for diversion and dancing on Sundays, when the black domestic servants had their day off. Other Chocoanos dispersed straight out into the more outlying consolidated *barrios populares*, and, of
course, a great many were live-in domestic servants in middle- and upper-class
barrios. With the slow transformation of the inner-city tenement zone and the
transfer of people and activities between it and Barrio Antioquia, the latter became a new focus for Chocoano settlement, although others clung on to islands
of tenement buildings which still survive today, and some, along with Antioqueños, invaded the nearby Alpujarra land belonging to the railway station and
built shacks that were only finally removed in 1982 in a resettlement program.

Chocoano settlement in Barrio Antioquia was accelerated by the location
there in 1963 of the headquarters of the Association of Chocoanos Resident in
Antioquia, founded in 1962 by a group of Chocoano professionals as a social,
mutual aid, and educational society. The association held dances and other functions and gave classes in sewing, first aid, and so on, directed principally at the
black domestic servants. Shortly after, other Chocoanos in the barrio started up
dance halls, and the neighborhood became a focus for Chocoanos, who would
come from all over the city to dance and meet their paisanos on Sundays. Many
also rented rooms in the tenements that were increasingly appearing. The black
servants suffered a good deal of abuse on the streets of the barrio from the local
youth, who would shout racist insults, run off with the women's umbrellas, and
generally make life unpleasant for them. Things came to a head in the late 1960s
when Chocoano settlement was at its peak, and the civic leaders of the barrio,
who had already fought strongly, but with only partial success, against the 1952
decree making their neighborhood a red-light district, started a quiet campaign
among the owners of tenements and rooms-to-let to restrict Chocoano settlement
there. The civic leaders considered the young women in particular to be loud,
foul-mouthed, and bad mannered, and the landlords had already had problems
with several women crowding into a room let out to one person. This campaign
braked Chocoano settlement, while many of those who already lived there, like
other tenement dwellers and rentees, began to move out in search of their own
homes, whether on invaded land or in pirate urbanizations. Barrio Antioquia had
passed a phase of its life: from a quiet working-class neighborhood of the thirties
and forties, it was suddenly converted, in the 1950s, into a red-light district, becoming a barrio with a noisy and energetic nightlife, full of bars, cheap tenements, prostitutes, and high livers; towards the end of this period, in the 1960s,
figured the Chocoano dance halls and the crowds of blacks who came to dance
on Sundays. By 1986, all the black dance halls had closed, and only a score of

Chocoano families remained; equally, the barrio's status as a red-light district had passed—it had since become a center for petty drug dealing and small-time drug mafiosos, whose vendettas still occasionally rack the neighborhood.

Nowadays, Chocoanos are distributed widely over the city, a process of dispersal which has always existed alongside their concentration, temporary or long term, in certain areas such as Guayaquil or Barrio Antioquia. They live mostly in the *barrios populares*, in the more consolidated areas; they also live in less consolidated, more peripheral barrios formed by accretive invasion or illegal subdivision and pirate urbanization (barrios that, in time, tend to consolidate and upgrade themselves with help from the municipal authorities and political patronage); and they also live in the two remaining city center invasions that have not been eradicated, La Iguaná and the zone known as Moravia, in the center of which is located what was until recently the municipal garbage dump. A small minority also live in middle-class areas that roughly correspond to their economic status. Nevertheless, the sociospatial relationship of the Chocoanos to the city is not simply a result of their primary condition as poor immigrants, most of whom have little education or city experience. The Chocoanos also form ethnic enclaves in some of the barrios where they live, and, as was the case in Barrio Antioquia, music and dance are often a focus, sometimes simply in the form of a private house commercially used for dances on weekends. These ethnic enclaves are points of congregation and exchange of information, and they can also act as places where Chocoano culture is reproduced, albeit in forms that would appear altered to a Chocoano "back home." In this sense, these enclaves are foci where a new urban form of black culture is being elaborated.

The localized concentrations in the outlying barrios or in the city center invasions may be noticeable only to those who live or work thereabouts, but the concentrations in El Centro are visible to all. There on Sundays many Chocoanos, especially the domestic servants, congregate on the steps and low walls around and in the Parque Berrío to pass the time of day and exchange news. Nearby, a few bars have been colonized by them, and the strains of *vallenato* accordion music from *la Costa* blast from jukeboxes over tables where hardly a white face is to be seen, except for those of the Antioqueño staff. Along the way a little, another group of bars vibrates with earsplitting salsa music, and again the blacks congregate there, although as salsa has become fashionable music among the younger Antioqueños as well, there are more white faces to be seen in these places. It is in the very heart of Medellín that the black presence is felt most publicly: the usually invisible army of black maids dispersed around the city suddenly becomes apparent (while their Antioqueño sisters remain unnoticed in the Sunday crowds); the groups of black men loafing on corners—as are so many other Antioqueños—spring to the eye. Right where all "self-respecting" Antioqueños can claim to trace their roots, there also are the Chocoanos, a contrast that has not failed to attract the attention of the local press. A reporter in *El Colombiano*, a Medellín newspaper, wrote thus: "The Chocó has inundated our main recreational centers in Medellín, above all at weekends and on holidays. On these days, they take over the steps of the Banco de la República, the Parque Berrío and the Parque Bolívar, the Zoological Gardens, the shopping malls and other places of recreation throughout the city, where the dirtiness of the streets and avenues can now be noticed." Further on, he refers to "the bad habits, excesses, lack of culture and the vulgarity of some Chocoanos . . . with no curb on their instincts" (16 July 1986, 13A).

I would occasionally drink with Chocoano and Costeño friends in one of the Chocoano bars, El Salón Suizo, and on one occasion took some photos there for purposes of illustration—an act that could not help but draw attention to me, especially as a white. Twice I was challenged by Chocoanos who objected to the sensationalist reports they had seen in the papers and which poked fun at the blacks: luckily, I was able to convince them of my serious intentions. Recalling how, a few minutes after I entered the Suizo for the first time, gunshots were puncturing a ceiling already peppered with bullet holes and how a knife or two appeared shortly after—all of which was noise and no action—or recalling the odd fight I had witnessed between a couple of young Chocoano women over some romantic attachment, I could see the scope for cheap sensationalism if the newspapers wanted to pick on the blacks' supposed lack of culture, even though in Medellín such incidents are of daily occurrence all over town.

El Centro is a critical focus for the city and has been ever since the Spanish imposed on Hispanic America their classic town plan with a central plaza around which were located the main institutions of power and authority: the church, the administration, and the houses of the wealthy citizens. In Medellín, El Centro has seen the class conflict between the "ancestral Medellín" and the new, pushy Guayaquil, in which the rich finally moved out of an increasingly congested and polluted center to quieter, leafier suburbs, leaving to commerce, the banks, and the city authorities the job of pushing out the less prestigious elements to more peripheral barrios. But El Centro is still a zone where these divisions are acted out: Guayaquil is not dead but still full of loud cantinas, cheap hotels, and prostitutes; Calle del Sapo, Toad Street, near the old railway station and a few minutes' walk from the Parque Berrío, is still full of decrepit tenement blocks where poverty-stricken people live, eking a living out of the city center. And El Centro is, naturally, the scene for public political discourse—union rallies, party political meetings, demonstrations. Everyone must pass through El Centro, not just because all the buses pass through there, not only because the city administration is there along with a hundred other city institutions, but also because it is the city in its essence. And just as it has reflected the city's class divisions in its spatial arrangements, so now it reflects racial divisions: it is in El Centro that temporary black enclaves form and blacks claim their own space in the city and its life. It is here that they are seen by the city's "owners" as alien and even as a threat to public morals. Naturally, what one sees in El Centro hides as much as it reveals. In the same way that the division between ancestral Medellín and Guayaquil hid the real interdependence of the two and the latter's increasing power to define the nature of urbanism, so the apparent segregation of the Chocoanos in the city center masks their dispersal into the city's economy and urban space and their impact on its culture in terms of the spread of music and dance from the Caribbean and *la Costa*.

### CHOCOANOS AND HOUSING IN MEDELLÍN

For most people in Medellín, as in other Third World cities, buying a finished house is not a standard procedure: whether one invades land, purchases a plot, or buys a concrete base or a skeleton dwelling from a pirate urbanizer, a legal urbanizer, or the state, housing oneself and one's family is a slow process of consolidation and, often, expansion as the dwelling grows to accommodate more people. This creates a tremendous variety of housing in the city which nevertheless obeys a basic sectoral zoned pattern.

Locating the Chocoanos in this variety is by no means easy, since they appear over the whole spectrum of that variety: the places where they are obviously concentrated in small nuclei of settlement are in the poorest areas of the city, but this is deceptive because, proportionally, there are more Chocoanos dispersed around the city in reasonably consolidated working-class barrios. Generally speaking, the greater the concentration, the poorer the area, whereas the greater the dispersion, the higher up the urban scale the barrio, until middle-class levels are reached where blacks are a tiny, widely scattered minority.

*Housing Quality: The Chocoanos' Position.* Chocoanos in Medellín live in broadly similar housing conditions compared with other immigrants. However, the data show that Chocoanos live in slightly worse, or more insecure, housing than Antioqueño immigrants, even when some other intervening variables are controlled for, such as time in the barrio, age, and education. But it is ultimately unclear how much of this is due to lack of capital or income and how much to discrimination in the housing market, or certain preferences on their part. My own conclusion is that the major factor is lack of disposable resources; discrimination does exist in the realm of housing, but it has a particular form characteristic of Latin America. I found evidence of it in sensitive areas such as the room-renting market, where renters lived at close quarters with rentees and had close control over the allocation of accommodations. I also found some evidence of it directed against better-off Chocoanos who tried to locate in higher-class barrios, although this seems to have been more characteristic of an earlier period of Chocoano immigration. And finally, as the case studies in the following section demonstrate, I found it manifested against black communities that made their cultural presence felt.

In La Iguaná, it is clear that many Chocoanos live in the worst-housed areas of the barrio: 40 percent of them live in the area upriver from Seventieth Avenue, and another 30 percent downriver from Sixty-fifth Avenue. These are both recent areas of invasion and contain the least-consolidated housing. However, the Chocoanos' concentration in these areas is primarily due to their relatively recent arrival in the barrio, and if this is controlled for, the discrepancies in general housing conditions between them and Antioqueño immigrants become statistically insignificant. General housing conditions in this context refers to the census enumerators' classification of dwellings as rancho (shack made out of planks, waste materials, etc.), "transitional," or "consolidated."

The Moravia data are similar in some respects and different in others. The zone comprises different sectors, with two rather older invasion areas dating from the 1960s, a new invasion area actually on top of the central garbage dump which dates from about 1976, and several other areas dating from about 1975 which were illegally subdivided and sold off by a family that was renting the land at the time. The first of these sectors, called Fidel Castro, is one of the oldest and most consolidated sectors: only 20 percent of the dwellings are ranchos. Of the 108 Chocoano families in Moravia, 25 families (23%) lived in Fidel Castro. Sixteen of these lived in three adjacent houses, the owners of two of which rented out accommodations. The second sector, El Bosque, despite its age, had some of the worst housing in the zone, with 60 percent ranchos and only 25 percent of houses in a consolidated state; it was very overcrowded and haphazard in layout, with open sewers running alongside and under dwellings: 30 percent of the Chocoanos lived there. The third, La Montaña, is on top of the now disused and grassed-over "mountain" of garbage which, at the time of the census in 1983, was still the municipal rubbish dump: the housing there was 90 percent ranchos. The rubbish hill itself is, of course, an unstable base for housing, and the authorities, who were upgrading this barrio, have tried to remove much of this housing. Thirty-four percent of the Chocoanos lived in this sector. Although Chocoanos are not overrepresented as invaders, having bought much of their housing even in sectors originally invaded, their general housing conditions are significantly worse since, despite being overrepresented in Fidel Castro where housing is relatively good, their presence there is in overcrowded rented accommodations, and they are also overrepresented on La Montaña and in El Bosque where housing is very bad. If we look at homeowners, Chocoanos are more frequently housed in ranchos than others (66% vs. 54%) and have less dwellings in a "transitional" phase (16% vs. 18%) or in a consolidated state (18% vs. 28%). With these data, no controls are applicable, since the Chocoanos' profiles in terms of time in the barrio, age, education, and declared income are broadly the same as for others.

The city sample census allocates every block to a socioeconomic stratum, graded one to six. The data show that, while the Chocoanos broadly follow the pattern for immigrant Antioqueños, they are marginally worse off. (For all the following figures, domestic servants living in their employers' houses are excluded.) While almost half (46%) of both categories live in stratum three, "medium-low," Chocoanos are overrepresented compared with the other category in stratum one, "low-low" (6% vs. 3%), marginally so in stratum two, "low" (32% vs. 30%), and are underrepresented in stratum four, "medium" (15% vs. 17%), and in strata five and six, "medium-high and high" (1.5% vs. 2.6%). Both categories are worse off than city-born dwellers. Controlling for age and education does little to alter this pattern; especially noticeable is the fact that the percentage of Chocoanos in stratum one is consistently twice that for Antioqueño immigrants, except for people with secondary or some further education, among whom there are no Chocoano stratum-one dwellers. It is also noticeable that these Chocoanos are overrepresented in stratum-three housing and underrepresented in stratum four, suggesting that even well-educated Chocoanos are living in areas not entirely consonant with their educational status. A critical shortcoming here is the absence of data on time spent in the city, which must affect housing standards in an important fashion: controlling for age is the only available alternative, and its relevance is shown by the fact that older Chocoanos' housing is better that that of their younger fellows, as is the case for everybody in the sample. The data also show that Chocoanos legally own their own home less often (56% vs. 62% for immigrant Antioqueños) and rely more on renting and de facto possession (i.e., invasion, etc.). Last, the data show that working Chocoanos are more frequently in the inner-city tenements (5% versus 0.5% for immigrant Antioqueños) and in ranchos and *viviendas de desechos*, dwellings made from waste materials (4% vs. 2%), and that less live in a private house (74% vs. 82%). Although the numbers are small, this last pattern remains when age and education are controlled for. Virtually all the Chocoanos living in tenements live in two houses in a small inner-city area, Colón, a surviving remnant of the Guayaquil tenement areas.

In sum, leaving aside domestics living in their employers' houses, although most Chocoanos live in what is, for Medellín, average housing—that is, strata two and three in the one-to-six hierarchy—their overall situation is rather worse than that of Antioqueño immigrants, even when age and education are controlled for. The only data on income available from the city sample indicate that, outside domestic service, Chocoanos earn almost on a par with Antioqueño immigrants, so controlling for income would have little effect. In fact, controlling for income is almost meaningless, since the numbers of those who declared an income are too small to allow significant results. The data from La Iguaná show that Chocoanos have bad housing in the barrio as a whole, but probably not when compared with other immigrants who arrived there at the same time as them: however, more of them did invade their plots. The data from Moravia show that the Chocoanos have inferior housing, even in the context of this generally poorly housed zone.

There are a number of possible explanations for these patterns. First, time in the city could be a crucial control that the citywide data do not include and which is not adequately compensated for by controlling for age. The Iguaná data show the importance of controlling for time in this way, but even here hints of discrepancies remain, and in any case the Moravia data are independent of time.

Second, Chocoanos are a poorer group and can spend less on housing than can Antioqueños of similar age and education, despite partial evidence to the contrary from the incomplete income-earning data. It may be that housing itself is a better indicator of economic status than declarations about income. Third, Chocoanos are not poorer but attach less importance to housing or have different housing preferences and thus appear as a more poorly housed group. Coming from a region where a good deal of housing consists of wooden structures on stilts, they may be less averse than Antioqueños to living in a wooden dwelling classifiable by census takers as a rancho. Connected to preference is the possibility that an ethnic network of information and solidarity draws some Chocoanos to live near one another, despite inferior housing conditions. Four, various discriminatory mechanisms restrict their access to the housing opportunities appropriate to their age, education, and income.

Trying to assess racial discrimination in distributive processes from the results of those processes is, of course, notoriously difficult, since many factors intervene in distribution outcomes. Eliminating all other factors, such as time in the city, income, or access to capital, is impossible with the data I have. The wide spread of Chocoanos through much of the city in conditions broadly similar to those of other migrants suggests that direct discrimination does not operate to any great extent in such areas of the housing market as house renting, house purchase, accretive invasion, or pirate urbanization. The differences noted above are probably due primarily to lack of disposable income among Chocoanos. However, by investigating one allocation process itself, I did find evidence of direct discrimination in the room-renting market, probably one of the most sensitive areas of the housing market, since these rooms are often in private houses. I recruited a group of eight blacks, made up of Chocoanos, children of Chocoanos born in Medellín (who therefore spoke with Antioqueño accents), and one Costeño; and a group of eight Antioqueños. As far as possible, I matched these two groups for age, educational status, and social status as apparent from their general appearance (color aside, of course); there were equal numbers of men and women in each group. I then gave each person a number of room-to-rent advertisements and left them to telephone the house and, if possible, arrange a visit. They were instructed to leave the renter with the impression that they would take the room and would phone later to confirm. After leaving, they filled in a short questionnaire about the visit. Later I phoned every house, partly to check that it had been visited and partly to cancel their offer. The idea was to see if the blacks got more refusals than the Antioqueños, assuming that the rate of refusals for reasons unconnected with color (e.g., the room had been taken between the initial phone call and the visit) would be randomly distributed. The experiment was conducted on two successive Saturdays. The results showed that out of forty-one visits made by blacks, they encountered eight refusals (20%), while the Antioqueños made thirty-four visits and were refused only once (3%). The black men encountered slightly more refusals than the women. Several times the refusals toward the blacks were reported as being done evasively or with some hostility and rudeness.

This simple experiment is important because it gives direct evidence of discrimination by some Antioqueños against people whom they could easily classify as "black." Even though these individuals were clearly not rough country folk fresh from the Chocó, there was a significant tendency to simply reject them. The conditionality barrier of acceptance in this context was quite high. And although it goes beyond the limits of this experiment, the suggestion arises that other Antioqueños discriminate in other contexts in a similar fashion. The crucial point does not seem to be simply admitting blacks into the home, since black domestics are widely accepted. Rather, it is a matter of admitting people stereotyped as "black" into socially autonomous and equal positions, as opposed to servile, dependent, and symbolically "junior" positions. This admission is not excluded—as we have seen, racial discrimination is not systematic—but it is restricted. It also tends to be conditional, and in Medellín, especially in the earlier years of Chocoano immigration, the conditions could be quite stiff. One of the few middle-class Chocoanos, for example, gave the following testimony:

> When I came from Quibdó, I'd bought a house in El Estadio [mostly stratum-four housing], and I had to leave the area because frankly they made life impossible for me there. I'd gone into a white barrio . . . people who had a certain economic status and who looked down on me. And I had to sell the house and go somewhere else. My children would go out, and they'd make life impossible for them. When I arrived, they'd shut their doors, despite the fact that economically I had what was needed. I had a house, a car, my children were studying, and I was a professional like any of them. I realized that that wasn't my milieu, and I had to leave. And that's happened to a lot of paisanos. Of course, nowadays, many have prospered: there are blacks, paisanos of mine, who are economically well-off and live in very select areas.

This man now lives in a stratum-three neighborhood farther away from El Centro. At that time, then, middle-class Medellín residents had no time even for someone roughly on their own economic level.

#### BLACK COMMUNITIES IN MEDELLÍN

Discrimination in the housing market is typical of Latin American racial discrimination against blacks in general: it is individualistic, unsystematic, and nongeneralized. As the case of Barrio Antioquia and the following case studies show, it is also tied into the overall dynamics of the racial order, which means that discrimination is generally directed at black community, which is perceived by nonblacks as not assimilated to their cultural mores.

*La Iguaná.* La Iguaná is the most obvious and dense concentration of Chocoanos in the city. There are barrios where there is a greater number of families present, but they do not represent such a large proportion, nor are they so densely concentrated. The barrio began as a settlement in the 1940s. The first settlers were gravel diggers who extracted sands and gravels from the river La Iguaná and who built dwellings on land near the river ceded to them by a local owner. Gradually, others invaded the land along the river's banks, and by 1963 the settlement had expanded to include about one hundred families. Municipal attempts to control invasion and restrict dwellings to easily removable wooden structures coexisted with community organization and attempts to consolidate. In this, the residents had various allies, including the municipality itself, which, although it never officially recognized their title to the land, grudgingly gave permits to build in certain zones after a flood wiped out part of the barrio in 1971 and then in 1973 to build permanent dwellings. Between 1972 and 1974, after many petitions to the secretary for health and to the Public Services Department, electricity, water, and sewerage were installed in a rudimentary fashion in the community using the inhabitants' labor. The church helped from an early date to finance a community building that functioned as a chapel and a school, and in 1983 a new school was built with community labor and finance from the Conservative party politicians, the archdiocese of Medellín, the drug trafficker Pablo Escobar, the city council, the city's Community Action Department, the armed forces, and a Swiss charity.

By this time the barrio had a tripartite structure, according to time of invasion. The settlement followed the river's banks and was crossed by Sixty-fifth and Seventieth avenues, between which was the oldest, most consolidated sector, with the school, the church, and most of the shops. Downriver from Sixty-fifth Avenue was a rather newer area that nevertheless had some consolidated dwellings, since Sixty-fifth had only been pushed through the barrio in 1984. Upriver from Seventieth Avenue was a sector called La Playita (literally "Little Beach"), a substantial part of which consisted of wooden shacks on stilts, practically over the river itself, although, where possible, residents had constructed in more solid materials.

In 1986, when I was living there, the municipality, through its agency Desarrollo Comunitario (Community Development), was trying to negotiate an upgrading plan for the barrio which consisted of canaling the river to obviate its periodic and disastrous floodings, reorganizing the layout of the barrio, installing proper services, and giving legal title to land. There were also plans to build two roads on either side of the barrio, for which the river's canalization was an obvious prerequisite. The left-wing housing action organization, Provivienda, which had a branch committee in the barrio, saw this as a long-term plan to make this little working-class nucleus accessible to the city's commercial interests, valorize the land, and open it up to pressure from urban developers and other capitalist ventures, thus eventually pushing out the present inhabitants, who would no longer be able to afford to live there or would succumb to attractive cash offers for their land. Every community in Colombia has a Junta de Acción Comunal, a Community Action group, a body elected locally but instituted and constituted on a national basis by government prescription. This group in La Iguaná took a more moderate line, seeking to negotiate a settlement that would guarantee as much protection as possible for low-income inhabitants and restrict disturbance of the barrio's actual layout. They tended to argue over specific details rather than contest the plan as a whole. Canalizing the river, for example, inevitably meant relocating the dwellings situated right on its banks, and there was discussion about exactly how this should be done. Moreover, La Playita was not included at all in the plan, mostly, it seems, because a planned road went right through it, and there were demands—albeit rather muted since the local Community Action group members all lived in the part that was to be upgraded—that this area be included.

During the time I lived in La Iguaná, it was still regarded as an alien element, dangerous and immoral, by the surrounding areas, which mostly contained middle-class residential units, commercial areas, and some light industry. Whatever the real benefits that had been handed over by the city authorities after extensive lobbying by the community, the feeling of the place was that of confrontation, whether with the nearby National University, which had fenced off land previously used by the barrio's soccer team; or with the nearest residential unit, the guards of which ejected Iguaná children from its playgrounds; or with the state, which sent in, alternately, teams of social workers and surveyors, or armed raids of military jeeps, mounted with machine guns. An island of poverty in a sea of middle-class plenty, only a ten-minute walk from the city center, the barrio has grown up and progressed in spite of, or at most with the grudging and opportunist acquiescence of, its neighbors and the state, and the feeling one had when descending into its huddle of houses and huts—with symbolic aptness, the place was physically as well as socially lower than its surroundings—was that of entering a different world.

The first Chocoano family arrived in La Iguaná in 1966: Luis Durán Urrutia Mosquera, his wife Delfa, and their three children. It was in his house that I lived during the several months that I was in the barrio, and he told me about his decision to move from Barrio Antioquia on the suggestion of a compadre of his who lived there.

So my compadre says to me, "Compadre, why don't you find a way . . . paying rent is very tough. . . . I live there, so let's go there." The first year, the second year, I didn't want to; the third year, I came over to have a look—it was a Saturday—and after, I convinced my wife to come too. Listen, you know how much I got for the first ten years' *liquidación* [a retirement-cum-severance fund, cashable during employment]? Just over five thousand pesos. With that I bought the first roof tiles, and I'd come in the evenings and every Saturday to work on the house.

The secretary of the barrio's Junta de Acción Communal, Octavio Palacio, wrote a history of La Iguaná for a people's write-the-history-of-your-barrio competition run by Desarrollo Comunitario in 1986. In this Urrutia is quoted as saying, "As is the custom of our race, I took to having parties at the weekends. People would have a good time, because before, there was nothing like that to be seen. There was just a little shop run by Pablo Beltrán."

The arrival of the first Chocoano thus saw the establishment of the first *bailadero*, or dance hall, in the barrio. He would play music, sell beer and *aguardiente*, while Delfa cooked and sold fried food to the customers. This initiative excited the moral indignation of some Antioqueños who thought the place encouraged drunkenness and licentiousness among the young, but Urrutia carried on until about 1976 when he tired of the enterprise and because people were using the house to consume drugs. A more explosive source of conflict was his decision to participate actively in the local civil defense group in an effort to combat crime and vice in the barrio: he became a central figure in the group and was seen by some as little more than a police informer. Some attempts were made to kill or injure him, and his front door still bears the marks of the impact of many stones. Significantly, others in the group, Antioqueños, did not suffer these attacks, and it seems clear that the fact that it was a black man, an outsider—who seemed in any case to be encouraging new and immoral activities—who was setting himself up as the barrio's moral authority exaggerated the antagonism felt against him. Nowadays, he leads a quieter life, having also given up working with the civil defense group, and continues to work as a welder in the light engineering firm that has employed him for the last thirty years. He has one of the best houses in the barrio, and he rents out the second floor as four single rooms; the rentees tend to be Chocoanos, not due to a particular preference on his part, since Antioqueños also live there from time to time, but because the ethnic information network creates a steady flow of Chocoano tenants.

The next Chocoanos to arrive were to be the center of a collection of kinsfolk which developed over the seventies and the early eighties. The first members of this aggregate came in the late sixties, from rented accommodations in an outlying barrio called Zafra, also a nucleus of Chocoano settlement. Over time, various other kinspeople arrived until, by 1984, there were some twenty-five adult members of the Rivas family, from Condoto, Chocó, who together with their children made up a group of some seventy-five blacks. In the chapter on the economy of Unguía, I noted how people moving around the Chocó make use of a flexible and widespread network of bilateral kin links in order to facilitate travel and subsistence (see also Whitten 1969, 1974; Friedemann 1985b). In the emergence of this localized aggregate of kin in La Iguaná can be seen the continuing use of these wide-ranging kin networks. Once a couple of members of the family were established in the barrio, others could use their presence there as a pied-à-terre. Naturally, the rights that could be claimed in this situation were not over land or mining territory, as in the Chocó itself, but having a relative in place made things that much easier, and in a couple of cases an incoming member had a piece of land ceded by an established relative. The connections between the Rivas who live in La Iguaná are as follows: The first to arrive were the two related sibling sets made up of Socrates, Rómulo, and Alfredo Rivas Rivas and their cousins Manuel Santiago, Leofanor, and Gorgoño Rivas Rivas. Jesús Ibarguen Rivas is generally spoken of as one of the latter sibling set, being an *hermano de padre*, that is, a sibling who has a common father but a different mother. He, like some others (e.g., Fabiola Rivas Hinestroza), has taken his mother's surname, a practice not uncommon in the Chocó, where consensual unions are very common and people may change partners a number of times during their lifetime. Mercedes Maya (1987, 92) notes the same phenomenon for the village of Bebará, Chocó, and attributes it variously to personal choice, a conscious rejection of the father if the latter was disliked or perhaps hardly known, a maternal decision stemming from conjugal animosity, and lastly, an imposition by the clergy who did not, and sometimes still do not, recognize the social paternity of an absent father. Other members of the Rivas family then joined these sibling sets, and the links that join them to the original invaders are flexible, wide-ranging, bilateral, and both affinal and consanguineal. In some cases, these links were of material advantage: Francisco Mosquera Benítez was ceded a piece of land by Gorgoño Rivas Rivas, who is his *tío* (uncle) by virtue of the half-sibling relation between Gorgoño and Francisco's mother. Sometimes the actual links are not known, although a distant relationship is recognized: Juan Lucio Asprilla Rivas, for example, is known to be related, but I could not ascertain the precise link even from well-placed informants. Despite the complexity of the actual relationships involved, people use a small number of basic kin terms: *primo/prima*, cousin, *tío/tía*, uncle/aunt, and *sobrino/sobrina*, nephew/niece, are very frequent terms and include a great number of kinsfolk, while given the plethora of half-sibling relations, *hermano/hermana*, brother/sister, can also include many relations. The terms *cuñado/cuñada*, brother-/sister-in-law, include most affinal relatives of the same generation. This classificatory use of a few kin terms eases the tracing of relationships in a kinship system whose complexity stems partly from the many half-sibling relationships caused by patterns of serial unions; it also facilitates the use of kin links to legitimate residence and claims on networks of reciprocity.

Kinship is, of course, important for the Antioqueños in the barrio too, but it is noticeable that virtually no Chocoano is without some kin in La Iguaná or arrived there without some kinship link, whereas this is not so common among the others. Moreover, the largest Antioqueño family in La Iguaná, comprising some seventy-five people, has a completely different structure, being made up of most of the bilateral descendants of an initial conjugal pair who arrived in the barrio in 1958 from a rural Antioqueño village: their offspring have dispersed throughout, and beyond, the barrio in a style very different from the accretive growth of the Rivas family by the addition of *primos* and *sobrinos* who migrate from the Chocó.

The Rivas formed part of the major influx of Chocoanos which occurred around 1978: according to the Desarrollo Comunitario census, 70 percent of the Chocoanos arrived after this date. And just as Urrutia had brought the first *bailadero* to the barrio in the form of his front room on the weekends, with this new influx several more houses began to take on this function. Both Manuel Santiago and Gorgoño Rivas had small-scale *bailaderos* in their houses in the late seventies, and the latter's still functioned in 1987. Altogether, of the eight *bailaderos* that the barrio has had, six have been in Chocoano houses. The owners of the houses have generally been well-known, older figures who have been in the barrio several years and who have dwellings made out of brick rather than planks. These houses are particular in the sense that there tends to be minimal separation between domestic, ordinary social, and *bailadero* functions. The *bailadero* operates in the main room of the house on the weekend, usually only in the evenings and during the day on Sunday as well; sleeping and cooking areas are therefore very close by. When the *bailadero* is not operating, the main room acts as a kind of "open house" where people, mostly Chocoanos, collect to play cards and dominoes, share cigarettes, talk, watch television if there is one, and just sit around. These *bailaderos* were, during the late seventies, a focus of ethnic conflict that both Chocoanos and Antioqueños remember. This took the form of attacks by the Antioqueños, usually the younger men, who would throw stones at the roofs of the houses when the *bailadero* was operating. Occasionally, they would enter to provoke incidents; equally, some Chocoanos would retaliate against the stone throwers. Clearly, the Chocoanos were seen initially as a foreign and disliked element. Not only were they building their houses there, but their *bailaderos* attracted other Chocoanos from all over the city as well, just as the *bailaderos* of Barrio Antioquia had done in the 1960s; and just as this provoked a reaction there, so it did in La Iguaná. With time, conflict has quietened down, and I came across no overt antagonism of this kind. However, the Chocoano *bailaderos* in the central, consolidated part of the barrio, which is overwhelmingly Antioqueño, no longer function, except for that of Gorgoño Rivas, which is right on the edge of this sector. Instead, the other three current Chocoano *bailaderos* are in La Playita, where 40 percent of the Chocoanos live, and in the sector below Sixty-fifth where another third of them live. So reduction in conflict has been accompanied by a de facto segregation process: even though the Chocoanos do not form a majority in any of the barrio's three sectors, they form concentrations within each sector, and the *bailaderos* are precisely within these nuclei.

This history demonstrates in a specific and local way the establishment of a black community, structured largely around characteristic patterns of Chocoano kinship and also around the institution of the *bailadero*. Nonblack reaction was hostile and antagonistic when faced with this community in its midst, and the outcome was a certain degree of de facto segregation, with the *bailaderos* locating in areas of the settlement where the Chocoano presence was strongest. As always, black community coexists with patterns of black adaptation to the nonblack world, and by no means do all La Iguaná's Chocoanos live in La Playita or the sector below Sixty-fifth, nor do they all participate in the *bailaderos* and associated activities. Typically, it is the younger, more recent immigrants who concentrate in La Playita and its *bailaderos*, while those living in the central sector tend to be older migrants. Nearly 80 percent of Chocoanos living in La Playita are under 30 years old, while of those living in the more consolidated central area, only 44 percent are under 30. Equally, 81 percent of Playita Chocoanos have been in Medellín for less than ten years, while the figure drops to 47 percent for those living in the central area. La Playita represents a niche in which black Chocoano culture is reelaborated in an urban context principally by younger, quite recent migrants and in which it is differentiated from Antioqueño culture.

The *bailaderos* are a focus of cultural differentiation. The atmosphere in Chocoano *bailaderos* is very different from that in the only Antioqueño *bailadero*—which would in any case prefer to be styled a *discoteca*, since the word *bailadero* has rather low-status connotations. The Chocoano places have a freezer, a sound system, and a couple of rough tables with a few stools and the odd upturned crate; they play only salsa and *vallenato* music, and most of the clientele is black. Often a good deal of the social activity takes place in the street outside the *bailadero*, where people talk and stand around, going inside to dance. This is especially true of young single women who do not have money to buy a drink: they will accept a *gaseosa* (fizzy drink)—or sometimes a beer, or more rarely *aguardiente*—from a man, who will then invite them inside to dance. The men who are at tables or standing inside tend to have more money to spend on drink for themselves and the women they have invited. Occasionally, one also sees women together paying for their own drinks, although this is more common in the city center bars such as El Suizo. (Compare Whitten's [1974, 103] description of the "saloon context" of the Pacific littoral.) In contrast, the Antioqueño establishment is a place specifically set up as a *discoteca* with colored lighting, chairs, tables, a separate dance floor, and waiter service; it plays a mixture of salsa, *vallenato*, ballads, and *música tropical* (usually popularized versions of traditional Costeño music, played by groups from both *la Costa* and the interior). The social activity associated with dancing takes place within the confines of the *discoteca*; although there are young men hanging around outside watching the action on the street and inside, there is not the same constant interchange of people from inside to outside, and women do not stand outside and expect to be invited to a drink outside and then a dance inside; lastly, the clientele is mostly Antioqueño.

The Antioqueño *discoteca* attempted to follow patterns defined by the city at large, from the center out to more peripheral neighborhoods. These are partly concerned with establishing divisions—inside and outside the premises, on and off the dance floor—which bound behavior. In the Chocoano *bailaderos*, the boundaries were far less obvious, with the limits of the dance hall itself spilling onto the street and there being little division between dance floor and a sitting area. These places seemed to transgress the urban norms of propriety to which the Antioqueño *discoteca* was aspiring.

The atmosphere in La Playita likewise has a distinctive flavor. The oldest part of this sector is on the highest and driest land and is mostly Antioqueño; the newer part is right down on the river and is mixed Antioqueño and Chocoano, with the latter predominating by about fifty to thirty households. One of the daughters of Urrutia, whom I knew from her frequent visits to her father's house, lived with her *marido*, common-law husband, and her child in a rancho in La Playita, and I used to go and see her there, since she was a main informant for kinship relations and general gossip and a facilitator for interviews with local residents. In the mornings, one could feel the Chocoano dominance of that little section with its houses and ranchos crowded along the narrow, muddy pathway. The women were out and about, sitting in their doorways, exchanging news, going to the corner shop, walking up and down with bundles of clothes to wash and with children hanging on to their skirts; they shouted at one another from their doorways, made barbed comments about their neighbors' sex lives, laughed uproariously; some walked around dressed in nightdresses, and if these were a little translucent, the odd loud comment might pass about that woman's knickers being a little on the skimpy side. Equally, in the afternoon card games there would be noise and shouting, loud disputes about scoring and betting transactions, rebukes yelled at importunate children. This type of behavior is *part of* lower-class black culture, although not necessarily synonymous with it, and appears to many Antioqueño residents to be typically *escandaloso* and *alborotado*, boisterous, noisy, rough, excitable, scandalous, and often too sexually explicit. For the Chocoanos, however, loudness is often the expression of well-being or confidence in oneself, and quietness is seen as indicating unhappiness or being ill at ease.

La Iguaná is a point of concentration for the Chocoanos, but in practice it is La Playita and, to a lesser extent, the part of the barrio below Sixty-fifth Avenue which take on this function. La Playita—also the name of a barrio in Quibdó—has a tightly knit group of Chocoanos, interlinked by kinship; it has two *bailaderos*—open houses that attract Chocoano visitors from all over the city on weekends, not to mention those who come to visit kin and friends; there Chocoanos feel at ease to behave in ways classified as *alborotado* by their Antioqueño neighbors; there one can find cases of Chocoano men with polygynous relations—in one instance, a man, a construction laborer, had two women living in adjacent houses, an unusual arrangement even by Chocoano standards. In short, it is a Chocoano community in Medellín.

*Zafra.* Despite being on the urban periphery and physically distant from La Iguaná, and despite a different history of settlement through the subdivision of a small landowner's territory for sale as individual housing plots, Zafra is a barrio that has a number of links with it. First, some of the Iguaná's Chocoano inhabitants rented there before moving to La Iguaná. Second, the process of its formation shares some similar features.

The barrio was originally a small, rural, agricultural settlement. In the 1970s, the area was caught up in processes of pirate urbanization, as landowners sold off plots to people who constructed their dwellings as they saw fit on the steep slopes of the hillsides. In the 1980s, there was some invasion on the margins of Zafra, but recently the area has found itself increasingly surrounded by middle-class housing schemes that, as in the case of La Iguaná, have isolated Zafra and its older neighbor, Sucre, as islands of poverty, looked down on as nests of petty drug dealing and crime by their richer neighbors.

The first Chocoano resident was a woman, Neila Ibarguen, cousin of La Iguaná's Luis Durán Urrutia Mosquera. Her brother lived in rented accommodations nearby in Sucre. She and her husband rented a house from an Antioqueño in Zafra in 1968, and she started a Sunday *bailadero* that attracted Chocoanos from other barrios. Her sister Dora, who had been working as a domestic, married a Chocoano man, a bus driver, and rented in a nearby barrio, helping her sister on Sundays. Soon after, Leofanor Rivas (now of La Iguaná) arrived, followed by some of his brothers and nephews and, of course, other Chocoanos. While many of these moved to La Iguaná after a few years, around 1975 Neila and Dora and their husbands bought their own houses, and in the latter's the Sunday dances continued. In 1973, another family, the Martínez, moved from Barrio Antioquia to Zafra, and between 1978 and 1981 the mother of the family rented a small place from the barrio's Community Action group to have dances on the weekends. As in La Iguaná, Chocoanos from all over the city would come to drink and dance.

The Antioqueños' reaction to this was similar to that in La Iguaná: young Antioqueños would throw stones and pick fights, a few local thieves would try their luck on the incoming crowd, and the Chocoanos retaliated and defended themselves. Both Antioqueño and Chocoano informants identified Antioqueños as the initial aggressors. Eventually, Community Action refused to continue renting to the Martínez family, who then moved their dances to a more peripheral location in a place rented from a big Antioqueño family. But already the influx of Chocoanos had been braked: not long after this, the *bailaderos* all stopped functioning.

Another point of disagreement was the Chocoano *velorio*, or wake, in which the deceased's coffin is watched over before burial: thereafter, every night until *la novena*, the ninth night, some people congregate in the family's house and perhaps pray or more usually sit around and talk, tell stories, or play dominoes. The Chocoano version of this is traditionally more celebratory than the more pious Antioqueño version and especially on *la novena* includes more noisy dominoes, storytelling, drinking, and so on. In Zafra there was general disapproval of the way these *velorios* were carried on: as one Antioqueño graphically put it, "The bottle of *aguardiente* on top of the coffin—that was too much." Again, the Chocoanos were seen as *alborotados*, and this was also *falta de respeto*, lack of respect, not only for the dead but for the morals of the community at large. Older Chocoano residents remember occasions when the necessary permit from the local *inspección de policía*, a civil authority despite its name, was refused for Chocoano *velorios*. With time, the Chocoanos adapted their *velorios* to a form that provoked less censure from the Antioqueños.

However, the Chocoano presence still causes the odd ripple of discontent in the barrio. Outside the Martínez house, men gather, especially on Sundays, to play dominoes, and given the close proximity of the houses in this area, one or two of the Antioqueño neighbors regularly lodge complaints with the police about the noise this involves.

In contrast with La Iguaná, where a certain degree of segregation facilitated the persistence of black community, in Zafra the original Chocoano nucleus basically adapted its behavior to local cultural mores. This black adaptation, generally accepted by the Antioqueños there, was influenced in part by the fact that the number of recent young Chocoano immigrants to the barrio was then less than in La Iguaná and that many of the original black residents had moved away.

The same kind of reaction occurred in the case of a municipal relocation project in Kennedy for the inhabitants of the old city center Alpujarra invasion, in which there were about thirty Chocoano families out of a total of about one hundred fifty. In the new housing, there were complaints to the municipal agency from Antioqueños who alleged that the Chocoano women would come out of their houses in petticoats or the men in their underwear and so on. One Antioqueño woman recounted to me how she had seen a black man naked, washing himself in his backyard; she rushed into her house and bolted the door. The agency put pressure on the Chocoanos, and they adapted accordingly. The Antioqueño woman observed: *"Ya les da pena hacer todo eso"* (Now they're ashamed to do all that).

### NUCLEATION AND DISPERSAL

The stories of these two barrios, La Iguaná and Zafra, contain more ethnic hostility and antagonism than those of other Chocoano nuclei (with the exception of the older Barrio Antioquia nucleus), but in other respects they are typical: in all cases, chain migration based on loose and wide-ranging kinship is a fundamental feature; also very common is the presence of a *bailadero* or open house belonging to a well-known figure which acts as a center for social activities, including parties and dancing. In the other Chocoano nuclei I investigated— Moravia, El Rincón, San Pablo, Kennedy—these two features also appear.

But to talk of Chocoano settlement in Medellín simply in terms of nuclei would be highly misleading, since a majority of Chocoanos live in a much more dispersed fashion. Even many of the nuclei have adapted culturally more than in La Iguaná, and most of them are not as tightly knit as La Iguaná: in San Pablo, for example, there are two well-established Chocoano families, one of which ran a *bailadero* for six years and the other of which rents out rooms to tenants who are almost entirely blacks, but the other Chocoano families in the barrio are not linked by kinship to these families. And the majority of Chocoanos live in barrios where there is little in the way of black community, where contacts with the ethnic network are more occasional, the inflow of young migrants from the Chocó is reduced, and an Antioqueño milieu clearly predominates. So La Playita in La Iguaná, although a critical focus of Chocoano activity in Medellín, is an extreme case on a continuum that ranges from tight nucleation to dispersal.

Nucleation and dispersal are clearly intimately related to processes of black community and black adaptation. They are analytically distinct because simple physical disposal does not inevitably lead to cultural assimilation into the new cultural milieu, nor does the latter necessitate the former. But, as the previous clusters have demonstrated several times, black community and adaptation, and likewise race mixture, are facilitated by nucleation and dispersal. In the context of a hierarchical racial order that nevertheless allows conditional acceptance, being surrounded by nonblacks and being immersed in a nonblack world increase the ease and likelihood of cultural change and race mixture. In this sense, spatial dispersal, genetic duration, and cultural adaptation go together in the overall process that I term black adaptation to the nonblack world, just as spatial nucleation, the absence of race mixture, and the continuity of black identity together constitute what I term black community.

As in previous instances, the dynamics of the racial order in Medellín are structured by the local political economy and by the processes of living in the city as an urban space. The urban processes that concern us here are: first, the city's residential differentiation per se, the economic position of immigrant Chocoanos, and the processes of economic consolidation over time (which do not necessarily mean upward mobility out of the working classes); second, dependence on the ethnic network for practical purposes, as against gradual familiarization with urban networks and institutions; and third, the family cycle.

First, Chocoanos, like any others, are subject to the constraints imposed on them by the availability of housing. Chocoanos cannot necessarily live near one another or with relatives, friends, or paisanos simply because they so choose. This in itself restricts the possibility of nucleation and inhibits black community, especially given the small numbers of Chocoanos in the city. However, within the housing market there are certain sectors within which nucleation can occur more easily, and these are the sectors that tend to attract the poorer and more recent arrivals. In tenement blocks, in invasions that are in the process of formation, and in developing pirate urbanizations, there is sufficient flexibility to allow

ethnically oriented locational choices to operate, whether these be actual preferences for living near other Chocoanos or choices made with information gar-
nered from the ethnic network (see below). In these types of housing environment, people can effectively choose to locate near one another more easily than
in already consolidated housing or in housing allocated via bureaucratic procedures. Thus poverty and recent arrival are conditions that facilitate the formation
of Chocoano nuclei.

On the other hand, there are factors that encourage dispersal. In essence,
greater purchasing power implies a relationship to the city's pattern of residential
differentiation and the housing market that generally militates against forming
residential nuclei. People tend to locate more in areas where Chocoano density
of settlement is lower, not only because there are fewer Chocoanos at their economic level but also because there is less flexibility in the more consolidated sectors of the housing market into which they tend to move. Evidence from the
citywide sample backs up the general relationship between more dispersed settlement and higher economic status; there is also a slight correlation between dispersal and age. (For these figures, domestic servants are excluded, since their residence in middle- and upper-class households distorts any analysis of spatial
patterns.) For example, working Chocoanos living in "high-density" survey tracts
(i.e., those with more than 1% Chocoanos) are under 30 years old in 50 percent
of cases, compared with only 33 percent of Chocoanos living in "low-density"
tracts (i.e., those with between 0.1% and 0.5% Chocoanos). In terms of occupation, whereas 25 percent of Chocoanos in low-density tracts work in professional-
technical occupations or as teachers, only 8 percent of Chocoanos in high- or
middle-density tracts do so. Not surprisingly, housing quality for Chocoanos in
the low-density tracts is higher than for the high- and middle-density dwellers.
About 50 percent of each category lives in stratum-three housing, but a full 40
percent of Chocoanos in high-density tracts live in strata-one and -two housing,
compared with 32 percent of Chocoanos in both middle- and low-density tracts.
Accordingly, 29 percent of Chocoanos in low-density tracts live in strata-four and
-five housing, compared with only 3 percent of Chocoanos in high-density and
20 percent in middle-density tracts. In sum, then, Chocoanos who live in areas
with low densities of Chocoano settlement tend to be better off, have better housing, and be slightly older than Chocoanos who live in areas of high-density Chocoano settlement. These differences can be due to variations in economic means
on arrival in the city, or they can be a result of processes of economic consolidation while in the city. The chances of economic consolidation, of course, depend
on the relationship to the labor market, and, as I showed in the last chapter, these
chances are limited. Generally, such consolidation as there is rarely means upward mobility out of the working class, and more usually it means securing a
reasonably stable place in it, getting one's own home, and improving it over time.
For example, many of the Chocoanos I interviewed in reasonably well consoli-

dated areas had started life in the city in areas such as La Bayadera or Barrio Antioquia, barrios of dense Chocoano settlement, before moving to other areas. Both initial and emergent differences in economic status impinge on the Chocoanos in Medellín, and their impact leads to the same result. Greater access to economic resources or economic consolidation leads to physical dispersal: Chocoanos find themselves living in barrios with relatively few other Chocoano families and surrounded by Antioqueño neighbors. In the context of the Colombian racial order, these circumstances clearly facilitate black adaptation to the Antioqueño milieu.

The second factor that structures the Chocoanos' relation to the local racial order is their familiarization with the city and its institutions and the degree to which this facilitates independence from the ethnic network of contacts with other Chocoanos. The ethnic network is important because it supplies, or supplies information about, a great many things of fundamental importance, especially, but not only, to the recent immigrant. It can supply contacts, orientation in a strange geography of streets, avenues, "transversals," "diagonals," and "circulars"; it can supply work, accommodations on a temporary basis, and information about more long-term housing strategies; it can supply advice, loans, friends, potential spouses, a Chocoano doctor, places to have fun, laborers and employers, helpers for a communal work party for one's house, parties, music, and somewhere to get one's hair plaited *en trensitas* (in little plaits or cornrows). Chocoanos make use of the ethnic network to obtain these goods and services, and, especially among recent immigrants, this induces them to regroup with their paisanos. As we have already seen, most Chocoanos come via a kin link or, failing that, a link with someone from the same village or river as themselves. This immediately links them into an ethnic network. Of course, both these features are fairly typical of immigrants per se: they often migrate in a chain fashion and depend on kin and people from the same village and town to orient them and help them settle in. There are, however, some differences between the Chocoanos and others here. Kinship is more important for them than for other migrants, a factor that tends to create a tighter network. In addition, whereas the network for Antioqueño immigrants is basically village or town based, the network for the Chocoanos spreads out to encompass all Chocoanos—a phenomenon that also occurs among Antioqueño migrants to Quibdó or Unguía.

Over time, however, Chocoanos become familiar with the city and how to cope with it: they learn how to move around, about danger spots, buses, and the grid system of the city; which institutions deal with what; and how to go about getting work and looking for housing. The network of ethnic contacts which initially tends to supply information and assistance begins to become less fundamental in a utilitarian sense, although it can remain important for information about scarce resources such as work and housing or for loans and other critical resources. Thus a Chocoano, if he or she chooses, can begin to leave the ethnic network behind as time gives him or her the experience to manage city life. It is significant in this respect that in a nucleus such as La Playita, 50 percent of the Chocoanos arrived after 1975, a fact that reinforces the relation noted above between recent arrival and nucleation.

The network is particularly relevant to patterns of nucleation because it mediates the relation between nucleation/dispersal and patterns of residential differentiation discussed above: it provides much of the information about housing with which people make the choices that are opened to them by their economic means. Gilbert and Ward (1982), for example, found that migrants in Bogotá tended to begin to concentrate in certain barrios according to their region of origin because of the way information about housing moved through regional networks after the migrants had arrived and initially settled. Equally, in the nuclei of Chocoano settlement in Medellín, I found that people had generally located through contacts with other Chocoanos, often relatives. In this sense, although the relation to the ethnic network is structured by the nature of the city's residential differentiation, the ethnic network itself feeds back into those patterns by supplying information about housing.

The third factor that structures processes of black community and black adaptation is the family cycle, which operates by influencing the impact of residential differentiation, although in a contingent fashion. Many Chocoanos who came as single migrants form unions with other Chocoanos and with Antioqueños and have families over time. The impact of this process on nucleation and dispersal can cut both ways, depending essentially on economic status. A couple with small children may decide to move out of rented accommodations and invade, or perhaps purchase, in a location that they learned about through the ethnic network. The Chocoano community in La Iguaná was indeed formed mainly by young families. Equally, a single mother will probably depend more than ever on the ethnic network for help with child care and economic assistance. On the other hand, a couple that has a relatively stable income may also be seeking extra living space to accommodate children. This may be an incentive to enter a more consolidated housing market, where, as before, there is less flexibility. It is only the decision to enter a more consolidated housing market—a choice ruled principally by economic status—which induces dispersal.

Black community and adaptation are thus structured by urban processes, and what emerges quite clearly from an investigation of the phenomenon of nucleation and black community is that it occurs in the poorest zones. Economic means are a crucial factor here and affect nucleation in two ways. First, it is in the context of settlements such as La Iguaná, Moravia, and Zafra that there exists the flexibility of choice of housing which allows a nucleus to develop. When people have greater purchasing power and want to move into more consolidated housing, they are more restricted in their choice of where they can go and the people near whom they can live. Second, the more recent immigrants tend to depend more on a network of other Chocoanos to find work, housing, information, friends, and diversion; as poor migrants their housing possibilities equally tend to be in the poorest, newest zones. Therefore, there is a tendency for more recent Chocoano immigrants to collect together in poor areas, due to their economic means and the operation of the ethnic network. Hence La Playita, Moravia, and Zafra are all fairly recent settlements, dating from the late seventies in terms of major Chocoano settlement. Youth, recent migration, and poverty are particularly evident in La Playita, and this is also clearly connected to its role as a vibrant focal point of Chocoano culture.

## References

Beavon, K., and C. Rogerson.
   1986    The Changing Role of Women in the Urban Informal Sector of Johannes-
           burg. In David Drakakis-Smith (editor). Urbanization in the Developing
           World. London: Croom Helm.

Bohman, Kristina
   1984    Women of the Barrio: Class and Gender in a Colombian City. Stockholm:
           At the University Press.

Boserup, Ester
   1974    Women's Role in Economic Development. London: George Allen and
           Unwin.

Bromley, Ray
   1979    Organization, Regulation and Exploitation of the So-called Urban Infor-
           mal Sector: The Street Traders of Cali, Colombia. In Ray Bromley (edi-
           tor). The Urban Informal Sector. London: Pergamon.

Bunster, Ximena, and Elsa Chaney (editors)
   1985    Sellers and Servants: Working Women in Lima, Peru. New York: Praeger.

Burgess, Rod
   1979    Petty Commodity Housing or Dweller Control: A Critique of John
           Turner's Views on Housing Policy. In Ray Bromley (editor). The Urban In-
           formal Sector. London: Pergamon.

Burton, Clare
   1985    Subordination: Feminism and Social Theory. London: George Allen and
           Unwin.

Camacol (Cámara de Construcción Colombiana)
   1986    Estudio metropolitano de vivienda y otras edificaciones. Report prepared
           by the Cámara de Construcción Colombiana (Camacol) and the Servicio
           Nacional de Aprendizaje (SENA), Medellín.

CEHAP (Centro de Estudios del Habitat Popular)
   1986    La calidad espacial urbana de los barrios para sectores de bajos ingresos en
           Medellín. Medellín: CEHAP, Universidad Nacional.

Chaney, Elsa, and Mary García Castro (editors)
  1989    Muchachas No More: Household Workers in Latin America and the
          Caribbean. Philadelphia: Temple University Press.
Cock, Jacklyn
  1980    Maids and Madams: A Study in the Politics of Exploitation. Johannesburg:
          Raven Press.
DANE (Departamento Administrativo Nacional de Estadística)
  1985b   Colombia estadística, 1985. Bogotá: DANE.
De Soto, Hernando
  1989    The Other Path: The Invisible Revolution in the Third World. New York:
          Harper and Row.
Friedemann, Nina S. de.
  1974    Minería del oro y descendencia: Güelmambí, Nariño. Revista Colombi-
          ana de Antropología 16:9–86.
  1985b   "Troncos" Among Black Miners in Colombia. In T. Greaves and W.
          Culver (editors). Miners and Mining in the Americas. Manchester: At the
          University Press.
Gaitskell, Deborah et al.
  1983    Class, Race and Gender: Domestic Workers in South Africa. Review of Af-
          rican Political Economy 27/28: 86–109.
García Castro, Mary
  1982    Qué se compra y qué se paga en el servicio doméstico? El caso de Bogotá.
          In Magdalena Léon (editor). Debate sobre la mujer en América Latina y
          el Caribe. Vol. 1, La realidad colombiana. Bogotá: Asociación Colombiana
          para el Estudio de la Población.
  1989    What Is Bought and What Is Sold in Domestic Service? The Case of
          Bogotá: A Critical Review. In Elsa Chaney and Mary García Castro (edi-
          tors). Muchachas No More: Household Workers in Latin America and the
          Caribbean. Philadelphia: Temple University Press.
Gilbert, Alan, and Josef Gugler
  1981    Cities, Poverty and Development: Urbanization in the Third World. Ox-
          ford: At the University Press.
Gilbert, Alan, and Peter Ward
  1982    Residential Movement Among the Poor: Constraints on Housing Choice
          in Latin American Cities. Transactions of the Institute of British Geogra-
          phers, n.s.7:129–149.
Gutiérrez de Pineda, Virginia.
  1975    Familia y cultura en Colombia. Bogotá: Colcultura.
Hansen, Karen Tranberg
  1986    Domestic Service in Zambia. Journal of African Studies 13.1:57–81.
León, Magdalena
  1989    Domestic Labor and Domestic Service in Colombia. In Elsa Chaney and
          Mary García Castro (editors). Muchachas No More: Household Workers

in Latin America and the Caribbean. Philadelphia: Temple University Press.

Maya, Luz Mercedes
1987    Familia, parentesco y explotación minera desde el fin de la esclavitud hasta hoy. Field Report. Ecole des Hautes Etudes en Sciences Sociales, Paris.

Mena, María
1975    Estudio sociológico sobre la marginalidad de las trabajadoras chocoanas en Medellín. Graduate Thesis, Universidad Pontificia Bolivariana, Medellín.

Moser, Caroline
1979    Informal Sector or Petty Commodity Production: Dualism or Dependence in Urban Development. In Ray Bromley (editor). The Urban Informal Sector. London: Pergamon.

Mosquera, Gilma
1976    Diagnóstico general sobre el problema de la vivienda en Medellín. Report of the Departamento Administrativo de Planeación, Medellín.

Olano, Ricardo
1939    Historia y crónicas de la Plaza de Berrío. Revista Progreso, 3d ser., 1:267–283.

Planeación Metropolitana
1985    Inventario de barrios subnormales. Report, Medellín.

Planeación Municipal
1980    La Alpujarra. Report, Medellín.

Portes, Alejandro, Manuel Castells, and Lauren Benton (editors)
1989    The Informal Economy: Studies in Advanced and Less Developed Countries. Baltimore: At the University Press.

Radcliffe, Sarah
1990    Ethnicity, Patriarchy, and Incorporation into the Nation: Female Migrants as Domestic Servants in Southern Peru. Environment and Planning D: Society and Space 8:379–393.

Roberts, Bryan
1978    Cities of Peasants: The Political Economy of Urbanization in the Third World. London: Edward Arnold.

Saffioti, Heleieth
1978    Emprego Doméstico e Capitalismo. Petrópolis, Brazil: Editorial Vozes.

Smith, Margo
1973    Domestic Service as a Channel of Upward Mobility. In Ann Pescatello (editor). Male and Female in Latin America. Pittsburgh: At the University Press.
1989    Where Is María Now? Former Domestic Workers in Peru. In Elsa Chaney and Mary García Castro (editors). Muchachas No More: Household Work-

ers in Latin America and the Caribbean. Philadelphia: Temple University Press.

Smith, Paul
    1978    Domestic Labor and Marx's Theory of Value. In Annette Kuhn and Ann Marie Wolpe (editors). Feminism and Materialism. London: Routledge and Kegan Paul.

Upeguí Benítez, Alberto
    1957    Guayaquil: Síntesis del poderío de una raza. Medellín: Carpel.

Viviescas, Fernando
    1983    Medellín: El centro de la ciudad y el ciudadano. Revista de Extensión Cultural de la Universidad Nacional de Colombia 15:46–56.

Vogel, Lise
    1983    Marxism and the Oppression of Women. London: Pluto Press.

Whitten, Norman
    1969    Strategies of Adaptive Mobility in the Ecuadorian-Colombian Littoral. American Anthropologist 71:228–242.
    1974    Black Frontiersmen: A South American Case. New York: John Wiley and Sons.

Wolpe, Harold
    1972    Capitalism and Cheap Labor Power in South Africa. Economy and Society 1:425–456.

# 16. "WE ARE PEOPLE OF THE *YUNGAS*, WE ARE THE *SAYA* RACE"

## Robert Whitney Templeman

Since the late 1970s, black people living in the Department of La Paz, Bolivia, have been working to recover cultural practices that they proclaim to
be *netamente Africano* (purely African). Among these are *zemba*, a lively song
and dance genre; their wedding music, called *la cueca negra* (the black *cueca*)
and *mauchi*, a solemn funeral music that they put forth in remembrance of a
once unique religion. Their most publicized cultural recuperation, however,
is *saya*, a song genre that black Bolivians traditionally used as a vehicle for
the transmission of their oral history and as festive dance music for their village celebrations (Templeman 1994).[1] Afro-Bolivians now deploy *saya* as the
collective voice and symbol of what they call Movimiento Negro (Black Movement).

The cultural practices of many black Bolivians, their music, dance, and religion, all but vanished in the decades following Bolivia's Agrarian Reform of 1953.
Through the 1960s and 1970s, black people, like indigenous people all over
Bolivia, migrated in large numbers out of their rural agricultural villages to the
cities of La Paz, Cochabamba, and Santa Cruz in search of better educational
and employment opportunities. Related to this, black individuals participated
in the dominant ideologies of *mestizaje* (cultural mixing) and *blanqueamiento*
(racial whitening) by intermarrying with people of lighter skin coloring, such
as *blancos* (whites) and mestizos, as a means of better integrating themselves—
and especially their children—into Bolivian society (M. Léons 1978, W. Léons
1977).

In this chapter I introduce two communities of black Bolivians from the Department of La Paz, one rural and the other urban. More than a decade ago,
musicians and political leaders from these communities reconstructed *saya* music. Through public performances of *saya*, they embarked on a grassroots social
movement aimed at raising the level of state and public consciousness about the
roles that black people played in Bolivia's political history and economy. They
elevated *saya* to the level of collective voice and symbol for their movement, and
they expanded to other departments of Bolivia by singing out and informing other
Afro-Bolivians of their mission. They sang *saya* texts that explicitly invited other
black Bolivians to "take a turn" and join them in recognizing the unique beauty
of their cultural heritage and of themselves.

## El Rey Negro (The Black King)

Black Bolivians of the Department of La Paz, Nor Yungas Province, have a unique ritualistic monarchy that they call *el rey negro*, their black king. People of the province recall one specific king, Rey Bonifacio Pinedo, who died in the 1960s. Bonifaz, as people remember him, was a benevolent black leader who lived in the small agricultural village of Mururata, Nor Yungas Province. The people of Mururata and surrounding black communities crowned him Rey Negro, but not until he was in his sixties. Although he was not recognized by the Bolivian state or even local authorities as being "king" of anything, black people throughout his province adored him and Afro-Bolivians still revere him. According to elder black people whom I interviewed and who knew him well, Bonifaz counseled youths about marriage and families about domestic matters. He was a disciplinarian who assisted the Catholic priest from Coroico during mass, and in the absence of a priest, Bonifaz said mass.

Following mass on Easter Sunday of each year, local Afro-Bolivians told me, Rey Bonifaz was carried out of the church on a special chair accompanied by 12 young men and 12 young women. He wore a European-style crown and cape, but only on that day. These garments remained guarded in Mururata's small Catholic church during the remainder of the year. Musicians and dancers celebrated their king on Easter by performing *zemba*, a uniquely Afro-Bolivian drumming, song, and dance genre in his honor (Templeman 1994, Flores 1989). At one point, the priest from Coroico, Padre Casimiro Crespo, objected to Rey Bonifaz being carried on a palanquin and being treated as a saint, and the priest demanded that these aspects of the institution end (Pizarroso Cuenca 1977:73). Rey Bonifaz died when he was in his eighties, having outlived even his children, and no successor was crowned.

Bolivian folklorist Max Portugal Zamora made an effigy of Rey Bonifaz based on his own ethnographic data (i.e., having visited him). People say that the effigy along with the crown and robes that Bonifaz wore were donated to the Casa de Murillo Museum in La Paz after his death in the 1960s (Pizarroso Cuenca 1977:69). The effigy clearly shows Rey Bonifaz in his crown and robe, and that he was a black man (see Portugal Ortiz 1977 for a reproduction of the effigy). Sometime after 1977 this effigy, along with his crown and robe, was stolen from the Casa de Murillo and has never been recovered.

The cessation of the cultural institution of the black king in the 1960s coincided with the disappearance of other black cultural practices, such as music, dance, dress, and religion. It seems that black people had forsaken their unique practices for more popular and dominant cultural trends. Like indigenous and mestizo people throughout Bolivia, black people consumed commercially recorded music. They hired brass bands for their local fiestas, and some individuals even joined and played instruments in these popular bands.

It was not until the latter part of the 1970s that high school–aged black students began actively rediscovering and rebuilding the nearly forgotten traditions of their parents and ancestors. Beginning with only a few key individuals, they started promoting an ideology to overcome *mestizaje* and *blanqueamiento*, one of constructing and mobilizing a new black historical identity, that of becoming "el Afroboliviano" (Afro-Bolivian).[2]

By 1992 the tremendous efforts put into recovering social and cultural practices reached Julio Pinedo, grandson of King Bonifacio Pinedo, and on Easter of that year Julio Primero (Julio I), as people refer to him, was crowned *el rey negro* (Montaño Aragón 1992:12). Upon being crowned and blessed by the black priest Benjamín, Julio I spoke to his followers as well as the press, promising:

> *luchar en defensa de la naturaleza, combatir de manera decidida por hacer posible que las riquezas del país sirven principalmente a los mismos bolivianos y evitar que nuestro país se convierta en una hacienda donde los ciudadanos no sean vasallos miserables, sino hombres libres y dueños de su destino.* (Montaño Aragón 1992)

> to decisively combat oppression by protecting the [natural] resources of the country so that Bolivians themselves are benefited and to prevent the conversion of our country into a plantation where the citizens will not be miserable vassals but rather free people in control of their destiny.

The coronation of Julio Pinedo, along with the recovery of *saya* and other Afro-Bolivian cultural practices, progressively became the foundation for an identity-based, pan-departmental social movement, "el Movimiento Negro" (Black Movement) in Bolivia. By the late 1990s, black individuals across Bolivia were valuing rather than shunning *lo Afro* (Africanness) in their cultural practices and institutions. These practices ranged from dialect, dress, dance, and hairstyle to the black monarch and all of the majesty formerly associated with him, including the *zemba* dance, and honoring him in his long robes and crown in the Easter parade.

### Rural and Urban Afro-Bolivians

The largest concentrations of Afro-Bolivians are in the city of La Paz, the capital of Bolivia, and in the nearby agricultural provinces of Nor and Sud Yungas. Situated on the eastern slopes of the Andes mountain range, the yungas are semitropical valleys that descend to the lowland Amazon basin. Published estimates on the numbers of black people in Bolivia vary too widely to be meaningful, between 6,000 and 158,000 (e.g., Monge Oviedo 1993). The Bolivian census does not count people by race or skin color but rather by language spoken. In 1994, Víctor Hugo Cárdenas, vice president of Bolivia, unofficially estimated the population of Afro-Bolivians to be on the order of 10,000, a number that echoes the discourse of the leaders of the Black Movement.

Afro-Bolivians most commonly self-identify as *negros* (blacks). They employ the terms *mulato* (mulatto), *medio mulato* (part mulatto) and *medio blanco* (part white) when referring to other Afro-Bolivians of lighter skin coloring. They use *zambo* when referring to someone of mixed black and indigenous (e.g., Aymara) descent. Both *zambo* and *mulato* are sometimes used teasingly by black people, but in the political discourse of the Black Movement in the late 1990s, *zambo* projected implications of racial dilution and cultural ambiguity.

In 1996, *prieto* (dark) and *negro prieto* (dark black) emerged among some in-dividuals to describe and identify other black people, but only of the darkest skin coloring. Although these terms do not directly refer to cultural behaviors (e.g., dialect, dress, hairstyle, or musicianship), their emphasis on blackness ascribes at-tractive cultural attributes to being *prieto* (dark). In using *prieto* and *negro prieto*, Afro-Bolivians not only assert positive associations of blackness onto others; they also embrace their own color. In this sense, terms such as these form and main-tain social bonds of resistance to *mestizaje* and *blanqueamiento*.

According to the spoken discourse of leaders of the Black Movement, people are expected to refer to Afro-Bolivians as *negros*, *afrobolivianos*, or *gente de color* (people of color). When white and indigenous people refer to them as *negri-tos* (cute blacks), *mulatos*, or *zambos*, Afro-Bolivians take offense. One of the most derogatory and unacceptable terms that a black Bolivian can be called is *rubio* (blond). Another label, offensive only when used by a nonblack refer-ring to a black woman, is *awicha* (grandmother, from the Afro-Bolivian's own dia-lect).

### The Village of Tocaña

Neighboring the village of Mururata in La Paz's Nor Yungas Province is Tocaña. Tocaña is smaller than Mururata, but its population is primarily black while Mururata has a large Aymara and mixed population. Tocaña has a popula-tion of 135 making it one of the largest rural villages of black people in Bolivia. The village comprises 35 single-family adobe households. Among the house-holds there are 31 families that self-identify as *negros*, three Aymara households, and one mixed black-Aymara family in which an Afro-Bolivian man married an Aymara woman from the neighboring village of Perolani.[3]

Tocañans (people from Tocaña) farm coca leaf, coffee beans, bananas, and cit-rus fruits. Their primary cash crop is coca leaf, as is the case with other yungas villages (see Spedding 1994). The Nor Yungas is one of the last remaining prov-inces in Bolivia where coca leaf can be legally grown. Afro-Bolivians sell the small quantities of coca leaf they produce at legal markets where it is dedicated to the commercial production of *mate* (tea), toothpaste, and homeopathic drugs, and its cultural preservation more generally. Tocañans sell their other cash crops at weekly markets in the nearby regional town of Coroico as well as in Caranavi, a larger yungas market town, and in the city of La Paz (Templeman 1994).

Tocañans speak a dialect of Spanish. Their vocabulary consists of a mixture of Spanish, Aymara, and African-derived words (see also Montaño Aragón). Words that are exclusive to their dialect include *awicha*, *cuancha* (scraper, played in *saya*), *ganjengo* (small *saya* drum), *mauchi* (mourning song for funerals), and *zemba* (song/dance genre traditionally associated with the black king). Until the mid–twentieth century, Afro-Bolivians spoke the Aymara indigenous language that predominates in the Department of La Paz. Elder black people of Nor Yungas villages remember and can still speak Aymara, but they rarely admit this. In over two years of ethnographic research, I never heard black Bolivians, from any department, converse among themselves in Aymara.[4] Tocañans still use Aymara terms such as *wachu* (a narrow terrace of dirt and stone behind which coca seedlings are planted) and *hawqaña* (drum stick). Other, more common indigenous terms such as *chakra* (agricultural field) and *rutucha* (first hair cutting), while being an important part of the Afro-Bolivian vocabulary, are used and understood by people throughout Bolivia and most of the central and northern Andes.

As of early 1997, there was neither running water nor electricity in Tocaña; even latrines were scarce. Tocañans have been offered AID projects contingent on their eradication of coca leaf farming, but they refuse to give up this primary means of subsistence. Coca is a hardy plant, they argue, better withstanding droughts, heavy rains, and diseases than coffee and citrus fruits. Coca plants are harvested year-round, generating steady income (see also Spedding 1994).

Following the Agrarian Reform of 1953, the first schoolhouse was built in Tocaña. When asked how Tocañans learned history before teachers were sent and the first schoolhouse was built, Sr. Manuel Barra (approximate age 71), the eldest and most prolific *saya* composer and musician told me "*solamente saya*" (there was only *saya*). An elder Afro-Bolivian woman recalled a *saya* that black schoolchildren sang around this time:

> Me mandan a la escuela,
> me mandan a la escuela.
> ¿Pero sin paper ni lápiz,
> con que voy a escribir?

> They send me to school,
> they send me to school.
> But without paper or pencil,
> with what am I going to write?

On the surface this song seems to address a need for school supplies; however, the underlying text may reveal confusion caused by a state-imposed logocentric teaching method onto a people who maintained a knowledge of their history through sung *saya* lyrics. By the late 1990s Tocañans were raising still other complex political issues regarding the education of their children. The schoolteachers sent to Tocaña by the state, parents argue, are not black; they are most often Aymara or mestizos of Aymara cultural descent. Because their principle language is not Spanish, Tocañans feel these grade school–level instructors are not qualified to teach Afro-Bolivian children language or history.

Following grade school, Tocañan teenagers are sent to Coroico, an arduous three-hour hike across a steep valley. There they reside during the school week in rented rooms, cooking and taking care of themselves, while attending the regional public high school, Guerrilleros Lanza. Tocañan parents say that because of the educational circumstances in Tocaña and Coroico, they would rather send their children to the city of La Paz to study and to become *profesionales* (professionals) rather than staying in the *campo* (rural countryside) where farming is the only means of survival. *Sayas* like "Me Mandan a la Escuela" are an important vehicle for voicing anything from grievances to praise and for informing and educating the state, the public, and more recently, uninitiated Afro-Bolivians about the Black Movement in Bolivia.

*Afro-Bolivian Migrants in La Paz*

The population of black migrants living in the city of La Paz exceeds that of any other Bolivian metropolis. Black people live in and around the city center, but especially in rapidly growing migrant neighborhoods on the outskirts of La Paz like Villa Fátima and Río Seco in El Alto. No part of the city has a significant concentration of Afro-Bolivians and there are no black neighborhoods.

Some Afro-Bolivians living in La Paz who are from villages near Coroico in the Nor Yungas province maintain a sense of community by participating as *socios* (members) of a *saya* music ensemble. To participate in this *saya* music ensemble is to be an active member in the Movimiento Negro (Black Movement); musical participation and political activism are one and the same for many of these individuals. Before joining forces in 1994 with other similar black identity movements from around the country, this group went by the name Movimiento Cultural Grupo Afroboliviano La Paz (Afro-Bolivian Cultural Movement, La Paz).

Membership in the *saya* ensemble of La Paz is open to any person self-identifying as *negro* (black), excluding no one, but as of early 1997, only Nor Yungueños composed this group. There is an equally large population of Afro-Bolivian migrants from the Sud Yungas; but none had joined the *saya*, and there was no equivalent Sud Yungueño club or *saya* ensemble in the city.[5] With few exceptions, the individuals who comprise the *saya* share a history of growing up in a Nor Yungas agricultural village, attending high school in Coroico, and migrating to the city as teenagers. They all share similar negative experiences of racial discrimination in the city. Besides creating a community, membership in the *saya* ensemble and in the Movimiento Negro provides Afro-Bolivian migrants with tangibles such as financial support, help in locating employment, and strength in numbers for cultural and political resistance.

Women make up the leadership of the Black Movement in La Paz. They manage nearly all of the organizational, economic, and political responsibilities. Since its inception, the position of president has always been filled by a woman. For years it was Sra. Julia Pinedo and later Sra. Fortunata Medina Pinedo de Pérez (distantly related to Sra. Julia Pinedo), both of whom were active in the recuperation of *saya* music in the early 1980s. Women find employment in the city as domestic servants, shop clerks, and secretaries; they are the primary bread winners and centers of urban households.

With few exceptions, the migrant men who participate in the *saya* ensemble limit their roles to musical composition and drumming. These men find it more difficult than the women to obtain steady employment. As one consequence, men often must return to the lowland yungas during harvest periods to earn money and bring produce back to the city. Once in the yungas, it is not uncommon for them to contract themselves to clean or plant large fields, which delays their return to the city for up to several months or even a year.

The cost of transportation and the economic situation faced by these migrants forces movement leaders to locate a centralized meeting place accessible to all members. Few Afro-Bolivian migrants are able to afford telephones in their homes. *Saya* meetings are one of the only means by which members get information about the times and locations of musical and political events. The other means by which communication takes place within the community of members, and by extension the broader social network of black migrants, is by word of mouth. This informal system is not always reliable enough to guarantee that everyone is well informed about events. Communicative problems together with group factionalism resulted in several near-dissolutions of the *saya* ensemble and as many attempts to completely restructure the membership and leadership of the organization from 1992 through early 1997.

Besides communicational difficulties, since its inception the social movement leaders have been struggling to locate and obtain a permanent place to meet. There was a period of several months in 1992 when they had no centralized meeting place and were forced to get together in the crowded plaza of Pérez Velasco, which is situated right at the intersection of La Paz's busiest pedestrian and automobile arteries. After a brief respite in the Museo Tambo Quirquincho (Museum), changes in city politics resulted in their being ousted once again to the streets of La Paz in early 1994. In 1996 the *saya* group received permission to meet in the Sede de los Strongest (the Strongest soccer team's central office and reception hall), but they were not permitted to sing, dance, or drum there.

Because of this and the limited role that men play in ensemble organization and politics, their participation and attendance rapidly diminished.

## (Re)Discovering the "Saya Race"

There are two versions—two different histories endorsed by Afro-Bolivians of Tocaña and La Paz—for the recuperation of *saya*. The first chronologically, but not the most agreed upon within Afro-Bolivian discourse, comes from Vicente Gemio, a Tocañan farmer and prominent *saya* musician and composer. According to Sr. Gemio, *saya* was first revitalized when, in 1976, the sponsor of a coffee festival in Coroico asked village leaders from Tocaña if they would dance *saya* for his fiesta. Although it was not a popular idea among the black people of Tocaña at the time, they agreed to perform. Gemio's father, along with Manuel Barra and other village elders, taught him and only a few other teenagers to sing, drum, and dance *saya* so that they would have enough drummers and dancers to perform. That year, according to Gemio, the group, made up of elders and inexperienced teenagers, danced *saya* publicly for the first time in decades.

This was a pivotal moment in Gemio's career as a *saya* musician and leader. From then on, he was recognized by black musicians throughout Bolivia as the most prolific composer of *sayas*. From 1995–1997 he was the *capitán* (captain) of the *saya batería* (drumming group) in Tocaña. In February 1995, Gemio was elected president of Tocaña's *saya* music ensemble. Natalio Russell, a wealthy mestizo hotel owner in Coroico and a longtime supporter and historian of Afro-Bolivian culture, refers to him as one of the *reyes de la saya* (*saya* kings).[6]

The second and remarkably different version of the *saya* recuperation story is told by the leaders of the Black Movement in La Paz, who are migrants originally from Tocaña and other small villages surrounding Coroico. According to migrants such as Fortunata Medina de Pérez, in October 1982, six years after the coffee festival in Coroico, she, along with junior-level students attending Coroico's public high school, Guerrilleros Lanza, decided to reconstruct *saya* for the town's annual patron saint fiesta dedicated to the Virgen de la Candelaria.

Local legend has it that during Bolivia's struggle for independence (1809–1825), the Virgen de la Candelaria miraculously saved the people of Coroico from encroaching Royalist armies sent by the Spanish Crown. With nowhere to hide, the people of Coroico fled into their church and prayed. When all hope was gone and the people of Coroico were completely surrounded, the Virgen de la Candelaria is said to have descended from the sky on a cloud. She commanded armies of Patriotas (Patriots) that drove the Spanish Royalists away (see Templeman 1994:9–10). Along with most people of the region, on October 20 of each year Afro-Bolivians celebrate Candelaria in Coroico.

For Fortunata Medina de Pérez, who was one of these students and who was the president (until December 1996) of the Afro-Bolivian *saya* ensemble in La

Paz, this reconstruction represented the rebirth of *saya* in particular and of Afro-Bolivian culture more generally. As she recounts the story, high school students had not previously danced in the *entrada* (entrance parade) of their town's annual festival. The idea to dance in Coroico's parade was suggested by Oscar Gisbert, secretary of Coroico's high school. Before this, the only representations of Bolivian black people to be found at regional festivals such as this were parodies like *los negritos* (pejorative: "the cute Blacks") and *tundiki*, which comprises black-faced mockeries of stereotyped colonial slaves performed by Aymara dance troupes (Templeman 1996). Sra. Fortunata Medina de Pérez, along with other Afro-Bolivians, says that to dance *saya* back then was to expose one's cultural features to the enacted discourse of disparagement leading to mockery and ridicule.

Following the instructions of village elders in Tocaña, the students borrowed and built the musical instruments they needed to dance *saya*. These included differently tuned and sized drums, bamboo scrapers, and sets of bells worn around the legs of *guías*, the lead dancers. Sra. Fortunata Medina de Pérez was led by her mother to what was perhaps the last remaining *saya* blouse, which one woman was preserving for her mother's eventual burial. It was a white blouse decorated with figures on the front and back made from brightly colored fringes and lace. Using this blouse as a pattern, the students contracted seamstresses in Coroico to sew 35 men's and women's *saya* dance uniforms. The men wore similarly decorated white shirts with red-bordered slacks. Women wore the white blouses along with white, red-bordered *polleras* (broad skirts commonly associated with Aymara market women in La Paz), and they carried sky-blue shawls draped over their arms. Men learned how to drum from Sr. Manuel Barra, one of the oldest *saya compositores* (composers), *capitanes* (captains), and *guías* (guides). Sra. Angélica Pinedo, the only able and willing *saya* dancer still living from Barra's generation, taught the women *saya* dance steps and choreography (Templeman 1996).

On October 20, 1982, these high school juniors entered Coroico's parade to publicly dance *saya* in honor of the Virgen de la Candelaria. Fortunata Medina, one of the members of that high school class and one of the founders of the Movimiento Negro, told me that "the people of Coroico cheered with delight when we entered the plaza dancing *saya*." Also present, but less enthused, were Afro-Bolivians from the yungas and La Paz who were shocked and embarrassed by the display. Sixteen years later, one of these individuals explained to me that she felt ashamed to see her brothers and sisters dancing *saya*. She, along with many others, felt that dancing *saya* was fueling the continued mockery of black people by *indios* (Indians, but with a definite pejorative connotation) and *tundiki* dance troupes (Templeman 1996).[7]

Medina danced again her senior year, and after graduating she moved to La Paz. In the following years, she, along with other migrants, returned to Coroico and continued dancing for the October 20 celebration and for what was becoming a reclamation of Afro-Bolivian culture and an acknowledgment of a new Afro-Bolivian identity.

## The Black Movement in Bolivia

Initially calling themselves the Movimiento Cultural Grupo Afro-Boliviano and, since January 1995, the Movimiento Negro, Afro-Bolivians have organized themselves throughout the country into a unified and expanding social movement. They have raised *saya* to emblematic level for the movement, and *saya* has become the voice and key means of generating income that sustains the movement. At the broadest level, the objective of the Movimiento Negro is to raise public consciousness, nationally and internationally, about the presence, history, and culture of black people and about the forms of racism in Bolivia. Besides La Paz and Tocaña, the movement has active membership organizations in the cities of Santa Cruz and Cochabamba and in the rural village of Chicaloma in Sud Yungas. Black activist musicians from La Paz and Tocaña founded the movement. Now these two groups work closely together, joining forces to perform *saya* at regional and national folklore festivals where they disseminate information while competing against other dance troupes for cash prizes.

Afro-Bolivian poets and composers transmit movement messages through their poetry and *saya* lyrics. Besides taking home cash prizes, the members sell cassette tape recordings they make of their music and poetry at fiestas nationwide, and most recently, internationally.[8] Reinforcing these powerful media are the organizers and leaders of the Movimiento Negro, who articulate their goals, accomplishments, and grievances over public address systems during parade performances and through newspaper, television, and radio interviews.

Afro-Bolivian political activists educate themselves through any available media about other black situations and social movements throughout the African diaspora. They have attended leadership conferences in Peru, Bolivia, and the United States, where experiences of racism and discrimination have been shared and where strategies for combating these oppressive forces have been established.

### Saya Music

To Afro-Bolivians, the word *saya* has several meanings. *Saya* refers to a dance genre, an ensemble of musicians and dancers who sing the genre, or any song of the genre. Perhaps most important, *saya* refers to the sung chorus; it is the choral response of an overall call-and-response cyclical form.

To accompany *saya* singing, drummers interlock three differently voiced drums. The *asentador* (setter) leads the drummers with a duple pulse, dampening the second beat. A slightly smaller and higher-pitched drum, the *cambiador* (changer), interlocks a varying triplet pattern over the duple set by the captain. The smallest and highest pitched drum, the *gangengo* (Afro-Bolivian word of unknown origins) interlaces a quick upbeat one-stick roll.

Guías (guides) of the saya ensemble wear bells around their legs. They wrap lower-pitched sets around their right legs and higher-pitched sets around their left legs. They guide the men dancers with their right legs, sounding the lower macho (male) set on the downbeats. The women dancers follow the higher-pitched hembra (female) bells, which the guías wear on their left legs, and they swing their hips to the offbeats. Elder Afro-Bolivians informed me that besides leading the separate men and women dancers, these bells are a reminder of the chains and shackles worn by their enslaved African ancestors.

The cuancha (an Afro-Bolivian word of unknown origins), a large bamboo scraper, binds the polyrhythmic texture together with an eighth, two-sixteenths rhythmic ostinato. Cambiadores (those who change) and asentadores (those who set) further fill out the texture with a responsorial drumming exchange: the cambiador occasionally calls out four accented eighths; his partner, an asentador, answers with the same or a variation, but at a lower pitch.

Sayas generally begin with the captain of the drummers calling out to the chorus a single couplet praise to, and reminder of, Manuel Isidoro Belzu, the president of Bolivia revered for having freed blacks from slavery.

> Isidoro Belzu, bandera ganó.
> Ganó la bandera, el altar mayor.
>
> Isidoro Belzu won our freedom.
> He won our freedom, the highest altar.

The leader of the women then joins in thirds with the captain of the drummers and the two repeat the praise. All of the women and men dancers then join in and sing the saya, as a choral response.

Saya verses are made up of a pair of melodically formulaic eight-syllable couplets. These couplets are called out by one or more copleros (couplet singers). The lyrics of these couplets can be improvised, but they are more often drawn from old repertoires. Copleros express deeply felt emotions through these verses, and coplas carry a hidden message. The lead coplero is generally the eldest man dancing; he holds the largest repertoire. As an example:

> ¿Hermanos como les cuento,
> una muerte lastimosa?
> Una mosca por volar,
> se rompió la calavera.
>
> Brothers how do I tell you,
> about a sad death?
> In trying to fly,
> [the fly] broke someone's head.

The students, who are now farmers in Tocaña and working migrants in La Paz, enjoy singing this copla. Many of them mentioned it to me as being among their favorites. It is both humorous and troubling; rather bittersweet. They appreciate its antiquity and laugh at the idea that a tiny fly could kill someone. The message that lies within, however, is one of mortality from a tropical bottfly, which resembles a large housefly, and lays its eggs beneath the scalp of its host. The cyst of larvae swells and becomes infected. With no sanitation or medical facilities, as is the case in the rural yungas, this *saya* verse reminds Afro-Bolivians of their loved ones who have died from any cause.

Responding to each verse is a chorus, the *saya* proper. All of the men and women, drummers and dancers, sing the *saya* in unison, while the best musicians occasionally harmonize by singing at a third or fifth above the chorus melody. As with the verse, it is the text that is central to the *saya* chorus. Sr. Vicente Gemio, a prolific composer from Tocaña, explained to me, "there is not a lot of time [in the *saya* chorus], every word counts, nothing can be wasted."

Since 1982—with tremendous organizational, financial, and political work on the parts of these students—*saya* has become the musical emblem and key symbol of black people throughout Bolivia. By 1994, the students, together with black activists, had elevated *saya* to be the central communicative medium for disseminating information to the state and public regarding their social movement. While the principle educational role of *saya* has shifted, the importance of text in *saya* lyrics has not. This younger generation of Afro-Bolivians has converted *saya* from a vehicle for the transmission of oral history to a political tool designed to raise the level of public consciousness regarding the social plight of Bolivian black people.

### Broadcasting Movement Messages

The direction of the Movimiento Negro shifted considerably between 1992 and 1996 as the social, economic, and political landscapes in Bolivia changed, but also as leaders learned about other African-American movements in adjacent Peru, elsewhere in Latin America, and throughout the African diaspora. The initial goals of the movement's founders were to rescue lost Afro-Bolivian cultural practices and to unite black people nationwide by inviting their *hermanos* (brothers) to join them in celebrating the *raza negra* (black race) by participating in *saya*. Perhaps the best-known *saya* is "Si Yo Fuera Presidente (If I Were President)," composed by Manuel Barra:

> Si yo fuera presidente,
> formaría un puente.
> Formaría un puente,
> de Tocaña hasta La Paz.

> If I were president,
> I would build a bridge.
> I would build a bridge,
> from Tocaña to La Paz.

Barra told me that he wanted a "bridge" that would span the widening gap in communications between Tocañans and their absent friends and family members who migrated to La Paz. He composed this *saya* at a time when communication had completely failed between the *saya* groups, and hence the communities, of Tocaña and La Paz. A misunderstanding about the participation of Tocañan women in joint *saya* performances resulted in the two groups going their separate ways in August 1992. Barra's bridge was intended to prevent this sort of internal fighting and reduce factionalism among Afro-Bolivians.

Barra's metaphoric bridge, however, was quickly appropriated and politicized by the young musicians of the Afro-Bolivian Cultural Movement. When they sang it in towns and cities throughout Bolivia, the message became one of joining all black people together, reducing their spatial distance and also reducing their ideological differences, so that they, as a tiny minority, could work as a unified group toward the advancement of common goals. Everywhere they went they sang "Si Yo Fuera Presidente," but always substituting the name of the village, city, or department in which they performed for "Tocaña" as a means of inviting black people from there to join the movement (e.g., "formaría un puente, de Cochabamba hasta La Paz").

"La Vueltita (The Little Turn)," another *saya* from this period, composed by Vicente Gemio, reaches out to black people all over Bolivia.

> *Cantaremos, bailaremos,*
> *todos de la saya,*
> *nuestra cultura.*
> *Alegría chicas,*
> *dense una vueltita,*
> *se ve bonita.*

> We will sing, we will dance,
> everyone of the *saya*,
> our culture.
> Be happy girls,
> take a turn,
> you look beautiful.

Like "Si Yo Fuera Presidente," through this *saya*, the Afro-Bolivian musicians transmitted fundamental movement messages to other Bolivian black people, "*saya* is our culture," and "it is beautiful to see you dancing [*saya*]." Beneath the simple dance turn there is a profound message challenging black people to change their ideological direction from one of rejection of black culture implicit in *blanqueamiento* and *mestizaje*, to an emergent ideology that celebrates being Afro-Bolivian. The *saya* encourages black people to be proud of their cultural heritage and it tells them that they are beautiful. As such, it is an aesthetic song and dance performance that takes place with cognate Afro-Latin American movements worldwide.

These essential aesthetic messages conveyed by the Black Movement continued through the 1980s and 1990s while another aim began to take shape: a more
formal demand to be recognized by the state as a *raza legítima* (legitimate race or
people) and to be counted as such in the national census. This trajectory resulted
in late 1994 in an invitation to the governmental palace in La Paz to meet Bolivia's vice president, Víctor Hugo Cárdenas. At that time, Cárdenas made an
informal promise to the movement leaders that Afro-Bolivians would be counted
in Bolivia's next census.

As of late 1996 no *sayas* had been composed that explicitly addressed the issue
of black representation in the national census. There were, however, a variety of
*sayas* performed that were intended to educate the state and the public about
Afro-Bolivians, their history, and their experiences in Bolivia. "Todo Es de Fruta
(Everything Comes from Fruit)" is one such *saya* composed by Vicente Gemio.
It introduces the group itself to its audience, and through it, Afro-Bolivians tell
the public about themselves:

> *Todo es de fruta,*
> *café y coca,*
> *el lugar donde vivimos,*
> *se llama Coroico.*
> *De nuestra cultura,*
> *hemos traído la saya*
> *pueblo Boliviano.*

> Everything comes from fruit,
> coffee and coca,
> the place where we live,
> is called Coroico.
> From our culture,
> we have brought *saya*,
> Bolivian people.

Through this song black performers present *saya* to other Bolivian people. In doing so, they open a space for their new ethnic voice to be heard. They tell people
that they are farmers, or that they come from farming villages like Tocaña. By informing people of their agriculturist backgrounds, Afro-Bolivians reveal the significant economic and historical roles that they continue to play in their country.

Another *saya* of this type, "Somos Yungueñitos (We Are People of the Yungas),"
advances the work of creating a space for a new racial identity:

> *Somos yungueñitos,*
> *señores presentes,*
> *somos de la raza de la saya.*
> *Trayendo lindas tonadas,*
> *para salir de Bolivia.*

We are people of the yungas,
[all of you] people present,
we are of the *saya* race.
Bringing beautiful melodies,
to go outside Bolivia.

"Somos Yungueñitos" goes one step further than "Todo es de Fruta" by "bring-ing" *saya* and Afro-Bolivian culture to people "outside Bolivia."

### The Struggle to Reclaim Saya

The most popular dance in Bolivia from 1994 through 1996 was *el caporal* (the slave foreman), a dance genre that is accompanied by brass band music. Bolivians commonly refer to this music as "*saya*" and to its rhythm as "*ritmo de saya*" (saya rhythm) and "*el ritmo negro*" (the black rhythm). While *caporal* is not related musically (i.e., melodically or rhythmically) to the *saya* that Afro-Bolivians sing and dance, it is directly linked to the history of black people and their presence in Bolivia since the early sixteenth century. *Caporal* is a colorful, energetic, and syncopated mestizo *comparsa* (dance genre) based on the character of a black colonial slave overseer. I estimate that between 1994 and 1996 more than one-third of all of the dance troupes participating in regional and national fiestas across Bolivia were *caporales*.

Topping the recording industry charts and driven by a similar "*ritmo de saya*" (*saya* rhythm) that is danced by *caporales*, are "*sayas*" by professional folkloric bands such as Los Kjarkas and, as of 1996, Pacha, a spin-off of Los Kjarkas aimed at a more international audience (Fernando Torrico, personal communication). These professional folkloric groups typically adopt native instruments such as panpipes and other indigenous flutes, and they make their living by performing "authentic" Andean music in hotels and at tourist night clubs and by selling tapes and CDs. This style of Andean folkloric music has joined the international mar-ket attracting consumers of world beat and new age music.

Like popular culture throughout Latin America, Bolivian popular culture has been dominated by these economic tides (i.e., world beat), and black music has become a commodity. "*Sayas*" appeared on the last three Los Kjarkas CDs and then on the first Pacha CD, "each one sounding more African than the previous," according to Los Kjarkas and later Pacha *saya* composer Fernando Torrico. Tor-rico told me in a recorded interview that he heard *sayas* for the first time from his grandmother, who used to sing them to him, and that they had the same *ritmo de saya* to which the *caporales* now dance. About a decade ago, Torrico was walk-ing through the streets of La Paz when he heard the Afro-Bolivians drumming and singing *saya*, and in it, he felt the same *ritmo de saya* that his grandmother sang and that he now uses in his *saya* compositions. Torrico believes that the *saya* rhythm of his popular compositions was brought to Bolivia by colonial slaves.

When asked what the difference between *saya* and *caporal* is, Torrico told me, "*saya* refers to the *ritmo negro, caporal* is the dance."

Participation in these musical forms, whether by joining a *caporal* dance troupe or by purchasing Los Kjarkas and Pacha CDs, works as an identity marker for young Bolivians interested in participating in world beat and the celebration of blackness throughout the diaspora. Unfortunately, both of these forms of *saya* have undermined the grassroots political and educational efforts of the Movimiento. By 1995 Afro-Bolivians viewed these popular "*sayas*" as a direct assault on their culture and as an obstacle to their consciousness-raising goals. By misrepresenting that which Afro-Bolivians present as "*cultura netamente Africano*" (purely African culture), they had dwarfed the Afro-Bolivian mission to demonstrate an authentically African cultural heritage.

Fighting against *tundikis* (Aymara black-faced mockeries of stereotyped colonial slaves) and commercial folkloric groups like Los Kjarkas quickly became the raison d'être for the Movimiento Negro. As viewed by black activists, the distraction and misinformation caused by these "*sayas*" was debilitating. The Movimiento Negro, determined to reclaim the word *saya*, began calling their *saya* "*la saya original*" (the original *saya*), and "*la saya auténtica*" (the authentic *saya*). "What these other groups play and dance to is not *saya*," they announce; "it is *caporal*, it is *tundiki*." In early 1995 a young Afro-Bolivian named Santos Reynal Reynal from Chicaloma, a village in La Paz's Sud Yungas Province, composed a *saya* that solidified and articulated the message needed by black people all over Bolivia:

> *Después de 500 años,*
> *no me vayas a cambiar,*
> *el bello ritmo de saya,*
> *con ritmo de caporal.*
> *Los Kjarkas están confundiendo,*
> *la saya y el caporal,*
> *lo que ahora están escuchando,*
> *es saya original.*

> After 500 years,
> you will not change it,
> the beautiful rhythm of *saya*,
> with the rhythm of *caporal*.
> Los Kjarkas are confusing,
> *saya* and *caporal*,
> what you are now hearing
> is the original *saya*.

Santos Reynal Reynal told me that he was inspired to write these lyrics when he was in La Paz and happened across a Festival de Saya a 500 Años (*Saya* Festival to 500 Years) sponsored by Los Kjarkas. It was the words "a 500 años" that stuck in his head and he felt he had to say something.

"Después de 500 Años" is the product of individual and Afro-Bolivian group creativity. In it the composer speaks out to Los Kjarkas and Los Caporales, but also to the Bolivian public and state, and perhaps most important, to Afro-Bolivians nationwide. The underlying text is one of resistance to *mestizaje* and *blanqueamiento*. Besides capturing the attention of audiences and the media, this *saya* became a powerful mover around which Afro-Bolivians united. Its message resonated with Afro-Bolivian voices across Bolivia, and it became indicative of the new direction of the expanding Black Movement. Although it was composed in Chicaloma, the *saya* ensembles of Tocaña and La Paz learned it and began performing it around the country. It is unusual for ensembles of the Nor Yungas province to perform *sayas* of the Sud Yungas; this became a notable exception.

By February 1996 the combined *saya* ensembles of La Paz and Tocaña were using this as their entrance and emblematic piece for parades. Activist black musicians and dancers throughout the country publicized this *saya* like no other in the history of black people in Bolivia. It came to represent that for which Afro-Bolivians were fighting and the Movimiento Negro in Bolivia. During a ten-day Lenten tour beginning on Carnaval and ending with Tentación, they sang it in Oruro's world-renowned Carnaval parade; two days later they performed it through the crowded streets of La Paz's Carnaval celebration; and a week later they sang at Bolivia's largest annual dance festival, the Corso de Corsos (Competition of Competitions) in Cochabamba. The movement leaders granted radio, newspaper, and television interviews as they sang and danced past reviewing stands. For each interview, the message was the same, "what you are now hearing is the original *saya* brought to Bolivia by our enslaved African ancestors."

*Notes*

I would like to thank Debra Lynn Van Engen, the people of Tocaña and Coroico, and the community of Afro-Bolivian migrants in La Paz for their encouragement and friendship, and all of the black people throughout Bolivia for their participation and support. I am grateful to Norman E. Whitten, Jr., and Arlene Torres for inviting me to participate in this volume and for their patience and editorial suggestions. I also wish to thank the Wenner-Gren Foundation for Anthropological Research, Fulbright (IIE), the Center for Latin American and Caribbean Studies at the University of Illinois, the Tinker Foundation, the Inter-American Foundation (IAF), and SEMILLA in La Paz for their contributions.

1. Afro-Bolivians self-identify as *negros* while the political leaders and intellectuals of the social movement also refer to themselves as Afrobolivianos. I use "black people" and "Afro-Bolivians" interchangeably, for stylistic reasons.

2. See the general introduction by Whitten and Torres for the significance of the article *el* as employed by Afro-Bolivians.

3. This demographic data changed little from December 1994 through January 1997.
4. In June 1996 I recorded an elder black man, Don Manuel Barra, engaged in conversation with an Aymara schoolteacher. I did not solicit this conversation; however, they did agree to be video taped as part of my ethnographic work. These video and musical recordings are available through the Ethnomusicology Archives, School of Music, University of Illinois, Urbana, Illinois, and through MUSEF (Museo Nacional de Etnografía y Folklore) in La Paz, Bolivia.
5. *Saya* was revitalized in the Nor Yungas town of Coroico by black students from the surrounding villages. By 1995 *saya* was also being reconstructed in Sud Yungas villages like Chicaloma. I would be surprised if the Afro-Bolivian migrants from the Sud Yungas *did not* form their own *saya* music ensemble and political base in the city of La Paz by the late 1990s.
6. This is not the same as Mururata's ritualistic kings (i.e., Bonifacio Pinedo and Julio Pinedo); it is, however, related. People from Coroico know of the black monarchy and in this case Sr. Russell is flattering Vicente Gemio, acknowledging his leadership and talent by alluding to it.
7. The use of the term *indios* is derogatory in Bolivia and illustrates racist sentiments.
8. Sra. Fortunata Medina de Pérez, the president of the La Paz movement, sold several cases of *saya* cassette tapes in the United States while participating at an international conference, La Mujer en el Activismo Político y Social (Women in Political and Social Action) in September and October 1996. Afro-Bolivians have also sold tapes to Canadians, Brazilians, Ghanaians, Angolans, Peruvians, and other people who support them from around the world.

## References

Flores, Rose Mary
  1989    Folklore de la Cultura Negra en Bolivia y su Aprovechamiento Turístico. Tesis de Grado, UMSA, La Paz.

Grupo Afro-Boliviano
  1991    Saya. Siembra Producciones, Prefectura de La Paz, CFB-4003. La Paz.

Léons, Madeline Barbara
  1978    Race, Ethnicity, and Political Mobilization in the Andes. American Ethnologist 5(3):484–494.

Léons, William
  1977    Pluralism and Mobility in a Bolivian Community. El Dorado 11(3).

Monge Oviedo, Rodolfo
  1993    Are We or Aren't We? Inset in The Black Americas, 1492–1992. NACLA Report on the Americas, 25:19.

Montaño Aragón, Mario
  1992    El Rey Negro de Bolivia fue Coronado en Coroico. Derecho, La Paz, September 4, 1992, p. 12.
  1993    La Familia Negra en Bolivia. Guía Etnográfica Lingüística de Bolivia. La Paz: Don Bosco.

Ortiz, Maz Portugal
    1977    La Esclavitud en las Épocas Colonial y Nacional de Bolivia. La Paz: Insti-
            tuto Boliviano de Cultura.
Pizarroso Cuenca, Arturo
    1977    La Cultura Negra en Bolivia. La Paz: Ediciones ISLA.
    1992    La familia negra en Bolivia. Guía etnográfica lingüística de Bolivia, Tomo
            III. La Paz: Don Bosco.
Spedding, Allison
    1994    Wachu Wachu: Cultivo de coca e identidad en los yunkas de La Paz. La
            Paz: Hisbol.
Templeman, Robert W.
    1996    Renacimiento de la Saya: El Rol que Juega Música en el Movimiento Ne-
            gro en Bolivia. Reunión Anual de Etnología 1996. La Paz: MUSEF.
    1994    Afro-Bolivians. Encyclopedia of World Cultures. Volume 7, South Amer-
            ica. Johannes Wilbert, ed. New York: G.K. Hall/Macmillan.

# 17. FOLK HEALING AND THE STRUCTURE
# OF CONQUEST IN SOUTHWEST COLOMBIA

## Michael Taussig

### Preamble

Folk healing and magic in today's Third World are not bizarre and meaningless discourse, but specialized forms of folk art and wisdom addressing the perplexity and mystery of daily life in the modern world. This poetic wisdom is rooted in the antiquity of an enchanted world whose spirit spoke to man through the story-teller, the conjurer, and the healer. Modern commodity production has not disenchanted the world of the lower classes in the modern Third World. The formal rationality of the capitalist market has not created the same void of meaning that afflicts mature capitalist cultures. Instead, capitalist development of the Third World has added to the power of its sorcerers and magicians. Hence, I wish to inquire into some of the ways by which folk healing, magic, and sorcery embody the history of imperialism in the Third World, and how they mediate contradictions associated with capitalist development. My ethnographic focus is on the vast network of folk healers splayed across the cities, mountains, valleys, and jungles of southwest Colombia in South America. The issues entailed by this inquiry are legion and include: (1) relations between magical medicine and popular culture, (2) the explanation of the efficacy of magical medicine in the context of neocolonial capitalist development, (3) the processes and effects of the commoditization of magic, (4) the role of magic in forging colonial and neocolonial hegemony, and (5) the social history of popular culture in Latin America and its constant replication into the present.

The speculations and themes developed in this article derive from almost four years of fieldwork experience as an anthropologist and physician in southwest Colombia between 1970 and 1977 (see Afterword). This work began in the plantation towns in the Cauca valley, near the city of Cali which is the principal financial and population center of the southwest of Colombia. My initial concern was with the history of economic development of the valley, focusing on the commercialization of agriculture from the Spanish conquest to the present day. This led me to an increasing interest in the history of the hinterlands and their connection with the plantation areas, as all of these, in their different and combined ways,

Originally published in *Journal of Latin American Lore* 6:2 (1980), pp. 217–78. Copyright © by The Regents of the University of California. Reprinted by permission of the UCLA Latin American Center.

were progressively enmeshed in the web of the international economy, cash crop production, and wage labor. It was impossible to live long in the plantation areas without becoming involved in the myriad interconnections binding them to the hinterlands: the jungles of the Pacific coast to the west, the jungles of the upper Amazon drainage to the southwest, and the slopes and plateaus of the Andes in between.

Archaeological research indicates that there were extensive connections among the inhabitants of these areas before the Spanish conquest. During the colonial epoch, from the mid-sixteenth century to the early nineteenth, the indigenous inhabitants were dispersed and sought refuge in hinterland areas, African slaves were circulated between the Cauca valley and mining camps on the coast, and the Spaniards and their descendants ruled over a mixed economy based on gold mining radiating throughout the vast and variegated region. Beginning with the railroad built in 1914, connecting the Cauca valley to the coast and thence to international markets, large-scale commercial agriculture developed apace, and following World War II migrant wage labor from the hinterlands flooded the plantations of the valley. The majority of these wage laborers (men) and servants (women) come from the jungles of the Pacific coast, but there are also many mestizo peasants from the Andean highlands to the south. In both cases the migration flow has a significantly large circular component, the migrants moving back and forth from their areas of provenience. This flow of population can be analyzed in terms of the development of a wage labor force responding to the growth of the capitalist economy. It can, in addition, be analyzed in terms of its salient ideological or phenomenological associations, as a synchronic representation of age-old myths about civilization and social development.

To the locals, born in the cities and plantation towns, the hinterland areas are places of mystery and the people who live there are thought of as primitive. Migration to the agribusiness sphere and the city is a process whereby these primitive people pass into the civilizing influence of town life and the cash nexus. The town and the plantations act as a sponge, absorbing the strata underlying history, embodied in the cultures of the hinterlands. To locally born residents, the blacks from the Pacific coast and the Indians from the highlands bear intimations of an earlier epoch of human history: they are close to nature, privy to her secrets, intertwined with the beginnings of time, and likely to possess stupendous magical powers to kill, to heal, and to dramatically change the course of misery and affliction. At the same time these people are derided as less than civilized, as ignorant about modern ways, as naïve and unable to read and write. "They sleep twelve to a room, on the floor. They can't speak properly. Back home they live in trees. They look like apes. . . ." So, locally born blacks will speak of their black brethren from the coast. Yet their magicians and healers are sought after by locals to cure the misfortunes attributed to sorcery that plagues life in the plantation towns. A similar pattern of paradoxical attributions is made with regard to the Indians from the mountains and from the upper Amazon basin. This pattern lies embedded in and is concretized by a vast network of healers (and patients) splayed across the land.

Healing and sorcery express significant ideological features of social relations and of the meaning of the world, ranging from the meaning of nature and of human nature to popular conceptions of civilization, race, and history. The practices and theories involved in folk healing sustain the general cultural foundations of knowing and of existence. They speak to what is just and to what is evil in the reciprocity that binds man to man and to his place in the cosmos. Furthermore, folk healing provides by far the commonest form by which lower-class people in so-called developing countries partake in rite and magic. The problems they bring to these rites are, in their own eyes, economic, political, and social, as well as those of bodily disease. The ritual and magic brought to bear on these problems open up to the people concerned metaphysical questions which always have a direct influence on everyday life. Moreover, the folk healing system that I wish to consider is not located within the confines of a single tradition, a single healer, or a single community. Instead it is constituted by a ramifying constellation of social and mental relations which crisscrosses the mosaic of contemporary landscapes that historical development evokes. Indeed, this network of relations as embodied in the practice of folk healing extends far beyond the southwest to the national capital and further still across international boundaries. Its inner constitution, which is at once historical and metahistorical, deserves our closest attention, because in it we find the coalition of magic and economic development upon which the social history of Latin American popular culture and ideological hegemony rest.

My interest here also extends to explaining, or at least partially explaining, the efficacy of folk healing within the broad context of the social relations established by neocolonial capitalist development. This inquiry raises many issues associated with the effects of the commercialization of magic and magical medicine. In this connection it should be pointed out that although the spread and intensification of the market economy is often said by social historians to promote rationalism and materialism (as these terms have generally been understood since the European Enlightenment), in a wide range of circumstances of capitalist development, the spread of market relations seems just as likely to promote or intensify magical beliefs.[1] This is particularly apparent in the flourishing healing cults that abound in today's Third World cities. It is my impression that such cults are proliferating in the cities of the southwest of Colombia. They generally bear a markedly commercial and "quackish" character, yet they meet a widespread social need which cannot be satisfied either by the Church or by the institutions of modern medicine. Furthermore, these cults are not sui generis, but owe much of their form, vigor, and appeal to older shamanic forms of healing still existing in the countryside from which, in fact, they derive much of their magical power and medicines.

In his essays on New World shamanic healing rites, Claude Lévi-Strauss has argued that they actively sustain myths central to a society's culture. Through the interaction of the healer and the patient, a structure of ideas immanent in the culture is actively elaborated and brought to consciousness, cathecting otherwise inarticulable conflicts and emotions. It is the affect embodied in the patient's affliction, initiating the shamanic seance, that energizes the elaboration of ideas developed in the ritual. These ideas constitute a structure which is vividly experienced as a new reality which gives meaning to the affliction and thereby resolves it, if only for a short time. In this way, through the dramatic intensity of the ritual and through the narrative skills of the shaman, culture provides the myth necessary for healing, and, conversely, healing provides a privileged means for sustaining culture (Lévi-Strauss 1967a; 1967b).

Further emphasis on the creative quality of shamanism is provided by Paul Radin. He argues that the shaman is the intellectual of many "primitive" societies and that it is the shaman's function to organize and synthesize the cognitive complex of culture with a view to providing interpretations. Radin stresses, as we must too, that complete systematization is impossible. As metaphysical ideas pass through the layman and as new elements are added from the inexhaustible magico-folkloric background, so the religious complex changes continually. "If we regard religion as the association of a religious emotion with certain concepts and folkloristic elements," he writes, "then it is essential to realize exactly how the religious emotion may be extended to new folkloristic elements. It is just in this connection," he concludes, "that the role of the shaman shows itself. It is he who extends them" (1914:351).

The Spanish conquest, Christianity, and modern economic organization tested the inventiveness of the South American shaman to the full. Moreover, in the situation discussed below, and by a surprising irony of history, the shaman is called upon to reelaborate the culture of the colonizer by the colonizers themselves.

Before analyzing this, it is apposite to make passing reference to the shaman's role as *mediator* because too much romantic nostalgia and misty exultation pervade analyses or the phenomenology of the shaman's mediation of the spirit world and transcendence of alienation. What must not be overlooked is that the shaman in colonial society and today's Third World mediates oppressive class and caste divisions as well. It is true, as Barbara Myerhoff writes, that the shaman mediates the "loss of bliss which occurs at the moment of primordial splitting, after which nothing can be the same" (1976:103). But unless we recognize the equally blissless and primordial split occasioned by European conquest and subsequent economic tyranny, we surely make a cruel mockery of what is at stake in the shadowy essence of shamanism in the postprimordial colonial world—after which nothing can be the same. There is no escaping the power of history which forces shamanism into the political sphere of violent conflicts between colonizer and colonized, white and native, oppressors and oppressed. In this situation, shamanism and magic mediate not only relations with spirits, but also the relations of class and caste that constitute the new social formation. To understand this it is first necessary to consider some of the relations between colonialism, religion, and magical medicine.

## THE COLONIAL EVOLUTION FROM
## RELIGION TO MAGICAL MEDICINE

The Spanish conquest in the New World stripped indigenous religion of its formal institutional covering, but by no means destroyed its basis in thought. Religion passed "underground" into what Europeans call "magic," especially healing magic. It befalls contemporary folk healers and shamans to sustain this system of thought, linked to the precolonial past as much as it is mixed with the religion of the conquerors. The manifestations of this system are constantly changing, partly because the system is in the hands of so many independent specialists, and partly because the social conditions to which it refers and from which it springs are constantly changing. Nevertheless, underlying the accretion or added elements and transformations, something essential in the precolonial structure of ideas continues, not as a mere survival or relic from the irretrievable past, but as an active force mediating history. My aim is to explore the details of this structure and its role in history. It has no Church or formal institutional expression and lies instead in the loose structure of ideas and activities that constitute popular culture. To the extent that it achieves some formalization it is, above all, in the quasi-underground networks linking healers (and patients). These networks are vast, and are, perhaps, continental in scope, spanning subcultures, regions, and national boundaries. They articulate diverse and widely separated eco-zones, modes of production, and ways of life, and they course between the city and the countryside. We can trace them on a map and reconstruct their geography, yet at the same time we must realize that this geography is also a map of social history and a cosmological charter represented in topography. The physical space articulated by these networks is also a semantic space—a mosaic of articulated differences in which heaven and hell, virtue and corruption, caste and class distinctions, and the mnemonic function of landscape in sustaining collective memory create the strange power of the outsider and traveler, particularly that of the nomadic medicine man. Before we attempt to trace this map, it will be useful to make passing reference to two illustrations of the colonial evolution from religion to magical medicine outside of South America.[2]

In his study of acculturation among the eastern Cherokee, R. D. Fogelson states that with Christianization completed by the first third of the nineteenth century, the medicine men became the repository of what he refers to as the remaining fragments of a "quite complex" (sic) religious system. All the medicine men consider themselves to be good Christians and their work consistent with Christian doctrine. He also notes that whites sometimes place great faith in these medicine men, especially when they suffer from incurable illnesses, and that a few medicine men have traveled far from the reservation at the invitation of whites. One medicine man has a regular circuit of white clients whom he visits sometimes for a few months at a time (Fogelson 1961:215–225).

In her book dealing with religion and medicine among the Gã people of modern West Africa, Margaret Field describes a similar situation. The ancient unified structure of the religion loosens and comes to pieces, she writes; but the pieces are by no means destroyed. Some of the old gods are exchanged for new ones. "In the words of one of my Gã friends, 'Many of them have gone inland into the forest and some have gone underground: they have run away from the Europeans.' " Owing to Christianity and colonialism, the high priests' authority is decaying. Religion and magic now have what she calls a "vagrant, questing quality," which is reflected in the worship of very many little yam-eating gods and in the ownership of private medicines. In place of the high priests surge the private medicine men. The "conscientious" and "decent" medicine man is dominant, but he is increasingly threatened to be displaced by cheats, quacks, and "preachers of little new religions." She thinks that the traditional medicine man is more prosperous now than ever before, but that villainous quacks will replace him. And the most gullible victims of these quacks are not the uneducated but the literate Africans. In a similar vein she notes that there is far more true superstition in the average European's attitude toward the mysteries of so-called fetish practice than there is in all the average medicine man's business (Field 1937:132–134).

### COLONIZATION AND THE MORAL
### NATURE OF ITS HEGEMONY

To the marvels of the New World and the occult practices of the African slave and the Native American, the credulous Spaniards brought their own rich store of preternatural beliefs and mythology. The mental universe of the common foot soldier, adventurer, priest, trader, and minor official was a world in which folk Catholicism and European paganism played a vital role. Inevitably they projected their superstitions onto their colonized subjects, and with equal inevitability their subjects responded with their own fabulations regarding the Europeans. The sixteenth and seventeenth centuries were the era of the European witch craze. The cosmic rupture of good and evil and the apocalyptic dualism of God and the devil divided all things—especially the character of the empire's new subjects, inhuman beings, both superhuman and less than human at one and the same time. "They were gods or demons," writes Richard Comstock (1976:62), "unfallen creatures possessing an original innocence or devils with a brutish evil beyond human ken. In the early encounters of European settlers with native

Americans we see both images operating in the white man's imagination." These images encompassed wider terms of reference than the Aristotelian ones so famously disputed by Juan Ginés de Sepúlveda and the Dominicans Bartolomé de Las Casas and Francisco de Vittoria concerning the application of the Aristotelian doctrine of "natural slavery." In the passionate complexity of their dialectical dualism, these opposed images of the Indian as God-like and as devil-like struck deeper chords of the popular imagination than these disputes among the literati can possibly convey. At the very least, in trying to understand that popular imagination, we would have to also consider those millennial notions expressed by the Franciscan Gerónimo de Mendieta who supplied (in John Leddy Phelan's words) the mystical interpretation of conquest: the third of the "three main axes around which revolved most of the ideas of that huge corpus of politico-ecclesiastical theory which enveloped the creation of Spain's overseas empire" (1956:5). (And we should not forget that it was the Franciscans who missionized the Putamayo lowlands in the seventeenth and eighteenth centuries, and their allied order, the Capuchins, in the twentieth.) The image that appealed to Mendieta to describe the Indians, the image of childlike innocence, stressed their defenselessness and their being the children of God—the simple, innocent, and pure who would inherit the kingdom of Heaven. "With a little help from the friars," writes Phelan, "the Indians could become sinless, that is, angelic" (1956:63–64).

Further on, where I describe the visionary journeys undertaken *today* by whites to the kingdom of God, when they are being cured by Indian shamans on the Amazonian frontier, we shall see how pertinent these sixteenth-century millennial notions of Mendieta still are. Nevertheless, these notions, like those of Sepúlveda and of Las Casas, are too "theoretical," one section of the intelligentsia talking to another and to the Spanish court. As such they reflect but dimly that rich complexity of dialectical attribution and counter-attribution with which the more humble colonist and the colonized wrought the identity of each other, fusing the God-like and the devil-like features into the one explosive charge.[3]

In the popular imagination of those times and in the specific circumstances of European conquest, it was common to attribute to the "primitive" African and Native American extraordinary magical powers, very much including the inseparable dyad of powers to kill and powers to heal. Partly human and partly beast, close to the secrets of nature and far from the pale of civilization and the sacraments of the Church, the "primitive" was decidedly inferior and even childish in all respects but this one, which, despite their fears and misgivings, the Europeans were not loathe to use. Having invested their conquered subjects with this macabre and contradictory power, the colonists undertook an equally contradictory strategy for the finding of gold and the founding of the City of God in the New World. As a moral endeavor promising salvation, colonization and the bestowing of (European) civilization found in this attribution of magical power its rationale and motive for Christian proselytism and destruction of paganism. But on the other hand, could not pagan magic be exploited as a stepping-stone to that high realm of purity and sacred power which the colonist was incapable of achieving alone? Historical evidence, and the contemporary ethnography that I will discuss in detail later on, do indeed show that the colonizer reifies his own myths concerning the pagan, becomes subject to their power, and in doing so seeks salvation from the civilization which torments him as much as the pagan on whom he has projected his anti-self. In this regard it is appropriate to refer to the mythology of the "wild man" in the later European Middle Ages.

In his book *Wild Men in the Middle Ages*, Richard Bernheimer describes the mythology concerning wild men said to live in the forests separating villages and towns. Becoming prominent in art and literature around the twelfth century, descendant from pre-Christian beliefs, and still to be found in secluded villages in western Europe, this wild man prefigures the mythology of the primitive and the shaman that was elaborated in the culture of colonialism. Half-human, half-animal, bereft of the powers of reason and of speech, this hairy monster of the woods was feared for his terrible temper and magical strength. Easily angered, his impulse is to tear trespassers to pieces. In revenge he may make lakes disappear and towns sink into the ground. He abducts women and devours human beings, preferring unbaptized children. He has control over the weather, seems happiest with tempests and gales, and has close kinship with animals and plants whose well-being is entrusted to him. He has the power to subdue the most ferocious animals, monsters and dragons included, and cares for nature's other creatures.

Most significantly he can be befriended by man, or caught and tamed in the hope that he will reveal and offer his secret powers. Especially desirable are his powers to heal, to provide plant medicines, and to assist the peasant in his livelihood. Bernheimer draws attention to a sculpture of a wild man on the portal of a thirteenth-century church in Provence, with his hand through the arm of a man counting money into a sack. He suggests that this is meant to show the profit that man can reap from an intimate and friendly association with the wild man (Bernheimer 1952: 21–26).[4]

Discussing the Malay concept of spirits, whose goodwill is sought by magicians, Kirk Endicott notes that they are thought to be stupid and that their emotional reactions are simple and basic. They are easily tricked by bribes or threats in return for their gifts. Although easily controlled, they are also very sensitive to insult, and even a thoughtless, disparaging remark can madden them to revenge. "Thus," he concludes, "spirits are generally regarded as inferior to man, but are still afforded a respect born of fear. In this respect they are like members of aboriginal tribes with whom they are grouped in some contexts" (Endicott 1970:55).

E. B. Tylor drew attention to the ubiquity with which a group of people regarded as primitive are alleged by their self-proclaimed superiors to possess extraordinary magical powers. In his book *Primitive Culture* (first published in 1871) he lists a number of examples, preceded by the comment: "The modern educated world, rejecting occult science as a contemptible superstition, has practically committed itself to the opinion that magic belongs to a lower level of civilization. It is very instructive to find the soundness of that judgment undesignedly confirmed by nations whose education has not advanced far enough to destroy their belief in magic itself. In any country an isolated or outlying race, the lingering survivor of an older nationality, is liable to the reputation of sorcery" (1958, I:113). Among his examples he includes the Hinduized Dravidians of southern India, who, in times past, he asserts, lived in fear of the demoniacal powers of the slave-caste below them. From contemporaneous ethnographic reports he noted that certain Dravidian tribes were in mortal fear of the Kurumbas, whom he described as "wretched forest outcasts, but gifted, it is believed, with powers of destroying men and animals and property by witchcraft." Tylor makes very specific mention of curing superiority attributed to the primitive. At the end of his examples he notes that many a white man in the West Indies and in Africa at the time of his writing dreaded the power of the Obiaman (1958:I, 114).

In contemporary industrialized societies, such as that of the United States or those of western Europe, the myth of the primitive as inferior yet endowed with mystical potency survives, and surely provides the metaphysical basis of modern racism.

Yet this same pattern of antithesis can also prod the notion of and the desire for a common humanity, joining the civilized and the primitive in a bond that will transcend the alienation of the former. In 1911 while partaking in a spiritualist seance, William Butler Yeats was visited by a spirit he identified as Leo Africanus, a Moorish writer and explorer who had been held captive at the court of Pope Leo X. Yeats maintained a correspondence with this spirit, in deliberately disguised handwriting, and, according to Mary Flannery, this experience was a powerful stimulus for one of his major poems, *Ego Dominus Tuus*. There is a small section of the first (1912) draft that I wish to quote, and I choose the draft version because, as Flannery asserts, it is in this version that Yeats is clearly describing the spiritualist experience which led to his summoning Leo Africanus (Flannery 1977:129–130):

ILLE     By the help of images
           I could call up my anti-self, summon all
           That I have least handled, look upon them all
           Because I am most weary of myself.

HIC     I'd rather seek a form of myself

ILLE     This is our modern hope and by this light
           We have found the gentle sensitive mind
           And lost the old nonchalance of this hand
           Whether we choose chisel, or pen or brush
           We are but critics; or but half create
           Timid, entangled and abashed and (empty)
           Lacking the countenance of our friends

In a famous passage in *The Heart of Darkness* Joseph Conrad describes the paddle steamer toiling up the Congo with its ivory tusk merchants (1973:51–52):

> The steamer toiled along slowly on the edge of a black and incomprehensible frenzy. The prehistoric man was cursing us, praying to us, welcoming us—who could tell? We were cut off from the comprehension of our surroundings; we glided past like phantoms, wondering and secretly appalled, as sane men would be before an enthusiastic outbreak in a madhouse. We could not understand because we were too far and could not remember, because we were travelling in the night of first ages, of those ages that are gone, leaving hardly a sign—and no memories.
>
> The earth seemed unearthly. We are accustomed to look upon the shackled form of a conquered monster, but there—there you could look at a thing monstrous and free. It was unearthly, and the men were—No, they were not inhuman. Well, you know, that was the worst of it—this suspicion of their not being inhuman. It would come slowly to one. They howled and yelped, and spun, and made horrid faces; but what thrilled you was just the thought of their humanity—like yours—the thought of your remote kinship with this wild and passionate uproar. Ugly. Yes, it was ugly enough; but if you were man enough you would admit to yourself that there was in you just the faintest trace of a response to the terrible frankness of that noise, a dim suspicion of there being a meaning in it which you— you so remote from the night of first ages—could comprehend. And why not? The mind of man is capable of anything—because everything is in it, all the past as well as all the future.

We will meet up again with these sentiments when we turn to the ethnography of contemporary southwest Colombia, in the forces that drive colonists to Indian healing rites, and in the drug-induced visions that befall the colonists on those miraculous occasions.

With regard to the Spanish conquest of South America, I wish to very briefly and schematically refer to two "cases" which I suggest are paradigmatic of the formation of its colonial and postcolonial moral hegemony. I do not intend to rest my argument on these illustrations in quite the same way as an empirically minded historian would, although I believe that could be done. Rather, they serve as guides for a general thesis that tries to make sense of contemporary social relations as historically rooted. The first concerns the famous slave entrepôt of Cartagena, on the Caribbean coast of what is today called Colombia, and this pertains mainly to the relations between the Spanish and their African slaves. The second example concerns the formation of colonial culture in the Andean highlands and the long-standing relationship between the societies of those highlands and the inhabitants of the hot slopes and jungles to the east of the Andes. In both cases, it is to the pattern of reciprocal attributions of magical power between conqueror and conquered, and to their consequent effects, that I wish to draw attention.

Accounts culled from Inquisition and Crown records, as well as from the memoirs of a leading Jesuit at the beginning of the seventeenth century, reveal the following picture of Cartagena (Lea 1908; Tejado Fernández 1954; Sandoval 1956; Borrego Pla 1973; Toribio Medina 1978; Taussig 1980). The blacks were generally alleged to be liable to possess special magical powers, to heal and to ensorcell ("bewitch"). In the opinion of the Jesuit Alonso de Sandoval, the blacks worshiped the devil and killed defenseless Christians with sorcery and with poison. A crucially important element in his strategy of gaining Christian converts was to utilize the miracles of the Church and its spiritual pantheon in tending to sick slaves. But as his own testimony betrays, this merely reinforced their pagan beliefs. Female slaves served as healers, attending their masters and even the chief Inquisitor and the Bishop. Yet the magic to heal was inseparable from the power to ensorcell, and blacks were often held to be exercising their evil power in a wide range of situations ranging from love magic and the personal intrigues that plagued the colonists, to the waves of sorcery and slave rebellions that ravaged it as well. The Inquisition claimed to have unearthed covens of witches, and even in those of Spanish women the blacks were said to play a crucial role. Significantly, it was also said that the blacks acquired some of their magical medicines from hinterland Indians.

In his monograph on the famous Qollahuaya medicine men of the Bolivian Andes, Gustavo Otero points to a similar pattern of magical attributions between conqueror and conquered. In this conjunction, which he refers to as a "mutual bedazzlement" and as a "trance," he goes so far as to assert that "the conqueror became the conquered"—surely a rhetorical exaggeration, but nevertheless one which clarifies the basic dynamic. The Spaniards projected onto the indigenous medicine men the fables and magical folklore of the late Middle Ages, wildly elaborated by the growing mythology concerning the alleged marvels of the New World. A notable illustration of this is the Bezoar stone, extracted from the stomach of alpacas and llamas. To the Spaniards this stone "was the compendium of all the magic that serves to cure illness, create wealth, bring in goods, and eliminate evil in all its forms" (Otero 1951:16–18). The Spaniards had few materially effective medical resources and relied heavily on magical medicine associated with the Church and with folk religion. In the strange conditions of the New World they availed themselves of indigenous medicines and indigenous practitioners, and they did so in accord with a metaphysical system that allowed for or even encouraged the ascription of marvelous magical powers to the indigenous people. The conquest of indigenous culture led to an indigenization of the culture of conquest in which the magic of medicine and its colonial transformation played a crucial role.[5]

In this regard it should not be overlooked that the Qollahuayas' fame as doctors predates the Spanish conquest. According to the chroniclers, they were specially favored in this role by the Inca Emperor himself (Wassén 1972:16). Furthermore, the Qollahuaya medicine men are still highly respected. They are sought out by whites and mestizos as well as by native Andeans, and they undertake extensive healing tours lasting up to many years through Bolivia and the adjoining republics including Argentina and even Brazil.

Moreover, their magical prowess lies not only in their long-standing pattern of magical attributions imposed by the Spanish conquerors, but also in a similar, if not identical, pattern of attributions which the Qollahuayas themselves impose on people they regard as inferior—namely, the lowlanders of the hot eastern slopes of the Andes and of the jungles of the upper Amazon. From these people they obtain coca and other medicines essential to their materia medica, just as they did almost 2000 years ago according to recent archaeological discoveries (Wassén 1972). It is from them that they obtain some of the magical medicines essential to their well-being and professional pursuits, and yet they regard these people, under the rubric of "*chunchos*," as uncivilized, unbaptized, naked Indians who don't eat salt and live from hunting with bows and arrows. In their legends, the Qollahuayas equate the chunchos with the devils and Jews that Jesus allegedly fought, and to them baptism is a rite of passage converting one from being a chuncho to being a Qollahuaya. In this regard, the primitive of the lowland jungles stands to the highland medicine men as the latter stand to the European conqueror and his descendants, while the hierarchy of magical power parallels but inverts this structure.

With reference to the chunchos and to the general theme I am developing in this essay it is rewarding to read José María Arguedas's novel *Los ríos profundos* (Deep Rivers), which is set in the valley town of Abancay in the Peruvian Andes, some forty years ago. The Pachachaca river flows close by this town on its way down to the Amazon jungles. Because of hoarding by merchants there is an acute shortage of salt, and the local *chicheras* (women who make and sell corn beer) lead a rebellion aimed at securing this salt and distributing it, free, to the women of the town and to the Indian serfs on the surrounding haciendas. The army steps in to brutally quell the insurrection, and the figurehead of the struggle, Doña Felipa, flees to the river and thence, so it is rumored, down to the jungle from where she promises to return with the chunchos and set fire to the haciendas. The authorities fear that if this happens the serfs will run away and join the chicheras. The chunchos are said to get awfully angry, and the boys in the college speculate that the Pachachaca river may take sides with the chunchos and Doña Felipa, reverse his current, bring them up on the chunchos' rafts to burn the valley and the sugarcane of the hacienda owners, and kill all the Christians and their animals. In the Abancay church, the rector of the college, who is also a priest, announces that a detachment of *guardias civiles*, made up of police well trained to maintain order, would be installed permanently in the barracks, and continues with the following sermon (in Spanish, rather than in Quechua):

> "The rabble is conjuring up a specter to frighten the Christians. And that is a ridiculous farce. The serfs on all the haciendas have innocent souls, they're bet-

ter Christians than we are; and the chunchos are savages who will never leave
the bounds of the jungle. And if, by the devil's handiwork, they should come,
their arrows would prove powerless against cannons. We must remember Ca-
jamarca . . . !" he exclaimed, and turning his eyes toward the Virgin, he begged in
his high metallic voice, for forgiveness for the fugitives, for those who had gone
astray. "You, dearly beloved Mother, will know how to cast out the devil from their
bodies," he said. (Arguedas 1978:159)

The distinction between the highland and eastern lowland cultures is obviously a significant and long-established one. H. Wassén notes its importance in
a creation myth about Tiahuanaco (ca. A.D. 900), in which it is clearly implied
that these were two utterly distinct cultural universes, so much so that the animals
and people of each area were created differently. Ethnobotanists and archaeolo-
gists have found much evidence testifying to the traffic in medicines from the
eastern lowlands to the highlands all the way along the Andean chain at the time
of conquest and long before. In his study of the political economy of the north
Andean chiefdoms, Frank Salomon cites research which indicates the antiquity
of these links as far back as 400 B.C., and he asserts that the great lowland shamans
were (and still are) figures of awe to the highlanders. In his account one sees how
the political power of the highland chiefs rested in part on their control over the
specialized trade with the eastern lowlands, and that the main influence of this
connection lay in the channel of curing and visionary experiences undergone by
highlanders in contact with jungle shamans (Salomon 1978:163–164).
    Doubtless, the highland chiefs used this magic acquired from the lowland sha-
mans to sustain their authority over the commoners in their own domains in the
highlands. We may even speculate that the institution of Inca kingship was itself
so indebted, if not throughout the duration of the Empire, at least, perhaps, at
its inception. The historic role of the Qollahuaya medicine men, mediating the
magical power of the lowland shamans with the authority of the Inca king, may
be relevant to this possible connection. It is exceedingly important to note that
later on we shall see how, in contemporary southwest Colombia, the highland Indian shamans channel the magical power of the lowland shamans into the hands
of rich peasants and hacienda owners so that the latter may more easily exploit
their peons. Yet before leaving this topic it should also be noted that lowland
shamanism was intimately associated with millenarian-type revolts of the lowlands against both Inca and Spanish imperialism, and, as suggested in the afore-
mentioned novel of Arguedas, the ever-present likelihood of this sort of revolt, in
alliance with highland Indian serfs, persists to the present day.[6]
    In summary, therefore, before embarking on an ethnographic analysis of the
contemporary folk healing network of southwest Colombia, and of the ways by
which it mediates class and caste relationships in the context of modern market development, it must be emphasized that this network owes much of its character to a structure of great antiquity. This structure is essentially a metaphysical

and moral one, mapped onto or represented by innumerable physical patterns such as racial and topographic ones. Its central feature lies in its contradictory or paradoxical organization, and it was established long before European conquest of the New World. Historical development has not so much changed this structure as worked through it. Indeed, we could cautiously formulate this process in stronger terms by stating that history itself is realized by this structure.

European conquest had the effect of adding new elements to the constitution of this structure and of widening its fan of referents and representations in such things as a broader topography, in postconquest racial classifications, in trans-Atlantic magical traditions, and, of course, in the specificities of colonial administration and rule. Contemporary folk healing, as we shall see below, provides dramatic testimony of the ways in which Spanish colonialism interacted with this structure in the formation of colonial hegemony. Native Americans, Africans, and their European masters forged a popular culture not through the flux of a "melting pot," nor through the one-sided imposition of European authority, but through the elaboration of a contradictory pattern of relations inherited from a far older world history. Ultimately these relations can be traced back from their point of convergence in the New World to three broad lines of social development: the shamanic complex of Siberia brought to the New World some thirty to fifty thousand years ago; the evolution underlying Spanish society from ancient Egypt through Greece, Rome, medieval Europe, and Islam; and the history of West Africans, enslaved and transported to the New World. Needless to say, I can only deal with a minute moment of this immense history, but nevertheless the ethnographic material to be presented insists that this moment be understood as one that is systematically "informed" by the historical process of which it is part and which it expresses.

Christianity and the civilization brought by the Spaniards, together with their African slaves, blended with a preestablished structure of relations. The power of the colonists was impressive, but it was also, in material terms, minute in comparison with the basis upon which it rested and depended. The colonies were vast, the colonists were few, and their subject populations were relatively enormous. European conquest did not by itself create colonial society nor the moral hegemony necessary to its existence. Conquest absorbed the power of the colonized and was in a crucial sense constantly dependent on that power, as the attribution of magical prowess to the "savage" curiously testifies to the present day. Whether we are more impressed by the changes history has wrought, or by the perpetuation of a structure of relations through which history is realized, we must remain alert to the interplay and be prepared for the startling inversions of good and evil that restlessly revolve in its midst.

*The Informal Folk Healing Network of Southwest Colombia*

Individuality and secrecy stamp the folk healers' practice. Yet every healer is the repository of a socially developed discourse and elaborates on a social product.

Every healer is dependent on other healers, for the acquisition of knowledge, and for protection. Although there exists no formal corporation or written rules, the folk healers of southwest Colombia constitute a system, loose and informal as it is. I regard this network as the material expression of a system of ideas, as a force for integrating at the same time as it is created by cultural and economic diversity, and as the source of the basic categories upon which popular culture rests.

Folk healers carry magical power from one part of the country to another. In what does this power reside? In large measure it is the power of difference. The practitioner of magical medicines mediates the differences that both divide and constitute the wholeness of society—its class divisions, its racial divisions, the division between town and country, and above all, the distinctions in the system of mental classification that sustains popular culture.

The significance of this popular culture is easily overlooked. It possesses no formal organizations or organs like schools, churches, clinics, or newspapers. All these lie in the hands of the state and the ruling classes. By contrast the popular institutions depend on personal relationships and informal contexts, very much including those provided by folk healing. The popular institutions are antithetical to the formal organization of power by the slate and to the formal organization of the economy by the market exchange of equivalents in the form of commodities. Yet all social relations and the totality of the social formation itself depend upon this contradiction, the conjunction of the informal and personal popular institutions with those formal ones controlled by the ruling classes. Folk healing manifests this contradiction in dramatic ways, as we shall see below, and gives voice to what Julian Pitt-Rivers calls the "social infrastructure"—"the network of interpersonal relations within the community which depends upon the memories and cultural traditions of the *pueblo* rather than on the written word" (1974:200).

We can schematically outline the social geography of the healing network in southwest Colombia in the following way. At one pole we find the vigorous and dynamic social life of the cities and the agribusiness zones. Here are migrants from all parts of the countryside confronting new problems and faced with the need for constant readjustment. Blacks from the jungles of the Pacific coast rub shoulders with blacks from the interior, Indians from the mountains, mestizos from small farms, long-established urban dwellers, and so forth. Into this flux enter healers, nomadic or permanent, representing all the different folk medical traditions, as well as the new healing cults generated by conditions specific to the Third World city and the new rural agribusiness towns.

At the other pole we find the Amazonian frontier, connected to the cities and agribusiness zones by tortuous roads and the constantly expanding flow of commerce, capital, raw materials, and migrants moving in both directions. Like the cities and the agribusiness zones, the frontier is also marked by dynamism, growth, and cultural pluralism—in contrast to the more stable and more homogeneous villages and social units lying between the city and the frontier.

A graphic manifestation of this bipolar pattern is given by the two raw materials that have underlain the economic development of southwest Colombia since the end of World War II: sugar from the Cauca valley plantations adjoining the city of Cali lying between the western and central chains of the Andes, and petroleum extraction initiated by the Texaco Oil Company on the Amazon frontier along the drainage of the Putumayo river. The recent history and prevailing social structure of southwest Colombia are in large measure constituted by the axis of the immense changes wrought by sugar plantation production in the interior, and oil extraction opening up the frontier. It is in terms of this social history and social geography that we can trace out the healing network of southwest Colombia.

We can begin with the agribusiness zone in the southern Cauca valley, closely and intimately connected to Cali, the principal city of southwest Colombia. Here we find large plantations, owned by Colombians but heavily financed by loans from the World Bank and other international agencies. The predominant crop is sugar, but some cotton, soya, beans, and corn are also produced. A proportion of this production is destined for international markets. The plantation owners have expanded over cattle-raising lands and appropriated the small plots of peasant farmers, descendants of African slaves, who are thereby forced to work as wage laborers on the large estates which they detest. There is probably no other part of rural Colombia where capitalist relations of production are as developed. To this area come temporary migrants seeking wage work. The majority are blacks from the far-off jungles of the relatively isolated and self-sufficient Pacific coastal communities. There are also some poor mestizo peasants from the highlands of Nariño, and other blacks from the Patía valley, driven out by expanding cattle ranches funded by the World Bank.

Locally born blacks regard the blacks from the coastal jungles as inferior to themselves. The jungle migrants do the hardest and least desirable work, such as cane cutting and loading, and the locals call them "savages" and laugh at their ignorance of town life and at their way of speaking. Yet the locals also regard the immigrant workers from the coast as likely to be adept sorcerers and healers. The coastal blacks are very sensitive to envy and accusations by kin of not sharing wealth gained from their employment. They claim that sorcery is rife as a means for getting even with those who fail to reciprocate. Their magic hails from the slave traditions and the colonial Church established on the coast and isolated after the abolition of slavery in 1851, from which time coastal society became even more of a backwater than during the colonial epoch. On the coast, the blacks also utilize local Indian healers, so-called *cholos*, who cure with the aid of an assistant female visionary who drinks small doses of a hallucinogenic called *pildé*. Numerically, the coastal people predominate among the plantation towns' healers. Yet, it is noteworthy that coastal people themselves place high status on the healers and new healing cults originating from the city.

In fact, these new cultists pay periodic visits to the plantation towns where they are immensely popular. Chief of these is the cult of the "brother" José Gregorio Hernández, a famous Venezuelan surgeon who was killed in a car accident in Caracas in the early 1920s. Renowned for his charity, Christian righteousness, and great healing power, he is now a popular saint throughout Venezuela and Colombia, although he is not recognized as a saint by the Church. Pictures and medallions of his image can be bought in marketplaces everywhere. The ritualists who devote themselves to his cult are generally white women, and they divine and heal by invoking his spirit in trance and performing "psycho-surgery." Their practice is characterized by very rapid, assembly-line procedures, by means of which they can minister to scores, if not hundreds, of patients daily.

The plantation towns have many university-trained doctors, pharmacies, clinics, and even a small hospital. Furthermore, the permanently employed plantation wage workers have social security benefits which pay their medical expenses. People do not flock to the folk healers because of an insufficiency of modern doctors or because folk healers are cheaper. Quite often, in fact, folk healers are much more expensive. There are two reasons why people resort to folk healers. First, the modern medical institutions are rather ineffectual even in the treatment of specifically organic diseases. The essential causes of organic disease lie in the high degree of malnutrition and in the lack of unpolluted drinking water. Treatment with drugs does little to alleviate the diseases associated with these causes. Moreover, the modern doctors are generally brusque and thoughtless in their treatment. Second, patients bring to folk healers diseases that modern doctors have failed to cure, and diseases that fall outside of the compass recognized by modern medicine. Folk healers are appealed to as people who can purify and work magic. People come because they have problems with a spouse or lover. A child may be suffering from the "evil eye." They cannot find work. Their small business may be floundering. Their home may be ensorcelled. They cannot save money or make ends meet. They require a charm or a talisman. They need magic to influence events and people. And so forth. So long as people persist in believing that interpersonal tensions have material effects through the medium of magic, and so long as healers exist to deal with such forces, this system will survive and play an important role in social and cultural life.

A most significant (although numerically small) component of the plantation towns' folk healing system is provided by largely nomadic Indian herbalists and healers, Inganos, from the eastern ridge of the far-off Andes overlooking the Amazon basin. These men sometimes travel with their spouse and children, sometimes with other close kin or friends, and sometimes alone. They set up stalls in the local marketplaces which they visit periodically, or else they wander the streets seeking clients or old contacts. In their medicine bags they have rare herbs and plant medicines from all over Colombia, from the Amazon lowlands, from the high plateaus of the Andes, from the temperate slopes, and from the jungles of the Pacific coast. In addition, they sell charms, along with iron filings, blocks of sulfur, beaks and feathers of jungle birds, and desiccated paws of the jaguar and the bear.

They function not only as herbalists, concentrating and distributing all the magical medicines of northern South America, but also as healers. In some men this healing function will be rather limited. A client buying herbs will ask for advice and in this discussion the herbalist will begin to assume the role of healer as well. At the other extreme, it is the healing function which is paramount, and the traveling medicine man will have an established clientele whom he visits regularly on his healing tours.

It is very important to note that these regular clients are often healers themselves. They depend on the traveler for herbs and for treatment of their own misfortunes. All folk healers require the services of a healer more powerful than themselves, because a healer is always likely to be stricken with sorcery as part of the profession of magical medicine. In attempting to heal victims of sorcery, a healer is liable to become attacked from the same source that afflicted the patient, usually another medicine man, and this may prove more than the healer can cope with alone. This is one of the leading reasons why a network exists among practitioners, and why it has a subtle hierarchical form extending from less to more powerful healers.

Resident medicine men in these predominantly black plantation towns tend to regard the nomadic Indian medicine men from the mountains overlooking the Amazon as great healers and sorcerers, and this high esteem is associated with regarding them as "primitive" and therefore as close both to nature and the beginning of time. The Indians do not dissuade them of such romantic ideas. Indeed they emphasize their ethnic status. They speak their native language in addition to Spanish. They may wear the clothes that unmistakably mark their special identity, including special ponchos and in many instances the skirt and specific hairstyle as well. Most importantly, they make enticing reference to their unique and master remedy, the hallucinogen called *yagé*, and in very special situations will even use it. In doing so, they invoke the presence of the great medicine men of the Amazon lowlands from whom they acquired their healing powers, and the hallucinogenic brew, and the property of being *cerrado*—"closed off" from sorcery attacks.

In this way they impart something of the magical lore of the Amazon basin and the mountain slopes overlooking it to folk healers all over the southwest of Colombia, and beyond to the hamlets and cities of the interior including the national capital of Bogotá. For several years many have traveled as far as Venezuela. In the course of these journeys they learn to modify their practice in accord with the problems and beliefs specific to different localities. They themselves learn of different traditions, just as they influence those traditions. In particular, they learn of modern drugs, of different disease entities and classifications, and of other sources of healing and sorcery power. To the evil magic acquired back home, they learn to add the powerful sorcery of European origin that afflicts the cities and towns of the interior, and the sorcerer's arts possessed by the blacks from the Pacific coast. Through this system of exchanges, magical power is diffused across the land following the contours of the new institutions and new problems associated with the capitalist development of agriculture and the frontier.

THE AMAZONIAN FRONTIER

If we follow the wandering Indian medicine men to their homes, we find that they live in an Andean valley perched high and directly above the immense Amazon basin. At any one time perhaps up to half of the Inganos of this valley are absent, pursuing their profession. They try to return once a year for the annual fiesta of Carnival. The wealthier may even fly part of the way, from Venezuela. Another reason for returning may be to partake in healing rituals with their shaman-teachers who live in the jungles below. For a healer's life is fraught with danger. His work places him at the center of sorcery conflicts, and he fears the envy of other healers. He needs dependable access to a trusted healer even stronger that himself, and he needs to constantly replenish his power so as to withstand the perils of his profession and travels.

The highland Indian healers claim that they learned their skills and acquired their power from a lowland jungle shaman. Their first contact is usually when they are seriously ill, with sorcery or spirit attacks. Beginning thus as patients, they then become apprentices, spending weeks to years, constantly or intermittently, with their teacher. In their eyes, the source of magical power lies in the Amazon jungle, in the jungle shamans, and in their master remedy, the hallucinogen that they call yagé which only grows in the dank fastness of the jungle.

The curing rites of the highland Indians are identical to or closely modeled on those of the lowland shamans. They have the Spanish language in common, but the native languages can be quite different. Like the lowlanders, the highland healers base their treatment on the group drinking of yagé, singing, and sucking out sickness and evil from the patient's body. The highland healers adorn themselves with the symbols of the jungle and the jungle shamans. High above the jungle and close to the arid and near-freezing *páramo* (tundra-like plateau) of the Andes, they put on the crown and train of jungle birds' feathers; "these are from the birds of the jungles, they make the visions come." Around their necks they wear the pods of the cascabel which tinkle as they move. "These are the sounds of the jungle, they bring the sounds when you take yagé." They wear the necklace of jaguar's teeth, for the jaguar is the owner of yagé.

Yet in the eyes of the highlanders, the jungle shamans and the jungle Indians in general are inferior, albeit in a highly ambiguous way. They commonly refer to them as uncivilized, as savages, as cannibals, as unbaptized, as illiterate, and non-Christian.

To these contrasts are added fear and tension. The highland healers depend on the patronage of the jungle shamans and fear their lack of reciprocity and greater power. The jungle shamans belittle the highland healers, claiming that they are given to vain boasting and quackery. They are critical of the prestige and commercial success which accrue to the highlanders as a result of their healing tours across the nation. And they fear a weapon that the highlanders acquire as a result of such tours and closer proximity to non-Indian society—the weapon of *magia*—European-derived black magic. The highland healers acquire this art from non-Indian healers in other parts of the country and from books bought in the marketplaces. The jungle shamans are rarely literate and are nonplussed and scared of magia. Their power is based on oral tradition and cannot be bought. Only very few people can acquire it, those born with the vocation and possessed of the courage necessary to withstand the ordeals and fear that taking large amounts of yagé implies. Yagé is revered and one can die, it is said, from taking it wrongly and from not observing the taboos associated with it. On the other hand, magia can be acquired by anyone literate, simply through buying a book of magic. The use of magic from this source implies making a pact with the devil (see Appendix). Through magia, especially when mixed with yagé magic or with Datura, the highlanders have the potential to overpower the mastery of their jungle masters.

The book and literacy are very important; they stand as symbols of the power of the Church and the state and all that is called civilized. The book becomes mythic. One highland healer, an Ingano, now resident in the Cauca valley, tells me that he owns a book of magic weighing around thirty pounds and that it swells with the phases of the moon. From it he learned to make his pact with the devil by sacrificing a black cat in the fields of the sugar plantation zone.

To an important extent we can understand this series of oppositions between jungle shamans and highland healers as elaborations upon and derivations from the contradictory features of the shaman-novice relationship. This is an extremely sensitive relationship, requiring reciprocity and trust. The novice is totally dependent on the goodwill of the shaman who may kill the novice or destroy his growing power if moved by anger or envy. The novice acquires power from the shaman, just as the shaman acquired his power from his teacher, through the medium of the master remedy, yagé. This extraordinarily ambivalent power is imparted by the shaman in his breath and songs chanted over the yagé before it is given to the novice. As he begins his shamanic flight into the heavens and the spirit world, the novice is utterly dependent on the guidance of the shaman. This power may be spoken of as a material substance which grows in the body as one's wisdom grows. This substance is the materialization of yagé-derived wisdom. It is matter, knowledge, and power, all in one. It represents the materialization of wisdom-in-action. It can kill and heal. It can exert harm and even death merely when the teacher feels angry. It is the substance of sorcery attack itself, taking various forms such a thorns, glass, blowpipe darts (*chonta*), and butterflies sent into the victim's body. It is also the power within the shaman that heals and with which he extracts sorcery objects, and is referred to (in Spanish) as something like a magnet.

Above all, this power is very delicate and easily damaged. It is loaded with paradox and dialectical propensities. The more one has of it, the more susceptible one is to danger. It is when a shaman is taking yagé that he is most open to attack. It is here, when he is communing with the spirits and gaining power, that he is also most susceptible to his enemies. To protect himself he has to take yagé. This is his medium for seeing, for attack, and for defense. But it also entails his exposure. Yagé grants power, but at the cost of becoming more *delicado* or delicate.

It is this pattern of tension that characterizes the shaman's relation to yagé and the spirits. The pattern is replicated in the relation between the shaman and the novice. The novice acquires power from the shaman in the nature of a gift, and reciprocates with gifts of pigs, cloth, money, and loyalty. The novice literally acquires some of the spirit of the shaman, just as the shaman acquired his power from a previous teacher and from the power of yagé. This highly personalized and spiritualized exchange relationship is a form of reciprocal gift-exchange which exhibits the tensions and ambivalencies of gift-exchange to the highest degree. Exposure to market forms of exchange and the social entailments of market economies markedly exacerbate these tensions, as we shall see below.

## COLONIZATION

The Putumayo lowlands were subject to sporadic Spanish incursions from 1542 onward. Some *encomiendas* (Indian trusteeships) were granted by the Crown, in the Andean foothills around the settlement of Mocoa for instance, and desultory expeditions in search of gold were made during the century of conquest also. The first sustained campaign of Catholic missionization was undertaken by Franciscans, operating out of Quito and Popayán, in 1632. There were few missions, they were small, and their records indicate that Indians often fought and killed missionaries. Nevertheless it is very likely that a transmuted form of Catholicism did penetrate into many Indian groups.

During the last quarter of the eighteenth century and all of the nineteenth, the area was abandoned by Churchmen and largely free of Spaniards and *criollos* except for those associated with a trickle of trade (which included lowland medicines) connecting the lowlands to the highland cities. Then, at the turn of the century, the infamous rubber boom brought untold misery and "the devil's paradise" to the Putumayo lowlands for some two decades—much worse, so it appears, for Indians such as the Huitotos living in the jungles to the east, than for those living in the *montaña* or foothills of cloud forest which unite the Amazon lowlands with the steep flanks of the Andes.

With the return to power of the Colombian Conservative Party in the late nineteenth century, a party that zealously advanced the Church's cause, missionary activity was vigorously renewed all over Colombia.[7] In 1896, Capuchin missionaries from Spain entered the Caquetá and Putumayo region "with no obligation other than the desire to spiritually help the Indians and whites dispersed in these immense, secular jungles," as one missionary later wrote (Canet de Mar 1924:24). At that time the missionaries estimated that there were approximately 9,000 Catholics (of whom 3,000 were whites and the rest Indians), and about 40,000 *infieles* (unfaithfuls) disseminated along the rivers and tributaries of the lower Caquetá and the lower Putumayo down to the Amazonas, and between the Aguarico and Napo rivers. By 1899 there were but five missionaries (three Fathers and two Sisters), based in the montaña settlement of Mocoa. In those first two and one half years they had already performed 1,010 baptisms and 263 marriages. By 1927 there were 62 missionaries, controlling 29 churches, 61 schools, 2 hospitals, and 5 dispensaries.

Supported with money and very liberal concessions from the national government, the Capuchins erected a network of churches, schools, and clinics in a determined attempt to open up the western Amazon basin of Colombia to their version of Christianity and to allow Colombia "to capture the major part of the commerce of the Amazon rivers, commerce that would be worth many millions," as they wrote at the time (Las Misones en Colombia 1912:111). If their published writings are faithful testimony, these missionaries saw their work as a continuation of the *reconquista* that the Spaniards had prosecuted against the Moors, driven out of the Iberian peninsula in the fifteenth century. Extending Christianity into the upper Amazon also meshed with the Colombian government's desire to drive the Peruvian rubber baron, Julio César Arana, and with him Peruvian claims to the Putumayo, out of an enormous tract of rubber-rich yet disputed jungle, claimed both by Peru and Colombia.

The missionaries saw their chief necessity as the construction of a road from the highland city of Pasto across the cold páramo, down the precipitous mountainsides to Mocoa, and from there through the jungle to Puerto Asís on the left bank of the Putumayo river—gateway to the Amazon, the Atlantic, and western Europe. The missionaries labored mightily to construct this road, and one imagines that the 1,600 men they daily employed labored even more. To the missionaries the road became an idée fixe—a glorious obsession entailing passions no less fabulous than those associated with salvation. In their own words they saw the road as the tie between Civilized Colombia and Savage Colombia, as the descent into the inferno of jungles enveloping the Indian in the darkness of infidelity. Being an allegory of the descent into and salvation from hell, as much as a decided material convenience for white domination, the eschatological image of the road seeped into the subconscious of popular culture—as we shall see when we consider the vision-trips of Indians and poor colonists taking hallucinogens in the curing rites conducted by Indian shamans today.

In addition to facilitating commerce and relieving the missionaries from the discomfort of riding several days on the backs of Indians, the missionaries also saw the road as a way of fulfilling their desire to flood this vast area with white colonists. They wistfully looked abroad to Europe as a source of such settlers, and European politics were central to their missionizing zeal. The Capuchins nearly all came from Barcelona, and Indians in the Putumayo lowlands still today remember the fury of their anticommunist and antianarchist sermons from the decade of the Spanish civil war, in part because many of the priests persist with their vitriolic anticommunist preaching, assuring the Indians that their poverty comes from their being lazy.

The road was begun in 1909, and within a few years was completed. The migration of poor white colonists from the highlands to the lowlands increased, forming a society which one missionary later on described like this:

> They were two antagonistic races persecuting each other to the death. The whites treated the Indians as slaves, and sometimes as beasts. The Indians had to serve them with everything and just in the ways that the whites wanted. . . . For their part, the Indians, upon seeing the tyrannical conduct of the whites, returned it with interest and with all the force of their savage nature. As a consequence there was constant and bloody struggle, requiring only the smallest spark to light up a terrifying outburst that was only extinguished with the blood of some of the combatants. (Canet de Mar 1924:52)

With the outbreak of war between Peru and Colombia in the Putumayo lowlands in 1932, a war that some knowledgeable observers said was a government-inspired strategy to divert energy from a growing socialist-revolutionary movement in the interior of Colombia, the Putumayo jungles were decisively opened to the rest of the country by a wider road passable to motorized vehicles. In 1906 there had been 2,200 colonists. By 1938 there were an estimated 31,775 (CILEAC 1940:29). In the 1950s the Texaco Oil Company began pumping out oil and the road system was vastly improved. Peasants forced off their lands in the interior and fleeing the nationwide and horrendous civil war known as the Violencia came now in droves, raising cash crops, cutting back the jungle and the Indians with it. Owing to this immigration the population of Puerto Asís, on the Putumayo river, doubled between 1957 and 1964.

These colonists are desperately poor blacks and whites. They represent the most impoverished and exploited classes of Colombian society. In the jungle Indians they find a foil by which they define themselves and rest secure as superior and civilized. They tend to despise the Indians and see in them everything that is outside civilization and progress. Yet they also regard the Indian shamans as extraordinarily powerful healers and will go to them for help, joining in the Indian yagé healing rites. In the words of one colonist:

> the peasants here say they take yagé with a shaman for distraction or when they are sick. They say that they are dañados [i.e., ensorcelled]. I am sick. Thus I go to the jungle, hunting. Then I shoot an animal. But I don't kill it. The gun doesn't fire, or whatever. Thus I don't kill it. Then I say, "No, I'm dañado. I can't kill anything hunting!" Well, after that, what next? . . . I'll go to the shaman to cure me . . . to the Indians, because with yagé they can cure one, so that I can kill when hunting. This is the custom at times for people; they go and drink yagé with the Indians. . . . They take yagé with the Indians to cure maleficio [sorcery]. . . . Many

people take yagé for that. Many come from far away, very far away, from different places. They come to take yagé with Roberto.

The colonists tell people back in the interior from where they came about the shamans and their wonderful rites. They thereby stimulate the flow of patients from the interior. Often the shamans do not understand the illnesses of which these patients complain, but grudgingly or not they comply. By treating non-Indian outsiders and including them in their rites, the shamans preserve much of their power and also modulate the conflict between Indians and outsiders.

Some of the colonists are so fascinated and enthralled by the Indian healing rites that they try to apprentice themselves to a shaman. I know two such men, utterly dedicated to this spiritual quest. Both are blacks from the far-off Pacific coast. One lives with his shaman-teacher and serves as his assistant. The other visits for long periods, and adopts Indian dress. He has taken cuttings of yagé and the other plants necessary for visions back to the coast, across the Andes, and cultivates them there. Both these men sing during the yagé ritual. This is a sign of great importance because only the elect gain the power to sing. In singing, one is giving voice to the singing of the yagé people whom one sees and hears in one's vision. One materializes their music in this way, as an intermediary, putting it into the world.

Yet despite their curious dependence on the shamans, the colonists exert a very destructive effect on the Indians. They take their land and encourage a feeling among the young Indians that their culture is shameful. Land disputes between colonists and Indians lead to disputes among the Indians themselves. Colonization forces Indians to adapt their land usage and landowning practices to those favored by the national market and national law. Conflicts develop within Indian communities as to whether to opt for individual private property holdings or communal land under the aegis of the shaman. Many young Indians react by deserting the shaman and attendance at healing rites. They say that the shaman is no longer powerful or that they fear his aggression. It appears that young men are increasingly disinclined to become shamans. Many of them say they are too frightened because now it is very difficult to maintain the taboos and special restrictions that a shaman must abide by. Furthermore, it is said that whites and blacks are polluting; a shaman who treats them frequently is thereby running the risk of losing his power and even his life. The highland healers, whose work involves constant curing of non-Indians, claim that they can circumvent this risk by taking special medicines. But the lowland shamans make no such claim.

The tragic irony of this overall situation is that while the younger Indians respond to the internal enmity destroying their community by deserting the shamanic mode of political and religious organization, the colonists resort to the shamans as a way of alleviating the tensions that corrode their society. The colonists are seeking aid from the very people they are destroying and look down on, in order to cope with the forces that make their own lives so miserable.

## Mediations

I have drawn attention to a series of oppositions that constitute the basic terms and structure of a vast healing network that extends between town and country in the evolving context of capitalist development. These oppositions (civilized/primitive, Church/pagan, literary/oral leaning, etc.) form a structure of relations that is loaded with ambivalency and power. To better understand this power, let us pause to consider some ways by which these oppositions are mediated.

### THE PRIORITY OF THE LOWLAND SPIRITS

The highland shamans take every opportunity to claim their superiority over the lowland shamans. But in their yagé healing chants, when they invoke the most powerful healing spirits to their side, they sing to the dead shamans or tribes of the lowlands. In the songs of the highland shaman I work with, he invokes ancient times and ancient tribes whose source lies in the jungles. In his own words, he makes a compact with the "people from below," with the Huitotos, for example (the tribe whom the Capuchins singled out as truly primitive savages). The spirit of yagé, Indian lowland tribes, and dead lowland shamans blend together in the appeals made in the chants to cure yagé and to cure the patient. In effect, a great chain of being and becoming is evoked, passing back to presumed origins and forward to the highland shaman crouched singing over the brew, uplifted with the visions tumbling forth and thereby empowered to exorcise evil. The highlander blends with the lowlanders, owners or masters of the chief remedy.

### FATHER BARTOLOMÉ

Father Bartolomé de Igualada is now legendary in both the highlands and lowlands. In contemporary mythology he was the foremost twentieth-century missionary in the area and is acclaimed as having baptized and converted countless ferocious Indians. Both highland and lowland Indians revere his memory and many possess his picture. Nearly everyone, white and Indian, remembers him, especially for his healing powers and great generosity in dispensing remedies. He studied medicine in Barcelona, performed good deeds in the clinic in the main church in the highlands, and is credited with saving many lives. Most importantly, the lowland shamans treasure his memory for stopping the Church from persecuting them on account of their yagé rites. This was the Indians' medicine, he is alleged to have argued, and it was good. It is said that he himself took yagé on many occasions, usually alone in his room—yagé prepared by the "savage"

Indians, *no-civilizados*. I have heard this story many times, nowhere more dramatically than in the depths of the jungle at night, taking yagé with an Indian
shaman and his neighbors. This legend of Father Bartolomé blends the tradition
of the Catholic priest with that of the Indian shaman, assimilates yagé to Christianity and "civilization," and this blending is sanctified by the fact that Father
Bartolomé is popularly held to be a saint.

### THE ORIGIN OF YAGÉ (KOFAN ACCOUNT)

The Kofan-speaking Indians of the lowlands have a story about the origin of
yagé which strives for a similar mediation but more pointedly maintains the tensions between Indian and Christian traditions. When God created the world he
plucked a hair from the crown of his head with his left hand and planted it in
the ground for the Indians only. He blessed this with his left hand. The Indians
discovered its properties and thereby developed the yagé rites and the entire
shamanic complex. Seeing this, God was incredulous and said they were lying.
He asked and was given some yagé brew. He trembled, vomited, defecated, and
cried profusely, overcome by the many wonderful things he saw. In the morning
he declared, "It is true what these Indians say. The person who takes this suffers.
But that person is distinguished. That is how one learns, through suffering." The
Kofan say yagé is their gift from God, and it is meant only for the indigenous
people.

### VISIONS: 1. SIONA

Jean Langdon has described what she believes to be a typical sequence of yagé
visions experienced by novices (1974). These were told to her by elderly members
of a Siona Indian community in the Putumayo lowlands, referring to a generation
or so past. The cosmos is composed of interconnected layers or realms. Beings of
the earthly realm can journey to other realms, and frequently become transformed when they do. Plants and animals may become human, and vice versa.
Practically everything in the earthly realm has its spirit double or essence, and
classes of beings have their prototypical spirit master. By taking yagé one can enter into this spirit realm and converse with the spirit masters, the masters of game
animals, of the fish, of the disease-inflicting spirits, and so on. The spirits of
yagé—the yagé people—guide one in these journeys. With their aid, the shaman
can divine the cause and treatment of illnesses, and determine communitywide
responses to social problems.

After weeks or months of preparation and isolation from the community, the
novices are ready to take yagé with the shaman. Night falls and they retire to the
jungle. Taking yagé with the shaman, listening to his constant chanting, the novices first feel drunk, drowsy, disoriented, and fearful. Vomiting and defecating,

the body is cleansed "for traveling." The visions begin. The shaman sings of the visions they will see and of those he sees—at least in rough outline. One feels very frightened and expects to die. The yagé people appear. They are like the shaman, only tiny. They are crying. They say you are going to die. Fire comes, followed by snakes wrapping themselves around you. If you have the courage to persist, then you meet the jaguar mother. She is large, big-breasted, and beautiful, dressed in white. She is the mother of the shamans. She takes the novice to her breast and wraps him in the blanket in which the Siona wrap their babies. Then she throws you away, crying, "Why did you take yagé? Now you are going to die!" Hundreds of snakes appear (which the Siona say are also the leaves of the yagé vine) and then they form into one enormous boa, which is the owner of yagé. He may wind himself around you. Death is imminent. Then the boa straightens out and carries you up into the heavens where the yagé people come to teach you about the hidden realms and introduce you to the spirits who live there. You have left your body. You are dead. Then you become reborn. After many such trips, the novice may finally reach the penultimate heaven and meet with God who bears the Hispanicized name of Diusu (cf. the Spanish word for God, Dios) and lives there with the "living God people," the angels. In his house God keeps his book—the book of "remedies" (no doubt a reference to the Bible?). Above God in the highest heaven exist doves who write on paper, a lonely tree branch from which a spirit hangs (Christ crucified?), and a door opening to nothingness. God asks the novice, "You have arrived. What were you thinking of?" The novice replies, "Only in God," and is given a beautiful staff—like the Spanish used in bestowing authority on Indian chiefs in colonial times. God tells the novice to always drink yagé and to care for his people, correcting them in their wrongdoing and curing them when they are sick.[8]

### VISIONS: 2. AN OLD INGANO MAN AND THE HEAVENLY CITY

An old Ingano lowland Native American friend of mine, Florencio, described the following yagé trip to me when we were both living for a short time with an Ingano shaman. Florencio lives deep in the forest. In his youth, in the 1920s, he served as the sacristan in a tiny church built by the Capuchins along the Caquetá river. He was once appointed "governor" by the national government, and was selected by the Church to witness the Pope's visit in Bogotá some fifteen years ago. I quote verbatim (translating from a tape recording in Spanish).

I saw clouds and flames, and these angels came and placed on my forehead the crystals that they carry so as to diagnose my illness, in order to get the experience of my illness so they can cure me and after that on my breast so that I would have good spirit with the people without any malice. To have good spirit. In my hands also, those crystals that they carry . . . the same crystals that the shamans have. These they place so that one will have a good consciousness with all that happens, here in the mouth so that one can talk with whatever person, to talk well.

This is what the yagé make one see.

And following that came the *tentes*, forming a queue, other birds of the jungle came behind them and the room filled up with them, nothing but birds everywhere, all around. It looks like it's real, doesn't it? But it's because of the yagé!

And after that came a street like in the city, and in each house and in each room there was a different *pinta* (vision), with their own songs and music.

First comes along an Indian from the (highland) Sibundoy valley, and then others with their crowns of feathers that the shamans use when curing. They all form up in the streets, some coming out of the houses, others going back in, each one with his own song, and dressed in their feathers and mirrors—yagé people—and still others dressed in gold, pure gold, and finally comes the army, a batallion—how wonderful they are. How enchanting it was to see them, dressed like the very rich, only far superior, in pants and boots of pure gold and with their arms. And I try to get up to sing with them, with them the shaman cures. I ask him, "With them you cure?" And the shaman says, "Yes! Seeing them, you can cure!" And after the last of the batallion passes by, I was in the street, a very beautiful street without any garbage, without anything . . . the pure firmament, let us say . . . and I found a house the color of the firmament with crosses all over it. It looked closed up, but I found a way in and there were three men like . . . like . . . bishops or archbishops surrounded by books spewing out gold, a waterfall of gold, and these books are pure crosses. And there are seated these three men, but all in one, all the same color, and with a staff. And so I went up to them, with *la chuma* (the drunkenness) in order to be acquainted, and they said, "You have come to get acquainted, to know; but you already know!" said to me the man in the middle, face to face. "All you have seen is what God gives to life, allows to life, for you. But you have to believe in evil and respect all. Take this staff!" And I took it, and his blessing and left . . . up till there no more!

VISIONS: 3. A WHITE COLONIST AND THE DEVIL

A white colonist some forty years old recounted the following yagé vision to me. He regards the Indians and the shamans as primitive inferiors. He has never returned to take yagé after this experience, but his two teenage sons do so every few months. He took yagé when he was around fifteen years of age, accompanying his uncle. I quote verbatim:

I took my cupful and nothing much happened. The shaman gave me a second, and still nothing much. Shortly after that a third. Then the *borrachera* (drunkenness) came; strong!

Suddenly some Indians came in *guahuco*, whistling, rattling their *ramas*, whoosh, woosh, woosh—which means "come come strongly the *borrachera*." And then they blew (*soplaban*); "oof, oof," like that, so that the *borrachera* comes strongly. Then I was asleep, my eyes closed. Then suddenly came a troop of *sainos* (wild pigs). Then a hurricane, lights and dark shades, like in a movie film. Darkness. Then suddenly I saw the devil. Oh!

I forgot to say that after I saw the pigs I saw jaguars. They went away, growling and chattering. They didn't come back. But it was all so awful, so ugly. Suddenly some snakes came, you know, out of my own mouth, coming out of my mouth . . . but it was lies, nothing but *borrachera*.

Well, as I was saying, I was sitting, half asleep, when I heard someone talking to me, singing rather, and I saw something there, it was frightening, it was the devil himself. But how could that be? Sitting there; right behind me. But when it wasn't the devil; it was the shaman. It was he who had been the devil.

Then I opened my eyes and saw all the Indians sitting there with the shaman. He's put on his feathers, his crown too, sitting by the fire chewing tobacco. Taita Martín. . . . The jaguar, the devil, it was Taita Martín. The devil, he had horns and . . . *colorada* (heated and red)—you should have seen him—with a long tail down to his knees . . . like they paint him—with spurs and everything . . . but *ugly!*

Well, it was the *borrachera!* I looked again and there was the shaman dressed in his crown of feathers, beautiful, with his necklace of jaguar teeth and all the other things that they dress themselves with. You know. So there I was seated and there I stayed. Then the *taita* ("father" = shaman) said, "What are you thinking friend?" "Nothing," I said. "Is the *borrachera* hard?" he asked. "No," I answered, "a little, just a little." "You're not scared?" "No. Just a little scared."

So things went by and went by, and then came these Indians (yagé people) blowing and sucking. You know. Strongly. Singing their chants, their "heh, heh, heh . . . " and sucking and blowing, and they did that to me . . . and then I knew I was going to die.

It was then clear to me that I was going to die. I was already dead. And after my death, who would see me? My uncle? He was already dead. Who was going to tell people that I had died? Dying, I left. My soul went up a staircase, up and up. Ooh. It was beautiful. The staircase was like that in a palace of the very rich, with gold. And beneath and around it was a beautiful landscape. I was seeing beauty, like when the night is full of stars. It was so beautiful. Up, up, up, always moving upwards, fast. And I was thinking I was dead. But it was only the *borrachera*.

I went up. I got to the top. There was a salon, sort of like a balcony, with a raised portion. I went up to the top part. I was then in air. There was nowhere more to go to. I'd finished, and at the end I saw God. He was on that side, in the air, in his palace, alone, bearded and with a crown—like they paint him.

So I'd arrived. I'd finished. And then he gave me his blessing. And so I thought, "What's this? Aren't I dead?" And my God said to me, "No. Nobody called you. You should go down." Well, I just turned around and went down backwards, step by step backwards descending until I was well down and when I got to the end of the steps I turned around and continued going down.

I went down and down and everything was incredibly beautiful like when the day is dawning and the night is clearing. It was a beautiful plain of grass, still a long way but I knew it was the earth, but it wasn't dark. It was shafts of light with the dawn coming. And the mists were rising. And further down I saw the green of the jungle. And so I reached the earth, and the *borrachera* was over. Then I was happy. All was clear. Now we had arrived. I spent the night—*borracho*.

When I told the shaman he said, "Now you could be a shaman."

"Did God resemble Taita Martín?"

"No! God is God! What are you coming at? He's not a shaman! But my Blessed God! There was no shaman there! When the devil appeared, then there was the shaman. But I only saw that he was the shaman later. When I turned around and when there was that change in the staircase, coming down and I turned around, and everything was changed, everything was clear; I arrived. Then I had arrived. Below."[9]

The inferior, pagan, and primitive Indian shaman not only acquires the form of the devil, but also provides the privileged stairway to the kingdom of God, the spiritual center of power and justice. Christian iconography is made emotionally real and stamped with a vivid conviction that the Church could never achieve. The hidden dimensions of the cosmos are literally traversed in this journey of death, flight of the soul, salvation, and rebirth. Cosmogony is reenacted. Darkness is lifted from the world. Clarity and happiness ensue.

The Ingano Indian makes his flight not to heaven but to the city; a golden city more like the center of the secular realm of white, state, and ruling-class power with its marching armies, riches, and book knowledge, spewing gold. And when he arrives, it is only to find that "he already knows."

The structure of ideas and sentiments created by the Spanish conquest of the New World in the sixteenth century, pertaining to the ideology of caste and class relations, lives on today as an active force. Folk healing sustains this structure of ideas. The efficacy of healing lies in its exploitation of the patterned ambivalence that is central to this structure. The evil and magic invested in the exploited people, essential to colonial hegemony, become the means by which the colonizer seeks release from the civilization which assails him.

### Colonization and Spiritualization of the Gift

Some colonists wish to become shamans or shaman-like healers and diviners, grafting shamanism to other modes of healing. Such is the white, José García, who came to the lowland frontier with his parents from the highlands in 1950 at the age of ten. With his future brother-in-law he cleared virgin forest from the lowermost slopes of the Andes, and he now possesses some sixty head of cattle and a small ranch which he largely works with his family (see Appendix).

He first became involved with shamanism around 1960 when he accompanied his sorcery-stricken sister to a nearby Indian shaman. He was very impressed and returned to take yagé many times with this man, partly because of his fascination with this new world, and partly to rid himself of the sorcery that he came to believe was afflicting him and reducing his life to one of remorseless poverty and misfortune. In the course of this quest he has visited many of the jungle shamans, within close reach of his small town. When I first met him, at the home of Luciano, a famous Ingano shaman, he was introduced as a *curandero* or healer. He takes yagé with Luciano very frequently, up to once or even twice a week. He sends patients whose problems are beyond his power to Luciano, and lately has begun to cure patients in their homes by taking yagé with them, while Luciano stays at his home and takes yagé on the same evening, thereby making the connection necessary for spirit contact. Furthermore, José García often tries to cure his own misfortunes by himself, while taking yagé in company with this shaman. His visions and developing system are marvelously syncretic. In his own words:

> To take yagé you have to consecrate it in the name of the Father, the Son, and the Holy Ghost, and ask our Father and the most Holy Virgin to help us. You also have to appeal to the spirits of the *médicos*; for example, the Indian shamans who have died, who were good people, and who are now entering into the spirit centers doing good for humanity. For example, take Andrés Hinchoa. He was a compadre of mine. He was the first to teach me to take yagé. He gave me the first pinta so that I experienced things that I had never seen before. He told me, "Good. I am going to give you a cup of yagé for your good fortune so that you will remember me. But you will have to be tough, compadre!" So he gave me the first cup and then came the *chuma* (visions). But ave María! . . . I was dying. I saw another world. I was in another life. I was on a rather narrow path, long, endlessly long. And I was in agony, in agony. I had left for eternity. I was on this path, walking and walking along this path, and then I came to an immense plain, a beautiful plain like a savanna. The fields were green. And then there was a painting of the Virgin of Carmen and I said to myself, "Now I am going there, to the Virgin of Carmen." Then I saw a tiny bridge with a hole in the middle of it; nothing more than this tiny bridge no thicker than a finger, and I thought to myself, "I'm afraid to cross; most Holy Virgin don't let me fall here! Don't let anything bad happen here!" In the name of God and of the Virgin I crossed and blessed myself and started to traverse the bridge. But then I started to fall off. Suddenly I was scared. Right there and then I called on the most Holy Virgin of Carmen to help me pass. Then I reached the most Holy Virgin of Carmen and said, "I've come so that all my sins shall be pardoned!" Because I was dead, no? And then she said, "I'm not going to pardon anything!" Then I began to cry ever so bitterly, yelping, looking for that salvation that the most Holy Virgin was denying me, crying and crying, imploring her for salvation. Then she told me that "Yes! I was pardoned. Yes! I was saved!" Then I was happy and I returned to this world, sitting here, my face bathed in tears.

He believes that the spirits of certain noble Indian shamans, now dead, are intermingled with the spirits of popular saints, famous as curers also. All these spirits live together in a community headed by God and the Virgin. He calls them brothers or saints. It is to them that one appeals when healing. They live together in a celestial spirit center or house, which is directly attached to earthly spirit centers (possibly in the city of Pasto) which replicate the divine one. Presiding over them is the mother of God, connected in ways I do not understand to the famous Virgin of Las Lajas whose shrine lies near the highland city of Ipiales. These healing brothers and saints require permission from her to come down to the earthly realm to assist the healer.

Among these spirits is the Indian shaman who first introduced him to yagé, noted for his charity, generosity, and skill. Other Indian shaman spirits are entering this spirit center, undergoing a process of purification before they are acknowledged. Among the non-Indian spirits are those of Francisco Montebello, a popular mulatto saint noted for his healing prowess, and that of the famous Venezuelan surgeon, brother José Gregorio Hernández, for whom cults have formed all over Venezuela and Colombia. These are saints of the "common" people and are not officially recognized by the Church.

When José García takes yagé he deems it essential to "consecrate" it (as he says) by invoking this spiritual pantheon of dead Indian shamans, popular saints, the Virgin, and the Trinity. "You have to become a trustee of God. It is like going to church. God helps you to take yagé, in order to see with yagé, to see the evil actions of men."

Shamans say that their songs come to them from yagé, from the yagé people. José García occasionally sings too. He says:

> I don't sing like the shamans, but another song that comes with yagé; for example, with a music that I hear. The very yagé teaches you what to sing . . . low or high, or whatever. You see prayers, but sung . . . prayers with the song of yagé. Thus you do your curing with this; singing . . . for example, the Magnifica. You are singing the Magnifica under the influence of yagé, curing the sick, or under the influence of one who is curing. The Magnifica says, "My soul is full of grace from Our Lord and my spirit is lifted to God, my Savior. In the light of his eyes, now all the generations call me, 'Welcome!' since in me great things have been made and here in me is the power almighty whose mercy extends from generation to generation to those who fear it, and his arms from my heart extend to those exposed. The humble also come in their need to seek your mercy like Israel your servant who made our father Abraham and all his descendants; for the centuries and centuries, Amen."
>
> This is what I sing, *borracho*, with yagé, singing the Magnifica and curing. With this you cure sorcery (*maleficio*), no matter how serious. With this you are singing, developing the Magnifica, with this, calming the illness.

In addition to his constant attendance at Indian shaman healing and yagé-taking, José García makes annual visits to a spirit center in the largest highland city. This center is run by a woman, the "sister" Carmela (an intimate friend of the Bishop, people say). She heals hundreds of people each week by invoking the spirit of the dead Venezuelan surgeon, José Gregorio Hernández. José García has learned much from her, and once took her down into the jungles to drink yagé with his favorite Indian teacher, whose home she cured. She cautions José García from drinking too much yagé, but so long as he stays within the bounds of twice

a month, she says this can help the development of his powers. Other white spiri-
tualists from the same city come to the jungle shamans to drink yagé and to take
some back to their own establishments to give to patients in very small doses. In
this way the new and flourishing urban healing cults are connected to the jungle
Indians, and folk Catholicism is invigorated.

In discussing his overall philosophy about yagé and the lessons it has taught
him, José García says:

> Yes! I have seen the greatness of this world, and one remembers, takes account of
> it, and manages one's life accordingly. That's why God helps me. God has spe-
> cially chosen me to succeed in anything I want, but not too much; to do great
> things, to perform great cures . . . according to my faith and how I conduct myself.
> Thus yagé helps me. . . . With yagé I have seen much wealth. But do you know
> that it is not mine. I am only the administrator of the goods of this world. Of pride,
> I have none. You don't find me like the rich, proud, like those rich people to
> whom you say hello and they don't answer back. I am only an administrator. The
> day that my Father esteems me, he calls me to account for all; "Come *mayordomo!*
> Come here *mayordomo!* Give me your account!"

He states that the power he acquires rests on the obligation to heal others.
Healers can never refuse this call. Generosity and good deeds are their watch-
words. Healing prowess and even some measure of material self-advancement
follow, but only so long as this rule is scrupulously observed. Moreover, as he
declares, any wealth obtained by means of this power is never truly one's personal
property. It is not owned, but cared for. The healer is but the steward of worldly
goods. This ideology can serve to justify a healer's wealth, but then healers are
not generally wealthy, and what is at stake here is a concern to combat greed and
the temptation to use one's power to exploit the afflicted.

To understand this better one has to appreciate that a healer is continually dependent on the spirits because his great power is also fragile and in constant need
of replenishment. This is in accord with the Indian metaphysics of shamanic
power and is also testimony to the fact that healers are subject to and afraid of
sorcery attacks leveled against themselves because their work constantly exposes
them to envy and sorcery disputes. A healer lives on a razor's edge between life
and death. In healing others, he is also healing himself. This is a persistent process, and lowland healers are never happier than when they are healing; they need
to heal in the same way as other people need to eat. In healing, one engages with
and exploits the forces of evil, converting them into life-giving powers. This is
achieved by finding the meaning of affliction, and to do this requires the visions
that come from entering into the spiritual realm. Poised delicately between defeat
and success, forever entangled in the mire of the underworld and the shining
clarity of spiritual enlightenment, the healer is in the constant process of ascend-
ing a hierarchy of purity and power from which he can be easily toppled. Receiv-

ing power "from above" is contingent upon giving it "to below," to the afflicted. It is only through helping the afflicted and thereby engaging with the powers of evil that a healer can ascend.

Power comes from this chain of reciprocal exchanges. And these exchanges of reciprocity, so it would seem, assume connections going back to the beginning of time through the spirits of generations of Indian shamans and folk Catholic saints. The phenomenology of the yagé experience is basic to this, because the wisdom and worlds it reveals, so sensuously and vividly, cascade into ever-widening cycles of understanding of cosmic history and one's place in that history.

To a colonist like José García, these themes of reciprocity are clear. He reveres the Indian shamans for their skill and generosity, and they respect him. In his spiritual quest and efforts to acquire magical power and success in life he mediates the city and the jungle, the highlands and the lowlands, the civilized and the primitive, the Church and paganism. In an important sense he is creating a new cultural form, but does not his creation also replicate the historical creation of Latin American folk culture as a whole?

### Commoditization of the Gift

Among the clients who come to the Indian shamans are rich peasants and small hacienda owners. Some journey hundreds of miles. They feel they have been afflicted with sorcery. Their harvests are poor. Their cattle fail to fatten. Their debts to the bank mount. Prices for their products are ruinous. They are sick with diseases that fail to respond to treatment. And the sorcery? They feel that it comes from their peons or poor neighbors, envious of their wealth and wrathful of their failure to share it. To deal with this they go to live with an Indian shaman and take yagé. This cures them and their economic enterprises, and grants them immunity from further attack for six to twelve months.

One man I know, a white with a hacienda of 500 hectares in the mountains just south of the Cauca valley, has made many such trips to the Sibundoy and Upper Amazonian shamans. He completed secondary school and has a son working as a mechanic in the Colombian navy. He works hard at manual labor on the land and also relies on some eight households of Páez Indian serfs who work half the week for him, and the rest of the time on the small plots he has relinquished to them in return for their labor dues. He is convinced that these serfs, who are also his fictive kin through ties of compadrazgo (god-parenthood), ensorcell him. His only way of alleviating or preventing the effect of this sorcery is to make recourse to an Indian shaman adept at yagé healing, to whom he brings samples of the hacienda's soil and other items for divination, often accompanied by his son. The serfs have neither the time nor the money to do this. The class war in this mountain hacienda is being fought through sorcery, and the landlord has the money to buy superior magic to keep it at bay and maintain the pattern and intensity of labor exploitation. I know the landlord and some of the serfs, dating

from the time I visited the hacienda with two leaders of the local peasant syndicate in 1972. Later on when I got to know the serfs better, amidst the camaraderie
of peasant gatherings and political meetings in the nearest market town, away
from the hacienda, I asked one of them about this and who was doing the sorcery.
"Why," he answered with a beaming face, "*los mismos compadres*" (the landlord's
serfs).

In the highlands alongside the one road that leads to the Amazon lowlands,
commercial farming has received a great boost in recent years. In the late 1960s
the World Bank instituted a cattle-raising program and through the rural bank
has organized credit facilities which reach the rich peasant stratum. Furthermore,
potato farming now requires large amounts of capital for fertilizer and pesticides,
and the rich peasants are the only ones who can keep up with rising costs. Invariably they employ their poor neighbors as field hands, and invariably they fear
their envy and sorcery. This is rationalized by their saying things like, "My neighbors (or my workers) are too lazy to make anything out of life. Instead they are
envious of my success, which is due to my hard work, and then they prepare a
*maleficio* or *capacho*. . . . " It would be naïve to assume that it is the introduction
or the intensification of capitalist relations of production through more commer-
cialized farming that causes this situation of inequality, exploitation, and envy.
No doubt inequality, envy, and fear of magical retaliation date from the remote
past. But there is also no doubt that the capitalist economy both creates new
forms and intensifies the socioeconomic conflicts among the peasantry.

I know a rich peasant embroiled in these conflicts, through my having taken
yagé with him on several occasions, and staying with him at his highland farm.
He regards himself as a white and is desperate to rid himself of the sorcery he
feels one of his neighbor-peons is deploying against him. Every two weeks or so
he attends the yagé healing ritual conducted by an Indian in a highland village
some two hours' bus journey away. The costs of that journey and the shaman's
fees put such recourse beyond the bounds of his peons. He cultivates some of the
magical medicines that Indian shamans use and has pretensions of becoming a
great curer himself. He attempts to cure the minor ailments of his neighbors, and
plans to buy divining crystals and feathers from lowland shamans. But it is the
singing that lies beyond his reach, and until he receives that power he must patiently wait.

"When you take yagé," he explains, "you acquire some of the power of the
shaman. The shaman gives you this gift and this is what cures people, cattle, . . .
everything, including sorcery of the soil and of the crops." He continues with a
statement which enables us to better grasp the vast system of magical exchanges
as a whole; "The highland shamans sing and they call the spirit of the lowland
shaman, the shaman that taught them, to come and help. They do this because
he has given the gift to them."

In his eyes, so it would seem, the highlands and the jungles as much as the
civilized and the primitive are connected by a chain of spiritual discourse stretch-

ing back through time, a chain of discourse which is based on successive gift-exchanges replicating the exchanges found between spirits and people, shaman and novice, teacher and pupil, healer and patient. As gift exchanges they embody and transfer the personality and spirit of the giver, and demand reciprocity. This form of exchange is the antithesis of the market exchange of commodities which is impersonal, separates persons from things, and is animated by the competitive desire for profit. But, as we see in the case of the rich peasant employer afflicted with sorcery alleged to come from his laborers, the power and the spirit of the gift is utilized to introduce and sustain its antithesis, the market organization of crop and cattle production, together with the commoditization of labor. The gift becomes a tool of labor exploitation and facilitates the spread of the market economy. Gift exchanges here terminate in and empower commodity exchanges, and one man's gift becomes another man's capital.

Just as he buys the exchange-value of his peons' labor power, in order to utilize its use-value, so the rich peasant is buying yagé-derived shamanic power in order to profit from its use-value. The latter transaction facilitates the former one, and in both instances it is human creativity, transformed from a gift to a commodity, that suffers.

In this situation, the highland shamans stand as intermediaries articulating two opposed systems of exchange and production, gift-exchange with market-exchange, and precapitalist with a developing capitalist mode of production. Yagé healing ritual becomes an agent for transforming gifts into commodities. A powerful source of conflict is established by this contradiction which threatens the chain of reciprocal exchanges linking jungle shamans with their more commercial highland counterparts. Progressive incorporation of jungle shamanism into the market economy may kill the shamanic source of magical power, while at the same time it is these very market relations which drive people to that source, to exploit the gift that allows them to exploit others and withstand their enmity. It is to the phenomenology of this destructive dialectic, as exemplified in the case of a sick lowland shaman, that I now have to turn.

*The Struggle for Life*

In January of 1976, José García's great teacher-shaman, the Ingano Luciano, lost sight in his left eye. While fishing one night he saw a veil of mist descending while casting his line, and soon lost all vision with that eye. A few months later he could not stand or walk without feeling weak. This progressed until he became almost totally incapacitated. He became dizzy while standing or walking, would vomit if he exerted himself, and would fall down in a dead faint. He was sure that he had been ensorcelled by Esteban, a highland Ingano Indian shaman.

Of late, Luciano has been finding it increasingly difficult to obtain crude yagé. Colonization has stripped back the jungle and the yagé vine with it. The highland shamans are coming down and paying suppliers high prices for liter con-

tainers of prepared yagé brew, and this means that there is less for lowland shamans who live at the edge of the jungle and who also have to get their yagé from
forest dwellers. Healers like Esteban are blamed for adding to the shortage.

It is also said that the highland shamans are using their knowledge of European-derived black magic (magia) to put pressure on lowland suppliers of yagé.
Lowland shamans do not understand this magic very well and are afraid of it. It
is because of their travels across the nation, their learning to mix different traditions of magic, and their involvement with more commercial problems that the
highlanders have acquired magia. Esteban exemplifies this. He is said to mix yagé
and black magic, and throw in Datura (Jimsonweed) for good measure.

Added to this, Luciano felt that Esteban was seized with envy by his prestige
as a healer and material success as a farmer. On his journeys to the lowlands for
yagé, Esteban has watched Luciano's farm develop from a small patch of corn,
beans, and plantains, to its present state of fifteen head of cattle. To some degree,
Esteban is being used here as a condensed symbol of many of the social conflicts
that commercialization of lowland agriculture brings. With the new livestock
credit programs established by the World Bank, cattle raising for export to the
cities has developed apace. This creates a host of serious problems. It encourages
the slashing back of the jungle, the unintensive use of land, and the displacement
of the poor peasant. It heightens the dependency of the small farmer on the credit
agencies and on the politicians who never hesitate to exploit that dependency.
The people without cattle feel envious of those who raise them. Theft is common. Fences have to be erected and maintained. The cattle become sick or hard
to control—a fairly sure sign of sorcery. Selling them raises anxiety because the
urban buyers cheat on the weight or fail to pay. When I first met Luciano he was
embroiled in a dispute involving a distant cousin who had stolen some of his
cattle and had been arrested by the police. A few days later, the morning after
taking yagé, Luciano said that he had had difficulty moving around the room
attending to patients. Cattle, beautiful cattle, kept getting in his way, mooing,
nudging, waiting to be patted, and nuzzling him. In that same healing session he
had been asked to heal some cattle of sorcery, mixing yagé with fodder and singing over the mixture. In short, cattle raising has now become a troublesome preoccupation. It features dramatically in social conflicts, heightens preexisting ani-
mosities between people, and raises the risks and amount of money involved in
farming to a very high degree. Esteban's name had been raised earlier in disputes
over cattle trading. He had tried to force some lowland Indians into selling him
cattle which he wished to sell in highland markets. When refused, it was said that
he had used his magic to kill the entire herd. (It is worth noting that this dispute
is perfectly analogous to those that occur between highland and lowland Indians
concerning the trading of yagé.)

Significantly adding to the factors implicating Esteban was the fact that Luciano had recently tried to cure a neighboring poor household from sorcery.
Upon taking yagé it was revealed that Esteban was to blame. This clinched the

argument that Esteban was the cause of Luciano's fearful illness, and in this claim we see the overdetermined expression of all the tensions and contradictions that enter into highland-lowland relations (and beyond them we also see the conflicts associated with the commercialization of agriculture and of magic).

At this point help arrived from an unexpected quarter. Convinced of Esteban's guilt, and his deployment of black magic in addition to yagé-empowered chonta darts, José García made a trip up to the highlands to visit the "sister" Carmela who is the head of a flourishing healing cult in the city. He did this because he believes that yagé shamans can only rarely overcome magia. He wanted Carmela to visit Luciano or for Luciano to visit her. She confirmed his suspicions and gave him medicines for Luciano.

Luciano took the medicines. He also called in Roberto, the shaman in whom he places all his trust. Roberto is a Kofan-speaking shaman with whom he studied long ago under the tutelage of the great Siona shaman, Patricio. Luciano took yagé with Roberto and his illness subsided a little. By thus involving himself, however, Roberto became ill too. Over the past few years Roberto has been having trouble with his throat and, most frighteningly, with his singing. Now it became a lot worse. Shamans from the Napo river in Ecuador are said to be sending their darts into him, out of envy, and his endurance is being sapped because he is healing too many non-Indians. This exposes him to the danger of breaking dietary and other taboos associated with menstruation and pregnancy. To deal with this, Roberto has been visiting the greatest shaman in the area, a Kofan hidden up one of the most isolated rivers, said to be living completely alone on the far side of a mountain range, refusing to treat anyone but lowland Indians.

By June of 1976, Luciano's illness worsened and to me and everyone else his death seemed imminent. Word was sent to Roberto to come immediately. He responded with a sanguine message that he would come soon and that he thought he could cure the illness because he now suspected it was not due to the highlander but to his own former teacher's son. It was being said that with yagé darts Roberto had killed his teacher, the great Patricio, and that now his son was bent on vengeance. If this was true, terrible as it would be, the battle would at least be fought out with the familiar weapon of magical chonta darts and not against the mysterious magia. Yet, Roberto delayed. It appears he was frightened of further involvement. People around Luciano speculated that Roberto had to wait until his rice was harvested, and that the heavy rains slowed his journey. With his typical insight into personal relations, Luciano said it was Roberto's wife who was reluctant to let him go. She fears for his health and knows that the Inganos drink vast amounts of liquor. The Kofans around Roberto do not. When they visit the Inganos they are plied with liquor and are sick for days.

In this suspenseful situation Luciano sat and waited. At times he would sing softly, alone, trying to cure himself. Each day brought more visitors. The word had circulated that he was dying and friends from far afield came to sit with him. It was the wet season. Torrential rains pelted down. Heavy clouds and mist filled the air. People sat all day reminiscing and drinking brandy and *chicha*. The river roared, full-throated. Clouds swirled effervescently, clinging to the tree-topped foothills and drastically changing their silhouette minute by minute. Nature itself was drunk; a yagé-imbued landscape, transforming constantly. Luciano was going to die as he had lived and liked to live, partially drunk, drinking, laughing, joking, and storytelling. There is always this atmosphere around his home, and almost all the healers I know share this ability to laugh and make others laugh as they tell their stories. His courage never left him, and he had no cheap comfort in the idea of a life after death. As far as he is concerned, death is the end.

In the midst of this he kept on healing people, and they came in droves. He would listen to their stories, sing over them, and exorcise evil, even though he was unable to take yagé. This is the worst of being ensorcelled; it stops yagé from taking effect, or one may die taking it. It is when he takes yagé that a shaman is most *delicado*.

But the temptation was great. Maybe he could master his weakness. Maybe he would see something. How else could he deflect his enemy? José García tells the story:

I went up to his place one afternoon and he was terribly drunk and his wife implored me to cure him saying that he was fearfully bad-tempered with her and everyone else around. So we sat around talking and drinking and when night came Luciano said we would take yagé, he, his nephew Esais, his son-in-law Evaristo, and I. "Good, we're all here," he said. He poured out the yagé and sang over it and gave each person a cupful, but at first forgot me. Then he remembered and gave me the largest cupful I had ever taken. "Ah!," I said, "in the name of the Holy Virgin this will do something." And I consecrated the yagé and called on god and the spirits of the Indian shamans, Tomás Becerra and Andrés Hinchoa, to come and help me, to cure this yagé in the name of Tomás Becerra and so on because they were yagé-takers and of the best. Then Luciano said, "But who is going to sing? Nobody? Well, you sing don José! Aren't you always singing to yourself under your poncho? All these times you've been taking yagé up here you've been singing and curing hidden under your poncho, no? Well come out into the public so that we can see if you really know or not!"

"All right, señor," I replied, "that's what we'll do." And in that instant he fell to the floor, as if dead. We jumped up and put him back in his hammock, but he stayed like he was dead, with only his hands moving, mute, speaking with nothing but his hands, mute. The others thought they were going to die. His son-in-law implored me to try to cure them. Now the yagé was catching me. I took up a curing broom and started to cure. The *chuma* was taking me. It was beautiful and I began to see what state the house was in. It was a complete cemetery. There was a burial. It was a total annihilation going on. Okay! So I got busy with my medicines and then the chuma caught everyone else, and it was terrible! His son-in-law was crying, "Don José please please come and cure me because I am dying!" I bent over him and exorcised, cleaning and sweeping and sucking. Then his nephew, the same thing. It was awful. I went from one to the other, and back again. Those two soon got better and then I attended to the friend Luciano. I worked on him till three in the morning and then he began to revive, to speak again. "Ya, ha ha ha." And he would whistle and scream. "We're not just anybody, don José," he said. "For we *know*, isn't that right don José?" And then he would become unconscious again. "We *know*. They can't get us! Isn't that right don José?" He also saw the cemetery, all of it. "Ave María," he said, "dead people putrefying everywhere," he said. Others in agony, about to die. The whole house was a graveyard. Ave María!

So we kept on taking yagé. And finally he said, "Good! Come again on Tuesday. If they're going to kill us, then they too will die!"

On Tuesday we took yagé again and he was beginning to sing when he cried out that he had an illness deep within and that he was going into the other room to see if he could cure it. He took his curing broom and we could hear him singing. Suddenly the candle went out and it was completely dark. I stayed there, jittering with the yagé, frightened, sure I was about to die. And the friend Luciano became silent. He stopped singing. I cured myself with my medicines, over my body, blowing incense and eventually I got better after an hour or so. When my force returned I began to sing and cure the others, singing and curing, singing and curing. "Ah, don José," said Luciano, "looks like they are trying to kill us, no? But they can't! So, let's take some more and see if they can kill us. Take more yagé!"

So we took another cup and when the chuma came, "pow"—he fell to the floor again. This time it only lasted for half an hour. He got up and started singing and said, "On Friday we'll take some more." So on Friday I went again and the chuma was good. I went to Pasto and came back with holy water and incense. I cured cattle and went a second time to Pasto and got medicines for Luciano from the sister Carmela. So we finished.

Luciano remained the same. He did not die, nor did he get any better. Finally, after I had gone (back to my university to teach), Roberto arrived with members of his family, including his mother-in-law, widow of a Siona shaman. She is old, the *mama señora*, and can now drink yagé with impunity and sings beautifully, says Luciano. It is she and only she who knows how to prepare the very special chicha of pineapple and corn and manioc that Roberto uses to sing to and call the game animals to the hunters, with yagé. Many other people came, so I was told, and they all took yagé. Roberto sang. The mama señora sang. "My betrothed (*novia*)" is what Luciano calls her, with a giggle. And don Apolinar sang too. He is a Correguaje shaman from the far-off Caquetá river drainage, married to one of Luciano's daughters. It is very hard to travel from the Caquetá nowadays because the army has militarized the area and a vicious guerrilla war has sown terror across the land.

After two nights of ritual Luciano improved dramatically. His eyesight remained impaired but his giddy spells, fainting, and vomiting all ceased. He was able to walk and work, and life resumed its normal pattern.

In December a man came, with his son, from Cúcuta on the Colombian-

Venezuelan border, all the way across Colombia. He was a rich middle-class man, owner of a large dance hall. He had heard about Luciano from one of his employees. His dance hall was ensorcelled by the owner of a rival dance hall. Now Christmas was coming and he stood to lose a fortune. He needed the "*indio*" from the Amazon lowlands to cure his business. Luciano flew there with his son. They planned to stay there four weeks. He came back, well paid, after two, late at night, grumbling and disgusted. He had had to cure all twenty-two rooms. There was no chicha, only bottled beer. The owner and his family kept asking him if he was baptized. He laughs uproariously: "I told them I was baptized before even those priests in the cities were!" They kept asking for magic to make money and to find gold. They asked him to cure jewelry. They wanted him to stay. But he left, saying that they were rich. They had laborers and everything. They needed no more, while he had his farm and they were waiting for him at home. And if his wife sickened, who would look after her? She couldn't go to the pharmacy or the hospital; they would kill her. Then, late as it was and tired as he was, he sat in his hammock and began singing, healing a patient, a *campesino* from the highlands who had been awaiting his return.

And his savior and great friend, Roberto? His powers are said to be waning. His singing grows weaker. He says he will die before his time. Attacked by Indians from Ecuador, polluted by too much healing of non-Indians, he is also traveling, to the lone Kofan up a far-off river deep in the jungle, hidden on the other side of the mountain and refusing treatment to any but the people for whom yagé was created.

He did die before his time, a year later, vomiting uncontrollably. One sensed the beginning of the end. There would be no more gifts from the jungle to stem the sweeping tide of colonization and of commerce. They had tried so hard, with humor and nobility, these jungle shamans, to accommodate themselves, their visions, and their songs, to conflicting pressures. They had been called upon by the white national society going crazy with fear to exorcise its demons, and it was Roberto who had paid for this with his life. Yet, he had saved Luciano.

It was at Luciano's home, later on, that we were looking intently at a photograph of Roberto, trying, without saying so, to decipher the meaning of his death and its implications for all of us. Luciano looked strong and confident, but the meaning of that death was terrible. A nephew of Luciano, up for a visit together with his wife and sons from a lonely stretch of jungle along the banks of the Putumayo, gazed at the picture a long time and said, "I never saw him—but there was a man." I remembered what he had said a little earlier when we were talking about what it took to become a shaman. In Luciano's words, "To become a tiger, to learn to kill people with chonta darts, and to cure, also." We talked about the courage and type of strength that were required to take yagé in vast quantities, until finally one drank an entire potful. "And does the power then come with a rush, all at once?," I asked. Luciano laughed. "To sing . . . that comes all at once. But the wisdom (*sabiduría*) . . . ," and his voice trailed off into the gusts of wind and the river's crescendo. They both laughed, and his nephew, leaning forward, suddenly exclaimed, "God illuminates it. The gift is given."

Next day I went with that man's twenty-year-old son, Luis Antonio, to a grove beside the river to prepare a yagé remedy. The rain had stopped. Birds chirruped. Insects picked at our feet and red drops of blood rose. The river thundered by. Two bats darted out of the dilapidated cooking hut as we approached, veering right in perfect unison seeking a path out through the jungle. We settled down to work. Ferns tickled my feet. Ants kept crawling into the mash of yagé stems and its female companion of *chagropanga* leaves that we were pounding. We talked, meanderingly, from topic to topic, as we became absorbed in the routine of our tasks in the fastness of the forest, excited with the expectation of the pleasure that our work would yield to others. Luis Antonio told me that his family had come to visit Luciano to be cured. A neighboring Ingano had "damaged" them, out of envy that the boys all stayed home and helped their parents, and had ensorcelled them in such a way that they made enemies all the time. His mother's arm is deeply cut open right now, from a machete blow delivered in a fight. He himself had been crazy when twelve years old. He would fall unconscious for half an hour or so and see horrible things such as snakes and spiders crawling over him. Upon waking he would run into the jungle, alone. Eventually he was cured after many yagé sessions conducted by an Ingano shaman. His mother's father had been a shaman. We sweated, joking and laughing, retelling Luciano's stories about the suffering yagé cooks undergo, especially galling when they prepare yagé for outsiders who know nothing of yagé. Luis Antonio was very thorough, a meticulous cook.

And then suddenly I was jolted by what he was saying into recognizing that he was not only a cook. He was learning to become a shaman. Luciano had told him just two weeks before, after taking yagé together, "*Perhaps* you could learn." But once you have started to learn you have to keep on taking yagé—or else the yagé itself will kill or seriously damage you.

He has flown up into the sky, pulled up very, very slowly. He has seen beautiful houses, small and pure blue. There is music, but no people, and he sees god, like the sun, illuminating, pure fire, singing, not talking. And in the nights when they take yagé together, even when Luciano stops singing, Luis Antonio hears the singing, continuing, like the river flowing on into the depths of the jungle.

### *Afterword*

The experiences on which this chapter is based come from the fieldwork and trips I made beginning in 1970 with Anna Rubbo in and around the Cauca valley in the southwest of Colombia. I visited the Putumayo lowlands for the first time in 1972, in part because of certain events in the Cauca valley, which I shall relate below, and in part owing to the kindness and urging of Jean Langdon and Scott Robinson—anthropologists to whom I am eternally grateful. It was Scott, known to many Kofans as Sakara, who introduced us to the great Kofan healer whom, in this chapter, I have named Roberto. And it was Roberto who introduced me to Luciano. Both these men showered me with the same kindness and generosity they grant any sufferer of misfortune who comes to their home. It is to them and their families that I owe my greatest debts, and I can only hope that this article in some small way serves to recognize those debts, and adds to their work. Needless to say Scott and Jean know far more about lowland Putumayo shamanism than I do, and I have benefited enormously from their guidance.

I have made nine trips to the Putumayo highlands and lowlands, ranging from three weeks to three months at a time. Apart from Spanish, four languages are spoken in the areas where I have resided—Kamsá, Inga, Kofan, and Siona—and my knowledge of these is very rudimentary. Everyone I met spoke Spanish, sometimes as their second language.

My field trips always consist in staying with three healers. Anthropologists would term them "shamans"; the local term is *curaca*. To help insure their survival I have had to change their names and deliberately obscure some geographical details. P.C. lives in the Sibundoy valley, 2,220 m high in the Andes, overlooking the Amazon jungles in a town alongside the one and only road connecting the jungle to the cities and highlands. Kamsá is his first language. Luciano lives just where the cloud-forested slopes of the Andes abruptly meet the foothills, the montaña or "eyebrow" (*ceja*) as it is sometimes called. He lives about four miles outside of a town with a population of some 20,000, and his first language is Inga. The third curaca with whom I stayed many times was the late Roberto M., probably the most respected and feared shaman of the Putumayo montaña. He lived along a tributary of the Putumayo, deep in the forest and far from any town or hamlet. His first language was Kofan, although, like that other great Kofan shaman, Pacho Quintero, his father was a white who had come down to the jungle during the rubber boom at the turn of the century and had married a Kofan woman.

Pacho Quintero died in 1977. He was a ferociously tough Indian Nationalist, sui generis, without knowledge of pro-Indian struggles and ideology in other parts of the country. "Yagé is our study!" he would scornfully say, deriding the government's schools. It is surely significant that the two strongest shamans in that area both had white fathers. It was these two men who took it upon themselves (and were granted that right by the communities in which they lived), to learn, explore, and develop shamanism more than any Kofan Indian. Furthermore, because Roberto's two most promising pupils were black colonists, from the Pacific coast, and because Luciano played such a decisively important influence in the career of a white, José García, is it not likely that shamanism is far from being a spent force and that its future development will encompass all marginal men—Indian, white, and black?

At first I had no desire to work as a field anthropologist and I considered journeys to those enchanting places in a quite different light. Note taking, photogra-

phy, and tape recording seemed to me to trivialize and to debase what the shamans and their sick clients were undergoing. In addition, the situation per se
militated against anthropological inquisitiveness and diverted one's curiosity into
other channels. One became something ephemeral, yet flowing, akin to the
streams rushing through the forest and to the mists rising from them to gambol
as clouds on the mountainsides, transforming the line between earth and sky into
a swirling but calm threshold of uncertainty. When you begin the working day
drinking chicha in the early morning and are surrounded by the cloud forest or
the river, and have been taking yagé over the past few days, then anthropological
concerns give way to others. Roberto once told me about becoming invisible.
When strangers came to be cured, when he was a child, and the shaman wanted
nothing to do with them, he would give all the people living in the house a special medicine to make them invisible, until the strangers left.

Moreover, what I became involved in was for a long time too foreign for me to
make honest and significant connections with anything else in my experience—
except that as a result of my almost two years of fieldwork in the interior I knew
that *in some way* these shamans were connected with the problems of peasants
facing capitalist development and with the philosophic infrastructure of the
popular culture of those peasants. So, I waited and joined in the daily rhythms of
work and healing. I felt that the fundamental issues would emerge, if ever they
would, not through my questioning but through the thickening tissue of enveloping human relationships creating historical understanding of an experience
"from within," rather than, or in addition to, the understanding of a neatly cata-
loged "system of belief" or "symbol-system" of another society.

The most pointed illustration of this problem is the shaman's singing—that
enthralling, night-long singing of yagé sounds which defies description. Yet, without an awareness of the power and the extraordinary beauty of this singing, one
cannot begin to understand how these yagé rites move and transform people. The
song is where the breath of the shaman, the breath which is spirit, fuses with the
songs of the yagé people, the spirits of yagé, to give voice to the patterns of connections lying mute and fragmented in the objective world. The shaman's spirit
pours forth in breath, and the song is his action on the world. Yet in coming
forward and in acting in this way, he provides but the medium for the transmission of a voice far greater than his own. "And in the vast jungle filling with night
terrors," writes Alejo Carpentier describing his impression of the shaman's song
in his novel *The Lost Steps*, "there arose the Word. A word that was more than
word. . . . This was something far beyond language and yet still far from song.
Something that had not yet discovered vocalization but was more than word . . .
blinding me with the realization that I had just witnessed the Birth of Music"
(1974:184–185). One is driven into sad despair, also beyond words, when one
hears these songs and realizes with plummeting foreboding that the present generation of shamans may be the last and that the world may lose this voice forever.

Surely, to understand yagé ritual and the meaning of that ritual to outsiders like myself who came down from the highlands, it was first necessary to absorb the quite frightening reality of moving into one's self and one's own history, and moving way out of one's body at the same time. For as far as I am concerned it is this epistemic flip-flop which is central to the yagé experience and from which its cathartic properties and healing function derive. One literally *is* the emotional involvement conjured up by the objects and the qualities of the objects beheld, felt, and heard, while at the same time one is outside of this frame of reference, way outside and looking at it from afar with a sometimes nervous and sometimes cool detachment. The assurance necessary to keep going, to drink more yagé, comes not so much from the shaman as a guide as from the knowledge that all the others with you are human and are going through the same sort of thing, and that their particular and different life histories are now unfolding in this collective event.

It also became apparent that no shaman had a "system" in the sense of having a neatly packaged set of doctrines, symbol dictionary, or answers to the issues confronting them. Instead, they too were plagued by uncertainty. Their lives were ones of intellectual as much as political quests, and their dilemma was that of having to communicate their vision, as the only way of making it real and clear, to a world whose historical development denied history and in so doing increasingly branded them as mystics.

The thought world of the shamans has nothing in common with the vaporous and uncritical idealism labeled as "mysticism" and nourished by the alienating conditions of modern life now so prevalent in industrialized societies as well as in Third World cities—an idealism which is as likely to romanticize and "spiritualize" the Indians as to kill them in the name of civilization. There is a solid, earthy, practicality to Putumayo shamanism, spiced with humor and all too human passions. It is this very monism—this unfractured blending of the sacred and the secular—that makes shamanism so potent in sustaining popular culture and such a powerful hindrance to the spread of the market culture of utilitarianism as well as to the hegemony of the state and the hierarchically organized "great" religions such as Christianity.

It was only much later, in 1977, that I began to feel a responsibility that demanded taking notes and recording conversations. In part this was due to my need to overcome the assault made on my analytic memory and sense of reality by moving in and out of the yagé world, which displaces one form of memory by another. This need turned on a greater one to make sense of the entangled and evolving life histories which led me like so many colonists, traveling healers, and damaged people from the highlands and "the city" to "the country," and back through history, so to speak. I now felt I was beginning to understand the grip of that ideological pilgrimage in which city and country as much as civilization and primitiveness stand as a web of interrelated metaphors in a society's expression of a specific form of development and of the contradictory human experience of that development. Together with that dawning understanding came the necessity to socially express it, as in writing and publishing, both as a way of drawing out its implications and of making it clearer to myself, as well as to publicly bring attention to the fragile virtues *and* the illusory and destructive aspects of this vast network of ideas and practices constituting the landscape of the historically formed popular imagination in southwest Colombia. Let me try to explain at least some of this.

Our dear friend, Marlene, in whose house we lived in the sugar plantation town in the Cauca valley, was killed by her lover, who then tried to kill her children and shot himself dead through the ear. We were in Mexico at the time. It was 1972 and our son was born. Marlene was a radical and a member of several political organizations in which she took an active part. She was very black. Her brother had been assassinated in the Violencia of the 1950s, and her mother and father had been peasants. She had inherited the land of her mother's family, as the sole survivor, and was relatively well-off. She had spent a year at the national university before returning to the town, now somewhat a misfit. She was convinced that someone, presumably her lover's wife, was ensorcelling her home and she spent most of her time and a lot of money on curers trying unsuccessfully to cure it. Her lover shot her and himself dead, I believe, because he could neither stand the terror of her leaving him, which was what she wanted to do, nor the circling charges of sorcery in which his image loomed large. His wife? He was after Marlene's land and money? These were misty charges, but acidic. He scorned Marlene's fears, yet it was obvious that he was overprotesting, and he was anxious about her father, who was a curer. He lived in a neighboring village, had one hand chopped off, was rather eccentric, and trusted nobody. He carried a huge bunch of keys and had a markedly asymmetrical walk because of the bags of medicines he always wore concealed under his shirt and pants. He was run out of town, I once heard, for molesting small girls. His lover ensorcelled him and he became awfully sick. No curer could help him until he came across a wandering Indian healer from the Putumayo and they took yagé together. I vividly recall his telling us in Marlene's home how he had traveled to heaven and talked with angels and saints. He learned something of the songs and chants of the fabled Putumayo which neither he nor I had ever visited. And I could never forget the first political meeting I attended in the plantation town. It was in Marlene's home. She had had the house ritually exercised for the occasion, and at night we stood while someone wound up the Gramophone and we listened to the scratchy voice of the great populist leader Jorge Eliécer Gaitán, assassinated in 1948. We were by the patio and the flowers reflected the light of the moon.

Later on the camp cooks in the sugarcane plantation fields introduced me to strange stories of the devil contracts allegedly made by a few plantation workers in order to increase their productivity and hence their piece-rate wages—wages of the devil and useless as a source of human well-being. Such compacts were said to be only made (and then, rarely) by men engaged in wage labor on the large capitalist estates, and never by peasants working their own plots or those of neighboring peasants because they would kill the crops, just as it killed the plantations' sugarcane. Here, indeed, was an interesting commentary on the magic of political economy and the change in a mode of production whereby peasants were forced into proletarian status. And who was assisting the wage laborers in making these alleged compacts? Sorcerers and curers, of course, like (but not only) the Putumayo Indian who now lived permanently in that narrow defile where the Cauca river thundered into the broad plains of the valley to which it gives its name. I had heard of him before when a friend of mine working on the plantations as a ditchdigger had asked him to use his occult power to "dispose" of a recalcitrant foreman who was giving the work gang a hard time and had refused to accept a bribe. This Putumayo curer had himself been ensorcelled as a young adult, had descended from the Sibundoy valley to the jungles to be cured, and had learned the art of shamanism there. Now he also practiced magia or European-style black magic, in the context of plantation life and plantation problems. Marlene's father, too, was often asked by plantation workers to effect magical solutions to labor problems, while in and around these activities a fairly vigorous trade union movement and a very modern political consciousness were also present.

In 1971 in the midst of rising peasant and landless day laborer militancy aimed at invading and taking control of plantation land, I accompanied two black peasant union leaders up the mountains. They wished to enlist Indian serfs on a hacienda to their union. It was there that I learned from the hacienda owner that he believed his serfs to be ensorcelling him and that he would cure himself and his hacienda's soils, crops, and animals by making the long pilgrimage across the mountain and down to the Putumayo shamans. It was obvious after talking with his serfs, away from the hacienda, that they knew this too, and that sorcery or alleged sorcery was an important weapon in the class struggle on the mountain haciendas. The Putumayo now beckoned me, irresistibly.

So, this article is written around these connections and begins from these starting points. I only wish Marlene were here to waggishly add her interpretation. I wonder if she would understand the demon of interpretation that drives at least some of us foreign wanderers to ask about the roots of popular consciousness and about local histories of good and evil. In any event, it is with the sense of justice and of envy in everyday life that this article deals, together with the understanding of good and evil as mediated by folk healers and the role of that mediation in the commoditization of magic and of human affairs. Therein, so it seems to me, lie many of the tropes and chords with which the political imagination composes its poetic wisdom in today's Third World.

*Appendix*

*Iconographic Dualities in Yagé Visions:*
*The Virgin and the Sorcerer*

José García's son, Pedro, made two drawings after telling me about the things he saw with yagé. We had been walking along the road from the town to Luciano's house, and night was falling. He is fourteen years of age, and has taken yagé since the age of eight. We passed his father's farm. He told me how their cattle, as well as plantains and other crops, faced constant risk of being stolen. He told me how his father had been attacked recently by a laborer demanding higher wages. His father fought back with his machete. The laborer retired, then stole their favorite dog, castrated it, and cut off its ears. Pedro fears sorcery constantly, so it seems. Why does he take yagé? He says that one takes it to see who is ensorcelling you, to clarify "one's situation," and at the same time to "clean" oneself of the "evil" (the *males* or bad things) that have been inflicted. He is afraid to walk along this road at night. Then we leave the road and take the trail into the jungle. It is almost night. We reach the river and cross the bridge. The bridge is made of bamboo and wire slung thirty feet over a cataract of rushing water and rocks. It is about ten inches wide and sways above the glistening water.

PEDRO: I saw a man making what here we call *brujerías* [sorcery] in our farm. He wanted to see all our cattle dead, and us begging alms. He wanted to see us like I was seeing. Later I saw my father, and his bad friends wanted to see him as a sorcerer like them. Then I saw my father in his underpants with a tail [like the devil] like a chain, and his body naked. I saw that. The others said that was how they wanted to see him. And they laughed when they saw that I saw. They wanted to take him off. They said they wanted me to see it like that, like them, doing evil.

Later on the sister Carmela [the spiritualist from the highland city] also said that the man I saw doing sorcery was the sorcerer. She hears that from the spirits, and with them she can cure. She calls the spirits . . . like Tomás Becerra [the Indian shaman who first gave Pedro's father yagé, now dead].

Later on, taking yagé, I saw my father curing the farm. The *chuma* caught me and took me there. I thought I was going to suffer too. Then I saw my father converting himself into a dove, and in the yagé I saw the sister Carmela and my uncle Antonio, all dressed in white, cleaning the farm.

Once I saw the Virgin. I passed to the other side and found her, mounted, like a statue. I prayed and I cried. Then after a little while the chuma changed and I saw her as a person like any other. Then I called my father and said "Look! Look! The Virgin of Carmen!" And he said, "Where is she?" And he also wanted to cry. But he said to me, "Don't cry. Why are you crying? Don't you see the Virgin of Carmen?" And she was there blessing me with the rosary in her hands. And from then the chuma changed and I saw no more.

I was crying because I was asking her pardon . . . for all of us. Thus she gave me her blessing [*la bendición*]. . . . My father told me that the same happened to him, except that he passed over a chasm with a tiny staff and he couldn't see the bottom and that he was about to fall but she got him over safely.

Pedro's commentary on his drawings

The Virgin
This is the river where I was walking and which I had to pass. This is the bamboo

bridge I had to cross. I wanted to turn around halfway across. This is the sun which lights everything up—which illuminates where we were. The face of the sun was in front of the Virgin. In front is the soil, yellow soil. There is the rock-face (*peña*)—on which the Virgin is standing. All that is peña. And that's where I met the Virgin . . . like a statue of the Saints in plaster. And then she converted, thus, like into a woman, alive, and then she gave me the blessing.

The wire in the front of the drawing is a fence of a farm. It seems to him, on questioning, that she is in the farm (in the fields where the cattle go).

The Sorcerer

This drawing consists of three parts; (1) top left, (2) top right, and (3) bottom:

(1) This is the face of one of those evil Indians (*indios malos*). I saw three, all with the same face, like those Indians from the highlands, from the Sibundoy valley.

(2) Then I turned to the farm—and saw a neighbor placing sorcery stuff (a *capacho*, or sorcery bundle) into a black, rotting tree trunk.

(3) This man is dressed in his underpants only, and has the tail of the devil and a broom in his left hand, and the *capacho* in his right. The capacho contains powdered human bones from the cemetery, soil from the cemetery, human hair, "and so on. . . . This is the man, Sánchez [a neighbor], who wanted to see my father doing sorcery; thus he wanted to see it like he saw it."

Now let us turn to a short extract from a tape-recorded conversation I had with Pedro's mother (i.e., José García's wife). Like José García she is a "white," born and raised in the Sibundoy valley before coming to live in this foothill town. Short as it is, this extract captures many salient issues.

The Indian is a brute! The Indian understands nothing. When they get drunk, reason stops falling on them. Wherever they want to puke, they puke, and there they fall and there they sleep. Not like educated people! The Indian! Ha! . . . That's why I want nothing to do with them. I stay away; apart . . .

*And José [her husband]?*

Ha! Well! He's happy with Luciano. He's caught their ideas. And that chokes me. That really chokes me, because I'm not for that. He's carrying the idea [of the Indians]; they are old friends. It's the yagé.

*What ideas?*

It's that he's caught their customs, no? The feeling [*genio*, temperament, brilliance, genius] . . . that's what.

In Sibundoy there's an Indian who speaks fourteen languages. I forget his name. He's very expert. But when the Carnival comes, he's the piggiest of all the Indians. He piggifies himself, falls into mud and becomes filth, or he dances on the mud, singing. He puts on one of those Indian masks because normally he wears the clothes of a white, no? And then comes the time of Carnival and the Indians put on masks of Indians and they dance, they drink chicha, they fight, and they wallow in the mud like pigs. That's why I say that education is wasted on Indians. What else! Fourteen languages; that's not a little!

*Magic and sorcery?*

There are Indians who do sorcery. Don Luciano doesn't. He cures, but only the sorcery that goes between Indians [i.e, only Indian-made sorcery]. Sorcery made with magia—very little! They [the Indians] can't cure that. Because for the magia, only the person who works with magia. . . . The Indians don't know magia. They can't cure it. The people who know it are the *compactados* [those who have made a pact], those who have studied the book of magic, those who have made a pact with Satan. They're the ones who know magia!

All that the Indians know is yagé and the plants with which they cure and do sorcery. The sorcerers place capachos; that's what they call it. It's very special. And the white person makes crosses with soil from the cemetery, with the soil of the dead. What else will there be? No?

She goes on to say that the blacks, "so they say, are the ones who experiment most with magia."

*Highland Indian curers compared to lowland Indian curers?*

The highlanders know another system—that gets one more money, no? They go and traverse the nations and wander here and there with their berries and nuts and things saying that they can cure when really they are swindling. They are the most cunning! With this they maintain themselves with good money! They go to Venezuela, to Peru. There's one that they call Silvestre that has gone off, he's the biggest, but he's not a sorcerer. . . . He's the son of a Spaniard and an indigenous woman (*indígena*). . . . Their system is different because they get money easier, and because their curing is a lie and but a way to get rich with filth!

*And the people here [in the lowlands]?*

Ha! No! No! The people from here, NO! From here, no! Those others [the highland Indian curers] are so given to traveling. They love traveling. They are so cunning! They wander here and they wander there, saying that they can cure. And they cure nothing. What they do is swindle and ensorcell.

## Notes

1. Of course, if "rationality" and "materialism" are to be understood in terms of the web of interconnected principles woven by Enlightenment philosophy and free-market ideology, then this sort of "irrational" reaction should cause little surprise. Neither the "rationality" based on the concept of the maximizing, autonomous subject, nor the Newtonian and atomistic version of "materialism" associated with free-market culture are rational outside of the social context they reflect and mystify. Hence, the contradiction established in peasant cultures by the market economy partakes more of that between rival metaphysical systems than that connoted by the loose usage of terms like rationality versus irrationality. In situations where market culture is greatly intensifying its hegemony over peasant life, the magical element inherent in the laws of capitalist economics may emerge

with great force, as is partially illustrated in the last sections of this chapter, entitled "The Commoditization of the Gift" and "The Struggle for Life."

2. The role of landscape (i.e., mythologized landscape and its associated folklore) in serving as a memorial or historical "text" laden with moral significance deserves far more elaboration than I can give here. The spirits (owners or Lords) of the mountains, for example, in both the Andes and Mesoamerica constitute a veritable iconography of both pre-Columbian and postconquest history, as the Catholic friars were quick to appreciate. (See, for example, Correa 1960; Albó 1972; Arguedas 1975, 1978; Clendinnen 1980; Taussig 1980, chapters 9–11). In our recent discussions Silvia Rivera C. has further impressed upon me the way and degree to which the semanticization of space (and of time), particularly as encoded in ritual (for the ancestors, the sick, the crops, and sorcery, etc.), sustains collective memory and its florescence in times of popular movements and rebellion.

3. Most, if not all, of the famous chroniclers of the Spanish conquest of South America quite unhesitatingly referred to the Indian gods and Indian religions as subject to the devil. Images of Paradise, such as that of Columbus in which the Orinoco river was seen to be one of the four rivers flowing from the garden of Eden, were soon turned upside down. In Edmundo O'Gorman's words, "The dream of concord that was to have governed the life of the new colony gave way to hate, misrule, and dissidence, while the gentle, innocent native population of this fictitious paradise, the supposed friends of the Christian, made patent their savage nature: indolent and perverse, good for murder should the occasion arise but poor for labor and the payment of tribute. The blissful image of a restored Golden Age gave way to an actual Age of Iron; the conviction grew that these native sons of the ocean were part of that vast empire of barbarians, the domain, avowed or not, of the Prince of Darkness, the enemy of mankind" (1961:90–91). Extremely interesting and pertinent testimony regarding the early Spaniards' identification of the devil with Indian shamans and their hallucinogens in northern South America is provided by Gerardo Reichel-Dolmatoff (1975:3–24).

4. For a brief introduction to the relevance of "wild man" in Spanish America, see Robe (1972).

5. By way of illustration, chosen almost randomly from an enormous number of similar references, see the fascinating chapter, "Algebristas, curanderos, herbolarios," in Constantino Bayle (1943). Bayle quotes from a lecture given at the inauguration of two professors of medicine in the University of San Marcos, Lima, in 1637, by Alonso de Huerta who disputed the need for such professors because "In this kingdom there are many medicinal herbs for many sicknesses and wounds which the Indians know better than the doctors. With these one can be cured without doctors. Experience shows that many people who have given up hope in the doctors go to Cercado or to Surco [Indian quarters in Lima] where they are cured by Indian women and men, whereby they regain the health that the doctors cannot provide" (1943:98).

6. Further indications of the more or less contemporary flow of magical power from the Amazonian lowlands to the Andean highlands are presented by Udo Oberem, Patricia Lyon, and Elsie Clews Parsons. No doubt these indications constitute no more than a tiny fraction of the underlying reality they express. According to Oberem (1974:351) the Quijos of the Ecuadorian montaña are called into the highlands to heal the sick, and it is generally believed in the highlands that these Amazonian *brujos* (sorcerers and healers) are more powerful than those of the highlands. He also asserts that highland Indians in the area are receiving training from the lowlanders and obtain their medicines from them.

Lyon (1974:345) mentions that the belief in the superior (i.e., magical) powers of the lowland Amazonian Indians also exists in highland Peru. Parsons (1945:65) notes that yagé was regularly sold in the highland market of the Otaveleños in northern Ecuador at the time of her fieldwork in the late 1930s. I should also mention that prisons can function as centers for the diffusion and syncretism of magical skills and traditions drawn from all across the land. A famous Páez wizard I came to know in the western cordillera of Colombia learned his art not from a venerable Páez shaman as I had at first suspected, but from a down-at-heel black, a fellow prisoner in the jail at Popayán.

7. For a valuable and very detailed account of the history of missions in the Putumayo, concentrating on the Sibundoy valley, see Bonilla (1972).

8. Robinson (1979) provided extremely rich and evocative accounts of yagé healing rites among Kofan people living several miles upstream from the Siona community referred to here. With regard to the shamanism of the jungle Quichua in the Ecuadorian *montaña*, several rivers to the south of these Siona and Kofan, Norman Whitten (1976) has written a masterful study, emphasizing the resurgence of that shamanism and its associated culture as a process of "ethnogenesis."

9. In their article "A Visit to God," T. Zuidema and U. Quispe M. describe and analyze a somewhat similar vision as told to them by an old woman in the river Pampas area in the Department of Ayacucho, Peru. She beheld this vision, as if she were dreaming, when she was seriously ill at the age of twenty, probably in a coma. "What makes her account so valuable," the authors state, "is its clearly discernible structure, which relates it to other ideas in Inca religion and social organization; ideas that still survive, as this account proves" (Zuidema and Quispe, 1968:22). This interpretation of Zuidema and Quispe is extremely valuable. Yet I am disinclined to adopt the static form of structuralism they use for the interpretation of the vision-texts I present above, because that form of structuralism (like Lévi-Strauss's) makes it very difficult to do justice to the tensions, contradictions, and self-transforming properties that colonial history has endowed to the subconscious structure of popular culture.

## References

Albó, Javier
  1972    "Dinámica en la estructura inter-comunitaria de Jesús de Machaca." América Indígena 32(3):773–816.

Arguedas, José María
  1975    "Puquio, una cultura en proceso de cambio. La religión local." In Formación de una cultura nacional indoamericana. Mexico City, Madrid, Buenos Aires: Siglo Veintiuno.
  1978    Deep Rivers. Translated by Frances Barraclough. Austin: University of Texas Press.

Bastien, Joseph
  1978    Mountain of the Condor: Metaphor and Ritual in an Andean Ayllu. American Ethnological Society. Monograph 64. St. Paul: West Publishing.

Bayle, Constantino
  1943    El dorado fantasma. Madrid: Publicaciones del Consejo de la Hispanidad.

Bernheimer, Richard
    1952    Wild Men in the Middle Ages. Cambridge, Mass.: Harvard University Press.

Bonilla, Victor Daniel
    1972    Servants of God or Masters of Men? The Story of a Capuchin Mission in Amazonia. Harmondsworth: Penguin.

Borrego Pla, María del Carmen
    1973    Palenques de negros en Cartagena de Indias a fines del siglo XVII. No. 216. Seville: Escuela Estudios Hispano-Americanos de Sevilla.

Canet de Mar, Benigno de
    1924    Relaciones interesantes y datos históricos sobre las misiones católicas del Caquetá y Putumayo desde el año 1632 hasta el presente. Bogotá: Imp. Nacional.

Carpentier, Alejo
    1974    The Lost Steps. Translated by Harriet de Onís. New York: Alfred A. Knopf.

CILEAC (Centro de Investigaciones Lingüísticas y Etnográficas de la Amazonia Colombiana. Bogotá.)
    1940    Amazonia Colombiana Americanista, vol. 1, nos. 2 and 3.

Clendinnen, Inga
    1980    "Landscape and World View: The Survival of Yucatec Maya Culture under Spanish Conquest." Comparative Studies in Society and History 22(3):374–393.

Comstock, Richard W.
    1976    "On Seeing with the Eye of the Native European." In Walter H. Capps, ed., Seeing with a Native Eye. New York: Harper and Row.

Conrad, Joseph
    1973    The Heart of Darkness. Harmondsworth: Penguin.

Correa, Gustavo
    1960    "El espíritu de mal en Guatemala." In Nativism and Syncretism. Middle American Research Institute, Publication No. 19. New Orleans: Tulane University Press. Pp. 41–103.

Endicott, Kirk Michael
    1970    An Analysis of Malay Magic. Oxford: Clarendon Press.

Field, Margaret Joyce
    1937    Religion and Medicine of the Gā People. London, New York, Toronto: Oxford University Press.

Flannery, Mary Cathleen
    1977    Yeats and Magic: The Earlier Works. Irish Literary Studies, 2. New York: Barnes and Noble.

Fogelson, R. D.
    1961    "Change, Persistence, and Accommodation in Cherokee Medico-Magical Beliefs." In William N. Fenton and John Glick, eds., Symposium on Cherokee and Iroquois Culture. Smithsonian Institution Bureau of Ameri-

can Ethnology. Bulletin 180. Washington, D.C.: U.S. Govt. Printing Office. Pp. 215–225.

Langdon, Jean
    1974    "The Siona Medical System: Beliefs and Behavior." Ph.D. dissertation, Tulane University.

Las Misiones en Colombia
    1912    Obra de los misioneros Capuchinos de la delegación apostólica del gobierno y de la junta arquidiocesana nacional en el Caquetá y Putumayo. Bogotá: Imp. de la Cruzada.

Lea, Henry Charles
    1908    The Inquisition in the Spanish Dependencies. New York: Macmillan.

Lévi-Strauss, Claude
    1967a    "The Sorcerer and His Magic." In Structural Anthropology. Garden City: Anchor Books. Pp. 161–180.
    1967b    "The Effectiveness of Symbols." In Structural Anthropology. Garden City: Anchor Books. Pp. 181–201.

Lyon, Patricia, ed.
    1974    Native South Americans. Boston, Toronto: Little, Brown and Company.

Myerhoff, Barbara
    1976    "Shamanic Equilibrium: Balance and Mediation in Known and Unknown Worlds." In American Folk Culture. Edited by Wayland D. Hand. Berkeley, Los Angeles, London: University of California Press. Pp. 99–108.

Oberem, Udo
    1974    "Trade and Trade Goods in the Ecuadorian Montaña." In Patricia Lyon, ed., Native South Americans. Boston, Toronto: Little, Brown and Company. Pp. 346–357.

O'Gorman, Edmundo
    1961    The Invention of America. Bloomington: Indiana University Press.

Otero, Gustavo Adolfo
    1951    La piedra mágica: Vida y costumbres de los Collahuayas. Mexico: Instituto Indigenista Interamericano.

Parsons, Elsie Clews
    1945    Peguche. Chicago: University of Chicago Press.

Phelan, John Leddy
    1956    The Millennial Kingdom of the Franciscans in the New World: A Study of the Writings of Gerónimo de Mendieta, 1525–1604. University of California Publications in History, vol. 52. Pp. 1–160.

Pitt-Rivers, Julian A.
    1974    The People of the Sierra. Chicago: University of Chicago Press.

Radin, Paul
    1914    "Religion of the North American Indians." The Journal of American Folklore 27:335–373.

Reichel-Dolmatoff, Gerardo
 1975 The Shaman and the Jaguar: A Study of Narcotic Drugs among the Indians of Colombia. Philadelphia: Temple University Press.

Robe, Stanley L.
 1972 "Wild Men and Spain's Brave New World." In Edward Dudley and Maximillian Novak, eds., The Wild Man Within. Pittsburgh: University of Pittsburgh Press. Pp. 39–53.

Robinson, Scott
 1979 "Toward an Understanding of Kofan Shamanism." Latin American Studies Program Dissertation Series. Ithaca, N.Y.: Cornell University.

Salomon, Frank Loewen
 1978 "Ethnic Lords of Quito in the Age of the Incas: The Political Economy of North Andean Chiefdoms." Ph.D. dissertation, Cornell University.

Sandoval, Alonso de, S. J.
 1956 De Instauranda Aethiopium Salute: El mundo de la esclavitud negra en América. (First published 1627.) Bogotá: Empresa Nacional de Publicaciones.

Taussig, Michael
 1980 The Devil and Commodity Fetishism in South America. Chapel Hill: University of North Carolina Press.

Tejado Fernández, Manuel
 1954 Aspectos de la vida social en Cartagena de Indias durante el seiscientos. No. 87. Seville: Escuela de Estudios Hispano-Americanos de Sevilla.

Toribio Medina, José
 1978 La inquisición en Cartagena de Indias. Bogotá: Carlos Valencia.

Tylor, Edward Burnett
 1958 Primitive Culture. 2 vols. New York: Harper and Brothers.

Wassén, S. Henry
 1972 "A Medicine-Man's Implements and Plants in a Tiahuanacoid Tomb in Highland Bolivia." Etnologiska Studier 32.

Whitten, Norman E.
 1976 Sacha Runa: Ethnicity and Adaptation of Ecuadorian Jungle Quichua. Urbana: University of Illinois Press.

Zuidema, R. T., and U. Quispe M.
 1968 "A Visit to God." Bidragen Tot de Taal, Land en Volkerunde 124:22–39.

# CONTRIBUTORS TO VOLUME I

REBECCA B. BATEMAN, Program Director of Community Outreach in Continuing Studies at Simon Fraser University, has undertaken serious ethnographic field research with the Black Seminoles of Oklahoma. She has also done comparative research on Caribbean and United States cultures, focusing on the relationships between indigenous and African American identities.

PHILIPPE BOURGOIS, Professor of Anthropology at San Francisco State University, has undertaken extensive field research in Central America, the western Caribbean, and the urban United States, focusing on ethnicity, immigration, the work process, and substance abuse.

R. S. BRYCE-LAPORTE, Director of the Center for African and African-American Studies and Professor of Anthropology at Colgate University, is a specialist in African-diaspora studies. His background as a Panamanian–West Indian adds personal depth to his interests in racism in plural societies.

NINA S. DE FRIEDEMANN, Professor of Anthropology at the Universidad Javeriana in Bogotá, Colombia, has undertaken extensive field research on black Colombians in many regions, including the Pacific Lowlands and the Atlantic Littoral. Her publications on this research are widely disseminated.

DAVID M. GUSS, Associate Professor of Anthropology at Tufts University, who specializes in urban and rural Venezuela, is one of the few scholars to undertake extensive ethnography with both African American and indigenous peoples of South America.

CAROL L. JENKINS, head of the Social Science Unit of the International Centre for Diarrhoeal Disease Research in Dhaka, Bangladesh, worked for fifteen years in Papua New Guinea following her research in Central America. Her sustained research in medical anthropology in Central America led to extensive work in Melanesia and now in South Asia.

VIRGINIA KERNS, Professor of Anthropology and past chair of the Department of Anthropology at the College of William and Mary, has conducted extended ethnographic and ethnohistorical research with the Garífuna in Belize, Central America. She has complemented this work with cross-cultural studies of women and aging.

KATHLEEN KLUMPP has undertaken field research in Colombia and Ecuador, working with indigenous and mestizo people in Ecuador, as well as with Afro–Latin Americans there. Her ethnohistorical and ethnographic work includes serious study of ritual enactment, textile design, and ceramic manufacture.

MADELINE BARBARA LÉONS, Professor of Anthropology at Towson State University, has long conducted field research on the subject of plural societies. Her work, often done jointly with her husband William Léons, focuses on the northern and southern *yungas* valleys of Bolivia.

BERTA PÉREZ, Research Anthropologist at the Instituto Venezolano de Investigaciones Científicas in Caracas, Venezuela, is the only scholar to have undertaken ethnographic field research with black people of the Amazonas Province of Venezuela, which is inhabited primarily by indigenous people.

DIEGO QUIROGA, Professor of Anthropology and Dean of the Social Sciences and Humanities at the Universidad San Francisco de Quito in Quito, Ecuador, has undertaken extensive ethnographic studies in western Ecuador, complemented by ethnography in Colombia. He is currently working in the area of Devil beliefs and practices.

JOEL STREICKER, of the Institute for Community and Religion in San Francisco, specializes in ethnographic urban field research. He combines the study of social interaction and discourse analysis to understand the gendering of racist and class stereotypes.

MICHAEL TAUSSIG, Professor of Anthropology at Columbia University, specializes in medical anthropology, folklore of resistance, and magicality and the state. These subjects, among others, have involved him in serious field research with black, indigenous, and mestizo peoples of Colombia and Venezuela.

ROBERT WHITNEY TEMPLEMAN is Assistant Professor of Music at the College-Conservatory of Music at the University of Cincinnati. He has conducted field research among black people of the Department of La Paz, Bolivia. This work was preceded by equally extensive field research with Quechua-speaking people of Andean Bolivia.

ARLENE TORRES, Assistant Professor of Anthropology and African American Studies at the University of Illinois at Urbana-Champaign, specializes in Afro-American and Latino/a Studies in the Caribbean and in the United States. She has conducted long-term ethnography in Puerto Rico and Barbados.

PETER WADE, Associate Professor of Anthropology at the University of Manchester, England, specializes in African-diaspora research. His studies in Colombia include extended ethnography with black people of the Atlantic Littoral, the Chocó region, and in Medellín and Cali.

NORMAN E. WHITTEN, JR., Professor of Anthropology and Latin American Studies, Affiliate of Afro-American Studies, and Senior University Scholar at the University of Illinois at Urbana-Champaign, has conducted extensive research in African American and Native American settings, principally in northern South America, since the early 1960s.

# INDEX

Abakua religion (Cuba), 49

Abangares gold mines (Costa Rica), 130n.13

Abeng (Jamaica), 315

ACADESAN (Peasant Association of the San Juan River), 317

ACIA (Integral Peasant Association of the Atrato River), 317

Acosta Saignes, Miguel, 271n.31

Adams, Richard, 343

Africa: symbolism and language of power in societies and cultures of, 33; and concept of trickster, 49–50; Senegambian region and Afro-Hispanic culture of Ecuador, 80. *See also* African diaspora; Language and languages; Shangó

African diaspora: discussion of concept of, 15–22; sources of power in, 31; slavery and historiography of, 35; class and ethnic discrimination in Costa Rica, 119–28

Afro-American culture: and the exotic in literature on ritual life, 168; and Black Seminole, 209. *See also* Black culture; Blackness

Afro-American Pastoral Program (Colombia), 317

Afro-Bolivian culture: and *saya* music, 426–42; and use of term *negro*, 442n.1

Afro-Colombian culture: and Champetudo music, 290–91

*Afro-ecuatoriano*: use of term, 84

Afro-Hispanic culture: in lowlands of Ecuador and Colombia, 80; and sex role enactment, 169–80; and integration of daily life and worldview, 173–75; social organization and sex roles, 180

Afro–Latin American culture: concept of and blackness in Ecuador, 94

*Afro-latinoamericano*: use of term in Ecuador, 84–85

Afro-Venezuelan culture, and Fiesta de San Juan as performance of history, 244–65

Agrarian Reform Law of 1964 (Ecuador), 81, 360, 375n.4

Agriculture: Chota–Mira Valley of Ecuador,

81–82, 359–60; and black population of Atlantic Coast of Costa Rica, 122–24; and work patterns of Black Caribs in Belize, 137, 141; Native American techniques of, 198n.4; in Amazon lowlands of Colombia, 479, 481

*Alabado-Novenario*: as sacred ritual context for sex role enactment, 175, 179

Alliance for Progress (Venezuela), 252

Alvarado, Pedro de, 84

Amazon: and Loja region of Ecuador, 92; race and politics in Colombian, 328n.13; and folk healing in southwest Colombia, 463–69

American Revolution: and history of Black Seminole, 202

Ancestral cults, and *dugu* ceremony of Garífuna in Belize, 149–64

Anderson, Benedict, 311

Andes: colonial culture of and relations with inhabitants of lowlands, 454–58. *See also* Bolivia; Ecuador

Andrés Pérez, Carlos, 256

Andros Island (Bahamas): and Black Seminoles, 207–208

Anglero, Roberto, 42

Animals, use of imagery to portray blacks in Cartagena, Colombia, 293–96

Appadurai, Arjun, 244

Arana, Julio César, 466

Arawaks. *See* Garífuna; Taíno

Archaeology, in southwest Colombia, 446, 457

Arens, William, 31, 33

Argentina: and Fiesta de San Juan, 245

Arguedas, José María, 456–57

Aripao: and maroon communities in Venezuela, 225–27

Arocha, Jaime, 36–37, 319, 327

*Arrullo* (music form): and black culture in Ecuador, 88; as sacred context for sex role enactment, 177–79

Art: representations of blacks in medieval European, 18; and Afro-American cultural traditions, 32; blackness and culture of Ecuador, 91–92